BLITZKRIEG IN THE WEST
THEN AND NOW

When the news came that the enemy was advancing along the whole front,
I could have wept for joy: they'd fallen into the trap!

ADOLF HITLER, OCTOBER 18, 1941

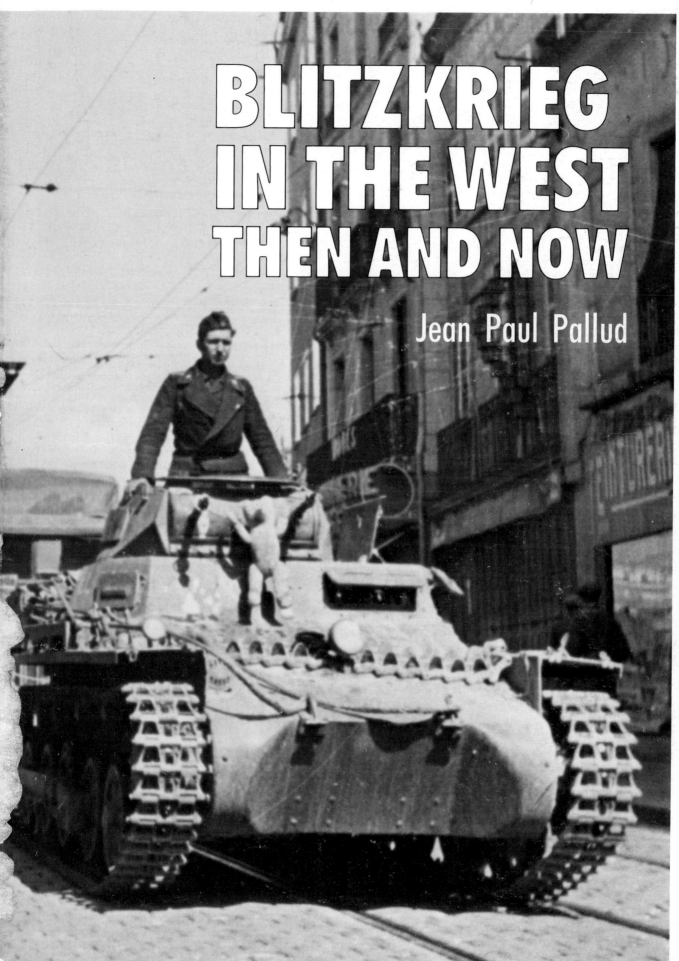

BLITZKRIEG
IN THE WEST
THEN AND NOW

Jean Paul Pallud

Credits

© *After the Battle* 1991
ISBN: 0 900913 68 1
Printed in Great Britain

Editor: Winston G. Ramsey
Sub-editor: Andrew Holmwood
Design: Jean Paul Pallud/
        Winston G. Ramsey

PUBLISHERS
Battle of Britain Prints
International Limited,
Church House, Church Street,
London E15 3JA, England
An *After the Battle* publication

PRINTERS
Plaistow Press Limited,
Church House, Church Street,
London E15 3JA, England

PHOTOGRAPHS
Copyright is indicated for all original illustrations where known. Present day photographs are the copyright of the author or *After the Battle* magazine unless stated otherwise. (See Picture Credits.)

EXTRACTS
Acknowledgement is given to the following authors and their publishers for permission to quote from published works:
Panzer Leader by H. Guderian, Futura, 1976.
Rommel Papers by B. H. Liddel-Hart, Collins, 1953.
Le temps des armes by P. Billotte, Plon, 1972.
En auto-mitrailleuses à travers les batailles de mai by Guy de Chézal, Plon, 1941.
Quelques-uns des chars by R. Bardel, Arthaud, 1945.
Hitler's War Directives: 1939–1945 by H. R. Trevor-Roper, Sidgwick and Jackson, 1964.
Opmars naar Rotterdam by E. Brongers, Baarn, 1982.
Finest Hour Winston Churchill 1939–1941 by Martin Gilbert, Heinemann, 1983.

FRONT COVER
Reproduced from a painting by George A. Campbell of Hitler receiving an enthusiastic send off after visiting Heeresgruppe A headquarters in Bastogne on May 17, 1940.

BACK COVER
'Ein grosser Tag in der deutschen Heeresgeschichte'. A great day in the history of the German Army noted General Franz Halder, Chief of the OKH, on June 14, 1940 as German troops entered Paris. Here a column marches down the Avenue de la Grande Armée.

FRONTISPIECE
The brilliant German victory in the west in May and June 1940 ensured everlasting fame to 'Blitzkrieg' and the panzers which made it a success. A PzKpfw II Ausf B of 4. Panzer-Division (complete with teddy bear mascot) rumbles down the Rue de la Liberté in Dijon on June 18, 1940.

FRONT ENDPAPER
The 'impregnable' Maginot Line. The GFM cupola (foreground) with a Mi turret (retracted) behind of Block 15 at Hochwald. The other two outlets are ventilation shafts.

REAR ENDPAPER
The battle lost, another column of French prisoners is marched towards their prisoner of war camp in Germany. In all, nearly a million and a half soldiers of the French Army were captured.

'The news from France is very bad, and I grieve for the gallant French people who have fallen into this terrible misfortune. Nothing will alter our feelings towards them or our faith that the genius of France will rise again. What has happened in France makes no difference to our actions and purpose. We have become the sole champions now in arms to defend the world cause. We shall do our best to be worthy of this high honour. We shall defend our Island home, and with the British Empire we shall fight on unconquerable until the curse of Hitler is lifted from the brows of mankind. We are sure that in the end all will come right.' Winston Churchill, June 17, 1940

AUTHOR'S ACKNOWLEDGEMENTS
The author would like to express his appreciation and thanks to the following: William Anhorn, Roger Avignon, Denis Bateman, Roger Bell, Pierre Coene, Claude Damm, Alain Dantoing, Jacques van Dijke, Pierre Gosset, Gérard Grégoire, Jacques Guérold, Albert Haas, Gérard Hénaut, Karel Margry, Georges Mazy, Stefan Meyer, Peter Mühlschlegel, Meinrad Nilges, André d'Olne, Régis Potié, Horst Riebensthal, Helmut Ritgen, Jean Louis Roba, Francis Sallaberry, Ian Sayer, Hubert Stembert, Francis Tirtiat, Jean Vanwelkenhuyzen, François Vasselle, Michel Viatour, Wolfgang Vopersal, Jean Bernard Wahl, and Henri de Wailly. Also to the American Battle Monuments Commission, the Commonwealth War Graves Commission, the Bundesarchiv in Freiburg and Koblenz, WASt archives in Berlin, the Volksbund Deutsche Kriegsgräberfürsorge in Kassel, ECPArmées in Paris, the Imperial War Museum in London, National Archives in Washington, Centre de Documentation Historique of the Belgian Army in Brussels, Centre de Recherches et d'Etudes sur la Seconde Guerre Mondiale in Brussels, Sectie Krijgseschiedenis ven der Generale Staf in The Hague and the Services Historiques de l'Armée in Vincennes.

Then . . . and now. With French forces reeling backwards in the face of the inexorable advance of the German spearheads, Général Antoine Besson, commanding Groupe d'Armees No. 3, tried to establish a new defence line behind the River Cher. However, on June 19, two days after Churchill's fateful broadcast, Besson had to fall back even further to the Indre. This German anti-tank crew overlook the Cher at Saint-Florent, 15 kilometres south-west of Bourges.

Contents

Introduction

On the morning of June 14, 1940, Soldat Sylvain Pallud — my father — a machine-gunner loader with the 108ème Régiment d'Infanterie Alpine, lay exhausted in a ditch at the side of the N19 near La Belle Etoile, 25 kilometres north-west of Troyes. For days he had fought across northern France, throughout a hectic withdrawal from the Aisne front where his gunner had been killed at his side near Cernay. Now, having been caught by panzers of 4. Panzer-Division pushing south wards, he lay with the surviving members of his unit on the edge of the forest. A German tank was driving up and down the road spraying the trees with machine gun fire while a French prisoner standing on the engine decking shouted again and again: 'Surrender! For you the war is over!'

Bullets were whistling above their heads and leaves and branches cut by the withering fire were falling on them. A soldier lying just behind my father was tugging at his feet and implored repeatedly: 'Go on Pallud! Tell them that we will surrender.'

Further down the road someone stood up, then another and another before the whole section came out of the wood. For Sylvain Pallud the war *was* over.

Fifty years later I motored across France on one of the many trips I have undertaken to take the comparison photographs for this book. Leaving Troyes on the N19 I tried to imagine the days in 1940 when this whole region of France was in turmoil, my country brought to its knees after barely four weeks fighting with nearly two million men killed, wounded, missing or prisoners of war.

At last La Belle Etoile came into view and the thoughts that here my father fought his last fight came flooding back. All was now at peace, the forest still, the road deserted. It was a moving moment and one which meant so much more to me after my five years study of Blitzkrieg in the West.

La Belle Etoile where Sylvain Pallud was forced to surrender on Friday, June 14, 1940, pictured fifty years later by a son following his father's footsteps.

To paint a clear, understandable picture of those dramatic six weeks which saw six nations battling across four countries is a daunting challenge, especially for the hectic first two weeks when Dutch, Belgian, German, French and British troops were involved; in the air, at sea, on land with paratroopers and panzers, armoured trains, cavalry, gunboats, et al.

As the battle progressed, although two combatants — Belgium and the Netherlands — dropped out, the area of the battlefield widened until it stretched from the Rhine valley on the frontier with Germany to the Spanish border on the Atlantic coast, and from the polders of the Netherlands in the north to the mountains of the Alps on the frontier with Italy.

I have drawn on the photographic archives of the Wehrmacht held in Koblenz, the National Archives in Washington, the French Army's own collection in Paris and British official pictures held in London. To these have been added a large number of 'private' photographs taken by soldiers on the move, the most well-known probably those of Rommel himself. I then found that on many occasions, the still photographers were working in conjunction with newsreel teams. This was true for both French and German reporters — the news films of both countries in May and June 1940 show actions that are pictured in this book. Typical examples appear on page 171 with the fording of the Amblève river, the attack across the Sûre river at Echternach on page 198, the shelling of the Maginot Line at Boussois on 304 and the BEF at Louvain on page 338.

The vast majority of the 5,000 photographs at my disposal were uncaptioned as to time or place and much midnight oil had to be burned to pinpoint the location concerned. Once this had been done the picture could be slotted into its rightful place in the overall canvas, with a detailed caption, rather than being used as just another 'Panzer on the Western Front'!

In spite of the culling of every known source of photographs, there are some aspects or areas that were not covered pictorially. The fact that I have not been able to include photographs of a particular action is not meant in any way to detract from its importance but is merely the consequence of the constraints imposed on me by the available photographs of the period. The heart of a strategic battle is not the easiest place to film — even if it is recognised as such at the time — and inevitably war photographers concentrated on photogenic scenes whatever they were. Thulin on pages 315–324 is a good example yet the coverage given this small village by Eric Borchert might easily tend to give it an undue importance of what was, in effect, just one small, local action.

War crimes is one aspect of war rarely covered pictorially and seldom adequately documented. The shameful behaviour of some German units is certainly proven, but isolated transgressions by some Allied personnel remain in the shadow of the victor's desire to suppress any suggestion of war crimes by its own armies. To the objective author, writing nearly half a century later, it appears that the record in this respect is still incomplete.

Though the German armour played a decisive part in the campaign, the panzers were not so numerous as the pictures in this book might suggest. Inevitably, the armour was much photographed at the expense of other facets of the battle, be it Guderian's panzers or Rommel's spearheads, or knocked out Allied tanks. In the latter category the French Renault B1 bis particularly impressed German photographers and the knocked out hulks, like whales stranded on a beach, featured predominantly in many of their pictures. Were we to have accurately reflected the historic balance, then more infantry pictures and much horse-drawn equipment should have been featured.

The Maginot Line in France, and, to a lesser extent the Belgian forts at Liège and Namur, have their own special place although they failed to achieve the rôle for which they had been constructed. The Belgian fortresses and the Maginot Line were simply bypassed by the main German attacks and even the secondary action against the fortresses was more in the nature of a holding action. Although the Blitzkrieg war of 1940 proved the impregnable forts to be colossal steel and concrete white elephants, nevertheless they remain the major relics of the battle to be seen today.

With such a vast area to cover photographically, I obtained the help of local contributors including Jacques van Dijke and Karel Margry in the Netherlands, Jean-Louis Roba and Francis Tirtiat in Belgium, Régis Potié in the north of France and Henri de Wailly on the Somme. Even so I have taken more than 90 percent of the comparisons myself, a task which has allowed me — perhaps the first time anyone has done so in such detail — to explore every corner of the battlefield: from the wooded valleys of the Ardennes, so significant for the breakthrough of the Allied line at Sedan; to the plains of the Gembloux gap in Belgium and the largest tank battle of the campaign; to the unspoilt countryside of France where the panzers sometimes clocked up 100 kilometres a day in their march to the sea.

One major difficulty was to sort out the time problem. Since the end of February 1940, Britain, France and Belgium were all on the same time — GMT

Father and son discuss the Blitzkrieg war: Pallud Senior with author Jean Paul.

plus one hour — while the Germans were one hour ahead (GMT plus two hours) and the Netherlands an unbelievable 40 minutes and 28 seconds behind (GMT plus 19 minutes 32 seconds). This meant that the neighbouring Belgians were also living 40 minutes and 28 seconds ahead of the Dutch — a somewhat ridiculous situation! Therefore, to be consistent throughout the book, I have chosen the most common time, GMT plus one hour, then in use in Britain, Belgium and France but where necessary the German equivalent is also given. Undoubtedly, this time inconsistency has led in the past to many errors or ambiguity in the various books or documents consulted, depending on their origination. I trust that I, too, have not erred in this direction.

There are arguments for and against using modern maps of the battlefield. Motorways of course did not exist then and clutter the countryside today. However, in view of *After the Battle's* particular approach to show the battlefields as they are today, on balance we have decided to use the modern version of the appropriate Michelin map. In this way, the visitor is not only guided to the area in the best way, but also the battles can be viewed in the context of today, rather than fifty years ago.

The past five years for me have been a very rewarding experience. Not only have I learned much of my own country's recent history but my efforts have resulted in a book that presents the Blitzkrieg in the West in a way never before attempted. To me, 'then and now' photographs bring history alive. To stand on the precise spot where men once fought and died is an emotional experience not easily forgotten. I hope in the following pages that you too can experience what I saw and felt as I moved in the tracks of the panzers — now faded but not yet forgotten.

JEAN PAUL PALLUD

Part I
AT WAR AGAIN

Peace for our time

In 1919, France tried to persuade her allies to agree to the permanent occupation of the Rhineland to guard against a renewal of German aggression, but she failed to convince them.

In September 1939, only twenty years since France and Britain had emerged victorious from the 'war to end wars', the two nations once more found themselves allies in another war with Germany. This time no popular excitement greeted its declaration. The carnage of 1914-18 was of too recent memory, the prospect of future horrors too ghastly to contemplate. If Hitler was to be stopped and war was the only way of stopping him, then so be it. In fighting a war that had become inevitable, however, tragically for France and Britain, neither of them possessed the capacity for waging an all out war of aggression.

Germany had been defeated in 1918, but had suffered comparatively less than victorious France. Although German economy had been disrupted by the blockade, most of her factories, mines and steelworks remained intact. Germany had lost some 2,000,000 men, about 9.8 percent of her active male population while France, with 'only' 1,385,000 dead, had lost 10 percent of hers. A large part of France had been ravaged by the fighting; hundreds of towns had to be completely rebuilt; the mines, steelworks and factories of the north-east were devastated.

France had received only a fraction of her 52 percent share of the 132 millions of gold marks that Germany was required to pay in reparation for the damage she had caused. In 1923, in default of German payments, France and Belgium had occupied the Ruhr. Payments were kept up until 1928 when they defaulted and in 1929 the Young

Plan cut reparations by 75 percent. By 1932, with Germany unable and unwilling to pay, reparation payments had been abolished altogether.

In 1919, to guard against a renewal of German aggression, France had tried hard to get Britain and the United States to agree to a permanent Allied occupation of the Rhineland, but all she could obtain was demilitarisation and a fifteen-year occupation as a temporary measure of security. Under the clear impression that she had been abandoned by her former Allies, France was left dispirited in the thirties when she was badly depleted in manpower. Her losses in the Great War (as World War I was generally known prior to 1939) had

France could only achieve demilitarisation and temporary occupation. Her War Minister, M. André Maginot, went on an inspection of the Allied troops in the Rhineland in the spring of 1922. Here he is pictured in front of the railway station in Koblenz on April 25. The Hotel Höhmann was still in business when we took this comparison on the Bahnhofsplatz in April 1989, 67 years later.

The fifteen-year occupation of the Rhineland, agreed at last by Britain and the United States, was far from the long-term security measure desired by France. Under the impression that she had been abandoned by her allies, France was dispirited. On July 14, 1922, Général Jean-Marie Degoutte led the parade in Mayence (Mainz), one of the main towns of the Rhineland.

been so shattering that a whole generation of unborn sons was lost and in 1939, there were 300,000 fewer Frenchmen to defend their homeland than there were in 1914.

Victory had bred complacency and stagnation. The Allies had preferred to believe that their eventual victory proved that their methods were right; the Germans had sought the reasons for the failure of theirs. Though the German High Command had found scapegoats to explain away defeat to the people, and blamed politicians for having 'stabbed the Army in the back', they had looked hard at the lessons to be learned and had developed new

techniques and tactics. Except for a handful of officers, radical thinking was not for the French and British generals who viewed fresh theories and new ideas with caution.

France had retained a large conscript army, but while the High Command lived on its former glory and became increasingly outdated in its thinking, financial strictures did little to encourage re-equipment and modernisation. Since the early twenties military spending was angled towards defence, and in 1925 the then Minister of War, Paul Painlevé, had expressed the aim of achieving 'a rational system of national defence, adequate in times of danger

but unsuited to adventures and conquests'. Apart from the strong anti-war sentiment induced by the squandering of lives in the Great War, there were other reasons for this essentially defensive posture, not least, that as a result of the war, France had regained Alsace and Lorraine from Germany and wished only to remain secure within her own borders. Practical expression of the policy to which Painlevé referred, and the security which France sought, was to be found in the fortifications built along the frontier with Germany — a 'line' which was to become known by the name of Painlevé's successor at the War Ministry, André Maginot.

In 1923, in response to Germany's default over the war reparations she had to pay for the damage she had caused during the war, France and Belgium occupied the Ruhr. *Left:* These French soldiers were pictured in front of the main post office in Essen, on January 15, 1923. *Right:* The post office has disappeared, probably destroyed during the Second World War, but the buildings opposite were still unchanged when we took this comparison in 1989.

With the increasing international tension created by Hitler's abrogation of the Versailles Treaty in 1935, followed by the occupation of the Rhineland in 1936, and take-over of Austria in March 1938, the British Prime Minister sought a meeting with the German Chancellor. *Left:* Here on September 15, Neville Chamberlain is escorted from Berchtesgaden station by the German Foreign Minister, Joachim von Ribbentrop (on the left) and Minister of State, Otto Meissner.

In March 1935, Hitler had asserted his will by denouncing the military clauses of the Versailles Treaty; conscription was decreed, an army of 36 divisions and a Luftwaffe were to be established and the construction of two battleships, two heavy cruisers, 16 destroyers and 28 submarines was announced. In turn, France signed a treaty with the Soviet Union and Hitler, claiming this as contrary to the Locarno Treaty, chose the opportunity to re-occupy the demilitarised zone of the Rhineland in defiance of the Locarno Treaty. Signs of what was going on had been clear since the beginning of 1936 and the French government debated the launching of a military operation if ever Hitler sent troops into the Rhineland. In reply, the French High Command explained that the Army was organised only for defence and not ready for any offensive operations. Nevertheless plans were drawn up for the occupation of the left bank of the Sarre river up to Merzig.

While Britain did not wish to see France engaged in what was seen to be a hazardous operation, nevertheless proposals for a naval blockade also foundered in the face of Britain's conciliatory attitude. When Hitler finally sent in his troops on March 7, both Britain and France contented themselves with verbal protests only.

At a rally on September 12 Hitler had stated his next territorial claim — against the part of Czechoslovakia called the Sudetenland — and so precipitated the 'Munich Crisis'. Chamberlain's first meeting failed to resolve the problem, neither did a second held at Bad Godesberg a few days later. However, Italy proposed an international conference to help defuse the situation, to which Hitler agreed. On September 29 representatives of Britain, France, Italy and Germany met at the Nazi party headquarters in Munich although Czechoslovakia was not invited.

Consultations between Britain and France at this time, which the British had suddenly asked for during the crisis over Italy and Abyssinia in October

Left: The first session over, the French and British delegations returned to their hotels to study the proposals but Mussolini, as honoured guest, enjoyed lunch with Hitler. *Right:* The Führerbau building now houses the State High School for Music.

The final drama came at 1.30 a.m. on Friday morning, September 30. The document sealing the fate of Czechosolvakia had been already dated September 29 but by now everyone was too tired to worry about the error. Hitler signed first, followed by Chamberlain, Mussolini and Daladier. The Czechs had no say in the matter and it was another bloodless coup for Hitler.

1935, amounted to little more than the occasional exchange of technical information. Although it was virtually taken for granted by the late 1930s that if there was to be another war, both countries would be in it together, Britain was wary of anything that might be construed as indicative of a military alliance with France whilst pursuing a policy of appeasement towards Germany.

In March 1938, Hitler marched into Austria, but France and Britain did nothing more than proclaim their indignant disapproval. The 'Anschluss' was proclaimed after a plebiscite and Austria was soon absorbed into the 'Greater Reich'. Agitation by German minorities in the Sudeteland then increased, and it appeared that Czechoslovakia was the next victim, but once again France and Britain failed to agree on a united stand in the face of aggression. France, which had just recovered some semblance of political stability when Daladier formed a new government on April 10, was willing to take some action but had to confess that her Army was not ready to bring direct help — by invading Germany — if ever Hitler invaded Czechoslovakia. In London, Chamberlain was still clinging to his policy of appeasement — a word which then did not have the same overtones that it does today. In September, Britain and France yielded once more and signed the Munich agreement which effectively dismembered Czechoslovakia — the Czechs having no say in the matter.

Chamberlain, exuberant in the thought that he had just secured the peace of the world, proposed to Hitler an Anglo-German Declaration which stated that both countries were 'determined to continue our efforts to remove possible sources of difference and thus to contribute to assure the peace of Europe'. This was the declaration he waved aloft when he returned to Heston. Later, speaking from 10 Downing Street, he announced that it was 'Peace for our time'.

Edouard Daladier, the French Prime Minister, was not so enthusiastic and was somewhat surprised to be greeted by a cheerful crowd at Le Bourget airfield. Descending from his aircraft, he is reported to have commented dejectedly 'Les Cons!' (Fools!). Today, with the advantage of access to the records of both sides, it is believed that Germany would have only survived a matter of days in September 1938 had her 12 divisions had to fight the 100 French divisions then in being.

At the end of the First World War France had the most powerful army in the world, but the High Command lived on its glory and was increasingly outdated in its thinking. Here Maréchal Philippe Pétain inspects the 231ème R.A. in 1921. Successive governments of the Republic did little to modernise the army, and by the thirties it was a far cry from what it had been.

At the end of World War I, France was considered to have the most powerful army in the world; since then it seemed to have gone unnoticed that the French Army of the thirties was a far cry from what it had been in 1918. For years French governments had been careful to prevent an offensive capacity being built into the Army, and had remained deaf to demands by the High Command for modernisation. It was not until 1934 that rearmament was at last agreed, but the period of political instability that followed — eight governments between 1934 and 1939 — and social and economic difficulties did little to support it. In 1938, after the 'Anschluss', the urgency was finally perceived, and renewed efforts made to increase the pace but by then it was far too late.

In Britain, defence spending was governed from 1919 to 1928 by the assumption of Lloyd George's Coalition War Cabinet that there would be no major war for ten years — this belief being then reviewed annually. The Royal Air Force was under strength, the Army bereft of weapons and equipment. Although the 'ten-year rule' was reappraised by the MacDonald government in 1932, no real attempt at rearmament came before 1936: people wanted peace, not arms. Once war was declared, however, despite the Labour and Liberal parties' refusal to enter into a coalition with Chamberlain's Conservative government, Parliament and the country as a whole were united in their opposition to Hitler.

France, then under the 108th Prime Minister of the Third Republic, Edouard Daladier, entered the war with mixed feelings. Understandably, there was a widespread dread of war as people shuddered at the thought of

country having to endure another blood-letting like that of 1914-18. Anti-German sentiments were strong and widespread in France but, on the extreme Right, a small minority saw Hitler as a bulwark against Bolshevism, while another, larger though less

extreme, of the right wing groups admired Mussolini as a shining example of what the power of leadership could achieve. On the far Left, the Communist party had long proclaimed its part in the struggle against Fascism but now performed a volte-face to accomodate Stalin and Hitler's non-aggression pact. Insidious Communist propaganda, in opposition to an 'imperialist, capitalist' war, had its effect, and accompanying subversion came acts of sabotage against the war effort.

If war had come in with a bang, it might have helped attain national unity; when it came in with a yawn, eight months of 'drôle de guerre' did nothing to help bring that about. The Finance Minister in Daladier's government, Paul Reynaud, was called upon to form a government in March 1940. Although more of a 'fighter', he could count on only a bare minimum of party political support and was to be no better served in his choice of Ministers for a politically-balanced government in the national interest.

Relations between the 'Western Allies' had been put to the test by serious differences in foreign policy since the end of the Great War. The Entente Cordiale had not forged feelings of great affection in war; in the ensuing peace there was a fundamental difference of attitude between the two nations towards their former enemy: the French motivated by the need for security; the British conciliatory in spite of the evidence. Mutual fear of German domination had ultimately brought them back into partnership. Their

On the eve of the Second World War the equipment of the French soldier was not so different from that of the victorious 'poilus' of 1918. The 8mm Hotchkiss Modèle 14 had seen service during the Great War but it was still the standard machine gun in 1940. A sturdy and efficient weapon, it nevertheless lacked punch.

Meanwhile the Germans had developed new techniques and tactics, the grouping of their tanks into mobile and powerful panzer formations being the decisive weapon of the 'lightning war' (Blitzkrieg) philosophy. However, they possessed only ten armoured divisions in May 1940. This is the 6. Panzer-Division with a PzKpfw 35(t) in the lead, followed by PzKpfw IVs.

peoples — the majority of them — viewed each other with, at best, suspicion. As late as March 1940, Winston Churchill, a devoted friend of France, was to lament on there being 'no effective intimacy with the French'.

Detailed talks between the two staffs were agreed by the British in February 1939. The first round took place on March 29, in the wake of the failure of the Munich agreement to prevent Hitler dismembering those parts of Czechoslovakia not ceded to him by Chamberlain and Daladier the previous September.

In France and Britain the scales belatedly began to fall from eyes blind to the fact that Hitler's word counted for nothing — that appeasing his demands would not deter him. In the two months that followed his taking the

Czech provinces of Bohemia and Moravia under German 'protection', and the disappearance of Czechoslovakia as an independent state, Hitler seized Memel, denounced the Anglo-German Naval Treaty and his non-aggression pact with Poland and signed a 'Pact of Steel' with Italy, which had in the meantime invaded Albania.

Compared with Germany, France's inferiority in manpower in the armed forces was alarming. The French Command had calculated in 1936 that the number of potential German soldiers (about 13,100,000 mobilisable men) would be by 1940 about twice as large as the French total (about 6,700,000). In 1939, current estimates were that France would be able to mobilise 100 divisions with fortress troops amounting

to another 16 divisions. With about ten divisions needed to man the Italian frontier and a dozen or so for North Africa, France would thus have the equivalent of about 95 divisions to garrison the Maginot Line on the north-east front and to deploy against Germany. With the addition of the four British divisions, the Allies would have a total of less than 100 divisions on the north-east front while Germany was thought to be able to mobilise at least 116 divisions by the middle of September, plus fifty or so over the months to follow.

The French Army units were of variable quality, reflecting the breadth of national conscription. They ranged from excellent for the Active units to poor, or less than poor, for the Series B

It must also be remembered that the bulk of the German Army was still composed of infantry divisions, albeit equipped with reasonably modern weapons like the MG 34 machine gun.

However the army still depended heavily on railways or marching on foot for deployment, and on horse-drawn transport for moving supplies in the field.

Nevertheless the French Army had developed a sizeable tank force like these Renault R-35s of the 12ème B.C.C. *(above)*, pictured during a parade in the winter of 1939. However the tank tactics favoured by the High Command were obsolete, parcelling them out in penny packets in close support of the infantry. Only a handful of officers emphasised the principle of concentration of armour, and the vital importance of mobility, one being Colonel Charles de Gaulle *(right)* in October 1939 when he was in command of the tanks of the 5ème Armée. This shot was taken during a visit by President Albert Lebrun. The cavalry was the first to adopt — though cautiously — these new ideas, and since 1935 it had developed a mechanised division, the D.L.M. The infantry followed and designated an armoured divison, termed the D.C.R. By May 1940 the French Army had three D.L.M.s, each with about 160 tanks and about 100 armoured cars, and three D.C.R. with 160 tanks apiece.

Britain had seven mechanised divisional cavalry regiments on the Continent with the British Expeditionary Force in May 1940, each regiment being equipped with 28 light tanks and 44 carriers. This shot of the 1st Fife and Forfar Yeomanry on manoeuvres shows Mark VI light tanks in the foreground with carriers behind.

units. The Active divisions, about a third of the available divisions at the time of the mobilisation, had mainly regular officers and NCOs and most of the men were regulars except for a number who had recently passed to the reserve. Next in quality were the Series A divisions which had a slightly smaller complement of regular officers and NCOs but which were basically made up of reservists. The Series B divisions had an even lower complement of trained men, only a few regular officers per regiment, and were made up of the oldest military classes, their ranks having an average age of 36.

The most that Britain had been in a position to send to the Continent was a mere two regular divisions. By the end of April this was doubled to four, to be sent to France within 33 days of mobilisation as an Expeditionary Force, which was to have an Air Component. In addition, an Advanced Air Striking Force of bombers was to be despatched at the outset. In February, a decision had been taken in principle to create an army of 32 divisions within a year of war breaking out. The following month it was decided to double the size of the Territorial Army and on April 27 the intention to introduce conscription was announced.

Within three months of mobilisation, Britain despatched five regular divisions to France, and in January 1940 the first Territorial division arrived. *Left:* A carrier of the 2nd Infantry Division traversing rough terrain near Arras in October 1939. *Right:* These officers were pictured in April in the Sarre, that area of France directly opposite the Saar.

The Allies and Poland

Propaganda on the Rhine! German signs on the eastern bank asking the French to 'help' the Germans make peace and to 'send the British back home'.

The population of the Danzig area, once part of Prussia, was overwhelmingly ethnically German. The port of Danzig had been declared a 'Free City' with a League of Nations Commissioner when Poland had been re-established under the terms of the Versailles Treaty, the new state's boundaries being extended to provide access to the Baltic. This creation of what was later to be termed the 'Danzig Corridor' cut off East Prussia from Germany and created an obvious source of future conflict. Poland had been given responsibility for Danzig's foreign policy, commerce and customs controls. From 1933 onwards the Nazi party controlled the city's senate.

The Polish-German non-aggression pact which Hitler denounced in April had been signed in 1934. In fact, Hitler nurtured hopes of Poland aligning herself with Germany against the Soviet Union; the Poles, much as they loathed the Russians, had no desire to compromise their own future. In November 1938 they rejected German proposals for Danzig to be incorporated into the Reich and for a German-controlled road and rail link with the city, in return for which Germany would guarantee her border with Poland and extend the non-aggression pact for twenty-five years. Hitler put forward the same proposals in January 1939 and Foreign Minister Ribbentrop tried again. The most that the 'colonels' who governed Poland would consent to were talks on a road-rail link, but not to extra-territorial rights, and on replacing Danzig's League of Nations status by a Polish-German arrangement, but not to the city becoming a part of Germany.

By the end of March this private stalemate had erupted into a public row. The Poles took up an offer of a guarantee from Britain to come to their support if Polish independence was threatened, and in April emissaries went to London where they offered to reciprocate in support of Belgium, the Netherlands, Denmark and Switzerland, and negotiations were started. In May, they went to Paris for discussions with the French. Like the British, the French baulked at what the Poles defined as being in their 'national interest'; for the idea of a guarantee had been to deter Hitler, not to encourage the Poles in their belief that they had a strong case over the Danzig question. At the conclusion of the Paris talks, a military agreement between France and Poland, subject to a political accord, was left unsigned when the Polish War Minister, General Thaddeusz Kasprzycki, returned home.

Tension mounted throughout the summer, the passionately-proud Polish leaders doing nothing to ease the tensions with Germany, and a crisis was reached in early August when the Polish representative in Danzig informed the local German authorities that henceforth Polish customs officials would be armed. Any attempt, he said, to obstruct them in carrying out their duties and the Polish government would 'retaliate without delay against the Free City'. To the Poles, this was a firm response to further provocation by the

When Hitler attacked Poland it was the final straw and Britain and France responded by declaring war on Germany. It was a brave act for neither country was really prepared for a major conflict. Winston Churchill, First Lord of the Admiralty, came to Arras in January 1940 with General Sir Edmund Ironside, the Chief of the Imperial General Staff (left in this picture) to meet General Lord Gort (right), the commander of the BEF. Also present were Général Alphonse Georges, Commander-in-Chief North-East Front, and Général Maurice Gamelin, the French Chief of the General Staff.

Although Général Gamelin believed that the best way of threatening Germany was through aggressive action launched 'between the Moselle and the Meuse', this option was ruled out by the neutral stance which had been adopted by Belgium.

Left: A commandant of a recce cavalry unit of the 1ère Armée inspects his squadron of Panhard P-178 scout cars. *Right:* A sentinel from the 2ème Armée stands guard at a road block — impotently waiting on the Belgian border.

Danzig people; to the Germans, another instance of the repression of their compatriots. The Polish press and radio blazed national resolve. Hitler, who had drawn up contingency plans long ago, decided that it was time to crush Poland and her arrogant leaders, and on August 25 he issued orders for the attack to begin.

Hitler gambled on France and Britain opting out of going to war over Danzig. He gambled too on their not attacking Germany in the West while the Wehrmacht was occupied in the East. For a moment he wavered, postponing the attack on Poland following the news that Italy would not follow him in the event of war and that Britain had signed and intended to stand by the Anglo-Polish mutual assistance pact. If it came to a war involving France and Britain, he knew though that the odds were in

favour of there being no threat to Germany's rear. Belgian neutrality was one factor of which he could be certain. In the flurry of diplomatic exchanges at the eleventh hour, the German ambassador to Belgium had met King Leopold and told him what he most wanted to hear: that Germany would respect Belgium's neutrality, while the King assured the ambassador that Belgium would remain uncommitted. Belgium would also resist any intrusion along her frontiers, including that with France. His rear assured, Hitler ordered the attack on Poland to commence on September 1.

The same day, the French Chief of the General Staff, Général Maurice Gamelin, wrote to Prime Minister Daladier to the effect that 'the present attitude of Belgium is playing entirely into German hands' and stating that the

best way to attack Germany would be 'between the Moselle and Meuse'. Any aggressive intentions along these lines that might have been entertained by Général Gamelin were ruled out for the time being and the means of rendering assistance to the Poles lay in a limited operation in a far less favourable sector, the Sarre (Saar).

The bulk of the Wehrmacht was then deployed against Poland but the Third Reich had not committed all its forces to the East, and a few days after the outbreak of war, when reserves had been brought up, there were 43 German divisions on the Western Front. In front of them the North-East Front commander, Général Alphonse Georges, could dispose of 57 divisions, all of them French, for the first British troops, I Corps, would not arrive in the Lille sector until the beginning of October.

The French decided to mount an attack on the Sarre (Saar), in which the 4ème Armée was given the main rôle. *Left:* Here the army commander, Général Edouard Requin, visits the 62ème

Division d'Infanterie at Hellimer, 18 kilometres south of Saint-Avold. *Right:* Hellimer in 1987 — a rainy day reminiscent of that winter's day in 1939.

France's Sarre Offensive

On September 9, a communiqué triumphantly announced that the greater part of the Warndt area of the Saar was in French hands. Here French troops stroll in Lauterbach.

Orders to prepare for an attack in the Sarre and the Palatinate intended by the French High Command to relieve the pressure on Poland if she were invaded, had been issued to the commander of Groupe d'Armées No. 2, Général Gaston Prételat, in May. The 4ème Armée of Général Edouard Requin was to have the main rôle in the offensive planned by the army group but the 3ème Armée of Général Charles-Marie Condé and the 5ème Armée of Général Victor Bourret were to play their parts on both flanks. In the opening stages, units of the 4ème and 5ème Armées were to attack east of Saarbrücken on a 35-kilometre-wide front and the 3ème Armée was to follow in attacking west of the town; the intention being to capture, as a basis for 'further operations', the heights east of Saarbrücken and the whole south bank of the Sarre river from Merzig to Bübingen. Despite visions of smashing through the Siegfried Line at a subsequent stage, there was little enthusiasm for looking that far ahead. Besides, Général Prételat could only base the offensive on the build-up of his forces: on September 8, five days after the outbreak of war, the army group had only 10 divisions available in addition to the fortress troops manning the Maginot Line, these troops having no offensive capacity.

Commanding the German 1. Armee holding this sector, General Erwin von Witzleben, had 13 divisions as well as various frontier units, and the efficiency of the German mobilisation plan meant that his reinforcements had begun to arrive as soon as war broke out — at a faster rate than the French facing him.

To declare war was one thing but to fire the first shot was another and the first days of war on the Sarre front were uneventful. In a number of places, the border guards of both countries had continued to chat and swop cigarettes for some time after war had been declared as if nothing had happened. The French knew well enough that the Germans desperately needed to keep things quiet in the West and were not fooled by German efforts to avoid any provocation. As Général Requin, in his General Order No. 1 issued on September 7, 1939, admonished his men: 'There is only one way to conduct war for the Germans and their current behaviour in front of us is only aimed at gaining time to crush Poland. The time has come to hit hard and answer with guns and machine guns all attempts at fraternisation. Any of the enemy to show up will be killed or captured . . . Everybody must be convinced that the present war knows neither weakness nor pity'.

The atmosphere at the border changed rapidly, although in some places it was to take a few more days yet for years-old patterns of behaviour to be broken. Thus while the men of Détachement Marion — a 4ème Armée mobile force assembled under Colonel Pierre Marion — entered Germany and occupied the village of Emmersweiler on September 7, the customs officials were still chatting away at la Vieille-Verrerie, a few kilometres to the north.

This shot of men of the 42ème Division d'Infanterie chatting in front of the Gasthaus Josef Siegwart enabled us to take a superb comparison in Lauterbach. Although the inn is no more, otherwise time has stood still for fifty years.

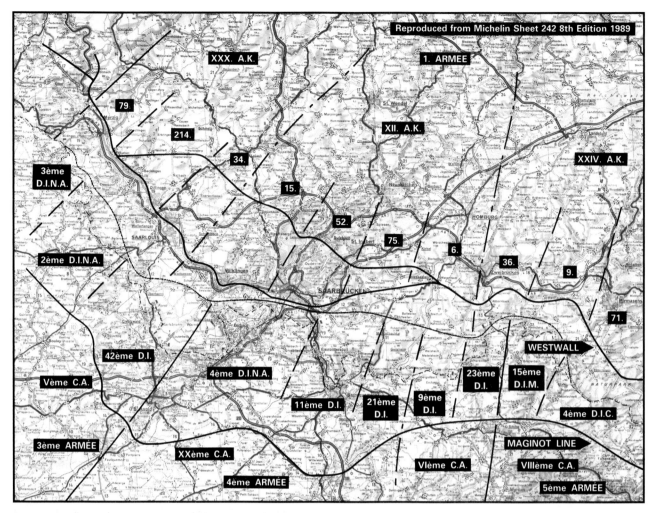

XXX. A.K.

1. ARMEE

79.

214.

34.

3ème
D.I.N.A.

XII. A.K.

15.

XXIV. A.K.

52.

75.

2ème D.I.N.A.

6.

36.

9.

71.

WESTWALL

42ème D.I.

4ème D.I.N.A.

Vème C.A.

23ème
D.I.

15ème
D.I.M.

11ème D.I.

21ème
D.I.

9ème
D.I.

4ème D.I.C.

3ème ARMEE

XXème C.A.

MAGINOT LINE

4ème ARMEE

VIème C.A.

VIIIème C.A.

5ème ARMEE

The Sarre offensive was fought in the 15-kilometre-wide strip of land that lay between the two main defence lines: the German Westwall in the north, the French Maginot Line in the south. The French advanced into Germany but proceeded cautiously and the gains were relatively small: some 200 square kilometres of ground and fifty villages. This was the situation by mid-September when the French 'offensive' halted and orders were issued to take up defensive positions.

This relaxed atmosphere and the swopping of cigarettes was not to end there until September 14, eleven days after the declaration of war, when a French NCO, fed up with it all, let fly with his rifle just over the heads of the German officials. Away they scurried, never attempting to fraternise again.

On September 3, conscious of the swift advances being made by the Wehrmacht in Poland, Gamelin urged Prételat to launch the planned operation in the Sarre the next day. The necessary troops had not yet all arrived; although units of the 3ème Armée attacked in the Warndt, a wooded area to the southwest of Saarbrücken, on September 4 and strong patrols were sent into Germany all along the front, it was not until September 6 that Général Prételat felt that he had the forces to enable him to issue the general order to attack. On September 7 the German Chief of the Army Staff, General Franz Halder, noted in his diary Hitler's view conveyed to the Army C-in-C, Generaloberst Walther von Brauchitsch: 'Operations in the West not yet clear. Some indications that there is no real intention of waging war . . .'

Between September 7 and 9, various French attacks got under way, and on the latter date eight Active divisions,

A soldier of the 151ème R.I., 42ème Division d'Infanterie, examines the plate on the Colonial Office in Lauterbach, perhaps debating whether it was worth lifting as a souvenir.

The capture of Lauterbach had, in fact, been easy, for the Germans had evacuated the village! The 'Am 13 Januar' sign referred to the plebiscite of January 13, 1935, which returned the Saar to Germany with an overwhelming majority vote.

two of them motorised, five battalions of tanks and numerous artillery units were assigned to the operation. Moving forward was seldom easy and not without casualties, for the Germans had erected a huge number of obstacles, sown mines everywhere and left booby traps behind in all the villages as they withdrew.

In the 4ème Armée sector, units of the 11ème Division d'Infanterie crossed the Sarre river and reached Eschringen while troops of the 21ème Division d'Infanterie were soon seven kilometres inside Germany on the heights overlooking the Blies valley. In the 3ème Armée sector, the 42ème Division d'Infanterie occupied the Warndt salient and soon reached Differten, only about two kilometres south of the Sarre river. It was a measured, cautious advance.

On September 9, a French communiqué triumphantly announced that the greater part of the Warndt salient was in French hands and referred to the success of the offensive. While French and British newspapers told of great victories as the offensive moved deeper into Germany, the 'limited' and 'methodical' operations that had been initiated were in fact already beginning to peter out. The idea of attacking the Siegfried Line or of launching an offensive through it into the heart of Germany had never really been contemplated by the French High Command.

On September 12, because of the way in which Poland was rapidly being overwhelmed, Général Gamelin decided that the 4ème and 5ème Armées were to keep far enough away from the German defences so that these could

not be used as a base for counter-attacks. Army commanders, he advised, should bear in mind withdrawal as an eventuality in view of a possible German move through Belgium. Two days later, Général Prételat issued orders to take up defensive positions on the ground that had been won; the 3ème Armée maintained the pressure in the Moselle valley up to the end of the month, but that was the extent of offensive operations. The gains, such as they were, consisted of about 200 square kilometres of ground and some 50 German villages.

The 1. Armee continued to reinforce and was planning a counterstroke to recover the ground lost to the French. A new division, the 73. Infanterie-Division, was inserted on the right flank of the XII. Armeekorps between Volklingen and Saarlautern. In the East, during the last two weeks of September, Germany and the Soviet Union were carving up Poland between them; soon it would be possible for the bulk of the German units to be brought back to the West.

On September 30, the North-East Front commander, Général Georges, arrived at Général Prételat's headquarters at Villers-les-Nancy to tell Prételat and his three army commanders what they already knew — that to remain in enemy territory, in front of the Maginot Line, with no aggressive plan in mind no longer served any purpose — and to inform them that the time had come for a general withdrawal to the frontier defences. So ended the vaunted Sarre 'offensive', which cost the French Army, 27 killed, 22 wounded and 28 missing and the French Air Force, 9 fighters and 18 reconnaissance aircraft, and which brought little relief to Poland.

The French withdrawal went more or less as planned in spite of a general attack launched by the 1. Armee on October 16. That morning 3ème Armée units came under fire as they were pulling back, and other attacks followed in the afternoon in the 4ème and 5ème Armée sectors. With the Germans close on the heels of the French, these had no appreciable effect except for bagging a few troops whose units had not adhered strictly to the timetable laid down.

Further to the west, in the Moselle valley, on the fringe of where the offensive had been mounted, a local attack launched by the XXIII. Armeekorps achieved a little more as it surprised the 36ème Division d'Infanterie in the Perl sector; in a somewhat disorganised withdrawal a strip of French soil had been given up to the Germans. This was of no real importance anyway, and after a couple of weeks of moves and countermoves, with the odd firefights erupting, by the end of October all the French troops were back on the frontier defences. Having reoccupied the terrain abandoned by the French, the Germans made no attempt to continue their advance and over the ensuing weeks the French relinquished even more when the High Command ordered some awkward salients to be given up.

Recaptured by the French in 1945, after two years of argument the Saar voted once again to be a part of Germany, finally becoming the tenth 'Land' of the Federal Republic in June 1959.

The Maginot Line

All along France's north-eastern frontier the Maginot Line stood guard. *Above:* The 75mm turret of Block 8 at Simserhof and *below* the barbed wire and tank obstacles at Hackenberg.

Along the Maginot Line, the 75mm howitzers of Block 7b of Hochwald-Est fired the first shots in anger on the night of September 8 in support of an infantry attack in the Schweigen area. These turned out to be the opening shots of the 'drôle de guerre' for the troops along the Line. In this 'queer kind of war' the two major battles that they were called on to face were on the propaganda front and against boredom. The Germans, by radio, loudspeaker broadcasts and the use of huge posters, waged a concerted campaign. One of the themes frequently employed concentrated on asking what the war was about and why anyone should be fighting it, and another harped on the British fighting to the last Frenchman. Shots broke the silence occasionally when test-firing was carried out, starting on September 10 at the Schoenenbourg fortress, continuing at Bréhain and Latiremont on October 3 and 21, and at Métrich in November. Patrols were sent out at night and some of the fortresses fired occasionally at German troop concentrations, as when the 75mm turret of Block 8 in the Simserhof fortress fired 79 shells at Hill 370 on January 10. Likewise on January 18, when Block 2's 75mm turret of Four-à-Chaux fired a similar number of shells at the village of Nothweiler, near where a German unit had shown up about eight kilometres to the north.

ORIGIN AND DEVELOPMENT

After the disaster in the war between France and Germany in 1870 and the loss of Alsace and Lorraine, France had decided to protect its border and build a powerful fortified line facing Germany. Constructed under the direction of Général Raymond Séré de Rivière, this line was essentially two arcs of fortifications, each being based on a powerful fortified position at either end and having six fortresses at intervals. The first of these arcs ran between Belfort and Epinal, the second between Toul and Verdun. The gap separating the two arcs was controlled by a fortress at Manonviller.

The line was obsolete when war broke out in 1914 with some of the forts already unfortified, but this fact was not appreciated, and when individual strongpoints fell in the first months of the war, it reinforced criticism over the uselessness of permanent fortifications. Consequently most of the forts remaining in French hands were partly disarmed in 1915. However the success of the defence at Verdun, and the part

Although the original commission had been set up by his predecessor at the War Ministry, it was M. André Maginot (pictured here in the Rhineland with Général Jean-Marie Degoutte on July 14, 1922) who presented the final project and hence became the 'Father of the Line'.

Above: **By the early thirties, the Maginot Line became a reality. This 'birth date' was cast into the concrete of the Mi turret of Block 15 at Hochwald.** *Below:* **France was proud of the Line, and Allied delegations made frequent inspection visits. Here Capitaine François Tari (second from the left), commanding Mont-des-Welches, shows British officers the 75mm turret of his fortress's Block 4 in 1939.**

played by the forts at Douaumont and Vaux in 1916, did much to compensate for the initial disappointments and gave a new lease of life for permanent fortification.

Back in the early twenties, the security of France's frontier with Germany, which had been re-drawn to the extent of including Alsace and Lorraine and thus placing most of the old fortified line far back from the border, had come in for examination by a commission appointed to consider the whole issue of France's defensive organisation.

The members of this commission, the Commission de Défense du Territoire, included the illustrious Maréchals of the Great War — Foch, Joffre and Pétain. The three men did not see eye to eye. The theory of a 'continuous front' — planned battlefield defences, derived from the experience of trench warfare — advanced by Pétain ran contrary to the thinking of Foch, who distrusted any static defences, and to those who thought, as Joffre did, in terms of the infantry's contribution to victory and of a series of fortified areas enabling the infantry to manoeuvre for attack. Joffre eventually resigned from the commission and over the years Petain's views were to carry a good deal of weight.

In December 1925, only a month after he had been made Minister of War, Paul Painlevé appointed a Frontier Defence Commission (Commission de Défense des Frontières) to take matters a stage further — to decide on the basic principles and establish the nature and layout of the future line. The commission took into account the protection of the whole length of the front, including the Alps. After considering where the evident weaknesses lay, it decided that there were three dangerous sectors that had to be fortified: the Metz, Lauter and Belfort areas. The rest of the north-eastern frontier was regarded as difficult for an invader and was to be made impassable by demolitions and defended by infantry.

It was made abundantly clear that the fortifications were intended to ensure that, if the Germans invaded France again, any frontal attack would be a costly business. Should they seek to invade France again and should they attempt an outflanking movement, France would have a new ally in either Belgium or Switzerland, whichever country the Germans invaded, who could expect France to fight in support of the violation of their neutrality. The thinking behind the fortifications was also that they would enable an invasion to be held in check and provide time for the French Army to be mobilised. Not least, it would conserve manpower, scarce as it was and due to become scarcer as the 'lean years' arrived in the 1930s, when the drop in the birthrate during the Great War began to manifest itself in a decreasing number of conscripts.

The detailed proposals arrived at by the Frontier Defence Commission were then passed to an Organising Commission for Fortified Regions (Commission d'Organisation des Régions Fortifiées, or CORF) which was set up in September 1927 to deal with the practical details of siting, basic design and construction priorities.

Work began on two small-scale experimental sites at Rimplas in February 1928, the Higher War Council adopting a five-year programme at an estimated cost of 3,760 million francs. To render it more financially attractive, this figure was reduced further and further before the project was put before Parliament, the major victim being the Belfort area, which was scaled down from an intended strongly fortified line to a row of casemates. The proposals cost 'only' 2,900 million francs when they were passed by a large majority in both Parliament and Senate in late 1929, the project being presented by the new Minister of War, André Maginot, who gave it his backing.

Well to the rear were the entrance blocks to each major fortress. There were usually two: one for personnel and one for munitions and supplies. *Above:* **This British delegation is at the munitions entrance of the formidable Hackenberg fortress, sometime in 1939.** *Below:* **A present-day visit to the fortress also begins at this spot.**

Four of the major fortresses located on the north-eastern front had only one dual-purpose entrance: those at Chesnois, Billig, Michelsberg and Velosnes *(above).*

By the time the plans were finalised, becoming law on January 14, 1930, a start had already been made the previous month on four fortresses that were considered to be essential: Rochonvillers, Hackenberg, Simserhof and Hochwald. Symbolic of how the fortifications had to be scaled down in succeeding years because of budget problems in a world stricken by grave economic difficulties, these four initial fortresses would turn out to be the strongest and most developed of the whole line.

Work proceeded with varying degrees of priority, the construction of casemates along the Rhine beginning in 1931 and measures in the Alps being introduced at a somewhat slower pace. With the completion of the first phase in 1933, the 'old fronts' (anciens fronts) were defended by 20 major and 27 minor fortresses plus hundreds of casemates and shelters.

But as impressive as it then was, the Maginot Line hardly represented a continuous defensive wall as it stopped far short of the coast, and this problem had yet to be solved. As early as September

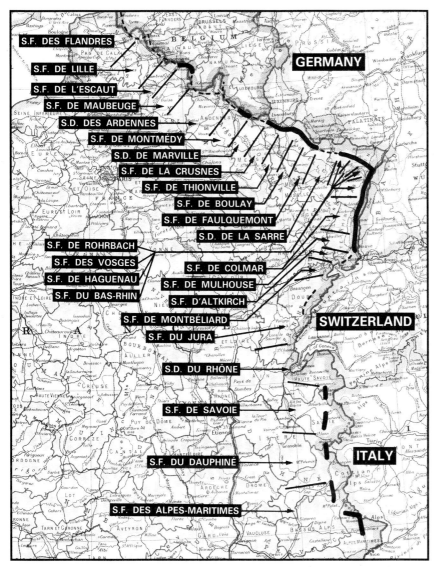

S.F. DES FLANDRES
S.F. DE LILLE
S.F. DE L'ESCAUT
S.F. DE MAUBEUGE
S.D. DES ARDENNES
S.F. DE MONTMÉDY
S.D. DE MARVILLE
S.F. DE LA CRUSNES
S.F. DE THIONVILLE
S.F. DE BOULAY
S.F. DE FAULQUEMONT
S.D. DE LA SARRE
S.F. DE ROHRBACH
S.F. DES VOSGES
S.F. DE HAGUENAU
S.F. DU BAS-RHIN
S.F. DE COLMAR
S.F. DE MULHOUSE
S.F. D'ALTKIRCH
S.F. DE MONTBÉLIARD
S.F. DU JURA
S.D. DU RHÔNE
S.F. DE SAVOIE
S.F. DU DAUPHINÉ
S.F. DES ALPES-MARITIMES

GERMANY
SWITZERLAND
ITALY

Stretching for about 1500 kilometres along the north, east and south-east borders of France, the Maginot Line consisted of 25 sectors. The strongest, equipped with fortresses, were designated 'Secteur Fortifié' (S.F.), the remainder, only lightly fortified, being called 'Secteur Défensif' (S.D.).

of casemates was also considerably reduced. Along the border with the Belgian province of Luxembourg, four fortresses and twelve casemates were built in the Montmédy area, but the two fortresses classified as major were not that strong and the sector was made still weaker by the existence of the Marville gap and the fact that the major fortress that was due to anchor its left at Vaux-les-Mouzons was not built. Further to the east, the Lauter front was extended westwards by the construction of two minor fortresses, the Haut-Poirier and the Welschoff, but with no artillery block, these two fortresses were far too weak considering their advanced position on the eastern flank of the Sarre gap.

At the end of 1935 the rôle of the Organising Commission had come to an end, except for the Alps where it was still dealing with work to be completed. The CORF undertakings along the north-eastern frontier amounted to 22 major fortresses, 36 minor fortresses, 348 casemates and blockhouses, 78 shelters and 14 observation posts. On the Alpine front, by 1940 22 artillery fortresses, 26 minor fortresses, 17 casemates (of which 16 were in Corsica), 11 shelters and 3 observation posts had been finished.

Between 1936 and 1940, when the CORF-designed works were being completed, construction continued under the Army regional commands. This third phase, when intentions were dissipated by restrictions in time and money, is often known as the 'plugging' phase. Hastily contrived on a local basis and not to any overall plan, these late efforts were to make no real contribution towards reinforcing the Maginot Line. As testified by Général Julien Dufieux at the Riom trial which was held after the French defeat of 1940, 'they were built at the lowest cost and quality was sacrificed for quantity'.

Although the infantry and artillery casemates designed by the Army's

1928 Painlevé was quoted as saying during an inspection tour that, 'the fortification of the Belgian frontier will be less important because we cannot build up impregnable obstacles in the face of our friends the Belgians, though it must be remembered that we were attacked once before by an enemy who violated Belgium and marched through that State into France.'

In 1934, after the new Chief of the General Staff, Général Maurice Gamelin, had carried out an general review of the fortifications, an extension of the Line was begun between Montmédy and Sedan, between Valenciennes and Maubeuge in the north and in the Sarre gap. The protection of these 'new fronts' (nouveaux fronts) posed impossible requirements — that of making the defences sufficiently strong, in such a short time, and within a limited budget. A strongly fortified position was planned near Maubeuge, five major fortresses being intended between Valenciennes and Trélon, but the ambitious project was watered down to just five minor fortresses and the elaborate line

Most of the fortresses were built to defend France's north-eastern frontier, but the Alpine front was also protected. This is Block 5 of Le Lavoir, constructed 2000 metres up in the French Alps in the Savoie.

Above: **In each of the major fortresses (save five of them which had a relatively short main passage), three or four Vetra or S.W. electric locomotives, developing a maximum of 40hp, operated on the narrow-gauge railway.** *Below:* **At Four-à-Chaux, the munitions entrance was located about 50 metres below the main thoroughfare level and from it a gallery 90 metres long ascended the 1-in-4 slope — a unique feature on the north-eastern front. Loads were hauled up and down the slope on a lift and a 215-step staircase ran alongside.**

Technical Engineering Services (Services Techniques du Génie, STG) had some value, most of the other bunkers built at this time were of relatively little significance and had nothing to do with the substantial CORF undertakings.

The number of blockhouses built during this latter phase is not precisely known but an approximate figure of about 5,000 can be arrived at from the data provided by a German report published by the OKH in 1941. Accord-ing to this report, the 'Denkschrift über die französische Landesbefestigung', the German investigators listed some 5,800 concrete constructions on the north-eastern frontier. The way in which they classified them, however, was not the same as that of the engineers responsible for building them, so that it is impossible to tell exactly how the statistics apply to CORF undertakings and how many of these were STG casemates.

Fortifications

From the Channel coast across France to the Rhine on the Swiss border, the defence of the north-eastern frontier was organised into fifteen Fortified Sectors (Secteurs Fortifiés) and four Defensive Sectors (Secteurs Défensifs). Each sector had under command all the troops manning the defences in the area and this amounted in peacetime, to one regiment of fortress troops (Régiment d'Infanterie de Forteresse, or R.I.F.). In wartime, each regiment was to be reinforced to form three regiments, the sector being then divided into three sub-sectors (sous-secteurs), each of them manned by one of the regiments.

At first the fortress regiment had a double rôle, to garrison the fortresses and casemates and to man the positions in between, but it soon became apparent that the units lacked mobility and were ill-suited to their second task. Reorganisation in December 1939 left the fortress troops to their main task within the fortresses, casemates and blockhouses, and entrusted the intervening areas (the 'intervals', hence interval troops) to normal field units. This shift of responsibility came somewhat late and it resulted not only in a sizeable increase in the number of men along the Line but also created a number of communication and command problems.

Though varying in strength, the Rhine defences, and the 'new fronts' on a lesser scale, were organised in depth. First came the small front line strong points built on the border itself, permanently manned by troops whose primary rôle was to sound the alarm. The main defences began about two or three kilometres back from the border with a series of advanced posts — garrisoned casemates with defensive armament.

To prevent a catastrophic explosion, either accidental or as a result of enemy action, the fortress's main magazine, M1, was built near the entrance, away from the main battle blocks. In an emergency, the main passage could be closed off just beyond the two M1 gallery openings by a huge eight-ton armoured door.

The power-house of each major fortress was equipped with four generators and, according to the size of the fortification, the power output of each of the generators varied from 75KVA to 300KVA. *Left:* The largest was that at Hackenberg, with four generators of 300KVA each, the No. 2 generator being seen here. *Right:* Also at Hackenberg, these were some of the filters designed to purify the air ventilated down into the fortress in the event of a gas attack.

The M1 magazine was set back off the main passage and access to and from it was via a gallery which ran right round it in a loop. At each end, where the gallery joined the passage, the ends of the loop were curved in the direction of the entrance so that, should an explosion occur, the blast would be directed outwards, towards the entrance. *Left:* At Hackenberg this nicely staged shot of two NCOs leading their sections shows, on the left, the curved gallery leading into the magazine and, right, the main passageway. The entrance is situated behind the photographer. *Right:* The same position photographed in 1987. When we took the comparison we discovered that a part of the wiring has since been removed.

The main line of resistance, the fortress line, ran about ten kilometres behind the border, accentuated by an anti-tank barrier of rails embedded in concrete in the ground. Where the terrain allowed, dams and reservoirs were built to enable flooding to be carried out, and a number of casemates and blockhouses were built to cover the inundations. In particular such schemes were developed on two sectors of the Line, the Schwarz-bach valley in the Vosges fortified sector and the Sarre gap, where inundations were actually the basis of the defences for about fifteen kilometres.

About one kilometre behind the main line of resistance were shelters for the infantry. A second line of resistance, of casemates and bunkers about fifteen kilometres from the border, came into being mainly during the third phase of building but was weak and badly organised. Interval artillery units — heavy batteries which the fortresses lacked, mobile or rail-mounted — were on this line.

Finally to the rear, between ten to twenty-five kilometres from the border, were the support and supply facilities: barracks for the bulk of the infantry, ammunition and food dumps, narrow-gauge railway lines feeding the major fortresses, the broad-gauge lines of the railway guns; underground communication networks, buried power lines supplying electricity from the main grid to the fortress power-house, buried telephone cables . . . all the various ingredients of a defensive system in which, as a feat of military engineering, the French could take justifiable pride.

Shelters

These were built to shelter the infantry operating between the fortresses and to provide an adequately equipped command post for their officers. Essentially passive, they were not taken into account in the fire plan and were only provided for their defence with one or two GFM cupolas and some embrasures for light machine guns. Rare exceptions had a JM cupola or an embrasure for a 37mm AT/Reibel JM.

Fortresses

There were five grades of fortress classified according to their armament and the size of their garrison but this was often simplified into two categories: the infantry fortress, known as the minor fortress (Petit Ouvrage) and the artillery fortress, known as the major fortress (Gros Ouvrage). Both had the same basic layout, with their battle blocks forward and entrance blocks some distance behind the firing line. Linked by galleries, the command post, power-house, sleeping quarters, storage areas, etc, were all sited far below the surface. Often however, because of the need to cut costs, plans had to be modified and a good many fortresses differed in their actual specifications. This applied particularly to the minor fortresses, which were sometimes built minus the entrance block to the rear or with fewer galleries so that not all their blocks were linked as planned. All the fortresses on the 'old fronts' with the exception of those in the Lauter area were numbered: eastwards from A1, Ferme de Chappy, to A38, Teting.

A minor fortress had two or three battle blocks, each mounting one MI turret, and one or two flanking blocks. The crew of a minor fortress of the north-eastern front — 'crew' because their existence was so much like that aboard a warship — numbered between 65 and 250 men with an average of 125. The minor fortresses had no artillery and the experience of June 1940 was to show that they were in fact unable to defend themselves when on their own. Thus after the withdrawal of the interval troops, the Germans were able to approach them from the rear to fire on them without opposition. This could only be prevented, and the attackers stand a chance of being repelled, if a minor fortress was within range of the artillery of a major fortress (or of the 81mm mortars of a minor fortress as demonstrated by Laudrefang, which effectively covered its neighbours Einseling and Teting).

The railway ran along the looped gallery of the magazine but, because of the ever-present fire hazard, the electricity supply did not extend to this area, the flat-cars being winched in and out. This picture shows ammunition crates — metallic cases holding fifty 75mm shells — being loaded onto flat-cars in the M1 at Hackenberg.

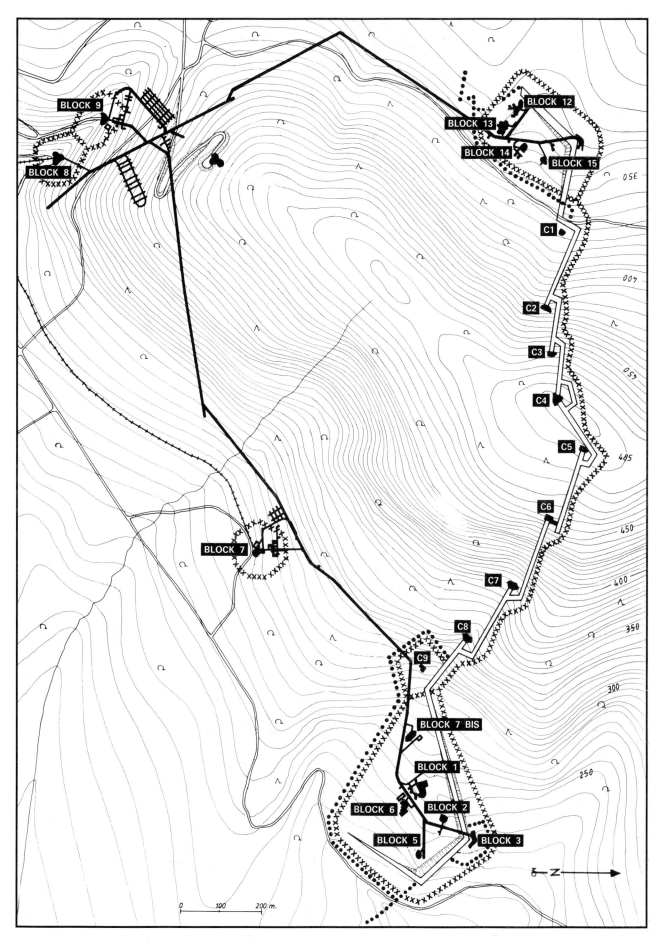

BLOCK 9

BLOCK 8

BLOCK 12

BLOCK 13

BLOCK 14

BLOCK 15

C1

C2

C3

C4

C5

C6

C7

BLOCK 7

C8

C9

BLOCK 7 BIS

BLOCK 1

BLOCK 6

BLOCK 2

BLOCK 5

BLOCK 3

0   100   200 m.

With Hackenberg, the Hochwald was the strongest of the Maginot Line fortresses. Hochwald Est (with six battle blocks) was linked to Hochwald Ouest (five battle blocks) by an anti-tank ditch controlled by a chain of nine casemates (G1 to G9). Hochwald had one supply entrance (Block 8) and was the only fortress to have two personnel entrances (Blocks 7 and 9).

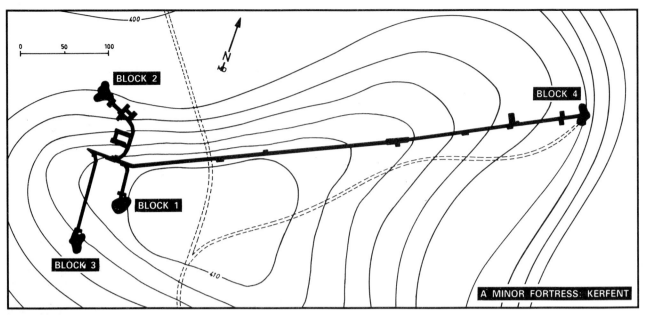

A MINOR FORTRESS: KERFENT

A major fortress had the same disposition of infantry blocks in front to ensure the defence of the fort but these were supplemented somewhat to the rear by one or several artillery blocks mounting 75mm howitzers, 135mm heavy mortars and 81mm mortars. Still farther to the rear, sometimes as far as two kilometres away, were the two entrance blocks to the fortress, one for personnel, one for munitions and supplies. According to the nature of the terrain, these entrances were either on a level with the main underground thoroughfare, connecting directly with it, or they were shafts sunk to this thoroughfare from above, with a lift at the munitions and supplies entrance and stairwell at the personnel entrance. The battle blocks being far from the entrances, the main thoroughfare of a major fortress was usually equipped with a narrow-gauge electric railway to bring up the ammunition to them. On the north-eastern front, a major fortress was garrisoned by between 450 and 1,000 men; on average about 500, of whom more than a third were gunners, and the others infantry and engineers in about equal numbers.

In the huge Hochwald fortress, comprising 11 battle blocks, 9 casemates and with a complement of 1,071 officers and men, Sous-Lieutenant Coquard, the commander of Block 1, stands at his command post, preparing a test firing of its 135mm gun.

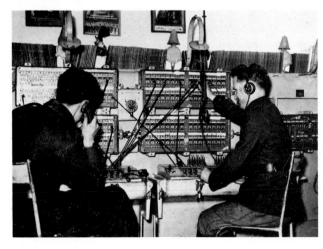

At Hackenberg, another huge fortress with 19 battle blocks and a nominal crew of 1,082 officers and men, there was a flurry of activity on the telephone switchboard (left) during a training exercise. This was orchestrated from the fortress artillery command post, controlled by Commandant Henri Ebrard, visible on the right, standing through the open doorway.

Left: **The STG casemate at Francaltroff in June 1940 with seven German graves in the foreground.** *Right:* **The casemate remains** but the dead have since been transferred to the Deutsche Soldatenfriedhof at Niederbronn.

Casemates

These concrete structures, providing sheltered firing positions for infantry weapons, were of various types according to the date of their construction.

The basic design of the initial casemate designed by the Organising Commission in 1930 — known as the CORF casemate — was fairly similar to the infantry block of a fortress; being independent, it had however to be self-sufficient and possessed its own generator, a ventilation system in case of gas attack, a water well, food and supplies. . . The forward-facing wall and the roof were about 3.5 metres thick; the others only half that. The CORF casemate usually had two levels, the upper one being the 'fighting deck', the lower housing the generators, supplies, and providing accomodation for the crew of about thirty men. They were sited every 1,200 metres or so, often as couples covering each other and which were sometimes linked by an underground gallery. There were either single or double, with one or two firing chambers, and usually armed with anti-tank guns (25mm, 37mm or 47mm), Reibel machine guns and light machine guns firing from embrasures and with GFM, JM and AM cupolas (see below). A few had variations of their own: five of the late casemates built in the Maubeuge area were armed with an AM turret with a 50mm mortar, a casemate near Havange was armed with a 50mm mortar firing from an embrasure, and one in northern Alsace with two 81mm mortars firing from embrasures.

Of the casemates that were built later, the well-designed and valuable Technical Engineering Services version — known as the STG casemate — consisted of two firing chambers and a cupola, with no second level. The others — those that were built in haste and often without any regard to a co-ordinated fire plan — were mostly of a single firing chamber type. Depending on which sector they were built in, they bore the name of the army group or army commander — Block Garchery, Block Billotte, Block Barbeyrac, for example. Some artillery casemates were built on the 'new fronts'; although armed with one or two 75mm howitzers, these were far less sophisticated than the artillery blocks built on the 'old fronts'.

Another STG casemate, MM 421, pictured in a peaceful 1986 setting beside the N43 near Petit-Xivry, about six kilometres west of Longuyon. The casemate's two embrasures still face the Chiers river, a few hundred metres away across a gently sloping meadow from where the German attack was expected.

The ground or 'interval' between the fortresses was to be held by infantry, hence their title of 'interval' troops. This squad was pictured early in 1939 at Velosnes, a major fortress in the Montmédy Fortified Sector.

Armaments

These brief details are intended to provide an indication of the Line's basic armament.

Weapons in retractable, rotating turrets:
75mm turret. Two 75mm howitzers mounted in a turret 3.30 or 4.20 metres in diameter according to mark, the 3.30-metre turret weighing 265 tonnes. Thirty-four such turrets were installed in the Maginot Line; of these 29 were on the north-eastern front.

135mm turret. Two 135mm heavy mortars mounted in a turret 2.10 metres in diameter and weighing 165 tonnes. There were seventeen of these turrets in the whole of the Maginot Line and of these sixteen were on the north-eastern front.

81mm turret. Two 81mm mortars mounted in a turret 1.55 metres in diameter and weighing 125 tonnes. Twenty-one such turrets were emplaced in the north-eastern part of the Maginot Line.

Magic Mushrooms! *Above:* **The 75mm Model 32 turret on Block 7 at Schiesseck and** *below* **Block 1's AM turret at the smaller Rohrbach fortress.**

A 135mm turret pictured in its elevated position in 1987 on Block 9 at Hackenberg.

Above: **The 81mm turret (seen here retracted) of Block 5 at the major fortress of Fermont in 1987. Note the GFM cupola nestling snugly in its concrete mount in the background.**

Below: **The claustrophobic interior of another 81mm turret showing almost every inch taken up by the equipment. This is Block 3 at the minor Immerhof fortress, pictured in 1986.**

AM turret (Arme Mixte: mixed armament). Diameter about 2.60 metres; weight about 150 tonnes. The 'mixed armament' consisted of a 25mm anti-tank gun and a set of twinned machine guns (Reibel JM mounting). The 25mm AT gun had a rate of fire of fifteen rounds per minute; muzzle velocity 918 m/s. Being of a later design, there were only twelve of these AM turrets in the whole of the Maginot Line, all on the 'new fronts'.

AM turret with 50mm mortar. Fitted with a 25mm anti-tank gun, a Reibel JM and a 50mm mortar. Another late-design turret, of which there were only seven in the north-east, and five in casemates in the Maubeuge sector.

MI turret (Mitrailleuses: machine guns). For twinned Reibel-mounted 7.5mm machine guns, it was 1.20 metres in diameter and weighed about 96 tonnes. There were 61 such turrets in the Maginot line, all in the north-east.

The Mi turret (*left* on Block 4 at Simserhof) was quite a common feature, but the AM type mounting a 50mm mortar (*right* on Block 9 at Anzeling fortress) was a late design of which only a dozen were installed on the north-eastern front.

Weapons operated from fixed armoured cupolas:

GFM cupola (Guet et Fusil Mitrailleur: watch and light machine gun). For observation and from which 7.5mm FM Mdle 24/29 light machine guns could be fired. Also later developed for the 50mm mortar. A periscope could be raised through an aperture on the top. There were usually three slits around the side, though some had up to five. Nearly 450 of these cupolas surmounted the fortresses on the north-eastern front, and there were hundreds on the casemates.

AM cupola (Arme Mixte: mixed armament). A late design, appearing only in 1934, for a 25mm anti-tank gun and Reibel JM twinned machine guns. There were more than fifty such cupolas in the fortresses on the north-eastern front, plus several on the casemates.

Observation cupolas, or Observatories, were for observation only and not for firing from. These were of two basic types: one with three side apertures as well as an aperture on top for a periscope; the other, having a far lower profile rising no more than a few centimetres above the ground, with a periscope only.

A brace of armoured cupolas astride the crest of Block 3 at Fermont. On the left is the JM type with the GFM on the right.

Like a gargantuan set of motorway cat's eyes, this AM cupola Type B squats on the grass on Block 2 at Rohrbach.

An episcopic observation cupola pictured in 1987 on Block 6 at Simserhof. This one has five side apertures plus the one on top for the episcope.

A similar cupola pictured on Block 12 at Hackenberg. This type of cupola had a very low profile offering a very difficult target for enemy counter-fire.

Left: **A GFM cupola on the top of Block 2 at La Ferté. It was here that Roger Conraux, Paul Gomez and Joseph Koesters were killed inside when German artillery scored a direct hit on the** far side of the cupola on May 18, 1940. *Right:* **The interior of a GFM cupola on Block 9 at Schiesseck. A 7.5mm FM 24/29 light machine gun and an episcope are mounted in the slits.**

LG cupola (Lance Grenades: grenade launcher). Designed to receive a 60mm mortar, this cupola was very low, projecting only 26 centimetres as opposed to between 1 and 1.25 metres for the other type. The 60mm mortar was not produced and its 50mm mortar replacement had not in fact been installed by the outbreak of war. There were fifty-one such cupolas on the fortresses of the north-eastern front, plus several of them on the casemates.

JM cupola (Jumellage Mitrailleuses: twinned machine guns). Designed to receive Reibel JM twinned machine guns, this type had a large firing slit and two smaller observation slits on one side.

A JM cupola on Casemate No. 35/3 at Marckolsheim photographed in 1988. The twin Reibel JM machine guns are still in place in the central firing slot while the two smaller observation apertures are closed with light armoured shields.

Left: **Dwarfed by its concrete dome, this 135mm mortar (135 Modèle 1932) peeps out of its embrasure in Block 4 at Simserhof in 1987. When in use, this monster needed 250 litres of water per day to keep it cool.** *Right:* **This 47mm anti-tank gun** **(AC 47 Modèle 1934) still stands guard at the munitions entrance to Simserhof. In such an embrasure, the gun could be elevated between plus 10 degrees and minus 15 degrees, and laterally through 45 degrees.**

Weapons firing from embrasures:

75mm howitzer. With a range of about 9 to 12 kilometres according to mark, this had an impressive rate of fire of nearly thirty rounds per minute. There were 44 such howitzers in the fortresses on the north-eastern front.

135mm heavy mortar. This lobbed an 18-kilo shell up to 5.7 kilometres, having a rate of fire of up to eight rounds per minute. Seven heavy mortars were installed in the fortresses on the north-eastern front.

81mm mortar. This lobbed a 3-kilo shell up to 3.2 kilometres; the rate of fire was about ten rounds per minute. In the fortresses on the north-eastern front there were sixteen such mortars plus two in a casemate near Hoffen.

47mm (or 37mm) anti-tank gun. Rate of fire twenty rounds per minute, muzzle velocity about 900 m/s. Originally the threat of armour had not been taken into account. For anti-tank guns to be installed, an ingenious rail-mounting system was devised and mounted behind a Reibel JM embrasure so that either the anti-tank gun or the twinned machine guns could be fired from the same embrasure — this arrangement being referred to here as a 47mm AT/Reibel JM embrasure. There were nearly 150 such embrasures in the fortresses on the north-eastern front, most of them for 47mm guns, plus several hundred in the casemates.

7.5mm machine guns. Two twinned MAC 31 machine guns on a mounting referred to here as Reibel JM. Rate of fire per set about 750 rounds per minute; effective range 1,200 metres. There were a hundred embrasures of this type in the fortresses on the north-eastern front, plus several hundred in the casemates.

7.5mm FM 24/29 light machine gun. There were several hundred such embrasures in the fortresses and casemates.

50mm mortar. This close-range weapon lobbed a one-kilo shell up to about 320 metres. Although designed to be fired from a GFM cupola, some of them were mounted and fired from the embrasure designed for a light machine gun.

Sous-Lieutenant Albert Haas, the commander of Block 16 at Hochwald, and Lieutenant Charles Lefèbvre, the commander of Block 13 — a picture taken with Albert Haas' own camera.

The Allied strategy

With Poland defeated in the East, and the French Sarre offensive terminated in the West, the war entered a new phase . . . of inactivity . . . the Drôle de Guerre had begun.

The French and British staffs readily agreed that the Germans were better prepared for war and would have superiority on land and in the air. Therefore, Allied strategy would be based on defence and initially concentrated on defeating a German offensive. While continuing to contain the Wehrmacht on the battlefield, the Allies would exert rigorous economic pressure to weaken Germany's powers of resistance while they built up the strength of their own forces in order, eventually, to go over to the offensive. In view of the defensive strength of the Maginot Line, it was also agreed that the Germans might be impelled to turn this barrier in the north and attack through the Netherlands and Belgium. Covering their southern flank in front of the Maginot Line, they might direct their main attack towards Brussels and Cambrai to reach the French positions from Hirson to the coast. In so doing, they would gain control of the North Sea coast and obtain airfields to put them within range of vital French and British objectives.

Caught by surprise in 1914 by the 'Schlieffen Plan', the French had since produced countless studies and plans bent on preventing a repetition of such a disaster. The absence of a Maginot Line type of defence along the frontier with Belgium was not solely due to the fact that large-scale fortifications would have left a then-ally on the wrong side of them. Cost came into it, of course, as did the unsuitability of the low-lying

It was, to use a phrase of the time, 'a queer kind of war' in which patrols into no-man's-land along the border and odd artillery duels were the only breaks in the boredom. In fact the term 'Bore' War was how the period became known in Britain until the Americanism 'Phoney' War took its place. *Left:* This French 340mm Modèle 1912 railway gun was pictured somewhere in the 2ème Armée sector while these two prisoners *(right)* were captured by a patrol from the 3ème Armée.

and flat terrain of the area, and an added complication presented itself: the important mining and industrial region of northern France, overrun by the Germans in 1914 and thereafter denied to the French for the rest of the war, would have been turned into a potential battlefield. To spare the mines and the great industrial complex of the north from destruction, thought had even been given to relinquishing the region altogether and fighting to the south, along the line of the Somme; but clearly a far more attractive option was that of engaging the Germans in battle in Belgium.

Maréchal Pétain, for all his defensive-minded reputation, had been, since 1927 as President of the War Council, an advocate of advancing into Belgium and in 1932 he stressed the importance of having 'a mobile force near the frontier and to make sure of its swift advance into Belgium'. Originally, the French High Command and the Chief of the General Staff of National Defence, Général Gamelin, were not in favour of a move into Belgium. However Gamelin was brought round to the idea by Prime Minister Daladier and his government and soon became an increasingly strong advocate of it.

The British High Command, having backed the idea, had second thoughts by the time war broke out, but the fear of German submarines in Belgian harbours and German bombers on airfields within range of Britain gradually undermined the wise and realistic counsel of the Chiefs-of-Staff, who in September 1939 reported to the War Cabinet that 'unless plans are concerted with the Belgians for the occupation of this line in sufficient time before the German advance, it would be unsound to adopt this plan'.

Then came winter — a particularly severe one in 1939-40 — and with it the life of the men at the front became even more uncomfortable, but still nothing happened, except that the propaganda war was hotted up to boost the spirit of the civilian population. This picture was taken in the 5ème Armée sector.

Allowing for the certainty that Belgian soil would be fought over, two questions remained: would the Germans strike the main blow in northern Belgium or somewhere further south? The French had come to the conclusion that there was only one possible invasion route, the historic one to the north.

Southern Belgium appeared to them to be hopelessly blocked by the 'impassable' Ardennes. Pétain in 1934 had described the Ardennes as 'impenetrable provided special dispositions are effected there'. Mainly perhaps because from 1936 the Belgians refused to discuss their defence plans with the

Another 'action' picture for the folk at home, this time in the area of the front held by the 9ème Armée. This particular army was nowhere in contact with German forces, being deployed along the frontier with neutral Belgium. This is a 25mm Modèle 1934 anti-tank gun, a potent weapon for its time, able to pierce 40mm of armour at 400 metres.

On December 20 the French Farman 222 heavy bombers of G.B. I/15, the 1er Groupe de Bombardement of the 15ème Escadre [Wing] of the l'Armée de l'Air, had moved to the aerodrome at Reims and flew their first war mission two days later — a night leaflet drop to Munich. The four-engined Farman 222s could carry up to five tonnes of bombs having a maximum speed of 320 km/hr (200 mph).

French, none were. This conclusion seems to have been accepted without hesitation by the British and apparently no attempt was made to consider what might happen if, once the Allied armies had moved into Belgium, the Germans pierced the front further to the south.

Belgium and the Netherlands had each proclaimed its strict neutrality. Although it was obvious that either or both of them would be involved in any war between Germany and a Franco-British alliance, each made it clear that they would remain neutral unless their borders were violated. Neither would take part in staff talks with the French or British. This was not so much a problem for the Allies in the case of the Netherlands — which had remained neutral throughout the Great War — as they knew that in any event they would not be able to effectively intervene to assist her if attacked by Germany. Belgium, whose neutrality had been violated in 1914, was different; for, as war loomed nearer, in all the discussions between the French and British General Staffs it was taken for granted that Belgium would be the battlefield. France and Britain urged the Belgians to join in staff talks with them, but the Belgians legitimately argued that they could not enter into talks with one side while proclaiming their neutrality to the other.

On September 26, 1939, the French High Command drew up a plan for an advance into Belgium in which the British Expeditionary Force would move forward to the Tournai area, with the French XVIème Corps d'Armée moving forward on its left, to form a defensive line along the River Escaut (or Scheldt). The plan was simple and involved only a day's march for the left wing which had the furthest to go, although it would mean holding a line thirty kilometres longer than along the border with Belgium.

The success of such a manoeuvre would of course depend on whether the Belgians allowed the Allies to cross the frontier in good time, and behind the scenes the French and British tried to secure some degree of consultation or pre-planning with them. Meanwhile, at the end of October, fresh instructions were circulated; it was now proposed that the French 7ème Armée, which until then was to be held in reserve behind the Allies left, should be engaged on the left wing, taking over the role previously assigned to the XVIème Corps d'Armée. Reference was made to the possibility of advancing as far as the River Dyle if time permitted, but the main line was still envisaged as based on the Escaut.

Many of the French generals expressed concern about leaving prepared positions to advance into Belgium at too short notice, some of them even doubting the whole concept of the Belgian manoeuvre. The BEF corps commanders thought it foolhardy until they were reinforced and ready. Commanding II Corps, Lieutenant-General A. F. Brooke recorded in his diary on October 19 how he and the I Corps

During the Drôle de Guerre, the reconnaissance squadrons were very active, particularly those of the Luftwaffe which violated Belgian airspace without hesitation, showing great interest in the Ardennes sector. In April 1940 alone, the Belgians reported some 330 incursions by foreign aircraft of which nearly 300 were German and the remainder French or British. This Dornier Do 17P belonged to the 3. Staffel of Auf.Gr.22, the reconnaissance unit assigned to the 16. Armee.

Crewmen of G.R. I/22 (1er Groupe de Reconnaissance of the 22ème Escadre), working with the 3ème Armée, discussing last-minute details before boarding their Bloch 131 at Chatel-Chéhéry airfield, some 35 kilometres south-east of Vouziers.

Reconnaissance aircraft suffered most of the French losses in September — on the 17th a Bloch 131 from this same group was shot down over Morsbach by five Messerschmitt Bf 109s of JG53, all four crewmen being killed.

commander, Lieutenant-General Sir John Dill, had buttonholed their chief to try to 'make him realise the danger of leaving our present prepared position for one totally unprepared'. 'Gort', wrote Brooke, 'will take a very light-hearted view of the situation and is too inclined to underestimate the strength and efficiency of the Germans'.

Gamelin's orders showed his own recognition of the obvious need for the Allies to be allowed to enter Belgium in good time and for collaboration before-hand, which he sought. This did not detract from his intention to move into Belgium, however. On November 17

the inter-allied Supreme War Council were agreed that 'it is essential that every endeavour should be made to hold the line Antwerp-Namur in the event of a German invasion of Bel-gium'. Thus the Dyle was adopted as the basis for the Allied defensive line in Belgium, and that day the French Commander-in-Chief North-East Front, Général Georges, issued his Instruction Personelle et Secrète No. 8 defining the operation.

This was a far more ambitious under-taking than the 'Escaut Plan' and meant sending four Allied armies into Belgium instead of two. Their cavalry units

would have to rush east for 200 kilo-metres to engage the enemy as a screen-ing force along the Albert Canal while the main infantry forces would have to move forward almost a 100 kilometres to prepare positions along the Meuse and Dyle rivers. On the other hand, the resulting line would be about 60 kilo-metres shorter than that of the Escaut Plan and, with the Dendre and Escaut rivers and the prepared defences of the French frontier lying behind it, the Dyle Line would have far greater depth. The Escaut Plan, however, was not entirely discarded and details were required to be worked out for it too.

This Mureaux 115 of G.A.O. 507 (Groupe Aérien d'Observation), the recce group assigned to the 5ème D.L.C., was shot down near Obergailbach, ten kilometres east of Sarreguemines, by a

Bf 109E of JG53 on September 20. The pilot and observer were only slightly wounded and had already been taken to hospital when these soldiers posed for this picture.

On the morning of November 8 a patrol of Hurricanes of No. 73 Squadron, RAF, intercepted a high-flying Dornier Do 17P which Flying Officer Edgar 'Cobber' Kain succeeded in shooting down. The Dornier, on a reconnaissance mission from Auf.Gr.123 and piloted by Oberleutnant Hans Kutter, crashed in Lubey, a small town just west of Briey, all the crew being killed. When Jean Paul took this comparison in 1987 he found virtually every house remained unchanged.

By the end of November, Allied intelligence estimated that between 97 and 99 German divisions had assembled on the Western Front, some 20 of them on the border with Dutch Limburg. Early that month Dutch intelligence had received information from an Abwehr source which pointed to an attack being imminent. In 1914 the German planners had not included the Netherlands in their strategy, a decision criticised later for having left the invading armies insufficient room to manoeuvre; obviously this time not only Belgium and Luxembourg but the Netherlands too was going to be invaded — or at least the 'appendix' of Dutch territory between Germany and Belgium with the town of Maastricht in its centre. During this invasion scare the Allied armies were placed on alert but when no attack came they were stood down. However the warning had been genuine enough for on November 5 Hitler had issued orders for the offensive in the West to begin but then postponed it two days later.

The likely inclusion of the Netherlands in the German plan of attack posed a further danger to the Allies. Should the panzers advance from Venlo through the Noord-Brabant to reach Walcheren, from there they could deny access to the major Belgian port of Antwerp. To prevent this, Gamelin considered how to provide some support for the Dutch; hence the so-called 'Breda' manoeuvre which proposed sending the French 7ème Armée further north to the Breda area to join hands with the Dutch Army. Gamelin knew that this manoeuvre could not save the Dutch, whose resistance was not expected to last longer than a few days, but he hoped to see the 7ème Armée thus securing the mouth of the Escault and safeguarding the left flank of the Allied line.

Although not implemented, plans were drawn up at this time for a bold airborne assault, Operation 'Malacca', to gain control of Walcheren ahead of the panzers. The idea was for Farman 224 transports to drop one company of paratroops near Vlissingen and on the Arnemuiden isthmus; half an hour later about fifteen Bloch 220 were to land on Vlissingen airfield, by then in the paratroopers hands, and bring in one company of the 137ème Régiment d'Infanterie; later the rest of the regiment was to disembark in Vlissingen harbour, transported by destroyers from Dunkirk.

Général Georges protested at the 7ème Armée, formerly his main reserve force, being thrust so far northwards and opposed this enlargement of the Belgian undertaking. On December 5 he commented forcefully on the risk of the Allies being 'deprived of the necessary means' for a counter-attack should the main German thrust come in the centre while the bulk of the Allied reserves were committed in the north 'in the face of a German move which might be merely a diversion'.

The 7ème Armée commander, Général Henri Giraud, drew attention to the fact that his troops would be in great danger of being caught on the run while arriving as the German units had to cover a far shorter distance (about 135 kilometres) than the French (230 kilometres). The 1ère Armée commander, Général Georges Blanchard, also expressed reservations and stressed that it would take a week for his army to reach the positions assigned to it and some days more to get organised. 'We must', he insisted, 'be absolutely certain of not meeting the enemy for at least eight days. If not, it will mean a battle of encounter fought in the worst conditions.'

The British were also sceptical but raised no objection as all these developments tended to favour their interests. Lieutenant-General H. R. Pownall, the BEF's Chief-of-Staff, wrote in his diary that 'it is good of the French to worry about Walcheren, whose denial to the enemy is primarily a British interest'. They were aware too of how small their own contribution was on land and deferred to the French as to the course which operations should take.

On November 23, 'Cobber' inspected the wreck of another victory, this time a Dornier Do 17P from Auf.Gr.22 which he had brought down near La Besace, 30 kilometres north-east of Vouziers. The aircraft had caught fire but the crew were taken prisoner.

Belgium sits on the fence

The King of the Belgians, Léopold III, inspects the 9ème Division d'Infanterie sometime in 1936. The 'armed independence' of Belgium had just been proclaimed.

In 1914, neutral Belgium had become embroiled in the Great War and afterwards in reparations. They desired security in Europe although politically there had long existed a degree of unease at establishing too close an identity with the perceived interests of France (or indeed Britain). The neutrality that Belgium had declared on the outbreak of war was the logical conclusion of a policy of 'armed independence' proclaimed in 1936, an independent course 'firmly directed', in King Leopold III's words, 'towards keeping us out of conflicts between neighbours'. To quote his Foreign Minister, Paul-Henri Spaak, it was a policy 'exclusively and wholly Belgian' which could be put forward to obtain the support for rearmament of the majority of a nation divided by politics, language and religion. Consequently, in 1937, France and Britain accepted Belgium's withdrawal as a party to the (by now defunct) Locarno Treaty. France viewed the Belgian policy with regret; Britain saw merit in Belgium putting her defences in order, 'the completion of this', said the Chiefs-of-Staff, will 'increase her chances of remaining neutral, an attitude which, from the military point of view, is to the advantage of France and ourselves'.

Belgium's military efforts were real and the Army Commander-in-Chief, King Leopold, could, within weeks, count on the mobilisation of eighteen infantry divisions, two cavalry divisions and two divisions of Chasseurs Ardennais — a tremendous effort for a small country of about 8,000,000 people. Both France and Britain reaffirmed their guarantees to come to the aid of

Belgium if she were attacked and to respect her inviolability and integrity. Germany followed suit with similar solemn assurances.

Belgium had begun to mobilise on August 25, 1939, and when war came sixteen Belgian divisions were in position. To avoid any reproach from Hitler about an imbalanced neutrality, they had deployed about two-thirds of these along the French border. Not unnaturally, from the French and British point of view, neutrality did not prevent them from doing what they could to make the most of covert military contact with the Belgians. Their response, despite growing increasingly aware of the threat of attack by Germany, was to stick to the tenets of neutrality while secretly going beyond what this permitted.

From the end of September the Belgian Army had been redeployed, and at the time of the 'alerte' in early November, all but a fraction of its forces facing France had been transferred eastwards to meet the threat of attack. Of the 20 divisions of the Belgian Army, 14 were now facing east.

On November 7 King Leopold sped off by car to The Hague accompanied by his Foreign Minister, M. Spaak, and his ADC and principal military adviser, Général Raoul van Overstraeten, to concert peace efforts with the Dutch. On November 10 the Belgian Military Attaché in Paris, Général Maurice Delvoie, went to see Gamelin at his headquarters at Vincennes to ask what forces the Allies would be able to advance on the Albert Canal 'if Belgium called on Allied help'. In that case, Gamelin assured him, Allied

troops would not hesitate to advance into Belgium. The next day, Delvoie met Gamelin's Chief-of-Staff, Colonel Jean-Louis Petitbon, who informed him that Allied troops could be on the Albert Canal in less than six days. The Belgians were pleased with the response and contact with the Allies was discreetly reinforced, the French sending Colonel Auguste Hautcoeur to Brussels and the British Admiral Sir Roger Keyes of Zeebrugge fame.

The Belgians had planned a defence in depth; their positions to the east along the Albert Canal, the 'Position de Couverture', were to form only a first line of defence to hold the Germans while the bulk of their armies were able to establish themselves on the main defence line — the 'Position Centrale' — along a line Antwerp-Wavre-Namur. Neutral they might be, but the Belgians always had in mind that French and British troops would come and support them on this main line if Germany were to invade.

Since August 1939 they had built up their defences along these two lines, digging trenches and building blockhouses and anti-tank obstacles, but once again the price of neutrality had to be paid and time and energy were also sacrificed to fortify the defences along the French border. Even if the forces facing France could be swiftly moved east, and were no more than a token price paid to neutrality, trenches and blockhouses could not, and all these efforts were spent in vain.

The defences on the northern part of the main line (known to the Belgians as the K.W. Line as it ran through the towns of Koningshooikt and Wavre), were ready in October but the line was far more vulnerable to the south. Its weak spot was the Gembloux gap between Wavre on the Dyle and Namur on the Meuse, open country dangerously inviting for panzers. Defence works would not begin in this sector before April and few, if any, had been completed on May 10.

On January 10, at 11.33 a.m., a Messerschmidt Bf 108 liaison aircraft, D-NFAW, made a forced landing at Vucht in Belgian Limburg, about 15 kilometres north of Maastricht. On board was Major Helmuth Reinberger, an officer attached to the 7. Flieger-Division, who was carrying documents of the greatest importance.

The previous evening he was at Münster when ordered to attend a conference at Luftflotte 2 headquarters in Cologne, about 130 kilometres away. He was supposed to travel by train but a pilot from the staff of Luftgau VI based at Münster had offered to fly him there. At first Reinberger refused, then decided to make the most of this opportunity of going by air. Unfortunately for him, the pilot, Major Erich Hoenmans, was not too proficient and, after getting lost in the fog over the Ruhr basin, the aircraft ran out of fuel before Hoenmans could work out their position. They crash-landed near the Meuse at Vucht. Beyond the river, about 12 kilometres to the east, lay Germany; only about 300 metres to the east lay the Dutch-Belgian border. Major Reinberger tried to burn the documents he was carrying but Belgian troops arrived in time and prevented him from doing so. While being questioned, he tried again, shoving the papers into a stove, and they were three-quarters burnt before a Belgian officer of the 13ème Division d'Infanterie, Capitaine Arthur Rodrique, plunged his hands into the flames and pulled them out. Horrified, Reinberger made an abortive grab for the Belgian officer's revolver to kill himself. Although singed at the corners, many of the documents were still readable and they turned out to be operational orders for Luftflotte 2 units participating in an

Belgian troops on manoeuvres. Parked in the background are two T-13 and two T-15 light tanks.

attack to be made across Belgium. There were also detailed plans concerning an airborne operation west of the Meuse, between Charleroi and Dinant, where the 7. Flieger-Division was to drop and airborne troops of the 22. Infanterie-Division were to be landed.

The Belgian authorities came to the conclusion that the documents were authentic and they provided the French, British and Dutch with extracts.

On the day of the crash-landing, Allied intelligence again received information indicating that an offensive was imminent — and again it was correct, as on January 10 Hitler had issued orders for the offensive to begin on January 17. There was another general 'alerte', with troop movements taking place, and Général Delvoie rushed to Gamelin's headquarters at Vincennes in the early hours of January 14 to inform the French High Command that the attack was 'almost certain for today'. As yet, however, Delvoie explained, he had not received instructions from his government to call on the French for assistance.

Taking advantage of the closer relations which had been established since the November 'alerte', and now this still more serious one, the French once more tried to persuade the Belgians to go further. Gamelin sent a stiff message to Brussels in which he pointed out that, unless the Allied troops could enter Belgium preventatively, the Belgians ran the risk of seeing much of their country invaded before aid was possible. The Belgian Foreign Minister, M. Spaak, told the French on January 15 that such a request was 'unacceptable' and incompatible with the attitude to which his country intended to adhere. On January 16 he told the German Ambassador, Vicco von Bülow-Schwante, that the precautionary measures Belgium had taken were justified by the documents from the German aircraft containing 'clear proof of an intention to attack'; yet the ambassador was able to report to Berlin that Spaak assured him 'solemnly and most earnestly that the Belgian Government would never commit the folly of calling the Allies into the country'.

All the same, when confronted with the information which came into their hands at Vucht, the Belgians took steps to prepare for what might lie ahead and top secret contacts with the French and British became closer. Boundary lines between the Allied armies rushing into Belgium and the Belgian Army withdrawing from the Albert Canal were studied on maps; the Belgians provided maps and airfield plans for the Royal Air Force and the Armée de l'Air; the advance through Belgium of the French 7ème Armée was studied and the movement by rail of the tanks of the 1ère D.L.M. to the Netherlands was arranged. There was still a mass of detail to be settled, but it was hoped that much could be sorted out in the first few days of war. If there was any comfort to be gained from the thought that no preparations had been made before August 1914, this was certainly a situation which the French, not least Général Gamelin himself, had tried vainly for eight months to remedy.

Belgian soldiers on their eastern frontier with Germany during the winter of 1939-40. There were repeated alerts but Belgium adopted a strictly neutral stance.

Plan 'Dyle'

In the event of an attack, French and British forces would advance through Belgium to the Rivers Dyle and Meuse. Heading the 7ème Armée would be the 1ère D.L.M. [1st Mechanised Division] seen here on manoeuvres in February 1940.

It now seemed safe to assume, in the light of the Belgians' determined preparations, that there were positive prospects of a German invasion being delayed by the Belgians, and by the French and British cavalry screen sent forward in support long enough for the Allied armies to reach their positions along the Dyle and the Meuse. However this assumption was to prove generally to be at fault, and the lack of adequate co-ordination beforehand was to have particular significance for the French 9ème Armée in the Ardennes. Here the Belgian strategy was for demolitions to be carried out and their units to immediately withdraw northwards to link up with the main body of their forces; consequently the 9ème Armée units would not have time to take up their positions behind the Meuse.

On March 20, Général Georges issued his Instruction Personelle et Secrète No. 9 to the commander of Groupe d'Armées No. 1 and the com-

mander of the BEF. These instructions, which complemented those issued in November 1939, took into account the reinforcement of the BEF and recent defensive measures taken by the Belgians and Dutch and proposed to give 'more extensiveness to the planned operations'. The instructions were packed with 'if' related to the Belgian and Dutch attitude: 'if the Belgians abandon the Albert Canal . . . if the order to enter the Netherlands is given . . . if the circumstances are favourable'. In a précis that, in the event, was to prove faulty, it stated that 'in accordance with the Belgian High Command, the withdrawal of Belgian forces was to be canalised on clearly defined roads in order not to hamper the engagement of our vanguard elements or the installation of our forces'.

As it now stood, the Dyle Plan was based on four French armies, the British Expeditionary Force, and the Belgian and Netherlands Armies. The disposition of the Allied forces reflected

the expectation that the major German effort would come north of Namur, where it was intended to deploy the strongest of the French armies, the 7ème and 1ère Armées. These two armies were made up for the most part of Active and Series A units. Between them they incorporated three light armoured divisions and five motorised infantry divisions as well as a large part of the available motor transport, anti-aircraft groups, tractor-drawn artillery, tank battalions, etc. The weaker 9ème and 2ème Armées were committed on the right flank, in the Ardennes and river Meuse sector, where a major German effort was regarded as impracticable. They were made up chiefly of Series A and Series B divisions; their reinforcement from the general reserve had been on a smaller scale, and they were worse off for modern equipment.

Should the Dyle Plan be put into effect, and the Allied armies move forward into Belgium and up the coast into the Netherlands, the line-up from

Top: **The 4ème Cuirassiers are pictured with their Somua S-35s and the 78ème Dragons** *above* **with their Hotchkiss H-35s.**

the North Sea to the Maginot Line would be thus: the Netherlands Army; the French 7ème Armée as far as Antwerp; the Belgian Army down to Louvain; the British Expeditionary Force from there to Wavre; the French 1ère Armée from Wavre on to Namur, barring the vital Perwez-Gembloux gap; the French 9ème Armée to Pont-à-Bar (just west of Sedan) and the French 2ème Armée to Longuyon. From Antwerp to Longuyon, the French armies on this part of the front came under the command of Groupe d'Armées No. 1 of Général Gaston Billotte.

At the end of March, in a letter to Billotte, Giraud again complained of the difficulties of the far too ambitious rôle his 7ème Armée was expected to perform. Billotte backed him up, and on April 14, Georges, who remained unconvinced of the soundness of going so far out on a limb, requested that the 7ème Armée be kept in reserve. Gamelin's reply, the following day, made it clear that the plan would not be changed: 'It seemed impossible systematically to abandon the Netherlands to Germany'. The Allied Supreme Command was confident, certain that in attacking in the north the Germans would come through Belgium again, and certain that the Dyle-Breda Plan was the right response to halt the attack they were expected to make. In sticking to the plan, the appreciation of German intentions on which the Allied campaign was based held good in fact until

Time has stood still at Etain railway station, north-east of Verdun, where these Renault B1bis medium tanks were photographed being unloaded in 1939.

The tanks belonged to the 8ème B.C.C. (Bataillon de Chars de Combat or Tank Battalion) which, together with the 15ème B.C.C., formed the heavy brigade of the 2ème D.C.R. (Armoured Division). 'Typhon' belonged to the 2ème Compagnie.

the end of February — until, that is, the German plan of attack underwent drastic revision. Thereafter, the move forward into Belgium and the Netherlands had become a recipe for disaster.

On May 9, on the eve of the German attack and the implementation of the Dyle Plan, Groupe d'Armées No. 1 had four armies plus the BEF, with a strength equivalent to 39 divisions (30 French), with the 5 fortress units being taken as the equivalent of 3 field units,

Left: **Capitaine Marcel Deyber, commanding the 2nd Company, leaves the station riding 'Eclair' (in this sense translated as** 'Lightning') eastwards along the N3 towards Metz. *Right:* **The level crossing has since been automated.**

The commander of Groupe d'Armées No. 1, Général Gaston Billotte (left) with Général Georges Blanchard of the 1ère Armée.

The CO of the 7ème Armée, Général Henri Giraud, inspects the 13ème R.I. (Infantry Regiment) of the 9ème D.I.M. (Mechanised Infantry Division).

and 9 British. Except for the fortress units, each of its armies were to advance into Belgium to occupy a 250-kilometre front, the left wing wheeling forward about 200 kilometres, pivoting on the right.

Groupe d'Armées No. 2 of Général Gaston Prételat had three armies, its strength equivalent to 37 divisions (36 French, with the 10 fortress units being taken as the equivalent of 8 field divisions, and 1 British. The army group was holding the fortified sector of the border from Longuyon to Sélestat in Alsace, about 330 kilometres. A few cavalry units were to move forward into Luxembourg; otherwise the army group was mainly static in the first phase of the Allied plan.

From Sélestat to the border with Switzerland Groupe d'Armées No. 3 of Général Antoine Besson had only one army with the equivalent of 9 divisions, the 4 fortress units being taken as the equivalent of 2 field divisions. Its front was no more than about 80 kilometres wide but the army group was to oppose

any German attack through Switzerland and, in the event, to be ready to advance into that country.

With the 17 divisions held in reserve, the Commander-in-Chief North-East Front, Général Georges, disposed of 108 units on May 9, these amounting to an equivalent total of 102 divisions, the 19 fortress units being taken as the equivalent of 13 field divisions.

Criticism is frequently levelled at the French High Command for having distributed its forces in almost equal density, both where there were fortifications and where there were not. This criticism is partly justified, and undoubtedly Gamelin ought to have reinforced his left wing and allotted more forces to Groupe d'Armées No. 1, particularly to the 9ème and 2ème Armées. It is surprising that each was given only nine divisions or so, the 9ème Armée to advance into Belgium and occupy a front 85 kilometres wide along the Meuse, while along part of the static and heavily protected Maginot Line, the 4ème Armée had the same

number of divisions for about 55 kilometres of front and the 3ème Armée a dozen or so for a front of about 80 kilometres.

It must not be forgotten however, that French strategy was not limited to the Dyle Plan. The Maginot Line had been intended to force the Germans to mount either a costly frontal attack or attempt to outflank the fortifications through Belgium or Switzerland. The French strategists were calling for such a flanking attack of the Maginot Line for it would force either Belgium or Switzerland into the battle and give the French Army an opportunity to fight the Germans far forward of France. The Dyle Plan was the response to the more likely of the two ways of turning the Line, but Switzerland remained a possibility which was why Gamelin stationed sizeable forces with the Groupe d'Armées No. 3 on his far right wing. Though the official explanation for this was that the French Army had to be in position to help Switzerland in case of invasion, in so doing the French High

On the right flank of the Dyle — in the Ardennes where a major German effort was regarded as impracticable — were the

weaker 9ème and 2ème Armées, commanded respectively by Général André Corap *left* and Général Charles Huntziger *right*.

As winter gave way to spring, the Allied armies continued their waiting game, leaving the initiative for aggressive action to the Germans. Nevertheless the Allied generals remained firmly confident in the defensive provisions of the Dyle Plan. *Left:* Here the commander of the 1ère Armée, Général Blanchard (right), with Général Pierre Dame of the 2ème D.I.N.A. (Division d'Infanterie Nord-Africaine) confer after a parade held on the Place d'Armes in Valenciennes in north-east France.

Command was also inviting the Germans to see these forces as a dangerous threat and to decide to hit first and attack through Switzerland.

There was also the possibility that a German attack through Belgium might be a feint (as it in fact transpired) and that a major attack would be directed at the Maginot Line. To guard against this, and because as part of the concept of a fortified defensive system it was intended to be able to launch powerful counter-attacks from behind it, Gamelin had to leave the necessary forces under Groupe d'Armées No. 2. These contradictory requirements also explain why the reserves were placed in such a way that, once the panzers had broken through west of Sedan, it was practically impossible to gather enough of them together to close the breach.

Following the defeat of Poland, some 180,000 Polish troops managed to escape through neutral territory. Many reached France, which had signed a military treaty of mutual aid with Poland on September 9, and the first Polish infantry division was formed in October, followed by a second in March 1940. Each division comprised three regiments and was subordinated to the French Commander-in-Chief while remaining under the overall control of the Polish authorities — much the same position as the British Expeditionary Force. These men were pictured lined up on the Place des Héros in Arras early in 1940.

The British arrive: a carrier of the 4th/7th Royal Dragoon Guards at speed near Arras. *Below:* The commander of the British Expeditionary Force, General Lord Gort, with the French Commander-in-Chief, Général Gamelin, on October 13, 1939.

The BEF lands

From the British angle, by the time war was declared the general strategy of the Allies had been agreed with the French, an initial committment of four divisions (two to a corps) to be sent to France within 33 days of mobilisation, and forecasts provided of other forces likely to become available at a future date. Plans had been drawn up for the two corps' prompt despatch and for their supply and maintenance. Similarly, measures had been agreed for the stationing of Royal Air Force units to operate in France. In all this, collaboration with the French had been 'close and harmonious'.

Upon the outbreak of war, command of the British Expeditionary Force had been entrusted by the British government to the Chief of the Imperial General Staff, General Lord Gort, a Grenadier Guardsman who had served as a staff officer and a battalion commander in the Great War, in which he had been decorated several times and awarded the Victoria Cross. Gort's instructions from the British government specified that the role of the BEF was to 'co-operate with our Allies in the defeat of the common enemy', and advised him that he would come under the control of the French Commander-in-Chief North-East Theatre of Operations, Général Georges; at the same time, as agreed with the French government, in the unlikely event of his ever receiving an order which appeared to him to imperil his force, he possessed the right to appeal to London before carrying it out. Another of his instructions laid down that he was to avoid parts of his force being transferred (except on a purely temporary basis) to an area other than that in which the main body was operating.

On the day before war was declared a

Left: Men of the 1st Battalion, the Royal Irish Fusiliers, on the march in bad weather on October 17 at Gavrelle, just outside Arras to the north-east. The battalion belonged to the 25th Brigade of the 50th (Northumbrian) Division under Major-General G. le Q. Martel. *Right:* Today the A-26 autoroute slices across the background, yet the village has changed little.

small advance party of 18 officers and 31 other ranks was flown to France. Advance parties sailed from Portsmouth on September 4 and the first convoy of troopships left Southampton and the Bristol Channel ports on the 9th. Utilising merchant shipping the Royal Navy conveyed men, equipment, stores and supplies steadily across the Channel as planned. Apart from an occasional hiccup in the arrangements after landing, the forward planning worked out well and the divisions arrived to time.

The British were to take over a sector of the frontier defences from French troops to the east of Lille, from Maulde to Halluin. On their left was the 7ème Armée, on their right the 1ère Armée. I Corps, with the 1st and 2nd Divisions, began taking over the sector assigned to it on October 3 and II Corps, with the 3rd and 4th Divisions, moved into the line on October 12.

General Headquarters was opened in Arras, a military mission under Major-General Sir Richard Howard-Vyse being appointed to the French General Headquarters (Grand Quartier Général, or GQG) of Général Gamelin at Vincennes, and another under Brigadier J.G. des R. Swayne to the headquarters of Général Georges at La Ferté-sous-Jouarre.

In the build-up that followed, another regular division, the 5th was sent to

Tommy comes marching in . . . to the station at Bachy, just a few hundred metres from the frontier south of Tournai. *Right:* Save for the cobbles giving way to tarmac, a corner of France where time has stood still since the days of the BEF. Comparison by Régis Potié in 1986.

Crews of the 4th Royal Tank Regiment servicing their Matilda Is in a farmyard at Acq, some 12 kilometres north-west of Arras. From here it was barely 20 kilometres to reach the Belgian frontier.

France by the end of 1939 and five Territorial divisions arrived between January 1940 and April. In early April a third corps was formed, and by the beginning of May the strength of the main fighting force, ten divisions in three corps and GHQ reserve, amounted to 237,319 men.

Sunday sermon at the battlefront. The place is Rumegies, near the Belgian border on the right flank of the sector taken over by the BEF. The date is April 28 — almost time for the battle to begin. With the conflict less than two weeks away, Father Coughlin, senior Roman Catholic chaplain with the BEF, might well have chosen that most appropriate prayer of Sir Francis Drake: 'O Lord God, when Thou givest to Thy servants to endeavour any great matter, grant us also to know that it is not the beginning, but the continuing of the same unto the end, until it be thoroughly finished, which yieldeth the true glory.'

The German strategy

'Sitzkrieg' about to become Blitzkrieg! The infantry of the newly-created 6. Panzer-Division on exercise with its panzers — a PzKpfw 35(t) (right) and a PzKpfw IV behind — early in 1940.

On September 27, 1939, Poland was defeated, Warsaw had fallen, and Hitler informed the General Staff of his decision to attack the French and British in the West, in the process breaking every assurance of respecting Belgian and Dutch neutrality. The General Staff and the leading generals were mostly opposed to the opening of an offensive in the West at that time, arguing that it would be more profitable to wait for the Allies to take the offensive.

The Führer Directive No. 6 for the Conduct of the War, Hitler's directive ordering preparations for the attack in the West, was issued on October 9. In this Hitler explained that the purpose of the operation was to defeat 'as much as possible of the French Army and the allies fighting on their side' and to win 'as much territory as possible in the Netherlands, Belgium and Northern France, to serve as a base for the

successful prosecution of the air and sea war against England and as a wide protective area for the economically vital Ruhr'. The plan of attack was prepared by the Army High Command, the OKH, and was issued ten days later. This first version of 'Fall Gelb' (Plan Yellow), in several ways an updated Schlieffen Plan, stated that the attack would be made on the northern wing of the front, through the Netherlands, Belgium and Northern France, its main objective being to secure central Belgium, where Heeresgruppe B was to concentrate its three armies to advance westwards on Ghent and Bruges. Fall Gelb was about to commit Germany, once more, to an unpardonable breach of the neutrality of Belgium and Luxembourg, and of the Netherlands.

On October 25 the Commander-in-Chief of the OKH, Generaloberst Walther von Brauchitsch, was summoned

with his Chief-of-Staff and OKH Director of Operations, General Franz Halder, to discuss the forthcoming operation with Hitler. When Halder explained that he planned on concentrating all the armoured formations in the direction of Ghent, Hitler made it known that he was thinking of using them south of Liège with 'the idea of a breakthrough in the direction of Reims and Amiens'. Three days later, Hitler informed the OKH that the attack was to be mounted to the north as well as to the south of Liège, with armoured units deployed each side.

A revised plan was issued on October 29, the intention of this second version of Fall Gelb being 'to engage and defeat as strong a portion of the French and Allied Armies as possible in Northern France and Belgium'. The main attack was to be made by Heeresgruppe B, with the 4. Armee striking westwards to

Watched by Generalmajor Erwin Rommel (second from right), engineers practice crossing the Mosel . . . with the Meuse in mind! Next to Rommel on his right is Oberst Georg von

Bismarck, the commander of Schtz.Rgt.7, one of the two armoured infantry regiments of the 7. Panzer-Division that Rommel was to lead in the breakthrough in May.

It was not until late February that the invasion plan Fall Gelb (Plan Yellow), in its fifth and final version, adopted the 'left wing' concept. Now the whole weight of the attack — the Schwerpunkt — was to be shifted eastwards. *Left:* The brain behind the change of plan is generally regarded as being down to General Erich von Manstein — seen here in conference with

Hitler when he was in command of Heeresgruppe Süd on the Eastern Front in 1943. It took some time to convince Generaloberst Walther von Brauchitsch *(right)*, the C-in-C of OKH (the German Army High Command) of the merits but, having done so, both he and his Chief-of-Staff, General Franz Halder, gave it their whole-hearted support.

the south of Liège and the 6. Armee to the north of the town. Heeresgruppe A was to cover the left flank of the attacking armies and further south Heeresgruppe C was to make feint attacks on the Maginot Line to pin down French divisions there. Since the main emphasis of the attack was no longer on the extreme north wing, the invasion of the Netherlands was ommitted but for the 6. Armee to cross the 'appendix' of Dutch territory around Maastricht, leaving the Dutch to decide whether to regard this as a 'casus belli'. This was more or less the plan of attack that the Allies anticipated.

On October 30, Generalmajor Alfred Jodl, the Chief of Operations of the Armed Forces High Command, the OKW, noted in his diary that Hitler had come up with 'a new idea about having an armoured and a motorised division attack Sedan via Arlon'. The following day, von Brauchitsch received two communications from the commander of Heeresgruppe A, Generaloberst Gerd von Rundstedt, one expressing the view that it would be unwise to launch an offensive in the West prematurely and maintaining that the operation planned could not have a decisive effect on the war, the other criticising the plan in detail. Von Rundstedt contended that the success of such an offensive would depend on the annihilation of all enemy forces north of the Somme, that these should be cut off and not merely pushed back, and therefore that the 'main effort of the whole operation must be on the southern wing'. Hitler's orders for the offensive to be launched on November 12, issued on November 5

and cancelled two days later, were to be the first of almost thirty such postponements, ostensibly because of the weather.

A third version of Fall Gelb was issued on November 15 which took into account Hitler's 'new idea' of an attack through Sedan. The XIX. Armeekorps with two panzer divisions was allotted to Heeresgruppe A 'to gain by surprise the west bank of the Meuse at, and south-east of, Sedan, and thus establish favourable conditions for further operations'. Basically, the plan was still for the main attack to be launched through the Belgian plain. OKH had not been unduly responsive to the changes proposed by von Rundstedt, and it is unlikely that Hitler had as yet even been made aware of them.

Hitler issued his Führer Directive No. 8 on November 20. Displaying his passion for detail — and confirming Halder's remark that his military interest was confined to grand strategy and petty detail, while all the major decisions in war lie in the area between — he ordered that all preparations had to be made in such a way that the offensive could still be delayed even if orders to do so did not reach commands until 11.00 p.m. the day before A-Day (Angriffstag, or day of the attack). He made known that the codewords, which were previously 'Rhein' and 'Elbe', will now be 'Danzig' (proceed with offensive) and 'Augsburg' (delay offensive). He also insisted that the operational order of October 29 was to be supplemented by precautions being taken 'to enable the main weight of attack to be switched from Heeres-

gruppe B to Heeresgruppe A should the disposition of enemy forces at any time suggest that Heeresgruppe A could achieve greater success' and the Netherlands, 'including the West Frisian Islands but excluding Texel', having to be occupied 'in the first instance up to the Grebbe-Meuse Line'. Fears that the Dutch would react by allowing in Allied troops and aircraft had resulted in the plan's extension to include an all-out invasion of the Netherlands. However Hitler directed that, though 'the attitude of the Dutch forces cannot be foreseen', where no resistance was offered or encountered 'the invasion will assume the character of a peaceful occupation'.

Time and again von Rundstedt and his Chief-of-Staff, General Erich von Manstein, presented the case for a stronger left wing — at meetings, in memoranda to OKH, even at a conference attended by Hitler — but von Brauchitsch remained unconvinced and Fall Gelb unaltered. The OKH did, nonetheless, take the line that the emphasis of the weight of the attack would have to be determined by how the fighting developed. In a directive issued on December 28 for the offensive to be launched in mid-January, it was stated that Hitler would decide where the weight of the attack was to be concentrated once it was clear where initial success was greatest.

Von Rundstedt then sent another memorandum to the OKH urging that the left flank be made the Schwerpunkt from the outset, with a request that it be submitted to Hitler. This substantially reiterated the Heeresgruppe A concept of the offensive as intended to bring about a 'decision', rejecting what it referred to as the 'partial' aim of an Allied defeat in Belgium and northern France and the gaining of that part of the coastline as not worth the risks entailed or the political upheaval of invading three neutral states. For the war to be brought to a speedy conclusion, it was argued, France had to be conquered, the BEF, the 'continental sword of the English' be eliminated, and then Britain could be dealt with at sea and in the air. Von Brauchitsch refused to submit the memorandum to Hitler and repeated that the final decision about the focal point of the attack rested with the Führer, whom he would advise accordingly.

Although it was taken for granted that information of one kind or another would have come into the possession of the Allies after the forced landing of the aircraft with Major Reinberger aboard in Belgium on January 10, the plan was not changed after the date for the offensive had already been fixed for January 17. After another postponement because of the weather, the fourth version of Fall Gelb was issued on January 30; again, it did not differ fundamentally from the previous one, except in expanding Heeresgruppe B's role to include the whole of the Netherlands. The Allies' appreciation of German intentions still held good.

Von Rundstedt and von Manstein continued to press their views but von Brauchitsch remained unconvinced. On February 13, according to Jodl's diary, Hitler reopened the question of where the main weight of the attack should be placed and concluded that the armour 'should be concentrated in the direction of Sedan where the enemy does not expect our main thrust. The documents carried by the aircraft which made the landing' Jodl wrote, 'have still further confirmed their opinion that our only concern is to occupy the Channel coastline of the Netherlands and Belgium.' That day, Jodl put forward Hitler's ideas to von Brauchitsch and his staff. A war game held on February 14 at Mayen meanwhile confirmed what had been shown by one held a week earlier at Koblenz: that additional forces would be needed to sustain an attack in the Sedan area. It seems that the results of the games had shaken Halder's opposition and he then recommended to von Brauchitsch that they adopt the 'left wing' concept advocated by von Rundstedt and von Manstein.

Then, on February 17, von Manstein, who had just been appointed to command the XXXVIII. Armeekorps, used the opportunity of a lunch with Hitler to expound the views of Heeresgruppe A on the conduct of the offensive in the West. After the meal Hitler heard for the first time a detailed explanation of the Heeresgruppe A proposals for the main blow to be struck by the left wing, since von Brauchitsch had consistently refused to relay them to him. Whether von Brauchitsch had come to know of the after-lunch conference and saw which way the wind was now blowing is not known, but on February 22 Halder

held a conference at OKH to discuss the fifth and final version of Fall Gelb. This was issued on February 24; the 4. Armee was transferred from Heeresgruppe B to Heeresgruppe A, and the whole weight of the attack was shifted to the left wing. The entire plan was drawn up around the intention of delivering the main blow at Sedan. Everything else was secondary, if not diversionary, and Heeresgruppe A got all, and even more, than it had asked for. It had taken some time for von Brauchitsch and Halder to come round to the idea of making the left wing the Schwerpunkt of the offensive; but

having done so, they had not shrunk from bringing the strategy to its ultimate conclusion.

The Allies' appreciation of the German intentions had been correct up to the fourth version of Fall Gelb but this final plan left the Allies outguessed, their plan to move forward to the Dyle and to the Breda completely invalidated.

There were still doubts and misgivings among the staffs, however, and many a commanding general had yet to be convinced. At a top-level conference at the Reich Chancellery in mid-March, the XIX. Armeekorps commander,

There were still some doubts amongst the higher echelons of the Wehrmacht, and the adoption of the final version of Fall Gelb owed much to the success of Generaloberst Gerd von Rundstedt, *left* (who was to command Heeresgruppe A — Army Group A — in the coming battle), in convincing Hitler of its merits. *Right:* One doubting Thomas was Generaloberst Fedor von Bock, the commander of Heeresgruppe B.

MAP

FALL GELB FIRST PLAN OCTOBER 19, 1939

3 DIVISIONS

HEERESGRUPPE B
(37 DIVISIONS,
INCLUDING
8 ARMOURED)

HEERESGRUPPE A
(27 DIVISIONS,
INCLUDING
1 ARMOURED)

HEERESGRUPPE C
(25 DIVISIONS)

OKH RESERVES:
(9 DIVISIONS,
INCLUDING 1 ARMOURED)

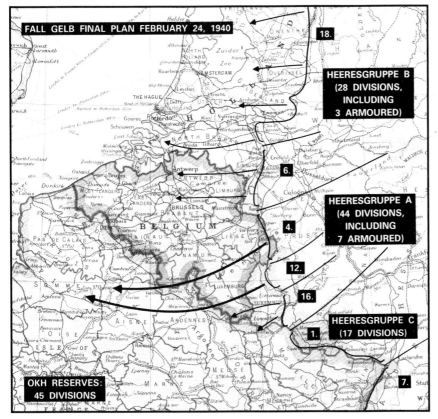

FALL GELB FINAL PLAN FEBRUARY 24, 1940

18.

HEERESGRUPPE B
(28 DIVISIONS,
INCLUDING
3 ARMOURED)

6.

HEERESGRUPPE A
(44 DIVISIONS,
INCLUDING
7 ARMOURED)

4.

12.

16.

HEERESGRUPPE C
(17 DIVISIONS)

1.

7.

OKH RESERVES:
45 DIVISIONS

General Heinz Guderian, having outlined his initial task and how he intended to carry it out, was asked by Hitler what he was going to do after establishing a bridgehead across the Meuse, at which point General Ernst Busch, commanding the 16. Armee, is said by Guderian to have cried out, 'Well, I don't think you will cross the river in the first place!' As late as April, the Heeresgruppe B commander, Generaloberst Fedor von Bock, was grumbling to Halder that, 'you will be creeping by ten kilometres from the Maginot Line with the flank of your breakthrough and hope that the French will watch inertly! You are cramming the mass of the panzer units together into the sparse roads of the Ardennes mountain country, as if there were no such thing as air power! And you then hope to be able to lead an operation as far as the coast with an open southern flank 300 kilometres long, where stands the mass of the French Army!' To von Bock this was 'transcending the bounds of reason'.

As to where the credit for the plan in its final form is due, Hitler undoubtedly sensed from the first the importance of striking south of Liège and he foresaw that concentrating the armour in the direction of Sedan could pay dividends. What he had not envisaged at the start but what Heeresgruppe A had continually pressed for, was making the Ardennes the point of the main effort of the entire offensive from the outset.

The basic concept of the strategy was that advocated by von Rundstedt and von Manstein — the brains behind it being generally regarded as von Manstein's. Hitler had never been over-enamoured with the second version of the plan and his imagination was only

really fired by the drastically revised final version. Von Brauchitsch and Halder, having produced the earlier plans, had held out for weeks against making further changes, although by the time von Manstein had expounded the Heeresgruppe A proposals to a receptive Führer they had begun to veer towards accepting the need to strengthen the left wing. To what extent this was as a direct result of the war games or the cumulative effects of Heeresgruppe A's persistence it is impossible to tell — probably a combination of the two, while the third, Hitler's dissatisfaction, was to tilt the balance. But once having adopted the idea of making the left wing the Schwerpunkt and of striking through the Ardennes to cut off and annihilate the mass of Allied armies to the north, von Brauchitsch and Halder went beyond the Heeresgruppe A proposals, so that in its final form the bold and inspired plan which emerged was the product of the OKH.

Aiming at the destruction of the enemy centre of gravity, the French 7ème, 1ère and 9ème Armées and the BEF in Belgium and northern France, Fall Gelb was now a superb realisation of Carl von Clausewitz's fundamental principle of the Schwerpunkt.

In the disposition of forces for the offensive, Heeresgruppe B, which faced the Netherlands and the Belgian plain north of Liège, had been reduced to two armies with 28 divisions, three of them armoured. The 18. Armee was to crush Dutch resistance, and to do so as soon as possible to free forces for action in Belgium or France. The 6. Armee was to attack through the Belgian plain, where the Allies were expecting the main German blow to fall; this being intended mainly as a diversion to draw

the Allied armies into Belgium and hold them while they were being encircled. The offensive in this sector was not to be followed up too rapidly in order to give the Allies enough time to advance as far into Belgium as they wanted to go, making it all the harder for them to get out.

South of Liège, opposite the Ardennes and Luxembourg, Heeresgruppe A totalled three armies with 44 divisions, including seven armoured. On the right was the 4. Armee, in the centre the 12. Armee, on the left the 16. Armee — the main effort spearheaded within the 12. Armee by five panzer divisions under the integrated command of Gruppe von Kleist driving for the Meuse between Sedan and Monthermé and beyond: the 'Sichelschnitt' — 'the cut of the sickle'.

Further to the south, Heeresgruppe C was to cover the Maginot Line from Longwy to the Swiss border with only 17 divisions and no armour. Its two armies, the 1. Armee and the 7. Armee, although essentially defensive, were to keep the Allies guessing whether a real or, at any rate, secondary attack would materialise — to tie down as many French units as possible. Facing them, in four French armies, were 36 divisions, not counting fortress units.

Forty-five German divisions, about three times the size of the ill-deployed French reserve, were positioned behind the two attacking army groups, to be engaged where needed.

May 5 was the date set by Hitler on May 1 for the attack to begin. From May 3 one postponement followed another, largely because of the weather but also while Hitler improved upon his justification for invading Belgium and the Netherlands, which were to be accused of having acted belligerently, until on May 8 Jodl noted in his diary that 'Göring wants postponement until May 10 at least'. Hitler, by now jittery over surprise being lost, 'against his intuition', consented: May 10, 'but not one day longer'.

One of the strongest supporters of Blitzkrieg — who now had the golden opportunity of putting theory into practice — was the XIX. Armeekorps commander, General Heinz Guderian.

55

The opposing forces

Tank-wise, the opposing forces were fairly evenly matched, both in quality and quantity. *Above:* **The panzers of 4. Panzer-Division and** *below* **the Hotchkiss H-39 of a French B.C.C.**

By May 10 the forces available to the Commander-in-Chief North-East Front had increased and Général Georges had 108 units at his disposal, amounting to a total of 102 divisions, but the Wehrmacht now disposed of 157 divisions — almost 50 more than at the beginning of September — of which 134 were deployed in the West. Although neutral, Belgium and the Netherlands were soon to be pushed onto the Allied side by the German invasion of their countries and this was to add about 20 Belgian divisions and 10 Dutch divisions to those facing the Wehrmacht.

These figures tell only part of the story for a precise estimate of strength is not obtained by simply adding up the

Neither was the morale or the ability of the men found wanting — it was simply the *way* the armour was used that made the panzers superior. Whereas the Germans concentrated their armour in mass attacks, the Allied tanks were scattered all along the front, proving again the old adage of 'safety in numbers'. *Above:* **A crew of the 6. Panzer-Division under training in their PzKpfw IV early in the year.** *Below:* **Commandant Louis Warabiot inspects men of the 24ème B.C.C., a few weeks before it became part of the new 4ème D.C.R. which fought at Montcornet and on the Somme.**

number of Allied divisions under command. Their value depends not only of their number, but also on the ability and effectiveness of their commanders.

The overall control of the Allied armies was very poor, for pre-war policies, particularly the Belgian adherence to neutrality and the earlier caution by the

British, had resulted in largely inadequate arrangements for the control and command of the force. The mere appointment of a supreme commander

At the beginning of May 1940, German armoured strength totalled some 3,500 tanks. All those available were deployed in ten panzer divisions which were themselves grouped together under four specialised army corps. Each panzer division was a fully integrated unit and comprised, in addition to its armoured brigade, a brigade of mechanised infantry; a regiment of mobile artillery with half-tracked prime-movers; a reconnaissance battalion equipped with armoured cars; an engineer battalion and a signals battalion. Elements of each could be tailored to the requirements of the battle and reassembled into battle groups, a typical 'Kampfgruppe' consisting of a panzer regiment, a mechanised infantry regiment, artillery, signals and engineers. *Right:* In May, General Heinz Guderian was in command of the XIX. Armeekorps, with three panzer divisions. In June, he commanded Gruppe Guderian and had two corps with four panzer and two mobile infantry divisions under him. This picture of Guderian's SdKfz 251 command vehicle was taken in June.

However, as integrated as the panzer forces were, the hardware still comprised several different tank types. After the Allied 'capitulation' at Munich, and the subsequent German take-over of Czechoslovakia, the Wehrmacht gained many valuable resources, and about one-third of the tanks available in May 1940 originated from Czech factories. Some 140 were PzKpfw 35(t) (the 't' standing for 'Tchechoslowakisch'). These two served with the 6. Panzer-Division.

The 1938-type tank of the Czech Army was designated the PzKpfw 38(t) as seen here on the right. The German's own light tank (apart from the machine gun-armed PzKpfw I on page 52) was the 10-tonne PzKpfw II — epitomised here by '243' of 7. Panzer-Division — equipped with a 20mm gun.

Weighing in at 15 tonnes, the PzKpfw III was considered in the medium tank bracket — its 37mm gun of German manufacture being more powerful than the Czech 37mm gun of the PzKpfw 38(t). This particular example was photographed with the 5. Panzer-Division.

ORDER OF BATTLE OF GERMAN PANZER DIVISIONS IN MAY 1940

1. Panzer-Division

Pz.Rgt. 1 and Pz.Rgt. 2:	161 light and command tanks 98 gun-armed tanks
Aufkl.Abt. 4:	50 armoured cars
Pi.Btl. 37:	13 PzKpfw I and PzKpfw II 4 bridgelayers on PzKpfw IV chassis
s.I.G. Kompanie 702:	6 self-propelled 150mm howitzers on PzKpfw I chassis

2. Panzer-Division

Pz.Rgt. 3 and Pz.Rgt. 4:	175 light and command tanks 90 gun-armed tanks
Aufkl.Abt. 5:	50 armoured cars
Pi.Btl. 38:	13 PzKpfw I and PzKpfw II 4 bridgelayers on PzKpfw IV chassis
s.I.G. Kompanie 703:	6 self-propelled 150mm howitzers on PzKpfw I chassis

3. Panzer-Division

Pz.Rgt. 5 and Pz.Rgt. 6:	273 light and command tanks 68 gun-armed tanks
Aufkl.Abt. 3:	50 armoured cars
Pi.Btl. 39:	13 PzKpfw I and PzKpfw II 4 bridgelayers on PzKpfw IV chassis

4. Panzer-Division

Pz.Rgt. 35 and Pz.Rgt. 36:	259 light and command tanks 64 gun-armed tanks
Aufkl.Abt. 7:	50 armoured cars
Pi.Btl. 79:	13 PzKpfw I and PzKpfw II

5. Panzer-Division

Pz.Rgt. 15 and Pz.Rgt. 31:	243 light and command tanks 84 gun-armed tanks
Aufkl.Abt. 8:	50 armoured cars
Pi.Btl. 89:	13 PzKpfw I and PzKpfw II 4 bridgelayers on PzKpfw IV chassis
s.I.G. Kompanie 704:	6 self-propelled 150mm howitzers on PzKpfw I chassis

6. Panzer-Division

Pz.Rgt. 11 and Pz.Abt. 65:	59 light and command tanks 159 gun-armed tanks
Aufkl.Abt. 57:	50 armoured cars
Pi.Btl. 57:	13 PzKpfw I and PzKpfw II

7. Panzer-Division

Pz.Rgt. 25:	109 light and command tanks 110 gun-armed tanks
Aufkl.Abt. 37:	50 armoured cars
Pi.Btl. 58:	13 PzKpfw I and PzKpfw II
s.I.G. Kompanie 705:	6 self-propelled 150mm howitzers on PzKpfw I chassis

8. Panzer-Division

Pz.Rgt. 10:	58 light and command tanks 154 gun-armed tanks
Aufkl.Abt. 59:	50 armoured cars
Pi.Btl. 59:	13 PzKpfw I and PzKpfw II

9. Panzer-Division

Pz.Rgt. 33:	97 light and command tanks 56 gun-armed tanks
Aufkl.Abt. 9:	50 armoured cars
Pi.Btl. 86:	13 PzKpfw I and PzKpfw II
s.I.G. Kompanie 701:	6 self-propelled 150mm howitzers on PzKpfw I chassis

10. Panzer-Division

Pz.Rgt. 7 and Pz.Rgt. 8:	185 light and command tanks 90 gun-armed tanks
Aufkl.Abt. 90:	50 armoured cars
Pi.Btl. 49:	13 PzKpfw I and PzKpfw II 4 bridgelayers on PzKpfw IV chassis
s.I.G. Kompanie 706:	6 self-propelled 150mm howitzers on PzKpfw I chassis

Apart from the tank strength in the panzer regiments and panzer abteilung which are given accurately (courtesy of Thomas L. Jentz and Steven J. Zaloga), these figures are the nominal strengths only. The 'light and command tanks' include PzKpfw I, PzKpfw II and Pz.Bef.Wg.; the 'gun-armed tanks' include PzKpfw III and PzKpfw IV, as well as PzKpfw 35(t) in the 6. Panzer-Division and PzKpfw 38(t) in the 7. Panzer-Division and 8. Panzer-Division.

The total armoured strength of the German forces was in excess of 3,000 units. For the attack, the Wehrmacht deployed 140 PzKpfw 35(t), 240 PzKpfw 38(t), 1,000 PzKpfw I, 1,000 PzKpfw II, 380 PzKpfw III, and 290 PzKpfw IV. Here a Kampf-gruppe of the 4. Panzer-Division is pictured in the field in May 1940 comprising trucks of infantry from Schtz. Rgt. 33, a SdKfz 221 recce armoured car of Aufkl. Abt. 7, and a prime-mover and 105mm howitzer from Art. Rgt. 103.

could not, in itself, weld the Allied armies into a whole when these armies were not organised on a common structure, their men not trained with a common doctrine, and not even speaking the same language! In this respect the Wehrmacht had a great advantage.

Beside this, the tactics of the two sides were very different. Technically, the Allies' outdated doctrines placed less reliance on armour and aircraft and, to a lesser extent, the application of anti-tank and anti-aircraft weapons. Unlike the French and British, the Germans were not fighting the last war, but the next, and their practice of the theory of 'Blitzkrieg' added tremendous power to their arms.

A balance sheet of the armoured forces engaged is not easy to produce for the exact figures are not known with certainty. Armament was varied: the PzKpfw I and the Mark VIB were armed only with machine guns; the PzKpfw III and the Renault R-35 had 37mm guns; the Matilda and Cruiser tanks were equipped with 2-pounder guns and the PzKpfw IV and Renault B1bis had 75mm guns.

Of the 3,132 modern tanks available to French forces in May 1940, about 900 were the Renault R-35 *(above)*, a light tank of 10 tonnes armed with a 37mm gun, which equipped 20 of the tank battalions. *Below:* Eight of the B.C.C.s were issued with the more numerous, yet antiquated, Renault FT, dating from the First World War, of which 1,500 remained serviceable.

ORDER OF BATTLE OF THE FRENCH ARMOURED UNITS
THE INDEPENDENT TANK BATTALIONS (BATAILLON DE CHARS DE COMBAT: B.C.C.)

1er B.C.C.*	45 Renault R-35	5ème Armée	21ème B.C.C.	45 Renault R-35	5ème Armée
2ème B.C.C.*	45 Renault R-35	5ème Armée	22ème B.C.C.	45 Renault R-35	7ème Armée
3ème B.C.C.	45 Renault R-35	2ème Armée	23ème B.C.C.	45 Renault R-35	3ème Armée
4ème B.C.C.	45 FCM 36	2ème Armée	24ème B.C.C.*	45 Renault R-35	4ème Armée
5ème B.C.C.	45 Renault R-35	3ème Armée	29ème B.C.C.	63 Renault FT-17	3ème Armée
6ème B.C.C.	45 Renault R-35	9ème Armée	30ème B.C.C.	63 Renault FT-17	3ème Armée
7ème B.C.C.	45 FCM 36	2ème Armée	31ème B.C.C.	63 Renault FT-17	5ème Armée
9ème B.C.C.	45 Renault R-35	7ème Armée	32ème B.C.C.	45 Renault R-35	9ème Armée
10ème B.C.C.*	45 Renault R-35	4ème Armée	33ème B.C.C.	63 Renault FT-17	9ème Armée
11ème B.C.C.	63 Renault FT-17	4ème Armée	34ème B.C.C.*	45 Renault R-35	5ème Armée
12ème B.C.C.	45 Renault R-35	3ème Armée	35ème B.C.C.	45 Renault R-35	1ère Armée
13ème B.C.C.	45 Hotchkiss H-35	1ère Armée	36ème B.C.C.	63 Renault FT-17	8ème Armée
16ème B.C.C.	45 Renault R-35	8ème Armée	38ème B.C.C.	45 Hotchkiss H-35	1ère Armée
17ème B.C.C.	45 Renault R-35	8ème Armée	39ème B.C.C.	45 Renault R-35	1ère Armée
18ème B.C.C.	63 Renault FT-17	8ème Armée	43ème B.C.C.	45 Renault R-35	3ème Armée
19ème B.C.C.*	45 Renault D-2	5ème Armée	51ème B.C.C.	9 FCM 2C	3ème Armée
20ème B.C.C.	45 Renault R-35	4ème Armée	B.C.T.C.	63 Renault FT-17	Armée des Alpes

These figures indicate the nominal establishment and do not include tank units in North Africa and the Levant, or depôt and training tanks. The subordination given is that at the beginning of May 1940. During the course of the battle in May and June, the battalions asterisked * were employed in the reconstruction of the D.C.R. to make good their losses.

Master of the French armed forces was the Renault B1bis — a 32-tonne monster whose main weapon was a 75mm, with a 47mm for secondary armament. Two battalions of the B1bis were assigned to each of the four armoured divisions (D.C.R.).

ORDER OF BATTLE OF THE FRENCH ARMOURED DIVISIONS (DIVISION CUIRASSÉE: D.C.R.)

1ère D.C.R.

1ère Demi-Brigade
28ème B.C.C. (35 Renault B1bis)
37ème B.C.C. (35 Renault B1bis)

3ème Demi-Brigade
25ème B.C.C. (45 Hotchkiss H-39)
26ème B.C.C. (45 Hotchkiss H-39)

5ème Bataillon de Chasseurs Portés

2ème D.C.R.

2ème Demi-Brigade
8ème B.C.C. (35 Renault B1bis)
15ème B.C.C. (35 Renault B1bis)

4ème Demi-Brigade
14ème B.C.C. (45 Hotchkiss H-39)
27ème B.C.C. (45 Hotchkiss H-39)

17ème Bataillon de Chasseurs Portés

3ème D.C.R.

5ème Demi-Brigade
41ème B.C.C. (35 Renault B1bis)
49ème B.C.C. (35 Renault B1bis)

7ème Demi-Brigade
42ème B.C.C. (45 Hotchkiss H-39)
45ème B.C.C. (45 Hotchkiss H-39)

16ème Bataillon de Chasseurs Portés

4ème D.C.R. (as on May 21)

6ème Demi-Brigade
46ème B.C.C. (35 Renault B1bis)
47ème B.C.C. (35 Renault B1bis)
19ème B.C.C. (45 Renault D-2)

8ème Demi-Brigade
2ème B.C.C. (45 Renault R-35)
24ème B.C.C. (45 Renault R-35)
44ème B.C.C. (45 Renault R-35)

4ème Bataillon de Chasseurs Portés
7ème Régiment de Dragons Portés

Attached cavalry units: 3ème Cuirassiers (40 Somua S-35)   10ème Cuirassiers (40 Panhard P-178)

The D.C.R. had two 'Demi-Brigades', one with two battalions of medium tanks, the other with two battalions of light tanks, and one battalion of mechanised infantry (Chasseurs Portés). The 4ème D.C.R. was created in May 15 on a stronger, though disparate, structure with an additional regiment of mechanised infantry from the cavalry. It also possessed two other cavalry units: one combat regiment with at first only two Somua S-35 squadrons (the two Hotchkiss H-39 squadrons of the 3ème Cuirassiers joined it on May 25) and one scout regiment. These figures are for nominal establishments only.

There were about 370 of the Hotchkiss H-39 in service, either with the D.C.R. or B.C.C.

The FCM 36, of which only 100 had been completed, equipped just two of the B.C.C.

1ère D.L.M.

  1ère B.L.M.
    4ème Cuirassiers (40 Hotchkiss H-35 and 40 Somua S-35)
    18ème Dragons (40 Hotchkiss H-35 and 40 Somua S-35)

  2ème B.L.M.
    6ème Cuirassiers (40 Panhard P-178)
    4ème Dragons Portés (60 A.M.R.)

2ème D.L.M.

  3ème B.L.M.
    13ème Dragons (40 Hotchkiss H-35 and 40 Somua S-35)
    29ème Dragons (40 Hotchkiss H-35 and 40 Somua S-35)

  4ème B.L.M.
    8ème Cuirassiers (40 Panhard P-178)
    1er Dragons Portés (60 A.M.R.)

3ème D.L.M.

  5ème B.L.M.
    1er Cuirassiers (40 Hotchkiss H-39 and 40 Somua S-35)
    2ème Cuirassiers (40 Hotchkiss H-39 and 40 Somua S-35)

  6ème B.L.M.
    12ème Cuirassiers (40 Panhard P-178)
    11ème Dragons Portés (60 Hotchkiss H-35)

1ère D.L.C.

  2ème B.C.
    1er Chasseurs
    19ème Dragons

  11ème B.L.M.
    1er R.A.M. (12 Panhard P-178 and 12 Hotchkiss H-35)
    5ème Dragons Portés (20 A.M.R.)

2ème D.L.C.

  3ème B.C.
    18ème Chasseurs
    5ème Cuirassiers

  12ème B.L.M.
    2ème R.A.M. (12 Panhard P-178 and 12 Hotchkiss H-35)
    3ème Dragons Portés (20 A.M.R.)

3ème D.L.C.

  5ème B.C.
    4ème Hussards
    6ème Dragons

  13ème B.L.M.
    3ème R.A.M. (12 Panhard P-178 and 12 Hotchkiss H-35)
    2ème Dragons Portés (A.M.R. not yet delivered)

4ème D.L.C.

  4ème B.C.
    8ème Dragons
    31ème Dragons

  14ème B.L.M.
    4ème R.A.M. (12 Panhard P-178 and 12 Hotchkiss H-35)
    14ème Dragons Portés (20 A.M.R.)

5ème D.L.C.

  6ème B.C.
    11ème Cuirassiers
    12ème Chasseurs

  15ème B.L.M.
    5ème R.A.M. (12 Panhard P-178 and 12 Hotchkiss H-35)
    15ème Dragons Portés (20 A.M.R.)

The D.L.M. had two light mechanised brigades (B.L.M.), one with two tank regiments, the other with one scout regiment (Régiment de Découverte) and one mechanised infantry regiment (Dragons Portés). The D.L.C. had two brigades, one true cavalry brigade (B.C.) with two horsed regiments and one light mechanised brigade with one armoured cars regiment (R.A.M.) and one mechanised infantry regiment. These figures are nominal establishments.

Altogether there were around 250 of the Somua S-35 with the D.L.M., this example being with the 18ème Dragons.

A Hotchkiss H-35 of the 4ème Cuirassiers, 1ère D.L.M., one of the 400 which equipped the D.L.M., D.L.C., and motorised G.R.D.I. (reconnaissance group) of the D.I.M.

The Light Mechanised and Light Cavalry Divisions also shared 300 Renault A.M.R. 33 light tanks *(above)* and 380 Panhard P-178 armoured cars *(below)*.

The 1st Armoured Division of the BEF had 143 Mk IV Cruiser tanks, these being from the 5th Battalion, Royal Tank Regiment.

The BEF's armoured cavalry regiments also had a nominal strength of 28 Mk VI light tanks each, like this example from the 13th/18th Royal Hussars.

In May 1940 the Wehrmacht had some 3,220 panzers, about one third of them the light PzKpfw I, another third, the PzKpfw II; and the remainder the heavier PzKpfw III, PzKpfw 35(t) and PzKpfw 38(t), all armed with 37mm gun, and the PzKpfw IV armed with a 75mm gun. To this figure must be added about 245 command tanks, giving a grand total of 3,465 panzers, of which one third only was armed with 37mm or larger calibre cannon. The six panzer divisions existing at the outbreak of the war had by now been supplemented by four more created by the conversion of light divisions into panzer divisions. The 35 panzer abteilungen, or tank units, of these ten divisions would be able to deploy 2,500 panzers in the first wave in the West (not including around 135 command tanks), of which 1,000 were armed with cannon of 37mm or above.

To oppose these the French Army had 3,132 modern tanks on May 10, and about 550 new tanks were to be brought in, most of them to replace losses, in the course of the battles to come. The French tanks, the Hotchkiss H-35 and H-39, Renault D-2 and R-35, Renault B1bis and Somua S-35, had generally thicker armour than the German tanks but their speed was less and their radius of action more limited. The Renault D-2, Somua S-35 and Renault B1bis were equipped with a potent 47mm gun, the latter having a 75mm in addition, while the Renault R-35, Hotchkiss H-35 and H-39 were equipped with a 37mm gun.

The BEF had about 300 tanks in France, some 200 being Mark VIB light cavalry tanks, the others Mark II infantry tanks equipped with a 2-pounder; of these 100 Matildas, only 23 were the more modern Matilda II. The 1st Armoured Division, which had started arriving in May, had six armoured battalions, in all 114 Mark VI light tanks and 143 Cruiser tanks equipped with a 2-pounder.

Like the French, who had spread out the available armour all along the front, the Belgians had split up their small armoured force of some 270 light tanks between their infantry, cavalry and border units. Each infantry division had a complement of a dozen T-13 light tanks *(above left)*; the two cavalry divisions had 18 T-13s each and a similar number of T-15 light tanks *(above right)*. The 1ère Division de Chasseurs Ardennais, had a complement of 48 T-13s.

To the Allied strength must be added the 270 or so light tanks of the Belgian armoured forces, of which most were the T-13 equipped with a 47mm gun in a semi-turret. These were split up among the infantry and cavalry divisions and would have little impact on the course of the battle. There were also the 24 Landsverk armoured cars of the Dutch Army.

These figures show that the available Allied armour was not inferior in quantity — about 3,500 for each side — nor really inferior in quality when compared to the panzers. It was the obsolete Allied tank tactics that really made them inferior and doomed them to certain destruction. Whereas the German doctrine emphasised the principle of the concentration of armour, all the available panzers being deployed within ten integrated panzer divisions, the French tanks were deployed into three armoured divisions (D.C.R.), a fourth being assembled; three mechanised (D.L.M.) and five cavalry (D.L.C.) divisions; plus 33 tank battalions and a dozen or so tank companies . . . all in all more than 60 independent units. At the same time, the BEF armour was scattered across eight cavalry regiments and two army tank battalions. While the panzer divisions were massed together under a few corps, the French armoured and cavalry divisions were distributed among several armies while the tank battalions were parcelled out all over the front. The words of the commander of the 1er Groupement Cuirassé, Général Charles Delestraint, well summarised the situation in 1940: 'We had 3,000 tanks and so did the Germans. We used them in a thousand packs of three, the Germans in three packs of a thousand.'

Of the four French armoured divisions, two were never given a chance because French tank doctrine condemned them into being outmanoeuvred and destroyed: the 1ère D.C.R. ran out of fuel in Belgium and the 2ème D.C.R., dispersed to begin with, was then blotted out piecemeal. 'In each army', wrote Général Louis Keller, Inspector General of Tanks, in a report on July 5, 1940, 'the tank battalions were scattered abroad, company by company, even section by section, on all the bridges, on all the roads, in the fringes of every wood, employed on casual or emergency errands.'

The Belgian Army also had eight Renault ACG-1s which equipped one Escadron d'Auto-Blindées (Armoured Car Squadron).

The Netherlands had only 24 Swedish armoured cars, 12 each of the Landsverk L-180 and L-181, called the M-36 and M-38 in Dutch service. A further dozen indigenous DAF M-39s *(above)* had just become operational by May 1940.

Although it is true that the skies were German in May and June 1940 and that few, if any, Allied aircraft were to be seen by the troops opposing the Germans, this was not only because of inferiority of numbers — the weakness of both the Armée de l'Air and the RAF in really efficient bombers being one of the most serious deficiencies — but mainly because the Luftwaffe did its best to support the ground troops, working its staffels hard, while the Allied air forces fought a largely static war, being outflown day after day. Taking into account the Dutch and Belgian Air Forces and those aircraft of the RAF based in France, it would seem that the Luftwaffe had a numerical superiority in May 1940 of about 10 to 6, which is somewhat less than has often been stated.

On May 10 the French Armée de l'Air had a first-line strength of about 1,400 aircraft, made up of about 650 fighters, about 250 bombers and 490 reconnaissance aircraft. Although most of the fighters were reasonably modern (Morane 406, Bloch 151 and 152, Curtiss H-75 or Dewoitine 520), the bomber and reconnaissance units were not. Only half the bombers were modern aircraft (LeO 451, Breguet 693, Amiot 354 or Martin 167); the rest were obsolete (Amiot 143, Bloch 200 and 210 or Farman 221 and 222), only fit for night missions.

Supporting the Groupe d'Armées No. 1 was Z.O.A. Nord with 12 fighter squadrons, 6 bomber squadrons and 23

In May 1940, the French Air Force — the Armée de l'Air — lacked an efficient bomber arm as half of its 250 aircraft were obsolete machines like the Amiot 143 *(above)*, of which 50 were still in service, and the Farman 222 *(bottom)*, some 20 strong. The Amiot 143 could carry 1½ tonnes of bombs at a maximum speed of 295 km/hr (185 mph), whereas the Farman 222 flew slightly faster and could operate with a bomb load of five tonnes.

Mardyck, April 22, 1940. Sous Lieutenant Victor Paquez, Adjutant François Dufour and Adjutant Laurent Legrand in front of '250'. This Potez 63/11 belonged to G.A.O. 501, the reconnaissance group assigned to Ier Corps d'Armée.

reconnaissance squadrons. Supporting the Groupe d'Armées No. 2 was Z.O.A. Est with 7 fighter squadrons, 4 bomber squadrons and 15 reconnaissance squadrons. On the morning of May 10 four bomber squadrons of the

Z.O.A. Est were subordinated to Z.O.A. Nord.

Other units were further south with Z.O.A. Sud, supporting the 8ème Armée in southern Alsace, or with Z.O.A. Alpes on the Italian front.

While the French fighter pilots were well-trained and motivated, their mounts, though not obsolete, were no real match for the Luftwaffe's Messerschmitt Bf 109.

The most numerous fighters were the Morane MS 406 *(top)*, of which 296 were in service, and the Curtiss H-75 *(above)*, 99 being on strength in May 1940.

Among these were 6 fighter squadrons, 13 bomber squadrons and 13 reconnaissance squadrons, most of these being committed to battle in the weeks that followed.

On May 10 the 19 fighter squadrons with Z.O.A. Nord and Z.O.A. Est comprised 531 fighters, of which about 400 were combat ready, plus 40 night fighters (of which 28 were combat ready). Nine of these squadrons were equipped with the ageing Morane 406, 6 with Bloch 151 and 152 and 4 with the Curtiss H-75. The night fighter squadrons were equipped with the twin-engined Potez 631. The two squadrons equipped with the superb Dewoitine 520 — G.C. I/3 and G.C. II/3 — were not to be committed before May 14.

To these figures must be added the 1,873 aircraft available to the RAF, of which 416 were stationed in France with the Air Component and Advanced Air Striking Force. The Air Component

Without doubt, the best of the French fighters was the Dewoitine D 520, which could fight on equal terms with the Bf 109, but there were only two fighter groups operational with the type: G.C. I/3 and G.C. II/3 (G.C. standing for Groupe de Chasse). Three more groups would be equipped with the aircraft before the Armistice, and the Dewoitine was to be credited with 147 victories in just over a month against the loss of 85 aircraft and 44 pilots.

had four fighter squadrons (two of Hurricanes, two of Gladiators), four bomber squadrons (Blenheims), five reconnaissance squadrons (Lysanders) and one liaison squadron (Dragon Rapides). The Advance Air Striking Force had two fighter squadrons (Hurricanes) and ten bomber squadrons (eight Battles and two Blenheims). Also seven Blenheim squadrons and two Whitley squadrons were available to support the BEF from their bases in England.

The Dutch Air Force consisted of 125 first-line aircraft organised in two regiments: the 1e LVR with four fighter squadrons (Fokker D-XXI and Fokker G-1A), one bomber squadron (Fokker T-V), and one reconnaissance squadron (Fokker C-X), and the 2e LVR with two fighter squadrons (Fokker D-XXI and Douglas DB-8A) and four reconnaissance squadrons (Fokker C-V, Fokker C-X and Koolkoven FK-51).

The Belgian Air Force's strength was about 180 first-line aircraft organised into three regiments: about 60 reconnaissance aircraft with the 1er Régiment (Fairey Fox and Renard R-31), about 80 fighters with the 2ème Régiment (Fiat CR-42, Hurricane, Gladiator and Fairey Fox) and about 50 bombers with the 3ème Régiment (Fairey Fox and Battle).

The rôle of the Royal Air Force in France was split between the Air Component of the British Expeditionary Force, responsible for the close support of the Army, and the Advanced Air Striking Force (AASF) which was to serve the needs of the whole front. This Blenheim IV of No. 139 Squadron, No. 71 Wing, was with the AASF and most probably photographed at Plivot.

The RAF had despatched four Hurricane squadrons to the Continent, two with the AASF and two with the Air Component. This is Flying Officer Dickie Martin of No. 73 Squadron.

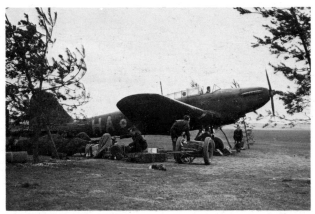

Left: **Servicing machines under improvised conditions in that bitter winter was no joke, and one feels for those mechanics working on a Lysander II of No. 13 Squadron of the Air** Component at Mons-en-Chaussée. *Right:* Spring in Champagne — rather more pleasant conditions for this ground crew of No. 218 Squadron with a Battle I of the AASF.

Although the Allied air forces had a theoretical strength of some 3,500 aircraft, they were faced by 4,000 German machines of the most modern types from a young air force not constrained by outdated thinking. The Luftwaffe's tactics and equipment had already been tested in action in Spain and fine tuned in Poland just a few months earlier. Now they were ready to demonstrate a new form of 'lightning' war in which ground and air forces worked together as one. *Above:* Of the 1,200 fighters in the West, 355 were the twin-engined Messerschmitt Bf 110 like this machine from ZG26.

The Luftwaffe units ranged in the West for Fall Gelb consisted of about 3,950 aircraft. Of these about 1,120 were bombers (half of them Heinkel He 111, the others Dornier Do 17 and Junkers Ju 88); 340 were Ju 87 — the famed 'Stuka' — dive-bombers and 40 elderly Henschel Hs 123 close-support aircraft (all these 380 aircraft were concentrated with VIII. Fliegerkorps — a Nahkampffliegerkorps (close-support air corps)). There were 860 Messerschmitt Bf 109 fighters and 355 Messerschmitt Bf 110 twin-engined fighters. The long-range and tactical reconnaissance squadrons had a strength of 640 aircraft and for the airborne operations, particularly those planned in the Netherlands, there were about 475 Junkers Ju 52 transport aircraft and 45 D.F.S. 230 assault gliders. To these

A superb picture of the Dornier Do 17Ps of 4. Staffel, Auf.Gr. 121, on their base at Stuttgart. Reconnaissance flights were quite numerous during the months of the 'Sitzkrieg' and the recce squadrons suffered most of the losses during this period.

The Luftwaffe fielded over 850 of its much-vaunted single-seat fighter, the Bf 109.

totals could be added the maritime aircraft and liaison aircraft.

On the right wing of the German attack, Luftflotte 2 was to support Heeresgruppe B with IV. Fliegerkorps, VIII. Fliegerkorps and IX. Flieger-korps, the role of the latter being sea-mining and anti-shipping operations in the North Sea. The fighter forces were under Jafü 2 (Jagdfliegerführer: Commander, Fighters) and the anti-aircraft arms, three regiments, under Flakkorps II.

Luftflotte 3 was to support Heeres-gruppe A and Heeresgruppe C with I. Fliegerkorps, II. Fliegerkorps, whose role was particularly to support the panzers of Gruppe von Kleist, and V. Fliegerkorps which was to support Heeresgruppe C on the left wing of the front. The VIII. Fliegerkorps was to be transferred from Luftflotte 2 after a few days, when the feint in Belgium had succeeded and was to support Gruppe von Kleist, the panzer schwerpunkt, in breaking out at Sedan. The fighter forces were under Jafü 3 and the three regiments of anti-aircraft troops under Flakkorps I.

Nevertheless it was the dive-bomber — the Sturzkampfflugzeug epitomised by the Ju 87 — which coloured the images and skies of France in May 1940. Formed into Stukageschwader (StG for short), the 'Stukas' were used as mobile artillery batteries where the ground forces required close support out of range of the conventional guns. Aircraft against aircraft, it was slow and easy meat, but against defenceless ground targets it was a formidable and fearful weapon of terror — made even worse for those hunched below by the screaming wail of its siren. VIII. Fliegerkorps had 380 at its disposal for direct support of the panzers.

Part II
FALL GELB

Code-word 'Danzig'

At 4.35 a.m. on May 10, German troops crossed the borders of the Netherlands, Belgium and Luxembourg. This PzKpfw I and II of 2. Panzer-Division have just entered Belgium.

This time nothing would stop Hitler and the signal 'Fall Gelb, 10.5.40, 5.35 Uhr' went out in the afternoon of May 9. It was sent to all units involved and the 16. Armee war diary noted it as being received from Heeresgruppe A at 1.10 p.m. (German time). After a tense afternoon, for the code-word 'Augsburg' might well have meant yet another postponment and sent back the alerted units to their barracks, the final 'Go!' signal arrived in the evening. At 10.20 p.m. (German time), the diary of 16. Armee noted: 'Stichwort Danzig'.

That afternoon Hitler had boarded his private train, the Führersonderzug 'Amerika', at the small Finkenkrug station north of Berlin, allegedly for a trip to Schleswig-Holstein. The train headed north for a while but then branched westwards and arrived in the early hours of May 10 at Euskirchen. Hitler then proceeded by car and reached his 'Felsennest' (Rocky Nest) front headquarters near Rodert, a kilometre south of Bad Münstereifel, at about 4.30 a.m.

The staff of the various Wehrmacht High Commands had followed him westwards, mainly by train but some by aircraft, and had also reached their advanced command posts dispersed in the proximity of the 'Felsennest'. The OKH, Generaloberst von Brauchitsch and General Halder and staff, had also established quarters in Forsthaus von Haniel, about eight kilometres from 'Felsennest'. Part of the Führerhauptquartier, including Oberst Walter Warlimont's Abteilung L office of the OKW's Wehrmachtführungsstab (Armed Forces Operations Staff), was dispersed in the village of Rodert.

Once again Allied intelligence had sounded a warning of the coming German offensive and since the afternoon of May 9, the frontier posts all along the borders of the Netherlands, Belgium and Luxembourg were reporting the noise of engines, the rattle of arms and the tramp of marching feet. The Belgian Army had been on the alert since 11.35 p.m. on May 9, and Paul-Henry Spaak, the Belgian Foreign Minister, described this last night of fear and hope, with contradictary reports coming over the telephone, while the signs of attack became unmistakable. In spite of all this, by about 4.00 a.m. nothing had happened and the Belgian ministers assembled with Mr Spaak began to breathe again. At the very moment when the German attack was about to break out, they felt relieved: 'The Dutch airfields were not being bombed, in Luxembourg the news seemed to have been somewhat exaggerated and nothing had happened in Belgium. Already we began to regard ourselves as people who had escaped a great danger. Timid smiles appeared on our lips. To relieve the tension, one or another of us risked a joke. We began to speak about our ridiculous fears'.

The joy was to be short-lived. At 4.35 a.m., without warning or provocation, German troops crossed the borders of the Netherlands, Belgium and Luxembourg and German aircraft were all over the western skies. Unlike France or Britain, who were at war with Germany, the Netherlands and Belgium had trusted German promises and the

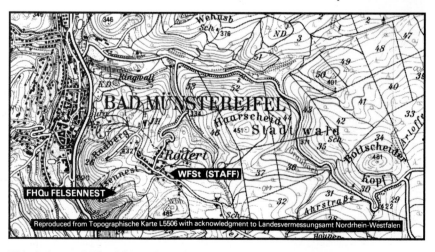

Hitler's forward HQ, dubbed Führerhauptquartier Felsennest (Rocky Nest) had been established just outside Bad Münstereifel, some 30 kilometres behind the frontier.

first attacks of the Luftwaffe shattered their dreams of undisturbed neutrality. Without regard for her own honour, Germany once again treated her pledge to respect their neutrality as 'scrap of paper'.

It was about an hour before the Belgians called the Allies for help but this delay was not reflecting hesitation but only the necessity to check that the invasion was real. Spaak called Paris and London to appeal for help in resisting the German invasion and then jumped into his car to take the message in person to the French and British embassies in Brussels. When Germany's Ambassador Vicco von Bülow-Schwante came to see him at about 8.30 a.m., Spaak read a few words of protest before the German envoy could say anything. Von Bülow listened in silence and then started to read a long note of apologia. In the middle, almost breathless with emotion and anger, Spaak impatiently took the paper from him and finished reading it himself. Von Bülow bowed and left.

The HQ, with camouflaged war room and living accommodation, was located on a hillside within walking distance of the nearest village of Rodert which had been taken over for the OKW's operations staff.

Only ruins today on 'Felsennest' Hill — once the nerve centre of one of the most successful military campaigns the world has ever seen.

Left: Here Hitler walks the few hundred metres down the lane to Rodert with, on his left, Oberst Rudolf Schmundt, his Wehrmacht adjutant, and Army adjutant, Hauptmann Gerhard Engel, on his right. Behind can be seen SS-Untersturmführer Hansgeorg Schulze, SS adjutant (left); SA-Obergruppenführer Wilhelm Brueckner, his chief adjutant (the tall chap in the centre), with Hauptmann Nicolaus von Below in the darker Luftwaffe uniform. Right: Today the whole landscape between Rodert and the hill has been changed, the road obliterated and re-aligned and new tracks cut in the forest which now encroaches on the hillside. Believe it or not, this is the exact comparison — just before the main gate to the compound.

A British Military Mission under Major-General H. Needham was appointed to Belgian Army Headquarters to keep the War Office informed of the Belgian situation, the French sending their own Military Mission under Général Pierre Champon with the same intention.

In London Neville Chamberlain's government resigned and a National Government was formed under Winston Churchill. The differences of opinion were, in Churchill's words, 'all drowned by cannonade' and Conservative, Liberal and Labour parties were all represented. However a similar con-

census was not possible in France and in Paris, Reynaud's government managed to survive the Allied debacle in Norway which had led to the fall of the Chamberlain government, but was forced to broaden his Cabinet further by bringing in two new Ministers of the Right, Louis Marin and Jean Ybarnégaray.

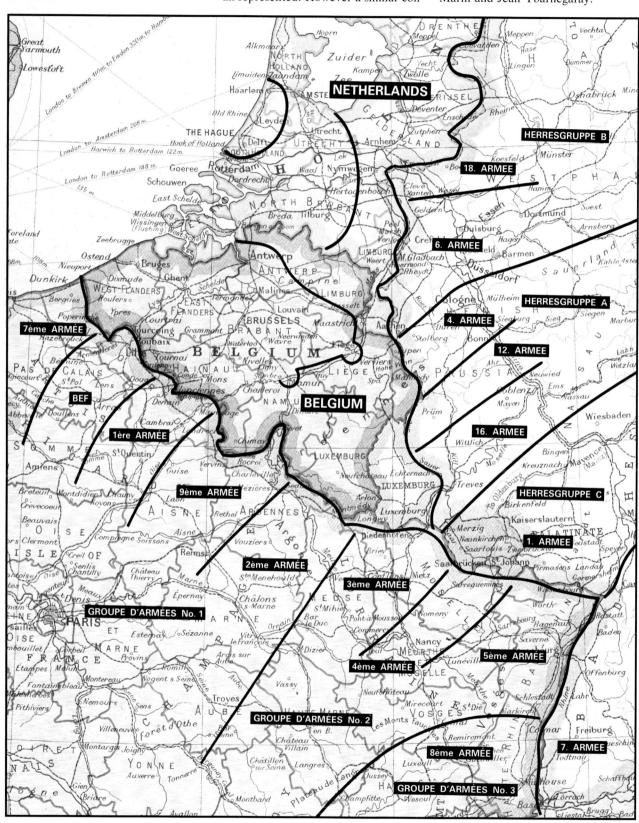

The opposing forces on the eve of Fall Gelb. Three German Army groups, deploying a total of 134 divisions, faced 92 French and 10 British divisions. As soon as neutral Belgium and the Netherlands entered the fight, an additional 20 Belgian and 10 Dutch divisions were added to the Allied side of the balance sheet.

The Brandenburg operations

The key to the success of Fall Gelb lay in the rapid advance of the panzer units of Heeresgruppe A, which was to strike the decisive blow, but a swift move in the Heeresgruppe B sector was also vital for it to appear that this was where the main attack was being made, and for the Allies to be lured into a trap. From the earliest planning stage, in the days when the offensive's schwerpunkt lay on the right, 'special operations' were devised along the whole length of the front to ensure success in the crucial opening phase of the offensive. These included the seizing of road junctions and crossings over canals and rivers just behind the Dutch and Belgian eastern border, particularly over the broad Meuse, and knocking out the strategically important Belgian fortress of Eben-Emael.

Imagination had been the watchword for these units: some would swoop down in gliders or descend by parachute or be delivered two at a time by light aircraft, some would ride into action by bicycle . . . or even commandeer a Rhine river-boat as happened in the attempt to capture the bridge at Nijmegen. In others cases deception and infiltration tactics meant wearing civilian clothes or enemy uniforms over their own.

In the attack on Poland, a few units, although not yet known as 'Brandenburg', had been engaged in commando-type activities, infiltrating before H-Hour in order to secure important installations against demolition. The

Left: **One of the very few action photos, if not the only one, of a 'Brandenburg' commando in operation. These men, dressed in uniforms of the Dutch military police, were members of the second section of 4. Kompanie of Bau-Lehr-Bataillon z.b.V. 800. Under Leutnant Siegfried Grabert, this section had the task of capturing four bridges over the Juliana Canal, but the Dutch** succeeded in blowing three of them. The fourth, here at Roosteren just east of Maaseik, was captured intact. *Right:* **This is not an exact comparison, as the bridge was rebuilt after the war, having been demolished by the Germans in 1944. Nearby stands a memorial to the men of the 6e Reserve Grens Compagnie who fell 'for Queen and Country' on May 10, 1940.**

best of these 'special forces' had been assembled at Brandenburg in the winter of 1939 and were formally organised into the inconspicuous Bau-Lehr-Bataillon z.b.V. 800. This 'training and construction' battalion was actually under the control of Section II of the Abwehr, the OKW Intelligence and Security Service. Section II being responsible for sabotage and special duties. (The z.b.V. of the battalion's designation stood for 'zur besonderen Verwendung' — for special purposes.)

Language skills and adaptability were prime attributes for recruitment into the unit. The men, quite a number of them from outside Germany, including Volksdeutsche and even foreigners, were trained to possess wide-ranging skills, from parachuting and skiing to handling small boats, moving silently at night and living off the land. Soon known as the 'Brandenburgers' after the town where their battalion was garrisoned, they rapidly developed into highly trained and competent commandos. The battalion was to become a regiment in 1940 and a division in 1943 whereupon it was soon reorganised into a conventional motorised unit. By then the Brandenburgers had lost most of their special status, the specially trained personnel having been either killed or dispersed to other units.

Most of the objectives assigned to Brandenburg units on the eve of Fall Gelb were bridges, which they had to capture intact. In the Heeresgruppe B part of the front, these were over the wide river Meuse or Juliana Canal while on Heeresgruppe A's front they were over the far smaller Our and Sûre rivers. In the centre, on the right wing of Heeresgruppe A, Brandenburg detachements had also to take important bridges and crossroads behind the Belgian border in the Losheim gap.

The skill and courage of the Brandenburgers were not always enough to triumph over sometimes impossible odds, especially when faced with capturing Meuse bridges deep inside Dutch territory. The Dutch engineers were successful in blowing in time the two bridges at Nijmegen, the one at Mook, at Roermond, and at Maaseik, and in the early hours of May 10, Halder recorded somewhat pessimistically in his diary: 'First reports: Trojan Horse not succeeding. Nijmegen bridge destroyed, Gennep bridge intact. Roermond and Maaseik bridge destroyed. Maastricht: bridge at Lanaken (to the north) and Kanne (to the south) destroyed. Situation at Veldwezelt and Vroenhoven yet unclear'. In fact, things were not quite as bad as that; Luftwaffe glider troops had taken the two bridges at Veldwezelt and Vroenhoven and the Brandenburg outfits had successfully accomplished many of their tasks.

In the north, at Nijmegen, the Dutch had actually blown all the bridges before they could be taken by the German commandos but south of the town the first section of 4. Kompanie had more success. This unit, four teams under Oberleutnant Wilhelm Walther, which had to seize two bridges in the XXVI. Armeekorps sector, had succeeded in

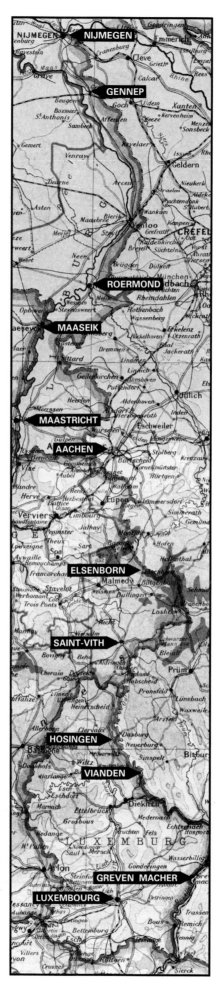

capturing the bridge over the Maas-Waal Canal near Heumen, the railway bridge over the Meuse and the railway station at Gennep.

Between Roermond and Maaseik, the second section of 4. Kompanie, under Leutnant Siegfried Grabert, had to capture four bridges over the Meuse and the Juliana Canal in the XI. Armeekorps sector. Theirs was an impossible task and they managed to take only the one, over the canal just east of Maaseik. The three over the Meuse, the road bridges at Maaseik and Roermond and the railway bridge at Roermond, were all successfully blown by the Dutch.

Between Maaseik and Maastricht, in the IV. Armeekorps sector, the Brandenburgers had more luck and the four teams of the 'Westzug' detachment under the command of Leutnant Kürschner, seized four bridges over the Juliana Canal intact. Unteroffizier Hans Landvogt led the commandos at Obbicht, Leutnant Kürschner those at Berg, Unteroffizier Klausmeier the group at Ormond and Unteroffizier Klein the one at Stein.

In the Losheim gap between Elsenborn and Saint-Vith, of the 24 targets which had been assigned to them, Hauptmann Rudloff's 3. Kompanie detachments had taken 19, including important bridges or crossroads at Bullange, Born and Saint-Vith.

On the eastern border of Luxembourg, 2. Kompanie detachments had to take control of the border. Those men under Oberleutnant Karl Schöller were to prevent the destruction of bridges over the Sûre; those under Feldwebel Eggers, bridges over the Our. Inside the Grand Duchy, there were also numerous Sonderkommandos — German residents who, wearing ordinary civilian clothes, achieved surprise and success in taking over and preventing the destruction of bridges, tunnels, viaducts, crossroads to help smooth the path of Gruppe von Kleist.

The Brandenburg teams had crossed the Our and Sûre rivers as planned. At various places, — Hosingen, Grevenmacher, Moestroff, Vianden to name but a few — shots were exchanged with gendarmes of the Grand Duchy, and grenades were thrown here and there; but although the bridges were not blown, the gendarmes often had time to close the barriers, for which orders were sent out at 3.10 a.m. Once closed, they could not be reopened and had to await demolition by the panzer divisions' engineers a few hours later. In the first of various incidents involving Brandenburgers not in uniform, five 'civilians' fired at gendarmes who challenged them near Grevenmacher at about about 1.30 a.m. and Gendarme Jean-Pierre Schammo was badly wounded. An hour later, gendarmes captured three injured men at the Felsmühle who turned out to be German soldiers and were taken to the hospital. The hospital records for 1940 reveal the identity of these peculiar 'patients' brought in that morning as Unteroffizier Herbert Switzy, Schütze Alfred Wolynl and Schütze Heinrich Kaczmarzik.

Having entered Holland just before midnight on May 9, the six-man 'Brandenburg' team under Oberleutant Wilhelm Walther, reached the Meuse without incident. However, one of the three Dutchmen from the Dutch Nazi Party with them showed signs of wavering and had to be sent back to Germany under guard. The team reached the Meuse near Gennep where they hid in bushes at the foot of the railway bridge embankment, photographed here by Karel Margry in 1988.

In order that the paratroops and air transported infantry which took part in the airborne assault on the Netherlands in the early hours of Fall Gelb should not have to carry on an unequal fight for too long, it was vital that they be relieved by conventional forces within the shortest possible time. To speed the advance of the relief troops, one of the vital bridges over the Meuse that the Brandenburgers had to capture was the 400-metre railway bridge near Gennep. This bridge, which was more than three kilometres from the border, carried a railway line into the west of Holland. Two troop trains, the one in front armoured, carrying a detachment of the 256. Infanterie-Division were to set off along it from Germany, heading for the Dutch defensive positions of the Peel Line, about 12 kilometres away, to take them by surprise. The Brandenburgers had to capture the railway station at Gennep and to prevent the Dutch from blowing up the bridge before the trains could cross it.

The capture of the bridge was to be carried out by a six-man section formed from 4. Kompanie led by the company commander, Oberleutnant Wilhelm Walther. Half an hour before midnight on May 9, this little outfit entered the Netherlands; with them were three Dutchmen from the N.S.B. (Nationaal Socialistische Beweging, a Dutch pro-Nazi party) dressed as Dutch military police. However one of them soon showed signs of uneasiness at the idea of having to fire on his countrymen; he was quickly disarmed and taken back to Germany under guard.

After crossing the road between Gennep and Heien without incident, the remainder of the party soon reached the Meuse where they hid in bushes at the foot of the railway embankment to await the dawn. Although the Netherlands Army had been on full alert since 10.00 p.m., there were no patrols to

challenge them. At the bridge, all was quiet.

Just before dawn, the two German trains moved across the border and approached the station which another team of Brandenburgers under Unteroffizier Günther Ziesold had just taken over. However the Dutch had switched the points and the first train ran onto the wrong tracks. Both had to be reversed before they could go forward onto the right ones towards the bridge. Meanwhile, Walther's commandos, wearing raincoats, and led by the two Dutchmen walking in front in their military police uniform, suddenly appeared at the eastern end of the bridge and approached the guardhouse. The three Dutch sentries were suspicious but the fact that two of these men obviously belonged to the Dutch Army allayed their suspicion long enough for

them to be taken by surprise and overpowered. Another guard speaking on the telephone was also captured.

The eastern end in their hands, the Brandenburgers now had to take the western end. One of the Dutchmen rang up the guardhouse at that end and told them that four German prisoners were being brought across the bridge. The prisoners and their escort started out and were met in the middle by sentries to whom the two 'Dutch' policemen handed over their 'prisoners', before returning to the eastern end of the bridge. The prisoners, after being searched, were marched away to a stone hut on the river bank at the western end. When the guard left on duty saw a train approaching from Germany, he telephoned a warning to the guard commander at the western end. The sergeant there hesitated as to the right course of action while the man on the detonator in the middle section of the bridge stood by waiting for instructions. Suddenly the Germans jumped down and grabbed both him and the detonator.

The small group of Dutch soldiers on the western bank hastily organised a defence, but in the confusion the Brandenburger prisoners soon overpowered their guards and started firing with weapons they had concealed about them and which had escaped the search by the Dutch sentries. Caught between the fire from the Brandenburgers and the troops from the train, the Dutch soon surrendered and watched in despair as the two troop trains picked up speed and continued on their way.

The commander of the 4. Kompanie, Oberleutnant Walther, led a subsequent operation at Nieuport and was the only Brandenburger to be decorated with the Ritterkreuz for participation in Fall Gelb, the award being announced on June 26. Possibly it was felt that with such an undercover unit, any wider accolade might have called attention to their rôle which would clearly have compromised the specialist nature of the unit.

The railway bridge was completely demolished in 1944, the abutments being used by the Royal Engineers to support temporary Bailey bridges for both road and rail traffic. Today the bridge has been reconstructed for road vehicles only.

The swoop on Fort Eben-Emael

In the German plan the panzer attack in the Gembloux gap was merely a feint aiming at preventing the Allied Command from discovering for as long as possible where the main blow was being struck. However, if the feint was to be a success, it had to be swift, which was not so easy because, although the gap was ideal for tank warfare, to reach it the panzers had first to cross the Meuse in the Maastricht sector and the Albert Canal which ran parallel to it. To gain a swift crossing, the Germans had not only to seize the bridges at Maas-

tricht and those over the canal just west of the town, they had also to cripple Fort Eben-Emael whose artillery controlled the whole sector. This was not an easy task as the fort was then regarded as one of the most impregnable of modern strong points.

Only twenty kilometres or so from the border, the Meuse bridges in Maastricht were to be captured by a special unit of Infanterie-Bataillon z.b.V. 100, the men approaching silently on bicycles in Dutch police uniform. To seize the bridges over the Albert Canal and

to cripple Fort Eben-Emael, a glider-borne operation was mounted by the Luftwaffe and this difficult and daring enterprise was assigned to the VIII. Fliegerkorps. To pull it off, a special assault detachment was formed under Hauptmann Walter Koch — Sturm-abteilung Koch.

The northernmost fortification of the Position Fortifiée de Liège, Fort Eben-Emael had been built between 1932 and 1935. Wedge-shaped, it measured some 900 metres from north to south and 800 metres at its southern end. The Albert

The two rotating turrets, Coupole Nord and Coupole Sud, covered the surrounding countryside with their 75mm guns with fields of fire out to a distance of 10 kilometres and the single Coupole de 120 (120mm gun) *above* to a range of 17 kilometres. Photographed by Francis Tirtiat in 1989, it still showed evidence of the penetrating explosive charge placed on it by German commandos on May 10, 1940. The concrete infilling was done post-war by the Belgian authorities.

Canal ran along one side, forming a huge moat, and another smaller waterway was dug between the canal and Block II, from where an anti-tank ditch and a wall about four metres high surrounded the rest of the fort.

Eben-Emael's armament fell into two main categories, offensive and defensive (German intelligence had its own numbers for each of the installations and these will appear in brackets here). The 1ère Batterie could be called the long-range battery as it controlled the four triple 75mm gun installations Maastricht 1 (12) and Maastricht 2 (18), ranged northward on the exits from Maastricht, and Visé 1 (26) and Visé 2 (9), southwards on the exits from Visé. It also controlled two retractable, revolving turrets, each with two 75mm rapid-fire guns, Coupole Nord (31) and Coupole Sud on Block V (23). Almost in the centre of the fort was Coupole 120 (24), a revolving but not retractable dome with twin 120mm guns.

The 2ème Batterie, intended for the defence of the fort itself, controlled Mi-Nord (19) and Mi-Sud (13) on top of the fort and the seven blockhouses set in the surrounding anti-tank wall: Block I (3), Block II (4), Block IV (30), Block V (23), Block VI (6), Canal Nord (17) and Canal Sud (35). The latter two, which had been constructed particularly for the defence of the locks on the Meuse Canal, faced the Albert Canal almost at water level. Each block was armed with several twin machine guns (21 altogether), one or two 60mm anti-tank guns (11 altogether, but none in Mi-Nord and Mi-Sud) and grenade throwers, and was equipped with observation cupolas and searchlights.

None of these casemates were protected by surface trenches, and no precautions had been taken on the large, flat top surface of the fort, either with mines or wire barricades, to prevent landings from the air. An air landing had obviously not been expected and only one small anti-aircraft battery (29) was situated on the south side.

All the individual blockhouses were linked by seven kilometres of underground tunnels with gas locks, beneath which were situated the barrack accomodation for the garrison. Entry was through Block I, in which a collapsible drawbridge was constructed to trap a tank trying to enter the fort. The entire fortress could be sealed off from the outside world and was self-sufficient, with its own electricity generators, water pumps, kitchens, washrooms, hospitals, fuel tanks, etc. The garrison totalled 1,200 men, but when the attack came about 500 men were still in their billets in the nearby village of Wonck, and because of the speed of the attack, could not be recalled in time. This left about 700 men to man the defences under the command of Major Jean Jottrand.

The attacking force, Sturmabteilung Koch, was divided into four assault groups, three of which were each assigned one of the Albert Canal bridges west of Maastricht. The fourth group was to incapacitate the Fort

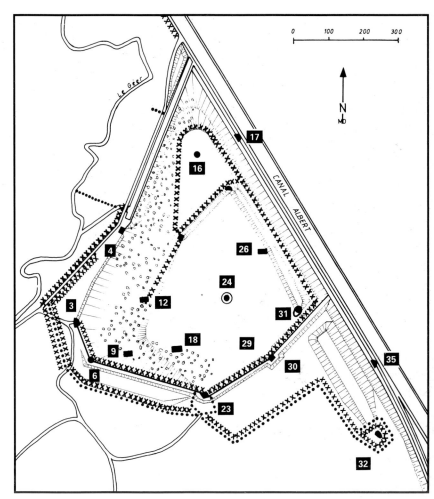

Coupole Nord and Coupole Sud, were, in addition, retractable. All the other guns were mounted in the various blockhouses, each covering particular targets like Visé, a town to the south, and Maastricht in the north.

Eben-Emael until strong ground troops could arrive to capture it. It was planned that Pionier-Bataillon 51 and Infanterie-Regiment 151, to which were to capture Eben-Emael, would arrive on the evening of the first day or the day after.

Hauptmann Koch had commanded the first company of Fallschirm-Jäger-Regiment 1, and his men were those of his own former unit, plus a platoon of engineers under Oberleutnant Rudolf Witzig which came from the second battalion of this same regiment. They had trained for six months at Hildesheim near Hanover without knowing

On its eastern boundary, the Fort is protected by the Albert Canal, which runs parallel to the Meuse between Liège and Maastricht, forming a 'moat' some 50 metres or so wide. These Belgian troops are repairing the wire barricade near Vroenhoven, just north of Eben-Emael.

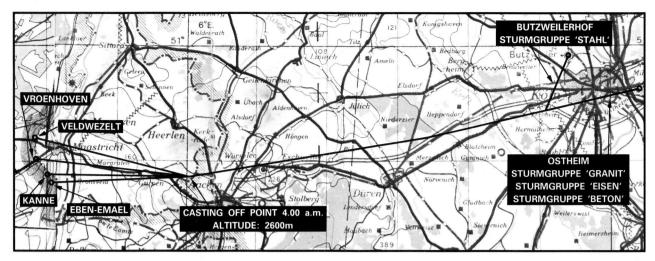

BUTZWEILERHOF
STURMGRUPPE 'STAHL'

VROENHOVEN

VELDWEZELT

OSTHEIM
STURMGRUPPE 'GRANIT'
STURMGRUPPE 'EISEN'
STURMGRUPPE 'BETON'

KANNE

EBEN-EMAEL

CASTING OFF POINT 4.00 a.m.
ALTITUDE: 2600m

the name of the intended objective, the glider pilots being trained to find a target and land nearby while the troops trained to scramble out of the gliders. Training moved later to the Sudetenland, where practice attacks were carried out on fortifications, intended in particular to familiarise the glider troops in the use of the 12.5kg and 50kg hollow charge, their most powerful weapon.

The LS-Versuchzug, the Luftwaffe experimental unit for the employment of gliders established in January 1939, was moved to Hildesheim in October and then took the inconspicious name of a 17. Staffel in K.Gr.z.b.V. 5. By March the unit had four groups of Junkers Ju 52s glider-towing aircraft under Leutnant Hans Schweitzer, Leutnant Günter Seide, Oberleutnant Hans-Günter Nevries and Oberleutnant Walter Steinweg and these were paired up with their gliders and with the four assault groups organised by Hauptmann Koch. On the eve of May 10 Sturmabteilung Koch had 50 D.F.S. 230 gliders, 42 Junkers Ju 52s towing aircraft plus four in reserve, six Junkers Ju 52s to drop parachute reinforcements and three Heinkel He 111s to drop supplies.

The plan was for the four assault groups, each of about 100 men, to descend silently on their objectives at 4.25 a.m., five minutes before the invading forces crossed the Dutch frontier:

Sturmgruppe 'Stahl' (Steel), in ten gliders, commanded by Oberleutnant Gustav Altmann, was to take the bridge at Veldwezelt.

Sturmgruppe 'Beton' (Concrete), in ten gliders, commanded by Leutnant Gerhardt Schacht, was to take the bridge at Vroenhoven. An eleventh glider was to land Hauptmann Koch and part of the detachment's staff.

Sturmgruppe 'Eisen' (Iron), in ten gliders, commanded by Oberleutnant Martin Schächter, was to take the bridge at Kanne.

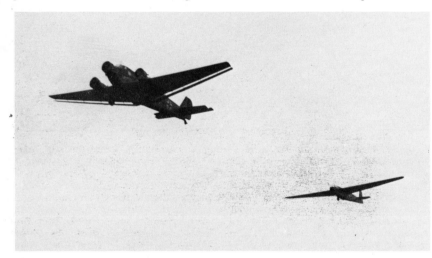

The weak link was that the Belgians had failed to obstruct the flat top of the fort to prevent airborne landings and the single anti-aircraft battery was an insufficient deterrent. At 3.15 a.m. on the morning of the 10th, Sturmabteilung Koch, the commando unit instructed to capture Eben-Emael and the bridges across the Meuse, began taking off in 42 D.F.S. 230 gliders towed by Ju 52s. After a flight of half an hour, the gliders were released to silently bear down on their targets.

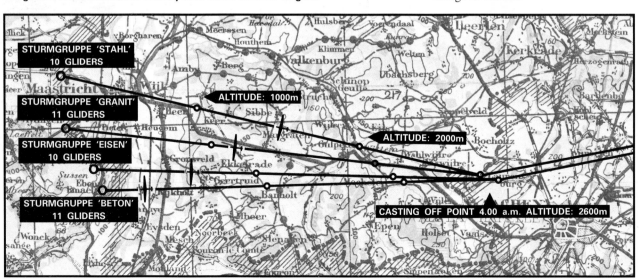

STURMGRUPPE 'STAHL'
10 GLIDERS

STURMGRUPPE 'GRANIT'
11 GLIDERS

ALTITUDE: 1000m

STURMGRUPPE 'EISEN'
10 GLIDERS

ALTITUDE: 2000m

STURMGRUPPE 'BETON'
11 GLIDERS

CASTING OFF POINT 4.00 a.m. ALTITUDE: 2600m

Sturmgruppe 'Granit', two officers and 84 men under the command of Oberleutnant Rudolf Witzig, in eleven gliders, was to assault Fort Eben-Emael. The whole of Witzig's engineer platoon and their bulky equipment was to land with this group, being armed with 6 machine guns, 16 sub-machine guns, 58 rifles, 85 pistols, 4 flame-throwers, 2½ tons of explosive and a radio set.

On the afternoon of May 9 Sturm-abteilung Koch, with 11 officers and 427 men, all of them highly trained, moved to their starting positions near Cologne where their fifty D.F.S. 230 gliders had been secretly assembled in January. The Stahl group was to stand by at Butzweilerhof airfield, the others at Ostheim. The towing Junkers Ju 52s arrived in the evening, one group landing at Butzweilerhof, the other three at Ostheim.

Starting soon after midnight on May 10, the ground crews prepared the aircraft and gliders, the tow-lines were attached and the men boarded their machines.

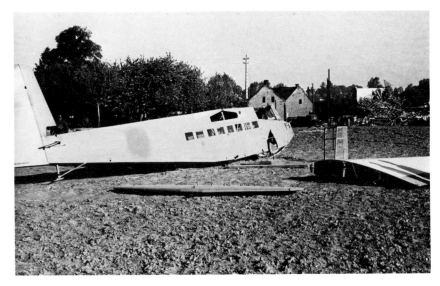

The 400-strong assault force was split into four Sturmgruppe: 'Granit' (Granite) to take the fort itself; 'Eisen' (Iron) the road bridge just to the north at Kanne; 'Beton' (Concrete) the important highway bridge at Vroenhoven, and 'Stahl' (Steel) the road bridge west of Maastricht. This glider has landed in the field beside the latter bridge at Veldwezelt. Note how its nationality markings have been obliterated.

Within a quarter of an hour of landing, the Stahl commando group had captured their objective and Oberleutnant Altmann was able to report the bridge intact. The men held the position until troops of 4. Panzer-Division arrived in the afternoon. Here an SdKfz 10/4 with 2cm Flak 38 provides anti-aircraft cover in the same field. Veltwezelt church is in the background.

At about 3.15 a.m. Koch received the word to go and the aircraft began taking off at 3.30 a.m. as planned, the last of the 42 aircraft-glider combinations being airborne ten minutes later. There were about 73 kilometres to the casting-off point near Vetschau, to the north-west of Aachen, and after flying for 31 minutes the gliders were released at an altitude of 2,600 metres. Having to fly further west, the Stahl and Beton gliders were released about a minute after those of the other two groups. Ten minutes after being released, the gliders were at an altitude of 500 metres and silently approaching their targets, then only a minute away to the west.

A second wave of six Ju 52s was meanwhile taking off from the Cologne airfields, carrying one and a half platoons of machine-gunners to be dropped at the three bridgeheads attacked by assault groups Stahl, Beton and Eisen about 40 minutes after the gliders had landed. This second wave was soon followed by a third consisting of three He 111s, which were to drop ammunition supplies to the attack force about 45 minutes after the gliders had landed.

Alongside lie the graves of six fallen commandos. Unteroffizier Karl-Heinz Gönner, the only name decipherable on the cross on the right, is now buried in Grave 150 of Block BZ in the German Soldatenfriedhof at Ijsselsteyn in the Netherlands.

Of the bridges assaulted by Sturmabteilung Koch, only that at Kanne was successfully blown by the Belgians prior to its capture.

Sturmgruppe Beton

Although one of the gliders broke its tow-line and had to land at Hottdorf, the ten remaining D.F.S. 230s emerged unscathed by anti-aircraft fire from Dutch batteries south of Maastricht. At 4.15 a.m. they came down at the bridge site at Vroenhoven, the assault troops taking it undamaged, and reporting 'objective taken' at 4.30 a.m. Half a platoon of paratroopers was successfully dropped one hour later and Hauptmann Koch established his command post near the bridge. At 10.32 a.m. he reported that all the objectives had been taken.

The Belgian unit in the sector, the 6ème Compagnie of 18ème Régiment de Ligne, 7ème Division d'Infanterie, fought back fiercely and launched a counter-attack to dislodge the glidermen. This failed but the Belgians held their ground and were only overhelmed the next morning by the relief troops. The attackers held the bridge until relieved in the evening by 4. Panzer-Division at about 8.00 p.m., and withdrew through Maastricht. Leutnant Schacht had lost ten men (one a glider pilot, Gefreiter Daum), with 29 wounded.

Sturmgruppe Eisen

One of the gliders failed to find the target, which left only nine for the assault on the bridge at Kanne at 4.35 a.m. The Belgians from the 2ème Régiment de Grenadiers of the 7ème Division d'Infanterie reacted quickly and fired at the gliders as they prepared to land. One was hit at an altitude of about thirty metres and caught fire; landing well alight, it completely burned out.

The troops assaulted the Belgians positions but the bridge was blown before they could do anything to cut the wires. At 4.40 a.m. they reported, 'Objective reached, opposition rather strong, bridge blown, but could be brought into use by engineers'. The group commander, Oberleutnant Schächter, was badly wounded and Leutnant Joachim Meissner took over. At about 3.00 p.m. the leaders of Infanterie-Regiment 151 arrived on the eastern bank of the canal but it was not until the evening that they could take over the bridgehead. The glider troops withdrew through Maastricht the following day. Losses were somewhat heavy: 22 killed, among them one of the glider pilots, Unteroffizier Seele, and 26 wounded.

Sturmgruppe Stahl

The gliders were fired at by Dutch anti-aircraft batteries as they flew over Maastricht but suffered no losses. They landed at Veldwezelt at 4.20 a.m. under fire from the Belgian defenders, the 2ème Régiment de Carabiniers of the 7ème Division d'Infanterie. One of the pilots, Unteroffizier Stuhr, was hit in the head and his D.F.S. 230 crashed from an altitude of about ten metres, most of the men inside being injured and put out of action. The troops assaulted the Belgian positions and by 4.35 a.m. Oberleutnant Altmann reported back 'Veldwezelt: objective taken'. The machine-gunners parachuted as planned at about 5.15 a.m. and an attack by Stukas later helped to subdue the Belgian defenders. Four Belgian T-13 light tanks approached the bridge site but the glidermen disabled two of them with their Panzerbüchsen (anti-tank rifle) and the remaining two withdrew.

In the afternoon the leading elements of the French 3ème D.L.M. — which had rushed 300 kilometres since morning — probed the positions but only after the glider troops had made their first contact with the 4. Panzer-Division. Late in the evening, they were relieved and withdrew through Maastricht. The group had lost 8 killed and 30 wounded.

Sturmgruppe Granit

Shortly after take-off, the group crossed the path of one of those that had started from Butzweilerhof, and the pilot of the Ju 52 towing Glider 11 (pilot Unteroffizier Pilz and team leader Unteroffizier Schwarz) had to take violent evasive action to avoid colliding with the tow-line of another glider. However the manoeuvre caused the rope to snap and the glider had to force-land in a field. This was a bad omen, as the commander of the group, Oberleutnant Rudolf Witzig, was aboard. Later another tow-line broke and Glider 2 (pilot Unteroffizier Bredenbeck and team leader Unteroffizier Maier) came down near Düren.

Fort Eben-Emael's anti-aircraft defences had spotted the gliders at 4.05 a.m. but did not open fire until 4.20 a.m., just as the nine gilders were actually landing. The gliders touched down and skidded across the top of the

Most bridges built in Belgium and Holland after the First World War had ready-made demolition chambers in the abutments. Here Belgian soldiers leave the western pier at Veldwezelt. The Germans subsequently blew the bridge in 1944.

Dated May 23, this picture shows German troopers on top of Mi-Nord, damaged by a demolition charge which had been detonated against one of its machine gun embrasures.

Undergrowth and trees have been allowed to reclaim much of the fort, but we were fortunate in photographing the blockhouse from nearly the same angle in 1974.

fort before coming to rest. Within seconds, the men poured out of the gliders and raced towards their objectives. At 4.42 a.m. Oberfeldwebel Helmut Wenzel, the leader of Glider 4 and who had taken charge in the absence of Oberleutnant Witzig, reported 'Eben-Emael: objective reached. Everything as planned'.

Two teams, Glider 6 (pilot Unteroffizier Ziller and team leader Unteroffizier Harlos) and Glider 7 (pilot Unteroffizier Scheidhauer and team leader Unteroffizier Heinemann), had landed as planned at the northern end of the fort to capture positions plotted on aerial photographs, which turned out to be dummy positions with tin domes. This, and the two gliders which had failed to reach Eben-Emael, left seven teams, totalling 55 men, to capture the vital parts of the fort.

The men from Glider 1 (pilot Feldwebel Raschke and team leader Feldwebel Niedermeier), under the command of Leutnant Egon Delica, attacked Maastricht 2 (18). They began by placing a 12.5kg charge on the end gun which blew it back in the casemate, killing one Belgian, Jean Verbois, and followed with a 50kg charge on the observation dome which killed two Belgians, René Marchoull and Martin David, throwing the interior into complete darkness. Grenades were dropped

The commandos used shaped explosive charges of 12.5kg and 50kg which could cut through, respectively, 7 inches and 12 inches of armoured steel. This is the devastating effect created by the explosion of a 50kg charge on the observation cupola of Block IV.

down the shaft, killing two more men inside, the survivors barricading themselves at the foot of the shaft.

The men from Glider 3 (pilot Unteroffizier Supper), led by Unteroffizier Peter Arent, attacked Maastricht 1 (12).

The glider had come down only 50 metres from its target and at 4.25 a.m., the glidermen blew up an embrasure with a 12.5kg charge which put out the lights inside and killed one man from the recoil of the destroyed gun.

Commandos from Glider 1 led by Feldwebel Niedermeier were responsible for knocking out Maastricht 2. A 12.5kg charge was fired on the left-hand embrasure, blowing the gun back inside.

Today two of the firing positions have been sealed with concrete, but a 75mm gun still remains to be seen in the centre embrasure.

Scene from a cine film of Pi.Btl. 51 crossing the Albert Canal in front of Eben-Emael 'under fire from the fortress'. The action was actually re-staged for the camera but the explosions of the 'shells' on the bank and in the canal were quite realistic!

With suffocating smoke penetrating the lift shaft, a second explosion from a 50kg charge put the other guns out of action. The crew retreated down the lift shaft and at 9.30 a.m. they started to construct a barrier out of girders at the bottom.

Glider 4 (pilot Unteroffizier Braüti-gam and team leader Oberfeldwebel Wenzel) was caught in barbed wire which brought it to a halt some 100 metres from its target, Mi-Nord (19). The embrasures were still shut and the men raced to the blockhouse unopposed. A 1kg charge was thrown through the observation dome whereupon one of the machine guns opened up. A 50kg charge was then exploded on the top of the cupola and a 12.5kg charge set off against one of the machine gun embrasures, killing the Belgian crew at their post. This opening was later enlarged with a 50kg charge and a command post set up behind the protection of the shattered concrete.

The men of Glider 5 (pilot Unteroffizier Lange and team leader Feldwebel Haus) had taken on the job of attacking Visé 1 (26) when Glider 2, whose objective it was, had come down near Düren. At about 5.00 a.m. they blew off the ventilators, which forced the Belgian crews to withdraw for lack of air. However they returned and started firing, causing the Germans, who had meanwhile moved on to take Block II (4), to turn their attention back to Visé 1 on which they detonated 1kg charges at about 9.00 a.m. An hour later the Belgians returned again to discover that only one gun had been put out of action. They began firing with minimum set fuses which made the shells explode just outside the barrel to deter the Germans who were assumed to be waiting outside but finally abandoned the position half an hour later.

Glider 8 (pilot Unteroffizier Distel-meier and team leader Unteroffizier Unger) was hit by machine gun fire and the troops inside had sustained casualties before it landed between its two objectives, the barrack hut (25) and Coupole Nord (31). Whilst the occupants of the barracks were pinned down by machine gun fire, the cupola of Coupole Nord was attacked with two consecutive 50kg hollow charges. Although these did not penetrate the large steel dome, they jammed it, and as the Belgians continued to fire from the emergency exit, it was blown up with a 12.5kg charge and partly buried.

Glider 9 (pilot Unteroffizier Schulz and team leader Unteroffizier Neuhaus) had landed only fifty metres from Mi-Sud (13) but a barbed wire entanglement protected the casemate which the engineers had to cut. They had just gone through when the Belgian crew arrived via the underground passage and began firing a machine gun. The gun was attacked at once with a flame-thrower and charges were detonated on the embrasure and observation dome. The entrance was then blown open with a 50kg charge and the casemate taken.

The men from Glider 10 (pilot Unteroffizier Kraft and team leader Unteroffizier Hübel) assaulted Coupole 120. At 4.40 a.m., rifle shots fired from the loophole of this turret had accidentally killed a Belgian who had been taken prisoner while manning the anti-aircraft battery (some of the Belgian prisoners later testified that the Germans were actually pushing them in front as shields). A 50kg charge was detonated on the six metre dome, but it failed to penetrate it and small 1kg charges were then stuffed up the twin barrels and set off at about 5.15 a.m. However it seems that the Belgian crew did not realise what had happened for at 9.00 a.m. they tried to fire the right-hand gun; there was a violent explosion and suffocating smoke drove them from the turret. At about 10.00 a.m. the crew was ordered to fire again but this

The terrain at Eben-Emael remained virtually unchanged until the mid-1970s when the opposite bank was completely removed — a major undertaking. Since this picture was taken in 1974 the canal itself has been widened to the east, and the original bank from where the German sappers set off has now been totally lost.

proved impossible; the turret was abandoned and a barrier erected at the foot of the tunnel.

Within an hour of landing, it was clear that Sturmgruppe Granit had been remarkably successful as most of the major objectives had been taken. When the Belgian Command realised that something was wrong at Eben-Emael, they ordered the other forts within range to fire on Eben-Emael to try to dislodge the paratroopers. Barchon reported firing its two 150mm cupolas for three hours from 4.55 a.m., followed five minutes later by Pontisse and Evegnée training their 105mm cupolas at Coupole 120, then at Visé 2, then the western side of the fort.

However, there was still some resistance left and two major installations which had not been attacked kept on firing but these had only nuisance value. Visé 2 (9), similar to Visé 1 in only being able to fire to the south and so not of prime importance to the Germans, was the only fortification not attacked by the German engineers. It fired minimum fused shells periodically and obtained covering fire from Coupole Sud (23).

Coupole Sud (23) on Block V caused the German commandos the most anxiety. At first they did not pay much attention to it as they thought it lay below the level of the top of the fort and therefore could not sweep its surface with fire. A 50kg charge was detonated on the dome by men from Glider 5 just as it rose but this had no effect and further attempts by the men from Glider 1 also failed. The turret continued to fire at the other casemates on which German engineers were 'working', also firing at the Kanne road and on Eijsden village. Stukas were called up but the turret was retracted when they attacked at 8.15 a.m. and it suffered no damage. It remained in working order until the fort surrendered.

Oberleutnant Witzig and the six men of Glider 11 finally arrived at about 7.30 a.m. After their forced-landing in Germany, Witzig had rushed to the nearest telephone to request another Ju 52 tug. While the aircraft was hurriedly dispatched he had worked frantically with his men to improvise a runway across the ploughed field and, although it

Another re-enacted sequence showed Oberfeldwebel Josef Portsteffen assaulting Block II with a flame-thrower.

looked impossible, they had managed to get airborne again. Near Düren, the men of Glider 2 had commandeered a truck and they also managed to reach the bridge at Kanne later in the day.

The battle now had to be taken inside the silenced casemates. The entrances were reconnoitred and installations penetrated but by this time the artillery had started shelling the fort and Belgian infantry were advancing up the north-west slope which was covered with thick undergrowth. Consequently Sturmgruppe Granit had to fall back to the northern part of the fort to defend itself. During the night 50kg charges were set off in the shafts of Maastricht 1 (12), Mi-Nord (19) and Mi-Sud (13).

At 9.45 a.m. a platoon of 40 men from the 7ème Division d'Infanterie reached the entrance to Block I with orders to wipe out the paratroopers. Major Jottrand sent two officers from the garrison to guide them and they advanced up the north-west slope. Colonel Maurice Modard, the commander of the Position Fortifiée de Liège, felt that the group was not strong enough and ordered Major Jottrand to assemble as many extra men as possible and send them out onto the top of the fort. However many of the men were demor-

alised and Major Jottrand had to come down and give them a pep talk before they would agree to move out. The forts of Barchon and Pontisse were asked to hold their covering fire and 80 men left Block II at about 12.30 p.m.

Under Commandant Léon van der Auwera, the second-in-command, they reached Maastricht 1 but failed to dislodge the German paratroopers inside. Under fierce air attacks from low-flying Stukas the men retreated, Commandant van der Auwera having to report back that his men showed a complete lack of moral fibre under strong fire.

At about 5.00 p.m. a third patrol, about 100 men strong, arrived from the barracks at Wonck and was sent forward, but soon retreated, reporting having been repulsed by air attacks. At 8.00 p.m. the first patrol, the one from the 7ème Division d'Infanterie, had to retreat to Block I, their supply of ammunition exhausted.

The men of Sturmgruppe Granit, who had fallen back to the northern part of the fort when confronted with the Belgian counter-attacks, resumed their demolition work and during the night 50kg charges were set off in the shafts of Maastricht 1 (12), Mi-Nord (19) and Mi-Sud (13).

Shortly after noon on May 11, Capitaine Georges Vamecq appeared at the entrance to Block I (left) with a trumpeter and a soldier carrying a white flag: the fortress that everyone had thought was impregnable had capitulated. In this picture taken twelve days later, the new management has already erected a 'Verboten' sign. Right: After being off limits to the general public for 50 years, Eben-Emael opened its doors to visitors in 1990.

Hitler decorated the heroes of Sturmabteilung Koch at a ceremony held at Felsennest. Here the commander, Hauptmann Walter Koch, is introduced to the Führer.

SATURDAY, MAY 11

Kampfgruppe A, the ground relief force for Eben-Emael, was under the command of the commander of Pi.Btl. 51, Oberstleutnant Hans Mikosch. He had organised three assault groups during the night of May 10-11, each made up of one company from Inf.Rgt. 151 and one company of engineers from Pi.Btl. 51. In the darkness of the early hours, the three groups launched their rubber boats into the water and assailed the Albert Canal, Group 2 some distance to the west of the Kanne bridge, Group 3 just east of the bridge and Group 1 farther to the south-east in front of Eben-Emael. Canal Nord (17) and Canal Sud (35) were not silenced and swept the canal with their fire, hitting the men from Group 1 as they

attempted to cross. To help them men from Glider 6 lowered charges from the top of the fort and detonated them in front of the observation dome of Canal Nord, hoping to block the slit. Under Oberfeldwebel Josef Portsteffen from Pi.Btl. 51, the leading platoon of Group 1 attacked Block II which, if knocked out, would leave the north side of the fort defenceless. The block's observation dome had already had a 50kg charge exploded on it by men from Glider 3 and later a 12.5kg by those from Glider 9. Porsteffen attacked Block II with a flame-thrower and, after a 50kg charge was exploded against the embrasure, killing one Belgian soldier and wounding six others, the position was silenced. The engineers pressed on and joined with men from Glider 9 at

about 6.00 a.m. It was said that Wenzel himself ran down the slope some time later to meet the engineers and performed a little dance with Portsteffen to celebrate the link-up.

At 10.00 a.m. Major Jottrand called the fort Defence Council together and explained the gravity of the situation, which was not helped by the pessimism displayed by most of the officers present. Major Jottrand tried to raise the morale of the garrison by addressing a large group of men assembled in a gallery but his spirited words were merely answered by repeated shouts for surrender.

He then selected Capitaine Alfred Hotermans to try to make contact with the enemy. However, when he reached Block I, Hotermans telephoned Jottrand to ask to be relieved of this duty and he was replaced by Capitaine Georges Vamecq.

Shortly after noon, when elements from Group 3 were approaching the fort from the west, a trumpet call was heard and a white flag appeared at Block I. Coupole Sud, Canal Nord and Canal Sud ceased firing and the Belgian emissary, Capitaine Vamecq, a trumpeter and a soldier carrying a white flag, appeared at the entrance of Block I. They were led to Hauptmann Heinrich Haubold, the commander of the 14. Kompanie of Inf.Rgt. 151.

The battle was over. The last telephone message from Major Jottrand had come at 11.00 a.m: 'Accept no more messages from Eben-Emael'. The Belgians had lost 23 dead and 59 wounded and some 750 emerged to be taken prisoner.

At about 3.00 p.m., the victorious glider troops left Eben-Emael and withdrew to Maastricht. Of the 86 men of Sturmgruppe Granit who had set out on the morning of May 10, six had been killed and 15 wounded, not counting those injured in the actual glider landings. On May 10 and 11, Inf.Rgt. 151 had lost 11 dead and 47 wounded and Pi.Btl. 51 one dead and 14 wounded.

Oberleutnant Witzig had the honour of being named in the official Wehrmacht report for May 11, 1940, which

Left: A delighted Hitler rewards Oberfeldwebel Portsteffen (right) and his commander, Oberstleutnant Hans Mikosch, with the Ritterkreuz. *Right:* History was made here: the scene of the award ceremony forty years later.

The commander of Sturmgruppe Granit, Oberleutnant Rudolf Witzig.

Leutnant Egon Delica, the leader of the team which assaulted Maastricht 2.

Oberleutnant Otto Zierach, Chief-of-Staff of Sturmabteilung Koch.

made known that 'the strongest fort of the Liège fortifications, Eben-Emael, had surrendered this Saturday afternoon. The commander and 1,000 men were taken prisoner. The fort had been incapacitated early on May 10 by a group selected from the Luftwaffe under Oberleutnant Witzig who had adopted new methods of attack'.

Hauptmann Walter Koch and the commander of the glider crews, Oberleutnant Walter Kiess, the four assault group commanders (Oberleutnants Gustav Altmann, Martin Schächter, Rudolf Witzig and Leutnant Gerhard Schacht) and six men from Sturmabteilung Koch were all awarded the Ritterkreuz, Koch and Witzig receiving the very first two awarded in the campaign in the west. These awards took place at FHQu Felsennest on May 15, Generalmajor Wolfram von Richthofen, the commander of VIII. Fliegerkorps, being awarded the decoration on May 17. Four days later, Oberfeldwebel Josef Portsteffen and the commander of Pi.Btl. 51, Oberstleutnant Hans Mikosch, also received the Knight's Cross for their part in the operation.

The heroes of Eben-Emael with their Knight's Crosses after the ceremony: Leutnant Egon Delica, Oberleutnant Rudolf Witzig, Hauptmann Walter Koch, Oberleutnant Otto Zierach, Leutnant Helmut Ringler, Leutnant Joachim Meissner, Oberleutnant Walter Kiess, Oberleutant Gustav Altmann and Oberartz Rolf Jäger.

The Sturmgruppe Stahl commander, Oberleutnant Gustav Altmann.

Oberartz Rolf Jäger, the doctor who landed with the Koch commandos.

Leutnant Joachim Meissner took over Sturmgruppe Eisen.

Airborne assaults in the Ardennes

Crailsheim on the morning of May 10: two Fieseler Fi 156s after having completed their first trip on Operation 'Niwi'.

In striking the decisive blow, two airborne special operations were planned for the vital Heeresgruppe A front: the larger of them, in the XIX. Armeekorps sector, to help smooth the progress of Gruppe von Kleist in traversing the Ardennes; the other, in the XXIII. Armeekorps sector, to protect the southern flank of the advancing armour by landing Luftlandekommando Hedderich in Luxembourg close to the French border.

The precise location where the troops were to land ahead of Gruppe von Kleist, either in Belgium roughly midway between Neufchâteau, Bastogne and the frontier town of Martelange in Operation 'Niwi', or in Luxembourg for Operation 'Rosa', was left to the last possible moment. The final decision plumped for 'Niwi', on the basis that demolition charges and road-blocks were less well prepared in Luxembourg and these could be safely left to be dealt with by the Brandenburgers.

OPERATION 'NIWI'

The broad intentions for Operation 'Niwi' were to keep open the roads east of Neufchâteau and impede any enemy move. Göring, keen as always for the Luftwaffe to gain as many of the laurels as possible, apparently put forward the idea of an airborne operation, to which Hitler agreed, so that on February 26, 1940, General Franz Halder was able to note in his diary that an airborne force of about 400 men was 'to open the way for XIX. Armeekorps'.

The Germans were not to know but, because Belgian intentions were for the Chasseurs Ardennais to destroy communications and then withdraw northwards to link up with the main body of their army, there was actually not much chance of the panzers coming up against too much opposition in this sector. The Belgian demolitions, being neither defended nor covered by artillery, were unlikely to slow the German advance for long.

As most of the air transport was committed with Heeresgruppe B, the daring plan relied on the use of some 100 Fieseler Fi 156 light aircraft carrying two apiece and making two trips to land all 400 men. Only three Ju 52s could be assigned to the operation, their rôle being to airdrop or land supplies once the troops were on the ground. This air fleet was under the command of Major Otto Förster.

The troops chosen for this difficult mission were from the élite Infanterie-Regiment 'Gross Deutschland', the bulk of which were to be engaged with the 10. Panzer-Division on the left wing of XIX. Armeekorps. The 400 men earmarked for 'Niwi' or 'Rosa' were from the regiment's third battalion — the battalion staff, 10. and 11. Kompanie and part of 12. Kompanie. They had been stationed at Crailsheim, where the light aircraft had been brought together, since February to train in the same conditions of secrecy that applied

at Hildesheim for Sturmabteilung Koch. Oberstleutnant Eugen Garski, the commander of III. Bataillon, was in charge of the operation.

Taking into account that they might have to face not only a regiment of the élite Belgian Chasseurs Ardennais but also French cavalry units, they were provided with extra firepower particularly in machine guns and anti-tank rifles, of which they had twice the normal complement.

The two landing sites chosen for 'Niwi' were near the villages of Nives and Witry — from which the operation took its name. Nives lay about six kilometres north of Witry. The Witry landings involved 56 aircraft and 240 men. Oberstleutnant Garski was to be with this group and, as the operation's commander, two radio sets were to be provided for him, one to communicate with the northern group, the other with XIX. Armeekorps. Some 160 men were to be landed near Nives by 42 aircraft;

Several of the Storchs — a remarkable observation and liaison aircraft which could land in as little as 18 yards — came to grief although for some reason this machine pictured at Petite Rosière near Nives has not been set alight as per orders.

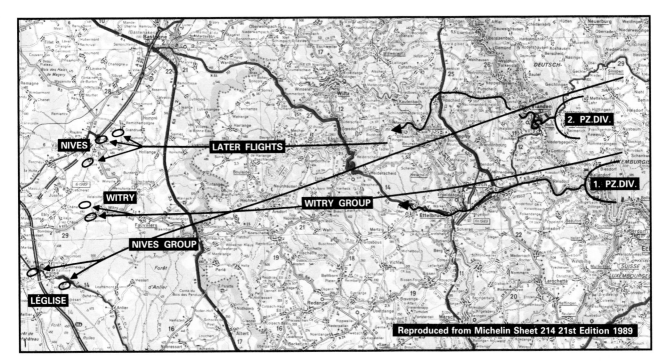

Reproduced from Michelin Sheet 214 21st Edition 1989

the northern group leader being Hauptmann Walther Krüger, with a single radio for communicating with his commander at Witry.

The two landing sites were about 10 kilometres to the west of the Luxembourg border and 60 kilometres west of the German border. It took about half an hour's flying time to get there from the two airfields in the Bitburg area where the men and aircraft assembled on the evening of May 9. This meant that the troops who were landed in the first lift would not to be joined by those in the second until at least an hour had elapsed.

At 4.20 a.m. on May 10 the 98 aircraft of the first lift took off as planned, those bound for Witry flying from Dockendorf and those for Nives from Pützhöhe. To avoid a massacre should enemy fighters be encountered, the aircraft flew in two loose formations and very low. They arrived over Luxembourg on schedule just after 4.30 a.m. Piloting the leading aircraft of the northern group, despite his rank and position, was Major Förster; with him was Hauptmann Krüger. Förster how-

ever made a drastic error, deviating southwards taking his formation with him. After some minutes, his aircraft passed between the fifth and sixth aircraft of Oberstleutnant Garski's southern group which were making for Witry. The pilot of the sixth aircraft took Förster's aircraft to be the one he was following; the other fifty aircraft of the southern group tagged on, and so Garski flew blithely on with only four aircraft behind him, while the northern group continued southwards! Having landed, Garski found that he had only nine men with him. His radio was with the other aircraft, so he could not contact either Krüger or headquarters to find out what had gone wrong. After waiting a short time to see what would happen, he decided to get on with the job with the puny force at hand.

Meanwhile Major Förster had realised the mistake he had made, and most of the second lift were able to keep to their correct course for Witry or to Nives, although a few aircraft were also sent to reinforce the troops that had gone astray under Hauptmann Krüger. A third lift was later organised for Witry

to compensate for this dispersion and the aircraft lost during the first.

However further confusion abounded as Krüger's first lift and the bulk of Garski's came down some 15 kilometres to the south of where they were intended to be — 93 aircraft cramming into the wrong area instead of 42. The pilots, with nothing to go by, put down as best they could and the troops were widely scattered. Several aircraft were damaged on landing, and eight which proved to be unable to take off again were set alight as per orders. Most of the aircraft had touched down near Rancimont. Krüger, with just four men, had landed about two kilometres away, near the village of Léglise. He was none too pleased to learn from two civilians where he really was, and he was in for another surprise when, after spending time gathering up the various groups, he saw that he had about 180 men with him, twice what he was supposed to have! Having set about cutting the telephone lines in the area, they started to requisition every passing car and truck in order to assemble a convoy to try to reach their comrades to the north.

Once they had arrived in Belgium — either at Witry or Nives as planned, or near Léglise where some landed by mistake — the

'Niwi' commandos promptly set about cutting telephone lines and blocking roads.

As soon as the Belgians realised what was happening — the sector was held by units from the 1er Régiment de Chasseurs Ardennais — they despatched two platoons of motor cyclists and two T-15 light tanks in the direction of the village. They were soon held up by German fire, and the tanks damaged, but the situation for the Germans was not too good. The Belgians were still a threat and when some French armoured cars from the 5ème D.L.C. appeared south of Léglise, Krüger decided not to linger. He had no specific purpose in this area and had already decided to move north to join up with Garski. A small Kampfgruppe was left in the village to cover the move, which started around nine o'clock. The rearguard pulled out an hour later and the Belgians entered the village at about 10.30 a.m. Having no orders to follow, they waited there until the end of the afternoon and then withdrew towards Neufchâteau.

To the north, Garski and his nine men got on with what more than ten times their number had been sent to do — cutting telephone wires, blocking roads and taking prisoner any Belgian soldiers in the cars they stopped. Fortunately for them, no opposition materialised before the arrival of the second lift at about 7.00 a.m. Two hours later, the third lift that was laid on for Witry after the mistaken landings at Léglise, brought Garski some more men and heavy weapons. The Belgians sent a patrol forward under Lieutenant Emile Schweicher, about ten men, a motor cycle and a T-13 light tank, which came upon the Germans near Traimont but they were forced to pull back in the face of an obviously stronger force. Garski then attacked Witry and took the village with ease as, contrary to expectations, it was undefended. At about midday, Krüger and his men arrived from Léglise and Garski was now in command of a sizeable detachment of about 300 men. Meanwhile, reinforced by another T-13, Lieutenant Schweicher was ordered to hold the crossroads east of Witry. During the afternoon, the patrol again clashed with Garski's men and then withdrew after having lost two men and one T-13 disabled by a Panzerbüchsen. Early that evening, Garski's men were joined by the advance elements of the 1. Panzer-Division.

Although the German airborne troops were threatened by advanced elements of the 5ème D.L.C., the French armoured cars were ordered to withdraw, and contact was soon established with the leaders of the panzer divisions. This column of SdKfz 251 half-tracks from 1. Panzer-Division was pictured moving through Witry.

The half-tracks were rolling westwards on the N45 — the main east-west road leading from the frontier crossing at Martelange.

It was after 7.00 a.m. when the first troops to actually land at Nives were brought in by the second lift. While his men attended to the telephone lines in the surrounding villages, Leutnant Andreas Obermeier went on an improvised patrol on an impressed motor cycle followed by a requisitioned car.

At Vaux they ran into advance elements of the French 5ème D.L.C. and were fired at, but managed to get quickly away and back to Nives. The Panzerbüchsen were effective enough to pierce the armour of the leading Panhard P-178 armoured car of 5ème R.A.M. which had raced for the village after

The obstacles thrown across the roads by the 'Niwi' teams proved more of a nuisance to their own troops!

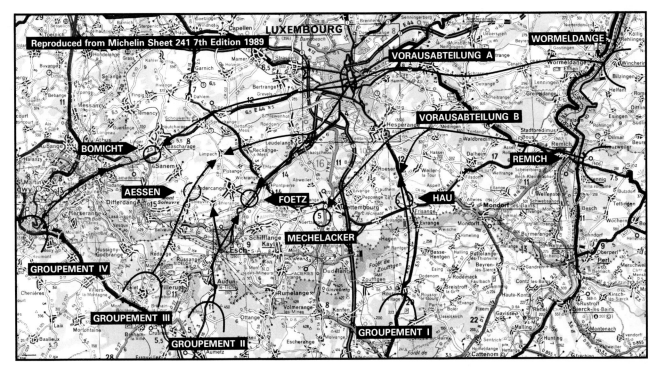

them. The French tried again but the armoured car was holed for the second time and the commander, Lieutenant Toussaint, was ordered to keep an eye on the situation.

A Belgian patrol, a few men and two T-13s, under Lieutenant Fernand Simonet, also probed the German positions and, just after midday, came upon a Ju 52 which had landed near Chaumont to unload supplies and equipment. Three shots from the T-13s disabled the aircraft which caught fire. Another Belgian patrol brushed with the Germans in the Bois de Cohet and lost one of its four T-13s and withdrew; an unlucky Ju 52 then overflew the Belgian patrol which promptly brought it down near Grande-Rosière. The 1er Régiment de Chasseurs Ardennais then withdrew northwards but the French, who had shot down two Fieseler Storchs flying supply missions to Nives, resumed their attack. Three Hotchkiss H-39s of the 5ème R.A.M. arrived at about 6.00 p.m. and together with three light tanks of the 15ème R.D.P., they drove out

the Germans, who had no anti-tank guns and whose Panzerbüchsen were useless in the face of reasonably armoured tanks. But without infantry support and cover for the night, the tanks were forced to withdraw when it began to grow dark whereupon the Germans reoccupied the village.

The night was uneventful but when the French tried to resume their advance the next morning they were met by determined opposition for at daylight, advance elements of the 2. Panzer-Division had made contact with the airborne troops.

Before long, the 5ème D.L.C. was involved in a general withdrawal of the advanced French cavalry units and Capitaine Ernest Fontant, who had taken command of the French advanced guard in the sector, was ordered to withdraw to Neufchâteau where they arrived by midday.

About 30 men had been killed on Operation 'Niwi', including Luftwaffe personnel. Sixteen Fi 156s were lost, besides the two Ju 52s out of the three

assigned to it. Not much fuss was made of the venture, understandable perhaps in view of the way it went wrong after Förster's error, and also the lessening of its significance with the melting away of the Chasseurs Ardennais it was designed to forestall. Even so, 46 Iron Crosses, 1st and 2nd Class, were awarded, but only Oberstleutnant Eugen Garski received the Ritterkreuz, awarded on July 19.

LUFTLANDEKOMMANDO HEDDERICH

In the south of Luxembourg, on the left wing of the 16. Armee, the XXIII. Armeekorps had the vital role of protecting the flank of Gruppe von Kleist against a possible attack by French forces. The 34. Infanterie-Division, on the corps' right, had the most difficult task on the first day as it had to cross the Moselle and dash about forty kilometres through the Grand Duchy to face southwards. Its initial objectives were only a few kilometres from the French border and speed was essential

Compared to the 'Niwi' operation, Luftlandekommando Hedderich was mounted on a much smaller scale. Just 25 Storchs were allocated to transport its 125 men to Luxembourg compared to the 100 aircraft provided for the Belgian operation.

as the French 3ème D.L.C. had orders to advance into the Grand Duchy from the south if the Germans invaded it. To get there as quickly as possible across southern Luxembourg, three advance units (Vorausabteilung) were formed by the 34. Infanterie-Division with motor cycle, bicycle or cavalry troops in the lead.

When the use of airborne troops had been decided upon ahead of the panzers (Operation 'Niwi'), Hitler himself had insisted on another airborne operation along the French border in the south of Luxembourg as part of the measures taken by the 16. Armee to provide flanking cover. The Chief-of-Staff of the 16. Armee, General Walther Model, was charged with the planning of the operation, the aim of which was the capture of five important crossroads on the major roads south of Luxembourg city.

Volunteers for a 'special mission' were obtained from the 34. Infanterie-Division, and early in March they were sent to Crailsheim and Böblingen on a tough selection course. The best 125 of them were then brought together at Crailsheim and trained in conditions of strict secrecy. They were organised into five groups, one for each of the objectives, and, like the troops trained for 'Niwi', received an extra quota of weapons, — each group of 25 men being allotted five machine guns, one anti-tank rifle and a number of Teller-mines in addition to their normal complement of rifles, sub-machine guns and hand grenades. Oberleutnant Werner

Although the war has commenced, protocol still had to be observed. Arriving at the border with Luxembourg, the leaders of the French 3ème D.L.C. wait patiently outside the customs post before receiving the OK to cross into Esch-sur-Alzette. Permission was granted around 8.00 a.m. — by which time Stosstrupp Oswald had entered the town from the north.

Virtually no change in nearly 50 years at the Grand Duchy border post with crossings now almost a formality with the EEC union.

Hedderich from the division's Inf.Rgt. 80 was in overall command — hence 'Luftlandekommando Hedderich'.

In April the men were moved to Trier, where training continued until the time came for the real thing.

Twenty-five Fieseler Storchs awaited them when they arrived at Trier-Euren airfield on the night of May 9, and by 4.30 a.m. the men of the first lift were on their way. Flying in one long column, the aircraft crossed the border

The men of the 31ème G.R.D.I. — in the van of the 3ème D.L.C. — soon came under fire from advanced elements of Leutnant Oswald's airborne group and some Frenchmen were wounded. However they pushed forward to reach the main square in front of the railway station *(above)* where they were greeted by an enthusiastic crowd and offered wine . . . flowers . . . and cigarettes!

near Wasserbillig without incident, and when over Luxembourg city, split into five smaller formations which each struck out for their objectives. These were the crossroads at Bomicht, near Pétange; at Aessen, north of Soleuvre; at Foetz, north of Esch; at Mechelacker, south of Bettembourg; and at Hau, just north of Frisange. Although all these locations were out in the open, and clearly visible from the French positions across the border, they were ideally placed to control the road network of southern Luxembourg. At 5.00 a.m. the 16. Armee reported to Heeresgruppe A that the first lift had landed 'as planned at the objectives'. Some of the aircraft were damaged on landing and had to be set alight, but most took off again and went back to make their second trip.

Bridges on the Moselle had been captured undamaged as the 34. Infanterie-Division advance elements started to cross as soon as the obstacles installed on the bridges had been removed, Vorausabteilung A taking the one at Wormeldange, and Vorausabteilung B that at Remich. Meanwhile, on the ground, a strange situation arose for the teams of Luftlandekommando Hedderich. As the airborne troops got busy, civilians began to gather, standing around like inquisitive tourists, watching what they were up to, while the Germans — only ten to a group to start with — set up their machine guns, erected road-blocks and sowed mines right before their eyes.

At Bomicht, the group landed there was joined by elements of Vorausabteilung A, and the one at Mechelacker by elements of Vorausabteilung B, before they were actually engaged by French troops. At Aessen, where Oberleutnant Hedderich himself had landed, the group was joined by elements of Vorausabteilung A which had brought up a 37mm anti-tank gun just in time to

stop the leading Panhard P-178 of the 3ème R.A.M. as they approached the crossroads. Another armoured car blew a mine and stopped, but by midday elements of the 4ème Regiment de Spahis supported by some Hotchkiss H-35s had taken the crossroads. The Germans had lost 16 killed and 13 captured in this action and Oberleutnant Hedderich had been forced to flee into a nearby wood with the four survivors. From here the Spahis advanced northwards through Sanem and Limpach, only to find the Reckange area packed with German troops and convoys; both flanks exposed, they were quickly ordered to pull back to Soleuvre.

The group which landed at Hau had

established itself at the crossroads it was to control when it was attacked in determined fashion by the leaders of the French force and overwhelmed. The group commander, Leutnant Hans Lauer, was killed and a number of his men captured but the French advance was stopped only a few kilometres to the north.

The group at Fetz had been joined at 6.30 a.m. by elements of Vorausabteilung B and had advanced southwards as far as a Luxembourg border control point where Leutnant Hubert Oswald established an outpost. At about 7.00 a.m. some of the bystanders shouted that the French were arriving and after a brief exchange of fire the Germans withdrew to the surprise of the French. The crowd vanished into thin air! The French troops advanced and crossed Esch to the cheers of the inhabitants but were halted at the edge of the town when the leading Panhard P-178 was disabled by a mine. The battle there was to last until evening when the French finally withdrew.

Meanwhile the French High Command, still waiting to be certain of what was happening, delayed issuing Alerte 4 until 6.45 a.m. — nearly two hours after the German troops had crossed the border. Thus the bold use of Luftlandekommando Hedderich and the swift advance of the 34. Infanterie-Division's Vorausabteilung had easily beaten the French to it in the Grand Duchy. The price of success had been minimal, 25 to 30 men killed and the loss of five Storchs.

The Luftlandekommando was officially disbanded on May 12 but before its dispersal, the entire unit was assembled at the Bascharage railway station on May 13 before the 16. Armee commander, General Ernst Busch. He congratulated them and each man was awarded the Iron Cross 2nd Class, with the 1st Class for Oberleutnant Werner Hedderich.

The welcome did not last long. By the time the French reached the northern end of the town they came across a barricade built by the Oswald group, and when the leading armoured car tried to pass, it struck a mine. Then the Germans manning the ambush opened fire. It was 8.10 a.m.

The Allies move forward

The BEF entered Belgium early on the afternoon of May 10; this patrol is walking towards the frontier between Wattrelos and Dottignies, just north of Roubaix.

The French Command reacted cautiously to the news of the expected invasion in spite of the fact that Général Gamelin and his staff had been warned by the Minister of National Defence that something was afoot at 1.00 a.m.. At about 4.30 a.m. they knew for certain that the Wehrmacht had crossed the borders of the Netherlands, Belgium and Luxembourg but still held back from issuing orders for Alerte 1 or Alerte 2, the first two steps in the execution of the Dyle Plan. It was 5.35 a.m. before the order was finally given for Alerte 3, the advance up to the border.

Alerte 4, the order for the entry into Belgium, was issued at 6.45 a.m. after it was certain that the Belgian government had asked for Allied intervention. This request had not come until 6.25 a.m., when the Germans had already been across the border for two hours. The order went out to the headquarters of Groupe d'Armées No.1, which was to be the main instrument of the plan, and to the Groupe d'Armées No.2, also involved to a lesser extent on the southern flank of the manoeuvre, its 3ème Armée due to enter Luxembourg. Général Georges put through a call to Gamelin: 'Well, Général, is it the Dyle manoeuvre?' asked Georges. 'Since the Belgians are calling on us', came the reply, 'do you see what else we can do?', 'Obviously not', said Georges.

Because it took some time to circulate the orders, the units were notified at different times, some having been placed on Alerte 3 as early as 5.30 a.m., others going straight to Alerte 4

at 7.00 a.m. At this time the very first units crossed the borders of Belgium and Luxembourg and within three hours all the armies were under way.

Because of the Belgian efforts to remain convincingly neutral right up to the end, the entry of the Allied troops into Belgium had not been prepared in detail. Some contacts at high level had been maintained, albeit in secret, but there was the greatest uncertainty

among the troops, particularly in Belgium where it took some time to pass the changed orders down to the lowest level. It was not until 7.00 a.m., two and a half hours after the first German units had crossed the border, that the Belgian Command gave orders to remove the barriers and open the roads in front of the Allied troops and even more time was to pass before the troops were told that the French and British aircraft must

Complete with their puppy mascot, convoys carrying the men of the BEF push on the 120 kilometres — about 75 miles — to their positions on the River Dyle. These ran from north of Louvain down to Wavre, a distance of 25 kilometres (15 miles).

not be fired at any more! When the orders did finally reach the units on the border, it still took some time to remove the road blocks, even though Belgian civilians enthusiastically lent a hand. All this lost time was to be paid for dearly by the cavalry units which hastened on ahead, in the words of the March 14 directive, to 'cover the move of our forces to the main defence line and their reinforcement, by rushing as fast as possible to make contact with the enemy, support the covering Belgian troops and slow the German advance'.

THE BEF

A message from the French Command was received at British General Headquarters in Arras at about 5.45 a.m. ordering the full alert and half an hour later a message arrived from Général Georges' headquarters about the immediate execution of the Dyle Plan. The BEF started to move as planned, the armoured cars of the 12th Royal Lancers crossing the border into Belgium at 1.00 p.m. There was one minor incident when a Belgian frontier guard tried to halt the passage of a 3rd Division unit for not being in possession of a 'permit to enter' — easily resolved by a truck charging the barrier.

Right: **On to Brussels and Louvain. The advance gets under way, supported by a number of the Belgian townspeople. This is a Light Dragon Mk II.**

Above left: **Further up the road, at the border itself, Royal Engineers demolish the frontier barrier to widen the roadway. Belgian and French soldiers look on. There appears to be a lack of urgency, almost a relaxed atmosphere. It would soon change.**
Above right: **Although 40-odd years have seen the liberalisation of frontiers and customs controls, some things never change. When Régis Potié took this comparison for us in Petit-Audenarde the Café Michel was still in business under the same name.**

And in come the cavalry! Its tracks clattering on the pavé, a Universal Carrier Mk I of 'A' Squadron, 15th/19th The King's Royal Hussars, crosses the level crossing at Petit-Audenarde at speed.

Here on the far right flank of the BEF line, some 30 kilometres east of Wavre, a Guy Mk I armoured car *(above)* and a Bedford lorry *(bottom)* of the 12th Royal Lancers carry out reconnaissance duties moving eastwards on the N37 at Thisnes. The track on the left is the local railway called the Chemin de Fer Vicinal.

The armoured cars of the Lancers arrived first on the Dyle Line, followed by the other armoured reconnaissance units allocated to the I Corps and II Corps, which began to deploy. The leading infantry divisions came up the next morning. The 3rd Division arrived to take over the left of the British sector, the Louvain area (already held by the Belgian 10ème Division d'Infanterie, which had to be dispossessed); the 1st Division took over the centre, and the 2nd Division the right, north of Wavre. General Gort had disposed his forces in depth, two divisions being in support to the north and south of Brussels, two in reserve and two more back on the Escaut river. As the main German effort was not directed at this part of the front, the BEF was able to occupy its sector without interference and to adequately organise its defences by the time the offensive reached its positions.

With the loss of the building on the right, now replaced by an extensive apple orchard, this was a tricky comparison to pinpoint.

The British and French troops were greeted warmly by the Belgian people, their implicit confidence far removed from the fear and confusion that would all too soon send thousands of refugees fleeing in the opposite direction. Lieutenant Louis Bounaix, a section commander in the 2ème Compagnie of the 37ème B.C.C. which arrived by train at Roux, just north of Charleroi, paints a nice picture of the enthusiasm of the Belgian people and the quiet confidence of the French élite units in these early days:

'We had nearly completed the off-loading when a sinister looking bird arrived on us from the far skyline. The crew disappeared into their tanks but my "Guynemer" was too far and I had to crawl behind a concrete block, my face between bits of old iron. Shame! It was a British aircraft. We quickly left this place that could become highly dangerous in the clear light.

'We crossed the canal over a narrow bridge, the tracks of our Renault B1bis tearing off some iron fittings under the stunned and respectful eyes of the locals. We drove along narrow climbing streets lined with terraced orchards, the walls of which reverberated with the roar of our engines. We then crossed the road to Gosselie and started to go downhill when the thing burst, unexpected, shy at first, then growing immensely. One of the Belgians looking at us passing by made a gesture and I got a pack of cigarettes on my knees. A few metres away, it was an orange. It was like a signal and every hand were now full of presents, chocolate, sweets, bottles . . . We were obliged to slow down and the officers were busily occupied in getting all the presents and giving them to their crew inside the tanks. An old women grabbed me to be certain that I could take her precious small paper-wrapped present, two sugar lumps. I felt deeply moved.

'The enthusiasm of the people grew higher and higher, their faces radiating more and more as we advanced. I heard them shouting "Vive la France et la Belgique. Vive les Français!"'

Compared with the scenes near the French border, the closer to the front, the less enthusiastic the welcome. The two sides would clash less than 15 kilometres from Vilvoorde.

'The Belgians have been wonderful to us all along the route,' said one of the BEF drivers on Saturday. 'Early this morning they brought out jugs of hot coffee which we gulped down as we stopped for a few minutes. The bakers brought us packets full of cakes and buns. At other places they gave us toffee and chocolates, and just outside this town they gave us a glass of beer. Though we have been on the road since late last night with no stop for a meal, it has not been at all bad.' This lorry from the 3rd Division is passing through the town of Vilvoorde to the north of Brussels on May 12 en route to Louvain.

On the western flank, Groupement Lestoquoi sped into Belgium on the afternoon of May 10 ahead of the 1ère D.L.M., and pushed on through the night towards the Dutch border. The reconnaissance group consisted of the 2ème G.R.C.A. and the 5ème G.R.D.I. These motor cyclists were pictured the following morning leaving their bivouac area.

They pointed to the names painted on the turrets of our tanks and I heard the explanation "Guynemer . . . a French pilot . . . "

'All these shouts, these smiles and these weeping eyes moved us to our deepest soul. The Belgians were counting on us, they would not be disappointed. An immense proudness was growing inside us, a huge confidence, strengthened by the admiration shown on these thousands of faces. Our Renault B1bis were beautiful and the Germans would learn to know them.

'A mother raised her baby in her hands, stretching him towards me as high as possible. A beautiful gesture of faith, hope and anxiety that asked to be reassured. "Yes Madame, we are going to defend your son" and I thought of all the mothers of Belgium and France that would have to flee with their children in their arms if we did not stop the German onslaught. But who could stop France and Great Britain?'

7ème ARMÉE

To the north, the 7ème Armée of Général Henri Giraud moved with all speed to carry out the role allotted to it north-east of Antwerp for the occupation of Zeeland. Preceding the army's six infantry divisions were the advance elements of the 1ère D.L.M. and, out in front, a number of reconnaissance units operating in two groups: Groupement Lestoquoi, making for beyond Antwerp ahead of the 1ère D.L.M., and Groupement de Beauchesne, making for Zeeland and the mainland at the neck of the South Beveland peninsula. This later group had been given the mission previously allotted to the airborne Operation 'Malacca' whereby French paratroopers were to drop on Vlissingen airfield and infantry landed there by aircraft some time later, to take control of Walcheren before the arrival of the panzers. The operation had been about to start during the alarm of November but it had been abandoned since and the

capture of Walcheren was left to the swift recce groups. It is interesting to note that the Germans had made virtually identical plans to take the Netherlands and these would prove to work.

The Alerte 3 had been given at 5.30 a.m. While the 1ère D.L.M. loaded its tanks onto trains, its advance elements, the 6ème Cuirassiers, crossed into Belgium at about 10.00 a.m. with Groupement Lestoquoi. These leading elements were at Turnhout that evening and by 9.30 p.m. had entered the Netherlands. Groupement de Beauchesne had embarked its three recce groups at Breskens in the afternoon and disembarked that evening at Vlissingen on the island of Walcheren, heading in the direction of Kapelle.

Early on May 11, the vanguard of Groupement de Beauchesne was at Roosendaal, elements of Groupement Lestoquoi had reached Breda and Tilburg, making contact with the enemy near there and at Moerdijk. The 1ère

Groupement Lestoquoi crossed into Belgium here at Callicanes, between Steenvoorde and Poperinge at about 10.00 a.m., before pushing on across the Albert Canal. This picture of the

border crossing was taken sometime later, probably on May 11, when Belgian refugees had massed there waiting for permission to enter France.

D.L.M. tanks were unloaded in the afternoon at Mechelen and south of Antwerp and the first elements of the 25ème D.I.M. arrived in the Netherlands that evening.

Far in front, the situation at the head of the column was uneasy and Sergent Marcel Berger, commander of a Panhard P-178 armoured car of the 2ème G.R.D.I. — he had disembarked on Walcheren as part of Groupement de Beauchesne and advanced eastwards — described (under his pen name of Sergent Guy de Chézal) how they were

Détachement Durand of the 68ème Division d'Infanterie was ferried by sea from Dunkirk to Vlissingen to occupy Walcheren. In these pictures, elements of the division's 224ème R.I. are pictured on board the ferry *Newhaven* then later in the Netherlands near Wilhelminadorp.

Down south, midway along the French-Belgian border, the 2ème D.L.M. crossed at Beaumont moving northwards towards Charleroi and the vulnerable Gembloux gap. This was the open country, between Brussels and Namur, north of the Meuse and Sambre rivers, possessing no natural defences, and was already a favoured European battleground since an Austrian army beat the Spaniards there in the 16th century. Waterloo lay on its northern extremity. It was the job of the 2ème D.L.M. with its 160 tanks and 100 armoured cars to help plug the gap. *Above:* Transport and a Hotchkiss H-35 pictured on May 10 in the Rue Madame in Beaumont, little changed since the trauma of May 1940.

quite alone, seeing only Belgian troops 'withdrawing at all speed' and Dutch troops 'talking of paratroopers'.

'Thousands of alarming stories circulated. How could we know the right from the wrong? What about the capture, true or not, of the Moerdijk bridge? And this farmer to whom I had asked by sign the way to Turnhout? He had answered in rather good French and sent us in the opposite direction. Our column had to turn back and we lost a lot of time. A British motor cyclist soon informed us that we were going the wrong way and I gave him the description of the farmer. Tapping his hand gun menacingly, he drove ahead. Having extricated ourselves, with great difficulty from the horde of refugees, we were surprised to see that the farmer was right! Who was this British motor cyclist who fooled us? Was he British? Or what?'

2ème ARMÉE

On the southern flank of the Groupe d'Armées No. 1, the 2ème Armée of Général Charles Huntziger had its five infantry divisions already in position on their main defence line. It, too, was to fan out cavalry units ahead in Belgium to slow the German advance, and the 5ème D.L.C., the 1ère B.C., the 2ème D.L.C. and several motorised reconnaissance groups moved forward into the Ardennes to continue the cavalry screen from the boundary with 9ème Armée near Saint-Hubert to the Luxembourg border.

Leaving the Sedan area, the 5ème D.L.C. reached the River Semois at Bouillon at about 8.00 a.m. and advanced to the north-east, hindered only by the demolitions carried out by the Belgian engineers. In the evening the division had reached the Libramont-Neufchâteau area, but its advance ele-ments were stopped in front of Houffalize by Belgian demolitions. During the afternoon contact with the enemy was made near Bertogne and Bastogne. The 2ème D.L.C. moved swiftly through Virton and reached Arlon and Habay-la-Neuve, but at 9.00 a.m. it had already come up against the enemy and was soon forced to withdraw.

In reserve, the 1ère Brigade de Cavalerie had moved as planned and taken up positions along the Semois in the Florenville area.

Already there were indications of poor liaison between the 9ème Armée and 2ème Armée, with Huntziger complaining that the 5ème D.L.C. and his left flank lay exposed as Corap's cavalry screen had not advanced as far east as planned. On the morning of May 11 elements of the 3ème Brigade de Spahis established contact with the 5ème D.L.C.

Having reached Charleroi, the column was pictured on Avenue Paul Pasteur near the La Villette bridge over the River Sambre.

1ère ARMÉE

In the centre was the 1ère Armée of Général Georges Blanchard, the strongest of all the French armies with eight infantry divisions, three of them motorised, plus the Corps de Cavalerie of Général René Prioux which spearheaded the army's move with two mechanised divisions, the 2ème and 3ème D.L.M.s, and several motorised reconnaissance groups. This was the army that was thought most likely to have to face a German panzer attack in the Gembloux gap.

The 3ème D.L.M. moved swiftly via Valenciennes, Bavay, Mons and Binche to reach the area north of Namur, its spearhead — Détachement de Découverte (DD) or discovery detachment — moving as far as the Albert Canal between Hasselt and the Maastricht area, the bridge at Hasselt being reached at about 5.40 p.m. One patrol

under Sous-Lieutenant du Chazeau crossed the canal at Diepenbeek and had advanced as far as Genk late that evening. Farther to the south, the DD Montardy made contact with the Germans holding the bridgehead captured early that morning at the Veldwezelt bridge by the glider troops of Sturmabteilung Koch.

The 2ème D.L.M. made its way through Maubeuge, Avesnes and Charleroi to the area north of Namur, its vanguard passing the western edge of Liège and crossing the Meuse at Amay and Engis. The DD Borie reached the Ourthe river at Durbuy while DD de Gastines arrived at Comblain-au-Pont.

The performance of the leading elements of these two mechanised divisions, in moving 300 kilometres in one day through unknown country and under hostile skies, was a considerable achievement.

9ème ARMÉE

Along the Ardennes area of the front — too 'inaccessible' to be considered a likely major field of operations — the 9ème Armée of Général André Corap had only seven infantry divisions with which to man a sector some 80 kilometres long between Namur and Pont-à-Bar. The army was already in position with the Meuse on its right wing but on its left it had to bring up two infantry corps behind the river between Givet and Namur. Three cavalry units, the 4ème D.L.C., the 1ère D.L.C. and the 3ème Brigade de Spahis, were to move forward east of the river into the Ardennes together with several motorised reconnaissance groups while the army was establishing its infantry along the Meuse.

The swift execution of the Dyle Plan was greatly impeded in the Ardennes, the vital sector where the Germans had planned to breakthrough, as the Belgians had devised plans of their own for this sector without taking the Dyle Plan into account. Général van Overstraeten, the Belgian strategist, had decided not to defend the Ardennes and the troops in this sector — Groupement K with the 1ère Division de Chasseurs Ardennais and the 1ère Division de Cavalerie — had the task of destroying communications from the River Salm area near Trois-Ponts down to the French border near Arlon before withdrawing to an intermediate position behind the River Ourthe to the south of Liège, thence to their main line of resistance behind the Meuse from Namur to Liège.

In April the French Command had asked to see a copy of the plans of the demolitions that the Belgians intended to carry out in the Ardennes. These Général van Overstraeten had refused to supply, although he had revealed to Colonel Hautcoeur, the French envoy, that they had been worked out so as not to impede the advance of the French cavalry units into Belgium. This was far from the truth as these plans were very rigid and timed only to coincide with the withdrawal of the Belgian troops: no precautions at all had been taken to ensure that the French units could move east to make contact with the Germans and then withdraw behind the Meuse.

The order given on February 12 to Groupement K made no mention at all of French units coming to support the Belgian troops. At the very beginning of May Général Jules Derousseaux had tried to persuade Général van Overstraeten of the necessity to amend the orders given to Groupement K but he failed to effect any change.

Alarmed by the news from Luxembourg, Général Maurice Keyaerts, the commander of Groupement K, had issued the order to blow some 90 'Ia' priority demolition charges at about 3.45 a.m. on May 10. He then ordered the 60 'Ib' priority charges to be blown at 5.12 a.m. Further to the west, the destruction of demolitions, classified with priorities II, III and IV, were all implemented as planned, timed at the Belgian withdrawal. In all, about 330 demolitions were carried out and an

Charleroi today. The city was originally called Charnoy but was renamed by the Spanish governor-general of the Low Countries in 1666 in honour of his king, Charles II. It was the scene of heavy fighting in the French Revolutionary wars at nearby Fleurus; the site of Napoleon's HQ before the Battle of Waterloo, and the location of the first battle between Germany and France in the First World War.

Travelling with its turret reversed, this Hotchkiss H-39 number 83 of the 3ème D.L.M. is passing through Thisnes, (see page 96) two kilometres west of Hannut. By the afternoon of May 10, Belgian refugees were beginning to flow westwards away from the forthcoming battle. German forces were then 45 kilometres (28 miles) to the east.

Crossing the Meuse south of them, advance elements of the 3ème Brigade de Spahis arrived on the l'Homme river between Grupont and Saint-Hubert between 8.00 p.m. and 9.30 p.m.

French officers tried to persuade the withdrawing Belgians 'to stay with them to share the battle' and on several occasions they had to remonstrate with Belgian troops whose orders were to blow up a road and withdraw without waiting for the Germans. There were even some occasions when they had to resort to actual threats to prevent the charges being detonated behind them.

The Chasseurs Ardennais did their job thoroughly, fulfilling their orders, and they gave very little assistance to French cavalry units in the Ardennes. Général Maurice Keyaerts, particularly, emerges in a very poor light when he insisted upon demolition La 5 near Maboge being carried out — in the rear of a French detachment that he himself had asked to advance eastwards to Nadrin! The commander of this French unit, Capitaine Henri Garnier, had to detach troops to guard against the possibilty of the Belgian engineers going ahead regardless of where this would leave his men. Strong language was to be heard at the Belgian command post in Laroche where French officers of the 1er R.A.M. strenuously objected to the idea of setting off charges that had been prepared, and revolvers were brandished. Capitaine Edouard de Verdelon, commanding the first group of the 1er R.A.M., was reported to have threatened 'If you blow the road, I will blow your head off!'

The French Corps de Cavalerie was then only a few kilometres from its objective — the line Opheylissem-Huy — on which the two D.L.M.s had to hold the German forces long enough for the main body of the 1ère Armée to reach the defence line in the Gembloux gap, 30 kilometres to their rear. *Below:* **Hotchkiss number 93 of the 3ème D.L.M. pictured on the Thisnes road.**

even larger number of road blocks constructed.

Well ahead of the advancing Germans, the speed with which the Belgians got on with blowing up roads in the Ardennes only made it more difficult for the French cavalry units to push forward their advance cover and reconnaissance screen over the Meuse, the 1ère D.L.C. and the 4ème D.L.C. advance elements being particularly impeded in their moves.

The 4ème D.L.C. moved through Trélon, Philippeville and Fraire and crossed the Meuse at Profondeville and Annevoie around 2.00 p.m. Advance elements reached the Ourthe at Durbuy and had got as far as Grandmenil when German patrols were encountered.

The 1ère D.L.C. moved through Philippeville and Givet to its bridges at Dinant. Heading for the Rochefort-Marche area, advance elements crossed the Meuse at 1.00 p.m. and the Ourthe at Laroche some three hours later to be at Bérismenil in the evening.

3ème ARMÉE

Eastwards, on the Groupe d'Armées No. 2 front, the lesser rôle of the 3ème Armée of Général Charles-Marie Condé in the creation of a forward screen beyond the main defence line consisted of sending a covering force into Luxembourg. It was made up of units from the 3ème D.L.C., the 1ère Brigade de Spahis, a tank company from the 5ème B.C.C. and various reconnaissance units, organised into four combat groups.

At 6.55 a.m. the force's commander, Général Robert Petiet, received the code-word 'Falguière' to enter Luxembourg as planned.

The combat commands passed the barriers at the border of the Grand Duchy at 7.30 a.m., i.e. three hours after the Germans had arrived, and just across the border they encountered the road-blocks established by the airborne troops of Luftlandekommando Hedderich. The French had kicked off so slowly that the Vorausabteilung of the 34. Infanterie-Division had even had enough time to make contact with the

Motorcyclists of the 3ème D.L.M. pass along Rue Neuve in Soignies, 15 kilometres to the north of Mons on the afternoon of May 10. The N7 runs on to Brussels but the mechanised division turned eastwards to its planned position at Gembloux. These pictures come from a photo album found at Soignies after the war. They had been taken by a local who, according to the numerous pictures included of Léon Degrelle, the leader of the pro-Nazi Rex Party, must have been one of his supporters.

A Somua S-35 now replaced by the ubiquitous Renaults and Citröens in Rue de la Station today.

weak airborne teams and to reinforce them.

On the left wing, Groupement IV — the 25ème G.R.C.A. — had soon found itself challenged just after the border near Rodange and was unable to break through. At the same time Groupement III — the reinforced 1ère Brigade de Spahis — had had to be pulled back to Soleuvre after making quite good progress and reaching the Limpach area. Groupement II — the strongest of the four task forces with the 13ème Brigade of the 3ème D.L.C. reinforced by the 31ème G.R.D.I. — halted on the northern edge of Esch-sur-Alzette had managed to push one of its columns to Mondercange, but had to withdraw that evening. On the right wing, Groupement I — the 5ème Brigade of the 3ème D.L.C. reinforced by the 22ème G.R.C.A., the 39ème G.R.D.I. and the 63ème G.R.D.I. — which had smashed

103

The D.I.M. — the motorised infantry division — still had a sizeable amount of horse-drawn equipment in its support and supply units. In the sector of the 7ème Armée, horses of the 9ème D.I.M. were ferried by lorry across Flanders to the division's planned operational area further east on the border with the Netherlands. Here they are pictured passing through Saint-Gillis, just south of Dendermonde, about 30 kilometres east of Gent.

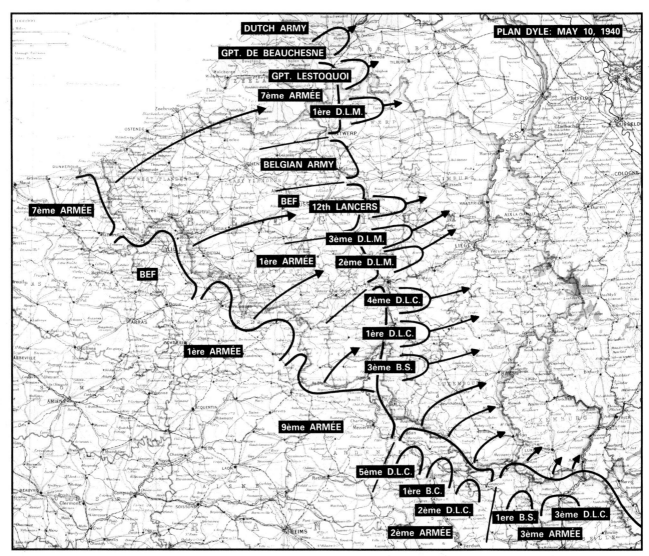

While the mobile units were rushing forward to screen their move, the bulk of the Allied armies, three French armies and the BEF, advanced to the planned defensive line from Antwerp to Namur then southwards along the Meuse river.

Setting out early on May 10, the 2ème R.D.P. (Régiment de Dragons Portés), leading the advance of Groupement II of the 3ème Armée, had reached the border of the Grand Duchy of Luxembourg at Esch-sur-Alzette by 7.30 a.m.

the airborne unit of Leutnant Hans Lauer at Hau, could only get five kilometres beyond the border.

Near Sanem, Vorausabteilung A clashed with advance elements of the 1ère Brigade de Spahis at about 9.00 a.m. and the abteilung commander, Major Theodor von und zu Aufsess, was wounded and only just escaped capture. Two hours later the 34. Infanterie-Division suffered another painful loss when the division commander himself, Generalleutnant Hans Behlendorff, was gravely wounded when his staff car ran smack into a small outfit of the 6ème Régiment de Spahis at the railway crossing between Sanem and Bascharage. The car stopped in front of the closed barrier and Behlendorff stood up to ask for it to be opened. At this point a shot rang out and he fell back in the car, severely wounded in the head. His driver fled across fields and his ADC, Major Manfred von Scheliha, jumped on a bicycle and pedalled furiously in the direction of Bascharage. A French NCO examined Behlendorff and, probably convinced in view of the head wounds that he would soon die, left him to the attention of a local man, Mr Albert Hopp. The NCO carried on but in failing to search Behlendorff's car missed a valuable prize: not only the orders for the 34. Infanterie-Divison but also those of the neighbouring divisions! (Behlendorff survived his injuries, and saw service again later in the war. He died in 1955.)

The motor cyclists were pictured on the D16 alongside the railway viaduct waiting for the final order to go.

Two kilometres to the south these motor cycles of the 2ème R.D.P. were photographed passing the French frontier post at

Audun-le-Tiche. Neither of these men knew that the Germans were then only five kilometres away!

By the end of the day, the Dyle Plan was in full swing, the infantry divisions having started to move, while to the east the advance elements of the cavalry units were in contact with the enemy. Apart from a report received from Colonel Hautcoeur, the French liaison officer attached to the Belgian High Command, which indicated that 'a rather serious incident' had occured at Fort Eben-Emael, the overall assessment of the day's events to the Allied High Command was 'favourable'. In the north, things also seemed to be going fairly well with the 7ème Armée, the BEF and the 1ère Armée. The Allied High Command was confident.

On the 9ème and 2ème Armée's fronts, an element of danger was recognised in part of Général Huntziger's cavalry screen having been forced to withdraw to the Semois, but there was no appreciation of the impending gravity of the situation in the Ardennes. Seemingly aware only of the purely tactical danger of the 2ème Armée's cavalry units being outflanked to the north, and not of the major strategic moves made by Gruppe von Kleist, the High Command urged the 9ème Armée to get its cavalry units moving as far east as possible during the night. Otherwise, the focus of attention was in the north where the main battle was expected.

Meanwhile, at Esch, whilst their officers were discussing the final details with customs officials for the entry of French forces into Luxembourg (see also page 92), the motor cyclists patiently waited behind the barrier. Standing in his Gnome-et-Rhône combination, the lieutenant in charge looks rather anxious to be off.

The German High Command were following developments intently. Late that night, the Army Chief-of-Staff, General Franz Halder, noted in his diary that clarification was required from the OKH intelligence section OQuIV: 'Is the enemy entering Belgium? Have the moves begun?'

Away at last! 'Simoun', a Renault R-35 of the 2ème Compagnie, 5ème B.C.C., races northwards through Esch. Firefights were

then already raging at the northern edge of the town with the airborne commandos of Leutnant Herbert Oswald.

The Fight for the Netherlands

Queen Wilhelmina reviews members of her armed forces preparing for the defence of the country.

In 1914, the Netherlands had been bypassed by the Imperial German armies and the then Chief of the General Staff, Generaloberst Helmuth von Moltke, had been criticised in German military circles after the war for not having struck across the Maastricht 'appendix' — the Dutch Limburg province — thus forcing German forces to squeeze westwards south of the Dutch border. The lesson had been learned but the intention shown at first in the Fall Gelb plan was not for an invasion of the Netherlands as such but only for the 6. Armee to cross the 'appendix' of Dutch territory. Fears that the Dutch would respond by allowing in French and British troops and aircraft were to result in the fourth version of Fall Gelb issued on January 30, 1940, which extended operations to include an all-out invasion of the Netherlands. Thus the Dutch, whose neutrality Hitler had solemnly guaranteed, found themselves at war after more than a hundred years of peace.

THE DUTCH PLAN

Defence spending had not been a priority in the Netherlands, defensive measures had been far less determined than in Belgium, and when war broke out in September 1939 the Dutch Army was small (about ten divisions) and its troops poorly trained and armed with ageing equipment. Neutrality prevented the Netherlands from entering into any military agreement even when the seriousness of the threat of an attack appeared certain, as it did in January 1940 after the crash-landing of the German aircraft in Belgium with the

The Dutch adhered strictly to their neutrality policy and deployed forces all along their frontiers, not only in the east against Germany, but also in the south to face Belgium. Coastal defence units guarded the coastline, like this unit at Scheveningen, to prevent possible invasion from the sea.

Light forces were deployed to guard vital river crossings, particularly along the IJssel, Waal and Maas. This impressive barrier was installed to block the southern access ramp to the road bridge at Nijmegen. A similar armoured gate was provided on the left-hand side of the road. As we have seen (page 75), the coup de main operation mounted to capture the bridge intact was foiled when the German commander found that the Dutch had already destroyed it.

Luftwaffe officer aboard carrying plans of Germany's intentions.

The defence of the Netherlands presented an extremely difficult problem. Knowing that the Army was too weak to stand a chance of defending the whole of the country, particularly the four northernmost provinces and the southernmost, Limburg, which were virtually indefensible, the Dutch Command had planned to defend only the central provinces of Noord-Holland,

The commander of the Dutch Army Air Defence Command (Commando Luchtverdediging), Generaal-Majoor Petrus Best, launched a modernisation plan for the anti-aircraft defences in 1938, and orders had been placed with Bofors, Skoda, Oerlikon and Vickers. In May 1940, the Dutch were able to deploy about 275 modern AA guns of 75mm, 40mm and 20mm, plus 450 AA machine guns. The Dutch Bofors, known in Holland as the '4 tl.' were purchased from Poland where they were built under licence. This particular example was pictured during the winter of 1939, the snowy scene more reminiscent of its country of manufacture than that of the Netherlands.

Some guns had been paid for by individual towns or factories. Advertisements such as this appeared in newspapers to raise funds: 'We ask for "silver rounds" for the protection of your city. It is to everyone's benefit if your city is protected by more AA guns! But has everyone contributed their share in order to achieve this security? Not until now! Send us your "silver rounds" on a Giro leaflet! Fl. 500,000 are needed! Pay your account on Giro No. 357 284 to the Air Defence Rotterdam Foundation.'

Zuid-Holland and Utrecht. The Dutch Army was intended to fight to the last for this 'Vesting Holland' — Fortress Holland — the economic and political heart of the country which included the major cities of The Hague, Rotterdam, Amsterdam and Utrecht. The defences of Vesting Holland, which could be made a virtual island by defensive inundations, ran from Muiden (just east of Amsterdam) on the IJsselmeer, east of Utrecht and along the Merwede Canal to Gorinchem on the Waal. Running westwards, the line then followed waterways, the Nieuwe Merwede, the Hollands Diep and the Haringvliet, up to the North Sea. Next to Vesting Holland, the Dutch Command had decided to defend the Zeeland province as a base from which France and Britain could assist the Netherlands in case of an invasion by the German Army.

In the centre of the country, from Baarn on the IJsselmeer to Rhenen on the Waal, an old defence line ran about 30 kilometres in front of the NHW Line (Nieuwe Hollandse Waterlinie), the Vesting Holland's eastern defence line. This Grebbe Line was in poor shape in 1939 but the Dutch Command saw in it an opportunity to gain time to implement the defences of Vesting Holland in case of attack and decided to reorganise the old defences and improve them. Two army corps were then deployed on the Grebbe Line, their task being to rebuild the defences and, in case of a German attack, to fight on it long enough for the necessary evacuations, flooding, and demolitions in front of Vesting Holland to be implemented. Then, on orders from the Commander-

in-Chief, these troops would fall back and withdraw in Vesting Holland to man the eastern defences there. It was then pointed out that the troops manning the Grebbe Line might have difficulty in withdrawing in time into Vesting Holland, and dissensions between the Dutch government and the Army Commander-in-Chief, Generaal Izaak Reynders, were such that he had to resign at the beginning of February 1940.

Meanwhile the defence works had proceeded efficiently on the Grebbe Line and, after the planned flooding had been achieved in November, by January 1940 it appeared that the defences of the Line now compared favourably with the ones of Vesting Holland. Consequently it was decided that the Grebbe Line was now strong enough to form the basis of the main defences and the new Commander-in-Chief, Generaal Henri Winkelman, then made this the eastern flank of Vesting Holland. This resulted in much more of the country being included in the 'fortress' area, and moved the front line farther away from some large towns like Utrecht but, in turn, added 40 kilometres to the 'fortress' walls.

In the south, along the Peel-Raam Line, the Dutch Command initially intended to deploy sizeable forces, one army corps with troops amounting to about three divisions, with orders to hold the Germans for a time before falling back into Vesting Holland. However, in spite of renewed efforts, it was not possible to agree on a common plan with the Belgians who rejected any idea of linking up with the Dutch there, and Winkelman realised that without

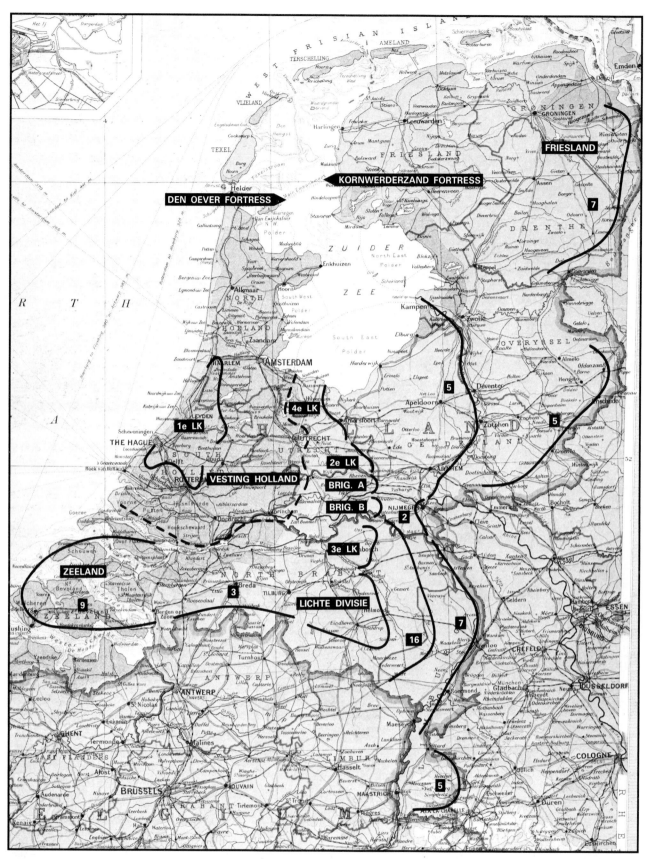

DEN OEVER FORTRESS

KORNWERDERZAND FORTRESS

FRIESLAND

7

5

5

4e LK

1e LK

2e LK

BRIG. A

BRIG. B

2

VESTING HOLLAND

3e LK

ZEELAND

9

3

LICHTE DIVISIE

16

7

5

In May 1940 the Dutch Army was deployed according to strategic plans drawn up by Generaal Henri Winkelman, the Dutch C-in-C. The Grebbe Line was the basis of the defence on the eastern flank of Vesting Holland (Fortress Holland), and two corps, the IVe Legerkorps and IIe Legerkorps, manned (with two divisions each) the line from the IJsselmeer to the Lek. Two brigades were responsible for the waterways sector: Brigade A from the Lek to the Waal, and Brigade B from the Waal to the Maas. South of the waterways, the IIIe Legerkorps, also with

two divisions, and the Lichte Divisie, were positioned to the rear of the Peel Line, ready to immediately fall back north-westwards behind the waterways in the face of an attack. The Ie Legerkorps, with the 1e Divisie and 3e Divisie, were in reserve in the heart of Vesting Holland. All along the borders, and particularly those in the east, light forces were stationed at battalion strength whose task it would be to sound the alert in the event of invasion and to delay the Germans for as long as possible along the axis of their withdrawal.

Generaal Winkelman became Commander-in-Chief following the resignation of Generaal Izaak Reynders in February 1940.

His adversary was General der Artillerie Georg von Küchler, commander of 18. Armee for the invasion of the Netherlands.

such co-operation, the troops manning the Peel sector would be in great danger and would not have enough time to withdraw north of the waterways. He therefore decided to forget all ideas of fighting on the Peel-Raam Line and to bring back most of the troops then south of the waterways into Vesting Holland. So as not to give away too much to the Germans, he decided to order these moves to start only at the very outset of a German invasion.

The Dutch defences east of Vesting Holland were based on inundations (i.e., flooding the land) and were not as sound as they should have been when the attack came for it took some time for the flood measures to come into effect. Because of the damage flooding caused to farming areas, there was understandable hesitation in ordering them too far in advance, but as it took several days, even weeks, before the water would rise to the required level to form an effective defence, most of the inundations did not constitute much of a barrier when the attack came on May 10. In some places local people even apparently tampered with the sluices to prevent their lands or homes from being flooded, and similarly there were people who were reluctant to see trees felled or barns demolished so fields of fire were often badly restricted.

In May 1940 two corps, the IVe Legerkorps and IIe Legerkorps, each of two divisions, defended the Grebbe Line from the IJsselmeer to the Lek, and two brigades were responsible for the waterways sector — Brigade A from the Rijn (Lower Rhine) to the Waal and

Brigade B from the Waal to the Maas (Meuse). South of the waterways, the IIIe Legerkorps was somewhat to the rear of the Peel Line with two infantry and one mobile 'light' division which were to fall back northwards behind the waterways immediately in the face of an attack. The Ie Legerkorps, with two divisions, was in reserve in the heart of Vesting Holland.

All along the eastern border, from the sea to the Maastricht sector, were light forces, about 25 battalions in all, most of them Grens-Bataljons, whose mission it was to sound the alarm, control and destroy the crossings on rivers, particularly the bridges and ferries of the wide Maas, to blow charges in front of the invaders to slow them down and then to withdraw westwards. A second line of seven battalions was also stationed along the IJssel river and the Pannerdens Canal in the centre, with another sixteen on the Peel Line in the south. To avoid any criticism of their neutrality being 'unbalanced', the Dutch had also deployed three battalions along the frontier with Belgium with nine battalions in Zeeland and many coastal defence units along the coastline

Although Général Gamelin had informed the Dutch attaché in Paris of his intention to send one of his best armies, the 7ème Armée, north through Belgium to assist the Netherlands, Generaal Winkelman knew very little about the French plans and, in accordance with the Dutch policy of neutrality, did not take these measures into account in formulating his own.

THE GERMAN PLAN

Fearful that each of the numerous Dutch waterways held by even a weak force could stop any advance for days, the German planners had devised an ambitious airborne operation to capture vital bridges over them, thus providing for a swift advance of the ground forces. Their tactical intention was to deploy airborne troops deep in the Netherlands, to unroll an airborne carpet right across the Maas and Rhine delta, from Moerdijk to Rotterdam, and north to The Hague. This was not only to give them vital bridges and centres of communication, but also to paralyse Dutch resistance and disrupt the movement of reserves. It seems that the idea was Hitler's own but the detailed operational planning had been carried out by Generalleutnant Kurt Student, the commander of the 7. Flieger-Division.

The actual invasion of the Netherlands was entrusted to the 18. Armee of General Georg von Küchler and was planned as a three pronged attack:

In the north, the 1. Kavalerie-Division was to advance across the Groningen and Drenthe provinces to reach Friesland in order to cross the IJsselmeer along the northern dyke (the Afsluitdijk) and come down on Vesting Holland from the north.

In the centre, the X. Armeekorps, with two divisions plus two regiments of Waffen-SS troops, was to attack north of Arnhem, to force the Grebbe Line and take Utrecht.

In the south, the XXVI. Armeekorps, with two divisions at first, was to cross the Maas, force the Peel Line,

The paratroops of the 7. Flieger-Division and the airborne infantry of the 22. Infanterie-Division were to be carried into action by the venerable, yet reliable, Junkers Ju 52 tri-motor transport. Eighteen men could be accommodated in each.

advance through the Noord-Brabant province and attack Vesting Holland from the south, in effect preventing the French from rendering any real assistance. This was to be the army's main attack and the 9. Panzer-Division, at first in army reserve, was to be subordinated to XXVI. Armeekorps once a breakthrough was reached. The advance elements of the 9. Panzer-Division were due to reach the Rotterdam area by the third day of the operation and, thrusting across the area secured by the airborne troops, rush to the heart of Vesting Holland.

THE AIRBORNE ASSAULT

The whole airborne operation was to be mounted under the responsibility of General Albert Kesselring's Luftflotte 2, and staffs were specially assembled to deal with all aspects of this ambitious and complex undertaking. Generalleutnant Student was entrusted with the actual conduct of the operation in the field and was assigned the command of the Luftlande-Korps, a specially assembled staff subordinated directly to Luftflotte 2. The corps was to employ about 3,500 paratroops from Student's 7. Flieger-Division who were to parachute into the heart of Vesting Holland and about 12,000 men from the 22. (Luftlande) Infanterie-Division who were to be air transported to supplement them.

General Wilhelm Speidel was made responsible for the transport force, about 430 Ju 52s assembled in two air transport wings, each having four groups: K.G.z.b.V. 1 of Oberst Friedrich-Wilhelm Morzik, with I. to IV. Gruppe and K.G.z.b.V. 2 of Oberst Gerhard Conrad, with K.Gr.z.b.V. 9, K.Gr.z.b.V. 11, K.Gr.z.b.V. 12 and K.Gr.z.b.V. 172. Each of these eight groups consisted of 53 aircraft and was able to transport what amounted to the equivalent of a full battalion in one flight.

Generalmajor Richard Putzier was appointed commander of a Fliegerkorps z.b.V., a staff assembled for the occasion, and was made responsible for the support of the operation by fighter and bomber units. He could deploy ten fighter groups — about 250 fighters —

Fallschirmjäger set up their MG 34 on the drop zone — a picture taken on a training exercise.

The negative for this picture of another MG team was removed from a camera found on a German paratrooper taken prisoner near The Hague. However, though the windmill is a typical feature of the Netherlands, this type of mill makes it more likely that the photo had been taken prior to May 10 in northern Germany.

and six bomber groups of which one was a Stuka group. In all about 170 bombers but most of these could be at hand only for a short time as Luftflotte 2 had to support the whole of Heeresgruppe B and had to share out its strength on the whole army group front.

Dropped as the first wave, the para-troops of the 7. Flieger-Division were to capture vital bridges between Moerdijk and Rotterdam and to seize airfields at Rotterdam and near The Hague. The Ju 52s were then to land companies of the 22. Infanterie-Division on the four airfields secured by the paratroops.

In the north, a reinforced battalion of paratroops from Fallschirm-Jäger-Regiment (F.J.R.) 2 was to capture three airfields surrounding The Hague, at Valkenburg (Landing Place I), Öck-enburg (Landing Place II) and Ypen-burg (Landing Place III), ready for two other regiments of the 22. Infanterie-Division to be landed there. The com-mander of the air-landing division, Generalleutnant Hans von Sponeck, was to be in charge of this northern group, with orders to take over the area and seize the Dutch government offices at The Hague, capture the Dutch High Command and important civil servants, and arrest the Royal Family.

In the south — in the Rotterdam sector — the paratroops of F.J.R. 1 were to be dropped at Moerdijk, near Dordrecht and at Waalhaven. One reg-iment of the 22. Infanterie-Division was then to be landed at Waalhaven (Land-ing Place IV), and was to secure the bridges and key points captured by the paratroops. This southern group was to be under the command of General Student himself, whose headquarters was to be at Waalhaven.

Though the scope of the German airborne operation was to be far greater than anyone could have anticipated at the time, the Dutch were not that surprised as they had the example of German tactics just a month earlier in the invasion of Denmark and Norway.

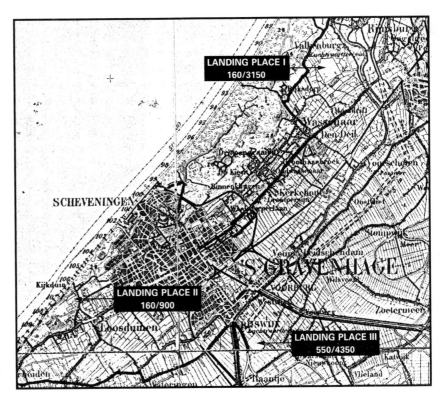

Generalleutnant von Sponeck had 9,300 men at his disposal, split into three groups, to encircle The Hague. The two figures given indicate the number of paratroops in the first wave and the size of the follow-up force which was to arrive in Ju 52s once the airfields had been secured.

The role played by the Luftwaffe in Operation 'Weserübung' had impressed the Dutch High Command which had taken measures to counter the threat of airborne operations aimed at the Dutch airfields. The landing strips had been covered by machine guns and a mobile force of armoured cars from the Lichte Divisie had been assembled on two airfields, with two platoons at Ypen-burg and two at Schiphol. These mea-sures would prove very effective and were to inflict heavy casualties on the attackers.

THE NORTHERN GROUP NEAR THE HAGUE

According to the plans, the comman-der of the northern group in The Hague sector, Generalleutnant von Sponeck, was to have about 9,300 men under command in three groups encircling The Hague by the evening of May 10:

a) one Staffel (12 aircraft) of Ju 52s from K.Gr.z.b.V. 172 was to drop the 6. Kompanie of F.J.R. 2, about 160 men, over Landing Place I at Valken-burg. Once the airfield was secured the first wave of transport aircraft, about 50 aircraft from K.Gr.z.b.V. 11, was then to land the staff and elements of Inf.Rgt. 47. Others flights would then follow and the five waves planned for the first day would bring in about 3,150 men in addition of the paratroops who had jumped first.

b) A Staffel of Ju 52s from IV./ K.G.z.b.V. 1 would drop 160 men of the 3. Kompanie of F.J.R. 2. over Landing Place II at Ockenburg. The first wave of 15 transports from K.Gr.z.b.V. 12, was then to land the second battalion of Inf.Rgt. 65. All in all, the six flights of transports sched-uled for this first day were to bring in 900 men in addition to the paratroops.

c) Some 40 Ju 52s from IV./ K.G.z.b.V. 1 were to drop the 1., 2. and 4. Kompanies of F.J.R. 2, compris-ing around 550 men, at Landing Place III at Ypenburg. The first flight of 38 transport aircraft from K.Gr.z.b.V. 12, was then to land elements of Inf.Rgt. 65, soon followed by a second wave bringing the staff of 22. Infanterie-Division. In total, the eight waves of transports were to bring 4,350 men as well as the paratroops on the first day.

The last hours of peace. The crews of the III. Gruppe of K.G.z.b.V.1 seen relaxing in front of their Junkers aircraft on May 9. Though they did not know it yet, they were to take off early next morning loaded with elements of Infanterie-Regiment 16 with orders to land them at Waalhaven.

In the early hours, while He 111s of K.Gr.126 mined the waters off the Dutch ports of Vlissingen, IJmuiden and Den Helder, and along the Nieuwe Waterweg near the Hook of Holland, the Luftwaffe bombed the airfields and areas containing the bridges where the paratroops were to be dropped. With airfields being the main targets, the Dutch Army Air Force suffered heavily in the early hours of May 10, losing about half of its 130 or so serviceable aircraft in the pre-emptive raids. Although most of the aircraft of the reconnaissance squadrons of 2e LVR [Luchtvaart Regiment] had escaped damage, the fighter squadrons of 1e LVR and 2e LVR were left with only 13 operational Fokker G-1As and Fokker D-XXIs out of 62.

As far as the parachute landings were concerned, things went badly from the beginning for von Sponeck's men as the first wave dropped as planned between 6.10 a.m. and 6.30 a.m. German time. The formations had been broken up by Dutch AA fire and many of the Fall-schirmjäger landed off target, particularly at Ypenburg and Ockenburg, so that when the Ju 52s arrived to land at about 7.00 a.m. the situation at all the three landing places was far from clear.

The Dutch air forces performed with great credit and accounted for 60 German aircraft during the campaign. The lumbering Ju 52s were easy meat for both flak and fighters, and in this remarkable shot a Dutch Fokker G-1A, with its characteristic twin-boom tail, of 1e LVR has been caught by the camera after making a firing pass at a Ju 52, just as the paratroops spill from their aircraft.

Landing Place I: Valkenburg

Although the paratroops had suc-ceeded in capturing the aerodrome, the surface was found to be too soft to support the heavy Ju 52s. When the 50 aircraft of the first wave landed they were unable to move off the runway and the crowded situation worsened when seven aircraft from K.Gr.z.b.V. 12, unable to land at Ypenburg, diverted to Valkenburg instead. Many aircraft were soon bogged down and the runway was blocked to such an extent that the airfield was soon unusable. When the second wave of 40 aircraft from I./ K.G.z.b.V. 1, arrived at about 9.30 a.m. they had to find somewhere else to put down. Some landed on the beach

between Katwijk and Scheveningen on the northern edge of The Hague but the others had to fly back to Werl with their load. Most of those which did land on the beach were unable to take off again. A last attempt at reinforcement was made in the afternoon when a flight of six aircraft from K.Gr.z.b.V. 9 was sent to Valkenburg but they failed, one aircraft managing to get down at Ock-enburg but the other five had to return to their base at Lippspringe.

The Dutch Army Air Force res-ponded with a bombing attack on Val-kenburg by five Fokker C-Xs which then strafed the beaches at Katwijk, followed by five Fokker D-XXIs from 2e JaVA [Jachtvliegtuig Afdeling].

The Dutch forces attacked the Ger-man positions near the airfield and their artillery began pounding them. The commander of Inf.Rgt. 47, Oberst Kurt Heyser, was wounded and the Germans were soon forced to withdraw to Valkenburg village just to the north-east where they found that they were only about 600 strong. Another group of around 350 men under Oberleutnant Hans Voigt, the commander of the regiment's 5. Kompanie, assembled near Wassenaar, a few kilometres west of the airfield, where they dug-in. The Dutch launched a powerful counter-attack to dislodge them, committing five battalions, but it failed, the Dutch losing 36 dead and many prisoners.

Left: **The airborne forces were under the command of General-leutnant Kurt Student: the Ritterkreuz he is wearing in this 1944 picture was awarded for his success in the Netherlands.**

Right: **About 3,500 paratroops from the 7. Flieger-Division were to parachute into Vesting Holland, and this picture is reputed to have been taken on the morning of May 10.**

Landing Place II: Ockenburg

Things were even worse at Ockenburg where the aircraft were badly dispersed with only about a quarter of the 3. Kompanie dropped as planned. Five aircraft released their men out to the west in the vicinity of 's-Gravenzande and three others as far away as Staalduinse Bos, near the Hook of Holland. While the 70 men dropped by the former flight did succeed in joining up with their comrades at Ockenburg, the 40 or so dropped by the latter flight remained in the wood there, being joined by some 100 men diverted from Ypenburg, until the end of the battle on Tuesday, May 14.

The first wave of Ju 52s, 17 aircraft from K.Gr.z.b.V. 12, landed without too much trouble at Ockenburg at about 7.00 a.m., although some bogged down and the situation soon turned out to be similar to that at Valkenburg. The first aircraft of the second wave landed at about 7.45 a.m. and blocked the airfield. The position worsened when three aircraft from K.Gr.z.b.V. 9 arrived from Ypenburg in the vain hope of finding an improvement at Ockenburg. Some aircraft then landed somewhat to the west, Generalleutnant von Sponeck being in one of them, while others landed on the beach or in meadows east of the dunes near Kijkduin or Ter Heijde. Some of these succeeded in taking off again, carrying with them the crews of those which had been stranded. When the 12 aircraft of the third wave arrived at 9.25 a.m. it was obviously impossible to land at Ockenburg and while two of them ventured to the north to land on the beaches near Wassenaar, the others chose to divert to Waalhaven.

Ockenburg was bombed by Fokker T-Vs from BomVA [Bombardeervliegtuig Afdeling] and in the evening Blenheims from Nos. 110 and 600 Squadrons of the RAF attacked the Ju 52s that had landed on the beaches at Kijkduin, reporting four aircraft destroyed.

On the ground a Dutch professional photographer (hence the use of a telephoto lens), Henk Lamme, pictured the paratroopers of Fallschirmjäger-Regiment 2 from the roof of his house on Helenastraat as they dropped over Ypenburg early Friday morning. The tower on the left marks Bosbad swimming pool with the floodlights of the V.U.C. stadium bottom right.

Dutch artillery had opened up at the German positions on the airfield in the afternoon, and by evening the Dutch had retaken the airfield, capturing 130 prisoners and liberating about 30 of their men who had earlier been captured. The Germans were forced to withdraw to Ockenrode, an estate some distance away, where von Sponeck organised the defence with a few hundred men.

Landing Place III: Ypenburg

Things turned out to be even worse at Ypenburg for the transport aircraft were badly dispersed by anti-aircraft fire even before approaching Landing Place III and most of the paratroops were dropped far off the drop zone. Then when the first of the 38 transport aircraft from K.Gr.z.b.V. 12 attempted to land on the unsecured airfield, a dozen were shot down and within ten minutes the airborne infantry had lost about 200 men. The aircraft now circled in complete confusion, some diverting to Valkenburg, others landing all over the area, two at Bleiswijk, one at Berkel and ten south of Delft on the Den Haag-Rotterdam highway or in the field beside. Most of them were unable to get off again and the first wave was a complete disaster, K.Gr.z.b.V. 12 being left with only two serviceable aircraft.

The second wave, of 40 aircraft from K.Gr.z.b.V. 9, ran into the same problems, some aircraft being shot down on the airfield and others diverting to Ockenburg or the highway south of

Two of the Ju 52s which diverted from Ypenburg to Ockenburg overflew The Hague, only to come under intense Dutch AA fire.

Both aircraft were shot down, one crashing in Tweede Adelheidstraat.

Delft. Oberfeldarzt Werner Wischhusen, the division medical officer, landed on the highway at about 7.15 a.m. and took command of all the forces there. Of the dozen or so aircraft of the second wave which had managed to get away from Ypenburg without being shot down and headed for Ockenburg, two overflew The Hague where they were brought down by Dutch anti-aircraft fire. Both aircraft were carrying members of the staff of the 22. Infanterie-Division; all were killed, but documents recovered from the wrecks gave first-hand details of the German plans. Among other things they revealed the intention to capture the Royal Family and key personalities in The Hague.

The confusion was completed at Ypenburg when the third wave of 30 aircraft from IV./K.G.z.b.V. 1, arrived at 10.00 a.m. Some aircraft landed where they could but others diverted to Waalhaven. Other pilots chose to land far to the west, on both sides of the Nieuwe Waterweg, three of them coming down on Rozenburg island to the south of the canal while six others landed north of the canal near Maasdijk. As K.Gr.z.b.V. 12 ceased to exist after the failure of the first wave, so the fourth wave was entrusted to K.Gr.z.b.V. 172, which arrived at 11.10 a.m. but had to divert to Waalhaven.

In spite of this disastrous beginning, the Fallschirmjäger at Ypenburg had still managed to capture most of the airfield but the situation worsened in the afternoon when the Dutch artillery started to hammer their positions. The Dutch put pressure on the airborne positions and soon regained control, but the news was not received in time to cancel a bombing raid by Blenheims of No. 40 Squadron. The twelve aircraft came in at 4.30 p.m., dropping their bombs on the Ju 52s immobilised on the field. A hangar was hit, but three of the bombers were shot down by the Luftwaffe in the vicinity of the airfield. The bombing caused the Germans to with-

draw to the southern edge of the airfield but Allied communications were poor and the raid also resulted in the Dutch pulling back to the northern edge. The Germans had however lost all control and their remaining strong point, north of the airfield at Johannahoeve, was forced to surrender in the evening, 30 men being captured.

The two platoons of armoured cars stationed at Ypenburg had played a significant part in the failure of the German assault. Corporal G. Mommaas, the commander of PAW 602 which was positioned in front of a large concrete hangar later recalled how 'the start of the war was terrible when a bomb fell on the hangar thereby covering the armoured car with debris.' 'Nevertheless,' said Mommaas, 'we must have recovered very quickly because before the next attack came Fikkers [Ale Fikkers, the forward

driver] operated the machine gun on the turret like an ape while I fired my first shots. The dive bombers attacked the hangar and this enabled us to aim at them very easily. We soon hit one of them, which resulted in a positive improvement in the morale of our crew. The heat of the burning hangar and the explosions of the fuel tanks from the aircraft parked inside forced us to change our position. As the nerve of van Breugel [the rear driver] had gone, Hummel [Karel Hummel, the co-driver] took over his place and drove the PAW on to a dirt track. After some time we went to the airstrip from where we fired at the diving aircraft, speeding ahead after each shot. From time to time we felt a great shock behind us but we had no time to determine whether it was caused by a crashed aircraft or by a bomb. During this episode of "hit and run" Cools [Jopie Cools, the gunner] claimed to have shot down one aircraft.'

While the bombing was still going on, the first paratroopers began to land and the crew of PAW 602 fired at them as they floated down. A little later the first Ju 52s approached. 'They were magnificent targets,' recalled Mommaas, 'as they landed at a ponderously slow speed. We shot at each aircraft and pumped them full with lead and iron. Our almost continuous firing caused some problems of overheating but Hummel very efficiently managed to clear the jams. Because the range was short we had first fired the anti-tank shells, then the HE, our last five rounds being fired at a Ju 52 which had come to a stop in front of the bombed hangar. It was so close that I had to aim the gun through the open breech as there was a deviation in the adjustment of the sights. Two shells hit that aircraft.'

Having used all their ammunition, they withdrew behind the hangar and Mommaas ran to try to get some more from the supply truck. He drove the truck back to the airfield, stopped near PAW 601 and started to carry a case of HE to it.

All 17 (some reports state 16) men on board were killed, but documents recovered from the blazing wreckage gave Dutch Intelligence an incredible windfall as the aircraft had been carrying members of the staff of 22. Infanterie-Division.

The Dutch scored a major coup when they recovered documents from the burning wreckage revealing German intentions, particularly concerning the capture of the Dutch High Command and Royal Family. Accurate intelligence was essential for such an operation, and the German military attaché had been feeding reports to Berlin on the location of key personnel and the strength of local Dutch units. In one report dated April 9 he revealed that when the two Royal heirs, Bernhard and Juliana, were in The Hague, they stayed in the Green Palace on Noordeinde Straat but, at the same time, the attaché had to confess that he had not yet been able to establish the whereabouts of the Dutch C-in-C, Generaal Winkelman. This plan, scorched from the flames, was one drawn up to guide von Sponeck's airborne troops from the 'Platz II' (Ockenburg) at the bottom left, along van Meerdervoort Laan, Waldeck-Pyrmont Kade, then Noord Wal to reach the Palace.

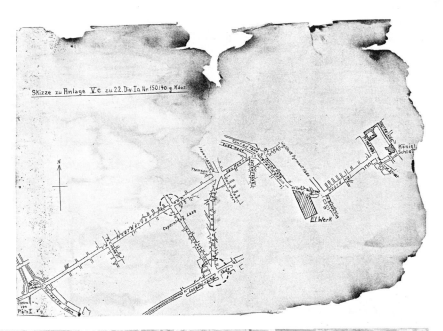

Today Tweede Adelheidstraat where the Junkers crashed has been completely redeveloped, as has Koningin Marialaan where the Bosbad swimming pool stood, and Helenastraat from where Henk Lamme took his pictures. What happened was that in March 1945 the RAF's 2nd Tactical Air Force sent a mixed force of Mitchells and Bostons to bomb the Haagse Bos, a forested area where V2 rockets were believed to be stored. By mistake, the aircraft bombed the wrong side of the road, completely razing the Bezuidenhout area of The Hague, killing 511 Dutch civilians and injuring another 344.

Two platoons of Dutch M-36 armoured cars were stationed at Ypenburg and six of the vehicles played a significant part in the failure of the German assault there. The PAWs were armed with a 37mm gun and three machine guns — this line-up being pictured in Brabant in 1936.

'After five metres or so, the soldier who helped me was fatally injured and I played dead myself. I noticed that the firing came from the other side of the highway to Delft and soon I saw a large group of paratroopers crossing the road, forcing Sergeant van der Horst and his crew (PAW 601) to surrender. From the direction of Delft came a group of Dutch soldiers, marching and shouting "Don't shoot! Don't shoot!" Behind them were Germans, their rifles pointing at the Dutch. Lying beside the camber of the highway I saw my PAW 602 approaching. Apparently they had no idea that the place was crawling with Germans. Cautiously I motioned them to drive on, because it was clear that if they stopped to pick me up it would have meant the end for all of us.'

PAW 602 then drove in front of the Germans, firing above their heads to force them to run for cover, thus allowing many of the Dutch prisoners to escape. (Corporal Mommaas avoided capture, reached Ypenburg and later rejoined his crew.)

In the evening of May 10 the situation of the northern group was catastrophic with only about 3,800 men being brought in, about one third of the planned figure, including crew members from the disabled aircraft. At Valkenburg, only 1,400 of the 3,300 men scheduled to land there had been assembled, and at Ockenburg only about 600 of the 1,050 men had been set down. At Ypenburg, out of an initial force of 4,900, only 1,550 were in the area, a large number not on the airfield but some distance away. Nothing had been secured; the Dutch had retaken all three airfields and, of the men brought in that evening, more than 2,000 were casualties, of which more than 1,500 had been captured. The remainder were dispersed in more than a dozen places around The Hague.

Of the 1,650 or so still in action, the largest group was at Valkenburg — about 600 men under Oberst Kurt Heyser, the commander of Inf.Rgt. 47.

Another group of 350 men from Landing Place I was near Wassenaar under Oberleutnant Hans Voigt. Generalleutnant von Sponeck was trapped in a wood south of Ockenburg with what was left of the force (some 360 men) brought in to Landing Place II, and about 140 men diverted from Landing Place III were in the wood east of the Hook of Holland. About 200 others were south of Delft under the command of Oberfeldarzt Werner Wischhusen.

Von Sponeck's men did succeed in one respect — that of drawing Dutch forces right into the heart of Vesting Holland. The Dutch Command had reacted swiftly and brought the whole of their Ie Legerkorps to bear against the German paratroops. This was a grave decision as the corps, with two divisions, was their main strategical reserve. They also decided to transfer troops back from the eastern flank of Vesting Holland and on this first day they committed nine battalions of infantry against the paratroops and numerous groups of artillery.

Dispersed by Dutch AA fire, the Ju 52s of the northern group landed in complete confusion. Many were shot down attempting to put down on the unsecured airfield at Ypenburg (above), while others diverted to Valkenburg or Ockenburg. Some tried, with mixed success, to land on the beach or get down in fields or even on the Delft to Rotterdam main road (below).

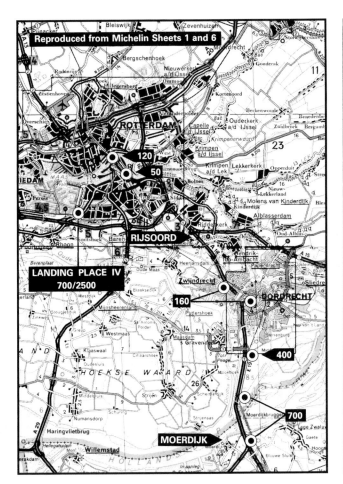

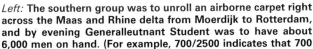

Left: **The southern group was to unroll an airborne carpet right across the Maas and Rhine delta from Moerdijk to Rotterdam, and by evening Generalleutnant Student was to have about 6,000 men on hand. (For example, 700/2500 indicates that 700** paratroopers were to be dropped on Landing Place IV, with another 2500 arriving later in transport aircraft.) *Right:* **Allegedly jumping in the Netherlands on May 10, these paratroopers were dropped at an incredibly low height of around 200 feet.**

THE SOUTHERN GROUP NEAR ROTTERDAM

According to the plan the commander of the southern group in the Rotterdam sector, Generalleutnant Student, was to have about 4,600 men at his disposal on the evening of May 10.

Firstly, 50 Ju 52s from I./K.G.z.b.V. 1 were to drop the II. Bataillon of F.J.R. 1, around 700 men, over Moerdijk, to the north and south of the bridges. Then another 30 Ju 52s from K.Gr.z.b.V. 172 were to drop the bulk of the I. Bataillon and the regimental staff, in all some 400 men, south of Dordrecht. Meanwhile a dozen aircraft from the same group were to drop the 3. Kompanie, about 170 men, on both ends of the Dordrecht bridges. Finally 50 transports from II./K.G.z.b.V. 1 were to drop the 700 men of III. Bataillon over Landing Place IV at Waalhaven. The first wave of 20 aircraft from III./K.Gr.z.b.V. 1, was then to land the first elements of Inf.Rgt. 16, the III. Bataillon, soon followed by a second wave bringing the staff of 7. Flieger-Division. Other flights would then follow and all together the six waves of transports scheduled for this first day were to bring in about 2,500 men at Waalhaven in addition to the paratroops.

The German plan was that the first elements of Inf.Rgt. 16 to land at Waalhaven were to fight their way through the suburbs to the heart of Rotterdam. This task was not easy, as in such surroundings a small number of determined men could easily stop a whole company. Therefore, in order to ease their advance and ensure the capture of the vital bridges in the town, Student had devised a bold plan of action: about 50 paratroopers would drop right into the town while 120 men

A flight of three Junkers Ju 52s (a Kette) has just disgorged their loads — about fifty men — who are coming down at the northern end of the Moerdijk bridges. The railway bridge can be seen in the background. Though the poor quality of this picture might lend credence to the claim that it was genuinely taken at first light on the morning of May 10, it is more than likely that it was taken during a re-enactment the following month to provide film for propaganda purposes.

Left: **A paratrooper from Fallschirmjäger-Regiment 1 at a defensive position at the southern end of the Moerdijk road bridge. The soldiers are manning a PzB 38 anti-tank rifle facing westwards from whence an attack from the Dutch, or even the** French, could materialise. *Right:* **The command post near the bridge with the regimental commander, Oberst Bruno Bräuer, standing. Leutnant Wolf-Werner von der Schulenburg sits behind, with Hauptmann Eberhard Rau lying on the right.**

Above: **Though this picture has obviously been taken some time later, it is an interesting shot which shows both bridges with the 14-span railway bridge on the left. Now the gun is a** **2cm Flak 30. Both bridges were blown in November 1944 as the Germans retreated, the present-day replacements *(below)* being completed in the 1970s.**

from 22. Infanterie-Division would be brought to the very heart of the town by a dozen seaplanes landing on the Maas river.

The paratroop unit, under the command of Oberleutnant Horst Kerfin, the commander of the regiment's 11. Kompanie, would be dropped from three Ju 52s of II./K.G.z.b.V. 1 directly over the Feyenoord football stadium which lay to the south of Rotterdam on the main road to the centre of the city.

The twelve Heinkel He 59s, Staffel Schwilden from K.Gr.z.b.V. 108 (a transport force of flying boats and seaplanes hastily organised a month earlier for operations in Denmark and Norway) was to land on the Maas bringing men from the 11. Kompanie of Inf.Rgt. 16 and some engineers from Pi.Btl. 22. These 120 men were under the command of Oberleutnant Hermann Schrader, the 11. Kompanie's commander.

Midway to Rotterdam lies Dordrecht where another vital road bridge had to be taken. *Above left:* This photo by Oberjäger

Januschowsky appeared in the Luftwaffe's house magazine *Der Adler* in August 1940.

SOUTH OF ROTTERDAM

The paratroops of F.J.R. 1 jumped as planned between 6.00 and 6.40 a.m. (German time) on the six zones assigned to them in the Rotterdam sector.

At Moerdijk about 700 paratroopers were dropped both north and south of the bridges. To the south they assaulted the bridges' access and soon took control. On the north side the paratroops had first to capture the Dutch garrison in the sector — an artillery battalion and three sections of infantry — before advancing towards the bridges, marching Dutch prisoners in front of them. The Dutch were unable to destroy the bridges, for although they were mined, the detonators were not in place and soon both the 1.2 kilometre-long road bridge and the 1.4 kilometre railway bridge were in German hands. Four Fokker C-Xs attacked the bridgeheads in the afternoon, bombing positions occupied by the paratroops at both ends of the bridges.

At Dordrecht, about 400 paratroops

Illustration by Propaganda-Kompanie war artist Richard Hess in the same issue.

Left: On May 12, the Dutch Lichte Divisie tried to recapture Dordrecht from the east, an attack which resulted in two days of confused street fighting in the town. The number of cartridges strewn across the southern end of the bridge

testifies to the fierceness of the battle. *Right:* The bridge has lost some of its strategic importance with the construction of the A16 motorway which runs in a tunnel under the Oude Maas, some hundred metres or so to the south.

ROTTERDAM
WAALHAVEN

Captioned only as 'Deutsche Fallschirmtruppen in den Niederlanden', this picture by PK war photographer Wiedemann proved difficult to pinpoint — even with the help of the road sign. In the end, Jacques van Dijke traced it to Waalhaven.

Today the old junction at Schulpweg and Hangarstraat has been widened, and the new access road to the Waalhaven industrial estate renamed Korperweg.

airfield for the transport aircraft to land. The Ju 52s bringing the first elements of the airborne troops — the third battalion of Inf.Rgt. 16 — soon appeared and they started to land around 7.00 a.m. However by the time the paratroops' commander, Hauptmann Karl-Lothar Schulz, greeted third battalion commander, Oberstleutnant Dietrich von Choltitz, the Dutch defences had not been entirely overwhelmed and some of the Ju 52s were brought down by Dutch AA fire. Others collided on the ground as they taxied in the confusion and the men on board suffered losses accordingly.

After the paratroops assaulted the last Dutch defences, the airfield was soon completely in German hands. In the morning about 50 aircraft brought in 570 men in three companies from von Choltitz's III. Bataillon, together with another 120 comprising the battalion staff, the staff of the 7. Flieger-Division and a section of divisional motor cyclists. However the airfield was still a highly uncomfortable place as two batteries of Dutch artillery in Kralingse Bos, a park north of the Maas in Rotterdam, began shelling it from midday.

Soon afterwards six RAF Blenheims of No. 600 Squadron attacked the airfield but they were themselves set on by a dozen Messerschmitt Bf 110s and only one of them regained Manston. In the afternoon nine Blenheim bombers of No. 15 Squadron attacked the airfield and all returned to Wyton claiming to have destroyed about 16 aircraft on the ground. Five Dutch Fokker C-Xs came in during the afternoon, damaging some of the transport aircraft on the ground, but were intercepted by Bf 109s, two of the Fokkers being forced down. The airfield suffered another air raid during the night when 36 Wellingtons carried out an attack between 11.30 p.m. and 3.00 a.m. next morning in preparation for a Dutch attempt to recapture the airfield on May 11. All aircraft returned safely and reported hits on buildings, hangars and aircraft.

were dropped as planned south of the town. They fell on the positions of a battalion of Dutch artillery and soon overwhelmed them. Meanwhile 12 Junkers had dropped the 3. Kompanie on both ends of the Dordrecht bridge, about 50 men landing at Zwijndrecht at the north end and about 120 men at Dordrecht on the opposite side. They suffered losses from Dutch AA machine guns, Oberleutnant Henning von Brandis, the commander of the 3. Kompanie being killed, but the survivors ran for the bridge and succeeded in taking it. Oberst Bruno Bräuer, the commander of F.J.R. 1, immediately sent a sizeable part of his reserve I. Bataillon towards Dordrecht where the paratroopers were in difficulties.

At Waalhaven 700 paratroops were dropped as planned south and east of the airfield. Some men landed in the water of the nearby harbour and were drowned, others fell into burning buildings, but after a short, sharp battle the paratroopers had enough hold on the

Waalhaven was soon firmly in German hands, enabling the transports to bring in the follow-up troops. However by lunchtime Dutch artillery was ranging on the airfield, the RAF and Dutch air force adding to the destruction during the afternoon.

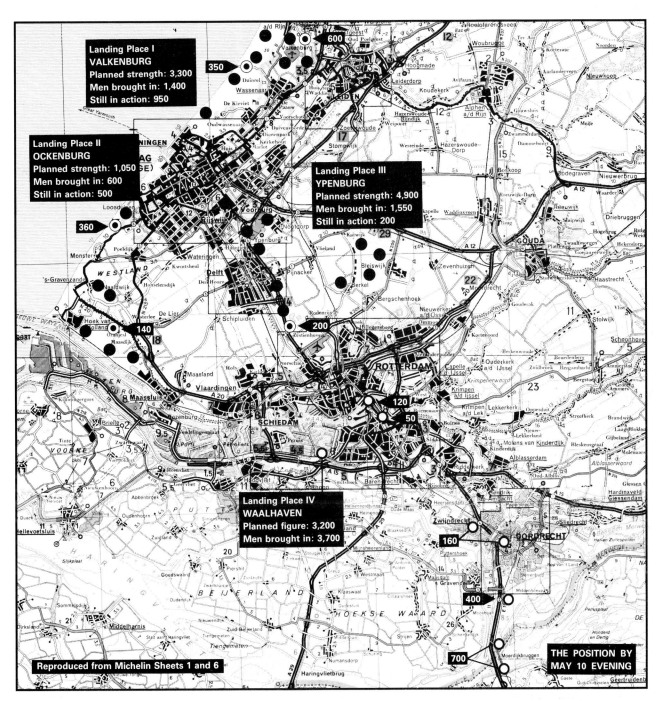

Landing Place I
VALKENBURG
Planned strength: 3,300
Men brought in: 1,400
Still in action: 950

Landing Place II
OCKENBURG
Planned strength: 1,050
Men brought in: 600
Still in action: 500

Landing Place III
YPENBURG
Planned strength: 4,900
Men brought in: 1,550
Still in action: 200

Landing Place IV
WAALHAVEN
Planned figure: 3,200
Men brought in: 3,700

THE POSITION BY
MAY 10 EVENING

Reproduced from Michelin Sheets 1 and 6

As far as the Germans were concerned, Friday had not been a good day in Holland, particularly for the northern group. The men had been badly dispersed when they came in (● on map). By the evening more than half were casualties and the Dutch still held the three airfields. The 1,650 or so men still in action had assembled by then into five separate groups (denoted with the symbol ◉). Things had gone better in the south in the Rotterdam area where the paratroops had landed as planned (at locations marked O) and some 250 Ju 52s had managed to bring reinforcements into Waalhaven.

AT ROTTERDAM

The twelve Heinkel He 59s of Staffel Schwilden had taken off from Zwischenahn Lake near Oldenburg early on May 10 and at 6.30 a.m. (4.50 a.m. Dutch time) they landed on the Maas, either side of the bridges. Because of its very boldness, the first part of the plan was completely successful and not a shot was fired at the seaplanes as they taxied slowly towards the bridge, bringing 120 men of Inf.Rgt. 16 right into the centre of Rotterdam.

Four of the He 59s had landed downstream of the bridges and then taxied upstream to make for the northern end of the bridges where the men disembarked. Of the eight which alighted upstream, some also taxied for the northern bank of the river, the men disembarking on the quay in front of the Maas railway station, while another group made for the Koningshaven, the southern arm of the Maas river, where the men went ashore on Nassau quay.

Under the gaze of astonished Dutchmen on their way to work, the Germans went on inflating their rubber boats and started to paddle for the quay. At one point on Ooster quay they were helped to clamber up by a Dutch sympathiser, a member of the N.S.B. Soon afterwards a policeman, Agent Ben Raes, arrived and tried to arrest this group but was killed, one of the first casualties of the day.

Those who disembarked in Koningshaven ran for the Koninginne Bridge, crossed it and reached Noordereiland, the island in the middle of the river; they took control of its northern side and then crossed the Willems Bridge to join up with those already ashore on the northern bank. Having secured the vital bridges they waited for Dutch counter-attacks, but Oberleutnant Kerfin's men, who had landed by parachute, were the first to arrive.

They had jumped as planned at about 6.30 a.m. directly over the Feyenoord football stadium. Once down, they

123

The capture of the four bridges in the heart of Rotterdam — two to the south of Noordereiland and two north of it — was entrusted to Kampfgruppe Schrader. The 120-man assault force was brought right to their objective in Heinkel He 59 seaplanes.

commandeered a local tram, ejected the surprised Dutch passengers and, piling inside, rode into battle on a unique form of transport without any difficulty for the kilometre or so to the bridges.

Unco-ordinated as they were, the initial reaction of the Dutch on the spot was quite successful. Without waiting for precise orders, Kapitein Jan van Rhijn launched his own company from 39e R.I. [Regiment Infanterie] and succeeded in breaking the whole left flank of the thinly-held German bridgehead at the north end of the bridges.

Meanwhile, a section of Dutch Marines made their way to the Maashotel and, throwing grenades from the roof, they soon succeeded in destroying some German machine gun positions which had been set up. The building was later set alight by German mortar fire and in the evening the Dutch were forced to leave. Nevertheless, the Marines frus-

trated the Germans on the right bank of the Maas, stopping dead their efforts to enlarge their hold northwards to the Beurs railway station, and forcing them to consolidate close around the end of the bridges.

Generaal Winkelman had asked for the assistance of the Navy, which sent a gun boat, the *Z-5*, from the Hook of Holland up the river. At about 8.00 a.m. the *Z-5* started to shell the German positions at close range with its two 7.5cm guns, hitting the four seaplanes as well as the men taking cover by the bridge. The Germans returned the fire, wounding some of the crew, and the *Z-5* withdrew for a while. She soon returned to the fray accompanied by a torpedo boat, the *TM-51*, although her torpedo tubes were of little use. She opened fire with her two 20mm cannon but by midday, having expended their ammunition, the two boats had to withdraw,

their superstructures riddled with bullet holes. The *TM-51* stopped at a naval yard in Schiedam and the *Z-5* sailed down the river to the Hook, both ships escaping to England on May 14.

Satisfied with the success of the naval attack by *Z-5* and *TM-51*, Vice-Admiraal Johannes Furstner ordered three more ships to Rotterdam, with orders to shell the infantry moving from the south and to stop them from crossing the river and linking up with the men trapped near the bridges. A destroyer, the *Van Galen*, slipped its moorings at the Hook and started to sail up the Nieuwe Waterweg in the afternoon. At Vlissingen, two gun boats, the *Johan Maurits van Nassau* and the *Flores*, were ordered to leave for Rotterdam. With orders to shell Waalhaven from a distance, the captain of the *Van Galen*, Luitenant Albert Pinke, decided that it would be far more effective to approach

Left: Early Friday morning, Jan van der Hoeven, a photographer for the *Voorwaarts* newspaper, took this scoop of German soldiers coming ashore from one of the Heinkels, still keeping its engines running to maintain its position in the middle of the Maas. The troops paddled towards the photographer standing on Oosterkade, on the northern bank of the river. Although the negative was destroyed later, during the bombing of the town, the picture had already appeared in print — hence this copy. *Right:* Today the twin towers of the old Hefbrug (lifting bridge) still stand beside a new replacement.

the German positions and pound them with his four 12cm guns at close range. But he never reached Waalhaven as the ships were attacked by Stukas when passing Vlaardingen. By taking frantic evasive action in the narrow river the ships avoided being hit, but the near misses were close enough to cause damage resulting in a loss of power which forced the *Van Galen* to retreat into Merwede harbour where she soon sank. The two gun boats, which by then had reached the entrance of the Nieuwe Waterweg, were recalled and ordered to return to harbour.

The bold German attack right into the heart of Rotterdam had been a success but the hours to follow would be far less easy. Even if the III. Bataillon could fight its way to the southern bank of the river, they would not be able to get across in force and relieve Schrader's and Kerfin's men who were to be cut off for the whole course of the battle on the northern bank, taking the full weight of repeated, if unco-ordinated, Dutch counter-attacks.

That evening Luftflotte 2 pessimistically reported to Heeresgruppe B on the airborne operations in the Netherlands, the operation by the 22. Infanterie-Division being acknowledged as a failure, with a statement on the heavy losses in transport aircraft.

In the field, Generalleutnant Student had landed with his staff at Waalhaven as planned but he had no contact at all with the northern group and was quite unable to act as commander of the whole Luftlande-Korps. By evening, although there was some concern about the outlook in the north, Student could still view the next few days with a degree of confidence for things had gone well for the southern group. On this first day of operations, some 250 Ju 52s had landed at Waalhaven, a number of them bound for the Hague sector but diverted because of the difficulties encountered there, and altogether he had about 5,000 men firmly established in various areas. Most of the 'island' south of Rotterdam was in German hands, as well as the bridges at Rotterdam, Dordrecht and Moerdijk. However, the situation at the airfield was far from easy as it was

Under the gaze of astonished Dutchmen surveying the scene from Maaskade on Noordereiland, a Heinkel taxies upstream to make for the Willems Bridge.

The part of the city in the background was destroyed in the subsequent air raid and has now been redeveloped on a grand scale.

suffering from air attacks and Dutch artillery shelling. On the other hand, reinforcement from the air was difficult and liaison with the elements holding the Dordrecht sector was poor. At the same time the Moerdijk bridgehead was menaced from the south by elements of the Dutch 6e Grens-Bataljon which had been ordered to recapture the bridges.

In the evening Student moved his command post to Rijsoord, half way between Rotterdam and Dordrecht.

Link-up between the air and ground forces close to the heart of Rotterdam. On the right is the school building in Zegenstraat where Generalleutnant Student established his first command post after landing at Waalhaven and before moving to Rijsoord.

THE DEFEAT OF THE NORTHERN GROUP

By the evening of the first day it was clear that the engagement of the 22. Infanterie-Division against The Hague was not going to succeed. The air transport groups and airborne infantry had suffered heavy losses, Dutch troops were pressing in on the attackers from every side, and German forces were far from having secured the approaches to The Hague. With little hope of anything further being achieved, late on May 10 Luftflotte 2 ordered von Sponeck to 'contract' and advance southwards with all those available and assemble his troops on the northern access to Rotterdam. However, because of communication difficulties, von Sponeck had received the order too late to move that same night and it was not until the following night that he could comply.

Communication was equally poor on the Allied side; demands for air operations against the airfields captured by the Germans had poured in throughout

This picture of containers dropping over Koningshaven was most probably taken on Friday afternoon during the attempt to resupply the 160 men holding out at the end of the bridges. These scenes appeared in the UFA newsreel for May 22.

The photo was taken from the Prins Hendrikkade on the southern side of Noordereiland, the island in the middle of the river (see picture page 124). The large building on the left is the Poortgebouw on Stieltjesstraat.

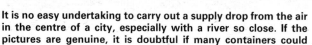

It is no easy undertaking to carry out a supply drop from the air in the centre of a city, especially with a river so close. If the pictures are genuine, it is doubtful if many containers could have been recovered. This one has fallen on the quayside between the Koninginne road bridge and the Hefbrug railway bridge.

May 10 and it was not clear that the Dutch had recaptured one airfield or another. Ockenburg was actually back in Dutch hands when Fighter Command sent the Hurricanes of No. 32 Squadron to raid the airfield at about 5.00 p.m., where they reported attacking 16 Ju 52s on the ground. The German airborne troops at Ockenburg were then emplaced in the wood south of the airfield; under the command of von Sponeck, these 360 men or so left with their 40 Dutch prisoners late in the evening. They marched southwards and were at Wateringen early on May 12 where they

Another container is recovered from the superstructure of the Hefbrug. Plans are afoot in Rotterdam for a new railway tunnel which would make this particular bridge superfluous after 1996, but the intention to demolish it is being resisted to preserve it as an historic monument.

exchanged shots with Dutch troops trying to encircle them. They captured some buses and, leaving a rearguard of about 80 men to cover the move, they successfully bypassed Delft to the west. On May 13 they were at Overschie, just to the north of Rotterdam, and joined with the Ypenburg group who had also moved on the previous day under the command of Oberfeldarzt Wischhusen.

Communication problems also prevented contact with the German troops in the Valkenburg sector and they never received the order to move southwards. Having held off repeated Dutch counter-attacks throughout May 11, the paratroops and the men from Inf.Rgt. 47 dispersed east of The Hague assembled on May 12 into two main pockets at Valkenburg and Wassenaar.

THE BATTLE SOUTH OF ROTTERDAM

On the morning of May 11 there was grave concern among the staff of the Luftlande-Korps about the situation of von Sponeck's northern group but it also appeared that problems were materialising all around Student's southern command.

To the south, at Moerdijk, the position had been contained though the Dutch 6e Grens-Bataljon was still pressing on, trying to eliminate the German bridgehead. However the Luftwaffe had managed to stop the French advancing on Moerdijk from the south with the intention of attacking the bridgehead in the afternoon.

A far graver threat was posed on the eastern flank where the Dutch Lichte Divisie retreating from the Peel Line was assembling north and east of Dordrecht. Consequently Student was forced to send all the available forces in the sector and employ two companies along the Noord river to cover his eastern flank. On the morning of May 11 the Dutch tried to cross the Noord near Alblasserdam but failed, partly because of the adverse effect on Dutch morale of a timely German air attack. The Dutch also pressed on at Dordrecht for the whole day but their efforts were poorly co-ordinated and were repulsed.

Another threat had to be dealt with on the southern flank in the morning for there the Dutch Command had planned another attack in co-ordination with the Lichte Divisie effort at Alblasserdam, the 3e Grens-Bataljon being given the job of taking the Barendrecht bridge and crossing the Oude Maas just south of Rotterdam. Having crossed the Hollands Diep from Willemstad the previous afternoon, and assembled east of Oud Beijerland, a three-pronged attack moved off at 6.00 a.m. (Dutch time). On the two flanks the Dutch succeeded in crossing the river but then hesitated and did not advance much further. In the centre the main attack was blocked by German elements defending the northern access to the bridge; Dutch artillery and mortar fire destroyed one of their strong points in a factory near the bridge access but that was all. After a last effort to cross the bridge, the whole Dutch attack bogged down and troops who had crossed withdrew south.

On the northern flank, in Rotterdam, von Choltitz's III. Bataillon had taken the southern bank of the river in the centre of the town but the small bridgehead held by the airborne north of the river was more and more threatened. Luckily for them the Dutch reinforcements were arriving piecemeal on the northern bank and were committed accordingly. Besides this, their efforts were poorly co-ordinated and in Rotterdam, the town commander, Kolonel Pieter Scharroo, had no authority over naval and air force units that were fighting in the town. At 10.30 a.m. (Dutch time) the air force sent two Fokker T-V bombers escorted by three Fokker D-XXIs to attack the German-held bridges at Rotterdam, but most of their bombs fell in the river. The formation went back to Schiphol to

At the urgent request of Generaal Winkelman, the torpedo boat *TM-51* (above) and the gunboat *Z-5* (below) were sent into the centre of Rotterdam to pound the bridge assault team at point-blank range although, in the circumstances, *TM-51* could only join in using her 20mm cannon.

rearm and repeated the attack at noon with the same results. On the return flight, they were attacked by a dozen Bf 110s and, in the combat that followed, the Dutch fighters claimed four Bf 110s destroyed for the loss of one Fokker T-V and two Fokker D-XXI.

Student was reinforced in the afternoon of May 11 when 36 Ju 52s from K.Gr.z.b.V. 9 landed on the main Moerdijk-Dordrecht road and brought in the 9. Kompanie of Inf.Rgt. 65 and one company of Inf.Rgt. 72, the latter regiment being brought in from the High Command reserve.

The Dutch resumed their efforts on May 12 to clear Dordrecht island, the Lichte Divisie having crossed the Merwede advancing south-west. The Dutch pressed on but Student committed all that he had (100 trucks bringing fresh troops had arrived in the afternoon from Waalhaven) and, with the support of the Luftwaffe which bombed the Dutch positions, the Germans succeeded in holding their ground.

In the afternoon Student was again reinforced when 40 more Ju 52s from K.Gr.z.b.V. 9 landed on the main road at Dordrecht and brought in more men from Inf.Rgt. 47 and elements from Art.Rgt. 22, the 22. Infanterie-Division artillery regiment. In the late evening RAF Coastal Command carried out its first bombing operation of the campaign. Six Beauforts of No. 22 Squadron supported by nine Swordfish of No. 815 Squadron, Fleet Air Arm, attacked Waalhaven, but no spectacular results were reported. It was too late anyway, for the transport aircraft were now landing on the highway and the total force airlifted to the southern group in the Rotterdam sector now amounted to a total of about 7,100 men; about 2,800 were from 7. Flieger-Division, some 4,200 from 22. Infanterie-Division and over 100 from Inf.Rgt. 72.

Meanwhile, in the Rotterdam sector, the Dutch had assembled as many troops as they could, planning to launch a strong counter-attack southwards

On Saturday morning (11th), two Fokker T-V bombers escorted by three Fokker D-XXIs attacked the German-held bridges in the city, repeating the attack at noon. However most of the bombs fell harmlessly into the river.

from the town. However, when Winkel-man found out that panzers were approaching from the south, he knew that he would have to settle for a defence of the northern bank of the Maas and he decided to commit the available force to break the Germans' hold on the bridges in Rotterdam. Their positions on the northern bank of the

Maas appeared hopeless, being held now by only 50 men.

The Dutch Marines made a determined attack on the morning of May 13 but their actions were once again poorly co-ordinated and they were forced to withdraw under mortar fire when they had all but overwhelmed the German defenders. It has been said that Ober-

leutnant Kerfin, who now led a party of only 20 paratroopers holed up in an insurance company building, was so close to surrendering that he had even had a white flag prepared.

South of the river on the morning of May 13 Student launched an attack from Hoogvliet to try to capture the refineries at Pernis to the west of Rotterdam. To avoid any major damage to the installations, the Germans were careful not to use their artillery and their attack was stopped at midday.

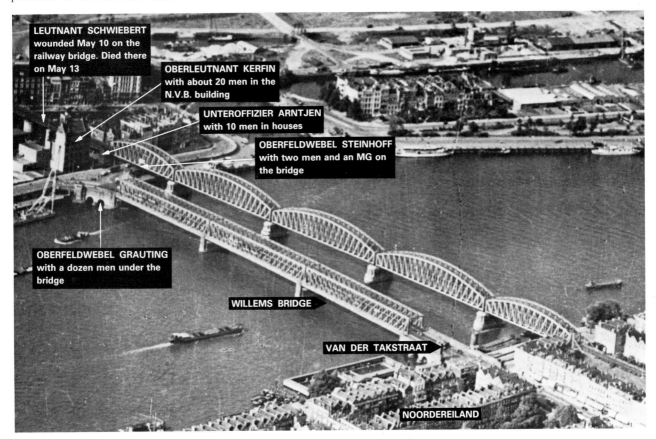

LEUTNANT SCHWIEBERT wounded May 10 on the railway bridge. Died there on May 13

OBERLEUTNANT KERFIN with about 20 men in the N.V.B. building

UNTEROFFIZIER ARNTJEN with 10 men in houses

OBERFELDWEBEL STEINHOFF with two men and an MG on the bridge

OBERFELDWEBEL GRAUTING with a dozen men under the bridge

WILLEMS BRIDGE

VAN DER TAKSTRAAT

NOORDEREILAND

Though the southern bank of the Maas and Noordereiland were in the hands of von Choltitz's III. Bataillon, the 50 or so airborne troops on the northern side were in an increasingly precarious position.

The advance elements of 9. Panzer-Division reached the Moerdijk bridgehead on Sunday afternoon (12th) being warmly greeted by the exhausted paratroopers. *Left:* A German cine cameraman was on hand to film the actual relief for the weekly

Wochenschau newsreel. *Right:* When the Moerdijk bridge was replaced, sections of the dismantled bridge were used to build this double carriageway for the new A27 motorway across the Bergse Maas 20 kilometres to the east.

A British demolition party backed by Dutch engineers started to blow up the plant, withdrawing northwards across the Nieuwe Maas in the evening.

By the late afternoon on May 12 advance elements of the 9. Panzer-Division had reached the Moerdijk bridgehead. They had stopped there to reinforce the position because although Student had his first contact with the panzer unit — a leutnant he met at Dordrecht — at 6.30 p.m. that day, the main body of the panzer division was not due to arrive before the following afternoon. Although every piece of available Dutch artillery shelled the Moerdijk sector, it was clear that the Germans were now too strong, and after a last counter-attack near Dordrecht on May 13, the Dutch withdrew.

This contemporary illustration somewhat over-dramatised the welcome.

The two leading armoured cars, an eight-wheeled SdKfz 232 and a four-wheeled SdKfz 221, crossed the river and made contact with the staff of Fallschirmjäger-Regiment 1 a few kilometres to the north at about 5.00 p.m. From L–R: Hauptmann Rau, Oberst Bräuer, the regiment's commander, and Leutnant von der Schulenburg. However the armoured cars did not stop and kept on northwards towards Dordrecht and Rotterdam.

THE LAND BATTLES

On the far right wing of the 18. Armee, advancing in a three-pronged attack, the 1. Kavallerie-Division had no difficulty in making progress in Friesland as the Dutch made little effort, if any, to defend their three northern provinces. The commander of the sector (termed in Dutch 'TB Friesland'), Kolonel Jacob Veenbaas, had only five

In the north the advance went smoothly, almost unopposed, and within 24 hours the 1. Kavallerie-Division was approaching the IJsselmeer. The cavalrymen in this picture appear to be in no hurry. Although the original print gave no clue as to location, in the end Johan Witteveen came up trumps with this beautiful comparison taken in the now-pedestrianised Drachtstraat in Heerenveen in August 1989.

battalions at hand, two of them border troops, whose task was simply to destroy bridges to slow the enemy advance. Explosives were so scarce that the men had been given axes and petrol to burn down the wooden ones and, because of this, some of the vital bridges could not be destroyed in time.

The attackers met the first real opposition on May 11 when they reached the Wons Line, on the eastern end of the Afsluitdijk which was covered by a belt of inundations. Because of the high water table, it was not possible to dig in and the Dutch positions were not too strong. They were soon forced north of Wons and withdrew along the Afsluitdijk towards Vesting Holland on May 12. When this main dyke cutting the IJsselmeer off from the sea had been built, it had been appreciated that it could provide an entry route to Vesting Holland and two fortresses had been incorporated to prevent it from being crossed. At the eastern end was the Kornwerderzand

The 1. Kavallerie-Division reached the first major Dutch defences when it approached the Wons Line — a belt of inundations to the north of the IJsselmeer. Here the cavalry are photographed passing Makkum.

fortress, supported by the Den Oever fortress at the western end. The former comprised 16 self-supporting casemates armed with 5cm guns and machine guns, and was manned by 220 defenders under Kapitein Christiaan Boers.

On May 13 the defenders, manning an AA gun evacuated from Leeuwarden, succeeded in shooting down a German aircraft and in the afternoon German artillery started to plaster the fortress but the assault that followed failed to make any progress. Confronted with this patently difficult

opposition, the Germans made plans to cross the IJsselmeer in small boats, but the IJssel flotilla — six minesweepers, gun boats and patrol boats, most of them old, plus some eight locally commandeered boats — was still a strong deterrent. An attack by the Luftwaffe the previous day had badly damaged the *Friso* and *Brinio* gun boats, the former being so badly damaged that it had to be scuttled. On the morning of May 14 another gun boat, the *Johan Maurits van Nassau*, shelled the German artillery positions from the Waddenzee and

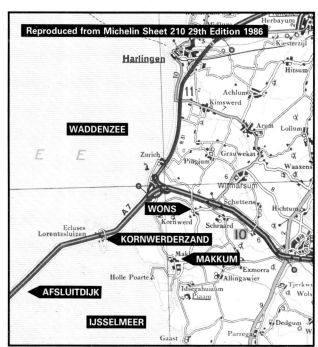

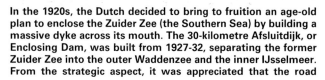

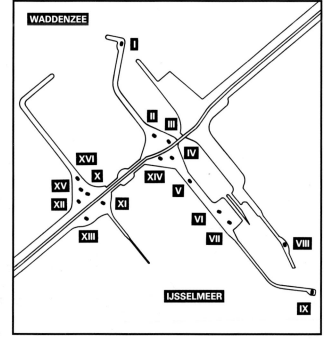

In the 1920s, the Dutch decided to bring to fruition an age-old plan to enclose the Zuider Zee (the Southern Sea) by building a massive dyke across its mouth. The 30-kilometre Afsluitdijk, or Enclosing Dam, was built from 1927-32, separating the former Zuider Zee into the outer Waddenzee and the inner IJsselmeer. From the strategic aspect, it was appreciated that the road

along the dam could provide a vulnerable back door entry route so fortresses were added at either end. At the northern end stood the Kornwerderzand comprising 16 self-supporting casemates armed with 21×7.9mm machine guns and 4×5cm guns, one of them anti-tank. In May 1940 the fortress was manned by over two hundred men under Kapitein Christiaan Boers.

returned to Den Helder before leaving for Britain in the evening.

The Germans never managed to get past the Kornwerderzand position, and thus were denied access to Vesting Holland from the north, but the premature capitulation of the Netherlands made the risky undertaking of a sea crossing unnecessary.

In the centre, the X. Armeekorps had to cross the IJssel and force the Grebbe Line. The 227. Infanterie-Division was on the corps' right wing, between Zwolle and Zutphen, with two battalions from the Leibstandarte SS-'Adolf Hitler' (the third battalion was in corps' reserve) and it was to advance in a three-pronged attack. The southern and middle arms were to cross at Zutphen, the latter backed by an armoured train, the E-Panzerzug 3. At the same time the northern thrust, also backed by an armoured train, E-Panzerzug 4, was to cross at Zwolle and Deventer. On the corps' left wing, between Zutphen and Arnhem, lay the 207. Infanterie-Division and the attached SS-Standarte 'Der Führer'.

Facing them the Dutch commander for the IJssel sector ('TB Overijssel') had only five battalions on the eastern border and five more behind the IJssel Line, whose task it was to blow demolition charges.

The 227. Infanterie-Division group arrived at Zwolle just before 10.00 a.m., only to find that the bridges had already been blown. Likewise the Deventer force also found its bridges demolished but when it received a spurious message stating that the Zwolle bridges were intact the group then marched northwards. They lost the rest of the day driving along the eastern bank of the IJssel and it was not before the late evening that it was confirmed that the bridges at Zwolle had in fact been destroyed.

Above: **The Germans brought forward artillery to shell the fortress (this is a 7.5cm leFk 18) but the Dutch retaliated by sending in a gunboat, the *Johan Maurits van Nassau* (below).**

Though they shelled the fortress, the Germans did not press home their attack and Kornwerderzand held out until the end. After the war, the fortress remained on the active list but since 1985 has been open as a museum. This is Block I at the end of the Waddenzee jetty. Several of the other casemates have been restored with a memorial erected between Blocks III and IV near the road, the latter formerly Kapitein Boers' command post in 1940.

Left: **When the Dutch government capitulated on May 15, Kornwerderzand was still holding the Germans at bay. This picture was taken late that Wednesday as parlementaires** approached the defenders through the anti-tank obstructions just east of the fortress complex. *Right:* **Next morning the 1. Kavallerie-Division moved off southwards along the dyke road.**

The bridges at Zutphen had also been blown when the troops in the centre reached the town. The Dutch resistance was fierce and it was not before the afternoon that a crossing of the IJssel became possible. A pontoon bridge was constructed and the main force of the 227. Infanterie-Division crossed the IJssel river next day.

Further to the north, though elements of Inf.Rgt. 328 dismounting from the E-Panzerzug 4 had succeeded in crossing the IJssel near Olst, bridging equipment was lacking and the division commander, Generalmajor Friedrich Zickwolff, ordered the whole of the northern arm to turn south and cross the IJssel at Zutphen.

Things went somewhat better on the German left wing between Zutphen and Arnhem. Here, although the bridges at Westervoort and Doesburg were blown, pontoon bridges had been completed by the afternoon. The advance element of SS-Standarte 'Der Führer' crossed over and assembled at Renkum, about ten kilometres west of Arnhem, prior to an attack on the Grebbe Line. In their wake came the 207. Infanterie-Division.

After an artillery barrage, two battalions from SS-Standarte 'Der Führer' attacked the Grebbeberg, the hill at the southern end of the Line, early on the morning of May 11, and by the end of the day the first line of defence of the Dutch 8e R.I. had been breached, the

regiment's third battalion had been forced back and the battalion commander, Majoor Christoffel Voigt, captured. A Dutch counter-attack was launched after dark but failed because of the inexperience of the men in operating at night. They succeeded, however in preventing the Germans from launching their own planned night attack.

Because of the destruction of all bridges on the Apeldoornsch Canal, in the sector covered by the 227. Infanterie-Division, only its light recce elements on bicycles had reached the Grebbe Line on the afternoon of May 11, followed in the evening by the first troops of the Leibstandarte SS-'Adolf Hitler'.

Above: **Cavalry approaching the camouflaged Block V from the sea end as the bridge on the main causeway had been blown and instead the Germans had to use the sluice bridge.** *Below:* **The same casemate today looking in the opposite direction towards the IJsselmeer with Block VI behind.**

After shelling throughout the morning, the battle resumed in the afternoon of May 12 and the main defences were breached. A counter-attack by the second battalion of 8e R.I. failed, its commander, Majoor Johannes Jacometti, being killed. The IIe Legerkorps then ordered three battalions from Brigade B to prepare to mount a strong counter-attack the next morning.

During the night, taking advantage of the confusion then prevailing on the Grebbeberg where the Dutch defenders were trying feverishly to organise their planned counter-attack, the commander of the III. Bataillon of SS-Standarte 'Der Führer', SS-Obersturmbannführer Hilmar Wäckerle, broke through near Rhenen with about 100 men, took several prisoners, and advanced as far as the railway line. Forced back, the SS troopers took shelter in a factory and the next morning some emerged behind a screen of Dutch prisoners dressed only in their shorts. This failed, as did another trick at about midday when some Germans came out in Dutch uniforms. This time it was their boots that betrayed their identity.

A dozen aircraft from 1e LVR of the Dutch air force attacked German artillery positions near Wageningen early in the morning and, although this boosted morale, the Dutch counter-attack bogged down and failed to prevent the Germans from opening their attack about midday. Stukas bombed the

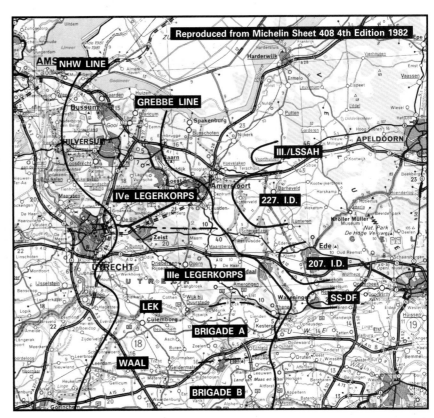

The main Dutch defence depended on holding the north-south Grebbe Line in the centre of the country with the Nieuwe Hollandse Waterlinie (NHW) behind it as a fallback position.

At the southern end of the Grebbe Line, just east of Rhenen, lay the commanding position of the Grebbeberg. Although only 150 feet high, it overlooked the Hoornwerk, an old bastion which had been modernised in the 'thirties, which itself controlled the bridge over the Grift river. Today the Dutch war cemetery for those killed in May 1940 lies on the hillside.

Left: **Majoor Willem Landzaat, the commander of the 1e Bataljon of 8e Regiment. On the afternoon of May 13 his command post in the Ouwehands Dierenpark, the zoo on the** Grebbeberg, **was surrounded but he refused to surrender and was killed. His widow had this memorial *(right)* erected on the spot where he made his last stand.**

Dutch positions near Rhenen and fighting during the afternoon isolated Dutch units east of the railway. During the battle the commander of the first battalion of 8e R.I., Majoor Willem Landzaat, was killed.

Further to the north, the 227. Infanterie-Division launched a two regiment attack against the Grebbe Line near Scherpenzeel in the afternoon but the Dutch held their ground and nowhere was the Line breached.

By now it was clear that the Grebbeberg was lost and at 4.15 p.m. the Dutch Command ordered a general withdrawal to the NHW Line to begin at 8.00 p.m. (Dutch time).

Meanwhile elements of SS-Standarte 'Der Führer' entered Achterberg but in the south the Inf.Rgt. 322 had some difficulty crossing the railway cutting and it was not until 9.30 p.m. that they entered Rhenen.

During the night the whole of the Grebbe Line was evacuated and the Dutch forces retreated into Vesting Holland. The units of IVe Legerkorps (on the Dutch left wing) and those of the IIIe Legerkorps (on the Dutch right) fell back in good order — the former with deep disappointment for they had not yet been in action — but in the centre the IIe Legerkorps retreat was a complete confusion. The corps

commander, Generaal-Majoor Jacob Harberts, who had not distinguished himself during the battle for the Grebbeberg, leaving in a hurry to rush westwards 'to inspect his new sector', was then relieved of his command.

Reaching their new positions, the withdrawing units found the NHW Line almost deserted for, in the meantime, the Dutch Command had scraped together every available unit to counter the threat from paratroopers in the heart of Vesting Holland. By the morning of May 14 the Dutch were in their new positions but this was effectively the end of the fighting in this sector due to the capitulation.

After the battle. A section of the Grebbe Line just south of Scherpenzeel, ten kilometres from Amersfoort, photographed in the summer of 1940 by Sergeant A. H. van der Hoek who had served there with the 15e Regiment Infanterie. The Germans made a determined attack in this sector on May 13 but failed to break through. Note the casemates built into the canal bank.

Remains of the Peel Line at Mill where it ran along the canal. Generaal Winkelman never intended to defend this part of the country but to withdraw north-westwards as soon as an invasion began. This is Pillbox No. 534, one of a series which had been sited to protect the railway bridge in the far background.

In the south, on the left wing of the 18. Armee, the XXVI. Armeekorps had to cross the Maas and force the Peel Line, both only lightly held by the Dutch. Up the railway line from the bridge over the Maas at Gennep already captured by a German assault team, two German trains, one of them armoured, loaded with men from the 256. Infanterie-Division, had rushed across into the Netherlands. On board were three companies of infantry from Inf.Rgt. 481, one company of heavy machine guns, plus one platoon of anti-tank guns and a platoon of engineers with four flame-throwers. At Mill, about 12 kilometres from the river, the Peel defences consisted of a canal manned by Dutch troops. They knew nothing about the seizure of the Gennep bridge and did nothing to stop the two trains. These halted about three kilometres further on for the troops to detrain and attack the Dutch positions from the rear. The trains were then driven on to the station at Zeeland, where the rear one was left on a siding while the lead train — the armoured one — went back to Mill to lend a hand with the few guns it carried. By now the Dutch had realised that something was wrong and had blocked the track, de-railing the train on the bridge over the canal. With the Peel Line breached at Mill and outflanked to the south after the Belgian withdrawal, Generaal Winkelman ordered the IIIe Leger-korps and the Lichte Divisie to be withdrawn as planned from the Noord-Brabant province into Vesting Holland, a move which began on the afternoon of May 10.

Although the 6. Armee was not actually involved in the initial invasion of the Netherlands, its right wing had

Having captured the bridge across the Maas at Gennep intact, the Germans cleverly outsmarted the Dutch defences at Mill by driving straight through them in an armoured train! However when it tried to return, the Dutch in this sector, belonging to the 1e Bataljon of the 3e Regiment Infanterie, were ready and the train was derailed.

The railway line between Goch in Germany and Uden in the Netherlands is now disused, enabling local enthusiasts to re-create history at Mill although unfortunately not at the exact spot where the derailment occurred. This should be just a little further to the west on the bridge visible in the distance.

also crossed the Maas and was advancing through the Dutch Limburg province (right in the south of the country) and into Belgium. Its IX. Armeekorps had three divisions in the Venlo sector, the XI. Armeekorps three divisions spread from Roermond to Born, and the IV. Armeekorps three divisions between Born and Maastricht, where the XVI. Armeekorps was advancing its two panzer divisions.

The withdrawal of the IIIe Legerkorps and its three divisions eased the way through the Noord-Brabant province for XXVI. Armeekorps. Elements of 254. Infanterie-Division soon followed the 256. Infanterie-Division and on May 11 both divisions were advancing across the Peel Line. The 9. Panzer-Division was crossing the Maas behind them, between Gennep and Mook, and the leading tanks were thundering westwards for the bridges at Moerdijk held by the paratroops. By the afternoon of May 11 the panzers had reached the Zuid-Willems Canal near Veghel and early next morning were just north of Tilburg.

They clashed with advanced French units around Tilburg and Breda, brushing aside these light reconnaissance forces, the 18. Armee noting with relief that the French were not pushing strong forces into the sector. Moerdijk was then only 40 kilometres away.

Late on May 12 the front of XXVI. Armeekorps had reached Moerdijk and linked with the paratroopers. At midday on May 13 the XXXIX. Armeekorps took command of these forces, particularly elements of the 9. Panzer-Division, which were crossing in force at Moerdijk and assembling on the southern edge of Rotterdam, together with units of both the 7. Flieger-Division and 22. Infanterie-Division, with the task of forcing Vesting Holland from the south. Meanwhile a bridge had been completed over the Wilhelmina Canal east of Tilburg and those parts of the 9. Panzer-Division south of the canal had crossed and reached the Moerdijk bridgehead in the afternoon of May 13. The next morning Student greeted Generalmajor Alfred von Hubicki, the commander of the 9. Panzer-Division, and Generalleutnant Rudolf Schmidt, the commander of the XXXIX. Armeekorps, at his command post at Rijsoord.

By Saturday afternoon the advanced elements of 9. Panzer-Division had reached the Zuid-Willems Canal near Veghel — an advance of 40 kilometres. These two SdKfz 6/2 self-propelled 3.7cm AA guns were pictured in front of the church.

Below left: By the evening of the first day Generalleutnant Student had landed at Waalhaven with his staff and had set up his headquarters in this café at Rijsoord, midway between Rotterdam and Dordrecht. There, three days later, he was able to greet the arrival of Generalleutnant Rudolf Schmidt of XXXIX. Armeekorps and Generalmajor Alfred von Hubicki, commander of the 9. Panzers. Some time later these Dutch prisoners were pictured passing the café which still stands today *(right)*.

A cheer for the benefit of the photographer from these men of the 224ème R.I., 68ème Division d'Infanterie, as they are shipped from Dunkirk to Vlissingen on the island of Walcheren on Saturday. The escort is the French destroyer *La Cordelière*.

THE FRENCH 7ème ARMÉE

Screening the 7ème Armée in its move northwards into the Netherlands, the reconnaissance units of Groupement Lestoquoi that deployed ahead of the army's spearhead, the 1ère D.L.M., consisted of two recce groups, the 2ème G.R.C.A. and the 5ème G.R.D.I. Those of Groupement de Beauchesne that had crossed the Scheldt estuary were the 2ème, 12ème and 27ème G.R.D.I.

Alerte No. 3 being given at 5.30 a.m. (French time), the two reconnaissance groups had crossed the border in the early hours of May 10. Groupement

Lestoquoi had rushed eastwards over the Albert Canal east of Antwerp in the afternoon and advanced during the night beyond Turnhout. The 2ème G.R.D.I. of Groupement de Beauchesne had been ferried from Breskens to Vlissingen, disembarking at about 7.00 p.m., and had soon made contact with the Dutch troops on Walcheren. The 12ème G.R.D.I. had followed during the night. From Terneuzen the 27ème G.R.D.I. had crossed to Zuid Beveland in the afternoon and moved eastwards in the direction of Woensdrecht.

The tanks of the 4ème Cuirassiers

and 18ème Dragons of the 1ère D.L.M. were loaded onto trains to be transported by rail directly to the Antwerp area but the rest of the division advanced behind Groupement Lestoquoi. Leading the way was the division's 'régiment de découverte', the 6ème Cuirassiers.

Chef d'Escadron Georges Michon, a squadron commander in 6ème Cuirassiers, relates how, having crossed the border at Steenvoorde at around 10.00 a.m., they made good progress that first day: 'In the afternoon, we stopped for about an hour at Overmere, fifteen kilometres east of Gent, to reorganise

The smiles did not last long for the Luftwaffe soon arrived to attack the transports while they were off the Belgian coast.

However no major damage was sustained and the ships continued on their way to bring reinforcements to Holland.

the column and enable all the vehicles to catch up. We advanced again until nightfall when we stopped at Emblem, just north of Lier, where Colonel Dario made contact with the commander of the Belgian 18ème Division d'Infanterie. We had to fill our tanks but it took a long time before the Belgians agreed to bring the fuel to us. We started again at about midnight and, knowing that the bridges in Turnhout were blown, we bypassed the town. At the border the road had to be cleared of the obstacles built by the Belgians and we reached Tilburg at first light on May 11. The 265 kilometres to Tilburg had been driven in one go, without incident from the enemy. We had seen numerous German aircraft, but no one had menaced us; neither had we seen any friendly planes.'

War stores are unloaded at Vlissingen docks from where a narrow isthmus gave access to the mainland near Bergen op Zoom. The NV Handelscompagnie warehouse *(above)* has since disappeared, but a similar one *below* still survives.

The Luftwaffe had not been too intrusive on the first day as Fliegerkorps z.b.V., the staff unit charged with the air support of the airborne operation in the Netherlands, had had to employ every available fighter and bomber group in support of the airborne assault on Vesting Holland. The following day Generalmajor Putzier turned a sizeable part of his force against the French threat on the southern flank of the airborne operation and, when the 1ère D.L.M. resumed its move early in the morning of May 11, the advance elements came under incessant attack from the air. Sergent Marcel Berger, commander of a Panhard P-178

armoured car with the 2ème G.R.D.I., relates how traumatic these attacks were: 'It was about 7.00 a.m. We drove along a nice road lined with trees when suddenly, in less than two minutes, the sky was filled with aircraft. The bombers flew over us at an altitude of about 1500 metres. Six by six, some ten metres apart, they dived on us, aiming at the road on which we were so easily visible. They dived with a fearful scream that made the plane itself a projectile more monstrous than a 310mm shell. The explosions of their bombs did not hurt us in our steel boxes. Our view was limited which was a relief as the sight of the explosions was frightening.

'Following our instructions, we left the road, bounced over the shallow ditch lining the road and spread out over the fields. We were lucky as only a few kilometres before, this same road was lined by a canal on each side. Our persecutors multiplied and persevered. They did not dive in lines of six any more, but in rows of 25 and 50. It was just like an huge wing which passed again and again above us, projecting its shadow on the ground, diving repeatedly at 45 degrees with a howling scream and incessant explosions.

'When a bomb went off near us, a hail of shrapnel hit our armoured car and we thanked our lucky stars for our relative safety, but were suffocated with a deep helplessness in the presence of the bombs that we imagined were aimed just at us. The armour plate surrounding us hugely amplified the roar of the aircraft and the whistle of the bombs. The incessant explosions tore at our guts and souls. All this went on for . . . was it four, five or six hours? At first, we hoped for the arrival of our own aircraft. But none came. Where were they?'

Though impeded and suffering losses

It is frustrating when illustrations for a particular action or battle cannot be found, but understandable as the last thing hard-pressed troops have on their minds is the taking of photographs. More often than not, war pictures are confined to those taken by the victors of the particular action and, although the picture *above* was taken later in France, it provides a good illustration of Panhard P-178s in action like that described by Sergent Marcel Berger. He reached Moerdijk only to find the road blocked by obstacles set up by the paratroops.

from the Luftwaffe attacks, the French forces nevertheless reached their objectives. Groupement de Beauchesne then pushed on to Roosendaal while Groupement Lestoquoi, whose 2ème G.R.C.A. had reached Breda, and 5ème G.R.D.I. Tilburg, was soon in contact with the enemy. Facing east, from Tilburg to the junction with the Belgian 18ème Division d'Infanterie east of Turnhout, the vanguard of the 1ère D.L.M. were on the Reusel river, the 6ème Cuirassiers in the Tilburg sector and the 4ème R.D.P. further south. That afternoon the 1ère D.L.M. tanks were off-loaded from their trains at Mechelen and on the southern outskirts of Antwerp. Two squadrons of Somua S-35s were held in reserve while the Hotchkiss H-35 squadrons moved off in order to support the Belgian 18ème Division d'Infanterie. Later in

the afternoon the Belgians started to withdraw on the Albert Canal which seriously threatened the right flank of the 1ère D.L.M. During the evening the leading troops of the 25ème D.I.M. were arriving on the Mark river in the Breda sector and those of the 9ème D.I.M. on the Albert Canal at Herentals.

Meanwhile, at midday elements of the 6ème Cuirassiers and 5ème G.R.D.I. had approached Moerdijk. Then the Luftwaffe struck. As Chef d'Escadron Michon recalls: 'The vanguard easily reached the railway crossing north of Zevenbergsenhoek while the main force entered the village. The detachment was then suddenly caught by a violent and seamingly endless air attack. The village was badly damaged by the bombs and the road between the platoon of Lieutenant André Martin in

Left: **This Panhard abandoned in Princenhage, just west of Breda, belonged quite probably to the 6ème Cuirassiers of the 1ère D.L.M., elements of which had reached Moerdijk on** Saturday. After being bombed by the Luftwaffe they were forced to withdraw to Breda. *Right:* **Jacques van Dijke traced the location in Dreefstraat,**

the van and the main body was completly blocked. At our rear, the bridge on the Mark had been demolished by the bombs, stopping any move from Terheijden to Breda. Now unable to keep up an offensive action against the bridges at Moerdijk, I gathered the main force and withdrew to Breda through Zevenbergen and Oudenbosch. Completely isolated by the destruction, Lieutenant Martin succeeded in extricating his platoon under fire from the German troops, and withdrew through Oosterhout.'

A unit of the 2ème G.R.D.I. advancing from Bergen op Zoom also approached the Moerdijk bridges late the next morning. Barriers blocked the roads, and these were forced, but it was not long before it was ordered to withdraw to Zevenbergen because of the uncertainity of the general situation. North of Turnhout Groupement Lestoquoi was also ordered to withdraw, and two platoons of Hotchkiss H-35s were sent to cover the threatened southern flank. That evening the army ordered a withdrawal of the 1ère D.L.M. and 25ème D.I.M. during the night on a line Wuustwezel-Wortel-Turnhout.

Out front, the reconnaissance groups were now under pressure on all sides. At 8.00 a.m. on May 13 the 2ème G.R.D.I., now the northernmost point of the army at Breda, was heavily bombed and was ordered to withdraw, having to fight off panzers which tried to outflank them to the south. The 9. Panzer-Division had pushed one battalion of panzers west of Breda in the afternoon but reconnaissance aircraft from G.A.O. 501 reported having seen about 20 panzers, camouflaged under the trees beside the road near Achtmaal, only about 20 kilometres east of Bergen op Zoom at 5.15 p.m.

In the vain hope of retaining control of the northern bank of the Scheldt and protecting access to the sea from Antwerp, Colonel de Beauchesne ordered Groupement Michon — the 12ème G.R.D.I. reinforced by some elements of the 6ème Cuirassiers and of the 4ème R.D.P. — to hold on around Bergen op Zoom, while the 2ème and 27ème G.R.D.I.s were ordered to defend the Huijbergen area a few kilometres to the south-east.

On May 14 the XXVI. Armeekorps launched a powerful attack aiming westwards at Antwerp. The 25ème D.I.M.

Left: **Groupement Lestoquoi came into contact with German forces near Tilburg, while further to the south the 1ère D.L.M. had reached the Reusel river. This AMR 35 of the 4ème R.D.P., 1ère D.L.M., was destroyed near the river at Diessen.** *Right:* **Jacques van Dijke took the comparison at the same place on Julianastraat. From here Tilburg is about ten kilometres to the north.**

Brotherhood in war. A French soldier from Détachement Durand, the advance guard from the 68ème Division d'Infanterie, shares a smoke with soldiers of Commando Zeeland, the Dutch force stationed in the province of Zeeland. However within a few days the fate of the Netherlands would be sealed and what could be saved of the Détachement Durand would be pulled out in somewhat indecent haste.

was then involved in heavy fighting near Wuustwezel; it counter-attacked and regained the lost ground, but to the north the recce units of Groupement de Beauchesne suffered badly as they fell back. Groupement Michon and all elements attached to it were surrounded at Bergen op Zoom.

Late that day the 7ème Armée ordered its divisions to withdraw in a line defending Antwerp. In the evening, at Boom and Puurs, to the west of Mechelen, the 1ère D.L.M. had loaded its two squadrons of Somua S-35s onto trains bound for France.

Although relations at grass-roots level may have been cordial, those between the French and Dutch commanders were not. Rear-Admiral Hendrik van der Stad, the Dutch commander in Zeeland, was annoyed that his French opposite number, Général Mary Durand, was looking to France for his orders rather than to him, and Durand disagreed with the Dutch commander over the choice of a defence line. By May 15, when Durand proved overly concerned about a French withdrawal, he had to be replaced to preserve unity, and Général Marcel Deslaurens of the 60ème Division d'Infanterie took his place the following day. Although the Netherlands had now thrown in the towel, because of the number of French troops still in the country, Zeeland was excluded from the provisions of the Armistice. On May 17 the Germans administered the coup de grâce with air attacks on Arnemuiden, Middelburg, Veere and Vlissingen, the historic centre of Middelburg being particularly badly hit. *Above:* In this picture, taken on the quay at Vlissingen, the offices of the Scheldt-Breskens ferry company have been damaged from a near miss. *Below:* Now the building of the Provinciale Stoombootdienst has been replaced by that of the local port radio station.

ROTTERDAM BOMBED

In Rotterdam the riverside had been badly damaged in the battle for the bridges and also from the shellfire of *Z-5* and *TM-51*. Dutch aircraft and artillery had contributed to the destruction the following day. The SS *Statendam* and SS *Boschdijk* anchored on Wilhelminakade were hit by artillery and set alight. Throughout May 12, the Dutch shelling had been intense. Smoke hung above burning buildings and the ships anchored on the Maas, the SS *Statendam* was to burn for another four days. On May 13, a Royal Engineers demolition party had blown up the fuel storage tanks at Pernis, just west of the town, adding still more smoke.

On May 14, in Führer Directive No. 11 (see page 241), Hitler noted that 'the Dutch Army has shown itself capable of a stronger resistance than had been supposed' and insisted that 'for political and military reasons, this resistance must be broken quickly'. German troops, particularly elements of the 9. Panzer-Division, had crossed in force at Moerdijk and had assembled on the southern edge of the town. At midday on May 13 the XXXIX. Armeekorps had taken command of these forces, and of both the 7. Flieger-Division and 22. Infanterie-Division, with the purpose of forcing Vesting Holland on its southern flank.

The corps now prepared a powerful attack to force a way through Rotterdam. On the afternoon of May 14, assembled at Feyenoord, just behind the southern ends of the Maas bridges, was Gruppe A, with panzers from Pz.Rgt. 33 and von Choltitz's third battalion of Inf.Rgt. 16, supported by two groups of artillery and two companies of engineers. Under the command of Oberst Wilhelm von Apell of the 9. Panzer-Division this group was to

After XXXIX. Armeekorps took command of the forces advancing on Rotterdam from the south at noon on Monday, a co-ordinated assault by air and ground forces was set in motion for the following day. Poised for the kill, Generalleutnant Schmidt planned to precede the attack with an ultimatum to the Dutch town commander, Kolonel Pieter Scharroo, to surrender. This was sent via Oberstleutnant von Choltitz, who had now moved his command post to a house near Van der Takstraat, to Scharroo's HQ at 147 Statenweg. A three-man delegation crossed the Willems bridge bearing a white flag at 10.40 a.m. on Tuesday morning, arriving at the Dutch HQ thirty minutes later. Here the German emissaries — Hauptmann Raymond Hoerst of the 9. Panzer-Division, Oberleutnant Friedrich Plutzar the interpreter, and Hauptmann Pessendorfer of a Propaganda Kompanie, arrive back on Noordereiland, believing that the Dutch will agree to surrender.

attack over the bridge and out of the small bridgehead held on the northern bank by Schrader's and Kerfin's men and advance towards Amsterdam. Further east was Gruppe B, lined up near IJsselmonde with three companies of Inf.Rgt. 16 and one company of engineers. Under the command of

Oberst Hans von Kreysing, the commander of Inf.Rgt. 16, this group was to cross the Maas on barges and disembark at Kralingen. On the southern edge of Rotterdam was Gruppe C comprising panzers from Pz.Rgt. 33 and the bulk of the Leibstandarte SS-'Adolf Hitler', ready to follow behind Gruppe A to try

A new bridge has since been built upstream from the original which was demolished in 1983 leaving Van der Takstraat a peaceful dead-end street.

Right: Kolonel Scharroo had his head-quarters at No. 147 Statenweg; now a monument nearby records the part it played in May 1940. However no mention is made of the fact that it was also here that Student was shot in the head and grievously wounded from a burst of gun-fire on Tuesday afternoon (see page 148). The bullet marks can still be seen on the walls today.

to relieve the few hundred paratroops assembled at Overschie before the Dutch could overwhelm them. They were then to advance towards The Hague. The land attack was to commence at 3.30 p.m. German time (1.50 p.m. Dutch time), preceded by an artillery barrage, then an air raid scheduled from 2.40 p.m. (1.00 p.m.).

Meanwhile the Dutch had mounted a three battalion attack to wipe out the airborne troops assembled at Overschie just north of Rotterdam. Under the

When Kolonel Scharroo conferred with Generaal Winkelman by telephone, the C-in-C seized on the technicality that the surrender ultimatum was not clearly signed and ordered that the document be rejected with a request for clarification, ignoring the plea from the Mayor to agree in order to save his city from further bloodshed and destruction. Kapitein Jan

Backer was detailed to take back the Dutch reply under the protection of a white flag. *Left:* Oberstleutnant von Choltitz came out personally to greet the Dutchman at the ad hoc conference room which had been established in an empty ice-cream parlour at No. 66 Prins Hendrikkade, no doubt expecting to receive an agreement to surrender.

command of Luitenant-Kolonel Hendrik Scherpenhuijzen, a three-pronged attack moved off in the morning on May 14 from the Delft sector, the major effort being in the centre along the main road. However the advance was slow — at walking pace — and contact with the Germans was not established until the early afternoon.

On the morning of May 14 the commander of XXXIX. Armeekorps, Generalleutnant Rudolf Schmidt, whose command post was then at Rijsoord, had sent a surrender ultimatum to Kolonel Scharroo, expiring at 2.10 p.m. (12.30 p.m. Dutch time), that is 50 minutes before the beginning of the air attack. At 10.40 a.m. German time (9.00 a.m.), three German emissaries left von Choltitz's HQ, crossed the Willems Bridge and arrived at Scharroo's CP at 147 Statenweg at 11.10 a.m. (10.30 a.m.). They were admitted to his office ten minutes later. Scharroo telephoned Winkelman who, probably eager to gain time for his counter-attack aimed at wiping out the airborne force assembled at Overschie, pointed out the

The former IJssalon on the right-hand side of the bank has now been converted into a private house.

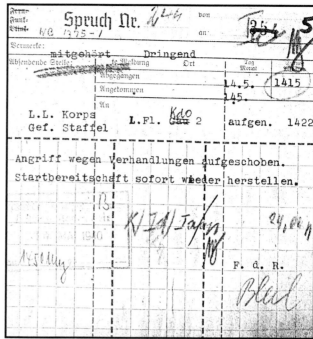

Left: **Generalleutnant Schmidt, accompanied by Generalleutnant Student (left), and his chief of staff, Major i.G. Heinrich Trettner (right), arrived at the command post shortly afterwards, no doubt banking on a positive response to his ultimatum. When Schmidt read the reply he wrote a new message on the back of Scharroo's paper, extending the deadline to 6.00 p.m. and clearly signing it with his name, rank and position.** *Right:* **Working on the presumption of a favourable reply, Schmidt sent a message to Luftflotte 2 to cancel their operation: 'Because of negotiations, attack is postponed. Renew preparations for take-off immediately.' This message was timed at 2.15 p.m. but it was already too late as the aircraft** were airborne. **(It must be remembered that during the Blitzkrieg the Germans were using their own clock time in the Netherlands which, from mid-March, was two hours ahead of GMT. Britain, France and Belgium were on GMT+1, but the Netherlands, incredible as it may seem, were on GMT+20 minutes! Ever since the 1920s, the Dutch had run their clocks 19 minutes 32 seconds out of synchronisation with GMT although, to their credit, they did at least round the difference to an even 20 minutes. Thus in May 1940 there was a 1 hour 40 minutes difference between German and Dutch time, and, if it appears confusing now, it was surely all the more so on that Tuesday when every minute counted.)**

fact that the document was not clearly signed and that a replacement document was required, clearly signed, with the name and rank of the German commander concerned. Scharroo, ignoring advice from the Mayor of Rotterdam, Pieter Oud, thereupon sent Kapitein Jan Backer back to the Germans with his answer. Meanwhile the three German emissaries had arrived back at the ice-cream parlour at No. 66 Prins Hendrikkade which was being used for negotiations at 1.30 a.m. (11.50 a.m.), giving the impression that the Dutch were about to surrender. Schmidt therefore decided to postpone the artillery barrage and sent a message to Luftflotte 2 at 2.15 p.m. (12.35 p.m.) requesting that the bombers be held back.

Kapitein Backer arrived at von Choltitz's command post at 1.55 p.m. (German time), Schmidt, with Student and von Hubicki, came 20 minutes later at 2.15 p.m. (12.35 p.m.). Schmidt then wrote a new message on the back of Scharroo's reply, requiring that the Germans be allowed to enter the northern part of the town and that Dutch troops were to lay down their weapons. Officers, on the other hand, would be permitted to retain sidearms.

This new ultimatum was clearly signed 'Schmidt, Generalleutnant und Kommandierender General eines Armeekorps', and would expire at 6.00 p.m. (4.20 p.m.). It made no mention of, nor did it threaten, bombing. Not that it would have made any difference,

The aiming point for the bombers was a triangle on the northern bank of the Maas facing Noordereiland. This picture, taken by the RAF in 1943, shows the devastated area of the city beyond the bridges.

for when Backer left with two Germans as escort at about 3.00 p.m. (1.20 p.m.) the bombers were already approaching. Communications between the field commanders in Rotterdam and Luftflotte 2 were poor and the chain of command too long for Schmidt's request to have reached it in time.

The target for the He 111s of KG54 was a triangular zone on the north side of the Maas, opposite the point held by German airborne troops, but the KG54 pilots had been warned to keep a careful look-out for signal flares to avoid bombing their own side. If they spotted red flares, they were to abort and bomb alternative targets.

Flying in two formations, the bombers approached Rotterdam from the east and south-east, the 54 aircraft in the eastern wave commanded by Oberst Wilhelm Lackner, the 36 aircraft in the south-eastern stream commanded by Oberstleutnant Otto Höhne. Red flares were fired — Höhne spotted them just after his three leading aircraft had dropped their bombs — and he quickly radioed the rest of his formation to turn away. However Lackner's aircraft apparently did not see the signal and released their entire bomb load. In all 57 He 111s dropped about 97 tons; the results were devastating and central Rotterdam was soon a mass of flames.

Having tried to join Winkelman at The Hague and failed, Scharroo now

Shocked by the air raid, and unable to reach Generaal Winkelman in The Hague, Kolonel Scharroo now made up his mind to surrender the city forthwith. *Left: Scharroo marches back across the Willems Bridge after having capitulated. By then Gruppe A had already started its advance to the north bank (right). A group of townspeople stand shocked at the southern end as the panzers roar northwards.*

made up his mind to surrender the city. He crossed Willems Bridge just before the leaders of Gruppe A and at 5.30 p.m. (3.50 p.m.) he met Schmidt at his command post on Prins Hendrikkade. After protesting strongly about the bombing, he signed the surrender. Schmidt told him that he was not responsible for the actions of the air force and expressed his regrets.

Gruppe A had already set out to cross the bridge at 5.25 p.m. (3.45 p.m.), von Choltitz's battalion leading the way. The motor cycle elements of Leibstandarte SS-'Adolf Hitler' which followed rushed northwards to relieve von Sponeck's men at Overschie. There, the airborne troops were by now in a difficult situation for the Dutch had increased the pressure during the afternoon. On the right flank they had forced the Germans to abandon their strongpoints in a factory and a mill from where they had controlled the highway; their left wing had reached Schiebroek

and their right wing was at a bridge on the Schie river. The Dutch troops then received the order to cease fire and the leaders of Leibstandarte SS-'Adolf Hitler' reached them in the evening.

Göring was apparently worried about the airborne troops still beleaguered at Overschie and a second raid on Rotterdam was planned for that evening. Schmidt, however, had sent a message in the afternoon to Luftflotte 2 in which he stated that the northern part of Rotterdam was occupied (which was then only partly true), and asked that no more bombs be dropped. This time the raid was cancelled in time. Utrecht, another major town under threat of bombing, and not wishing to suffer the fate of Rotterdam, had meanwhile surrendered to Generalleutnant Karl von Thiedemann, the commander of the 207. Infanterie-Division.

There is still much debate about the purpose of this air raid on Rotterdam: was it a 'terror' bombing aimed at

Below left: Men from von Choltitz's battalion advance amid the smoke and flames. These men have reached the Bolwerk on the northern side of the river where a ship is burning in the Oudehaven. Below right: War artist Alfred Steffmann gives his own impression of Gruppe A advancing through burning Rotterdam.

crushing what remained of the Dutch fighting spirit, in accordance with Führer Directive No. 11, or was it a close-support operation to enable the ground forces to break through the town? It is certain that the German Command was worried about the fate of its elite paratroopers as the remnants of von Sponeck's northern group was in great danger of being completely annihilated. A breakthrough at Rotterdam was then an urgent tactical necessity, and it is also clear that there were some among the German Command who had few scruples — indicated by the parallel threat to Utrecht. Communications were difficult, the messages between Schmidt and KG54 having to pass through Luftflotte 2 and then Fliegerkorps Putzier. Dutch indecision also indirectly affected the fate of Rotterdam.

What is certain is that the bombing of the city was unnecessary, for the Dutch were already on the point of surrender and this was to tarnish the German victory in the Netherlands. Allied propaganda made great capital of the price paid by Rotterdam in the overall violation of the neutrality of the Netherlands. Tragic as it was, this was greatly inflated by the Dutch to 30,000 dead ('4,000 unoffending men, women and children per minute'), whereas the actual figure was closer to 900.

Later in the afternoon, while Student and von Choltitz were conferring with Kapitein Backer in Kolonel Scharroo's command post at 147 Statenweg (Scharroo, shocked by the destruction of the town, had returned home), there was a sudden crackle of small arms fire just outside the apartment block. A squad of the Leibstandarte SS-'Adolf Hitler' coming along the street had been fired on by a Dutch soldier and immediately returned fire. Student walked to the window to see what all the commotion was about, only to receive a bullet in the head. Ironically the man who had planned and conducted the world's first ever large-scale airborne assault had fallen victim to his own troops. He was however to recover from his serious wound and to carry out another successful assault during the invasion of Crete. After the shooting of Student, a massacre of Dutch prisoners and civilians by the furious Waffen-SS was only avoided by the persuasive intervention of Oberstleutnant von Choltitz.

The rights and wrongs of the bombing, its timing and the recall signal, have kept historians arguing for the past 50 years, fuelled by greatly exaggerated figures of the number of deaths announced at the time. In 1940 the fear of aerial bombing was coloured by the horrific reports from Guernica destroyed in April 1937, and Warsaw razed in September 1939, although the figure of between 600 and 900 killed at Rotterdam pales by later standards. Nevertheless the bombing of the city stands as a milestone for a profoundly different reason — that, coupled with similar threats to other Dutch towns, it immediately led to national surrender — the only instance of the shock effect from aerial bombardent until the collapse of Japan five years later. Yet even there, the huge total of around 140,000 deaths in the Tokyo fire raid in March 1945 alone was not enough; it required the double cataclysmic blow of the atomic bomb to bring about what 97 tons of bombs had achieved in the Netherlands in May 1940. This picture of Generalfeldmarschall Göring touring the city was taken at the northern end of Willems Bridge with the Nationale Levensverzekering Bank building where Kerfin and his men held out just visible in the background.

Looking northwards from the top of Witte Huis — then and now. Notable are the Beurs station and Laurens church.

Left: On Wednesday morning Generaal Winkelman, escorted by Generaal-Majoor Herman van Voorst tot Voorst, arrived at Student's command post which had been set up in a school in Rijsoord. Waiting for them was General von Küchler, commanding the 18. Armee, and six other officers. *Right:* The De Poort institute building at No. 101 Rijksstraatweg today.

THE NETHERLANDS CAPITULATES

Having taken the advice of many commanders, among them Luitenant-Generaal Jacob van Andel, the commander of Vesting Holland, Generaal Winkelman decided to surrender and at 6.30 p.m. (4.50 p.m.) he sent out instructions to that effect to the main body of the forces under his command, ordering the destruction of arms and equipment, especially the guns of the coastal artillery. The forces in Zeeland, however, were excluded from the surrender because of the considerable number of French troops stationed there, and this was communicated to the Dutch commander for this sector, Schout-bij-Nacht (Rear-Admiral) Hendrik van der Stad. The surrender came as something of a shock to most of the Dutch field commanders, for a great many of them had not yet seen any real fighting and those who had did not regard themselves as beaten.

At 11.45 a.m. (10.05 a.m.) the following day the Armistice was signed between General von Küchler and Generaal Winkelman at the Rijsoord school where Student had established his command post. The Netherlands had been knocked out of the war in less than a week, which meant that most of the 18. Armee was now free for action against Belgium and France.

The Dutch government and Royal Family had escaped aboard British destroyers, HMS *Codrington* fetching the Crown Princess and her family from IJmuiden on May 12 and HMS *Hereward* evacuating Queen Wilhelmina, her entourage and the British Minister to the Netherlands, Sir Neville Bland, the following day. Later in the day, members of the Dutch government and Allied legation staffs sailed in HMS *Windsor*. The Queen had not, however, intended to leave her people. When she had boarded HMS *Hereward*, she had asked to be taken to Vlissingen, but the captain received orders while at sea to proceed directly to Harwich. After landing she was eventually persuaded, reluctantly, to travel on to London.

'Yielding to German superior forces, Generaal H. G. Winkelman, Commander-in-Chief of Land and Naval Forces, signed the capitulation agreement in this building on May 15 1940.'

With General Student fighting for his life in hospital, General von Küchler fronted the German delegation and the capitulation was signed at 11.45 a.m. *Left:* A few minutes later the two Dutch generals left the building. *Right:* Thirty-five years on, a monument was erected outside the school to record an inglorious day in Dutch history. A second inscription was added by the famous Dutch historian, Dr Louis de Jong: 'A people which neglects its defence puts its freedom at risk.'

THE END IN ZEELAND

With the capitulation of the Netherlands the 'Breda' variant of the Dyle Plan was rendered null and void for the 7ème Armée which was consequently ordered to pull back. The 1ère D.L.M. was directed to withdraw to Alost, 20 kilometres west of Brussels, and the 9ème and 25ème D.I.M. were assembled west of Antwerp soon to be transferred to the 1ère Armée and ordered south. The forward screen of Groupements de Beauchesne and Lestoquoi was disbanded on May 15, each of the reconnaissance outfits returning to its parent unit.

On May 15, while units of the XXXIX. Armeekorps, elements of the 9. Panzer-Division and Leibstandarte SS-'Adolf Hitler', were parading in Amsterdam after the successful occupation of Vesting Holland, the XXVI. Armeekorps prepared the final assault to capture the Zeeland province. On May 14 a demand for immediate surrender had been sent to Schout-bij-Nacht van der Stad, threatening him with shelling and air attack. The ultimatum stated that the Germans could bring to bear 21 artillery units to smash the Dutch and French positions and that the Luftwaffe would employ six Stuka and five bomber Geschwaders. The province's main defences were now manned by French troops, about one regiment each of the 60ème and 68ème Divisions d'Infanterie which had taken over the sector when the 7ème Armée had pulled back, plus some reconnaissance and artillery units. To enable these troops to be supported from Breskens and Terneuzen, and to secure their withdrawal, French minesweepers were busy trying to remove the mines sown in the Westerschelde by the Luftwaffe and two of these, *AD-16 Duquesne* and *AD-17 Henry Guégan*, were lost to magnetic mines on May 15.

On the morning of May 16, after dive-bombing by Stukas and intense artillery fire, the SS-Standarte 'Deutschland' forced the canal behind which the

The 9. Panzer-Division has reached Willemstad at the entrance of the Hollands Diep, about 15 kilometres west of Moerdijk, where a German photographer caught this officer rather haughtily confronting a Dutch captain on Benedenkade on May 14.

French defenders were established. At midday they were at Kapelle and soon at Goes. One battalion of the 68ème Division d'Infanterie was trapped on Zuid-Beveland and lost but otherwise the French made an orderly withdrawal and tried to build another defensive line on the Arnemuiden isthmus. Général Mary Durand, commander of the 68ème Division d'Infanterie, who was in charge of the advanced elements in Zeeland, showed signs of uneasiness and was dismissed for defeatism. Général Marcel Deslaurens, the commander of the 60ème Division d'Infanterie, arrived on Walcheren late on May 16 to take command of the defence. However there were far too few demolitions to enable them to create a solid defensive line and, as a result, the French decided to abandon the islands.

Heavy fighting continued throughout May 17, the French Navy evacuating as many of the troops as they could from Vlissingen. The last to leave were taken off at about 10.15 p.m. but Général Deslaurens was not among them,

Two days later, a Dutch policeman is symbolically pictured with the ubiquitous bicycle on the seafront at Scheveningen just north of The Hague. Behind stands a 9. Panzer-Division radio car (SdKfz 263).

With the collapse of the Netherlands, Hitler ordered an immediate victory parade in Amsterdam which took place on May 15 with Generalleutnant Schmidt taking the salute. Troops of the

9. Panzer-Division and Leibstandarte SS-'Adolf Hitler' took part — this SdKfz 231 armoured car of 'Hitler's Own' being pictured before the Royal Palace in the Dam square.

having been killed on Walcheren earlier that day while leading the rearguard protecting the withdrawal. Elements trapped near Veere on the northern coast of the island held out until mid-morning the following day before surrendering.

The 18. Armee lost no time in re-organising its forces for the attack on the fortified line defending Antwerp and the city fell on May 18. Fighting then ceased in that corner of the battlefield but further to the west the French 60ème and 68ème Divisions d'Infanterie, and the Belgian 2ème Division de Cavalerie, were to hold this part of the Netherlands along the southern coast of the Westerschelde until May 25.

The 7ème Armée had played its part in the Allied plan. It had moved rapidly into Belgium and the Netherlands to firm up the Belgian left and lend a hand to the Dutch troops at the mouth of the Scheldt. However, it could not have affected the outcome: the defeat of the Netherlands.

Nothing would better illustrate how the Allies had been outguessed than the deployment of the 7ème Armee in the Dyle Plan. Sent so far north on the assumption that the Schwerpunkt of the German offensive would be between

Antwerp and Namur, it was fighting a losing battle remote from the main arena when the full force of the offensive erupted far to the south. One of the best of the French armies, it had been sent on a fruitless venture, and its losses were not only those sustained in action but in the time lost dashing almost 250 kilometres through Belgium to the Netherlands and back. If it had been available to be rushed to where it was needed, in the Sedan sector, the entire balance of forces in the fight to stem the breakthrough would have been altered.

The parade was watched by a considerable crowd and German photographers were quick to capture on film any sign of enthusiasm being shown for the victorious SS warriors. This shot was taken on Rokin with Dam square in the background.

LOSSES

Up to May 18 the Dutch had lost 2,157 men killed, 1,957 from the Army, 75 from the Air Force and 125 of the Navy. Another 2,700 had surrendered. The total civilian death toll was 2,559.

For the Germans, the airborne operation had proved to be far more difficult than anticipated and the losses were heavy, particularly for the northern group where the engagement turned out to be a complete disaster. When the main pocket at Overschie was relieved on the evening of May 14 by the forward troops from the XXXIX. Armeekorps, the northern group was down to about 1,100 fighting men. About 500 were still fighting at Valkenburg and Wassenaar, 100 or so were playing cat and mouse in the Staalduinse Wood near the Hook of Holland and about 500 were at Overschie. Of the 3,800 men of the northern group airlifted into the Netherlands, some 1,100 had been killed or wounded and 1,600 were prisoners. Of the latter, 400 were liberated on May 15, but for the

On May 30 the Germans organised a joint burial ceremony at Crooswijk, Rotterdam, where, as well as their own dead, 115 Dutch soldiers were laid to rest. Alongside lay a mass grave for more than 550 of the civilians who had lost their lives in the air raid.

No German graves remain in Crooswijk today, all having since been moved to IJsselsteyn, between Helmond and Venlo.

1,200 others the war was already over as they had all been transported to Britain, 900 on May 13 in the SS *Phrontis* and 300 on May 14 in the SS *Texelstroom*.

Although a costly failure it was, nevertheless, a victory of sorts as von Sponeck's few thousand odd men had tied down the bulk of the Dutch reserves — the Ie Legerkorps with its two divisions — at a critical period of the battle for the Netherlands.

The southern group, which had benefited by the failure of the northern group and received more airborne troops than planned — around 7,100 men in all — had suffered some 1,200 casualties of whom about 250 were dead.

Of the 1,000 aircraft engaged by the Luftwaffe in the campaign, around 330 aircraft were lost, two thirds of them to the potent Dutch anti-aircraft defences. The slow and low-flying transport wings had paid the heaviest price and, of the 430 Ju 52s engaged, about 220 had been lost in the Netherlands — more than 50

Among the 31,000 dead there from the Second World War, Leutnant Heinrich Schwiebert of Infanterie-Regiment 16, mortally wounded in Rotterdam (see page 129).

percent of their strength. Of these 220, K.G.z.b.V. 1 had lost 63, its II. Gruppe having suffered the least with the loss of only 8 aircraft, while each of the other three groups had lost about 18 aircraft. K.G.z.b.V. 2 had suffered heavier losses in the Hague sector, losing 157 aircraft; K.Gr.z.b.V. 172 lost 12 aircraft; K.Gr.z.b.V. 9, 39 aircraft; with K.Gr.z.b.V. 11 and K.Gr.z.b.V. 12 about 50 aircraft each, virtually wiping them out. As a result, the remnants of these last two groups had to be disbanded.

However, as many of the aircraft were subsequently recovered — 53 proving to be repairable while 47 others were dismantled for spare parts — only 167 Ju 52s were recorded as being totally lost in the Netherlands. Had the Dutch been wise enough to destroy the aircraft they had taken when they had recaptured the airfields at Ockenburg and Valkenburg, this figure could have been increased by at least 50, but all they removed were the batteries!

The 6. Armee in Belgium: the feint

A PzKpfw III of Pz.Rgt. 36 (4. Panzer-Division) pushing into the Netherlands on the morning of May 10.

The 6. Armee attack, intended to deceive the Allies for as long as possible into believing that this was where the main blow was being struck, depended for its initial success on rapid progress across the 'Maastricht appendix', the narrow strip of the Netherlands dangling between Germany and Belgium. Beyond lay the gently rolling and relatively open terrain of the Gembloux gap, between Wavre and Namur; ideal country for the panzer divisions.

As the final minutes to zero hour slipped by, special operations were already underway to help the attack break through the Belgian positions along the line of the Albert Canal. The ruse to gain control of the vital Meuse bridges in Maastricht was in motion with men of the Infanterie-Bataillon z.b.V. 100 riding off on bicycles dressed in the uniform of Dutch policemen, as was the gliderborne operation mounted by Sturmabteilung Koch to seize the equally vital bridges on the canal just west of the town and cripple the formidable obstacle of Fort Eben-Emael.

To secure the crossings, 4. Panzer-Division was to follow up closely in support of these operations. On the second day of the attack, the XVI. Armeekorps of General der Kavallerie Erich Hoepner was to insert the 3. Panzer-Division on the right of the 4. Panzer-Division and take charge of their armoured thrust westwards.

Stationed in this strip of the Netherlands were only weak forces as the Dutch well knew that their southern province was undefendable and had therefore made no plans to defend it.

Kolonel A. Govers, the Dutch territorial commander for the Zuid-Limburg sector, whose command post was at Maastricht, had only five battalions of border troops at his disposal, armed with a total of seven anti-tank guns and four anti-tank rifles.

Across in Belgium, this sector of the Albert Canal came under the Belgian Ier Corps d'Armée with the 4ème and 7ème Divisions d'Infanterie; on its left was the 1ère Division d'Infanterie and on its right, to the northeast of Liège, was the 3ème Division d'Infanterie. These Belgian units were to be supported by French forces racing into Belgium as per the Dyle Plan as soon as the Germans attacked — in this case, the Corps de Cavalerie of the 1ère Armée, its advance elements arriving to screen the canal in the Belgian Ier and IIIème Corps d'Armée sectors.

Valkenburg lies in the centre of the sliver of Dutch territory which projects southwards below Roermond, forming a wedge between Belgium and Germany. At its widest part the 'appendix' is only 30 kilometres from east to west and no barrier to the German assault. Valkenburg lay on what was designated 'Strasse Gelb' — Yellow Route — with the Meuse at Maastricht just 10 kilometres to the west.

The leaders of 4. Panzer-Division reached Maastricht by about 6.00 a.m., only to see the bridges flying into the air right under their noses. While engineers hastily assembled the first of the pontoon barges to ferry the troops across, the rest of the division piled up in the city, its vehicles packing the streets. This is Hoogbrugstraat in 1940 *(left)* and 1986 *(right)*.

The Infanterie-Bataillon z.b.V. 100, which had the job of taking the Maastricht bridges intact for the leaders of the XVI. Armeekorps, was not a Brandenburg unit as it came from the Abwehrstelle Breslau, but it was an Abwehr unit and it fought on the same lines and with the same weapons. The battalion's 'Dutch policemen' had started at 3.20 a.m. but they had ridden only ten kilometres towards Maastricht when they were detected by Dutch troops who were probably on their guard as a result of the unusual amount of activity in the air with the anti-aircraft batteries at Maastricht firing at the Sturmabteilung Koch gliders. In the shooting that broke out their leader was killed. The motor cycle detachment of Infanterie-Bataillon z.b.V. 100 immediately took over the job, the men in German uniform this time, with elements of Aufkl.Abt. 7 of the 4. Panzer-Division. Surprise was now lost and the advanced elements arrived at Maastricht at about 6.00 a.m. only to see the bridges blown up as they approached. Heeresgruppe B regretfully reported that 'the Maastricht bridges had flown into the air just under the nose of the 4. Panzer-Division'.

At 8.30 a.m. the engineers of the 4. Panzer-Division started to ferry men and equipment across the river while the construction of a bridge proceeded at once, six bridging columns being assigned to the task. The first pontoon, an 8-tonner, operated as a ferry from midday and two 4-tonners followed within an hour. The commander of the 4. Panzer-Division, Generalmajor

Further along Hoogbrugstraat, a PzKpfw II — panzer '142' of the 1. Kompanie of Pz.Rgt. 36, 4. Panzer-Division — parks outside the local grocer's shop.

Left: The hieroglyphics on the turret of this PzKpfw III waiting on the opposite side of the street clearly show the addition of the small yet significant full stop after the number, denoting it as a tank of Pz.Rgt. 36 as opposed to Pz.Rgt. 35, the other tank regiment of 4. Panzer-Division. The number '156' identifies it as Tank No. 6 of the 5th Platoon (5. Zug) of the 1st Company (1. Kompanie). *Right:* All that part of Maastricht east of the Meuse was spared the ravages of war.

While men and light equipment like motor cycle combinations were shipped across the Meuse in rubber boats, the first available pontoons were utilised as barges to ferry heavier equipment, like this SdKfz 10. This picture was taken on the eastern bank of the river a few hundred metres upstream from the destroyed road bridge in Maastricht.

Johann Stever, organised two battle groups, to link up with the paratroops holding the bridges at Vroenhoven and Veldwezelt while Pi.Btl. 51 was sent towards Kanne. Contact was soon established with the men of Sturmabteilung Koch at the bridges over the Albert Canal and, in spite of the destruction of the bridges at Maastricht and Kanne, the day ended successfully. Earlier that morning, the commander of Heeresgruppe B, Generaloberst Fedor von Bock, had come to Maastricht to discuss the situation with the various field commanders.

SATURDAY, MAY 11

The destruction of the Meuse bridges at Maastricht had provided a day's respite for the Belgian Ier Corps d'Armée, but at 3.30 a.m. on May 11 the first of 4. Panzer-Division's panzers crossed the Meuse on pontoons and an hour later the first bridge, a 16-tonner, was ready. The XVI. Armeekorps took over 4. Panzer-Division at midday, though General Hoepner had to wait for 3. Panzer-Division which could only follow on behind, its first panzers starting to cross at 5.30 a.m.

On May 11 the Belgian Air Force sent nine of its sixteen bombers to attack the three vital bridges on the Albert Canal at Briedgen, Veldwezelt

On Saturday (May 11), Blenheims of No. 110 Squadron attacked the crossing sites at Maastricht and this salvo is pictured exploding in the Meuse at the same spot where the barges and rubber boats were photographed above. In the bottom left of the picture, below the destroyed railway bridge, the first 16-tonne pontoon bridge, just completed, can be seen.

Left: Meanwhile, in Maastricht itself, engineers had lashed rubber boats together to support a plank footbridge across the destroyed span of the road bridge. The access down the broken span was somewhat steep and the men had to use ladders or ropes to avoid slipping into the water. Right: The bridge was reconstructed and opened in December 1947.

Three bridges remained intact over the Albert Canal at Maastricht: the one to the north-west at Briedgen; the west at Veldwezelt, and the south-west at Vroenhoven. *Left:* On May 11, nine Battles of the Belgian 5ème Escadrille (3ème Régiment d'Aéronautique) were detailed for the attack, three aircraft per bridge. Battles numbers 58, 60 and 73 went for that at Veldwezelt; 61, 64 and 70 attacked Vroenhoven, while 62, 68 and 71 struck at Briedgen. Six aircraft failed to return with five men killed including Capitaine André Glorie *(right),* the second-in-command of the squadron.

and Vroenhoven. Nine Battles of 5/III (5ème Escadrille, IIIème Groupe) 3ème Régiment d'Aéronautique, took off at 5.30 a.m. from Aalter, about 20 kilometres west of Gent, the first flight of three aircraft aiming at Veldwezelt, the second at Vroenhoven and the third at Briedgen. This was a suicidal and useless mission as the Battles were far too slow and fragile for such an attack and although they each carried 400kg of bombs, these were 50kg bombs which were unable to do more than slightly damage the concrete structure of the bridges. Six of the aircraft attacked the bridges through an inferno of flak but in most cases, because of a malfunction of the bomb release, the bombs did not fall when the pilot pushed the button.

At Vroenhoven two pilots — Capitaine André Glorie and Adjudant Frans Delvigne — decided to make a second run at the bridge and both aircraft were shot down. After the attack at Briedgen, the pilot of Battle 68, Adjudant Gustave Wieseler, did not notice that his bombs were still aboard and crash-landed his badly damaged aircraft onto his eight bombs. In this instance, the crew was lucky that the safety on the bombs was better than the launching gear! Two aircraft were lost from each

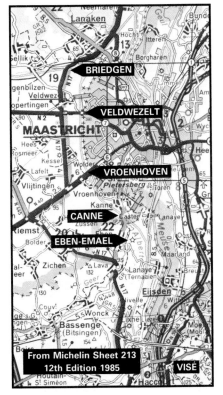

From Michelin Sheet 213
12th Edition 1985

of the three flights, five men had been killed and five others wounded yet the three bridges were still undamaged.

The Belgians had also asked for the assistance of the French and British air forces in the Maastricht area and the RAF committed two squadrons of Blenheims there in the afternoon. Twenty-three Blenheims delivered their bombs, No. 110 Squadron concentrating on the bridges at Maastricht and No. 21 Squadron on German columns between Maastricht and Tongeren; two of the Blenheims which attacked at Maastricht were shot down. In accordance with the timing arranged with the RAF French bombers arrived at about 6.30 p.m. Thirteen LeO 45s of the French 12ème Escadre, attacked the pontoon bridge at Maastricht but were greeted by an inferno of light flak: three aircraft were shot down and the others returned with so many shell holes that only one of them was airworthy the next day.

In spite of the relatively slow start of the German attack, the Belgian plan to fight a delaying action on the line of the Albert Canal had been totally wrecked after the loss of the bridges at Vroenhoven and Veldwezelt and the capture of Fort Eben-Emael, which had been intended to cover them. Pressed by the

Left: The following day it was the turn of the British. On Sunday six Battles (one aborted before take-off) of No. 12 Squadron, led by Flying Officer Donald Garland, left, with his observer, Sergeant Thomas Gray, were sent in to bomb Veldwezelt and Vroenhoven. Garland led the attack shortly after 9.00 a.m. on Sunday morning, but out of the five aircraft, only one returned, badly damaged. Flying Officer Garland and Sergeant Gray were both killed, each being awarded the Victoria Cross. *Right:* One of the Battles lost that day was P2332 flown by Flying Officer H. M. Thomas with Sergeants D. T. Carey and T. S. Campion.

157

The largest tank battle of the campaign in the West was fought in the Gembloux gap (between Brussels and Namur) by the XVI. Armeekorps and French Corps de Cavalerie, depicted here by a PzKpfw IV of the 4. Panzer-Division *(above)* and Hotchkiss H-39s of the 3ème D.L.M. The forces were unevenly matched yet the French were still a formidable force.

advanced elements of the 4. Panzer-Division, the Belgian 7ème Division d'Infanterie went to pieces in the morning and the panzers were soon at Grandville, on the main road between Saint-Trond and Liège. The Belgian Command had hoped that the Albert Canal could be held for five or six days, but was forced to accept the idea that the line had been broken in less that 48 hours and by midday they decided for a general withdrawal to the Dyle during the coming night. This was done but the 7ème Division d'Infanterie had been badly shaken, 7,307 of its men (includ-

ing 32 officers) were claimed as having been captured by the 4. Panzer-Division. The 3. Panzer-Division had started to cross the Meuse and assembled on the right flank of the corps in the afternoon; in the evening a second bridge was completed at Maastricht.

The Corps de Cavalerie of Général René Prioux had made such good time, only for the 2ème D.L.M. and 3ème D.L.M. to arrive in the Liège area just as the foremost Belgian units were falling back in confusion. For once, Allied troops advancing according to schedule arrived at the right place at the

right time and were strong enough to stop the panzers: the scene was set for the biggest tank battle of the entire campaign, and the only encounter in which the panzers did not have an overwhelming advantage. Although such comparisons are difficult, the French Corps de Cavalerie was not the equal of the German XVI. Armeekorps, which had almost twice the armour and men, but it was strong enough to exchange shot for shot with the panzers for a time; to encounter this level of opposition was a unique experience for the panzers in 1940.

Men, horses and artillery of the 253. Infanterie-Division of the XXVII. Armeekorps cross the Meuse at Visé on May 12 almost as if they are on a training exercise — the tranquility of the scene in 1940 being reflected in today's comparison *below*.

SUNDAY, MAY 12

The Belgians requested again and again urgent air support in the Maastricht area, particularly against the Albert Canal bridges west of the town. The first attack of the day was delivered by nine Blenheims of No. 139 Squadron soon after dawn, to columns on the Maastricht-Tongeren road but the German fighter cover accounted for seven of them. Sometime later six Battles of No. 12 Squadron were sent to bomb the Albert Canal bridges, each bridge at Vroenhoven and Veldwezelt to be attacked by a section of three Battles. At the last minute, the release on the bomb rack of one of the aircraft failed to function and only five aircraft actually took off. Manned by volunteer crews, the five attacked the bridges through withering flak and small arms fire at about 9.15 a.m. Only one aircraft

The second water obstacle — the Albert Canal — lay just to the west of the town where the road bridge now lay in pieces, having been successfully demolished by Belgian engineers before the Germans reached it.

— badly damaged — returned but the bridges were unharmed except for slight damage at Velwezelt. This action resulted in the posthumous award of the Victoria Cross to Flying Officer D.E. Garland leading the attack and his observer, Sergeant T. Gray: the first RAF VCs of the war.

The operation had been timed to coincide with an attack by Blenheims of No. 15 Squadron and No. 107 Squadron at crossings and columns in Maastricht. This attack was delivered between 9.20 and 9.30 a.m., only 15 out of 24 aircraft returning. French aircraft then took over, 10 LeO 45s from the 12ème Escadre and 20 Bréguet 693s from the 54ème Escadre, bombing and strafing the roads west of Maastricht. Eight of the aircraft committed did not return.

By no means insignificant, this Allied air activity was a thorn in the side of the advance elements of the XVI. Armeekorps and the corps war diary recorded how the columns were 'attacked by enemy bombers, causing considerable delays.' Because of these attacks, but mainly because the crossing of the river was still a bottleneck at Maastricht, the supply situation west of the Meuse for the advance elements was very difficult. The leaders of 4. Panzer-Division had to be re-supplied by air and about 20,000 litres of fuel were air-dropped to them near Lens-Saint-Remy on the morning of May 12.

Although the withdrawing Belgians had been engaged in some fierce rearguard fighting, the bulk of their Army was soon out of danger as the Corps de Cavalerie was about to bear the main

'Although this road is still in the line of fire, the detachment is having a rest while waiting for its replacement.' So runs the original caption to this picture, purported to have been taken in 'Grehen' (sic) on May 13. It is one picture in the series which follows but no such village exists in Belgium. It was only after we widened the search to consider alternative possibilities, and looked in and around *Crehen* which is located one kilometre south-west of Hannut, that we discovered they had been taken in Merdorp, four kilometres further to the west.

burden of the German attack which had veered south-west instead of northwest. Instead of trying to break through the northern end of the Dyle Line held by the BEF and the Belgian Army, the XVI. Armeekorps was aiming — as anticipated by those who had drawn the Dyle Plan — at the Gembloux gap.

The Corps de Cavalerie's advanced

elements, all in contact with the enemy, withdrew and that afternoon all these were safely behind a line Tirlemont-Huy with 3ème D.L.M. between Tirlemont and Hannut and the 2ème D.L.M. between Hannut and Huy. Here, across a broadly undulating landscape, with only scattered woods and villages well apart, armour was in its element.

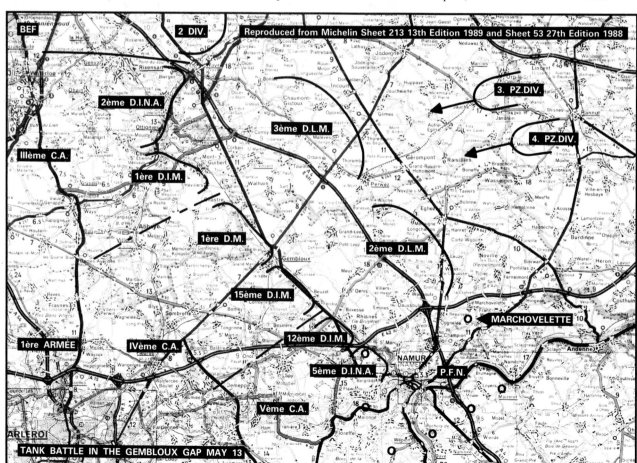

Schtz.Rgt. 33 reached Merdrop on Monday afternoon (the 13th) where the leaders of 4. Panzer-Division were embroiled with the 2ème D.L.M. Here reinforcements from the 3. Bataillon arrive aboard Krupp-Protze transport around 4.30 p.m.

Apart from the numerous conflicts between opposing reconnaissance units that had taken place since the previous day, the first engagement between the Corps de Cavalerie and the 4. Panzer-Division occurred at 8.00 a.m. on May 12 near Avesnes.

In the afternoon the Stukas came over to soften up the French positions and the 4. Panzer-Division, which had by now reached Waremme, started to seek out weak points in the French line. Lieutenant Robert Le Bel, from the 11ème R.D.P. of the 3ème D.L.M., described the sight from the turret of his Hotchkiss H-39 standing on the outskirts of Jandrain.

'I backed my tank and stopped under an apple tree. There I sat on the open turret door and observed through my field glasses the plain where I had wandered in a motor cycle only three hours ago. I saw an extraordinary show which was played out about three kilometres away: a panzer division shaping itself for battle. The massive gathering of this armoured armada was an unforgettable sight, the more so that it appeared even more terrifying through the glasses. How many were they? It was not possible to tell from so far way but they were numerous and their guns seemed to be potent.

'Some men, probably officers, walked to and fro gesticulating in front of the tanks. They were probably giving last minute orders to the tank commanders, the head and shoulders of whom I could see between the open two parts of the turret hatches. Suddenly, as if swept away by a magic stick, they all disappeared. No doubt the H-Hour was approaching. A dust cloud soon appeared on the skyline, disclosing the enemy move. I got down into the tank, closed the hatch and peered through the episcopes'.

The armour was soon in contact and the battle raged throughout the afternoon, particularly around Crehen and Thisnes where two squadrons of Hotchkiss H-39s of the 2ème Cuirassiers were heavily engaged before being ordered to withdraw in late evening. Adjudant Georges Hillion, of the 4ème Escadron of the 2ème Cuirassiers, later told his story of the battle:

'It was about 8.10 p.m. when I was excited to see two enemy tanks coming out of the dead ground and approaching the eastern extremity of Crehen, advancing slowly towards my position. It seemed they had not seen me; I took my time to aim, not wishing to miss such a beautiful target: my first target! I fired and saw the direct hit. The panzer

stopped and I saw a brilliant light and smoke pouring out of the tank. I turned and aimed at the second. The first shot seemed to ricochet on the turret. I fired a second shot slightly lower; this hit just under the turret and the panzer stopped.

'Until now nothing had hit my tank except perhaps some machine gun fire which might explain some suspicious knocking on the tank. Through the episcope on the left side of the turret I could see some infantrymen, ten or so, and four other panzers appearing on the right of those two I had just disabled. I turned to them but the branches of the tree behind which I was hiding prevented me from aiming accurately. We were hidden by the side of a track along which I ordered my driver, Corporal Phiz, to advance. While our tank broke through the hedge lining the track, I fired my machine gun at the group of infantry I had just seen, using up half my magazine in one long burst. Either they were hit or they took to the ground; in any case I could not see them any more.

'The enemy response hit us as soon as we were on the track. We received the first strike on the rear of the tank which immediately stopped. My driver tried to restart the engine but failed. We were

Left: This PzKpfw II of Pz.Rgt. 35 has been brought up to help overcome the resistance still being offered by groups of French soldiers in the village. Right: In spite of its brief brush with war, Merdrop remains today much as it was in 1940.

161

'Medical personnel approached while the street was still under fire.' The troopers are armed with the bolt action Mauser

Gew. 98, the standard German infantry rifle of 7.9mm calibre first introduced in 1898 but improved after World War I.

immobilised in the open some 300 metres in front of the enemy. A shell burst through the turret, I was wounded in the face and left arm; blood covered my face and I could not see any more from my left eye. I aimed my machine gun at the enemy who seemed to be advancing quickly, now only about 200 metres away, but when I was about to press the trigger a powerful shock struck just behind me. I felt a violent pain in the back and a burning sensation on the whole left side of my face. Dense smoke filled the tank. I fired but I was unable to see if I hit anything. I was suffocating. I leaned down to take off my scarf to try to wrap it around my face and in front of my mouth but another violent hit struck the turret as I took my shoulder from the butt of the machine gun. The main gun jerked violently to the left. I straightened up and from the breech which had remained open since our last shot I could see that the end of the barrel of my 47mm gun was broken. The aiming device was destroyed too, and only the machine gun appeared to be in good order.

'I decided to continue the fight from outside and started to remove the machine gun. I told Phiz to bring the

magazines and try to reach the tree behind which we had been hiding a few minutes ago, while I carried the machine gun. Two more shells shook the tank violently. The air inside was now unbreathable, I felt I was suffocating, my left eye was completely closed and I could feel my strength failing. With difficulty I got out of the turret, carrying the machine gun, when another terrific shock suddenly blew off my helmet and I fell down the side of the tank. I gathered what strength remained in me to crawl to the tree and then fainted. I do not know how long I was unconscious but as I came to felt an awful pain in my legs. I opened my right eye and saw a tank rolling over both my legs, the edge of the track just under my knees. The tank commander was standing in his turret, looking in the direction of the positions held by the first platoon. Fearing he might fire a mercy shot, I strove to keep quiet . . . The panzer advanced further, stopping at the hedgerow. Shells suddenly rained down on the ploughed field in front of me and clods of earth thrown up only a few metres away fell back on me, partially covering me. I got two splinters in my left hand . . . I was exhausted and fainted again.

'It was dark when I came to at last. I called for Phiz but got no answer. I tried to search for him but my physical state was such that I could not move a long way. My right leg was crushed and did not obey me any more but the left one was responding, albeit very painfully. I succeeded in rolling on my belly and crawling but my search for Phiz was in vain and I crawled along the track in the direction of the village. After 50 metres or so two Germans armed with sub-machine guns came up from behind the hegerow and asked me if I was French or British. They examined me, spoke together in German, and decided to carry me. Because of the pain in my legs I asked them to drag me, which they did up to a house. It was then about 11.30 p.m. or so.'

Some of the Hotchkiss tanks did come back from their advanced positions but others found themselves isolated and four Somua S-35s were also lost when the 1er Escadron launched a counter-attack to disengage those trapped. The losses had been heavy for the 2ème Cuirassiers, 11 Hotchkiss H-39s being lost at Crehen and 13 at Thisnes, and the commander of the 3ème Escadron, Capitaine Bernard Sainte Marie Perrin, had also been killed in Crehen.

To deal with the Somua S-35s of the 2ème D.L.M., a Pak 35/36 has been set up on the Rue de Straux although this German

anti-tank gun would have been unable to pierce the frontal armour of the French tanks.

Further to the south, the panzers had arrived at the Meuse and the 1ère Armée was ordered to withdraw behind the canal at Charleroi. This 155mm C Modèle 1917 field gun was pictured pulling back near Nivelles on the morning of May 16.

Pz.Rgt. 35, later described enthusiastically for the *Berliner Illustrirte Zeitung* how the Stukas 'buzzed around the enemy like hornets, searching out their targets and looking for where they could unload their lethal cargoes. The Stukas rarely missed their targets and the bombs fell where they were intended'.

The bombardment dragged on for more than an hour and the panzers launched their attack. They advanced as far as the outskirts of Merdrop, closely followed by infantry, but French tanks held the village and halted them there. In the resulting duel neither gained the upper hand and eventually the Germans decided to bypass the village, whereupon the French sallied out of Merdrop to attack the infantry which followed.

All this had forced both sides into close contact and von Jungenfeld described how the intensity of the fighting made it seem like being 'in a witch's cauldron' and revealed that the panzers had 'to work hard to get the better of' the French tanks. The cauldron seethed

Some panzers then tried to breakthrough near Crehen but the French tanks sharply drove them off and another breakthrough was stopped near Thisnes in the late afternoon.

By the end of the day, both sides had suffered sizeable losses and, inconclusive as the fighting had been, the panzers had gained ground and the two villages, as well as Hannut, were in German hands by evening. Meanwhile the 3. Panzer-Division had advanced beside the 4. Panzer-Division and was ready to make its weight felt on the morrow.

Since May 10 it had been clearly desirable that the operation of the Belgian Army, the BEF and the French 1ère Armée and 9ème Armée should be co-ordinated and the matter had been discussed at a meeting at Château Casteau, near Mons, on the afternoon of May 12. King Leopold with Général van Overstraeten, Lieutenant-General H. R. Pownall, Gort's Chief-of-Staff, was there with Brigadier J. G. des R. Swayne, the French being represented by Général Georges, Général Billotte and M. Daladier. All agreed that Général Billotte, the commander of Groupe d'Armées No. 1, should 'co-ordinate the operation of the Allied forces on Belgian territory'. This was not a completely satisfactory decision as Général Billotte was only to co-ordinate, not to command, and his responsibilities, from the Netherlands to Longuyon, were unreasonably great.

MONDAY, MAY 13

The night passed uneasily for the French as it was clear that the Germans were going to make a decisive effort the next day. The Germans remained relatively quiet during the morning but the Stukas arrived suddenly at 11.30 a.m., their attacks timed to coincide with a sudden artillery barrage.

Failing to mention the fact that the Luftwaffe had the skies to themselves, Hauptmann Ernst von Jungenfeld, commanding the second battalion of

Moving southwards, a Somua S-35 and two Hotchkiss H-39s of the 3ème D.L.M. enter Seneffe, 10 kilometres south of Nivelles, that Thursday morning. From here the canal is just a few kilometres further west.

all day and by evening the advance elements of the 4. Panzer-Division were at Ramillies, ten kilometres west of Hannut. The advance had been costly but the 2ème Cuirassiers had suffered heavily, losing 11 S-35s and 4 H-39s. But for one tank which had charged from the village and broken through the German ring, crushing men, anti-guns and machine gun nests under its tracks, the whole of the first platoon of the 1er Escadron had been destroyed at Merdrop and the platoon commander, Sous-Lieutenant Louis Jacquenot de Presles, had been killed.

To the north, the 3. Panzer-Division had forced the Gette river near Orp-le-Petit after fierce house-to-house fighting and had reached Jauche. The tanks of the 1er Cuirassiers fought back to comply with the regimental orders 'to hold without thought of withdrawal' and when the order arrived at last in the afternoon, the positions had been infiltrated, most of the tanks encircled, and the platoons isolated. The withdrawal was hectic but thanks to the efforts of some — such as three S-35s of the third platoon of the 2ème Escadron under the command of Sous-Lieutenant Jean-Paul Pasteur that advanced into Jandrenouille but never came back — most of the tanks managed to force their way out. The day had been costly anyway for the 1er Cuirassiers which had lost 25 tanks. In a few days Oberleutnant Bruno Nolde, the commander of 8. Kompanie of Pz.Rgt. 6, was to have the honour of being singled out in the Army Report of May 20 for 'his extraordinary coolness during the tank battles in recent days'.

A Hotchkiss followed by a Lattil personnel carrier cross the town as part of the 3ème D.L.M. convoy. This sequence of the 3ème D.L.M. pushing through Seneffe was shown on French newsreels during the week of May 29.

With the Tirlemont-Huy line broken, Général Prioux ordered his corps to withdraw to a new position about eight kilometres east of the main Wavre-Namur line on which the bulk of the 1ère Armée infantry was now assembled. There, the Corps de Cavalerie could take advantage of a line of Belgian anti-tank obstacles, although of doubtful value, being badly laid and with numerous gaps. The withdrawal was carried out with some difficulty during the night, the 3ème D.L.M. thereafter taking up positions between Beauvechain and Perwez, and the 2ème D.L.M. between Perwez and Marchovelette.

While tank fought tank in the clash to the east between the Corps de Cavalerie and the XVI. Armeekorps, the 1ère Armée had brought its six infantry divisions into position behind the railway line which represented the Wavre-Namur line. The IIIème Corps d'Armée

Ancient and modern. The 190 brake horsepower of a 3ème D.L.M. Somua contrasts with the deux chevaux of a mounted cavalry patrol turning west onto the road to Familleureux.

with two divisions was in the north, with the British I Corps at Wavre down to Chastre. The IVème Corps d'Armée, with two divisions, was in the centre between Ernage and Beuzet, while the Vème Corps d'Armée, with two divisions, was in the south, from Beuzet to the Meuse area, from where it was to link up with the Belgian Position Fortifiée de Namur and the northern corps of the 9ème Armée just south of the town. May 13 was spent in feverish activity, bringing the units forward and organising the defence under the constant threat of German aircraft.

TUESDAY, MAY 14

At 5.00 a.m. on May 14, the German artillery started to plaster the French positions while their engineers began to advance to clear paths through the steel anti-tank obstacles, blasting them to pieces one after another. After four hours of shelling, the panzers rolled through the breached line and soon reached Baudeset and Sauveniere, about five kilometres to its rear, making contact by midday with the French main line of defence. French tanks of the 3ème D.L.M. counter-attacked and stopped the panzers but the Corps de Cavalerie had now spent its strength, having lost half of its Hotchkiss and one-third of its Somuas. It was then ordered to pull back behind the infantry for reorganisation and the two D.L.M.s withdrew with the panzers on their heels. A confused situation occurred at about 10.00 a.m. near Ernage when some panzers followed tanks of the 2ème D.L.M. and found themselves inside the positions held by the IVème Corps d'Armée. Anti-tank guns of the 1ère Division Marocaine destroyed them and a swift counter-attack backed by tanks from the 35ème B.C.C. re-established the situation. French artillery opened up on the panzers, halting the assault, and at about 5.00 p.m. the Corps de Cavalerie was safely behind the main line of the 1ère Armée.

The great tank battle in the Gembloux gap was over but the panzers had still not broken through. They were now facing French infantry solidly established in their positions and the 1ère Armée was able to give a demonstration of what well-trained units of the French Army could do — standing their ground and holding back the panzers. It is worth noting that on this part of the battlefield the theory behind the Dyle Plan had worked in practice: the French leading elements had delayed the Germans long enough to enable the infantry to take up their positions on the main line of defence and the infantry then proved to be strong enough to hold the panzers. It was also ironic that it was precisely here that the German planners had hoped to see the best of the French troops engaged!

Having kept up the pressure, for no substantial gains, the XVI. Armeekorps called a halt at 7.50 p.m. preparatory to resuming the attack at 9.00 a.m. the following day with full artillery support.

The RAF sent two more raids to the Meuse bridges, six Whitleys from No. 58 Squadron attacking during the night of May 13 at Maastricht and Maaseik and six Wellingtons from No. 99 Squadron bombing Maastricht on May 14.

WEDNESDAY, MAY 15

But for the Gembloux gap where the battle was as exhausting for the Germans as well as the French, things were relatively quiet north of Namur. The Germans had made all their efforts against the 1ère Armée but had done nothing forceful either against the BEF or the Belgian Army. Some moves were made in front of the BEF near Louvain on May 14 and were renewed the next day, but with no great success. Another effort was made near Wavre on May 15, and was equally unsuccesful. On the Belgian front the Germans merely put out feelers.

In the Gembloux gap the battle resumed as planned early next morning when the German artillery started to hammer the French positions following a strict fire plan. At 8.00 a.m. the Stukas arrived and struck at the French line for half an hour. The panzers then attacked on a narrow front between Gembloux and Perbaix, the 3. Panzer-Division attacking north of Ernage, the 4. Panzer-Division south of the town. Backed by the panzers, the German infantry managed to obtain local successes in breaking through the solid French positions, particularly at Ernage and just to the north of Gembloux where the line held by the 2ème R.T.M. was breached. Otherwise the French units in the gap held their ground, fighting back in isolated groups, limiting the German advance and inflicting casualties. Consequently, at about midday, General

Lying not far from Mons, this area was no stranger to war for it was near here that the 'Old Contemptibles' of the British Expeditionary Force first clashed with the First German Army on August 22, 1914. Now, a quarter of a century later, their sons were to meet again on the same field of battle, yet the architecture appears timeless. Seneffe in 1989.

Erich Hoepner ordered that the panzers be withdrawn to their start line. However, the order was misunderstood and also taken to refer to the infantry with the result that part of the Schtz.Rgt. 12 also withdrew, soon to be followed by most of the infantry of the 4. Panzer-Division. The division's commander, Generalmajor Johann Stever, then came forward to clarify the situation only to be wounded by a shellburst. Things were now very confused and at around 2.30 p.m. the corps suspended further operations until the next morning when the attack resumed with the support of the 35. Infanterie-Division and the 20. Infanterie-Division (mot) which had crossed the Meuse and assembled just behind the panzer divisions. Taking advantage of the German confusion, at about 5.00 p.m. the IVème Corps d'Armée launched a battalion of the 2ème R.T.M. backed by tanks of the 35ème B.C.C. in a determined counter-attack which partially restored the line.

Nevertheless it was all in vain. To the south, the situation of the 9ème Armée had now become very precarious and,

Spoils of war. Although the Battle of the Gembloux gap was costly for both sides, the Germans came out on top. Here they are seen inspecting their prizes on the field of battle. This Hotchkiss of the 3ème D.L.M. has the newer long-barrelled 37mm gun.

These two Somua S-35s of the 2ème Cuirassiers (3ème D.L.M.), disabled near Wansin, were inspected by German soldiers immediately after the battle as this picture is stated to have been taken on the afternoon of May 13.

In the heat of the battle there had been little time to cope with major mechanical breakdowns and these two H-35s of the 2ème D.L.M. had to be left to their fate. This was in the 1ère
Armée area and, when the army retreated westwards, the tanks were left behind on the Place du Jeu de Balle at Soignies . . . still a parking place for the 'Hotchkiss' of the 1980s.

Late on May 18, the XVI. Armeekorps and its two panzer divisions was switched from the 6. Armee to the 4. Armee. These pictures were taken the following morning as elements of the 4. Panzer-Division crossed the Sambre at Montignies, on the southern edge of Charleroi, over a bridge which had been repaired by Pi.Btl. 62. *Left:* It was only just wide enough for the PzKpfw III with little room for error. *Right:* The gasworks still stands alongside the river.

faced with the risk of seeing it out-flanked, that morning Général Billotte had warned the 1ère Armée to be prepared to pull back. By evening the 1ère Armée had to order its three corps back on a line running from Waterloo to Charleroi. The Germans were not long in finding out what was going on, for Generalmajor Sigfried Henrici no less, the commander of Arko 30, was personally aloft in a balloon observing the artillery shelling, and as early as 6.10 p.m. he reported long columns of French vehicles moving south-west.

The retreat was carried out in an orderly fashion although, with the Germans following too close for comfort, much equipment, artillery and anti-tank weapons had to be abandoned — materiel which the already battered 1ère Armée could ill-afford to lose.

THURSDAY, MAY 16

It was not merely the 1ère Armée that was at risk of being outflanked. On the morning of May 16 Général Billotte, in his rôle as co-ordinator of all the Allied armies in Belgium, issued instructions for the whole Allied line in Belgium to be withdrawn to the Escault, the move to be made in three stages, beginning that night. The first part of the withdrawal took the 1ère Armée behind the Charleroi Canal. The XVI. Armeekorps followed and attacked on May 17 and 18 to force a crossing. By now, however, the situation to the south was evolving as hoped by the German planners; the deployment of the panzers in the Gembloux gap having clearly succeeded, their decoy rôle was about to end.

Late on May 18 the XVI. Armee-korps ordered its two panzer divisions and the 20. Infanterie-Division (mot) to disengage and turn southwards to cross the Sambre near Charleroi. Their sector on the canal was taken over by the XXVII. Armeekorps while the XVI. Armeekorps and its three mobile divisions was transferred to the 4. Armee to play a part in the Sichelschnitt Plan whereby, through its engagement with the 6. Armee in Belgium, it was to draw into the Gembloux gap a sizeable portion of the élite of the French Army.

The PzKpfw III *top left* and PzKpfw I *above* both belonged to Pz.Rgt. 36.

The Sambre river is canalised from its confluence with the Meuse at Namur through Charleroi and across north-western France to Landrecies where it joins the Sambre-Oise Canal. The road bridge at Montignies is on the Rue du Déversoir in the south-eastern quarter of Charleroi.

The 4. Armee on the Meuse

The spearhead of the 4. Armee was the XV. Armeekorps with the 7. Panzer-Division, seen here in Belgium . . .

The two corps of the left wing of Général André Corap's 9ème Armée began to assemble and move forward into Belgium to take up their positions along the Meuse: the IIème Corps d'Armée from south of Namur to Anhée, the XIème Corps d'Armée from Anhée to Givet. Already more or less in position, on French territory, the XXXXIème Corps d'Armée held the sector from Givet to the boundary with the 2ème Armée near Sedan. The Army Command thought it needed at least five days — more likely six or seven — in which to get the infantry divisions of the left wing into position behind the river.

Orders having arrived late in the afternoon from Groupe d'Armées No. 1 telling Corap to get on with his cavalry screen — the 2ème Armée's having promptly advanced far ahead of the 9ème Armée's — at about 1.00 a.m. the following morning the main body of Corap's screening force started to cross the Meuse. By dawn of May 11 the 3ème Brigade de Spahis had established contact with the 2ème Armée's 5ème D.L.C. while the bulk of the 1ère D.L.C. and the 4ème D.L.C. were following up their advance elements. The 9ème Armée, however, found itself in a potentially precarious situation —

. . . and the 5. Panzer-Division to which this PzKpfw III belonged. This picture was taken on May 10 in Saint-Vith — a Belgian town in the Ardennes only 10 kilometres or so from the German frontier. This part of Belgium had been German until 1918 but, in spite of the Treaty of Versailles, many people still felt their allegiance belonged to the East — hence the Nazi flags welcoming the invader. *Right:* The town was heavily bombed in December 1944, hence the new buildings on Grand Rue.

Some 20 kilometres further north along the winding N23 lay Malmédy — a town whose name was later to become synonymous with the massacre of American troops there in December 1944. It, too, was heavily bombed that same month but these pictures show remarkably little change between 1940 and 1987. It also had its pro-German element with the troops being greeted with the odd 'Sieg Heil' in their unopposed capture of this important road junction.

Proceeding west along the Rue Cavens, the men from the 267. Infanterie-Division reached the Place de Rome *above*. Here the decoratively scolloped mantlet of a 7.5cm IG 18 infantry gun appears to have attracted the attention of a young girl. Above the shop on the left with the striped awning, a portrait of Hitler looks down upon the proceedings.

its mobile units having been ordered forward beyond the Meuse, its infantry units still making their way on foot to establish a defensive line along the river. The Meuse itself, which it was the army's rôle to defend, lay unprotected, the infantry still somewhere to the west and the cavalry over to the east.

Even worse, the 9ème Armée staff had no idea what was going on east of the river, for the advance elements of the cavalry units which had earlier been sent on to reconnoitre had been prevented from going forward by the demolitions being carried out by the Belgians ahead of them, and sometimes behind them. Protesting angrily, they had been forced to return without being able to report on German movements.

Opposite the 9ème Armée, the 4. Armee had deployed as planned, advancing mostly unopposed as the Belgian Groupement K was under orders to withdraw from the Ardennes.

Left: While the main body of the division was marching westwards along the southern bank of the Warche, this cavalry platoon was pictured crossing the river to recce northwards.

Above: The same bridge to Outrelepont remains, having escaped the demolitions of 1944 when American engineers tried to stop Hitler's second coming in the Ardennes.

Reaching Trois-Ponts, the leaders of the division have just passed under the railway viaduct (just visible on the left in the comparison) and turned left towards the Amblève bridge only to find the road blocked by this barricade.

Elements of the 3ème Régiment de Chasseurs Ardennais clashed with the German advance guard in the Salm valley that Friday and some men were caught before they could withdraw. These Belgian soldiers who had manned a block-house near Trois-Ponts surrendered the following morning and were searched in front of a house near the Amblève bridge.

Just south of Trois-Ponts, near Rochelinval, other troops of the Chasseurs Ardennais put up a determined fight. Here in Spineux a German cameraman pictured German and Belgian soldiers evacuating their wounded, probably on May 11.

Left: Both the road and rail bridges were blown at Trois-Ponts, and photographer Hinz climbed up the railway embankment to take this shot. The Germans had wasted no time and a detachment from Pi.Btl. 48 was already well advanced in throwing a replacement across the river. *Right:* The bridges were rebuilt during the war but the road bridge was demolished once more, this time by American engineers trying desperately to halt Kampfgruppe Peiper in their spearhead thrust towards the Meuse in December 1944. Now they have been replaced rather more permanently.

The crossing was proceeding without difficulty — with the horse-drawn wagon it could almost be a scene from a Western of pioneers crossing the Rio Grande — save for the vehicle which displays on its left rear the Maltese cross insignia of the division. Then, all of a sudden, there was panic.

Above: Meanwhile, further downstream, elements of the 28. Infanterie-Division were fording the Amblève on the northern edge of Trois-Ponts. A propaganda cameraman found a perch to record the scene — a clip being included in the UFA newsreel for May 15. *Below:* Forty-seven years later we took this comparison from the same window.

A build-up of water behind the fallen bridge further upstream had suddenly been released with disastrous effect on the column caught in the middle of the river. The poor horse was rescued and lies exhausted on the bank. While efforts were made to save the wagon, the light Einheits-Pkw was swamped and at no time do we see the driver escape.

171

To the south-east of the Meuse Belgian mobile units were to form a first line of defence — the Position de Couverture — while the bulk of their armies established themselves on the main defence line. In the Ardennes, the sector from the Amblève valley to the border with France was held by Groupement K comprising the 1ère Division de Chasseurs Ardennais and the 1ère Division de Cavalerie. That from the Amblève valley to the border with the Netherlands was occupied by various units, among them the 1er Régiment de Lanciers from the 2ème Division de Cavalerie, and units of the Cyclistes-Frontière. This T-13, commanded by Sergent Edmond Jacob and abandoned north of Trois-Ponts, was from the 8ème Compagnie of the 2ème Régiment de Cyclistes, quartered at Stavelot when the Germans attacked.

The demolitions did slow the German advance but only marginally as the crossings were neither covered by artillery or infantry and could easily be overcome. Elements of the third company of the 3ème Régiment de Chasseurs Ardennais put up a determined fight at Chabrehez and stopped the advance of the 7. Panzer-Division for several hours until the last of them surrendered at about 9.00 p.m. The panzer division's commander, Generalmajor Erwin Rommel, was angered by all the time lost and reproached what he saw as a lack of initiative from some of his officers.

In the evening, four German infantry divisions were on the Amblève and Salm rivers while the 32. Infanterie-Division was at Houffalize and the leaders of the two panzer divisions of XV. Armeekorps were south-east of Baraque-de-Fraiture, ready to push on westwards. Further to the south, the 3. Infanterie-Division of the 12. Armee was at Bertogne and the 23. Infanterie-Division at Bastogne.

Curious soldiers from the 251. Infanterie-Division look over Sergent Jacob's T-13 which was abandoned in the yard of M. Mathieu's house in Moulin-du-Ruy. The picture was probably taken on May 11.

Left: 'For you the war is over!' Also captured at Ruy (on a minor road about 10 kilometres north of Trois-Ponts), these two Belgian soldiers appear to be doing all they can to relax the atmosphere and secure fair treatment. Their captors are most probably a party from the 251. Infanterie-Division. Right: The house in the background has been pleasantly modernised, but the old shed on the left has disappeared, being replaced by a new villa.

Demolitions effected by the Belgians in the Ardennes were numerous and these pictures taken along the Amblève valley show that even if the efforts of the engineers did not slow the German advance appreciably, they nevertheless had quite a nuisance value. *Left:* Here the road has been blown at the entrance to Stoumont with the vehicles of 251. Infanterie-Division, including this command car, having to bypass the huge crater across the field. *Right:* The view today is eastwards in the direction of La Gleize with no evidence or tell-tale repairs to mark the spot.

SATURDAY, MAY 11

While the infantry divisions of the 9ème Armée's IIème and XIème Corps d'Armée were on their way to the Meuse, the first troops having arrived at their positions behind the river, the vanguards of the 1ère D.L.C. and the 4ème D.L.C. clashed with advance elements of XV. Armeekorps. By the afternoon, the 4ème R.A.M. was fighting with forces of the 7. Panzer-Division in and around Marche while the 1er R.A.M. was also engaged near Rochefort.

Further south the cavalry units of the 2ème Armée had clashed with the leading forces of Gruppe von Kleist and were ordered to pull back behind the Semois. Consequently, at 3.00 p.m., the 9ème Armée told its 3ème Brigade de Spahis to withdraw its right wing to follow the retreat of the 2ème Armée's 5ème D.L.C. but to keep its left wing forward enough to tie in with the 1ère D.L.C. Two hours later the army informed its cavalry units that the 2ème Armée's cavalry was pulling back to the south and gave them permission to start withdrawing, which was carried out in the late afternoon. At about 10.30 p.m.,

Another cratered road is carefully negotiated near Trois-Ponts by a truck from a support unit of the 28. Infanterie-Division (note insignia on rear panel). The Belgian T-13 number 527 abandoned alongside is another tank-destroyer from the 11ème Compagnie, 3ème Régiment de Chasseurs Ardennais. The effectiveness of the prepared demolitions was later reported by the Belgian engineers with craters of 10 to 20 metres across blown to a depth of up to 8 metres.

The N33 runs alongside the river on the northern bank and if this artery could be cut, then the Germans would have been denied a vital east-west route. *Left:* Here, just to the west of Stoumont, an attempt has been made to blow the road at a vulnerable point which has not quite succeeded. *Right:* Nevertheless the damage was such that it took years before the road was restored to its full width — the place still being known today as 'La Destruction'.

A nice photographic study as well as a picture full of interest. *Above:* As the name implies, there were three bridges at Trois-Ponts, the third, the Glain bridge, being to the south of the town across the Salm river which runs into the Amblève. Destruction of this bridge (the photographer is standing on the remains) cut the north-south road from Vielsalm, but by the time this picture was taken German engineers had constructed a makeshift crossing utilising felled trees and had already commenced work on a second bridge. *Below:* The road bridge had been rebuilt by 1944 when Peiper's Kampfgruppe used the same route west during the Battle of the Bulge, but the bridge was reached first by men of the US 51st Engineers. They had it wired for demolition and blew it just after midday on December 18 as the leading German troops were on the bridge. Today it has been superseded by a new bridge a hundred metres or so downstream, and the old one sealed to traffic.

Above: **Some 25 kilometres to the west lies the larger Ourthe river — yet another obstacle on the line of advance to the Meuse. At Hamoir, 30 kilometres south of Liege, the Flak-Lehr-Regiment has set up a 2cm Flak 30 on the eastern bank to** provide cover against air attack on the pontoon bridge in the background which has been built by Pi.Btl. 48. *Bottom:* **Almost 50 years have passed, yet time has stood still, with the days of Blitzkrieg just a memory.**

The view looking eastwards from the opposite bank. For the technically-minded, the bridge is a Brückengerät B, the troops crossing being from 8. Infanterie-Division. The assault boat belongs to Pionier-Bataillon 48.

Aufklärungs-Abteilung 251, the reconnaissance battalion of the 251. Infanterie-Division, reached the Ourthe at Chanxhe, just north of its confluence with the Amblève, on May 12.

Although it was hoped that the bridge might still be intact, it had been well and truly destroyed and men and equipment had to be ferried across.

Within a few hours, engineers had constructed a wooden trestle bridge enabling the bulk of the division to cross dry-shod. For the moment, though, man and beast helped each other. *Below:* A timeless comparison by Jean Paul in April 1986.

faced with the danger of seeing his cavalry units isolated, Corap ordered them to fall back across the Meuse.

The two panzer divisions of XV. Armeekorps had crossed the Ourthe (the 5. Panzer-Division at Hotton, the 7. Panzer-Division at Beffe, Marcourt and Laroche), but had not advanced all out, contenting themselves merely with reconnaissance and in bringing more

elements across. Late in the morning the corps had ordered them to halt and regroup in the Marche area, for too much activity on this front would have forewarned the French Command whereas the Germans wanted as much as possible of the French armies advancing into Belgium to be trapped there when Gruppe von Kleist broke through at Sedan.

SUNDAY, MAY 12

The French cavalry began pulling back at 2.00 a.m. and their withdrawal was carried out without too much difficulty throughout the morning, the main nuisance being the Belgian demolitions. On one occasion, near Crupet, the Belgians even accidentally blew a railway bridge while a squadron of the 31ème Dragons was passing, several

Some 30 kilometres to the south, the 5. Panzer-Division had reached Hotton only to find that their bridge over the Ourthe had also been destroyed. While the river was shallow enough to be forded by the larger vehicles like this PzKpfw IV, all other equipment had to be laboriously manhandled across.

The Germans replaced the bridge with a wooden one in the summer of 1940 but blew it during their retreat in 1944. It was rebuilt by the US Army and survived the Battle of the Bulge (although the 116. Panzer-Division reached Hotton) and lasted until 1953 when the present one was constructed.

The leaders of the division had already outrun their supply units and an air-drop had to be laid on to cover their immediate requirements on May 12. The Ju 52s each carried three containers which were dropped in fields north of the town.

The 7. Panzer-Division advancing about 10 kilometres to the south found the Marcourt bridge demolished but the river still fordable. Here an SdKfz 223 light armoured radio car *(left)* is followed by an SdKfz 251/3 communications half-track.

men being wounded. The 4ème D.L.C. recrossed the Meuse at Profondeville, Annevoie and Yvoir; the 1ère D.L.C. at Dinant, Anseremme and Hastière; the southern three reconnaissance groups at Heer and Givet and the 3ème Brigade de Spahis at Charleville. All went according to the timetable, the advance elements covering the moves and withdrawing in the end. Taking the 1ère D.L.C. as an example, the 1er R.A.M. fought off the Germans in the Rochefort sector while the division's main force was pulling back, and the division commander, Général Jacques d'Arras, who was as far east as Ciergnon in the morning, crossed the Meuse with his staff at Dinant at about 1.00

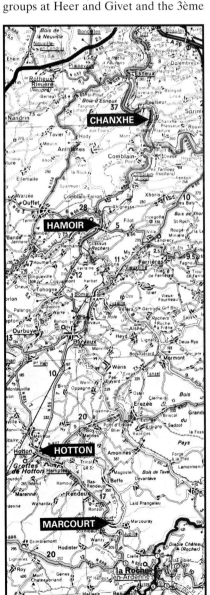

At the same time the engineers (pioniere in German) begin work to improve the temporary footbridge which has been laid across the ruined masonry.

The permanent post-war replacement on the same alignment was opened in 1947.

p.m. The 1er R.A.M., which fought as a rearguard, crossed at Dinant at about 4.00 p.m. By late afternoon, most of the cavalry units were back on the west bank of the river. Their experience east of it had been somewhat painful but nothing fatal had occured.

The XV. Armeekorps resumed its progress, two routes having been assigned to each of its panzer divisions, which were to advance alongside one another. Kampfgruppe Werner of the 5. Panzer-Division kept abreast of the 7. Panzer-Division, but Kampfgruppe

Blitzkrieg in the Ardennes . . . but where? Perseverance led to the identification of this uncaptioned picture of PzKpfw IIs as having been taken in the little hamlet of Forge-à-l'Aplé, 10 kilometres from Hotton, identifying the column as belonging to 5. Panzer-Division.

Once over the Ourthe, the panzers were within striking distance of the Meuse. However the Belgians had either removed all road signs or obliterated those not easily uprooted. *Left:* Here the paint is being scratched off to confirm the location. The signpost reveals the position as a junction on the N38 west of Leignon — the river is just 12 kilometres away at Dinant. *Right:* Although the house has since been demolished, the curve of the road in the background is unmistakable.

Lübbe fell far behind and its route was then 'loaned' to the 7. Panzer-Division, which was just to the south. At 9.14 a.m. Kampfgruppe Werner was subordinated to the 7. Panzer-Division until the Meuse was reached.

The railway bridge at Houx was blown at 2.45 p.m. and the road bridge at Yvoir at 4.30 p.m. when the advance guard of Kampfgruppe Werner, under the command of Leutnant Heinz Zobel, approached. Belgian engineers dropped the bridge as the leading armoured car was on it. Consequently Colonel Jean Taschet des Combes, the commander of the French 129ème R.I. which held the west bank, was trapped on the far side where he had gone to make contact with some cavalry officers, and was killed when trying to get back across.

It was the same story at Dinant when forces from 7. Panzer-Division, under the command of Hauptmann Horst Steffen, approached the town. The bridge was blown at 4.20 p.m. and the one at Bouvignes less than ten minutes later. Hauptmann Steffen was killed at the Meuse when the tank in which he was riding was hit by a 25mm shell from an anti-tank gun manned by the French 77ème R.I. on the far side.

The railway bridge at Anseremme was demolished at 4.20 p.m., the bridge at Profondeville at 6.40 p.m., that at Godinne at 7.24 p.m. and the one at Hastière at 9.00 p.m.

Four kilometres away at Ciney, the leaders of 5. Panzer-Division exchanged shots with the rearguard of the 4ème D.L.C. as they pulled back on May 12. In 1944 this was to be virtually the limit of Hitler's breakthrough . . .

. . . but in 1940 his troops swept on to the Channel. Vehicles of Kampfgruppe Werner pass in front of Ciney town hall in which Général Paul Barbe, commander of the 4ème D.L.C., had his HQ only the day before.

Left: **In the shadow of the blown road bridge across the Meuse at Bouvignes, just north of Dinant, a 10.5cm le FH 18 howitzer of Art.Rgt. 78 (7. Panzer-Division) shells French targets on the western bank. The picture was taken on May 13 by the** divisional commander, Generalmajor Erwin Rommel, the bridge having been demolished around 4.30 p.m. the previous afternoon. *Right:* **The bridge was never rebuilt — the only trace remaining today being part of the westernmost abutment.**

The five days at least which Corap thought he would have to establish his positions along the Meuse had turned out to be a mere two. Faced with this reality, the 9ème Armée had asked Général Jean Bouffet and Général Julien Martin, the commanders of the IIème and XIème Corps d'Armée, to hasten the moves of their infantry divisions. However this could not change the outcome and a considerable proportion of these never reached the Meuse in time to take part in the battle and those which did get there were never given the opportunity to prepare themselves for it. The motorised 5ème D.I.M. was actually taking over its positions from Dave to Anhée when the

Germans attacked. Further south, the situation of the two infantry divisions of the XIème Corps d'Armée (two Series B divisions) was much more of a problem. The 18ème Division d'Infanterie which was to hold the Meuse from Anhée to Hastière — the sector threatened by the two panzer divisions of XV. Armeekorps — had only five of its nine infantry battalions at hand late on May 12 and the men were exhausted after long approach marches on foot. From Hastière to Vireux-Molhain south of Givet the 22ème Division d'Infanterie was in the same situation and it was not until the morning of May 13 that five battalions were on the Meuse, most of the men having marched all through the

night. Also tired and somewhat disorganised after their distant and hasty commitment east of the river, the units of the 1ère D.L.C. and 4ème D.L.C. had been deployed along the length of the Meuse front as they were withdrawn.

MONDAY, MAY 13

Although the French Command was still debating whether or not the main German attack was in the Gembloux gap or in the Ardennes, by the evening of May 12 it was certain that the 9ème Armée was not on a secondary front as anticipated. Having asked the Groupe d'Armées No. 1 for reinforcements, Corap's headquarters issued that morning General Order No. 20. It was

Bouvignes burns — another picture from Rommel's personal photograph album. A keen photographer, copies of the pictures he took in 1940 and on later campaigns are now held in photo archives in London and Washington, yet without captions. Only after much research has it been possible to put names to many of the places depicted during his drive across France.

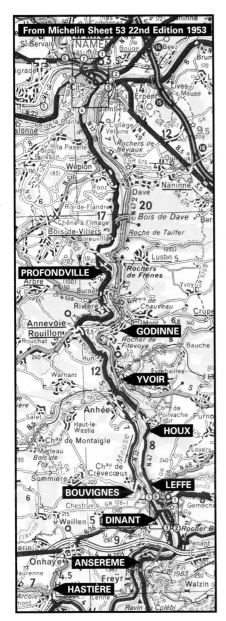

'I drove back along the Meuse to Leffe [a vilage on the outskirts of Dinant] to get the crossing moving there,' wrote Rommel (see page 187). 'I had already given orders for several Panzer IIIs and IVs and a troop of artillery to be at my disposal at the crossing point. We left the signals vehicle for the time being at a point some 500 yards east of the river and went forward on foot through deserted farms towards the Meuse. In Leffe we found a number of rubber boats, all more or less badly damaged by enemy fire, lying in the street where our men had left them. Eventually, after being bombed on the way by our own aircraft, we arrived at the river. At Leffe weir we took a quick look at the footbridge, which had been barred by the enemy with a spiked steel plate. The firing in the Meuse valley had ceased for the moment and we moved off to the right through some houses to the crossing point proper. . . . I now took over personal command of the 2. Bataillon of Schutz.Rgt. 7 and for some time directed operations myself. With Leutnant Most I crossed the Meuse in one of the first boats and at once joined the company which had been across since early morning. From the company command post we could see that Kompanie Enkefort and Lichter were making rapid progress. I then moved up north along a deep gully to Kompanie Enkefort. As we arrived an alarm came in: "Enemy tanks in front." The company had no anti-tank weapons, and I therefore gave orders for small arms fire to be opened on the tanks as quickly as possible, whereupon we saw them pull back into a hollow about a thousand yards north-west of Leffe. Large numbers of French stragglers came through the bushes and slowly laid down their arms.'

'crucial', the order proclaimed, that 'any German elements which had set foot on the left bank of the Meuse be immediately destroyed or thrown back into the river'.

Early in the morning the 5. Panzer-Division tried to cross the Meuse just south of Yvoir but the 129ème R.I. was in position on the west bank of the river and repulsed the assault. The panzer division's commander, Generalleutnant Max von Hartlieb, personally went forward to urge his men across but finally had to concede defeat: most of the assault boats having been sunk with very few men on the far bank.

At about the same time, elements of the division's Aufklärungs-Abteilung 8 had managed to cross the river at the lock at Houx, a few kilometres to the south, and Oberst Paul Werner, the

Left: Until a bridge could be completed, as much as possible was moved across on pontoon rafts. This SdKfz 221 armoured

car from the division's Aufkl. Abt. 5 crosses the river near Leffe. *Right:* The Auberge de Bouvignes still in business today.

commander of the 5. Panzer-Division's advance guard, immediately sent the three battalions he had at hand to reinforce the bridgehead. This was a lucky move, for the lock was right on the boundary between the two French corps which had hastily assumed responsibility for the west bank of the river. Also the second battalion of the 39ème R.I., 18ème Division d'Infanterie, which was supposed to hold that part of the line, was one of the division's four battalions still on its way.

Further south, between Houx and Dinant, the 7. Panzer-Division found itself in front of a sector where the 18ème Division d'Infanterie had actually taken up its positions. Consequently the attacking forces encountered problems in gaining a foothold on the west bank. When the division's

It is obvious that these pictures were taken after all opposition on the far bank had been eliminated. This PzKpfw II belonged to the recce platoon of the regiment's I. Abteilung.

Above and bottom: **Traffic jam beside the Meuse. Crews of 1. and 2. Kompanie of Pz.Rgt. 25 look over their mounts as they wait their turn to be ferried across. These tanks are PzKpfw 38(t).**

Having been ferried across, these two self-propelled guns have turned north along the N17, which runs beside the left bank of the Meuse, and have halted just outside Anhée, a kilometre or so from the crossing point. The guns are 15cm sIG 33s mounted on the chassis of a PzKpfw I. The forecourt of the Garage du Tourne Bride provided a useful parking spot although one doubts if sIG Kompanie 705 were paid-up members of the Royal Automobile Club de Belgique!

commander, Generalmajor Rommel, arrived about 2.00 a.m. at the spot the Schtz.Rgt. 6 were trying to force a crossing, the situation as he described it 'was none too pleasant'.

'Our boats were being destroyed one after the other by the French flanking fire', wrote Rommel, 'and the crossing eventually came to a standstill. The enemy infantry were so well concealed that they were impossible to locate even after a long search through glasses. A smoke screen in the Meuse valley would have prevented these infantry doing so much harm. But we had no smoke unit. So I now gave orders for a number of houses in the valley be set alight in order to supply the smoke we lacked.

'Minute by minute the enemy fire grew more unpleasant. From up river a damaged rubber boat came drifting down to us with a badly wounded man clinging to it, shouting and screaming for help — the poor fellow was near to drowning. But there was no help for him here, the enemy fire was too heavy.

'With Hauptmann Paul Schräpler [Rommel's adjutant], I now drove south down the Meuse valley road in a PzKpfw IV to see how things were going with Schtz.Rgt. 7. On the way we came under fire several times from the west bank and Schräpler was wounded in the arm from a number of shell splinters. Single French infantrymen surrendered as we approached.

'By the time we arrived Schtz.Rgt. 7 had already succeeded in getting a company across to the west bank, but

Meanwhile 7. Panzer-Division engineers were pressing on with the construction of a Brückengerät B pontoon bridge with a 16-tonne classification to span the river, at this point some 80 metres wide.

The bridge had been carefully sited to make use of this tunnel under the railway embankment which flanked the left-hand bank at this spot, and was completed by 7.00 p.m. on Tuesday, May 14. Here one of the division's Horch staff cars WH55575 has just reached the western bank as despatch riders wait to recross east.

Left: The day after the bridge had been opened, the bottleneck was still acute on the eastern bank — a perfect target had the Allies had any measure of air superiority. *Right:* The old bridge has been completely cleared yet the same weir survives.

186

Above: **Motor-cyclists of the 7. Panzer-Division race along the N36 down to Dinant. This picture was taken on the eastern** bank near Gemechenne at a place where the Belgians had attempted to erect a solid concrete road block.

Left: **As transport climbs up the hill from the river, another despatch rider returns to the bridge. This is still the N36 — then** as now *(right)* the main road out of the town to the west. Philippeville is just over 30 kilometres away.

the enemy fire had then become so heavy that their crossing equipment had been shot to pieces and the crossing had had to be halted. Large numbers of wounded were receiving treatment in a house close beside the demolished bridge. As at the northern crossing point, there was nothing to be seen of the enemy who were preventing the crossing. As there was clearly no hope of getting any more men across at this point without powerful artillery and tank support to deal with the enemy nests, I drove back to the division headquarters, where I met the army commander, Generaloberst von Kluge and the corps commander, General Hoth.

'After talking over the situation with Major Heidkämper the divisional Ia [first staff officer] and making the necessary arrangements, I drove back along the Meuse to Leffe to get the crossing moving there . . .

The N36 bridge in Dinant had also been blown although access from the river would have made it difficult to construct a pontoon bridge in the town — hence the decision to build it a kilometre to the north. This 2cm Flak 30 has been set up on the eastern pier giving a good overall vantage point against any Allied attack from the west.

Eight kilometres north of Dinant, the leaders of 5. Panzer-Division reached the heights overlooking the Meuse at Yvoir, where they saw that the bridge was still intact with French troops continuing to cross to the west. The Germans launched an immediate attack: while panzers shelled the western end in the hope of forcing the engineers responsible for its demolition to take cover, an armoured car sped down and onto the bridge. A Belgian engineer, René de Wispelaere, rushed forward to detonate the prepared charges, being shot down in the process, but when the smoke from the explosion cleared, the bridge lay in ruins and the armoured car had disappeared into the river. *Above:* In this shot of German engineers inspecting the damage, the photographer is standing on the eastern bank. *Below:* When it was rebuilt after the war, the bridge was moved a hundred metres upstream. *Right:* A plaque was erected on the old eastern abutment with a memorial to Lieutenant de Wispelaere on the far bank.

A crossing point for the 5. Panzer-Division was established just to the south at Houx where access from the bank was easier. The usual procedure was followed with the first light vehicles being taken across on rubber boats, followed by the construction of a pontoon raft. *Left:* Here a barge is unloaded on the eastern bank and *right* a PzKpfw III arrives on the western bank. *Below:* In our 1985 comparisons, both the buildings seen in the background have since disappeared.

'The crossing had now come to a complete standstill, with the officers badly shaken by the casualties which their men had suffered. On the opposite bank we could see several men of the company which was already across, among them many wounded. Numerous damaged boats and rubber dinghies lay on the opposite bank. The officers reported that nobody dared show himself outside cover, as the enemy opened fire immediately on anyone they spotted.

'Several of our tanks and heavy weapons were in position on the embankment east of the houses, but had seemingly already fired off almost all their ammunition. However, the tanks I had ordered to the crossing point soon arrived, to be followed shortly afterwards by two field howitzers from Bataillon Crasemann.

'All points on the western bank likely to hold enemy riflemen were now brought under fire, and soon the aimed fire of all weapons was pouring into

rocks and buildings. Leutnant Hanke knocked out a pill box on the bridge ramp with several rounds. The tanks, with turrets traversed left, drove slowly north at fifty metres' spacing along the Meuse valley, closely watching the opposite slopes.

'Under cover of this fire the crossing slowly got going again, and a cable ferry using several large pontoons was started. Rubber boats paddled backwards and forwards and brought back the wounded from the west bank.'

Initially, the bridging column only had sufficient material to construct an 8-tonne bridge which was in operation on May 13. However, Leutnant Heinz Zobel, commanding the division's advance guard, was impatient to get across and he drove his

PzKpfw IV onto a pontoon raft although it exceeded the design limit by more than 100 percent. Inevitably the raft collapsed, and the tank fell into the river. The body of the driver was never found.

It is interesting to note that, in his dramatic account of how he forced the Meuse, Rommel, always keen to portray himself in the best possible light, made no mention at all of the 5. Panzer-Division which had crossed the Meuse before him.

Even if the overall price was small compared with the advantage gained, nevertheless the Meuse crossings had been costly for the two panzer divisions. The XV. Armeekorps recorded 84 killed and 332 wounded that day, two-thirds of them from the 7. Panzer-Division. Among the officers killed were Hauptmann Horst Steffen of Pz.Rgt. 25 and Major Hans Binkau, the commander of Pi.Btl. 58; the wounded included Major Friedrich von Steinkeller, the commander of Kradschtz.Btl. 7.

In the evening, seven LeO 451 bombers of the 12ème Escadre attacked the bridges at Dinant and columns east of the town and later in the night five Amiot 143s of the 38ème Escadre bombed troop concentrations between Marche and Dinant.

TUESDAY, MAY 14

In the early hours a French counterattack — by two companies from the 129ème R.I. and the second battalion from the 14ème R.D.P. backed by eight armoured cars from the 1er G.R.D.I. — struck the second battalion of Schtz.Rgt. 14 at Haut-le-Wastia. There, although the Germans were initially forced back, the arrival of eight panzers from Pz.Rgt. 31 regained them the advantage.

By dawn the 7. Panzer-Division had erected a bridge across the Meuse. About thirty panzers were already on the west bank, including those ferried across during the night, when in the morning a message was received from Rommel's advanced guards. Misinterpreting the word 'eingeschlossen' (encircled) as 'eingetroffen' (arrived), He then promptly launched them westwards and captured Onhaye, five kilometres beyond the river. This was a risky undertaking which might have endangered the whole bridgehead had the French units been installed in their

Six kilometres north-east of the bridge at Houx lies the little village of Crupet, and it was here that a photographer came across these two French AMR33 tracked armoured cars which had most probably been left there by the 14ème R.D.P. of the 4ème D.L.C. They had carried out a reconnaissance along the far bank of the Meuse before withdrawing to the bridge at Profondeville on the afternoon of May 12. The bridge there was blown at 7.00 p.m.

A fine comparison but one very difficult to find with no location. We only succeeded when Pierre Gosset identified the picture as having been taken in Crupet.

Left: For these French prisoners of the 77ème R.I., 18ème Division d'Infanterie, the battle on the Meuse is over. Right: This one was a little easier to find — the railway station at

Spontin, south-east of Crupet. The road to Yvoir more or less marked the corps boundary between the XV. Armeekorps and the VIII. Armeekorps on its right flank.

190

Left: The infantry divisions of VIII. Armeekorps were advancing on the right of XV. Armeekorps and at Godinne, a dozen kilometres north of Dinant, an 8-tonne bridge was completed on May 15 for the 28. Infanterie-Division. When this picture was taken, another section of the Brückengerät B bridge had just been floated into position, bringing across at the same time a command car and some motor-cycles and horses. Right: So tranquil is the present-day scene that it is difficult to imagine that a bridgehead once existed across the Meuse at this precise spot some 48 years before.

Left: Three kilometres to the south at Yvoir, another 8-tonne pontoon bridge was built by Pi.Btl. 48, this time for the 8. Infanterie-Division which had advanced abreast of the 28. Infanterie-Division on the extreme left flank of the VIII. Armeekorps. The bridge was completed on May 19 and this transport was pictured bringing back some Belgian prisoners on its return from taking supplies up to the front. Right: The bridge stood just downstream from where the new replacement road bridge was built after the war to the south of the town.

Above: **This Hotchkiss H-39, abandoned in Sovet, belonged to the 4ème R.A.M. of the 4ème D.L.C. In the van of the division, the unit had crossed the Meuse at Godinne at 2.00 p.m. on May 10 and rushed eastwards to come into contact with the** Germans near Grandmenil. Following the withdrawal order, the 4ème R.A.M. pulled back behind the Meuse on May 12. *Below:* Nothing has changed in Sovet which lies about ten kilometres east of the river at Dinant.

positions. As it was, there was not much the XV. Armeekorps' staff could do about it; the operation had been a success and Rommel was one of Hitler's blue-eyed boys.

Meanwhile, the two infantry divisions of the VIII. Armeekorps had started to cross the Meuse, the 8. Infanterie-Division at Yvoir and the 28. Infanterie-Division near Annevoie.

The French High Command could see the danger created by the expansion of these bridgeheads, with the possibility of a breakthrough west of the Meuse, and so decided to bring up the

The build-up. A convoy comprising both two- and four-wheeled transport of the 8. Infanterie-Division at the level crossing in

Yvoir. At this point they are still several hundred metres short of the bridge.

Once the bridgehead was secured, the heavier equipment was ordered up to the front. This SdKfz 7 prime-mover towing an

8.8cm Flak 36 was photographed passing through Nassogne, some 50 kilometres from Dinant.

Left: In Thynes, some six kilometres back from the Bouvignes bridgehead, this building has been taken over as a field hospital

for both German and French wounded. Right: Another difficult comparison achieved thanks to Pierre Gosset.

Nevertheless the advance to the Meuse was not entirely one-sided. This PzKpfw IV from the 5. Panzer-Division has been well and truly stopped in its tracks by a direct hit from a Hotchkiss of the 4ème D.L.C. near Marche on May 11.

1ère D.C.R., an armoured division previously subordinated to the 1ère Armée, to support the threatened 9ème Armée. In the morning, Corap visited the XIème Corps d'Armée headquarters at Florennes and informed its commander, Général Julien Martin, that the corps had been given two new units, the 1ère D.C.R. and the 4ème D.I.N.A., until now in army reserve, to prepare a counter-attack towards Dinant. Martin was told that the 1ère D.C.R., which was in the Charleroi area, had been ordered to regroup in the vicinity of Ermeton, Flavion, Corenne and Stave, some 15 kilometres west of Dinant. The commander of the 4ème D.I.N.A., Général Charles Sancelme, soon arrived at corps headquarters to point out that his division was not as 'fresh' as announced, his men being exhausted by days of long marches, the last of these under incessant attacks from the Luftwaffe.

Beside it at the roadside lies the grave of one of the crew, Gefreiter Arthur Germann of the 7. Kompanie of Panzer-Regiment 15. From the violence of the explosion, it is probably safe to assume that he was not the only crewman killed.

Moved from his battlefield grave, he now lies in the company of nearly 40,000 of his countrymen in the huge German military cemetery near Lommel in the north of Belgium near the border with the Netherlands (Block 7, Grave 133).

The 12. Armee on the Meuse

On the right wing of the 9ème Armée, the sector held by the XXXXIème Corps d'Armée from Givet to just west of Sedan ended at the boundary with the 2ème Armée marked by the little River Bar. With its two divisions in place, the XXXXIème Corps d'Armée was in effect at the pivot of the wheeling movement of the Allied armies entering Belgium. On the other side of the junction, on the left wing of the 2ème Armée, the Xème Corps d'Armée of Général Pierre Grandsard was responsible for a front of 40 kilometres from Pont-à-Bar.

The XXXXIème Corps d'Armée's 61ème Division d'Infanterie, in the line from Givet to Revin, and the 102ème Division d'Infanterie de Forteresse, from Revin to Pont-à-Bar, had come to know their sectors well in the weeks they had been there. The corps' two divisions were not of the best, the 61ème Division d'Infanterie being a Series B and the 102ème Division de Forteresse a new formation having been created in January from the Ardennes

Wasserbillig lies just inside Luxembourg on the important border crossing with Germany where the River Moselle meets the Sûre (Sauer). The 16. Armee advanced across the southern part of the Grand Duchy to cover the flank of the 12. Armee.

The French Command had always considered that the Ardennes were 'impassable' to an enemy attack, and in this sector of the frontier the Maginot Line — in fact an extension of the Line northwards — was only lightly fortified with odd blockhouses built along the Meuse. This MOM-type casemate, which controlled the river just west of Sedan, at Donchery, survived the war and still overlooks the countryside where the 2. Panzer-Division crossed the river.

Defence Sector. The Ardennes having always been considered as 'impassable', the only 'forteresse' in this sector was the one in the name of the 102ème D.I.F. and a few blockhouses hastily built along the river.

The Xème Corps d'Armée front was held by the 55ème Division d'Infanterie on the left and the 3ème Division d'Infanterie Nord Africaine on the right. The 71ème Division d'Infanterie, which in April had been taken out of the line for further training and was ordered back on May 10, started to reach the front on the night of May 12 to be inserted between them. The 3ème D.I.N.A. was a good division, a Series A, but the 55ème Division d'Infanterie, like the 71ème Division, was poorer Series B material. Although nominally the left wing of the Montmédy Fortified Sector, this sector of the frontier was regarded as being behind the 'impassable' Ardennes and it had been only

The main German assault mounted by Gruppe von Kleist was to hit the 55ème Division d'Infanterie (a Series B formation) at Sedan, the city straddling the Meuse facing the south-eastern portion of Belgium. This second-rate unit had been rushed to the area to occupy unfinished positions along the river, but with every belief that their front would be by-passed for more favourable terrain further west. Here a squad poses with a Hotchkiss for a photographer in the 2ème Armée sector.

Left: **Marsch! Marsch! Having just received the order to move, the advance guard of the 2. Panzer-Division kicks off into the Our valley in the north-eastern quarter of Luxembourg.** *Right:* **The most northerly panzer road ran from Bitburg over the**

1400ft pass at Brimingen and across the Our river to Diekirch. When we pinpointed the spot it turned out to have been taken just a kilometre inside Germany on the descent to the frontier post at Roth.

lightly protected by casemates and blockhouses built on the high ground south of the river.

In the Belgian Ardennes, out in front of the 2ème Armée divisions in the line, Général Huntziger's cavalry units — the 5ème D.L.C., 1ère Brigade de Cavalerie and 2ème D.L.C. — were moving forward to cover the area from around Saint-Hubert to the Luxembourg border, on their left wing in liaison with those of the 9ème Armée.

General Ewald von Kleist, the commander of Gruppe von Kleist, whose task was to cut through the Ardennes to reach and cross the Meuse between its confluence with the Semois and Sedan, was to advance the three divisions of its XIX. Armeekorps abreast in the first wave. Four 'panzer' roads had been devised for XIX. Armeekorps, the most northerly having being assigned to the 2. Panzer-Division, the second to the 1. Panzer-Divison and the two southern ones to the 10. Panzer-Division. The XXXXI. Armeekorps was to follow with two panzer divisions to shift onto the group right wing as soon as the Ardennes was passed and cross the Meuse at Monthermé.

The tanks are PzKpfw IIs and are stocked up with extra fuel in jerrycans. Normal range would be about 200 kilometres, say 125 miles, at the normal consumption for road use of 4 miles per gallon. This would increase to less than 2 miles per gallon for hilly or cross-country work.

The uncommon white cross on the turrets and the letter 'K' — virtually hidden in this shot by the crewman's jackboots — denoted Gruppe von Kleist, it being a common German practice to name units or task forces after their commanders.

Obviously these tankers have nothing to declare as they roar past the customs post — unlike the reception which greeted us in 1987 when the German border guards suggested that the tanks in the photograph were American!

197

Left: Having just entered the Grand Duchy, these PzKpfw IIIs climb the steep road through Vianden. The vehicle with the K in the foreground is the battlefield recovery vehicle version of the PzKpfw I which consisted of the hull of the Ausf. B minus turret and superstructure. *Right:* This part of Vianden remains much as it was the day 2. Panzer-Division hit town.

Left: To the south, on the right wing of the 16. Armee, units of the VII. Armeekorps crossed the Sûre at Echternach. The bridge was captured intact with the obstacles which barred the way being blasted aside. *Right:* The town suffered grievously in the re-run four years later when Hitler tried to repeat his victory of 1940 with another breakthrough in the Ardennes. The only building to have survived in this picture is the customs post on the right.

Further south in the 16. Armee sector, a convoy of the XIII. Armeekorps pushes westwards along the southern bank of the Moselle. Although still in Germany (where the river should technically be called the Mosel) they are approaching Igel, five kilometres from the frontier. In the foreground is an SdKfz 10/4 mounting a 20mm Flak gun.

An SdKfz 11 prime-mover from Artillerie-Regiment 73 of the 1. Panzer-Division photographed on the afternoon of May 10 — but where? The gun is a 10.5cm leFH 18 howitzer and the tactical marking identifies it as belonging to the regiment's No. 1 Battery, the oak leaf being the divisional emblem. The original caption describes it as showing 'Vormarsch in Elsass' (Advance in Alsace) — somewhat misleading as Alsace is a hundred kilometres south of Luxembourg! However, the formation sign put us on the right track and we managed to trace Arthur Wolff, still in the fashion business in Ettelbruck.

Advancing abreast of the 1. Panzer-Division, and on its right, the 2. Panzer-Division had crossed Luxembourg and reached the Belgian border near Tintange by the afternoon of the first day. This Panzerbefehlswagen III Ausf. D was pictured ten kilometres from the frontier in Bavigne. It was a command vehicle which externally closely resembled the PzKpfw III in order to not unduly attract enemy fire, although it had no armament, the main gun being a dummy. The 'K' of course denotes Gruppe von Kleist, while the two dots below the lozenge indicate that it belongs to the 2. Panzer-Division.

FRIDAY, MAY 10

The panzers crossed Luxembourg during the early morning without difficulty thank to the efforts of the various 'Brandenburg' teams in successfully preventing demolitions. As the Ib of the 1. Panzer-Division, Hauptmann Friedrich von Kielmansegg, put it, 'the inhabitants did not have time to rub the sleep out of their eyes.' By about 6.30 a.m. the 1. Panzer-Division's advance guard had reached the Belgian border at Martelange but here they found the bridge across the Sûre river down. The division's Pi.Btl. 37 immediately began to erect a new one which would be completed during the afternoon. Just before noon a Potez 63/11 of G.A.O. 2/520 flying a reconnaissance mission for the 2ème D.L.C. met two Henschel Hs 126s of 2.(H)/Aufklärungsgruppe 23 near Martelange and shot down one of them.

Meanwhile, the 1. Panzer-Division's advance elements had had to fight a Belgian unit, the fifth company of 1er Régiment de Chasseurs Ardennais, out

off Bodange. The Belgians should have been withdrawn after having carried out demolition orders in its sector but, because all the telephone wires had been cut by the 'Niwi' commandos, they never received the order and they stayed put. After some hours' fighting, with two of the company's three officers killed, what remained of the Belgian company surrendered at about 6.00 p.m. The advance elements of the 1. Panzer-Division then established contact with the airborne elements of Operation 'Niwi' near Witry. To the north, the 2. Panzer-Division had reached Strainchamps but neither division was able to advance swiftly and deep into Belgium owing to the extensive road demolitions until they could be cleared during the night.

The delays imposed had enabled the 5ème D.L.C. to fulfil its objectives for May 10 without serious fighting. Sharp encounters had ensued when the 2ème D.L.C. ran smack into the advance elements of the 10. Panzer-Division in the open country west of Arlon late in the afternoon, forcing the cavalry to fall back on the Semois, the last natural barrier in the southern Ardennes before the French frontier.

As May 10 drew to a close, although the German panzer divisions had made good progress, Gruppe von Kleist had failed to reach its objectives for this first day, the line Libramont-Neufchâteau-Virton. At the same time, aerial reconnaissance reported strong French forces, including armour, crossing the Meuse at Mouzon while other moves were detected at Longwy and Montmédy. All this was viewed at German headquarters that night as a serious threat to the left flank of the panzer group which called for strong countermeasures.

That same night, although the French Command was unhappy at the 2ème D.L.C. being thrown back on the River Semois, it failed to appreciate the gravity of the situation in the Ardennes. The German moves there were seen only as a tactical danger for the cavalry units of the 2ème Armée, of their being outflanked to the north, and consequently the 9ème Armée was urged to

The obstacles and mines along the border having been cleared during the night, the 2. Panzer-Division resumed its move westwards on Saturday morning. This PzKpfw III was pictured passing a Krupp-Protze lorry mounting a 2cm Flak 30.

When a comparison is laid alongside the original it looks easy, yet hours of on the spot research are necessary to put names to uncaptioned pictures, and thereby make them more meaningful in the context of a battle. A church is often the best clue . . .

. . .and it enabled a location to be put to both these shots. The one at the top of the page proved to have been taken in Strainchamps, just west of the N4 south of Bastogne, and that above showing engineers working to construct a replacement for a bridge blown 20 kilometres further to the west at Neuvillers, just outside Libramont.

Rolling westwards across Luxembourg, through Diekirch and Ettelbruck on their designated 'Rollbahn', the 1. Panzer-Division reached the Belgian border at Martelange within hours. As Hauptmann von Kielmansegg, the division's intelligence officer, put it: 'the inhabitants did not have time to rub the sleep out of their eyes'. However, just inside Belgium at Bodange, the Chasseurs Ardennais had prepared their own welcome, holding up the Germans for most of the day. This picture shows PzKpfw IIs having broken through to Witry ten kilometres further down the N45 after joining the airborne elements of Operation Niwi.

push its cavalry units as quickly as possible east of the Meuse to flank those of the 2ème Armée on a line Marche-Rochefort. Corap's cavalry crossed the Meuse all through the night and by morning of May 11 his 3ème Brigade de Spahis had established contact with Huntziger's 5ème D.L.C. while his 1ère D.L.C. and 4ème D.L.C. had travelled as far as the sector east of Saint-Hubert, reaching the Ourthe river. While the names of Rotterdam and Maastricht were monopolising the communiqués and the attention of the French Command, the true danger was creeping undetected through the Ardennes.

SATURDAY, MAY 11

During the night, to counter the expected French threat on its left flank, Gruppe von Kleist had ordered the 10. Panzer-Division to change direction at once and face south. General Heinz Guderian asked for the cancellation of this order and instead, as a precaution, ordered this division to move along a road north of its designated route. This shifted units of the 10. Panzer-Division into the sector previously allocated to

The Chasseurs Ardennais had fulfilled their orders well, carrying out extensive demolitions and obstructing roads which successfully delayed the German advance. This PzKpfw III helps clear a road blocked by the Belgian demolitions but all this took time and by the evening of May 10 Gruppe von Kleist was still far from its planned objectives for the first day.

The pictures taken in Witry that day fail to show any airborne troops so perhaps they had left before the photographer travelling with 1. Panzer-Division arrived. Here the divisional artillery from Art.Rgt. 73 presses on towards Neufchâteau.

Witry also figured in the Wacht am Rhein offensive in December 1944 and today a memorial stone stands in the village, marking the limit of the German advance (by the 5. Fallschirm-Jäger-Division) in this part of the 'Bulge'.

Seventeen kilometres west of Neuf-château, a PzKpfw III of Panzer-Regiment 2 came to grief when it skidded into a crater blown in the N45 on the western edge of Bertrix. The tank was still firmly embedded in the mud when this picture was taken on May 12. Though the number is not visible in this shot, it was II01 indicating that it belonged to the commander of the regiment's II. Abteilung — a man no doubt not in the best humour that Sunday morning.

the 1. Panzer-Division, which then tangled into the advance route of the 2. Panzer-Division, whose units in turn became mixed with those of the 6. Panzer-Division. Had Allied aircraft attacked the traffic jams, the consequences might have been dramatic, but not so much as a reconnaissance aircraft appeared in the sky that day. Gruppe von Kleist went along with Guderian's measures but the threat to the flank did

PzKpfw IIs of the regiment's 2. Kompanie take a breather in the centre of the town.

On Saturday (May 11), Gruppe von Kleist wheeled southwards to rush the Semois to secure crossings for the advance on

Sedan. These motor-cycle troops were pictured in Nollevaux ten kilometres short of the river on Sunday morning.

not materialise as aerial reconnaissance had mistaken the three 2ème Armée cavalry units for more powerful armoured units.

The demolitions and minefields along the border having been cleared, the panzer divisions moved forward at noon. Withdrawing Belgian Chasseurs Ardennais, elements of the 3ème Brigade de Spahis and the 5ème D.L.C. lay in their path, and the 1. Panzer-Division had to fight for Neufchâteau and Bertrix, the French units being attacked incessantly by waves of Stukas. German air support, as described by Oberstleutnant Soldan, was at its 'most admirable' during this critical period, after much time had been lost by the foremost units because of the cratering of roads. 'Planes, watching the situation from above' wrote Soldan, 'promptly recognised any position where help was needed. Dive-bombers flung themselves on the enemy and opened the way for the countless vehicles whose engines were making a terrible noise as they laboured through this forest region of hills and mountains.'

After confused fighting which lasted for several hours, the hard-pressed 5ème D.L.C. was forced back on the Semois. To avoid being cut off the 9ème Armée's 3ème Brigade de Spahis had to pull back too and by 5.30 p.m. they were on the south bank of the river with the bridges blown behind them. The 1. Panzer-Division took Bertrix and then

By Saturday evening advance parties had actually reached the river at Bouillon. Oberst Johannes Nedtwig, the commander of Panzer-Regiment 1 (1. Panzer-Division) was pictured in his PzKpfw III command tank (hence the number R01) as he entered the town on Sunday.

moved west as far as Fays-les-Veneurs, to turn due south for Sedan, some 30 kilometres away, and as dusk was falling, it reached Bouillon only to find the

Semois bridge blown. Another destroyed bridge was taken at Frahan, a few kilometres to the west, and further to the west a ford was found at

Throughout the day transport from the division lined the streets of the town waiting for a bridge to be completed across

the Semois. Down in the town smoke drifts from houses damaged by French artillery.

Below: General Guderian personally came down to the crossing to check on the progress on the bridge-building. With him in this picture taken on Sunday is Leutnant Voss and Leutnant Munk (in the black panzer uniforms) of Pz.Aufkl.Abt. 4 and Major Alexander von Scheele, the commander of the recce

battalion. *Above left:* A 2cm Flak 38 has been positioned on the undamaged eastern span to cover the engineers at work about 200 metres downstream *(bottom)*. It was a wise precaution as the Royal Air Force sent three Battles to attack Bouillon during the afternoon.

One of the most remarkable pictures of the entire campaign in May 1940 was taken that Sunday morning by Lieutenant Lucien Saint-Genis flying at 2600 metres over Bouillon. His aircraft, a Potez 63/11 of G.R. II/22, the reconnaissance squadron attached to the French 2ème Armée, was piloted by Capitaine Fouché with Sergent Taieb as gunner. When they arrived over the town at 9.30 a.m., German transport was lining the river on the eastern side and some tanks were even caught in the very act of fording the river a few hundred metres west of the destroyed road bridge.

Mouzaive and elements of the recce battalion under Leutnant Werner Dürckess established themselves on the other side during cover of darkness.

That night, the German staffs had much to be satisfied with. Gruppe von Kleist had caught up with its timetable; it had taken its objectives for the second day, and those French cavalry units encountered by the panzers had been forced back.

For the French, the situation was

All day engineers worked to construct the trestle bridge seen here in the background. However, when completed at 6.00 p.m. on Sunday evening, its classification was only 8 tonnes — suitable for lighter wheeled vehicles only — tanks still having to make their way across under their own steam like this PzKpfw I *(above)* and PzKpfw III *(right)*. Later Brü.Bau-Btl. 531 moved in to build a 16-tonne bridge to cater for the panzers, although by then the division had all crossed to the west. *Below:* Fifty years after — the rebuilt bridge overlooks the site of the assault crossing.

worsening. Corap, who had ordered his cavalry units back behind the Meuse far earlier than anticipated, asked Général Billotte for reinforcements. Although the French Command reacted to the threat in the Ardennes, it did not panic as it viewed the German advance in terms of their own logistic abilities. As

yet the French had not begun to understand what was happening and the Command was still determined to follow the Dyle Plan in spite of the news from the 9ème and 2ème Armées. In fact, it was not easy to divine the Germans' intentions on May 11, for the Ardennes was by no means the only sector in which things were not going too well, the enemy having captured airfields and bridges in the Netherlands . . . taken Fort Eben-Emael . . . and attacked the Maginot Line in the 3ème Armée sector. These feint attacks on the Line, as part of the plan to discourage French reserves from being moved

Further to the west at Mouzaive, the 2. Panzer-Division was also crossing the Semois on Sunday. Tank No. 142 was a PzKpfw III.

Cavalry fording the river just upstream of the bridge (from which the picture was taken) with the village of Mouzaive on the right.

northwards, were to last for four days — long enough to assist the breakthrough. With more or less the entire front on the boil from Holland to Alsace, and the main blow expected for certain in northern Belgium, the French Command was not going be alarmed by what was happening on one of the other 'secondary' fronts. It also failed to appreciate the urgency, still thinking in terms of the rate of advance in the last war. As a result the first elements of the units sent to reinforce the Sedan sector would not arrive before May 14 and the main bodies would not be there before May 15 or 16.

SUNDAY, MAY 12

The three divisions of XIX. Armeekorps had now moved southwards in the direction of Sedan, having left enough room on the roads through Luxembourg and Belgium to enable the XXXXI. Armeekorps, which had set

The stone bridge at Mouzaive must be pretty unique in Western Europe as it was never destroyed, neither in 1940 nor in 1944. However the reason is simple: it was very narrow, barely a metre wide, and little more than a footbridge although it could have been used by men on horseback. In this shot, a SdKfz 11 demonstrates its prowess as a prime-mover by towing across a Magirus M206 as well as an artillery piece. By this time on Monday, the leading panzers had already reached Sedan, 15 kilometres to the south.

The main crossing point across the Semois for the 2. Panzer-Division was a couple of kilometres to the west at Vresse where a ford had been discovered late on Saturday by a platoon of Kradschützen-Bataillon 2, the divisional reconnaisance battalion, under Leutnant Werner Dürckess. *Above:* On Sunday, this column of PzKpfw IVs was pictured approaching the crossing site, passing in front of the Hôtel à la Glycine. The leading panzer was an Ausf. D, the followers Ausf. C. The double dot insignia identifying the division can be seen on the front armour plate and left-hand corner of the superstructure below the yellow rhomboid panzer emblem. The '5' indicates that these tanks belonged to the 5. Kompanie. *Below:* Today Vresse is a pleasant, peaceful village with the hotel still in business, having been enlarged. The beautiful wisteria, after which the hotel was named, has now grown so much that it covers most of the lower floors.

off behind it, to overtake on the right. The XXXXI. Armeekorps's two panzer divisions advanced in the path of the 2. Panzer-Division as far as the Paliseul area, continuing westwards when Guderian's armour turned southwards. The last French units east of the Meuse in the Monthermé sector having withdrawn the previous night, the bridges were blown in the morning of May 12: the road bridge at Monthermé at 6.15 a.m. and at Château-Regnault at about 7.00 a.m. However the railway bridge south of Monthermé could not be destroyed before evening as the last train from Givet was due that afternoon.

Further south the 3ème Brigade de Spahis had withdrawn behind the Meuse, the last elements crossing the river at Mézières at the first light on May 13. Late on May 12 the advance guard of the 32. Infanterie-Division of the II. Armeekorps reached the Meuse near Givet and those of the 6. Panzer-Division were on the heights overlooking the Meuse east of Monthermé.

Guderian had spent the night at Neufchâteau and on the morning of May 12 he drove to Bouillon to see for himself the progress of Schtz.Rgt. 1

Right: **While a BMW motor cycle combination from Flak-Abteilung 92 (a Luftwaffe anti-aircraft unit) splashes across the river, an SdKfz 263** *(below)* **of Pz.Aufkl. Abt. 5 crosses dryshod. The tubular structure is a large-frame antenna for its long-range radio.**

Above: Two bridges were built at Vresse by Brückenbau-Bataillon 521, an 8-tonne bridge followed by a 16-tonne Brückengerät K. This panorama gives a superb illustration of the 2. Panzer-Division crossing the Semois. From left to right we can see the destroyed road bridge, the 8-tonne bridge, the 16-tonne bridge and the ford. A Magirus truck is returning northwards from a supply trip across the 8-tonne bridge while two SdKfz 263 armoured cars move in the opposite direction across the 16-tonne bridge. Meanwhile a PzKpfw II is about to ford the river. Behind, a Panzerbefehlswagen III has halted, waiting its turn to cross. This was in fact the same command tank that we have already seen moving westwards through Bavigne (see page 200). A group of German soldiers can be seen working at the far end of the 8-tonne bridge, and appear to be struggling with a horse and cart! On the far bank a group of prisoners, probably French, are gathered together in the field. *Left:* No chances could be taken against British or French air attacks and these three SdKfz 6/2 half-tracks mounting 3.7cm Flak 36 weapons of Flak-Abteilung 92 have just forded across to take up positions in the field overlooking the crossing site. *Right:* The armoured might of the German Army has faded into the history books while man and nature have combined to restore tranquility.

While convoys of the 2. Panzers press on southwards in the direction of Sedan, these motor cyclists have pulled up beside a fortified 'house' which controlled the D6 north of Fleigneux. The Maison Forte was basically a large camouflaged pillbox, the upper floor providing accommodation for the crew in peacetime. The four ground-level embrasures permitted machine gun fire from the corners with a 25mm anti-tank firing position in the centre. This particular pillbox has taken some punishment.

which had launched an all-out attack at 6.45 a.m. to force the Semois. The town was captured but the bridge was down and the engineers had to start work on a new one; but French artillery found the range and made it a difficult job.

For the first time since the beginning of the attack Allied aircraft were in the air. Three Battles of the Advanced Air Striking Force attacked the bridge at Bouillon in the afternoon, all returning safely but, of two waves of six Battles which attacked columns on the road between Bouillon and Neufchâteau later in the afternoon, six were shot down by light flak.

At Bouillon the German advance guard had found a ford some 50 metres downstream from the destroyed bridge and here the infantry had forced a crossing, followed by some panzers and personnel carriers. At about 6.00 p.m. the bridge was ready; meanwhile French artillery was still firing accurately at Bouillon and causing problems. French troops offered occasional resistance behind road blocks but the Semois had been forced. To the west the 2. Panzer-Division was at Vresse and to the east the 10. Panzer-Division was at Herbeumont. Bursting into France, by evening, the vanguards of both 1. and 10. Panzer-Division had reached Fleigneux, Saint-Menges and La Chapelle. Down the road at Sedan all the bridges were blown at around 8.00 p.m.

That night the German Command had to choose whether to bring their forces up to full strength — most of the artillery and infantry were still far behind the advance guards and the supply units were strained because of the overextended lines — or to exploit the

Jean Paul found the pillbox still standing beside the road six kilometres or so south from the Franco-Belgian frontier. Although long abandoned and overgrown, making an exact comparison impossible, this picture shows the fourth embrasure facing the road for a light machine gun.

Sedan is now less than five kilometres ahead down the N77 and a traffic jam has already backed up through the village of Givonne. Both these vehicles display the 'K' of Gruppe von

Kleist although the rear truck has a civilian number plate. The formation sign indicates that they both belong to the I. Abteilung of an artillery unit.

element of surprise to the utmost, without waiting for rest and reinforcements. The strategy of Fall Gelb called for pressing on, which is what it was decided to do. It was the right decision, for the French Command was, according to a report sent by Air Marshal A. S. Barratt at 8.00 p.m., 'not yet able to decide which of the two following enemy thrusts is the main attack,

Above: **Further down the road, on the outskirts of Sedan, the same photographer pictured this seemingly endless column of BMWs.** *Below:* **A timeless comparison with even the old cobbles breaking through the tarmac surface just like in 1940.**

general axis Maastricht-Gembloux or attack in the Ardennes in general direction Mézières with purpose turning Maginot Line'. The Allies had, as yet, no conception of 'Blitzkrieg' and the French made no real effort to hasten the

reinforcement of this sector ordered the night before. Although one armoured and three infantry divisions had started their moves, the first units would only begin to arrive on May 14, and the rest over the days that followed.

MONDAY, MAY 13
Sedan

At Sedan the main German assault would hit the 55ème Division d'Infanterie, which had arrived only recently and hastily occupied the unfinished positions along the Meuse. The division was not a good one — another Series B unit — and its ranks were filled with over-age reservists. Only four percent of the officers were regulars and it was poorly trained and was badly lacking in equipment.

The spearhead of Gruppe von Kleist had spent the night in preparation for the assault on the Meuse. The point of main effort lay with the 1. Panzer-Division, which had been reinforced by Infanterie-Regiment 'Gross Deutschland', together with all the available artillery, including that of the other two panzer divisions. The 10. Panzer-Division was on the Meuse just east of Sedan but the 2. Panzer-Division had yet to close up and reach the river to the west and only its reconnnaissance and motor cycle battalions would be ready in time.

The previous evening, the operations officer of the 1. Panzer-Division, Major Walther Wenck, had noted the remarkable similarity of the actual course of events to one of the actual war games held previously. Consequently he pulled out an order issued during the Kriegsspiel held at Koblenz on February 14 and, after merely changing the date, he issued the same order to the division!

On May 12 the VIII. Fliegerkorps — the Luftwaffe tactical command which had under its control the bulk of the

On Sunday, May 12, the VIII. Fliegerkorps was transferred to Luftflotte 3 and assigned to support Gruppe von Kleist. This formation is from I./Stukageschwader 76.

For five solid hours on Monday morning, the Luftwaffe hammered the French positions south of the Meuse. The French anti-aircraft defences, illustrated here by a twin 8mm Hotchkiss machine gun and crew, were very weak, and the morale of the 55ème Division d'Infanterie, which bore the brunt of the main assault, suffered from the weight of the attack.

Above: In Sedan, the Pont de la Gare had already been destroyed by the French, and anti-tank obstacles barred the way. Here a PzKpfw I appears to have broken down at the eastern end of the bridge. *Bottom:* The replacement bridge was inaugurated in 1957. In the background of both pictures is the spire of Saint-Léger church.

Left: A PzKpfw III of Pz.Rgt. 8 (10. Panzer-Division) has come a cropper while driving along the river bank. *Right:* Fortunately the tower of the church is visible beneath the arm of a crewman and enabled this otherwise impossible comparison.

Left: **The 1. Panzer-Division crossed the Meuse at Sedan between Floing and Glaire. Here a PzKpfw II of 4. Kompanie of Panzer-Regiment 1 drives cautiously across the bridge (note the Hakenkreuz (Swastika) Flag spread on the engine decking to**

provide air recognition).** *Right:* **We discovered that the picture had been taken from the yard of the Draperie Sedanaise factory — still in business five decades later in the same building on the eastern bank. Behind stands the village of Glaire.**

Stukas as six of the nine existing Ju 87 groups were subordinated to it — had been transferred from Luftflotte 2 (for which the Stukas had attacked in the Netherlands and in the Maastricht and Gembloux sectors) to Luftflotte 3. The feint to the north having now succeeded, the hammer blow was about to fall on Sedan and the dive bombers were ready to support Gruppe von Kleist for the crossing of the Meuse and the following advance westwards.

On May 13 a powerful air support operation was mounted to soften up the French positions south of the Meuse, the first appearing suddenly over the Meuse valley at 11.00 a.m. For about five hours, during which more than 200 sorties were flown, the Stukas attacked the French positions, aiming at the pillboxes on the bank of the Meuse and the artillery positions just behind them. They were backed up by Dornier Do 17s and Heinkel He 111s of II. Fliegerkorps which put in 310 sorties.

A member of the 1. Panzer-Division, Unteroffizier Schulze, writing later for *Militär Wochenblatt*, described the scene: 'Suddenly they start to dive; a

On the far bank of the river Guderian was greeted, with the light-hearted cry: 'Pleasure boating on the Meuse is forbidden!' by Oberstleutnant Hermann Balck, the commander of Schtz.Rgt. 1. Here Balck (in forage cap looking at the camera) keeps a close eye on things as infantry walk down the access ramp to the pontoon bridge, passing French prisoners who have just reached the eastern bank.

The scene at the end of the bridge on the western bank. Although the Hague Convention on prisoners-of-war forbids their employment in an active war zone, these French soldiers have obviously been detailed to improve access to the crossing. (Article 3 of the Convention declares: 'The state may employ

the labours of prisoners-of-war ... the work shall not be excessive and shall have no connection with the operations of war.') Here they take a breather as an SdKfz 251 trundles across. In the background, then as now, the Draperie Sedanaise factory, although the chimney was demolished in the 1970s.

The frustrations of the Monday morning traffic jam show on the face of this tanker as he waits his turn to proceed in his PzKpfw II.

A few days later, Balck had the honour of being named in the Army daily report for having 'through tireless personal engagement, gained oustanding successes with his troops south-east of Sedan.'

At 5.30 p.m., the bridgehead at Glaire was firm enough for the engineers to start the construction of a 16-tonne pontoon bridge. An hour later the first pontoon ferry was ready and was operated non-stop to carry panzers, armoured cars and anti-aircraft guns across the river, while motor cycles and the lighter 3.7cm Pak 35/36 were shipped across in rubber boats. A second ferry was soon ready and the pontoon bridge being built at Glaire was completed at about midnight.

French artillery shelled the area but the batteries had no forward observers to correct their fire and it was not accurate enough to prevent the crossing. Although his men were exhausted, Guderian threw wave after wave over

screaming sets in and the dive becomes even steeper. Three or four bombs are loosed, the screaming grows shriller, there is an impact and a deafening detonation. Only a cloud of dust remains to be seen where the enemy position was. Meanwhile the planes are up and away, their mission accomplished. A new wave of Stukas comes roaring up, some sixty to a hundred of them over Sedan, preparing the infantry's decisive thrust.'

For the French Command, the sudden attack in this sector was a complete surprise. Only that morning Général Grandsard had agreed with his staff that the Germans would not be able to do anything for several days, there being 'time to bring heavy artillery and ammunition supplies forward.'

As the Stukas screamed over, softening up the defences on the southern bank, the rubber boats and rafts were brought across the fields and concealed near the water's edge. Artillery and panzers advanced up to the river bank and at about 3.00 p.m. they began firing at point-blank range at the French pillboxes and machine gun nests on the far side.

The crossing began with hundreds of men dashing for the river, pushing out into the water and paddling furiously across. There were some casualties but the majority reached the far bank unscathed. By 4.00 p.m. the 1. Panzer-Division had succeeded in getting across at Glaire, as had the 10. Panzer-Division east of it near Wadelincourt. However the 2. Panzer-Division assault was too weak and had been repulsed by heavy fire at Donchery. Guderian himself crossed the Meuse in one of the first assault boats of the second wave and was greeted cheerfully on the far bank at Glaire by the commander of Schtz.Rgt. 1, Oberstleutnant Hermann Balck, with the cry 'Pleasure boating on the Meuse is forbidden!' This was a take-off using the very words spoken by Guderian during an exercise some months earlier when it seemed to him that some of his young officers were taking things rather too light-heartedly.

In the jam at Floing on the 13th, this Sturmgeschütz Ausf. A was a very rare beast indeed as only 30 of the type had then been produced. The two crewmen just visible would have been wearing the special uniform which had been designed for assault gun crews based on the style of the black panzer suit but in green material.

A far cry from the activity of May 1940 — the same spot on the D5 today.

219

Above: **The crossing point for the 2. Panzer-Division was a couple of kilometres to the west at Donchery. As with all the bridges in the sector, the road bridge had been well and truly destroyed by French engineers.**

Below: **A perfect comparison by Jean Paul Pallud from the northern bank . . . but a view not to be seen for much longer as the factory on the far side has closed and is scheduled to be pulled down.**

the Meuse; in Schulze's words: 'The men, exhausted, drop into the grass. The troops that have not yet seen action now climb down from their vehicles and take up the pursuit.'

The bridgehead was widened to the west with the capture of Donchery but to the east, at Wadelincourt, progress was slow. La Marfée Woods were infiltrated in the evening and the French artillery batteries concentrated on the high ground there were attacked under cover of darkness eliminating the main threat to the bridgehead.

During the night Guderian sent a signal to General Ernst Busch, the commander of the 16. Armee, who, at the conference with Hitler in Berlin had questioned Guderian's ability to cross the Meuse, informing him of his success.

The efforts of the engineers to build a pontoon bridge at Donchery were harrassed by the repeated shelling from French artillery, and it was not until Tuesday that the Brückengerät B

pontoon bridge was completed. Two bridges, in fact, had to be constructed: one across the Meuse *(above)* and another across the canal parallel to it *(bottom)*.

With the French shelling the site all day on Monday, key elements were sent over to Floing to use the 1. Panzer's bridge. The 15cm self-propelled gun seen here — 'Edith' to her crew — was from the sIG Kompanie 703 which had been temporarily subordinated to 2. Panzer-Division.

TUESDAY, MAY 14
Sedan

During the night the 1. Panzer-Division had expanded the bridgehead and soon reached Chéhéry and Vendresse. At Glaire, elements of the 2. Panzer-Division crossed using the 1. Panzer-Division's bridge and started moving westwards along the bank of the Meuse. Meanwhile the 10. Panzer-Division had advanced southwards, taking the high ground south of Bulson, reaching Maisoncelle and easily blocked a counter-attack launched by the 55ème Division d'Infanterie in the morning.

Bridging the river with pontoons suitable for each of the panzer divisions was not an easy task as the Meuse at Sedan was very wide. In a study drawn up in April 1940 three 'probable' bridge sites at Sedan had been chosen. However it was found that the width of the river at the bridge site chosen for the '21. Panzer-Division' (code-name for the 1. Panzer-Division in the study) was between 60 to 70 metres; the one at Donchery at the site chosen for the '22. Panzer-Division' (2. Panzer-Division) was 80 metres; and the one at Balan chosen for the '210. Panzer-Division' (10. Panzer-Division) was between 60 to 70 metres.

By the evening of May 13 the French Command had at last understood the

Having manhandled their 8.8cm Flak 18 across the first bridge (in the picture at the top of the page), the gun crew push and

pull it the last few metres over the canal bridge *(above)*. Now its prime mover can take over again.

221

In service with the bridge-building units was a miscellany of equipment such as Brückengerät C, rated at just over 5 tonnes (see page 235), and Brückengerät K with a 16-tonne classification (see page 212). The 8-tonne Brückengerät B could be up-rated to 16 tonnes by doubling up the number of pontoons.

Even so, loads had to be split up to avoid mishaps from overloading (like the disaster which befell the impatient Leutnant Zobel at Houx on page 189). *Below:* Mirror on the Meuse — another fine comparison with an artistic flavour thrown in as well.

At 10.00 a.m. on Monday morning, Général Billotte, the C-in-C of the North-East Front, called his counterpart in Air Ops North (Z.O.A. Nord), Général François d'Astier de la Vigerie, to send every available aircraft against the bridges at Sedan. 'Victory or defeat depend on these bridges,' he implored.

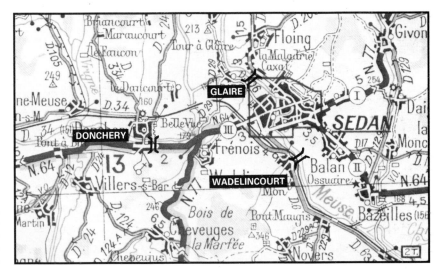

gravity of the situation in the Ardennes and had decided to send every available aircraft to attack the bridgehead. They also requested that Advanced Air Striking Force bombers be sent at first light the following morning to pontoon bridges in the Dinant and Sedan sectors. Two operations were prepared during the night but the projected one at Dinant was cancelled when news was received that the bridges here had already been destroyed by French

To defend the vital bridgehead, Flak-Regiment 102 was deployed in and around the town, this 2cm Flak 30 being set up right in the centre on the Place d'Alsace-Lorraine which gave it a good all-round field of fire.

engineers. The attack against Sedan was duly delivered at first light on May 14 by six Battles of No. 103 Squadron, this raid being followed at around 7.00 a.m. by another attack from four Battles of No. 150 Squadron. The RAF aircraft were followed at 10.00 a.m. by nine Bréguet 693s from the 54ème Escadre which attacked columns of the 10. Panzer-Division near Bazeilles and the pontoon bridge at Wadelincourt.

In the morning the news from the Sedan sector was very grave indeed. The Germans had greatly enlarged their bridgehead, and Général Georges and

Général Gamelin both asked Air Marshal A. S. Barratt for maximum air support. As we have seen, the operation planned in the Dinant area was cancelled, so the Advanced Air Striking Force was ordered to bring every bomber they could to bear on Sedan. In conjunction with the French Air Force, the day witnessed the heaviest series of daylight bombing attacks carried out by the RAF during the campaign. A plan was agreed for a four-wave attack, the first by the Armée de l'Air to be followed by three attacks by Advanced Air Striking Force bombers.

The first attack came just after midday, five LeO 451s of the 12ème Escadre attacking the Meuse crossing just east of Sedan at 12.30 a.m. One aircraft was shot down by a Bf 109, only two members of the crew escaping by parachute before the bomb load went off in the burning aircraft, the explosion killing the other three crewmen. At this same time, four Amiot 143s of the 34ème Escadre arrived with the same objectives: pontoon bridges and troop concentrations in the vicinity of Sedan. The antiquated Amiot 143s were obsolete by 1940, even more unsuited to their task than the Battles, and two were shot down, one by a Bf 110, another by flak. The latter was being flown by the commander of the second group of the 34ème Escadre, Commandant Dieudonné de Laubier, and he

Throughout Tuesday, desperate attempts were made by British and French aircraft to knock out the pioneer bridges at Sedan and ten Battles went in during the morning, followed by nine Bréguet 693s. Further attacks were made by five LeO 451s and four Amiot 143s in the afternoon, three of which were shot down including the machine of the CO of the second group of the 34ème Escadre. Commandant Dieudonné de Laubier (left) decided to led his men personally in Amiot No. 56 of Lieutenant Jean Vauzelle, piloted by Sergent-Chef Georges Occis. All three men lost their lives and now share a common grave in Floing Military Cemetery.

crashed not far from the bridge at Donchery.

Most bombers available to the Advanced Air Striking Force were committed in the afternoon, about 70 bombing bridges and troops columns in the Meuse valley in three attacks over a total of 45 minutes. No. 76 Wing sent 19

The RAF's Air Component, targetting both the bridges and troop concentrations in the Sedan area, lost 35 of the 63 Battles sent out, and five of the eight Blenheims. This Battle was photographed down somewhere in the Sedan sector on Tuesday. By nightfall the gunners of Flak-Regiment 102 had had a field day, a success which was to be recognised by the award of the Ritterkreuz to their commanding officer, Oberst Walter von Hippel.

Battles in the first wave of which 11 were lost; No. 71 Wing sent 15 Battles and 8 Blenheims in the second attack losing 10 Battles and 5 Blenheims, and No. 75 Wing sent 29 Battles in the third losing 14.

A further raid took place in the evening when 28 Blenheims of No. 21, No. 107 and No. 110 Squadrons, with strong fighter protection, bombed troop movements at Bouillon and east of Sedan. Six of the aircraft were shot down. Another attack was launched during the night by six Farman 222 heavy bombers from the 15ème Escadre which bombed the western edge of Sedan.

As Guderian noted, 'The extremely brave French and English pilots did not succeed in knocking out the bridges, despite the heavy casualties they had suffered. Our anti-aircraft gunners proved themselves on this day, and shot superbly.' The gunners from Flak-Regiment 102 defending the bridges near Sedan claimed later to have shot down 150 enemy aircraft, quite probably an inflated figure, and their commander, Oberst Walter von Hippel, was awarded the Ritterkreuz on July 29, 1940.

French positions along the river line were hammered mercilessly. In the wood on the southern bank this pillbox was shattered by a direct hit from artillery firing over open sights across the Meuse. A German photographer recorded the scene after the battle had passed over.

The 295ème Regiment of the 55ème Division d'Infanterie had occupied the heights above Wadelincourt and had fought vainly to hold the last major river line. This was another strongpoint knocked out on May 14.

With no recognisable background, Jean Paul could not believe his eyes when he found the same pillbox, still standing, amid a newly-planted field of maize. The damage was identical: the same two hits with the direct strike on the embrasure.

Only when he looked inside did he realise the significance of another of the pictures in his file — it was a deeply moving moment when he realised that he had found the location of this scene of carnage.

The very emptiness of the place where four men paid the supreme sacrifice for their country — Pour la France — added to the sanctity of the moment. Yet did anyone still really care, he wondered?

225

By Tuesday evening the battle of the Meuse had been lost for the French. Having failed to perceive the Ardennes force as the main threat, the French High Command had taken Hitler's bait hook, line and sinker, and had been caught in the trap. Outwitted and out-manoeuvred, from now on nothing could be done to stop the inexorable German war machine in its advance to the sea. *Above:* Resplendent in his all-black panzer uniform, the commander of the lead tank waits impatiently as the engineers put the finishing touches to the ramp to the pontoon bridge at Wadelincourt.

In view of the appalling losses suffered on May 14, the Battles of the Advanced Air Striking Force were switched to night bombing over Sedan the following day and, although the results were far from effective, all returned safely.

The commander of Heeresgruppe A, Generaloberst Gerd von Rundstedt, came to Sedan to have a look at the situation at about midday, Guderian reporting proudly to him in the very

Meanwhile one of the artillerymen captured on the south bank is escorted back by a wounded rifleman of Schützen-Brigade 10.

The breakout. This PzKpfw II Ausf. A of Panzer-Brigade 4 of 10. Panzer-Division advances south from the Wadelincourt bridgehead up the hill to the Bois de la Marfée. The motorbike is from Schützen-Brigade 10.

centre of the bridge then being completed at Donchery while the French Amiot 143's air raid was going on. When von Rundstedt asked drily, 'Is it always like this here?' Guderian smiled that it was.

Even for the Germans the day had not gone all their way and the XIX. Armeekorps' day summary noted in the evening that 'The completion of the pontoon bridge at Donchery had not yet been carried out owing to heavy flanking artillery fire and long bombing attacks on the bridging point . . . Throughout the day all three divisions have had to endure constant air attacks, especially at the crossings and bridging points.'

In the face of these attacks, the engineers had worked hard and by late evening all three panzer divisions had their own pontoon bridge in service, the 2. Panzer-Division's having finally been completed at Donchery and another near Wadelincourt for the 10. Panzer-Division.

The tell-tale 'Z' pattern of the hedges on the far hillside gave the clue as to where the shot had been taken . . .

. . . and from that it was possible to find this picture of an SdKfz 10 half-track with its accompanying 3.7cm Pak 36 anti-tank gun.

Now the expansion of the bridgehead was gaining momentum . . . breakout was just around the corner.

Moving westwards, Sugny lies midway between Bouillon and Charleville-Mézières, ten kilometres or so north of the Meuse, and it was here that this picture was taken on Monday. These SdKfz 263 radio cars could belong either to 2. Panzer-Division, in which case they would turn south to Sedan, or to 6. Panzer-Division, whereupon they would advance west to Nouzonville.

MONDAY, MAY 13
Monthermé

The 102ème Division de Forteresse was responsible for the Meuse from Anchamps, just east of Revin, to the River Bar. At Monthermé the German assault would hit the division's 42ème Demi-Brigade consisting of two battalions of colonial machine gunners.

The traffic jams on the narrow and meandering approach roads allocated to the XXXXI. Armeekorps had caused confusion and delay and at this stage the corps commander, General Georg-Hans Reinhardt, had very little of his two panzer divisions with which to force

the Meuse. When they arrived, the 6. Panzer-Division was to try to cross at Monthermé and the 8. Panzer-Division further south at Nouzonville.

In the early afternoon, as a thin mist floated down the Meuse valley, the third battalion of Schtz.Rgt. 4 was assembling on the heights overlooking Monthermé. Surveying the scene from the hill, the battalion's commander, Oberstleutnant Rudolf Höfer, observed the destroyed bridge, the extensive barbed wire entanglements along the river bank and some concrete pillboxes. His 11. Kompanie was to attack on the right of the bridge, the 9. Kompanie on

its left leaving the 10. Kompanie in reserve.

Carrying rubber boats, machine guns, mortars and ammunition down the steep, rocky slopes, men of Pi.Btl. 57 and Schtz.Rgt. 4 approached the river. At first they were not fired at by the French, possibly because they were hidden by the mist, but as they raced down the last fifty metres, they were caught in the open. Jumping into the boats the men paddled furiously across but the 9. Kompanie was unable to gain a foothold. The 11. Kompanie did however succeed in getting across and Höfer immediately reinforced it with

At Charleville, the Meuse turns almost at right angles to run northwards, and it was at Monthermé, ten kilometres north of the city, that Schtz.Rgt. 4 made an assault crossing on Monday afternoon under cover of an artillery barrage. *Left:* This is

11. Kompanie setting out for the French-held bank in a rubber assault craft. They succeeded in establishing a bridgehead and within two hours the 5ème Compagnie of the 42ème Demi-Brigade had been overwhelmed.

the 9. Kompanie. After two hours of fierce fighting on the river bank, the French 5ème Compagnie of the 42ème Demi-Brigade (which held the tip of the bend at Monthermé) had been overwhelmed and their commander, Lieutenant Paul Barbaste, killed when trying to force a way out. The French thereupon withdrew to their second line of defence which crossed the foot of the bend a few kilometres to the south, members of the 5ème Compagnie filtering back to the new line in the evening.

When viewed that evening, the position of XXXXI. Armeekorps was worrying. Its two panzer divisions were both stuck at their crossing places, although the 6. Panzer-Division did have a small bridgehead at Monthermé, but at Nouzonville the 8. Panzer-Division's efforts had come to naught in the face of stiff French resistance. This was even more frustrating as the neighbouring infantry corps, the II. Armeekorps to the right and the III. Armeekorps on the left, had reached the Meuse, the former in the Givet area, the latter near Mézières and Nouzonville, and were already all prepared to cross it.

While engineers of the 6. Panzer-Division were struggling to complete a pontoon bridge, the first available sections of the Brückengerät B were used as rafts to ferry panzers (like this PzKpfw IV of the 3. Kompanie) across on Wednesday. To ease the problem of access, the engineers had sited the bridge right in front of the Rue du Port leading down to the river bank.

Taken from the heights overlooking the town — the position from where the advanced elements of the 6. Panzers first overlooked the river on Sunday evening — this picture shows

the completed pontoon bridge just downstream of the demolished road bridge (visible on the left of the picture at the top of the page).

TUESDAY, MAY 14
Monthermé

At Monthermé, the engineers of 6. Panzer-Division had found that a safe crossing was possible along the metal girders of the road bridge which had fallen into the river, and a footbridge had been hastily improvised during the night with wooden planks and rubber boats lashed together and roped to the girders. Throughout the night French artillery fired at the bridge site, damaging the footbridge, but this did not stop the Germans from bringing up another battalion to support Höfer's weary

Further north, the swift advance meant that many towns and villages were now falling with barely a shot being fired. Thirty kilometres away to the north-east, in Belgium, the Aufklärungs-Abteilung of 32. Infanterie-Division, marching in the van of II. Armeekorps, had entered Beauraing on Sunday afternoon. Having arrived from the direction of Rochefort, this SdKfz 7 is pictured turning westwards in the direction of Givet, the next large town on the N40, but actually in France.

troops. In the afternoon, with Hoth's leading panzers having already advanced fifteen kilometres west of the Meuse, Reinhardt's armour was still pinned down in the Meuse valley. Consequently the commander of the 6. Panzer-Division, Generalmajor Werner Kempf, ordered an all out attack to be launched to break through the French line at the base of the Meuse bend at Monthermé. A Stuka attack had been arranged to precede the assault but when, after two hours, the aircraft failed to appear, the infantry went ahead on their own but still failing to break out of the bridgehead.

A group of refugees watch in despair as the Germans rumble past through the deserted streets.

Although the N40 from Beauraing runs more or less in a westerly direction, six kilometres further down the road a narrow finger of French territory bisects the road either side of Givet (see map page 74). The result is that two customs posts are encountered within ten kilometres of each other as the road enters and leaves France. *Left:* This SdKfz 7 — an early type built by Krauss-Maffei — ignores the formalities as it crosses the border. *Right:* As this is only a minor frontier post today, it is not surprising that the original French customs building is still in use.

Sitting astride the Meuse, and at the junction of the east-west N40 and the north-south N51/N96, Givet was a strategic objective. Aufkl.Abt. 32 reached the town on Monday afternoon and the following morning these stormtroopers were filmed clearing Petit Givet — that part of the town which lies east of the river. Jean Paul Pallud established that the first picture *(above)* had been taken in Rue Joly, although he found that the

street had since been turned into private property for half its length. With no other access, in the end he climbed the gate to the furious barking of guard dogs — strictly, of course, in the pursuit of history. *Below left:* Further down the street the troopers approach the burned-out Café du Coin, but 'JP', following in their footsteps, finds only an empty street corner *(below right)*.

At the other end of the street — in Rue Chantereine — JP takes his place in another of his remarkable comparisons. *Left:* Harrassed by French sniping, the stormtroopers have taken shelter in a doorway, although the man with the grenade in his

boot seems largely unconcerned for his safety. *Right:* The author 'on the spot' 50 years later. What had seemed an almost impossible picture to match before reaching Givet now looks easy. Take a bow, JP!

WEDNESDAY, MAY 15
Monthermé

During the night the pontoon bridge had been built at Monthermé and some panzers from Pz.Rgt. 11 had been brought forward to back up the infantry. Reinhardt knew that he had to break out that morning as von Rundstedt had ordered his corps to be moved into reserve at midday, and the Monthermé sector was to be taken over by the infantry of the III. Armeekorps.

Early in the morning, the grenadiers of the 6. Panzer-Division launched another attack, backed by some of their panzers, and managed to overcome the French defences. Isolated French units fought back but the panzers moved on westwards, leaving the task of eliminating them to the infantry. At about 9.00 a.m. the command post of Lieutenant-Colonel Henri de Pinsun, the commander of the 42ème Demi-Brigade, was overrun. Success at Monthermé had resolved the situation at Nouzonville and a solid bridgehead was soon established there.

In the afternoon Bréguet 693s from the 54ème Escadre attacked the bridge site at Monthermé and the columns on the roads in the sector, being followed at about 3.00 p.m. by 12 Blenheims of No. 82 Squadron, Bomber Command, operating under French fighter protection, and a few minutes later by four Blenheims from the Advanced Air Striking Force. These repeated air attacks did not helped the 8. Panzer-Division's panzers in extricating themselves from traffic jams but, by superhuman efforts, the engineers managed to get a pontoon bridge across for the 8. Panzer-Division that night.

Small, scattered groups from French units attempted to withdraw westwards, some of them evading capture for several days, a few for even longer. By evening, the 102ème D.I.F. had practically disappeared, Lieutenant-Colonel de Pinsun had been taken prisoner and the divisional commander himself, Général François Portzert, was captured the following morning.

The XXXXI. Armeekorps, after three days of being stalled at the Meuse, now more than made up for lost time. At the end of the day, its advance elements were further west than any

Above: **Having assaulted the western bank of the Meuse, the men of the reconnaissance unit scaled the hill to take Fort de Charlemont, built by Charles XV in the 16th century when Givet was equally of strategic importance. In this picture, taken from the northernmost corner of the fort, down in the valley the destroyed road and rail bridges can be seen, as well as the beginnings of the Brückengerät B bridge then under construction.**

Though the fortress is now disused as such, it is still owned by the French Army and used for commando training, although it can be visited during the summer break.

Having just been captured, the French garrison is marched away under guard. Here they are passing through the Philippeville Gate.

Left: On the outskirts of Givet, the bridge over the small Houille river had been blown and these engineers of Pi.Btl. 263, two companies of which had been attached to 32. Infanterie-Division to help in bridging the Meuse at Givet, have just completed the construction of a new trestle bridge. Right: A modern replacement now carries the French D949 eastwards to the border with Belgium, about three kilometres away, at which point it becomes the Belgian N46 to Beauraing.

As with all the vital bridge crossing sites, anti-aircraft guns had been brought in. This 2cm Flak 30 was positioned on the eastern embankment of the destroyed railway bridge at Givet, and belonged most probably to I./Flak-Regiment 61.

The engineers positioned the 16-tonne Brückengerät B pontoon bridge about 300 metres downstream from the road bridge.

Left: The 12. Infanterie-Division crossed the Meuse on Tuesday at Heer, about three kilometres north of Givet. The usual bridging methods were adopted: first the rubber boats to take across men and light equipment, followed by the rafting of heavier items on the actual sections of the bridge as they were floated into position. *Right:* The Brückengerät C pontoon bridge was constructed down a track which meets the river at a place called Les Sorbiers.

The railway bridge at Givet rose again after the war only to fall foul of declining demand and revenue. No longer commercially viable, the railway is now disused, with the track barred by a steel gate.

The Heer bridge, with a classification of just over 5 tonnes, was completed within two days. This view is taken looking east.

Left: Another frontier post little changed from 50 years ago. This is Pussemange, west of Sugny (see page 228), where no doubt the cellar of the Café à l'Arrêt de la Douane proved irresistible to the thirsty warriors. *Right:* JP's antics, driving back and forth across the border armed with a camera, soon attracted the attention of the customs guards and they came after him in the white car, taking a close interest in what he was doing, yet not interfering.

Aiglemont lies near the Meuse close to Charleville where these soldiers of 23. Infanterie-Division were photographed carrying their assault craft down to the river for a crossing just north of the city. From the attitude of the two men on the right, one suspects that there was some air activity going on overhead when this picture was taken.

Further north, the 1. Gebirgs-Division, advancing on the right flank of the XVIII. Armeekorps, reached Fumay on Wednesday.

A Brückengerät C with a 4-tonne capacity was sufficient for the mountain troops with their four-legged friends.

other German units. Once the stubborn French defences on the Meuse had been breached, the 6. Panzer-Division found itself in the 'empty' rear of the 9ème Armée. Its tanks were able to cover up to 60 kilometres in one day, something few armoured units could achieve even on a peacetime exercise, and they soon bumped into those of Guderian's XIX. Armeekorps at Montcornet. Meanwhile

After their headlong rush across Luxembourg and Belgium, the forces of the German Schwerpunkt were entering France. The frontier defences had been pierced in a score of places and breakthrough was now about to become break-out. The die had been cast but to the Allied commanders in their remote headquarters the position was far from clear. *Above:* Down at the front, Charles de Gonzagues surveys a deserted Place Ducale in Charleville-Mézières, the city he founded in 1606 . . . deserted that is save for the men of the 6. Panzers. This PzKpfw 35(t) belonged to Panzer-Regiment 65.

news was received of the award of the Ritterkreuz to the commander of

Gruppe von Kleist, General Ewald von Kleist.

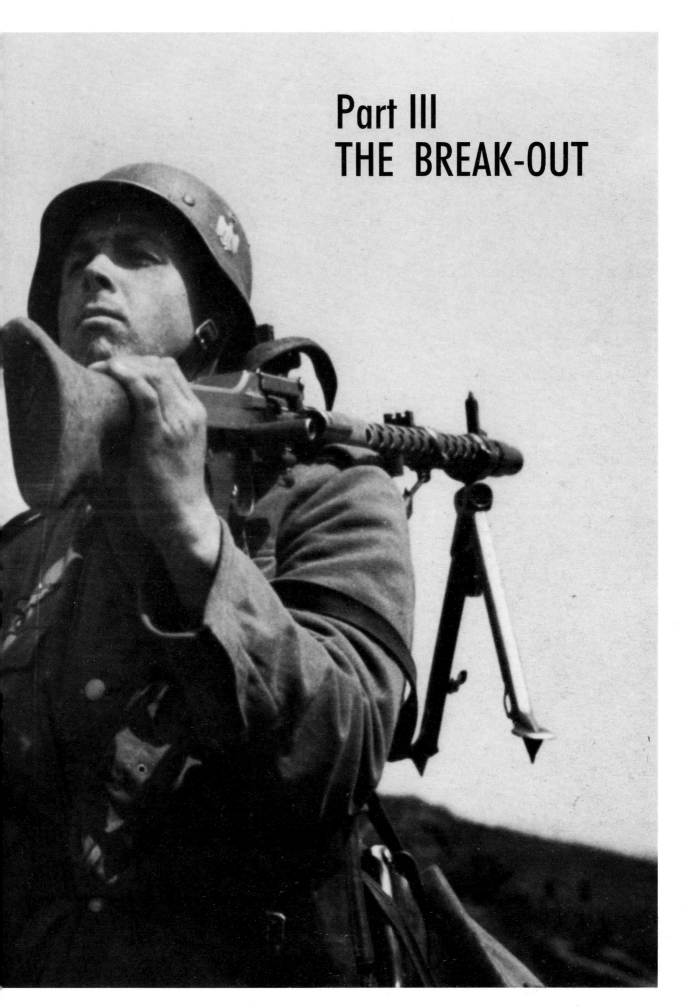

Part III
THE BREAK-OUT

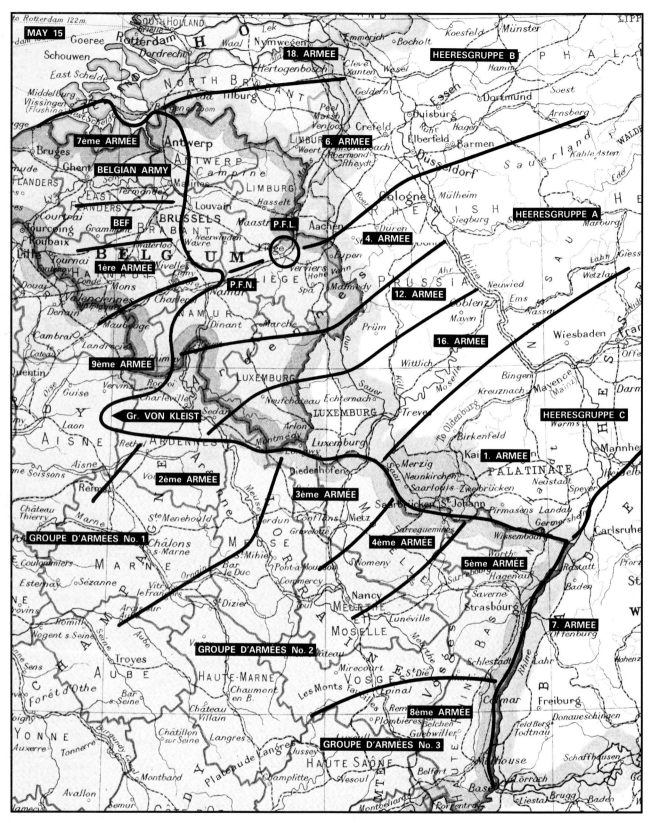

MAY 15

to Rotterdam 122 m.

18. ARMEE

HEERESGRUPPE B

7ème ARMÉE

6. ARMEE

BELGIAN ARMY

P.F.L.

HEERESGRUPPE A

BEF

4. ARMEE

1ère ARMÉE

12. ARMEE

P.F.N.

16. ARMEE

9ème ARMÉE

Gr. VON KLEIST

HEERESGRUPPE C

2ème ARMÉE

1. ARMEE

3ème ARMÉE

GROUPE D'ARMEES No. 1

4ème ARMÉE

5ème ARMÉE

7. ARMEE

GROUPE D'ARMEES No. 2

8ème ARMÉE

GROUPE D'ARMEES No. 3

On May 14 it was clear to the German Command that the Allies had so far failed to appreciate the strategic intentions of Fall Gelb. Hitler issued his Führer Directive No. 11 in which he stated that '. . . Heeresgruppe A have established the first essentials for a thrust in all possible strength north of the Aisne and in a north-westerly direction . . . Such a thrust might produce a major success . . . All available motorised divisions will be transferred to the operational area of Heeresgruppe A as soon as possible.' On May 15 the Netherlands capitulated and alarming reports of panzers having broken through and were advancing westwards, had reached Paris. Early that morning the French Prime Minister, Paul Reynaud, telephoned Churchill

in London and informed him that the counter-attacks had failed and that 'the road to Paris was open' and 'the battle was lost'. Churchill, in power now for just five days, could not accept that all could have been lost in less than a week's fighting, and he advised his Chiefs-of-Staff that he might have to fly to Paris 'to sustain the French Government'. His first visit to France took place on the afternoon of May 16 and at 5.30 p.m. he met with Reynaud, Daladier and Gamelin, 'utter dejection written on every face'. The acrimonious meeting led to the British acceding, in part, to the French request for more air support. Early on the 17th Churchill returned to London, depressed that the French were crumbling.

The XV. Armeekorps and the 9ème Armée

A grave threat was arising on the front of the 9ème Armée. Both panzer divisions of XV. Armeekorps had gained a bridgehead across the Meuse — the 5. Panzer-Division at Houx and the 7. Panzer-Division near Dinant — and on the morning of May 13 Général Corap issued his General Order No. 20 which proclaimed that it was 'crucial that any German elements which had set foot on the left bank of the Meuse be immediately destroyed or thrown back into the river'. However, a French counter-attack at Haut-le-Wastia early on May 14 failed to dislodge the Germans and the two panzer divisions continued to transfer more and more forces across the river. Just to the north, the two infantry divisions of VIII.

Armeekorps had started crossing the Meuse: the 8. Infanterie-Division at Yvoir and the 28. Infanterie-Division near Annevoie. Consequently Général Corap went to see the commander of the XIème Corps d'Armée, Général Julien Martin, at his command post at Florennes to brief him on the gravity of the situation, and inform him that he was being given two new units to prepare a counter-attack towards Dinant, the 1ère D.C.R. brought in from the 1ère Armée and the 4ème D.I.N.A. until now in army reserve.

On the morning of May 15 the French Command had a clear picture of the 9ème Armée situation and Général Billotte informed Général Gamelin that 'the 9ème Armée is in a very critical

situation, its whole front pushed back'. He also suggested that Général Corap should be relieved of his command and replaced by Général Giraud as 'the man best fitted to revive this failing army'.

During the night, the 1ère D.C.R., which had been assigned to the XIème Corps d'Armée, had advanced its armour in order to block the emergence of the German panzers from the Dinant-Yvoir bridgehead. The division, commanded by Général Marie-Germain Bruneau, consisted of two demi-brigades of two battalions of tanks each and one battalion of motorised infantry: the 1ère Demi-Brigade (Renault B1bis medium tanks), under Colonel Jean-Marie Rabanit, with the 28ème B.C.C. (Commandant Louis

The Führer and Supreme Commander of the Armed Forces

Headquarters, 14th May 1940

Directive No. 11

1. The progress of the offensive to date shows that the enemy has failed to appreciate in time the basic idea of our operations. He continues to throw strong forces against the line Namur–Antwerp and appears to be neglecting the sector facing Heeresgruppe A.

2. This fact and the swift forcing of the Meuse crossing in the sector of Heeresgruppe A have established the first essentials for a thrust in all possible strength north of the Aisne and in a north-westerly direction, as laid down in Directive No. 10. Such a thrust might produce a major success. It is the task of forces engaged north of the line Liège–Namur to deceive and hold down the greatest number of enemy forces by attacking them with their own resources.

3. On the northern flank the Dutch Army has shown itself capable of a stronger resistance than had been supposed. For political and military reasons, this resistance

*must be broken **quickly**. It is the task of the Army, by moving strong forces from the south in conjunction with an attack against the Eastern front, to bring about the speedy fall of Festung Holland.*

4. All available motorised divisions will be transferred to the operational area of Heeresgruppe A as soon as possible.

Armoured and motorised divisions of Heeresgruppe B will also be switched to the left flank as soon as there are no further prospects of effective operations in their own sector and as the situation allows.

*5. The task of the **Luftwaffe** is to concentrate strong offensive and defensive forces for action, with the focal point at Heeresgruppe A, in order to prevent the transfer of enemy reinforcements to the front and to give direct support to our own forces.*

In addition the rapid reduction of Festung Holland will be assisted by the deliberate weakening of forces hitherto operating ahead of 6. Armee.

*6. The **Kriegsmarine** will operate against sea traffic in the Hoofden and in the Channel as opportunity offers.*

ADOLF HITLER

Above: This French 155mm G.P.F. heavy artillery piece be-longed to the 219ème Régiment d'Artillerie of the 18ème Division d'Infanterie. The barrel appears to have been spiked before it was abandoned near Bioul, perhaps, as this picture was taken by Luftwaffe war photographer Stempka, after it had been stopped by dive-bombers. Below: At this point on the N532, we are five kilometres west of the Meuse. Now the dead straight, tree-lined road, typical of so many in provincial Belgium before the war, has been widened, losing the trees, yet the farm has survived virtually intact.

The wreck of 'Gard', a 2ème Compagnie Renault of the 37ème B.C.C., stands silent guardian over the graves of two French poilus in Belgium near Flavion. 'Gard' was knocked out on Wednesday, May 15, killing the entire crew.

Pinot) and 37ème B.C.C. (Commandant Jean-Marie de Cissey); the 3ème Demi-Brigade (Hotchkiss H-39 light tanks), under Colonel Charles Marc, with the 25ème B.C.C. (Commandant Maurice Pruvost) and the 26ème B.C.C. (Commandant Pierre Bonnot); and the 5ème Bataillon de Chasseurs Portés (Commandant Louis Perrodo).

Although accounts vary from one source to another, the 1ère D.C.R. had some 160 to 180 tanks — around 70 Renault B1bis with the 1ère Demi-Brigade and 90 or so Hotchkiss H-39s with the 3ème Demi-Brigade. The two German panzer divisions of XV. Armeekorps advancing towards it had a numerical superiority of something like three to one: the 7. Panzer-Division having some 200 panzers and the 5. Panzer-Division slightly over 300.

WEDNESDAY, MAY 15

The 28ème B.C.C. was at Flavion, just to the north of the main Dinant-Philippeville road, the 25ème B.C.C. near Corenne, the 26ème B.C.C. north-east of Flavion, and the 37ème B.C.C. just south of another east-west main road near Ermeton. Tactically the situation was good but many of the tanks were very low on fuel, especially the big and thirsty Renault B1bis of the 1ère Demi-Brigade. Although the 37ème B.C.C. received some more petrol on May 15 the 26ème B.C.C. had to go without.

By 8.30 a.m. the French tank crews noted panzers moving west near Anthée, just three kilometres east of Flavion. These were the leading elements of Pz.Rgt. 25 of 7. Panzer-Division. The French opened up to stop the advance, and for a time succeeded, but most of the panzers avoided a head-on, tank-versus-tank battle with the Renault B1bis and began to move through the wooded area to the south to skirt the French positions. The 7. Panzer-Division reconnaissance unit, Aufkl.Abt. 37, which followed them, maintained the pressure against the 26ème B.C.C. and 28ème B.C.C. while artillery was brought up into position. The French tanks mounted determined attacks and disabled some of the panzers and guns but they were greatly hampered by lack of fuel and, lacking mobility, they fell one by one under the German artillery barrage which soon opened up.

To the north the 37ème B.C.C. was ordered to counter-attack the panzers of Pz.Rgt. 31, 5. Panzer-Division,

The previous day 'Var', a Renault B1bis of the 2ème Compagnie, 37ème B.C.C., broke down in nearby Ermeton with mechanical problems. The crew were unable to get it going and withdrew, the tank commander, Sous-Lieutenant de la Romignière, remaining with the tank to guard it until he was picked up on Wednesday by 'Belfort II'. *Right:* When the Germans attempted to move the unwieldy vehicle, the house came off the worse for wear, the repair since being made with modern bricks.

243

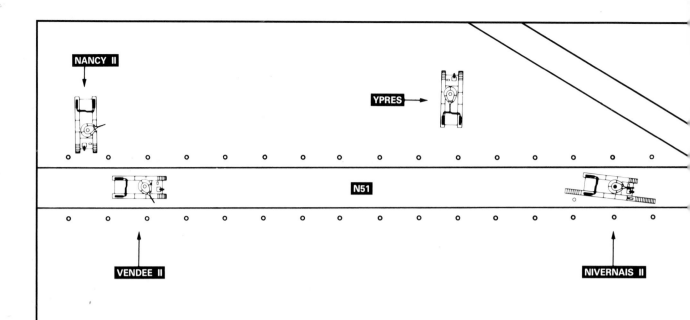

NANCY II

YPRES

N51

VENDEE II

NIVERNAIS II

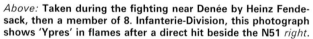

Above: Taken during the fighting near Denée by Heinz Fende-sack, then a member of 8. Infanterie-Division, this photograph shows 'Ypres' in flames after a direct hit beside the N51 *right.*

Below: After 'Ypres' stopped burning, the horrific sight of the dead crew was revealed: Lieutenant Michel Duhourceau, Caporal Gustave de Ridder and Caporal Paul Merger.

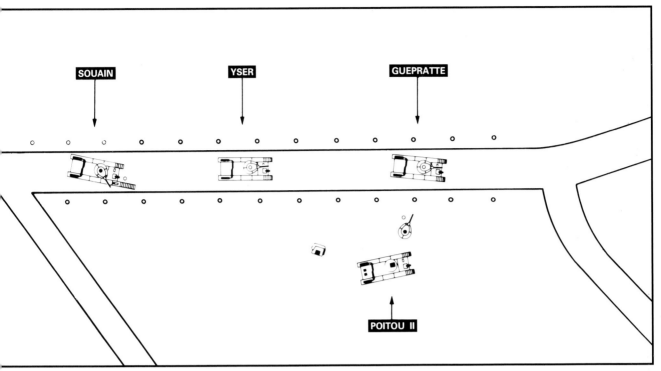

Lying some ten metres away from 'Yser' which can be seen in the background, this dead tanker might well be one of its crew, four men having been killed fighting in front of their stricken tank. Was he Sous-Lieutenant Georges Gossin, Sergent Jacques Stalin, Chasseur Maurice Josserand or Chasseur René Gicquel? We do not know.

which were moving west from the Houx bridgehead along the axis Sommiere-Faläen and thus threatening to outflank the 28ème B.C.C. Leading the counter-attack, the 2ème Compagnie of the 37ème B.C.C. hit the leading Germans hard but suffered heavily as a result. Fighting in his tank 'Guynemer' was Lieutenant Louis Bounaix, the 3ème Section leader, who describes what it was like:

'Hits rang against the armour on our left side but I could not identify our adversaries at first and I was searching to the south-east when my driver shouted, "There's a tank by the edge of this wood!" It was a PzKpfw IV and I targetted the 75mm gun. "Height 450" . . . too short. "Height 500" . . . too short again. "Height 550" . . . "We've got it!" A bright red light flashed on the enemy front armour and two or three men rolled down beneath nearby bushes. I realised then that the whole of our left flank was packed with German tanks but I could not see them clearly as these were motionless, camouflaged in the wood.

'Red flashes and a crash on our armour: one shot had struck the side door which banged open half mangled. Chasseur Millard, grasped it and kept it closed to the end of the fight. Sergent Reverberi, my driver, suddenly yelled to me that "Legac is here!" and, peering out of the half-opened turret door, I could see that this was right. Chasseur Legac was there standing in the middle of this hellish ground. He was riding "Adour", the tank of the company commander, and he shouted that Capitaine Gilbert had been wounded and I was to take command . . .

'We disabled another panzer but then the troubles started. "One hit into the radiator!" A shell, or some splinters pierced our radiator. Another shell hit the 75mm gun, jamming it into full recoil but we kept firing with the 47 . . .

245

Capitaine Jacques Lehoux, commander of the 3ème Compagnie, was riding in 'Poitou II' (coded 3C) which was destroyed by a violent explosion whilst crushing German foxholes hastily dug in the field by the roadside, killing the entire crew within the tank. The piece of wreckage is the armoured engine decking. On the road stands 'Guépratte'.

Left: 'Poitou II' was blown apart after a German anti-tank shell pierced the turret. Right: 'Mort pour la France.' The parents of Jacques Lehoux requested that their son's grave in Denée Cemetery be left untouched; all the other fifteen French casualties were exhumed in 1949 and the remains re-interred in their local churchyards.

'We moved a little and by the edge of a wood I saw the "Gard", its turret door open: through the aperture I could see the radio operator, Sergent Waslet, with a revolver in hand. What had happened? I could only guess . . . My right track was rattling very worryingly and my 47mm gun has been worked so hard that the bolt could not be closed because of the over-heated oil in the braking system . . . We withdrew slowly.'

By 2.00 pm the 2ème Compagnie had been all but annihilated. Of the seven tanks which had launched the attack, four had been disabled and the other three, 'Guynemer', 'Ourcq' and 'Isère', were in such a bad way — engines or tracks damaged, fuel tanks empty, ammunition spent — that they had to be destroyed by their crews after making it back to the start line. The company commander, Capitaine Pierre Gilbert, had been killed by machine gun fire together with most of his crew when getting out of his tank 'Adour', which

Top: **This famous picture of a French tank crewman surrendering is in all probability a re-creation for the camera some time later. When 'Guépratte' was hit, the driver, Caporal-Chef Roger Level, was killed and all the other crewmen wounded, two of them seriously. It is likely, therefore, that the 'Frenchman' is in fact a German stand-in!** *Left:* **The Renault B1bis displayed an elaborate set of markings and each tank bore its own number as well as its name. Each company of ten tanks was identified by a geometrical emblem (a square for the 1st, triangle for the 2nd, circle for the 3rd) while each section of three tanks displayed a letter and a playing-card symbol (spade, heart or diamond) placed within the company's geometrical design. Belonging to the 1ère Section, 'Guépratte' bears the code-letter 'T' in addition to the company circle/spade symbol. In the field lies the wreck of 'Poitou II'.**

247

'Nivernais II' was disabled just to the south of the little crossroads at Denée (which is off to the right). The right side of the Renault, facing the German batteries, has been badly damaged, one of the shots having struck a tree in front of the tank. The commander, Lieutenant Perrier, was wounded, the rest of the crew escaping unhurt. Unit markings: a heart (barely visible), for 2ème Section, within a circle, for 3ème Compagnie, and the section letter 'U'. 'Souain', 'Yser' and 'Guépratte' are further down the road, unchanged today but for the removal of some of the trees.

brewed up after being hit by artillery. At 4.00 p.m. the 1ère and 3ème Compagnies, which had carried out only flanking attacks and suffered few casualties, were ordered north to the Mettet area. The 3ème Compagnie was to move to the village of Somtet, about a kilometre south of Mettet.

To the south the 28ème B.C.C. was nearing the end with most of its Renault B1bis stranded without fuel and now vulnerable targets. By 5.30 p.m., when the 28ème B.C.C. received the order to withdraw to the line Mettet-Florennes, only seven Renault B1bis could actually be pulled back. The 26ème B.C.C., which had only some twenty Hotchkiss H-39s left, withdrew towards Mettet while the 25ème B.C.C., which had suffered less, followed in tow.

The 3ème Compagnie started its move north at about 4.30 p.m. The column reached the main road south of Ermeton and the two leading tanks, 'Poitou II' and 'Nivernais II', engaged

Top: '**Souain' was knocked out a few hundred yards further north in a similar situation: again it is the right-hand side of the vehicle that has suffered. One crewman was killed while the tank's commander, Sous-Lieutenant Pourtal, and another** crewman were wounded. Note the unit marking: a heart within a circle with the section letter 'U'. *Below:* **Four of the crew of 'Yser' were killed. (Unit marking: a spade in a circle with section letter 'T'.)**

and destroyed a German anti-tank gun which had challenged the column from a position some 200 metres east of the road. At Ermeton a small river hampered their progress and, instead of moving west towards Somtet as planned, the column headed northwards in order to reach the main road just north of Denée. Approaching this village, the French tankers spotted groups of infantry and attacked them. German guns immediately opened up; 'Amiral Guépratte' was hit and stopped west of the village and 'Belfort II' was hit a few hundred metres further north and started to burn. In spite of being under fire from German infantry, the crew managed to put out the flames with portable extinguishers. The company commander, Capitaine Jacques Lehoux, led his remaining seven tanks some distance to the west, regrouped

'Nancy II' and 'Vendée II' were disabled south of the crossroad; both Renaults belonged to 3ème Section of 3ème Compagnie — displaying the section code-letter 'X'. 'Vendée II' was disabled when a shell killed the driver, Caporal-Chef Charles Camus, seriously injuring the other two crew members. The tank commander, Lieutenant Baston, was wounded by another shell. 'Nancy II' was carrying three extra men in addition to the crew: Chasseur Armand Poulain, the driver of 'Ourcq', a 2ème Compagnie Renault which had been disabled near Flavion earlier that day, and two crewmen from 'Belfort II' of the company's 2ème Section, knocked out north-west of Denée at the beginning of the afternoon battle on the 15th. Three men were wounded when 'Nancy II' was hit; Chasseur Poulain was killed by an anti-tank shell and Sous-Lieutenant Alexandre Lecocq, the tank commander, was killed by a burst of machine gun fire.

and launched an attack towards Denée. Facing them was the vanguard of the VIII. Armeekorps, the second battalion of Inf.Rgt. 28, 8. Infanterie-Division, which had crossed the Meuse at Yvoir and advanced westwards out of the bridgehead. How things developed is described in an account by a member of this unit, a survivor of this French attack: 'Tanks to the left. Friend of foe? They approached the battalion CP. They were French heavies of 32 tonnes with an impressive front and a large white cross on the side. [This description applies to 'Vendée II' and 'Nancy II' which belonged to the compagnie's 3ème Section and displayed the section X letter code.] They moved from right

Two weeks later Luftwaffe photographer Stempka was on hand to record the interment of the victims of the battle at Denée. *Left:* A German infantryman is laid to rest, albeit temporarily, near 'Guépratte', while the three crew members of 'Ypres' are buried next to their tank *(right)*. German casualties from this part of Belgium are now concentrated at Lommel.

to left parallel to the road. The situation deteriorated and our 3.7cm PaK could not pierce their armour. The first three tanks ['Vendée II', 'Nancy II' and 'Ypres'] arrived near us . . . stopped for a while, then moved on to the left. Then things got even worse as they lined up along the road facing us.'

With the situation critical for II. Bataillon, the division's artillery opened up and saved the day. When news of the French force arrived, Major Friedrich

This memorial, just north of the battleground, lists the names of 24 French soldiers who 'fell for France and Belgium' on May 15.

A group of French prisoners, quite probably soldiers of the 18ème Division d'Infanterie, are marched eastwards through

Onhaye, a town just west of Dinant on the N36 highway to Philippeville.

Left: Six kilometres further down the road at the crossroads just west of Anthée, a 25mm Hotchkiss Modèle 1934 anti-tank gun stands amid a scene of carnage. A horse still in the shafts lies motionless while wreckage and shells from the ammunition limber it was towing lie scattered about. *Right:* White lines and garden swings — yesterday's battlefield transformed.

Left: This 75mm Modèle 1897 field gun — the famous French 'soixante-quinze' of the First World War — has been destroyed just north of the crossroads at a place called La Forge. There,

too, the horses towing the gun and limber have been struck down. *Right:* It is the very timelessness of the comparison which accentuates the horror.

We are now a little further to the west at Florennes, north-east of Philippeville, where these knocked-out Panhard armoured cars were pictured by an unknown German photographer near the crossroads. He also took a close-up of the ghastly sight of the burned body hanging out of the door of the nearest P-178 — a picture too awful to publish.

Filzinger, commander of the III. Bataillon of the division's Art.Rgt. 8, had been summoned urgently to his command post. Quickly he resited his batteries to counter the threat. The regiment's 10.5cm artillery, various anti-tank guns of the 14. Kompanie of Inf.Rgt. 28 and Pz.Jg.Abt. 8, anti-aircraft guns of the 1. Kompanie of Flak-Lehr-Regiment, all opened up at very short range against the French tanks and within a few minutes the seven remaining Renaults had been disabled. In the destruction of the 3ème Compagnie at Denée, 16 crewmen were killed, 16 wounded and 25 taken prisoner. Just three men, Sous Lieutenant

de Dufourcq, Caporal-Chef Briand and Caporal-Chef Bessou, all from the 'Belfort II', succeeded in rejoining the French forces.

For the 1ère D.C.R. May 15 was a costly defeat but, although some 60 tanks — about 45 Renault B1bis and about 15 Hotchkiss H-39s — had been lost in the sector, it cost the Germans between 30 to 40 panzers, mostly belonging to Pz.Rgt. 31. The experience of these encounters was not lost on the Germans, and on May 20 the commander of the VIII. Armeekorps, General Walter Heitz, issued the following instructions to the four divisions under his command:

'To the 8., 28., 87. and 267. Infanterie-Divisions. As it appears that the enemy heavy tanks are impervious to our PaK, one gun will be detached from each battery of the light artillery and will be loaned to the infantry for fighting back at the heavy tanks. These guns will advance with the infantry so that they will be ready to repulse any surprise tank attack.'

For his part in saving the day for Inf.Rgt. 28 at Denée, Major Friedrich Filzinger was decorated with the Ritterkreuz on June 5. On the French side, the 3ème Compagnie commander, Capitaine Jacques Lehoux, killed in 'Poitou II', was posthumously created a

Left: This H-35, probably from the 4ème R.A.M. of the 4ème D.L.C., came to grief after a near miss from a bomb caught it near Nalinnes. Général Bouffet, the 4ème D.L.C. commander, was killed during the same raid. *Right:* Jean-Louis Roba found the spot for us just outside the little village, six kilometres south of Charleroi.

Knight of the Légion d'Honneur on October 12, 1943.

The IIème and XIème Corps d'Armée — the 5ème D.I.M., 18ème Division d'Infanterie, 4ème D.L.C. and the newly committed 4ème D.I.N.A. — tried in vain to stop the advance of the Germans out of their bridgeheads. Fighting in unprepared positions, with little or no co-ordination, under incessant attacks from the Stukas, the French units were hopelessly outmanoeuvred. Conflicting orders to withdraw were received by some units and not by others, leaving them stranded only to be mopped up or forced to surrender the

next day. Around 5.00 p.m. the commander of the 4ème D.L.C., Général Paul Barbe, was killed near Mettet when his command car was shot up by aircraft. The following day the commander of the IIème Corps d'Armée, Général Jean Bouffet, was killed in front of the 4ème D.L.C. command post during a two-hour air raid when Stukas were sent in after a Henschel Hs 126 spotted a supply convoy of the 4ème D.L.C. near Nalinnes to which the division command post had by then withdrawn.

After the disastrous battles at Flavion and Denée, the 1ère D.C.R. ordered

what remained of its tanks to withdraw and assemble in the Beaumont area. By the evening of May 15 it had only about twenty battleworthy tanks left. These were spread over a large area and communications were very poor. The fuel situation was hopeless, with crews searching frantically — and mainly fruitlessly — for their supply columns. Without fuel, the 2ème Compagnie of the 26ème B.C.C. had to set light to its remaining Hotchkiss H-39s. Here and there, the tanks lent a hand in support of some infantry unit trying to stop the German advance, but only until they had to leave for the Beaumont area.

May 15 ended in disaster for the French 9ème Armée which by evening was withdrawing in disorder. The 1ère D.C.R. had left most of its tanks behind, as had the 6ème B.C.C. which had been subordinated to the IIème Corps d'Armée. *Left:* Hotchkiss H-39 of the 26ème B.C.C. and *right* a Renault R-35 of the 6ème B.C.C. disabled by the explosion of a bomb.

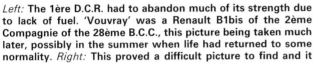

Left: The 1ère D.C.R. had to abandon much of its strength due to lack of fuel. 'Vouvray' was a Renault B1bis of the 2ème Compagnie of the 28ème B.C.C., this picture being taken much later, possibly in the summer when life had returned to some normality. Right: This proved a difficult picture to find and it was only with the help of Jean-Louis Roba with his detailed knowledge of the battlefield in this area of Belgium that the location was found. Even then the village of Pry, north of the N36 between Philippeville and Beaumont, has seen considerable change since 1940.

THURSDAY, MAY 16

The 37ème B.C.C., now reduced to seven tanks, had started to withdraw from its endangered positions north of Mettet at about 1.30 a.m. on May 16. Their supply column could not be found but by chance they met an outfit of the 1er G.R.D.I. at Aiseau which had some fuel and agreed to let them have some. The seven tanks, plus 'Simoun' of Colonel Jean-Marie Rabanit, the commander of the 1ère Demi-Brigade who with the brigade staff had joined up with the battalion, then moved towards Beaumont as ordered. On their way they passed other tanks of the 1ère D.C.R. which had been abandoned for lack of fuel: two Hotchkiss H-39s and two Renault B1bis, 'Vouvray' and 'Armagnac' at Pry, and more Renault B1bis, among them 'Kairouan' and 'Konakry', immobile and facing east on a hill near Rognée.

At Mertenne, Colonel Rabanit's command car leading the column was machine-gunned and disabled and so 'Escaut' moved alongside to cover the occupants as they transferred to the comparative safety of the tanks. Moving south they fell on the leading armour of the 5. Panzer-Division which was

The last five Renault B1bis of the 37ème B.C.C. were all left stranded in the centre of Beaumont. 'Cher' in the foreground belonged to the 1ère Section of the 1ère Compagnie as shown by the square company symbol surrounding the spade insignia of the section. The 'M' denotes the 1ère Section. Behind is 'Marne' of the 3ème Section of the 1ère Compagnie.

Left: When the command car belonging to Colonel Jean-Marie Rabanit, the CO of the 1ère Demi-Brigade, was destroyed, he transferred to this B1bis named 'Escaut' of the 37ème B.C.C. However, it too was hit by German artillery fire on the eastern outskirts of Beaumont where it was photographed on May 17 by Heinz Steurnagel, a member of the 8. Infanterie-Division. Right: This was another match only made possible by the historical studies of M. Roba and his associate, Jean Léotard.

255

The Battle of Beaumont. Their useful fighting life over, the five Renaults at least provided a final service in blocking the Rue Madame — the main road into the town from the east. 'Béarn II' and 'Meuse' are in the foreground ('O' signifying the 3ème Section), with 'Marne' behind and 'Rhône' and 'Cher' at the end of the street. The picture opposite shows the latter two tanks after they had been pulled out of the way as the Germans lost no time in clearing their route westwards.

approaching Beaumont on the main road. As soon as they opened fire German artillery replied, turning the French tanks west towards Beaumont. Approaching the town, 'Escaut' was damaged by a shell and forced to stop by the side of the road. 'Garonne' was also hit, plunging down a steep slope on its left. Those inside were all wounded — they included the battalion commander, Commandant Jean-Marie de Cissey who had boarded 'Garonne' after the command car had been disabled,

and Capitaine Henri Raberin, commanding the battalion's 2ème Compagnie. The wounded were evacuated to Maubeuge and the five remaining tanks took up positions in the centre of Beaumont early that afternoon.

When Kampfgruppe Haarde of the 5. Panzer-Division attacked Beaumont they let loose, forcing the panzers to skirt the town to the north. The French tanks soon found themselves trapped in Beaumont with panzers behind and in front of them. Out of fuel once again

and out of contact with the division, the crews decided to destroy their tanks and withdraw. 'Meuse' was driven beside 'Béarn II' to block the main road into the town from the east and the five tanks were set alight at about 4.00 p.m. Most of the local population had fled and the flames spread to nearby houses, starting fires that were to continue to burn until the evening of the following day.

In three days of battle, the 37ème B.C.C. had been completely wiped out.

'Béarn II', the mount of Commandant Jean-Marie de Cissey, the battalion commander, violently exploded after having been set on fire by its crew. The tank blew apart with a large section

of armour plate smashing through the wall of the house on the right (No. 6 Rue Madame next to the post office), ending up in the living room.

The worst damage was caused at the end of the street when 'Rhône' exploded with such violence that the turret was blown thirty feet from the tank. Then the flames from 'Cher' spread to the building alongside which was completely destroyed. The commander of 'Rhône' was Sous-Lieutenant André Marsais *(below left)*, seen here when a member of the 511ème R.C.C. (a tank regiment) whose second battalion had become the 37ème B.C.C. in 1939.

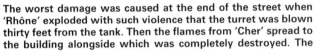

The road now clear, 5. Panzer-Division presses forward through Beaumont. Picture taken from the N6 looking towards the N36.

Symbol of the Blitzkrieg war. The rapid advance put the 32. Infanterie-Division at Couvin by Wednesday (May 15) with the leaders pushing further west towards Chimay. France now lay but a dozen kilometres away.

In another picture from the same series, taken just up the road from Couvin (the same house is visible in both photos), German troopers have pulled up to examine an abandoned Citroen cabriolet. In three weeks time, with the battle in the north virtually in the bag, Hitler would move his 'Felsennest' forward headquarters from Bad Münstereifel in Germany to the little Belgian hamlet of Brûly-de-Pesche just five miles to the south of this spot when the HQ was renamed 'Wolfsschlucht'.

Left: On the following day, May 16, another photographer reached Couvin to picture French prisoners assembled in the market place. *Right:* This shot gave us an opportunity to take this superb comparison, most of the structures remaining exactly as they were right down to the statue, the church and even the trees.

And on into La France! Having brushed aside the 4ème D.I.N.A. before they had had a chance to establish effective positions, the 7. Panzer-Division pressed on westwards and its leading tanks reached the border between Sivry and Clairfayts on May 16. *Above left:* This PzKpfw 38(t) of the 5. Kompanie of Panzer-

Regiment 25 thunders past the frontier without stopping for the usual formalities. The knife-rest barrier, hardly a deterrent to an armoured vehicle, has been pushed aside. *Right:* Though it is now disused, the border post can still be seen today, together with the remains of the barrier.

All its 35 Renault B1bis had been destroyed or abandoned and 31 men had been killed, including two company commanders, with another of them and the battalion commander among the badly wounded.

To the south, the 7. Panzer-Division had simply brushed aside the troops of the 4ème D.I.N.A. before they had a chance to establish an effective defence. The divisional headquarters found itself trapped at Neuville, just south of Philippeville, and the division's commander, Général Charles Sancelme, and his staff were taken prisoner the following night having got as far as La Capelle.

Rommel now had to cross the French border and force the northern extension of the Maginot Line. The Line here was in fact very weak, one of the weakest sectors of all. The major fortress that in 1934 was intended to be built at l'Epine, right on the route taken by the 7. Panzer-Division in 1940, was never actually constructed, and there were only a few casemates standing in the way of Rommel's tanks.

A PzKpfw II of the 1. Kompanie follows on. The emblem of the 7. Panzer-Division — an inverted Y with three dots alongside — can just be seen in the top right corner of the black cross, just below the '4' on the turret.

Left: This picture was taken at the same spot on Friday morning, May 17, as the supply columns of the 7. Panzer-Division formed an endless convoy moving westwards in the direction of Avesnes, 18 kilometres away. There the vanguard of the division had just overpowered the Hotchkiss H-39s of the

25ème B.C.C. following the desperate attempt by the French to block the road. *Right:* Who would imagine the drama this little back road witnessed in 1940? The left-hand D104 leads to Avesnes with the road on the right, the D27, running north to Maubeuge via Solre-le-Château.

'We had broken through the renowned Maginot Line', wrote Rommel but, in fact, on this sector of the frontier, the 'line' was nothing more than isolated blockhouses and an anti-tank ditch. *Left:* This was the anti-tank ditch as it appeared just west of Clairfayts in 1940. *Right:* No trace remains today, but the blockhouse is still there although it has nearly disappeared under the rampant growth which has softened its outline and merged it into the landscape.

Writing later, Rommel described the careful preparations for his attack on the Maginot Line on the evening of May 16, going on to describe how the panzers moved through the shallow belt of anti-tank obstacles and casemates. 'We had broken through the renowned Maginot Line' wrote Rommel triumphantly, 'and were driving deep into enemy territory'. At least the second part of the sentence was undeniable: after his engineers had captured the pillbox which directly controlled the road just west of Clairfayts and blown away the steel hedgehogs blocking it, Rommel sped westwards, travelling with the commander of Pz.Rgt. 25, Oberst Karl Rothenburg, in the regiment's command tank.

It was now dark. The panzers pressed on through l'Epine and turned north to reach the main road, passing groups of refugees and French troops sheltering alongside for the night, their vehicles and carts parked all over the place including the road itself. The panzers were fired at and Rommel gave the order to increase speed and fire broadsides to the right and left as they went. The column drove through Sars-Poteries and Beugnies with all guns blazing, and it took some time to get the firing stopped after it had outlived its usefulness. They reached the main road just north of Avesnes and Rommel noted that 'the nearer we came to Avesnes the greater was the crush of vehicles through which we had to fight our way'.

It was about 10.30 p.m. and shortly before Avesnes had been shelled by German artillery. Most of the people were on the move, jamming the streets and blocking the way not only for the German column but also for the numerous French troops who were in the town. The leading panzers in Rommel's column bypassed the town to reach the high ground to the west before stopping to round up French troops that were in the area.

Meanwhile the French in Avesnes had recovered from their surprise and at about midnight fighting broke out in the town. What remained of the Hotchkiss H-39s of the first company of 25ème

Men of the 7. Panzer-Division take time out to walk across to inspect another blockhouse. Not surprisingly, in view of the speed of the advance, all these casemates survived intact and can still be seen absolutely as they were in 1940. This is blockhouse No. 3/152 bis.

With the French military machine still firmly believing in the might of their fixed defences, born out of the experiences of 1914-1918, the fast-moving, ever-changing war of 1940 came as a severe shock. Although both sides still depended heavily on the horse, the advent of the new type of warfare was forged by the mechanised spearheads. Here, in a picture taken on May 17, primitive hedgehog obstacles have been swept aside on the D104 just west of Clairfayts.

B.C.C. attacked the Germans, and Rommel soon lost contact with his second battalion of panzers and Kradschtz.Btl. 7 which were following the advance guard. 'The second battalion of Pz.Rgt. 25 at once tried to overcome the enemy blocking the road, but their attempt failed with the loss of several tanks. The fighting in Avesnes grew steadily heavier.'

The battle lasted until 4.00 a.m. on May 17 when Rommel sent some PzKpfw IVs from the west against the French light tanks in Avesnes to crush the last resistance. Only a handful of Hotchkiss tanks managed to escape to the south. The commander of the 1ère D.C.R., Général Marie-Germain Bruneau, then ordered what remained of his division to take up positions south of Avesnes, although the 1ère D.C.R. was no more. Général Bruneau and his staff, including the commanders of the division's two demi-brigades, Colonel Jean-Marie Rabanit and Colonel Charles Marc, were to be taken prisoner on May 19 near Vendhuile, 15 kilometres south of Cambrai by elements of the 6. Panzer-Division.

Another innovation was the tracked bridgelayer — something the British had first developed on the Mk V** tank in 1918. The engineer battalion of the 7. Panzer-Division was Pionier-Bataillon 58 which possessed four prototypes of the two-part bridges mounted on the chassis of the PzKpfw II.

Left: Another aspect of the campaign, illustrated here for the first time in this picture, was the hopeless plight of the refugee. Terrified of being caught up in the fighting, or perhaps fleeing from an image of brutality given them by their parents' experiences in Belgium in 1914, this group has already been overtaken by events as the Germans pass them by. Now there is nowhere to run to. *Right:* We found that the picture had been taken at l'Epine (three kilometres west of Clairfayts), the same field beside the junction now being overlooked by modern villas on the road to Avesnes.

A little way to the north the 5. Panzer-Division approached the French border down the N21 to Grandrieu. There the French had blown the bridge across the Thure and, anticipating that the Germans would consequently attempt to drive across just downstream, they mined the river bank. Sure enough, the first panzer to try it — a PzKpfw III of Panzer-Regiment 15 — struck a mine and remained stranded minus a track at the water's edge. *Above:* Engineers having cleared a gap through the mines, an SdKfz 7 half-track pulls its charge — in this case an 8.8cm Flak 36 — across into France.

FRIDAY, MAY 17

Dawn was slowly breaking when the battle ended and Rommel soon re-established contact with his second echelon. He was out of wireless contact with his rear and received no reply from the XV. Armeekorps to his allegedly repeated pleas for permission to continue forward and seize a bridgehead on the Sambre. He therefore decided to resume the attack at dawn to take the bridge over the Sambre at Landrecies and issued orders by radio to the divisional units to follow the panzer regiment in its advance on the town. Without waiting for any acknowledgement, he moved off at about 4.00 a.m:

'As no supplies had come up during the night, we now had to be sparing with ammunition and drove westwards through the brightening day with guns silent. Soon we began to meet refugee columns and detachments of French troops preparing for the march. A chaos of guns, tanks and military vehicles of all kinds, inextricably entangled with horse-drawn refugee carts, covered the road and verges. By keeping our guns silent and occasionally driving our cross-country vehicles alongside the road, we managed to get past the column without great difficulty. The French troops were completely overcome by surprise at our sudden appearance, laid down their arms and marched off to the east beside our column. Nowhere was any resistance attempted. Any enemy tanks we met on the road were put out of action as we drove past. The advance went on without a halt to the west.

'Particularly irate over this sudden disturbance was a French lieutenant-colonel whom we overtook with his car jammed in the press of vehicles. I asked him for his rank and appointments. His eyes glowed hate and impotent fury and he gave me the impression of being a thoroughly fanatical type. There being every likelihood, with so much traffic on the road, that our columns would get split up from time to time, I decided on second thoughts to take him along with us. He was already fifty metres away to the east when he was fetched back to Oberst Rothenburg, who signed to him to get in his tank. But he curtly refused to come with us, so, after summoning him three times to get in, there was nothing for it but to shoot him.'

Above: **Withdrawing from Beaumont on the afternoon of May 16, the crew of 'Verdun II' halted at the crossroads north of Avesnes, hoping to make contact with the staff of the 1ère D.C.R. from which they had become separated. However, that evening the first panzers of the 7. Panzer-Division approached, forcing 'Verdun II' to move southwards in the direction of Avesnes. With the panzers on its heels, shots were exchanged (note the turret trained to the rear) and 'Verdun II' was hit in a track.** *Below:* **It took some time to establish the precise spot where the tank had been knocked out, as the N2 has seen considerable post-war development.**

On the move! The Thure has now been bridged and a Luftwaffe truck loaded with fuel moves on towards Sars-Poteries.

263

'A chaos of guns, tanks and military vehicles of all kinds covered the roads and verges,' wrote Rommel. This was the scene along the D962 just west of Sars-Poteries, with a 75mm Modèle 1897 field gun in the foreground.

The French troops surprised near Landrecies were elements of the 9ème D.I.M. moving from the Valenciennes sector southwards to the Oise river. The division, which was rushing back from the Netherlands after the unsuccessful adventure of the 7ème Armée, had just been transferred to the 9ème Armée and ordered to hold the Oise river between Hirson and Guise.

Because of the refugees crowding the road, progress became very slow; the panzers passed through Maroilles and arrived at Landrecies at about 5.45 a.m. Then they crossed the Sambre. Assuming he had his division behind him, Rommel continued towards Le Cateau where he stopped at 6.15 a.m. on a hill

We are told that the German Blitzkrieg across France relied largely on Michelin maps, and here is Oberst Karl Rothenburg, commander of Panzer-Regiment 25, proving the point. It would be nice to think he was holding Sheet 53 — an extract from the present-day edition is reproduced *below.*

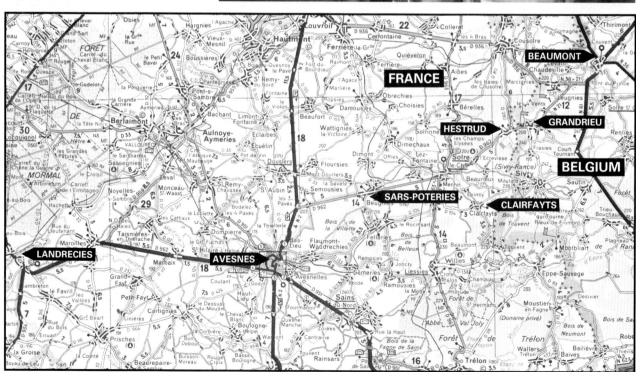

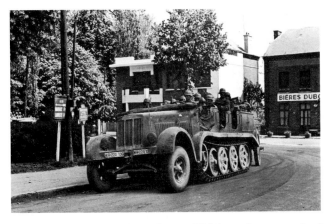

On reaching Avesnes, the 7. Panzer-Division, after a march of just seven days, was more or less at the mid-way point in its advance to the Channel coast. Here an SdKfz 8 prime-mover has stopped for a propaganda shot next to the signpost to Landrecies, its next port of call 24 kilometres away to the west along the D962.

Left: An interesting sequence of pictures was taken showing infantrymen breaking into a house on the corner of the main square in Avesnes. With no captions one can only speculate on the reason, although as the Germans came down heavily on looting, executing any of their men found guilty, such behaviour would hardly have been photographed in detail. *Right:* This was then, and still is now, the home of M. André Demoulin — No. 20 Avenue Jessé de Forest.

Although the photographer is now looking westwards towards Landrecies, some transport is pictured coming back from the front and passing the SdKfz 8, now seen to be towing a 15cm sFH18. About a kilometre further down the road, the prime-mover would pass the H-39s of the 25ème B.C.C. which had been knocked-out during the previous night's battle.

265

The last tank of the 25ème B.C.C. was disabled around 4.00 a.m. on Friday morning (May 17) and, with the coming of daylight, all was revealed. The photographer arrived just in time: as a

PzKpfw 38(t) moved off westwards, a group of French prisoners marched back to the town. The spade on the French tank denotes 1ère Section and the heart 2ème Section.

Above: Some days later another photographer pictured the same stretch of the D962, with the H-39s now pushed aside.

Below: It is remarkable after such an urban tank battle that no trace of damage remains to be seen today.

Above: The battle had not been entirely one-sided — in this shot we see a stranded PzKpfw IV from Panzer-Regiment 25 as refugees make their way back to the town. Dead horses lie on the left.

The bodies of the numerous horses killed in the battle have now been cleared away, leaving their mechanical counterparts to be either salvaged or scrapped, like these two Hotchkiss tanks, one from the 2ème Section (heart emblem) in the foreground, the other with the diamond motif from the 3ème Section. The field gun *(below left)* is a 105mm Modèle 1935.

Above: **Rommel was in Landrecies on Friday (May 17) to observe Panzer-Regiment 25 crossing the bridge over the Sambre. This is his own picture of PzKpfw 38(t) tanks taken while standing on top of a truck.** Bottom: **Unfortunately we** were unable to commandeer a similar vantage point for our comparison. Below: **The official German photographer meanwhile pictured these French prisoners being marched back through the town.**

just east of the town. Leaving Rothenburg in charge of the advance guard, which had meanwhile formed an all-round defence there, Rommel then attempted to return and bring the rest of the division forward but his first attempt to get through was halted by anti-tank fire. He tried again in his signals vehicle with a PzKpfw III as escort. Warned to go carefully, they took quite a time crossing Landrecies where the French units there had recovered from their surprise. Near Maroilles the escorting PzKpfw III broke down. There were no German troops to be seen but French troops lay in every field beside the road.

'There was no chance of getting them on the march as prisoners', wrote Rommel, 'as we had no men to form an escort. Where we did manage to get them moving, they marched only so long as our armoured car was with

Two decades before, Le Cateau had been the linch-pin of the first major battle of the Great War when the Old Contemptibles attempted to halt the German advance in August 1914. Their efforts failed and thereafter Le Cateau remained in German hands until liberated in August 1918. Now in 1940 Rommel stopped to photograph disabled French armour just east of the town.

them, and then vanished into the bushes the moment we drove on ahead.' At top speed, Rommel's car crossed Maroilles and, to his relief, east of the village they came across a PzKpfw IV which had been stranded there earlier that morning by mechanical trouble. A company of his motorised infantry then appeared, travelling fast down the road from the east. Thinking that further detachments would be following them, Rommel set off eastwards again 'but found nothing'. They halted a French convoy of lorries which came out of a side turning and turned it off towards Avesnes. At the head of the captured convoy they arrived at Avesnes where Rommel finally made contact with elements of Schtz.Rgt. 6.

The vehicles included a Panhard P-178 (left) of the 1ère D.L.M. and a Renault B1bis 'Indochine' of the 15ème B.C.C., 2ème D.C.R.

SATURDAY, MAY 18

Orders had come in shortly after midnight on May 17 for the advance to be continued towards Cambrai but at 7.00 a.m. the adjutant of Pz.Rgt. 25, Oberleutnant Student, arrived at headquarters and reported that the advance guard was in trouble. Student had managed to get through from Le Cateau in an armoured car and he reported that they were low on fuel and ammunition and since the previous afternoon had been cut off from the rear by French tanks and armoured cars. These were from the 1ère D.L.M. which were attacking from the north while odd tanks from the 2ème D.C.R. were menacing the roads and even launched a damaging raid into Landrecies itself.

Rommel promptly ordered his last available panzer battalion to force its way through to Le Cateau and get supplies forward to them. When the panzers failed to get near Pommereuil, Rommel went forward himself to find that a few Renault B1bis of the 2ème D.C.R. barred their way:

'Violent fighting developed on the road and there was no chance of out-flanking the enemy position on either side. Our guns seemed to be completely ineffective against the heavy armour of the French tanks. We stood for some time watching the battle from close range, until I finally decided to take the battalion south through the wood via Ors.' More French tanks were encountered south of the woods and the panzers had to fight their way through, it being midday before they reached Rothenburg's positions.

By 3.00 p.m. Rommel had a clear enough idea of the situation to risk going ahead with the attack on Cambrai, utilising the single infantry and panzer battalions to hand, relying on the two other panzer battalions to reach them shortly. In fact, the supply column took a long time to get through and by the time they had taken on fuel and ammunition, the first battalion of Schtz.Rgt. 6 was approaching Cambrai, supported only by a few panzers and two troops of self-propelled Flak. The great clouds of dust thrown up as they advanced on the northern edge of the built-up area were seen from Cambrai as indicating a large-scale panzer attack and the town was easily taken although the other two panzer battalions were still a long way behind.

Riding in the command car of Oberstleutnant Max Ilgen, the commander of the second battalion of Panzer-Regiment 25, Rommel took another shot looking along the main street. Whereas the town was badly damaged during the First War, it escaped lightly in the Second, many of the buildings seen standing in May 1940 still being in evidence today.

From Le Cateau the N39 runs as straight as a die towards Cambrai — the very names symbols of the carnage wrought across this area of France within recent memory. Now once again the town had fallen to the invader as Rommel's men pushed on westwards. This is another picture from his camera.

Gruppe von Kleist and the 2ème Armée

On May 10, in the certainty that there was nothing to fear in the Sedan area, the 2ème Armée had no forces to comprise a second line of defence. Two days later things were not so certain and the army was given the 3ème D.C.R. then in reserve near Reims, where it had been formed less than two months previously, together with the 3ème D.I.M. The following day, when the first panzers of XIX. Armeekorps began crossing the Meuse at Sedan, Général Charles Huntziger, the army commander, ordered the 3ème D.I.M. to move during the night to a second line of defence on the heights on either side of Stonne. From there he planned to launch a counter-attack northwards to re-establish the situation at Sedan using the 3ème D.I.M. and the 3ème D.C.R. which was assembling west of Le Chesne with about 60 Renault B1bis and 70 Hotchkiss H-39s.

On May 14 the 2ème Armée's first line of defence was broken, the 55ème Division d'Infanterie had been smashed away, the 71ème Division d'Infanterie was being routed and the army's mobile units were hastily committed along the second line, fighting dismounted, to hold it until the arrival of newly committed infantry divisions. To take charge of this line, the XXIème Corps d'Armée was brought in from reserve. This comprised the army's cavalry units, 2ème D.L.C., the 5ème D.L.C. and the 1ère Brigade de Cavalerie, which were to fight beside the newly arrived 3ème D.C.R. and 3ème D.I.M. to try to contain the German break-out.

Général Huntziger decided to launch his counter-attack in the early hours of May 14, but this was unrealistic as the fledgling 3ème D.C.R. — less than two months old and still in process of formation — was short of equipment and transport and could not possibly reach its assembly area in so short a time. Its commander, Général Georges Brocard managed to get the attack put back but it was still to be launched 'as soon as possible after 11.00 a.m.'. Early in the morning, the army ordered a tank battalion, the 7ème B.C.C., northwards to counter the 1. Panzer-Division.

By the evening of May 14 the battle of Sedan had been lost by 2ème Armée. While the German panzers were expanding from the bridgehead, elements of the French cavalry units trapped in Belgium had no choice other than to surrender. The examples reproduced here show *(top)* a PzKpfw II followed by a Panzerbefehlswagen of 10. Panzer-Division and *(above)* prisoners from the 5ème D.L.C. — ironically, the negatives for both pictures being captured by the French Army in 1945!

With the German forces on the point of achieving a mass break-out, the 2ème Armée hastily brought fresh units forward — the 3ème D.C.R. and 3ème D.I.M. — while its engineers mined bridges, obstructed roads and removed the road signs.

This picture was taken at Stenay, some 40 kilometres south of Sedan on the N64 to Verdun. We found that the sign destroyed with such vigour in May 1940 has never been replaced — the road since reclassified as the D964.

However the panzers were too many to be stopped and the battalion lost most of the 39 FCM 36s engaged.

In the afternoon the 3ème D.I.M. and the 3ème D.C.R. brought up a sizeable part of their strength and as a consequence Général Brocard and his staff were now confident in the feasibility of a powerful counter-attack. The 41ème B.C.C. was on the Le Chesne-Sedan road, north of Mont-Dieu, with the 42ème B.C.C. behind it; the 45ème B.C.C. was at Stonne with the 49ème B.C.C. arriving behind, and the 16ème B.C.P., the division's motorised infantry, was near Mont-Dieu. Two infantry regiments of the 3ème D.I.M. were also in position and a third was arriving.

Nevertheless any possibility of a counter-attack that day soon disappeared when the commander of the XXIème Corps d'Armée, Général Jean Flavigny, fearing that his infantry would not be strong enough on the new line when night came, decided to share out the tanks of the 3ème D.C.R. to reinforce the line. This was completed at around 9.00 p.m. and the tanks of the armoured division correspondingly found themselves dispersed over a front about 20 kilometres wide.

WEDNESDAY, MAY 15

At 1. Panzer-Division headquarters, the point was being raised whether the whole division could be turned westwards or if they should leave a flank guard facing south. Guderian was one of those present who heard the division chief-of-staff, Major Walther Wenck, come out with a slang expression of the XIX. Armeekorps commander, 'Klotzen, nicht Kleckern' — 'clobber them, don't dab at them', in other words 'attack in force, concentrate, don't disperse'. That clinched it. The 1. Panzer-Division and the 2. Panzer-Division were immediately ordered to change direction with all their forces, to cross the Ardennes Canal and push westwards, leaving the job of securing the dominating heights around Stonne to the 10. Panzer-Division and Infanterie-Regiment 'Gross Deutschland'.

Meanwhile on the left wing of the 2ème Armée the 1ère Brigade de Cavalerie and 3ème Brigade de Spahis were trying to stop the break-out westwards of Gruppe von Kleist but they were far too weak. The Spahis sacrificed themselves at La Horgne where, after ten hours of stout fighting against the 1. Panzer-Division on May 15, the brigade had suffered about 30 percent losses. Its commander, Colonel Olivier Marc, had been gravely wounded and taken prisoner, and the commanders of its two regiments, Colonel Emmanuel Burnol and Colonel Edouard Geoffroy, were

The 2ème Armée relieved the 7ème B.C.C. to counter-attack on the morning of May 14 but the light FCM 36s were not powerful enough and far too few to stop the panzers and, of the 39 tanks engaged, 29 were lost. Three of their number can be seen in this picture taken near Chémery, 15 kilometres south of Sedan. *Below:* Like so many roads in France, the felling of trees has transformed the D27 since the war.

That same day, the 3ème Brigade de Spahis had been moved into the Vendresse sector, 15 kilometres south of the Meuse, to cover the flank of the 53ème Division d'Infanterie. However, no matter how magnificent the horsemen looked in their North African setting, and although fighting bravely for ten hours, they were no match for the armoured might of 1. Panzer-Division, and sacrificed a third of their strength on the altar of the hamlet of La Horgne. This cavalryman was one of the lucky ones; although wounded in the battle, he has managed to escape capture to reach friendly lines further south.

Moving south from the Sedan bridgehead, this motor-cyclist was pictured at the Maison Schmitt crossroads in the Forêt d'Elan. It is a typical shot beloved of war photographers, with signposts in the background, although ostensibly the place-names mean little. However in 1940 memories of the Great War

would have been fresh, and the fact that the Germans were now entering former American-held territory would no doubt have been of propaganda value back home. In fact, the picture was taken virtually on the Armistice Line reached by French and American troops in the Meuse-Argonne in November 1918.

dead. During the night the 1ère Brigade de Cavalerie, down to one third of its nominal strength, was ordered to withdraw south of the Aisne river with the remnants of the 3ème Brigade de Spahis and the 5ème D.L.C. The XIX. Armeekorps kept on pushing west on the 9ème Armée's right wing, and caught the the 53ème Division d'Infanterie in the process of turning to face east.

To free the XIX. Armeekorps from having to deal with the situation on its left flank, the 10. Panzer-Division and Infanterie-Regiment 'Gross Deutschland', which were still involved near

Stonne, were subordinated to the XIV. Armeekorps until such time as units of the corps could take over from them.

Early in the morning, the Infanterie-Regiment 'Gross Deutschland' pressed on and took Stonne. The French counter-attacked and their tanks entered the village several times, only to see it reoccupied as soon as they departed. Finally a determined attack launched at about 10.00 a.m. by the 1ère Compagnie of 51ème R.I. cleared it. The village was held despite heavy shelling until nightfall, but when the French tanks withdrew, the Germans

immediately launched a powerful assault. The French infantry were forced back but managed to dig in about 400 metres to the south-east.

The night saw Battles of the Advanced Air Striking Force setting out on their first night bombing operation. Twenty aircraft were despatched and were timed to arrive over troop concentrations in the area between Bouillon, Sedan and Monthermé between 10.00 p.m. and 1.00 a.m. The targets were difficult to identify at night and, although the results were negligible, all aircraft returned safely.

With the bitter defeat of 1918 now well on the way to being redressed, German engineers work to clear a field of fire for a 2cm Flak 30 which has been set up to cover the crossroads. One

of the crewmen uses a range-finder to check the distance to the buildings of Maison Schmitt in the background although it is most probably a posed shot for the benefit of the cameraman.

THURSDAY, MAY 16

Early in the morning the French artillery started to pound Stonne and a new counter-attack was launched at 5.00 a.m. with two companies of Renault B1bis of the 41ème B.C.C. leading the way. The battalion commander, Commandant Michel Malaguti, led the attack from up front, followed by a company of Hotchkiss H-39s from the 45ème B.C.C. and two companies of infantry from the 51ème R.I. They entered Stonne, destroyed the panzers of the 10. Panzer-Division that were there and wiped out the grenadiers of the élite Infanterie-Regiment 'Gross Deutschland'. Capitaine Pierre Billotte, the commander of the 1ère Compagnie of the 41ème B.C.C., riding in 'Eure', describes what happened:

'I rushed for the centre of the village and when I entered the square from the south I suddenly saw a column of panzers arriving at the northern end,

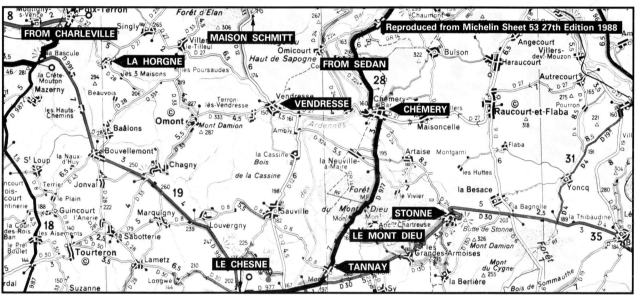

Top: **Stukas always hit hard, but sometimes struck the wrong place! This column from the 1. Panzer-Division was attacked in Chémery, 15 kilometres south of Sedan, on May 14. A rare 8.8cm Flak 18 (SFI) (only ten built) can be seen disabled on the left, together with a PzKpfw II and a PzKpfw III. The staff of** Panzer-Regiment 2 suffered heavily from this mistake with Oberleutnant Johannes Harrach, Leutnant Hartmut von Fritschen and Oberleutnant Josef von Fürstenberg being killed among many others. *Below:* **Chémery today, looking north along the D977 towards the crossroads with the D27.**

only fifty metres away. Because all the turret episcopes had been damaged in the previous battles, I was observing through my gun visor. I knew that my 47mm gun was loaded and I fired instantly at the leading tank, a PzKpfw IV, without having to train the gun. The panzers following it were spaced at regular intervals on a 200-metre climb, each of them being shielded by those in front. On the other hand, I was uphill and I could fire at them from above. The firing was intense and we later counted 140 impacts on our armour. In ten minutes, the panzers at the head of the column were all silenced, one after the other, and I could see the ones in the rear hastily withdrawing . . . We moved on and found ourself in front of an anti-tank gun that we destroyed at ten metres with the 75mm.'

Stonne was back in French hands but a violent bombardment by German artillery and aircraft soon resumed.

FRIDAY, MAY 17

During the night the 2. Infanterie-Division (mot), which had advanced on the previous day, relieved the 10. Panzer-Division and Infanterie-Regiment 'Gross Deutschland' and took over the Stonne sector. Next day these two units resumed their move westwards while the newcomers launched an all out attack which lasted the whole day. In the evening, after a last French counter-attack by three Renault B1bis of 49ème B.C.C., the battle subsided. The day had been somewhat successful for the Germans as Stonne was now in their hands, but it had also been very costly, and the commander of the 3ème D.I.M., Général Paul Bertin-Boussu, reported the capture of over 100 prisoners — a none too frequent occurrence at that time.

Eleven tanks of the 49ème B.C.C. and 45ème B.C.C. attacked once again on May 18, followed by infantry of the 51ème R.I., managing to enter Stonne

Above and bottom: **Two PzKpfw IVs of the 10. Panzer-Division, destroyed in Stonne by the Renault B1bis of the 41ème B.C.C. when they counter-attacked on May 16.**

Photographed nearly 50 years later, this is the D30 as it enters Stonne from the east. The village suffered heavily during the tank battle and subsequently much of it had to be rebuilt, although the end-most house was not replaced.

in the afternoon. They were then hammered by such heavy shelling that they had to withdraw that evening leaving the village in German hands. The VI. Armeekorps then brought in three infantry divisions and the battle for the Mont-Dieu-Stonne positions continued until the 3ème D.I.M. and its supporting units were ordered to withdraw on the night of May 24 behind a new line established to the south by the 35ème Division d'Infanterie.

With the first part of Fall Gelb proceeding as planned, on May 14 Hitler issued Führer Directive No. 11:

'The progress of the offensive to date shows that the enemy has failed to appreciate in time the basic idea of our operations. He continues to throw strong forces against the line Namur-Antwerp and appears to be neglecting the sector facing Heeresgruppe A. This fact and the swift forcing of the Meuse

The stubborn defence of Stonne by French armoured units was one bright light to set against the gloom of seeming German invincibility. However, the French success was not without cost to the 3ème D.C.R. which had to leave several of its precious Renault B1bis behind when they were finally ordered to

withdraw. *Left:* 'Hautvillers' from the 49ème B.C.C. was knocked out in Stonne, and 'Fleurie' *right* of the 41ème B.C.C. broke down near Tannay. Its crew attempted to hitch a tow but, when this failed, its commander, Sous-Lieutenant Rémy Klein, ordered the tank to be abandoned.

crossing in the sector of Heeresgruppe A have established the first essentials for a thrust in all possible strength north of the Aisne and in a north-westernly direction, as laid down in Directive No. 10. Such a thrust might produce a major success. It is the task of the forces engaged north of the line Liège-Namur to deceive and hold down the greatest number of enemy forces by attacking them with their own resources. . . . All available motorised divisions will be transferred to the operational area of Heeresgruppe A as soon as possible.'

The first sign that something was going very wrong with the Allied plan had come on May 14 when the French communiqué laconically announced that 'the enemy had reached the Meuse from Liège to Namur and Sedan. The latter towns have been evacuated.' The newspapers did their best to cover up the bad news but the French Command was only just beginning to wake up to the size of the spreading catastrophe.

On May 14 the 6ème Armée, until then in reserve far behind the front, was put in charge of all the forces the French

Several memorials to the battles of May 1940 can be seen at Stonne today. This 47mm Modèle 1937 anti-tank gun, behind which André Saïs of the 3ème D.I.M. was killed, is displayed in front of the village church.

Left: A memorial has also been erected on the edge of a field near the village where 'Chinon' of the 49ème B.C.C. was destroyed on May 15, the whole crew — four men and its

commander, Sous-Lieutenant Yves Rohou — being killed. *Right:* This plaque on the wall of Stonne church remembers the deeds of the 3ème D.I.M. and 3ème D.C.R.

277

High Command was scraping together to close the gap. At headquarters at Vincennes there were still fears of seeing the Germans attacking via Switzerland and even now, with panzers swarming in the rear at the boundary between the 2ème and 9ème Armées, the High Command could not bring themselves to order a drastic withdrawal from the Maginot Line but instead brought in several divisions from eastern France. With these newly committed divisions, plus units which had been withdrawn and transferred after their initial participation in Belgium, Général Robert Touchon, the army commander, had been given the impossible task of re-establishing a front between the 2ème Armée and 9ème Armée.

The French Command had missed a golden opportunity of disrupting the carefully laid plans of Fall Gelb when the 3ème Armée was in a position to threaten the left flank of the German units advancing westwards. However nothing was done and the chance slipped away.

At first Général Charles-Marie Condé and his staff had been taken in by the noisy pressure maintained by the Germans in the Longwy sector. Although it had been clear since May 15 that their main effort was directed westwards at the Meuse, Condé did not propose, nor was ordered, to attack northwards into Luxembourg and southern Belgium to strike into the flank of Heeresgruppe A whose units were just a few kilometres in front of his 3ème Armée. Instead he ordered the forces westwards to reinforce his left wing obviously endangered by what was happening on the Meuse.

Alarming reports were flowing into Paris and soon after 7.00 a.m. on the morning of May 16 Reynaud telephoned Churchill. The French Prime Minister was in an excited mood, informing his British opposite number that the counter-attack at Sedan had failed, 'the road to Paris was open' and that 'the battle was lost'. Churchill, who as he wrote in his memoirs 'did not comprehend the violence of the revolution effected since the last war by the incursion of a mass of fast-moving

Fanning out from the bridgehead, Gruppe von Kleist now pushed on virtually unopposed. The panzers were always further west than anticipated, leaving the French constantly one jump behind. Here in Faissault, over 50 kilometres south-west of Sedan, the leaders of 1. Panzer-Division have surprised the crews of these two Tracteur UE, capturing their bewildered crews without a fight.

We followed in the footsteps — or rather tracks — of the panzers. This is the N51 with Rethel 15 kilometres ahead.

heavy armour', could not accept the incredible idea that all had been decided in a few days. He flew to Paris that afternoon and by 5.30 p.m. was in Reynaud's study on the Quai d'Orsay.

Daladier and Gamelin were present, their faces 'the picture of misery and despair'. General Ismay's impression was that 'the French High Command are beaten already.'

Another Tracteur UE abandoned in Novion-Porcien on the D985, seven kilometres to the west. Many of the captured infantry supply carriers were later taken into German service with the designation 'Infanterie Schlepper UE 630(f)'.

At 5.30 p.m. on that fateful Thursday — May 16 — the British delegation led by Churchill faced their French opposite numbers in Paris for the first time since the German attack. According to one observer, throughout the meeting Churchill was 'aggressively trying to find out the exact state of affairs, which Reynaud, Gamelin and the others hardly knew themselves'. *Above:* Gruppe von Kleist knew exactly where they were going — even if they were stalled momentarily by heavy traffic. The scene in Mesmont, two kilometres west of Novion-Porcien.

Gamelin began the meeting by explaining the strength and position of the German breakthrough. Churchill then asked, after a considerable silence: 'Where is the strategic reserve?' breaking into his indifferent French: 'Où est la masse de manoeuvre?' Général Gamelin, who had already complained about 'inferiority in numbers, inferiority of equipment, inferiority of methods' simply replied with a shake of the head and a shrug: 'Aucune'.

The end of the 9ème Armée

One of the last tanks of the 1ère D.C.R. — 'Bourgueil' — was disabled near Bergues on May 16.

Early in the afternoon of May 15, following the suggestion made that morning by Général Billotte, the 7ème Armée commander, Général Henri Giraud, was ordered to replace Général André Corap at the head of the 9ème Armée, as from 4.00 p.m. An hour later Corap left for the 7ème Armée but four days later, his name a byword for the catastrophe on the Meuse, he would be dismissed.

Giraud was asked to save a situation which was growing more desperate by the hour. What was left of his 9ème Armée was now scattered inside a triangle formed by the Meuse on the east, the Aisne on the south and the Sambre on the north-west. Only in two places was there a recognisable front facing east but the panzers of XV. Armeekorps were forcing their way between them. On the broad southern flank there was no front at all as Gruppe von Kleist was racing westwards more or less unopposed.

While Giraud was taking over, the advance elements of both the 1. Panzer-Division and 6. Panzer-Division were entering Montcornet, twenty kilometres to the south of the army's headquarters at Vervins. Giraud decided that he could not afford to wait for reinforcements and drew up plans for an immediate counter-attack to be launched on May 17 with such forces as he could find. However the reality was somewhat different and in fact all that was available was the 2ème D.C.R. — supposedly assembling for a counter-stroke.

His name a byword for the catastrophic situation in which the 9ème Armée now found itself, Général André Corap (above) was dismissed his command and replaced by Général Henri Giraud.

Left: **At Oisy, a dozen kilometres south of Landrecies, French engineers primed the demolition charges on this bridge over the Oise-Sambre Canal but only one of them actually exploded. The bridge was not destroyed and the Germans were able to** use it without difficulty. Bergues, where 'Bourgueil' had been disabled *(see opposite)*, is only a kilometre to the east. *Right:* **Having survived the remainder of the war, the tell-tale repair work to the reinforced concrete remains.**

When the 2ème D.C.R. had started its move on May 13, partly by train, partly by road, it was due to be engaged with the 1ère Armée and sent to the Charleroi area. The surprising speed of the German advance had caused these plans to be cancelled and the 2ème D.C.R. had then been assigned to the 9ème Armée with orders to assemble near Signy-l'Abbaye. On the afternoon of May 14, while the first elements of his division were arriving, the 2ème D.C.R. commander, Général Albert Bruché, reported to 9ème Armée headquarters at Vervins. He explained that it was simply impossible to regroup an armoured division in such a confused situation and suggested an alternative assembly area south of Vervins. This

request was not granted as the division's units, although scattered and out of touch, were the only organised troops in front of the panzers which were now racing to the rear of the army, and the 2ème D.C.R. was ordered to attack and stop them regardless, at the latest on May 17. On the evening of May 15, the division hardly knew whether it was coming or going and it no longer represented a coherent fighting unit. Elements were at Nouvion, others at Hirson, yet more south of the Aisne. They clashed here and there, the panzers stopping them for a while, but suffered badly in these unco-ordinated actions. In one of them, the commander of the 14ème B.C.C., Commandant Marcel Cornic, was killed near Lislet.

THURSDAY, MAY 16

The pace at which the panzers advanced brought its own worries for the German Command, which noted the growing vulnerability of its southern flank. Early on May 16 von Rundstedt issued orders that the 2. Armee be brought forward with all speed to secure the southern flank while units of the 4. Armee and 12. Armee were closing up in preparation for a renewed advance.

The 1ère D.C.R., down to almost nothing after its costly commitment in Belgium, was ordered to attack south to Hirson, then down to the Oise to cover the arrival of the 2ème D.C.R. Général Bruneau tried to comply with the order but the few Hotchkiss tanks to reach La Capelle were to be destroyed there by

Left: **The defeat of the 9ème Armée epitomised in the burned-out wreckage lining the streets of Guise — a town on the main N30 route to Saint Quentin.** *Above:* **We found that the Garage Moderne was still in business in the same building on Place Meurisse.**

the 6. Panzer-Division the following morning.

Spread over a wide area, mostly broken up into small packets to guard the bridges of the Oise-Sambre Canal, the 2ème D.C.R. was about to be annihilated. Its misuse was perhaps the clearest example of what was wrong with French tank doctrine. To guard a bridge was a purely static mission which violated two of the fundamental principles of armoured warfare — massed force and mobility. Colonel Jean-Paul Perré, who was to take command of the 2ème D.C.R. on May 20 when it was hurriedly refitting, later had this to say:

'On the front from the Somme to the Aisne, certain generals had the strange idea of posting tanks on bridges and leaving them without support; instead of employing the armoured division according to a sound, clear plan in massive fashion, it was scattered and frittered away. This was the reason why, although we had more or less as many tanks and armoured vehicles in the field as the Germans had, their effectiveness was, alas, very different.'

'Certain generals had the strange idea of posting tanks on bridges . . . ' Two Renault B1bis of the 8ème B.C.C. were lost this way in Guise.

'Ouragan' *(top)* and 'Rapide' *(above)*, both of the 1ère Compagnie, were disabled trying to prevent the crossing of the Oise on May 17. 'Rapide' was destroyed on the river bank, at the end of the bridge.

MAY 17-19

The counter-stroke planned by 9ème Armée had to be cancelled, the 2ème D.C.R. never managing to assemble, its strength dissolving, tank by tank, in trying to oppose the panzers in the vast emptiness of the army rear areas. Some were disabled at Guise, others at Longchamps, at Moy-de-l'Aisne . . . They were far too dispersed to actually change the course of the battle but an example of what they could do was shown on May 17 and 18 when a few tanks from the 2ème D.C.R. attacked northwards from Wassigny in support of an intended counter-attack by the 1ère D.L.M., one of the divisions transferred south from the 7ème Armée, advancing southwards from the sector of Valenciennes. They took control of the road to the rear of the leaders of the 7. Panzer-Division, cutting it off, and fought back aggressively when Rommel tried to restore the situation. 'Mistral', 'Tunisie' and 'Indochine', three Renault B1bis of 15ème B.C.C., went to Landrecies on May 17 where hundreds of enemy vehicles had been reported. 'Indochine' never did reach Landrecies but

When we first obtained these pictures we had no idea where they had been taken, but a search on the name 'Buridant', which appeared over the door of the cake shop, in the computerised French telecommunications directory led us to the Rue Camille Demoulin at Guise.

Another Renault B1bis of the 8ème B.C.C. was sent to the vital bridge at Origny-Sainte-Benoite, a few kilometres south of Guise, where the N30 crossed the canal. 'Toulouse' was knocked out in the centre of the town, east of the canal, the picture *above* subsequently being used by the Germans for propaganda purposes, simply captioned: 'In der Strassen von Bapaume' although that town is miles away to the north-west and of no relevance to the picture!

'Mistral' and 'Tunisie' entered the town and created much havoc, smashing German vehicles and equipment which packed the streets. 'Tunisie' entered one road lined with German vehicles parked on both sides and, firing alternately to the left and right, set the entire street alight, destroying dozens of vehicles.

Like most of the third company of 15ème B.C.C. which had been destroyed in the sector of Le Cateau, 'Indochine' failed to return from the Landrecies mission but the tanks 'Tunisie' and 'Mistral' did get back unscathed to Wassigny, only to be destroyed on May 18 at Le Catelet. The counter-attack of the 1ère D.L.M. failed to achieve anything, for the division, hurrying back from the Netherlands, was somewhat disorganised, and

With its strength frittered away, tank by tank, in a forlorn attempt at a piecemeal defence of the Oise-Sambre Canal bridges and the vast emptiness of the 9ème Armée rear areas, by May 20 the 2ème D.C.R. had ceased to exist. Its once-powerful Renault tanks now lay scattered across the plains of Picardy: 'Aquitaine' *(left)* and 'Martinique' *(centre)*, both of the 15ème B.C.C. photographed near Hérie-la-Viéville, and 'Typhon' *(right)* of the 8ème B.C.C. near Guise.

although some of its tanks detrained at Le Quesnoy, the division had great difficulty in assembling. When it did counter-attack on the evening of May 18, its two columns faced strong opposition and were forced to withdraw.

By the evening of May 18 little was left of the 9ème Armée. Cut off from the south; its rear raided by the panzers of Gruppe von Kleist; isolated from the north by the breakthrough of XV. Armeekorps, and hammered from every direction, a wave of hopelessness swept through the ranks, from the top downwards. Regardless of which way they turned there was no front line any more and the Germans were always further west than anticipated.

The staff of the 9ème D.I.M., another division transferred south from the 7ème Armée, was caught in a surprise attack near Bohain on May 18. Some were captured and, although the division's commander, Général Henri Didelet, got away wounded and exhausted, he was caught the following morning.

Meanwhile Général Giraud had decided to withdraw his command post at Wassigny to Le Catelet. His small

The capture of Général Henri Giraud, the commander of the 9ème Armée, on May 19 marked the formal end of the army. This picture was also published in Germany as a propaganda postcard with the inscription 'Sieg im Westen' although the precise location was not stated.

Left: Another Renault B1bis of the 8ème B.C.C. 'Glorieux' was pictured in Moy-de-l'Aisne where it had fought on May 17 to hold another bridge across the canal. The tank received a direct hit and exploded, killing three members of the crew. *Right:* We discovered that the photo had been taken at the western end of the bridge.

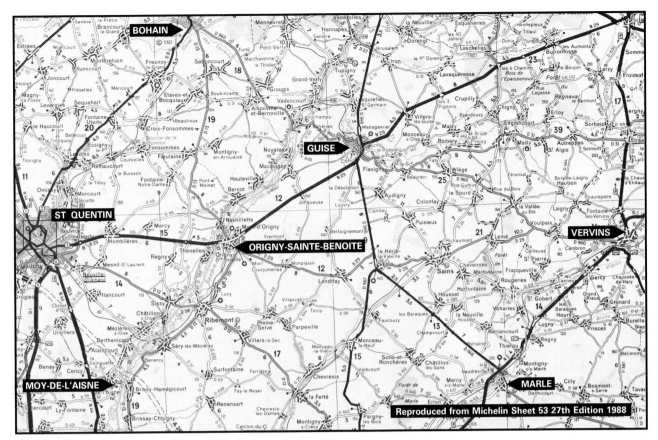

convoy found German armoured cars at every crossroads and they were forced to abandon their vehicles near Le Catelet late on May 18. They reached the town on foot during the night and even exchanged shots with some German troops. The party having split up, when daylight came Giraud stopped a small French column. He climbed aboard a gun-carrier but they soon ran into trouble. The carrier managed to knock out the first of the panzers that fired at them

but when three more appeared the passengers were forced to take refuge in a farm. A few of the panzers, belonging to Pz.Rgt. 11, 6. Panzer-Division, surrounded the farm. Troops came to search the place and as a result the commander of the 9ème Armée was taken prisoner. The next day, the 6. Panzer-Division proudly reported an impressive list of 'high level' prisoners including Général Giraud, his chief-of-staff and 50 officers.

Giraud's capture on May 19 marked the formal disappearance of the 9ème Armée. Some elements had succeeded in getting away to the south by crossing the Aisne; others went north to join the 1ère Armée, but a large part of the army had been shattered by Gruppe von Kleist and had surrendered. The 2ème D.C.R. itself, with only ten Renault B1bis and twelve Hotchkiss H-39s in fighting order on May 20, had practically ceased to exist.

Having broken through in the rear of the 9ème Armée sector, the forward troops of Gruppe von Kleist were now racing westwards towards the Channel coast with no French troops in front to oppose them. (The 'K' was borne by all elements of the Gruppe of which 1. Panzer-Division was a part. This SdKfz 221 belonged to its Aufkl.Abt. 4.)

Sichelschnitt

'On to the Channel!' *Above:* **Armoured personnel carriers of 1. Panzer-Division pound westwards while** *(below)* **General Georg-Hans Reinhardt, the commander of XXXXI. Armeekorps, halts at a crossroads near Aisonville, just west of Guise.**

Having broken through the French line of resistance, the panzers were now pushing forward inexorably in the rear of the 9ème Armée as it reeled back on the run. Alarm had turned to panic at Vincennes in the evening of May 15 when reports arrived about German forces having reached Rethel and preparing to cross the Aisne. Realising that he now had nothing to use to stop a German advance from the Aisne towards Paris, Gamelin finally appreciated

the extent to which he had been out-manoeuvered. The United States ambassador, William C. Bullitt, witnessed the moment at the French War Ministry when the War Minister, Edouard Daladier, received a telephone call from Gamelin to be informed of the disaster. Stunned by Gamelin's pessimism, hearing that there was 'not a single corps of soldiers' at his disposal 'between Laon and Paris', Daladier cried out: 'Then it

means the destruction of the French Army!' To which Gamelin slowly replied 'Yes . . . it means the destruction of the French Army'.

On the morning of May 16 plans were drawn up for moving the government to Tours. Although panic measures led to the burning of secret papers in the courtyard of the Foreign Ministry, things soon quietened down when there was no sign of the enemy. The Germans were actually at Rethel and, as far as

Paris was concerned, Gamelin was alarmed needlessly for their main thrust was aiming westwards at the Channel. The troops at Rethel were only flanking elements and, faced with dogged French defence, for five days they were unable to take even the part of the town which lay north of the river. Soon nerves were steadied and all plans for evacuation set aside. That evening in a radio broadcast, Reynaud complained of 'absurd rumours' and claimed that 'the Government is in Paris and stays in Paris'.

A huge gap had now been created between what remained of the 9ème Armée, swept aside in the north, and the 6ème Armée as it sought to create a line behind the Aisne with its left on the Ailette river near Laon. To block the

While the panzers were exploiting the disintegration of Corap's 9ème Armée, defences were being hastily thrown up by the 6ème Armée along the Aisne — the next river line to the south. Bridges were mined or blown and others barricaded, sometimes at the last moment.

approaches to Paris the High Command decided to create a 'new' 7ème Armée and insert it into the hole left by the vanishing 9ème Armée, with the intention of extending the line westwards up the Somme. This new army was placed under the command of Général Aubert Frère and on May 17 Généraux Gamelin and Georges called him to Georges' headquarters at La Ferté-sous-Jouarre to appraise him of his mission. Général

Corap, who had been transferred to command the 7ème Armée on May 15 to organise its transfer southwards out of the Netherlands, was told on May 18 that he had been dismissed.

By now, to the south and west of Gruppe von Kleist, a new French front was taking shape and units, albeit not all in the best shape, were arriving every day for the 6ème Armée and the 7ème Armée. The line was still very thin —

Further to the east, in the 2ème Armée sector, the front had become more stable after the Germans wheeled towards the Channel. This 155mm Schneider Modele 1917 field gun of the 6ème Division d'Infanterie was brought into action near Stenay on May 20.

Victor and vanquished. *Left:* **The driving force behind the massed mobility of the panzers, and the man to whom the success of the Blitzkrieg owed much, was General Heinz Guderian, the commander of XIX. Armeekorps, seen here on the left with Generalleutnant Friedrich Kirchner of 1. Panzer-Division.**

Right: **One of those who had not foreseen the violence of the revolution effected since the last war by the incursion on the battlefield of a mass of fast-moving armour was Général Maurice Gamelin, the Allied commander-in-chief, who was relieved of his command on May 18.**

the 6ème Armée had only six divisions on May 16 to hold about 100 kilometres of front — and the army could have no overall effect on the panzers' drive west as it was merely trying to cover the southern flank of the Aisne while the panzers were advancing north of it.

The moves of the French divisions were greatly hampered by the Luftwaffe which, since May 13, had concentrated its attacks against communications, the main weight being spread over a number of railways and towns in north-east and eastern France. Damage was reported at Chalons-sur-Marne, Hirson, Epernay, Rethel, Vouziers, Troyes, Lunéville and Vitry-le-François, all localities far to the rear as the Luftwaffe was actually aiming at lessening any possibility of the French switching forces from the rear to the 6ème Armée and 7ème Armée. The Armée de l'Air could not cope with such an air offensive and, not only the French, but also British senior officers in France, including Air Marshal Barratt and General Gort, had been pressing London since May 13 to release further fighter squadrons for France. The result of these representations was that a further 32 Hurricanes were ordered to proceed to France that afternoon to be distributed among the RAF Component fighter squadrons.

A strong request for further reinforcements was made the following

day from Reynaud to the War Cabinet: 'You were kind enough to send four squadrons, which is more than you promised, but if we are to win this battle, which might be decisive for the whole war, it is necessary to send at once, if possible today, ten more squadrons'. However, on the grounds that it

might prove to be against Britain's ultimate national interest to despatch more fighters to the Continent, the War Cabinet decided that 'no further fighter squadrons should for the present be sent to France'. Renewed requests, particularly from Air Marshal Barratt, flowed from France on the morning of

Marle lies on the main N2 highway (see map, page 285) which eventually reaches Paris. At the junction with the N46, the French defenders had set up this primitive

An exhausted soldier of the 102ème D.I.F. is helped along the main street of Marle by a tank crewman and a doctor of a Luftwaffe Flak unit. His division had been holding the Meuse in the Monthermé sector, but was defeated on May 15. The survivors were hastily pulled back, only to be overrun once again as the panzers caught up with them 80 kilometres further west.

May 16 and the War Cabinet decided to send the equivalent of four squadrons immediately. While this was being arranged, Churchill had himself left for France and from there he telegraphed later on May 16 to ask that six more squadrons be sent across in addition to the four promised. Pointing out the fact that the airfields in France could not efficiently handle all these squadrons, he suggested that six squadrons of Hurricanes should be concentrated in the south of England, three flying across to French bases for the morning work, with the other three relieving them in the afternoon. Arrangements were made during the night so that the squadrons were ready for operations on the morning of May 17.

By now Reynaud had recovered his nerve after the alarm of May 15-16, but the encirclement of the Allied armies in the north was clearly approaching and he had since decided that a government shake-up and a new Commander-in-Chief were paramount. In the changes announced on May 18, he himself took over as Minister for National Defence and War, ousting Edouard Daladier, the protector of Gamelin, from the post he had kept when he lost the premiership, transferring him to the Foreign Ministry. Georges Mandel, once Clémenceau's hatchet man, was transferred from the Colonies to the Interior, a key post when civilian morale was at stake; and from Madrid the French ambassador to Franco was recalled and invited to join the government as Minister of State and Vice-Premier — Maréchal Philippe Pétain, the 'Victor of Verdun', returning to France in the service of his country. Gamelin was thereupon relieved and Général Maxime Weygand, Foch's Chief-of-Staff in the last war, was summoned to Paris from his command in the Levant and appointed the new Commander-in-Chief.

Weygand arrived at Vincennes on May 20 to meet Gamelin and take over his command. Gamelin, whose name was thereafter to personalise the French defeat for which he was undoubtedly party responsible, departed — a convenient scapegoat also for the pre-war weakness of the French political system in opposing Hitler.

sand-bagged machine gun position which was easily brushed aside by the first few shots from the leading tanks of 1. Panzer-Division.

ON TO THE CHANNEL

In spite of the stunning success of its panzers, anxiety was beginning to be expressed at Heeresgruppe A headquarters and Hitler, who had approved the boldest aspects of the Manstein plan, was himself showing signs of cautiousness. Orders were soon issued to halt all further advances which, late on May 15, led to Guderian becoming involved in a heated discussion with von Kleist to get the orders cancelled. Finally von Kleist approved the advance being maintained for another 24 hours, but only so far as that sufficient space could be gained for the following infantry corps.

The drive westwards had therefore continued on May 16. Since Gruppe von Kleist had not laid down any corps boundary between the forces of Guderian and Reinhardt, Guderian had to agree on one with the commander of the 6. Panzer-Division, Generalmajor Werner Kempf. They encountered each other in the market place at Montcornet, and there and then worked out the allocation of roads between the three divisions which were pouring through the town. Guderian's orders for the day to his panzers were simply to drive on until the last drop of petrol had been used up. Early on May 17 they had reached Crécy on the River Serre and Ribemont on the Oise when orders arrived from Gruppe von Kleist for an immediate halt and for Guderian to report to the Panzergruppe commander. Guderian presented himself and, without a word of praise for the performance of the troops, von Kleist berated him for having disobeyed orders. Guderian thereupon asked to be relieved of his command. Later in the day Heeresgruppe A sent down Generaloberst List, the commander of the 12. Armee, to sort things out and to inform Guderian that his resignation would not be accepted.

It had now become apparent to the German Command that the immediate priority for the French on their southern flank was defence rather than attack. This being so, von Rundstedt ordered von Kleist to push forward 'strong advanced units' to the Cambrai and Saint-Quentin area on May 18 while he closed his main force up to the Oise. Hitler was fearful about possible counter-attacks on the southern flank and on May 18 Halder noted in his diary how 'the Führer has incomprehensible anxiety about the southern flank'. Visiting von Rundstedt's headquarters, Hitler insisted that decisive success 'at the moment depends not so much on a rapid thrust to the Channel as on the ability to secure as quickly as possible an absolutely sound defence on the Aisne in the Laon area', but he approved the orders that Gruppe von Kleist should push units forward in force.

Advancing from their bridgeheads on the Oise on May 18, the 2. Panzer-Division reached Saint-Quentin at 9.00 a.m. On its left the 1. Panzer-Division had crossed the Somme and was advancing on Péronne. In the evening the advance units of Gruppe von Kleist were along the Canal du Nord while on

This column from 1. Panzer-Division has stopped in Dercy, ten kilometres west of Marle. Identifiable are tractors of Art.Rgt. 73, an armoured personnel carrier, motor cycles of Schtz.Rgt. 1 and a Mercedes 170V with Westphalian licence plates.

When on the afternoon of May 19 General Hermann Hoth *(left)*, the commander of XV. Armeekorps, visited Rommel's command post, the Desert Fox convinced his chief that his tanks were ready and able to press on throughout the night.

On the morning of May 17 Hitler set out from Felsennest for the 75-mile drive to see von Rundstedt at the headquarters of Heeresgruppe A which had been established in Bastogne. The enthusiasm of the welcome belied Hitler's personal belief that von Kleist's panzers were moving too far, too fast, and he insisted that the southern flank be secured as quickly as possible. Von Rundstedt argued that with the French unbalanced, the initiative must be maintained, and Hitler, though he was nervous of a flank attack to this extended front, approved the order that Gruppe von Kleist should push forward.

their right the 7. Panzer-Division of the XV. Armeekorps was at Cambrai. In his corps orders for the following day, Guderian announced that Gruppe von Kleist had been given specific approval to further the advance.

The breakthrough had continued to lengthen the southern flank and the Aisne, Serre and Somme rivers, which had served until now to help protect it, were covered only by reconnaissance and engineer units. The danger on this open flank could not be ignored and on May 19, while the 1. Panzer-Division and the 2. Panzer-Division forced the canal, the 10. Panzer-Division was brought forward to take over the rôle of flank protection.

There was also some concern for the northern flank and here the XV. Armeekorps was held back until infantry divisions arrived to take over its protection. Hoth's two panzer divisions spent May 19 reorganising and bringing up supplies although Rommel was impatient to get moving again that night to seize the high ground south-east of Arras. He had however to convince his corps commander that such a move was feasible. The opportunity came to raise the subject when Hoth visited Rommel's command post that afternoon.

The Führer leaves the headquarters at No. 3 Avenue de la Gare — the inspiration for our dustjacket by George A. Campbell.

Although the corps commander believed that the troops were too tired to be pushed further, Rommel countered by saying that they had already spent twenty hours or so at the same place, and that a night attack would mean less casualties. Hoth demurred and Rommel began preparing his next move.

Whatever doubts he had inside, to the troops their god-like leader was all-victorious.

In September 1939, one month after the creation of the Fortified and Defensive Sectors, the 'new fronts' along the Belgian border from the sea to the La Crusnes Fortified Sector south of Luxembourg, were established. From the sea to the Lys river ran the Flandres Defence Sector (to be renamed Fortified Sector in January 1940). Then came the Lille Defence Sector (to be renamed Fortified Sector in March 1940) running from the Lys to the Maulde; from Maulde to Wargnies was the Escaut Fortified Sector with one minor fortress, Eth, fourteen casemates and a large number of hastily built blockhouses. From Wargnies to the Helpe river east of Avesnes lay the Maubeuge Fortified Sector; then came the Ardennes Defensive Sector (to become the 102ème Division de Forteresse (D.I.F.) in January 1940) holding the border behind the 'impassable' Ardennes from the Helpe river to Pont-à-Bar. Finally the Montmédy Fortified Sector continued down to the boundary with the La Crusnes Fortified Sector near Velosnes. Although the fortified sectors had some minor fortresses, the four defensive sectors had no fortress line except a few blockhouses and hurriedly constructed defences.

Enlarging the breach

The extension of the Maginot Line — the so-called 'New Fronts' — was far weaker than that fortified prior to 1933. This 47mm AT has been positioned at a 47mm AT/Reibel JM embrasure.

As the panzers rushed on westwards through the breach, the following infantry soon turned to the fortified sectors which flanked their breakthrough on its left and right flanks, preventing the widening of its base and threatening the flanks. The VII. Armeekorps was committed on the breached left flank, with the mission to capture the fortresses and casemates of the Montmédy Fortified Sector which controlled the Chiers valley. Further north, on the right flank of the breach, the VIII. Armeekorps was to deal with the Maubeuge Fortified Sector.

The most westerly fortress of the Montmédy Fortified Sector, La Ferté, stood on a hill overlooking the Chiers valley between Villy and La Ferté. The road which passed the hill just behind the fortress and this valley was defended at either end by a 75mm casemate. Casemate Ouest was angled towards Villy with Casemate Est (above) facing La Ferté.

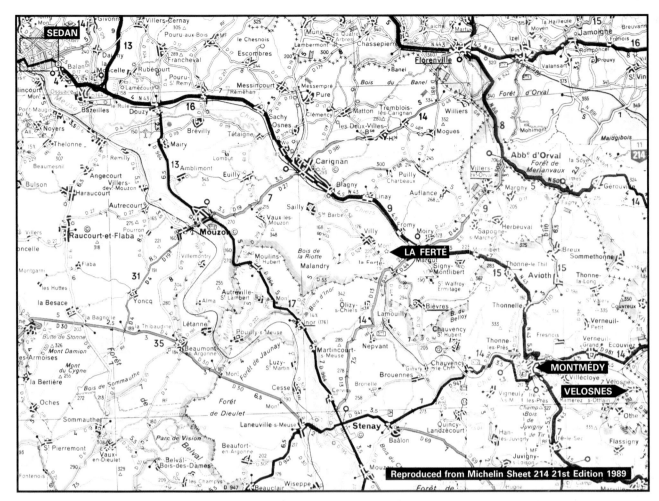

THE MONTMÉDY FORTIFIED SECTOR

The Montmédy Fortified Sector was responsible for the frontier from Pont-à-Bar, seven kilometres west of Sedan, to Velosnes, about six kilometres east of Montmédy. The sector fortifications consisted of two major fortresses, two minor fortresses and twelve casemates, stretching from La Ferté in the west to Veslosnes, a major fortress, in the east. This relative weakness was even more noticeable on both of the sector's flanks as the Ardennes Defensive Sector in the west and the Marville area in the east were only fortified with casemates.

The La Ferté fortress had two battle blocks:

Block 1: one 47mm AT/Reibel JM embrasure, one Reibel JM embrasure, two GFM cupolas and two AM cupolas.

Block 2: one AM turret, one GFM cupola, one AM cupola and one observation cupola.

Near the fortress were two casemates which controlled the road on both sides of the ridge, Casemate Ouest facing Villy and Casemate Est facing La Ferté.

The fortress was manned by 3 officers and 101 men of the fourth company of the 155ème R.I.F. under Lieutenant Maurice Bourguignon, and the two casemates by men of the 169ème R.A.P.

The most western fortress of the sector — La Ferté — was poorly designed. The gallery which linked its two

blocks provided neither long term accommodation nor an escape route; its two blocks were unable to support each other as well as they ought, this being even truer of the two casemates, and there were large areas of dead ground, particularly near Block 2 and the Casemate Est. To make things worse, the

The commander of Pi.Btl. 171, Oberleutnant Alfred Germer, was the leader of the assault group assembled to disable the fortress at La Ferté. Awarded the Ritterkreuz on May 26, 1940, he was to be killed in Russia in August 1944.

fortress and the two casemates were not under the same command.

In May 1940 the left wing of the Montmédy Sector was under the tactical command of the XVIIIème Corps d'Armée of the 2ème Armée. On May 14, after the German breakthrough at Sedan, the 3ème D.I.N.A. holding the Chiers river withdrew and the 71. Infanterie-Division was soon in contact with the left of the fortified line. As the fortress and casemates overlooking the Chiers valley prevented the widening of the VII. Armeekorps base and were a threat to its flank, it had to be dealt with. While Arko 7 was bringing its artillery batteries forward, the infantry of 71. Infanterie-Division pressed on. By the 16th the pressure mounted, particularly on the village of Villy which was resolutely defended by men of the 23ème R.I.C. On May 17 the crews of the two casemates were ordered to withdraw; the next day the last elements of the 23ème R.I.C. at Villy were overwhelmed and the La Ferté fortress — Panzerwerke 505 to the Germans — was alone.

Arko 7 having brought forward most of its batteries (three abteilung of heavy 210mm mortars, seven of 150mm howitzers, nine of 105mm howitzers, three of 100mm howitzers and one battery of 88mm Flak) the shelling of the fortress intensified. While 88mm Flak fired directly at the cupolas and embrasures, heavier guns, among them the 210mm heavy mortars, smashed gaps in the barbed wire and made craters that

293

Having taken La Ferté, these German troops relax to enjoy the view over the Chiers valley. Having already been jammed by an artillery round in the raised position, the AM turret was especially vulnerable to the explosive charges of Stosstrupp Germer's engineers as they picked their way cautiously over the fortress.

enabled the engineers to approach unseen. The AM turret of Block 2, probably hit when firing at German troops on Hill 311, jammed in a firing position on May 18, and this badly reduced the already weak armament of the fortress. The 75mm turret of the neighbouring fortress of Le Chesnois fired in support of La Ferté for several days, lobbing more than 4,000 shells towards the fortress and the surrounding area, although the fire was not all that accurate as the guns were at the limit of their range.

On May 18 a counter-attack by two battalions of the 6ème Division d'Infanterie backed by some Renault B1bis of the 41ème B.C.C. was mounted to try to relieve the pressure but it failed. Three tanks were lost, the 'Charente' being disabled by a German anti-tank gun, the 'Muscadet' by its own side mistaking it for German and the 'Tarn' by falling into the Chiers river, its entire crew being drowned.

The German infantry had now reached the rear of the fortress and took the Casemate Ouest, which had been abandoned the day before by the artillery but re-occupied by a few infantry. Stosstrupp Germer, the German assault group assembled to disable the fortress, advanced to the edge of Villy, waiting

Save for the removal of some earth from around the base, the turret remains virtually unaltered. We were quite alone when we took these comparison pictures in May 1987 — our only companion being a brisk wind, whistling through the barbed wire. ... The scars left by two direct hits, which have ricochetted off the thick, round steel plate, can still be seen as can the camouflage paintwork, although it is not quite so evident in this photograph.

Two German soldiers take a breather in a crater beside Block 2 at La Ferté. On May 18, engineers of Stosstrupp Germer managed to reach the block from this side with the idea of blowing off the turret and cupolas. They succeeded in knocking

the AM turret askew, leaving it dislodged from its mounting, so effectively that it remains in this position even to this day. The GFM cupola on the right was the one in which three members of the crew were killed by a direct hit on May 18.

for the artillery to stop. In the evening, when the shelling lifted and moved down to the Chiers valley at the appointed hour, Stosstrupp Germer engineers launched their assault on Block 2. Dodging from one crater to another, they reached the superstructures whereupon they blew off the turret and the cupolas. After replenishing their supplies of explosive charges during a renewed bout of shelling, they assaulted Block 1 during the night, blowing off three of its four cupolas, the last one at dawn on May 19.

At 6.15 a.m. on May 18 a direct hit on the GFM cupola on Block 2 had killed three men but because of the very short time between the end of the shelling and the first of the charges blown by the engineers, the block's crew thought that these explosions were part of the bombardment and had not rushed to their posts. Stunned by the incredible destruction of all their weapons in Block 2, they had withdrawn towards Block 1 only to see it destroyed just as quickly. For some unknown reason, they all then withdrew to the gallery, waiting for an order which never came. As the air became poisoned by the smoke and fumes which drifted down from the fires raging in the blocks they all suffocated,

The tranquil external appearance presented to the inquisitive Germans must have been quickly dispelled as they ventured inside, to be faced with a virtual chamber of horrors in the gallery where the fortress personnel had suffocated whilst awaiting orders during the Stosstrupp Germer attack. This snapshot was taken by one of those who dared to venture into the interior.

Left: View from the top of Block 2 looking out across the valley after the battle. The knocked-out AM turret and pair of cupolas (AM on the left and GFM on the right) remain almost

unchanged to this day, silent witnesses to those few dramatic hours in May 1940 in spite of the efforts of nature to soften the scars of the battle *(right).*

Lieutenant Maurice Bourguignon was the commander of the fourth company of 155ème R.I.F., about one hundred men strong, which manned La Ferté. He died alongside his men in their stricken fortress on May 19 but his remains were not recovered until July 1973 when the last missing bodies were discovered in a common grave dating from 1940 near Block 2. He now rests, with other members of his crew, in the small military cemetery that was built beside the D52, opposite the memorial erected near Block 2 to commemorate the tragic end of the fortress and its personnel.

the ventilation system being unable to cope amidst the damage. All telephone communication with Le Chesnois fortress ceased at 5.00 a.m. on May 19: the La Ferté crew had perished to a man in their stricken fortress.

A squad from the 16. Armee arrived at the fortress on June 8 and for three days worked hard to recover the dead, manhandling decaying corpses from within the depths of the blockhouses in the poisonous atmosphere before burying them in common graves. (Most of them were reburied after the war but not until 1973 were the last 17 missing bodies found in a grave in front of Block 2; among them was the fort commander, Lieutenant Maurice Bourguignon.)

In their propaganda the Germans made the most of this capture of a fortress of the Maginot Line and dropped leaflets headlined 'Maginot Line, a common grave for those who defend it' which described how the bodies 'of your comrades were found, badly mutilated and burnt' in La Ferté. On May 19 the commander of Pi.Btl. 171, Oberleutnant Alfred Germer, who had led the assault at La Ferté, had the honour of being named in the Army report which proudly made known that the 'strong Panzerwerk 505 had been taken', and on May 26 Germer was awarded the Ritterkreuz.

When a general withdrawal was ordered from the fortified line, the three other fortresses of the Montmédy sector, Le Chesnois, Thonnelle and Velosnes, which then lay in hopelessly exposed positions, were ordered to be booby-trapped and abandoned on June 13 and 14.

Above: This plaque from veterans of the 71. Infanterie-Division honouring their former adversaries can be seen on the memorial in front of Block 2. *Right:* The barbed wire defences at La Ferté have been left just as they were in 1940 — the gaps blown by German shell-fire now being augmented by gaps created by the ravages of time.

Above: **The battle of the Maubeuge Fortified Sector ended at 11.00 a.m. on May 23 with the capture of Fort les Sarts. This was Block 1 as it appeared just after the end of the battle. One of the block's two cupolas (it had one GFM and one AM cupola) can be seen as well as one of its two embrasures (it** had one 47mm AT/Reibel JM and one Reibel JM). *Below:* **Freshly-planted trees have mellowed the landscape at Les Sarts today and all the ironwork has been removed, yet the profile of the casemate is unmistakable, a few hundred metres from the N2.**

THE MAUBEUGE FORTIFIED SECTOR

Maubeuge had been a 'Place Forti-fiée' for centuries, although in the 1920s this part of the front was not included in the scheme drawn up for the system of fortifications which became known as the Ligne Maginot. As one of the 'new fronts' of the mid-1930s, the spending cuts which resulted in a drastic curtail-ment of the plans to build five major fortresses between Valenciennes and Trélon (plus some minor fortresses and

numbers of casemates) meant that none of the major fortresses initially planned were built. Had they been constructed, two of them would have stood in the way of the German breakthrough in 1940: at Quatre-Bras, impeding the 5. Panzer-Division, and at l'Epine, block-ing the 7. Panzer-Division.

The Maubeuge Fortified Sector was responsible for the frontier from Warg-nies, ten kilometres east of Bavay, to the Helpe river, east of Avesnes. This 50-kilometre front was protected with

four minor fortresses and twenty case-mates, stretching from the minor for-tress of Les Sarts to the west to another minor fortress, Boussois, to the east.

The four small fortresses of the sector had all been built on the foundations of old forts dating back from 1880 or 1890. North of Maubeuge, by the side of the road to Mons, was Les Sarts fortress, which had two blocks; to the east was Bersillies with two blocks; and further east was La Salmagne, also with two blocks. East of Maubeuge lay Boussois,

87ème R.I.F., between 70 to 100 men in each fortress, each fortress being armed with one 47mm AT/Reibel JM embrasure, one Reibel JM embrasure, one AM turret, three GFM cupolas (two only at Les Sarts), two AM cupolas and one LG cupola (none at Les Sarts).

On March 15, 1940, the Maubeuge Fortified Sector had become the 101ème Division d'Infanterie de Forteresse. When the Dyle Plan was activated on May 10, the units of the Vème Corps d'Armée in the Maubeuge sector had moved into Belgium with the 1ère Armée, leaving the 101ème Division de Forteresse with its two regiments, the 84ème R.I.F. and the 87ème R.I.F. to hold the Sambre sector. On the right wing of the 1ère Armée, the corps soon ordered the 5ème D.I.N.A. to detach Groupement Marioge — one battalion of infantry, one company of light tanks and one group of recce motor cyclists, all under Lieutenant-Colonel Eugène Marioge, the commander of the 6ème R.T.M. — south of the Sambre to maintain contact with the IIème Corps d'Armée on the left wing of the 9ème

Above and bottom: **On the N2 just south of the fort, men of 28. Infanterie-Division search the houses at La Banlieue on the morning of Sunday, May 21. Soon the French defenders in Maubeuge, a kilometre to the south, would be overwhelmed.**

Left: **As the last odd groups of defenders were being mopped up one by one down town in Maubeuge, victorious German infantrymen take a breather at the bottom of the Vauban** fortifications. *Right:* **Almost unchanged today, this is the junction of Rue Casimir Fournier (left) and Rue Vauban (right) on the northern edge of the town.**

the strongest fortress in the sector with three blocks. Seven of the sector's twenty casemates completed the defences of the Sambre valley, three being with the fortresses on the northern bank of the river and four south of it to the east of Maubeuge. A rare feature, typical of the late design of these fortifications, was that four of these casemates were armed with an AM+Mo turret.

Boussois, the strongest of the four fortresses, had three battle blocks:

Block 1: one 47mm AT/Reibel embrasure, one Reibel JM embrasure, one GFM cupola and one AM cupola.

Block 2: one AM turret and one GFM cupola.

Block 3: one 47mm AT/Reibel embrasure, one JM embrasure, one AM+Mo turret and two GFM cupolas.

In May 1940 the fortress was under the command of Capitaine Maurice Bertin with 5 officers and 195 men from the 84ème R.I.F.

The sector's other three fortresses were manned by garrisons from the

La Banlieue today, minus cobbles and tramlines. The N2 is the direct north-south route between Brussels and Paris, via Mons (in Belgium), Maubeuge and Laon. Fort des Sarts lies between the village and the Franco-Belgian frontier six kilometres to the north.

Above: Soldiers of 28. Infanterie-Division rest for a while in front of Maubeuge's northern gate, the Porte de Mons, on Sunday. Maubeuge had been a 'Place Forte' for centuries and in 1940 it was still surrounded by intricate fortifications of the Vauban era. *Below:* During the concentrated reconstruction years after the war, little thought was given to preservation and most of the old fortifications, including the superb Porte de Paris, were swept away. Fortunately on the northern side of the town, the Porte de Mons still survives, barely changed from the day it provided a backdrop for an invading army.

Sébastien Le Prestre de Vauban was a French engineer who revolutionised siege warfare and defensive fortifications to cope with the introduction of firearms to the battlefield. His fame rests on his work in the second half of the 17th century during the wars of Louis XIV, yet 300 years later his fortresses were still to play their part. These remarkable comparisons were achieved by the author in the remains of those spared the post-war demolitions. He is especially pleased with that *below*, at first sight a seemingly impossible match which turned out to have been taken near the Place Vauban.

Armée. Contact was made on May 15 with elements of the 5ème D.I.M. and Groupement Marioge was ordered in the evening to withdraw south of the Sambre in liaison with this division.

On May 16, the advance guards of the 7. Panzer-Division crossed the French border near Sivry and easily broke through the weak line of casemates thinly held by troops from the 84ème R.I.F. By the evening the situation south of the Sambre was desperate and the 84ème R.I.F. was ordered to withdraw north of the river, but one company was ordered to keep its positions in the casemates south of the Sambre at Rocq, Marpent Nord, Marpent Sud and Ostergnies.

FRIDAY, MAY 17

The two regiments of the 101ème D.I.F. which were in positions north of the Sambre in the sector of Maubeuge had now been reinforced by miscellaneous elements. Beside them there were now Groupement Marioge, with one battalion of the 6ème R.T.M. and one section of Renault R-35s from the 39ème B.C.C., plus elements from the 5ème D.I.M. and a few Hotchkiss H-39s and Renault R-35s from the 26ème B.C.C. and 6ème B.C.C. Although at first sight the strength appeared impressive, in reality the force available was not, for all these units were very

In spite of the relaxed atmosphere of the pictures at Place Vauban, the fortresses north of the town had not yet fallen. This shot shows a battery of 8.8cm Flak 18 guns preparing to move northwards through the southern suburbs at Louvroil. Having been in action against casemates south of the Sambre (which runs through the town), the guns were now being brought forward to pound those casemates still holding out.

Once captured, the Maubeuge defenders were assembled on the southern edge of the town before being marched eastwards to prisoner-of-war camps in Germany. This picture of a mixture of French infantry (most from the 43ème Division d'Infanterie) and tank crewmen from Groupement Marioge was taken on Sunday afternoon in Rue Ferrière.

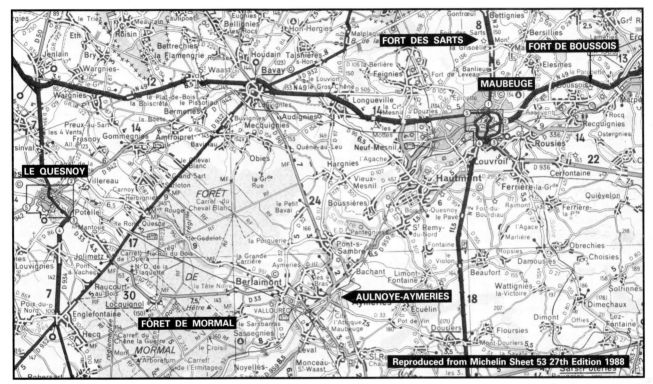

Reproduced from Michelin Sheet 53 27th Edition 1988

Due to the confused situation in the area, Lieutenant-Colonel Eugène Marioge, the commander of the 6ème R.T.M. of the 5ème D.I.M., suddenly found himself in charge of the entire Maubeuge sector. This picture was taken shortly after his capture as he is respectfully escorted along the Rue Ferrière to the German command post at Louvroil.

Above and bottom: **Having extricated his unit from Belgium with only four tanks left, the commander of 26ème B.C.C., Commandant Pierre Bonnot, then took part in the defence of Maubeuge. He was given 12 Renault R-35s — four from 6ème** **B.C.C. and eight from 39ème B.C.C. — and for three days they helped keep the Germans south of the Sambre before being finally overwhelmed on the afternoon of May 21. These six Renaults were captured in the Rue du Ponceau in Boussois.**

Human sentiment for animals being what it is, the sight of a foal waiting beside its dead mother for her to awake touches **the heartstrings with compassion. The sad scene in Rue de Valencienne in Maubeuge.**

Above: **As the fortresses were still holding out, artillery was brought forward to pound the block's embrasures and cupolas over open sights. This 10.5cm lFH 18 of Artillerie-Regiment 28 (28. Infanterie-Division) is seen being manhandled into position** at La Grisoëlle crossroads to enable it to be brought to bear on the rear of Les Sarts fortress. *Below:* **In the present day view, the memorial to Général Jean-Baptiste Gouvion, killed there in 1792, can be seen on the side of the N2.**

tired and low on ammunition, fuel and supplies after the failure of their initial mission in Belgium with Dyle Plan.

Early on May 17 Général Billotte had ordered that the 1ère D.L.M., which was then assembling in the Valenciennes sector after its hasty withdrawal from the Netherlands, be assigned to the 9ème Armée and to be engaged in a decisive attack southwards to cut off the advanced panzers from their rear. Two groupements were organised — each with two squadrons of tanks, one battalion of motorised infantry and one group of artillery — Groupement de Beauchesne to advance to Le Cateau and Groupement de Caussans to Landrecies. But with the German advance threatening the commander of the XIème Corps d'Armée which had just reached Le Quesnoy, Général Julien Martin, decided he could wait no longer. He ordered one squadron of Somua S-35s of the 1ère D.L.M. eastwards to recapture the Sambre bridges east of the Mormal Forest, between Maubeuge and Landrecies. The French tanks moved on and a fierce battle raged for several hours in the afternoon at Berlaimont between these Somuas of the 4ème Cuirassiers and infantry of the 7. Panzer-Division and panzers of the 5. Panzer-Division.

Left: **Further to the east (still in Boussois), another 10.5cm IFH 18 (the 'standard' German field piece) has been positioned on Rue Gabriel Péri just behind the fortress. Block 1 can actually be seen on the horizon just to the left of the gun mantlet.**

Right: **The IFH 18 (standing for 'light field howitzer' — leichte Feldhaubitze) fired two-piece ammunition and the shells and charges can be seen stacked ready for use. Normal range of the gun was 10,000 metres — about six miles — with a 32lb shell.**

SATURDAY, MAY 18

At Maubeuge, as some of the bridges — the one at Louvroil among them — had not been blown, advance elements of the 5. Panzer-Division had reached the northern bank of the Sambre during the night. The Hotchkiss H-39s and Renault R-35s of Groupement Marioge fought back against the panzers of Pz.Rgt. 31 for most of the day but the defenders were unable to prevent the Germans from expanding their bridge-head north of the river. The 28. Infanterie-Division of the VIII. Armee-korps then took over the sector and the panzers moved further west in the evening. The newly-arrived infantry immediately proceed to attack the forts, taking up positions all around the four casemates south of the river and starting to shell Boussois.

Further south in the Mormal forest, the battle had resumed, this time on its western edge at Jolimetz, between the Somua S-35s of the 1ère D.L.M. and the panzers of the 5. Panzer-Division. French infantry trying to reach the eastern edge of the forest were badly mauled by the Germans who already held the sector in force; the whole of one battalion of the 27ème R.T.A. was destroyed. Further south the leading

In this case the range was a mere 400 metres or so.

elements of Groupement de Caussans had succeeded in fighting their way to Landrecies but to the west, near Le Quesnoy, in a short but deadly encoun-ter with the artillery and Pak guns of the 5. Panzer-Division, most of the Hotch-kiss H-35s of the 4ème Cuirassiers were destroyed in the afternoon.

Left: **The capture of a Maginot Line fortress was of great propaganda value. Here, working in concert with the stills photographer (both from the Luftwaffe), a cine cameraman has** set up his equipment behind a barn on the corner of Rue Jean Jaurès, some 20 metres behind the gun. *Right:* **Our author Jean Paul re-photographs the scene and recreates history.**

What is now the Rue Gabriel Péri has been redeveloped yet the old building on the right remains to pinpoint the spot where three French soldiers once surrendered — no doubt to the delight of the waiting cameramen!

SUNDAY, MAY 19

Lieutenant-Colonel Marioge, who had organised the defence of the Maubeuge sector with the motley collection of units assembled there, had seen elements of the 43ème Division d'Infanterie taking positions on his right flank in the north and west of the town. The battle raged throughout the day on the northern edge of Maubeuge and in Assevent, the Germans pressing their attacks home against the forts. At Boussois, their artillery now began to fire point-blank at the rear of the blocks. Called on by Capitaine Yvon

Cariou, the commander of the 101ème Compagnie which was surrounded in the four casemates south of the Sambre, the guns of Block 3 fired at them to repulse the Germans approaching the casemates for the final assault. However they were not repulsed for long. At about 5.00 p.m. the 101ème Compagnie was forced to surrender its four casemates and from Boussois, the men of the 102ème Compagnie could see their comrades of the Marpent casemate come out one by one.

At Maubeuge, in the town itself, some grenadiers had been taken by surprise when fired at by the French defenders and they replied with grenades at suspected buildings and many in the Rue de Mons, Rue de l'Esplanade, Place de la Grisöelle were all in flames.

Leaving the Maubeuge Sector to the 28. Infanterie-Division, the 5. Panzer-Division had pushed on westwards and surrounded Le Quesnoy where elements of the 84ème R.I.F. and 5ème R.T.M. were barricaded in the old fortified town. With them were about 2,000 Dutch, Belgian and French refugees trapped in the besieged town. However with the piecemeal commitment of the 1ère D.L.M, its strength was spent and the powerful counter-attack planned by Général Billotte came to nothing. The division was then withdrawn and the mission to clear the Mormal Forest was then given to the 5ème D.I.N.A. Its commander, Général Auguste Agliany, was summoned to the command post of the Vème Corps d'Armée at Blaregnies and

ordered to clear the forest in the evening to enable the passage of the units of the 1ère Armée which were withdrawing from Belgium. For the operation he was to commit two of his own regiments, the 6ème R.T.M. and the 24ème R.T.T., two battalions of the 3ème R.T.M. of the 43ème Division d'Infanterie and the infantry was to be supported by four squadrons of tanks from the 2ème D.L.M. plus two sections of Renault R-35s from the 39ème B.C.C. (the third section was at Maubeuge with Lieutenant-Colonel Marioge). The counter-attack began as ordered but only the supporting tanks were ready in time; without infantry support, which was late, the tanks suffered heavy losses as they tried to force their way into the forest.

The fort's garrison of some 180 men clambered out from Block 3, being ordered to surrender their weapons in front of the casemate. The German artillery had achieved a number of direct hits, smashing the radio antenna supports and the 47mm AT gun in the centre. The right-hand position was a JM embrasure.

The battle of Maubeuge is over and columns of French prisoners are marched away eastwards to camps in Germany.

Above and bottom: This large group has reached les 4 Bras, six kilometres from the Belgian border on the D936.

Left: This group are pictured marching past the Café de la Bascule in Louvroil, still in business, *right*, on Route d'Avesnes.

The 4. Panzer-Division entered the battle of Mormal Forest on Monday, May 20. *Above:* The divisional insignia can be seen displayed on this PzKpfw II, the dot after '216' identifying it as belonging to Pz.Rgt. 36 (rather than Pz.Rgt. 35, the other regiment of the division). *Bottom:* Having established that the picture was taken on the D959 at Noyelles, just before the bridge over the Helpe river, it proves that this Kampfgruppe of the division was bypassing the forest to the south.

MONDAY, MAY 20

By now the situation of the defenders near Maubeuge was desperate. The fortresses of Boussois and La Salmagne were still shelling the Sambre crossing at Assevent and at Boussois, and the southern bank of the river near Recquignies, and the main road near Cerfontaine, but at 11.00 a.m. Stukas bombed Boussois, shaking the fort to its foundations but causing no serious damage. As soon as the aircraft had left, the artillery resumed its efforts to counter the German guns, but at such close range the fortress guns could not be depressed low enough to aim at most of them. At 11.00 p.m. Lieutenant-Colonel Marioge informed the Boussois

fortress commander, Capitaine Maurice Bertin, that his men had been forced out of Assevent. The Boussois garrison worked hard for most of the night to repair the damage, filling a crater caused by a Stuka bomb, and repairing the badly damaged access door on Block 1 and the radio antennas. The noise must have alerted the Germans as a heavy salvo crashed on the fort only a few minutes after the working parties had finished and had returned back inside.

Further west, in the Mormal Forest, infantry of the 5ème D.I.N.A. had made up for their lateness during the night and advanced into the forest supported by tanks from the 29ème Dragons and 39ème B.C.C., falling on strong German positions. North of the forest were elements of the 8. Infanterie-Division; the 4. Panzer-Division was in the centre and to the east; elements of the 5. Panzer-Division were to the west, and the advance guards of the 20. Infanterie-Division (mot) were to the south. The French

The 1ère D.L.M. fought desperately in the forest on May 18 but paid dearly for the losses its tanks had inflicted on the 5. Panzer Division. This Somua S-35 of the 18ème Dragons was disabled near Englefontaine, south-west of the forest.

In the final battle in the forest on May 21, gunners from Flak-Regiment 'General Göring' fired point-blank at the French tanks which were restricted to moving along the forest tracks. *Above left:* Here at the crossroads just east of Jolimetz, a 20mm

Flak gun has been emplaced to enfilade this particular track. Two Renault R-35s from the 39ème B.C.C. have just been hit. *Right:* Now nothing to mark the spot where brave men fought to their deaths.

were soon blocked in the middle of the forest where furious encounters raged for the whole day. The losses were heavy on both sides, the French tanks suffering particularly at the hands of the 88mm Flak of the 1. Bataillon of Flak-Regiment 'General Göring' attached to the 4. Panzer-Division.

TUESDAY, MAY 21

The battle in the Mormal Forest was lost and what remained of the 5ème D.I.N.A. was badly mauled trying to force a way out of the trap on the south-west edge of the forest. Near Englefontaine, the 24ème R.T.T. — most of them Moslems from Tunisia — had assaulted the panzers and the artillery positions, being decimated in the process, the third battalion disappearing almost to the last man into the inferno. A few men succeeded in breaking out but most of them were killed or captured, about 8,000 being taken prisoner. Most of the tanks of the 39ème B.C.C. and 29ème Dragons had been lost, many abandoned because of lack of fuel. The garrison of Le Quesnoy surrendered in the afternoon to the

Another Somua S-35 of the 1ère D.L.M. was destroyed at Berlaimont, on the eastern edge of the forest. It belonged to the 4ème Cuirassiers, the regiment's Joan of Arc emblem being visible on the side of the hull.

Left: Englefontaine lies on the western extremity of the forest and, according to the original caption to this photograph, this 8.8cm Flak 18 of Flak-Regiment 'General Göring' was 'protecting the divisional headquarters of the 4. Panzer-Division'. *Right:* We found that the gun had been positioned at the crossroads in the village, sited to cover the D932 to Le Cateau from where a possible attack by French armour could materialise. Note that the D934 — the Landrecies–Le Quesnoy road — has been hastily barricaded by the French yet it was hardly an obstacle which would impede the panzers.

commander of the 5. Panzer-Division units besieging the town, Oberst Paul Werner.

At Maubeuge the French defenders were also overwhelmed, Lieutenant-Colonel Marioge being captured. Nevertheless the fortresses were not yet defeated and, early in the morning, the men from Block 3 of Boussois gave some food and supplies to the exhausted men from a small unit of the 8ème R.I., about eighteen men plus a prisoner, who withdrew to the fortress. They then left only to be captured some distance away as they tried to rejoin their unit. The shelling of Boussois resumed in the morning, quickening in tempo, bringing each of the three blocks under attack. This barrage lasted throughout the day while the assault troops from Pi.Btl. 28 and Inf.Rgt. 83 took up positions south of the fort. At about 8.20 p.m. all firing suddenly stopped and the men in the fort waited for the inevitable assault. It came at about 8.45 p.m. The Frenchmen fired with everything they had at the German pioneers who rushed forward to clear a path through the barbed wire, followed closely by the grenadiers of Inf.Rgt. 83. One of the defenders remembered a trumpeter being out in front sounding a

One of that courageous breed of men to whom we owe a debt for all the pictures that illustrate this book. War photographer Heilmann was pictured in action by his team mate in Englefontaine on May 21 while filming from the turret of a PzKpfw II of the 4. Panzer-Division. In a few days time, Heilmann was to be gravely wounded while operating from this same turret.

The typical scene depicted in the newsreels of an invading army — whatever the nationality, period or country. Equipment and men move forward while the long columns of the defeated enemy are marched rearwards. Englefontaine on the afternoon of Tuesday, May 21 looking up the D934 towards Le Quesnoy. The road on the right is the D932 to Bavay.

Another picture, symbolic of the French defeat, was this shot of an abandoned 155mm G.P.F.T. heavy artillery piece . . . but where? The street name plate reads 'Place de la Gare' but there are hundreds of 'Railway Station Squares' in France. A better clue was provided by the name board of the restaurant owner: Balleux. The French telecommunications directory listing was called up on the author's computer terminal and indicated that a M. Balleux was living in Aulnoye-Aymeries — just east of the Mormal Forest and therefore of much relevance to this part of our story. A quick phone call confirmed the location.

Above: 'Surrender Field', May 1940. The remarkable sight in a meadow near Chemin aux Croix in Le Quesnoy on the 21st

where dozens of French prisoners had discarded their helmets . . . a view little changed fifty years on *bottom*.

Left: **Returning home after the panic of the previous week, refugees proceed slowly eastwards.** *Right:* **Although the road**

on the right was clearly signposted as a route to Neuville in 1940, today it would be classed as little more than a farm track.

call when he was hit and killed with the instrument to his lips. Boussois fired a red flare, the agreed signal to request supporting fire from La Salmagne to be brought down right on top of the fort. However, by a strange coincidence, this was also a prearranged German signal to request artillery support to cover a withdrawal! With both French and German shells exploding in their midst, the grenadiers had no option but to pull back.

During the night work parties again attempted to make good the damage while the occupants of the hard-pressed L'Epinette casemate, about two kilometres to the north-west, evacuated the fort as ordered after carrying out the necessary demolitions. Two days later they were taken prisoner.

On the morning of May 22 the artillery again set about the forts, wreaking still more damage, disabling one weapon after another, and destroying the ventilation systems. At 9.00 a.m. Stukas launched another attack against Boussois but Heeresgruppe A

A dozen kilometres west of Le Quesnoy a photographer came across this Hotchkiss H-35 of the 4ème Cuirassiers (1ère D.L.M.), abandoned by the side of the N342 (now the D942), just a kilometre outside Romeries.

Above: **There beside the road the cameraman found two graves: one of a French tanker, the other that of a German infantryman.** *Below:* **All battlefield dead were later exhumed for reburial in newly-established war cemeteries. However if, for whatever reason, the markers were removed or destroyed the graves would be 'lost' — save in cases like this where a photographic match is possible. The author's young son, Johan, learns another aspect of his country's recent history first-hand.**

noted that this attack was 'ill-advised' having apparently resulted in heavy casualties.

A general assault followed the Stuka attack and Bersillies was taken at 10.15 a.m. The situation at Boussois was now desperate. The air within was not fit to breathe and most of the weapons had been put out of commission. As any further attempt at resistance was out of the question, at 11.00 a.m. a white flag was shown from Block 3. The fort's garrison, some 180 men, clambered out to find their fort completely ploughed up by the explosions and covered with hundreds of German soldiers. While the prisoners were lined up, the commander of the 28. Infanterie-Division, General Hans von Obstfelder, arrived with some of his staff and made a brief speech to celebrate the victory, his men standing at attention all over the fort amidst the destruction. He awarded 15 of them with the Iron Cross on the spot and then talked with the French officers, congratulating Capitaine Bertin on the gallantry of his men.

The shelling of Les Sarts did not let up all day, being aimed particularly at Block 1 where the AM turret was jammed — later repaired during the night. La Salmagne surrendered at 8.30 p.m. and the casemate at Héronfontaine was ordered to be abandoned after all the weapons had been destroyed. On May 23 the shelling of Les Sarts resumed and the turret on Block 1 was put paid to once and for all. Then the shelling suddenly ceased as the grenadiers assaulted the fort, which surrendered at 11.00 a.m.

Two officers of the 28. Infanterie-Division, Oberst Hans Jordan, the commander of Inf.Rgt. 49, and Oberstleutnant Ernst Langenstrasse, a company commander with Pi.Btl. 28, were both named in the Wehrmachtbericht of May 25 which made known 'their extraordinary coolness during the battle in the recent few days near Maubeuge'. (Both were awarded the Ritterkreuz on June 5.)

313

This self-propelled anti-aircraft vehicle (SdKfz 6/2) mounted a 3.7cm Flak 36 gun. The entire crew — nine men — of this one from the 1. Batterie of Flak-Abteilung 77 were killed when their weapon was disabled, probably by a tank from the 1ère D.L.M., at Louvignies near Le Quesnoy on May 21. Their graves can be seen in the left background.

Further north the Escaut Fortified Sector — one minor fortress at Eth, the old fort of Maulde rejuvenated by some STG casemates built on its superstructures and fourteen casemates — manned by the 54ème R.I.F. fought back for several more days but all were finally overwhelmed on May 26. By the end of the month most of the 'new fronts' on the extension of the Maginot Line from the Montmédy Fortified Sector to the sea, had disappeared. But further east the 'old fronts' were yet unchallenged and the Maginot Line still ran continuously from the casemates west of Le Chesnois, now the most western fortress of the Montmédy Fortified Sector, to the Swiss border.

Left: Their first resting place was a common grave on the battlefield but the nine were later reburied in a temporary plot in the First World War German Soldatenfriedhof at Assevent.
Right: In 1956 they were moved to Block 28 of the permanent German War Cemetery established at Bourdon where the crew were split up into several graves: Gerhard Hanke (grave 558), Franz Tippelt (grave 621), Franz Stephan (grave 615), Friedrich Bünting (grave 645 — our picture), Erich Hüsgen (grave 665), Franz Lastovka (grave 657), Anton Nacke (grave 659) and Robert Küll (grave 651). The name of the ninth man, Zapouschek, was probably spelt incorrectly as we have been unable to trace his grave.

Thulin

The 43ème Division d'Infanterie had been kept in reserve near Epernay until May 13 when it was assigned to the 1ère Armée and ordered to the Maubeuge area for the defence of the Sambre. On May 17 the division was heavily engaged against the advance elements of the 5. Panzer-Divison and the next day it was ordered to withdraw and take up new positions near Bavay. However a sizeable part of the division, the 158ème Régiment d'Infanterie, the 10ème Bataillon de Chasseurs and the 12ème Régiment d'Artillerie, were trapped north of Maubeuge. Under Colonel Sylvain André, the commander of the 12ème R.A., these units fought stubbornly in this sector with Groupement Marioge but on May 21, after four days of battle, the situation was desperate and they were left with no other alternative but to withdraw north-westwards to try to join up with the French forces around Valenciennes. Groupement

Thulin is a small Belgian village mid-way between Mons and Valenciennes, situated just north of the N22. On Thursday, May 23 the French 158ème Regiment d'Infanterie under Colonel Pierre Puccinelli brushed aside the light German forces then in the area and advanced to the centre of the village hoping to find food and ammunition. However, a warning had already been relayed back to the HQ of the 269. Infanterie-Division reporting that the French had retaken Thulin and were therefore a threat to Infanterie-Regiment 469, then fighting south-west of the village. Oberst Rudolf von Tschüdi immediately ordered his first battalion to turn around and retake the village.

Where the Germans advanced. The field beside the Chemin du Grand Franquier (see map page 319) with the Quertinmont garage in the background.

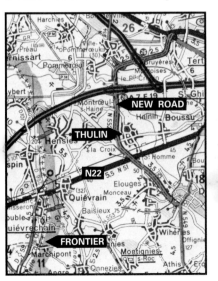

By the time the German attack reached the village proper, the French were out of ammunition.

A new road now bypasses Thulin to the west and the Rue des Canadiens, which was only a village street ending in a field track in 1940, now branches on this main road. Today this is the main access to the village.

A 3.7cm Pak 35/36 was brought forward to engage the last points of resistance.

After being unhitched, the gun was manhandled along the Rue Paul Pastur into a good firing position.

Meanwhile, men from Aufklärungs-Abteilung 269 had entered from the north, reaching Rue des Raulx. Unfortunately, a comparison of this view today would be rather meaningless for the wall on the right has been demolished and newly-planted conifers now totally mask the property along the Rue des Archers in the background.

However, a good 'then and now' match is possible for this shot of German infantrymen searching houses and gardens on Rue Paul Pastur from where they had been fired upon just minutes earlier.

One of the most poignant and often-used pictures of war. Approaching the centre of Thulin, a German patrol advances cautiously along the Grande Rue. As the infantrymen pass a wounded Frenchman lying on the pavement, one turns to look at him with concern while the other signals for caution against enemy snipers.

Although this picture (and those opposite) have been seen many times before, they have never been accurately captioned with time and place. The photographer was Eric Borchert, working for the Propaganda Kompanie, and he later published the series in his book in 1941 titled *Entscheidende Stunden* — Decisive Hours. Borchert's original negatives were captured by the French Army when they entered Strasbourg in 1945, the pictures now being retained by the ECP Armée in Paris.

The next frames in the sequence. The second soldier has stayed behind to help the fallen enemy soldier, freeing him from his helmet, accoutrements and overcoat. Meanwhile the rest of the group move on towards the Grande Place.

Marioge and two battalions of the 158ème R.I. failed to disengage and were overwhelmed but the 10ème B.C.P., the 12ème R.A. and the third battalion of the 158ème R.I. succeeded and assembled near Quévy.

Having only a few horse-drawn carts to carry supplies and ammunition, the men set out northwards on foot early on May 22 with what remained of the 158ème R.I. leading the way, followed by the 10ème B.C.P., the 12ème R.A. and other miscellaneous troops. That evening they came up against the Germans occupying Blaregnies and after a fierce fight the head of the column managed to force its way through the village but the rear elements were trapped. These men fought on throughout the night before being finally overwhelmed on May 23. The commander of the 12ème R.A., Colonel André, was killed fighting as an infantryman and the commander of the 10ème B.C.P., Commandant Jean Carlier, badly wounded. Those who had forced their way through, the third battalion of the

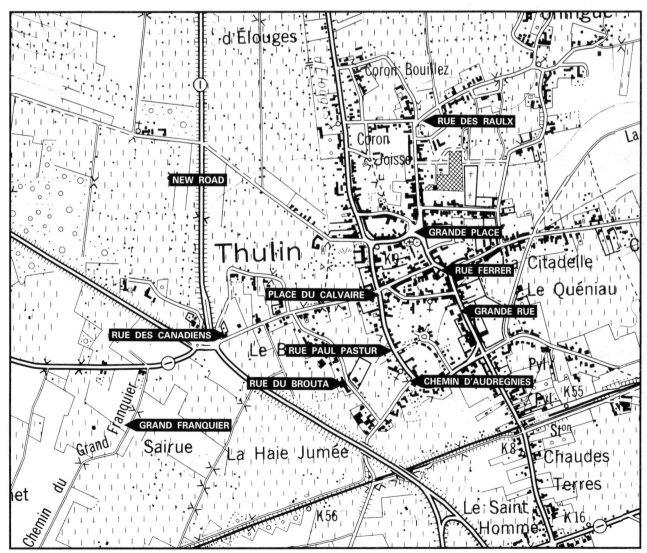

Blowing his own trumpet! Never was the phrase more apt than in the streets of Thulin that Thursday when the clarion call sounded out loud and clear on Rue Ferrer but was it just for the benefit of the photographer? Borchert took a great many pictures of this unidentified Obergefreiter and, according to the story which appeared in the *Berliner Illustrirte Zeitung* three weeks later (and retold in 1941 by Borchert in his book), this particular trumpeter had learned how to sound the French Army call to muster and he played it that day to encourage French soldiers to come out of hiding. It is a nice story but possibly somewhat exaggerated. The group in the background seem far too unconcerned and the number of photos taken would tend to indicate that the picture was posed as a nice publicity shot for home consumption.

The story in the *Berliner Illustrirte Zeitung* appeared on June 13 — a superb piece of clever propaganda with pictures which we now know show genuine action. For intelligence reasons the name of the village was not given, the story enigmatically being titled: 'The village of —— must be taken'. However, on May 23 there was little need for hyperbole to describe the incredible German advance in just two weeks. 'Holland over-run; four-fifths of Belgium occupied; the French Army hurled back towards Paris; and an Allied Army believed to number a million men, and including the élite of the Franco-British forces, trapped and encircled on the Channel.' So wrote William Shirer, the American war correspondent, in his diary on May 24.

Although the skirmish at Thulin was insignificant within the scale of the overall conflict raging across north-west Europe, photographically, the pictures taken there by Borchert are of such good graphic quality, rich in detail, that your editor makes no excuses for devoting more space to the sequence than is warranted by the battle itself. We are also fortunate that much of the village remains unchanged, improving Jean Paul's dramatic comparisons. This group of prisoners is on the corner of the Chemin d'Audregnies and Rue Paul Pastur. The house on the corner was No. 71 in 1940; now it's No. 3.

The awful scene in Rue du Calvaire where the innocent victims of war lie opposite the Rue Victor Delporte.

Another column marches along Rue du Brouta. In all some 300 French soldiers were captured in and around Thulin.

158ème R.I. and the third company of the 10ème B.C.P., arrived at Thulin the next morning.

The village was almost empty. For three days, between May 15 and May 17, the Luftwaffe had bombed and strafed the road to the south on which columns of refugees were fleeing westwards, carrying their belongings on every conceivable form of transport, certain that they would find sanctuary behind the invincible Maginot Line. Some of the inhabitants of Thulin had already followed the fugitives into France. Then, retreating French soldiers, some of them obviously from defeated units, were seen passing near the village. When the local gendarmes were ordered away to Flanders, panic set in with large numbers of the popula-

Wounded comrades are carried across the Place du Calvaire. On reaching the corner, they pass a French 25mm Hotchkiss anti-tank gun which has been damaged on the shield and trail.

tion fleeing in the teeth of the advancing onslaught. The morning of May 19 saw the last of the French troops retreating towards Hensies, followed by odd civilians. All became quiet and by midday less than ten percent of the population remained in Thulin.

Early next day the first German soldiers, a bicycle patrol from the 269. Infanterie-Division, entered the village asking for directions for Elouges. They were followed during the afternoon by more and more infantry, many of whom took over the best of the abandoned

houses, the staff officers occupying the home of the local notary.

On the morning of May 23 the German outpost of six or seven men from Aufkl.Abt. 269 stationed at the Saint-Homme crossroads on the main road south of Thulin was surprised to see a French motor cycle coming up the road from Elouges. Either genuinely surprised or as a ruse to capture the two men on the machine, the Germans threw up their hands and surrendered immediately. A few minutes later bursts of sub-machine gun fire came from the

Turning right, other prisoners move along a narrow path towards the centre ville.

323

Ten officers were also captured at Thulin. Here one of them still carrying his map case and wearing his sidearm is escorted into the Grande Place where many of the prisoners were congregated.

upper windows of nearby houses. The German prisoners dived to the ground while the two Frenchmen, Capitaine Jules Levresse and Caporal Richard Claus, jumped into a nearby ditch. Their machine was riddled and with its fuel tank punctured soon started to burn, the flames and smoke acting as a warning to the commander of the 158ème R.I., Colonel Pierre Puccinelli. Realising that the two men sent to recce the road ahead were obviously in trouble, Colonel Puccinelli immediately pushed forward and a few minutes later his troops recaptured the Saint-Homme

The guards soon relieved him of his 7.65mm 'Ruby' semi-automatic, the French WWI pistol made in Spain, copied loosely from the 1903 Browning.

crossroads and had taken prisoner the entire German unit holding the area.

Hoping to find food and ammunition in Thulin, Colonel Puccinelli decided to take the village and promptly launched an attack with what remained of his regiment. The road was easily taken as the Germans had set up their positions along the railway which ran parallel to the road some 600 metres north of it. The main French thrust broke through, reaching the station and the railway track, while on the right wing they attacked over open fields to reach the hamlet of Quéniau which they captured after fierce hand-to-hand fighting with

Of the 14 French soldiers of the 158ème Régiment d'Infanterie killed in Thulin on May 23, four are still buried in Belgium, in the French Military Cemetery of Chastre-Villeroux, 25 kilometres north-west of Namur. In Carré B, Paul Lepers (grave 89), Henri Michaud (grave 90), Guillaume Goeppner (grave 91) and Richard Schmitt (grave 92) repose side by side.

fixed bayonets. On the left wing the French pushed along the Grand Rue of Thulin to reach the Grand Place and the Rue du Calvaire.

At 6.15 a.m. a message sent from Aufkl.Abt. 269 had reached the head-quarters of the 269. Infanterie-Division reporting that a strong enemy unit moving north from the Bavai area had attacked Thulin, threatening the division's Inf.Rgt. 469 which was then fighting to the south-west of the village. At 6.30 a.m. the division ordered its artillery to fire at Thulin. Half an hour later the Aufkl.Abt. 269, which had by now been forced to retreat to the canal north of Thulin, reported the village in enemy hands, whereupon the commander of Inf.Rgt. 469, Oberst Rudolf von Tschüdi, ordered his first battalion to turn back and to retake the village.

The French now faced insurmountable odds. Arriving from the direction of Montrœul and Quiévrain, the I. Bataillon of Inf.Rgt. 469 entered the

In Thulin, the Place du Calvaire has now been renamed Place des Français where this monument has been erected by the Belgians to honour the French dead.

Of their opponents, we have traced these graves in the German Cemetery near Lommel. Schütze Arthur Schönbeck (Block 61, grave 270), Gefreiter Christel Rönnebeck (Block 56, grave 547) and Gefreiter Heinrich Windhorst (Block 56, grave 548).

battle, soon backed by elements of Inf.Rgt. 490. From Ville-Pommerœul the II. Bataillon of Art.Rgt. 59 started to pound Thulin. The French continued to fight back aggressively, but as more and more German troops were committed to the battle, they were soon outnumbered and overwhelmed. Colonel Puccinelli, who had been wounded at his command post near the Saint-Homme crossroads, was captured.

The last group fought on near the Sardon, the northern locality of Thulin, until 10.00 a.m. when, having exhausted all their small arms ammunition and expended their last mortar bombs, they were forced to surrender. However captivity was not something that Soldat Kleber Lebert, for one, was prepared to accept. Jumping on a motor cycle, he made a break for it, yelling at the top of his voice as he headed full tilt straight at the German positions, only to be cut down by a burst of automatic fire.

The last of the German prisoners were liberated, and the French soldiers who had now replaced them were lined up along the Rue du Calvaire. At 10.50 a.m. the 269. Infanterie-Division was informed that Thulin was back in German hands. By midday the 10 officers and over 300 men reported as having been taken prisoner had been marched away to Pommerœul.

The exact number of casualties in Thulin that day has never been precisely established, but 14 French and 12 German soldiers were buried in the village. Also, the 269. Infanterie-Division casualty list indicates that two officers were killed at Thulin on May 23: Leutnant Heinsohn of Inf.Rgt. 490 and Leutnant Steinhoff of Auf.Abt. 269.

According to some of the German soldiers who had remained prisoners of the French for the whole battle, two prisoners were killed by fire from their own side. The Germans held the French responsible for not having adequately protected their prisoners and Capitaine Levresse of the 158ème R.I. was tried by a German military court which sentenced him initially to 15 years; then the death penalty, but later commuted this to life imprisonment.

With the battle over, Eric Borchert continued on westwards. Four kilometres away in Hensies, on the Franco-Belgian border, he pictured this German troop asleep in the Rue de Villers. Blitzkrieg by bicycle was no doubt an exhausting business!

Left: Then, moving a couple of kilometres further to the north, he photographed the tank-hunters of Panzerjäger-Abteilung 570 as they crossed the canal between Pommerœul and Hensies. Their mounts were PzKpfw I chassis fitted with a 4.7cm Pak(t). *Right:* Although this was anticipated as being an easy shot to match, Jean Paul found that part of the canal had been diverted to build the E10 autoroute on its disused bed and that the old road had been straightened and widened and the Pont à l'Haine rebuilt! Only the house on the right remained. (See map page 315.)

The 4ème D.C.R: threat from the south

Colonel Charles de Gaulle, who on May 11 had been given command of the new 4ème D.C.R. then in process of formation, had been called to Général Georges' headquarters early on May 15 and was informed of the rôle assigned to the 6ème Armée. He was ordered to engage his 4ème D.C.R. in the Laon area to stop the panzer divisions and gain time for Général Touchon to form the new front. De Gaulle drove immediately to Laon and set up his command post at Bruyères. Waiting for his troops to arrive, he reconnoitred the area only to find that the French troops

there were both few and far between. His division would be alone. He had no idea when his troops would arrive but, even if they arrived in time, he knew that he would not have a real armoured division so much as a collection of various units which were not fully trained.

The first elements of the division reached him on May 16. They were the 345ème Compagnie de Chars from Versailles who detrained at Soissons and Crouy in the morning, followed in the evening by the 24ème B.C.C., the 46ème B.C.C. and one company from

the 2ème B.C.C. Although he had only a small proportion of his forces at hand, de Gaulle knew that he had to attack the next morning as the panzers' advance threatened the French positions. For the attack planned for May 17 de Gaulle had about 88 tanks plus the anticipated two battalions of tanks which were still on their way. However the 44ème B.C.C. and the 47ème B.C.C. did not arrive in time; neither did the four other tank companies, nor the artillery, two cavalry regiments and one regiment of supporting infantry. Only one battalion of infantry, the

Units destined for the 4ème D.C.R. under training in the spring of 1940. Renault D2s of the 19ème B.C.C. *(top)* on manoeuvres with R-35s of the 24ème B.C.C. *(above)*. The 4ème D.C.R. was created at the beginning of May and put under the command of

Colonel Charles de Gaulle *(right)*, the French contemporary of Guderian in the conduct of armoured warfare. This picture was taken of him in October 1939, when he was commanding the entire tank force of 5ème Armée.

Our story now has to go back in time and space to a point just a week after the offensive began in order to catch up with events in the Aisne sector. We left the area on page 290; now we return with de Gaulle's force as it pounds northwards to close with the enemy. This Renault D2 of the division's 345ème Compagnie de Chars was pictured near Laon on the afternoon of May 16 en route for the assembly area north-east of the city at Samoussy.

4ème B.C.P., became available, inserted on arrival straight from the trains into the battle. Lieutenant René Bibes, the commander of the first company of 46ème B.C.C., described the difficulty of the night march to the attack positions 'as we had to ride the road between two columns, one of fugitive soldiers, another of refugees'.

The units took up their attack positions on the northern edge of the Samoussy Forest during the night of May 16 to launch an all out attack in the direction of Montcornet. The 6ème Demi-Brigade under Colonel Aimé Sudre was to make the main thrust along the Laon-Montcornet road with 33 Renault B1bis of the 46ème B.C.C. and 14 Renault D2s of the 345ème Compagnie de Chars. Their left flank covered by the Renault D2s, the Renault B1bis were to lead the attack, the first company advancing on both sides of the road, the second company following closely on the road itself. The battalion's third company would not be involved as it had not yet arrived. The 8ème Demi-Brigade under Colonel Léon Simonin was to cover the right flank of the attack with about 40 Renault R-35s of the 2ème B.C.C. and 24ème B.C.C.

FRIDAY, MAY 17:
de Gaulle's armour attacks

The attack started as planned at 3.45 a.m. and made good progress despite the heavy Renault B1bis having some

difficulty negotiating the marshy ground south of Liesse. Six tanks bogged down but all but one were recovered by the support company in the evening. As they neared Chivres, the tanks attacked a German motorised column, and the trucks they destroyed on the road blocked their advance at a bridge south of the village for more than an hour. To clear the way, Commandant

The march to the attack position was difficult as the tanks had to ride the road between two columns, one of fugitive soldiers, another of refugees. Here another Renault D2 of the 345ème Compagnie de Chars pushes on to the rendezvous. By the evening, de Gaulle had only assembled a small proportion of his force — about 88 tanks. Nevertheless he decided to attack early the following morning, knowing that time was on the side of the Germans and running out for the Allies.

Meanwhile this convoy from 1. Panzer-Division had passed through Marle (only 20 kilometres north of Laon) and had halted outside a café at Dercy (10 kilometres to the south). Just a few minutes earlier 'Bourrasque' had surprised the Germans, bursting into the middle of the advancing columns and firing furiously (see page 334).

Jean Bescond, the commander of the 46ème B.C.C., advanced his Renault B1bis 'Berry-au-Bac' some fifty metres in front of the burning vehicles, blasting them apart with several shells from the tank's 75mm gun and forced a way through the flames. The Renault D2s followed and soon took the lead over the slower Renault B1bis. The tanks then moved through Chivres, destroying German vehicles on the way, before reaching Bucy where they had to

By the time the 4ème D.C.R. pulled back after the attack at Montcornet (20 kilometres east of Marle) late on May 17, it had lost about 20 Renault R-35s, a dozen B1bis and a handful of D2s. *Left:* This B1bis of the 46ème B.C.C. was knocked out right in the centre of Bucy-les-Pierrepont, ten kilometres or so south-west of Montcornet. *Right:* With no clue as to location, we consulted a local expert in church architecture in the Aisne area who was able to pinpoint the correct village.

stop to await refuelling. The support elements arrived as planned, having had to fight their way through Chivres where some German survivors had attacked their Lorraine tractors with small arms fire. Some Renault D2s soon reached Montcornet and shelled the German convoys moving on main roads to the south and west of the town.

To the south the 8ème Demi-Brigade advanced without opposition through Sissonne and approached Montcornet. The Renault R-35s of the 1ère Compagnie of the 24ème B.C.C. entered Montcornet at about midday only to have

their four leading tanks stopped by mines and anti-tank guns. Meanwhile the battalion's second company reached Lislet while the second company of the 2ème B.C.C. was approaching Dizy-le-Gros.

By about 3.00 p.m. the main force had been refuelled and had resumed its move eastwards. It passed Clermont and reached Montcornet, surprising and attacking German convoys on the roads south and west of the town. The Germans eventually started to react to the oncoming tanks and before long panzers were ordered up. Anti-tank guns

and artillery were hastily brought into action against them. A few French tanks were disabled at Lislet and Dizy-le-Gros, one of them 'Berry-au-Bac' being immobilised by mechanical problems. Commandant Bescond boarded another Renault B1bis, 'Sampiero-Corso', with some of his crew, but this was hit some time later near Clermont and exploded, killing all eight men inside. The too few supporting infantry had not been able to keep pace with the tanks and were still busy mopping up at Chivres, far to the rear. De Gaulle was then forced to call his tanks back behind

Left: **Another Renault B1bis of the 46ème B.C.C. 'Cambronne', was caught in an artillery barrage while withdrawing from Montcornet that same evening. It subsequently bogged down** in soft ground beside the road outside Chivres-en-Laonnois. *Right:* **Midway between Montcornet and Laon, Chivres lies at a point notorious for marshy, waterlogged ground.**

330

Another of the 4ème D.C.R.'s tanks destroyed near Laon. From the identification number '15' stencilled on the front armour and the serial number ('2068' in the centre), we realised that this was the same tank that we pictured on page 328 when it was on the march to the attack positions on May 16. One wonders what was the fate of the crew. The picture also has another significance as it was taken on the move during Hitler's tour of the battlefield in the last week of June.

the marshes which ran from Sissonne to Chivres. German aircraft, among them Stukas, attacked the French tanks during this withdrawal. By the time the 4ème D.C.R. was back on its new positions late in the evening, it had lost twelve Renault B1bis, a handful of Renault D2s and about twenty Renault R-35s: losses which nevertheless balanced against the large amount of enemy equipment and vehicles accounted for by the attack.

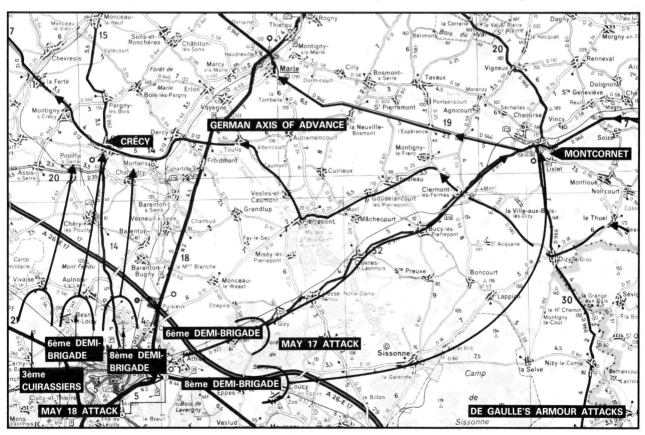

The leaders of de Gaulle's right wing — the Renault R-35s of the 1ère Compagnie of 24ème B.C.C. — had entered Montcornet by midday on Friday. However, the four leading tanks were soon disabled by mines and anti-tank guns firing from Montcornet up the road which plunged straight down to the town — a perfect firing range. This Renault (50059) belonged to the 4ème Section; the one further down the road (50135) to the 1ère Section. It is the same one that we saw on page 327.

SUNDAY, MAY 19
de Gaulle's second attack

On the evening of May 18, with the new elements that had reached the 4ème D.C.R. during the previous two days (two companies of the 2ème B.C.C., the third company of the 46ème B.C.C., two squadrons of Somua S-35s from the 3ème Cuirassiers, the 10ème Cuirassiers with its Panhard P-178 armoured cars) de Gaulle had command of about 155 tanks. He was ordered to launch another attack against the panzer divisions the next day, this time on the Serre river to the north-east of Laon. De Gaulle organised his three battle groups from west to east: the Somua S-35s of the 3ème Cuirassiers on the left, the Renault R-35s of the 8ème Demi-Brigade in the centre and the heavies of the 6ème

Demi-Brigade on the right. The armoured cars of the 10ème Cuirassiers were to cover the flank.

The 4ème D.C.R. moved into its assembly area to the north-west of Laon and attacked northwards at 4.00 a.m. on May 19. It was much the same story as at Montcornet two days earlier. The French tanks broke through but were far too few to be decisive and, as before, they were poorly supported. The tanks of the 6ème Demi-Brigade reached Mortiers, destroyed anti-tank guns covering the bridge but two Renault B1bis and two Renault D2s were knocked out. The crossing of the Serre river soon proved to be impossible, the Germans having blown the bridge.

Further west, the Renault R-35s of the 2ème B.C.C. reached Crécy but found that the village was held in force. They lost four tanks trying to break through before withdrawing. Coming from Mortiers, the heavier Renault D2s of the 345ème Compagnie forced the barrages, destroyed several artillery guns but were also compelled to pull back to the edge of the village.

On the left wing, the two squadrons of Somua S-35s had reached Chéry then Bouilly-sur-Serre. During the confused battle which followed, they mistook for Germans some Renault B1bis of the 46ème B.C.C. which had suddenly appeared from behind some German vehicles which the Somua S-35s had just chased away. Although the mix-up was soon corrected, it was too late for Sous-Lieutenant Michel Gohin who was grievously wounded and died some time later.

Some of the tanks had approached to within a mile of XIX. Armeekorps's advanced headquarters which 'had only some 20mm anti-aircraft guns for protection', and Guderian confessed to having 'passed a few uncomfortable hours until at last the threatening visitors moved off in another direction'.

For four hours that afternoon the Stukas repeatedly bombed de Gaulle's forces. The commander of the 345ème Compagnie de Chars, Capitaine Jean-

Above and below: **The view from the opposite direction up the D977 in the direction of Laon. In the foreground a third Renault (50040) of the 4ème Section. It had been the mount of Sous-Lieutenant Albert Mouchet before it, too, was knocked out.**

Left: **One for the war album! It would be interesting to know if this soldier had a personal rôle in knocking out Renault 50194 . . . or whether he merely stopped to pose for the photographer. This was the leading tank in which Capitaine André Penet, the commander of 1ère Compagnie, was riding and we can see that** it has received a 37mm shell hit between the turret and hull.
Right: **One never knows what to expect when taking comparison photographs and we can imagine Jean-Paul's astonishment to find that the same wooden shack had survived the rest of the war and fifty years besides!**

Though it was not part of the 4ème D.C.R., but from the 15ème B.C.C., 2ème D.C.R., the 'Bourrasque' was also embroiled in the same battle in the Serre river sector early that Friday morning. While withdrawing from the Vervins area, it came across a supply convoy for the 1. Panzer-Division near Dercy and drove right along the column shooting up numerous trucks, cars and motor cycles. However, with its tanks empty, it petered to a stop whereupon the crew were captured.

Charles Idée, described how 'the German aircraft, one hundred of them, were bombing and strafing everywhere. All the villages to a depth of about 20 kilometres were attacked, as well as every wood copse that we could see'. The Germans counter-attacked near Chambry, threatening to cut off the French line of retreat and at 6.00 p.m. de Gaulle was ordered to withdraw.

The 4ème D.C.R. pulled back southwards behind the Aisne river, losing tanks and men in further harassing counter-attacks. In its second engagement on the Serre, and the following

Jean-Paul discovered that 'Bourrasque' had ended its days on the D12 which joins Dercy with the N2. The house behind the tank still stands although it is now a gutted ruin having burned out in the 1960s.

Jean Bescond, the commander of the 46ème B.C.C., was killed the same day in the Renault B1bis 'Sampiero-Corso', which he had comandeered with his own crew after their own mount, the 'Berry-au-Bac', had been hit. Both crews were killed and now lie buried in the cemetery of Ville-au-Bois, about five kilometres south of Montcornet.

costly disengagement, the 4ème D.C.R. had lost a dozen Panhard armoured cars, ten Renault B1bis, about twenty Somua S-35s and nearly fifty Renault R-35s. Nevertheless de Gaulle knew how to employ armour and his 4ème D.C.R. had not been squandered like the 2ème D.C.R. Although lacking the necessary infantry and air support, he had attacked with what he possessed and twice penetrated the German flank, hit hard and been hit hard back by Stukas. In the prevailing shambles it was an impressive performance although it was of little consequence in the broader context of events.

MONDAY, MAY 20:
Germans reach the coast

In pressing on towards the Channel coast, the orders issued by the XIX. Armeekorps for May 20 were for the 1. Panzer-Division to advance on Amiens and the 2. Panzer-Division at Abbeville, to establish bridgeheads on the Somme. During the night of May 19 the 10. Panzer-Division was brought forward again to relieve the elements of the 1. Panzer-Division engaged on the flank. The manner in which the relief was carried out did not go down well with the commander of the 4. Panzer-Brigade whose units arrived to find that Schtz.Rgt. 4 of the 1. Panzer-Division had already pulled out so as not to be late for the attack on Amiens in the morning. An irate Oberst Franz Landgraf was not exactly mollified to be told by Oberstleutnant Hermann Balck that 'if we lose it you can always take it again', commenting that 'I had to capture it in the first place, didn't I?'

The head of the 2. Panzer-Division reached Noyelles-sur-Mer at about 8.00 p.m. on May 20 — the first German unit to reach the coast. The High Command was still acting as if surprised and frightened by its own success and on the evening of this momentous day Gruppe von Kleist had neither received, nor issued, any instructions for the development of operations. The day closed with the recognition of the efforts of the commander of the 1. Panzer-Division, Generalleutnant Friedrich Kirchner, with the award of the Ritterkreuz on May 20.

This memorial was erected at the side of the road between Ville-au-Bois and Clermont-les-Fermes, at the exact spot where 'Sampiero-Corso' met its end.

Sweeping pell-mell for the coast, 1. Panzer-Division passed through Péronne on Saturday (May 18) and then advanced towards Amiens through Albert. Following up a few days later, a photographer pictured the wreckage at the junction just east of the town where the N17 meets the D917 where the panzers had brushed aside a forlorn French attempt to stop them.

The situation north of the Somme was very fluid and confused with no organised defence and with the German vanguards always one step further west than anticipated. *Right:* The absence of any memorial or reminder of the forgotten few who once attempted to halt the tide makes the present day orderliness all the more poignant.

MAY 21-22:
The advance on the ports

The XXXXI. Armeekorps had now moved abreast on Guderian's right flank, the 6. Panzer-Division being on the Authie at Le Boisle and the 8. Panzer-Division at Hesdin, but for the XIX. Armeekorps most of May 21 was wasted waiting for orders. When they finally arrived they instructed that the advance be continued in a northerly direction with the capture of the Channel ports as the objective.

Guderian planned on making a three-pronged attack northwards but early on May 22 Gruppe von Kleist ordered that the 10. Panzer-Division be held back in reserve. Guderian's request to retain most of the division was refused and he was left with only two panzer divisions for the advance on the ports: the 1. Panzer-Division was to head for Calais while the 2. Panzer-Division was to proceed along the coast to Boulogne. However, neither of them could move forward in full strength as they both had to leave units behind to secure the Somme bridgeheads until relieved by follow-up forces from the XIV. Armeekorps.

The panzers reach the sea! What a breathtaking ride — 250 miles in ten days — and what a bracing view for the crew of this SdKfz 221 of Aufklärungs-Abteilung 5 from 2. Panzer-Division as they inch down the shingle at Ault. On May 21 patrols crossed the Somme and carried out reconnaissance as far as the River Bresle, 30 kilometres further south. Now the focus of attention switches again . . . this time to the north where the position of the Anglo-French forces in southern Belgium was becoming increasingly precarious as they constantly retreated. Soon it would be backs to the wall.

Gort favours evacuation

Flashback to May 14. The main square in Louvain is deserted save for a group of Belgian refugees and a British carrier driving towards the front.

In the early hours of May 19 Général Billotte visited General Gort at his headquarters and gave him an account of the situation, telling him as much as he knew about the German breakthrough but giving him no reason to hope that the German panzer divisions could be cut off and the gap closed. He told him that another attack from the south against the left flank of the breakthrough was not possible at present, the 4ème D.C.R. having tried and failed on May 17 and 18.

As they conferred Gort saw only two possibilities. The Allied forces in the north must withdraw from Belgium either to join the main body of the French Army south of the Somme or to be evacuated by sea. Apart from the fact that the Belgians would never agree to a proposition which meant giving up their country, the first alternative appeared unrealistic as the leaders of the panzer divisions were already in the Somme valley, driving hard on Abbeville. The second, evacuation by sea, appeared to Gort as the only feasible option open to him, although he was realistic enough to see that it would be difficult if not impossible.

No decision was made between Gort and Billotte although the British com-mander was now firmly of the opinion that that evacuation was the only way to save the BEF whatever the French or Belgians were to decide. That afternoon Gort's Chief-of-Staff, Lieutenant-General H. R. Pownall, telephoned the War Office to discuss the situation and told them that Gort was being forced to consider the possibility of a withdrawal to the northern coast. This led the War Office to contact the Admiralty about the possibility of evacuation, although Gort was far ahead of his superiors in London about the acceptance of such a course of action and it was to be some days yet before it was adopted.

Having spent four uneventful days deployed along the River Dyle, by the 14th the BEF was in contact with the enemy along its whole front. *Above:* Recent bombing or shelling had left its mark on this part of Louvain east of the river. This patrol from the 3rd Division marches along the deserted road which leads south-east to Tienen.

Above: Further along the street, sappers were preparing to demolish the bridge over the railway. This party relaxes on items of furniture borrowed from an evacuated house to await the order for the big bang. With units of the XI. Armeekorps already probing the area, the bridge was blown not a moment too soon *below*.

ARRAS: 'FRANKFORCE'

On the morning of May 20 the Chief of the Imperial General Staff, General Sir Edmund Ironside, having flown from England, came to see Gort bringing instructions from the British Cabinet. These were mainly based on information received from the British liaison officer attached to the French High Command and were somewhat optimistic. They ordered the BEF to 'move southwards upon Amiens, attacking all enemy forces encountered and to take station on the left of the French Army'. Gort objected strongly that his seven fighting divisions had just ended a difficult withdrawal to the Escaut where they were under constant pressure from the enemy. To strike in force towards Amiens they would have to disengage from the line of the Escaut, fight a rearguard action down to the Somme before attacking the German units there. He conceded that he 'already had plans in hand' for an attack southwards — but did not tell the CIGS that his own inclination was increasingly for moving in exactly the opposite direction! In the event the massive thrust specified in Ironside's instructions turned out to be a small operation by 'Frankforce' made up of reserves which were being assembled under the command of Major-General H. E. Franklyn to bolster the Arras defences. For this, the 1st Army Tank Brigade and the 5th Division had been ordered to join the 50th Division in the Vimy area. No mention was made

The withdrawal began on May 16 and, after crossing the Senne and Dendre, three days later the BEF lay behind the Escaut. The move was not executed without difficulty, but by midnight on the 19th it had been completed. During the following night, the 50th Division was ordered to concentrate north of Arras and to prepare for offensive action. It was soon joined by the 5th Division and the 1st Army Tank Brigade, the combined force becoming known as 'Frankforce' after its commander, Major-General Harold Franklyn — pictured here in 1941 when a Lieutenant-General.

The calm before the storm. The scene at the crossroads 16 kilometres outside Louvain on the road to Brussels. Less than a week after the German attack, the BEF would be ordered to retreat and pull back west of the Belgian capital to the Escaut river.

Meanwhile the leaders of Gruppe von Kleist were on the Somme with the two panzer divisions of the XVI. Armeekorps, back from their successful feint in the Gembloux gap (page 167), now pressing on westwards in the second phase of the Sichelschnitt Plan. *Above:* This panzer-jam was photographed at Maroilles on the road between Avesnes and Landrecies.

to General Franklyn of his force having any larger rôle than that originally given to it — 'to support the garrison of Arras and to block the roads south of Arras'.

Although Gort agreed with Ironside that the gap had to be closed if disaster were to be avoided, he explained that the BEF could do nothing about it and that a solution must rest chiefly with the French. Generals Ironside and Pownall then went to see Général Billotte at his headquarters in Lens. They told him of the action planned by the two British divisions near Arras on May 21 and

urged him of the need for French participation in the operation. Billotte acquiesced and promised to engage two French divisions towards Cambrai on the same day.

On the evening of May 20, the 1. Panzer-Division was at Amiens, the 2. Panzer-Division at Abbeville, while the 6. Panzer-Division was at Le Boisle. The 8. Panzer-Division was centred on Hesdin, with its vanguard approaching Montreuil. Meanwhile the 7. Panzer-Division and the SS-Totenkopf-Division were south of Arras with the

5. Panzer-Division south-east of the town.

Billotte's decision to attack on May 21 was somewhat over optimistic as the French units were far from ready to attack. It was soon apparent that the 25ème D.I.M., back from the Netherlands, could never be ready in time and the same applied to the divisions of the Corps de Cavalerie which were still disorganised after its hasty withdrawal from Belgium. Later in the day Général Blanchard, the commander of the 1ère Armée, sent word to Gort that the

promised French attack towards Cambrai could not be launched before May 22. General Franklyn had meanwhile met Général Prioux, the commander of the Corps de Cavalerie, and Prioux offered to place elements of the 3ème D.L.M. on the outer western flank of Frankforce in the May 21 operation.

Gort did not believe that a counter-attack to the south was really feasible but, having had to compromise with his superiors in London, Gort's intended large-scale mopping-up operation by Frankforce in support the garrison of Arras had consequently come to be thought of at his headquarters in terms of a 'counter-attack'. Although it gave the impression of being the first stage of a big counter-attack launched southwards by the French 1ère Armée, fresh orders were not issued to turn it into one. Faced with the question of attacking as planned without French support

When we found this sequence of pictures, they were without either caption or location. They could have been taken anywhere but, after much effort in trying to decipher the virtually unreadable wording on the signpost behind the PzKpfw III *(top)*, Jean Paul was able to narrow the search to the Avesnes area. It was then a case of driving along each road until the almost unchanged house and cemetery came into view at the junction of the D959 and D962. Once the location had been established the shots could be slotted into the correct position in the overall canvas of the Blitzkrieg in the West.

or waiting for the French, Gort left things as they stood; the actual operation that General Franklyn had been ordered to carry out made no mention of French participation, and Franklyn's plans did not depend on French collaboration beyond that that to be given by Général Prioux.

Command of the attacking forces had been given to Major-General G. le Q. Martel, the commander of the 50th Division. The attack was set for 2.00 p.m. on May 21, with the Cojeul river the objective for the first day, the Sensée river for the second, and then on to Bapaume and Cambrai. Instead of the two divisions and one tank brigade involved in Gort's original plan, by now the forces available for the attack had melted down to the 151st Brigade from the 50th Division and the 1st Army Tank Brigade. The 50th Division's first

A photograph has so much more significance when the place where it was taken is known. These pictures of 3. Panzer-Division armour are visible proof that it bypassed Cambrai to the south just as 4. Panzer-Division avoided the city by circling round it to the north. They proved to have been taken on the village main square in front of the town hall in Marcoing, eight kilometres to the south, but in this case luck played a considerable part in establishing the location.

brigade (the 150th) had been sent to strengthen the Arras garrison and hold the Scarpe river immediately east of the town, one brigade from the 5th Division was also committed on the Scarpe and the other was held in reserve for the second phase of the attack. The 1st Army Tank Brigade had also been much reduced by breakdowns along the way, having travelled almost 200 kilometres by road, and 58 Mark Is, 16 Mark IIs and 7 Mark VIs were all it could muster at its assembly area near Vimy that day.

Martel planned to attack with two columns which were to move forward west of Arras, about a kilometre apart. Each column consisted of a tank battalion, an infantry battalion from the 151st Brigade, a battery of field artillery, a battery of anti-tank guns and a company of motor cyclists for reconnaissance. Prioux's promise of cooperation was duly honoured and elements from the 3ème D.L.M. plus several companies of light tanks were to be engaged on the right flank of Frank-

force while the 2ème D.L.M. had orders to attack east of Arras as soon as the British attack reached the Sensée.

There was little time to organise the assault and none for reconnaissance, and maps of the area were scarce. Some

On one of Jean Paul's many trips across the Blitzkrieg battlefields, he missed the motorway entrance near Anneux and found himself in Marcoing. Although he did not have this picture with him on that occasion, the style of the church tower rang a bell. Returning home, 'JP's' visual memory proved correct but he had to return to take the comparisons.

of the troops were late in arriving and the attack started half an hour late, hitting at the flank of the 7. Panzer-Division and SS-Totenkopf-Division much to the Germans' surprise. Elements of Schtz.Rgt. 6 and Schtz.Rgt. 7 of the former and the SS-Inf.Rgt. 3 of the latter had concentrated in the area on the previous night and they were just resuming their advance when the British attack began.

The right-hand column advanced but fighting broke out almost immediately and it had to fight hard to take Duisans while the French tanks advancing on the right flank reported panzers further to the west. Two companies of the 8th Durham Light Infantry were left to hold Duisans and deal with the prisoners captured while the column pushed on

Left: This shot, however, was not easy. Even though JP's travels had covered hundreds of miles, criss-crossing the battle zone, he just could not find where this picture had been taken. In the end he had it published in the regional newspaper *La Voix du Nord* and received 15 correct answers — Escaudœuvres on the north-eastern outskirts of Cambrai — a place which today *(right)* proved to have little resemblance to the scene in May 1940. The tank is a PzKpfw II Ausf F of 4. Panzer-Division.

towards Walrus. German troops were in the village, which had to be cleared; prisoners were taken, and the advance continued through Berneville.

To the west, after having disabled a German convoy north of Agnez, the French tanks had moved south and reached Simencourt. A British advance guard crossed the main road and were approaching Wailly when they were pinned down by heavy mortar and machine gun fire. Rommel, who happened to be near Wailly at the time to urge his infantry forward, has described how they suddenly came under fire from the north. He and Oberleutnant Joachim Most, his dispatch rider, ran on ahead of their vehicles to a howitzer battery of Art.Rgt. 78 which was in position at the northern exit of Wailly:

'It did not look as though the battery would have much difficulty in dealing with the enemy tanks, for the gunners were calmly hurling round after round into them in complete disregard of the return fire. Running along the battery lines, we arrived at Wailly and then called up the vehicles. The enemy tank fire had created chaos and confusion among our troops in the village and they were jamming up the roads and metres with their vehicles instead of going into action with every available weapon to fight off the oncoming enemy. We tried to create order. After notifying the divisional staff of the critical situation in and around Wailly we drove off to a hill a thousand metres west of the village, where we found a light anti-aircraft

The Waffen-SS originated from the pre-war idea of forming an armed force from within the 'Schutzstaffeln' (the organisation created for the special protection of the Reich and its Führer) of volunteers who could fight in battle for their ideals and, under its leader, Reichsführer-SS Heinrich Himmler, the Waffen-SS was to wage aggressive war without mercy. The third division to be assembled incorporated many concentration camp guards from the SS-Totenkopf-Verbände — hence the adoption of the skull and crossbones (the Totenkopf or death's head) as its badge of office. By May 19 the SS-Totenkopf-Division was approaching Cambrai and here SS-Sturmbannführer Max Simon, the commander of SS-Infanterie-Regiment 1, is seen with his staff planning his advance into the Arras sector.

The picture was taken on the corner of the Rue du Cateau in Bazuel (25 kilometres east of Cambrai).

troop and several anti-tank guns located in hollows and a small wood, most of them totally under cover. The crew of a howitzer battery, some distance away, now left their guns, swept along by the retreating infantry. With Most's help, I brought every available gun into action

The death's head insignia is clearly visible on the headlight black-out cover on this motorcycle (a BMW R35) which has stopped in Adinfer, a small village 15 kilometres south of Arras. In the background stands a PzKpfw 38(t) of the 7. Panzer-Division.

at top speed against the tanks. Every gun, both anti-tank and anti-aircraft, was ordered to open rapid fire immedi-

ately and I personally gave each gun its target. With enemy tanks so perilously close, only rapid fire from every gun

could save the situation. We ran from gun to gun. The objections of gun commanders that the range was still too great to engage the tanks effectively, were overruled. We now directed our fire against the other group of tanks attacking from the direction of Bac du Nord, and succeeded in keeping the tanks off, setting fire to some, halting others and forcing the rest to retreat. Although we were under very heavy fire from the tanks during this action, the gun crews worked magnificently. The worst seemed to be over and the attack beaten off, when suddenly Most sank to the ground behind an anti-aircraft gun close beside me. He was mortally wounded and blood gushed from his mouth.'

The left-hand column also had to fight all the way, through Dainville, Agny and Beaurains, inflicting heavy losses in men and materièl on the surprised German units. A small advance party reached Wancourt. Rommel wrote how 'the anti-tank guns which we quickly deployed showed themselves to be far too light to be effective against the heavily armoured British tanks and the majority of them were put out of

Above and below: **Down the road in the next village, members of the Luftwaffe are on duty at the crossroads in Ransart ready to direct vehicles of their unit, probably a Flak battalion marching with the leading panzers, onto the correct road for the front.**

Just west of Arras, beside the N39, the SS observe artillery fire falling on Louez, most probably on May 22.

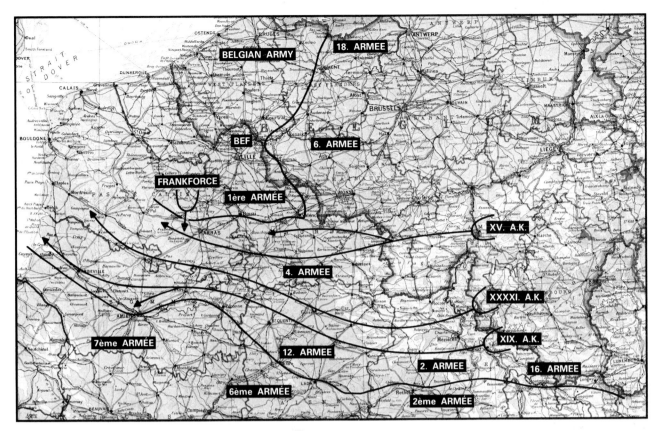

By May 21, the Sichelschnitt operation had achieved complete success. On the previous evening the head of XIX. Armeekorps had reached the coast at Noyelles with the XXXXI. Armeekorps abreast, its leaders having reached Hesdin. On the right flank of the breakthrough, XV. Armeekorps was following, with its vanguards advancing south-west of Arras. In this advantageous situation, the unexpected attack by Frankforce at Arras came as a shock to the Germans, who saw it as being much more powerful than it really was. Although the attack failed to achieve material gain on the battlefield, it made its mark as a psychological success — in Guderian's words, it made 'a considerable impression on the staff of Gruppe von Kleist'.

Burning Matildas: the end of the vain attempt by Frankforce to attack the flank of the German spearhead. 'Gloucester' and 'Glanton' belonged to the 7th Royal Tank Regiment — their crews died with honour fighting against overwhelming odds.

action by gun-fire, together with their crews, and then overrun by the enemy tanks. Many of our vehicles were burnt out. SS units close by also had to fall back to the south before the weight of the tank attack. Finally the division artillery and anti-aircraft batteries succeeded in bringing the enemy armour to a halt south of the line Beaurains-Agny.' In this area Rommel claimed 28 tanks for his artillery and 8 for his anti-aircraft batteries.

Sergeant T. Hepple, the commander of 'Guinivere', a Mark I of B Company of the 7th Royal Tank Regiment, later told his story:

'The level crossing at Dainville was closed, so I was compelled to break through it, and proceeded about half a mile at high speed. Seeing two men attempting to hide in a cornfield I pursued them and opened fire with the .303 Vickers. One man surrendered and the other was apparently killed. I put the prisoner in the rear of the tank, covering him with my revolver while we went down the road. Three wrecked motor-cars were passed and one dead civilian. A mile further on we ran into a village occupied by German forces who opened fire with rifles. I turned round and came back to report to Captain M. W. Fisher. I continued into Dainville and handed over the prisoner to a captain of the Durham Light Infantry. The troops displayed great animosity towards the prisoner and I was compelled to draw my revolver and order them off before I could reach their officer.

'I then followed two Mark II tanks of B Company intending to pass them and catch up with the Mark I vehicles. Odd groups of the enemy were seen and engaged, but near a main road west of Achicourt we came under anti-tank fire and sustained three direct hits. The effect was that of hitting a large stone at speed, and the track on the right-hand side was sent a metre or two in front of the tank. Two more shots followed, and then the guns were silenced by our fire,

The Arras battleground. Her luck run out, 'Good Luck', a Matilda II of the 7th Royal Tank Regiment, lies at the northern end of Wailly. T6751 was one of the tanks knocked out in the furious exchange of fire on the 21st described by Rommel.

Berneville lies about five kilometres north-west of Wailly across the N25, where this Somua S-35 of the 4ème Cuirassiers of the 1ère D.L.M. was disabled at the south-eastern end of the village.

Above and below: **The battle had been fought across ground which had already seen war in its most violent form. Here, amid the still-barren landscape near Notre Dame de Lorette, a Horch command car containing Luftwaffe personnel passes a Matilda abandoned in the Frankforce assembly area. In 1915 a chapel stood on the eastern spur of the ridge which was captured by** the French after heavy fighting. After the war it was chosen as the site of the French National Memorial. Its cemetery contains 20,000 individual graves with the remains of thousands more unidentified dead in the ossuary beneath the rebuilt chapel (its dome can be seen on the left). On the right stands the combined lighthouse/observation tower at the memorial.

and that of Mark I tanks which went on without seeing us.

'We were subjected to intense rifle fire for some minutes, and then left alone, apparently in the belief that we were all killed. After five or ten minutes about thirty to fifty Germans were congregated in groups on the road and to the right of us. We estimated the range of each group, and then opened fire. Many of the enemy fell, but some doubtless were unhurt. Later an abandoned anti-tank gun was remanned but was seen to be deserted after we fired upon it. Soon afterwards more tanks appeared, both Mark I and Mark II, and the firing died down. Infantry also appeared.

'I then got out to inspect the damage. About five track plates and pins were damaged, there was a hole about two inches in diameter in the right-hand sprocket which had two teeth missing, and the radiator, which could not be opened, was leaking. The engine would run, but smelt strongly of burning.

'At dusk most of the infantry had withdrawn and since it was obvious that a counter-attack was coming and that in the dark I could do no useful work against it I prepared to abandon the tank. All movable kit, including guns, wireless, pyrenes, was piled on an abandoned Bren carrier which we managed to start, and when it was obvious no help was coming, the tank was fired. It was soon blazing fiercely.'

On the right flank, the engagement of the French light tanks provided an unfortunate example of the lack of co-ordination. Hotchkisses of the 13ème B.C.C. had reached Simencourt and, seeing no British infantry, some of them decided at about 4.30 p.m. to go to Duisans to obtain some information and orders. As they approached the village

A Mk VI Light Tank still carrying its civil registration: HMC 573.

The quick . . . and the dead. Pictured somewhere in the Arras sector, they fought and died for King and Country.

the leading Hotchkiss, in which was Capitaine Achille Pentel, the commander of the battalion's second company, was hit by an anti-tank shell whereupon the tanks started to fire back. The leading tank was hit again and Capitaine Pentel jumped down to hear someone shouting: 'Ce sont des Anglais!'. Waving his map about, he cautiously approached under fire and finally made contact with British gunners who, because the tanks were not displaying large white identification squares, did not realise that they were friendly. The French remonstrated that

Two victims of the battle on May 21. Major Gerald Hedderwick, of the 7th Royal Tank Regiment, was reported missing in action and this grave in Beaurains Communal Cemetery (just south of Arras) bears the qualifying inscription: 'Believed to be'.

Rommel's despatch rider, Oberleutnant Joachim Most — promoted posthumously to the rank of Hauptmann — was killed beside him near Wailly. Most now lies in the German Military Cemetery at Bourdon, 20 kilometres west of Amiens.

the blue, white and red French cockades ought to be clear enough but in the brief encounter one Hotchkiss had been destroyed and three damaged, and two men killed.

The commander of the 13ème B.C.C., Commandant Maurice le Merre, could not understand why the British infantry refused to move on further and, complaining about their lack of spirit, he asked Général Prioux for infantry support. He was promised a squadron of dragoons from the 3ème D.L.M. and at 6.30 p.m. he sent his

Hotchkiss back to Simencourt. However at 9.30 p.m. a supply column trying to reach them found panzers blocking the road at Agnez: the tanks were obviously surrounded and it was apparent then that the promised support would not materialise. As a result the tanks were ordered back, most of them succeeding in extricating themselves, although no one from the 3ème Compagnie returned from Simencourt and the company commander, Capitaine Marcel Raoult, was taken prisoner.

With Frankforce unable to hold onto the ground it had won, still less reach the Sensée river, the operation was called off and with it the flank support of the 2ème D.L.M. for the second phase east of Arras. In the evening the two British columns were ordered to withdraw. As they started to move out the left-hand column suffered a 20-minute attack by the Luftwaffe which bombed Beaurains and Duisans. The Germans took advantage of the vacuum thus created and were hard on the heels of the withdrawing units as they moved

A foreign field forever England. *Left:* A German cameraman pictures the Imperial War Graves Commission Cemetery at Vis-en-Artois which had been completed in 1927. Here over 2,300 of those killed in the capture of this sector in August 1918 lie

buried, with another 10,000 names engraved on the Memorial to the Missing for those who fell in Picardy and who have no known grave. *Right:* Fifty years later the author's little daughter, Céline, stands in for the long-forgotten trooper.

When the British counter-attack failed, Gort realised that it would be impossible to hold the high ground north of Arras, and on the evening of the 23rd he withdrew what was left of Frankforce behind the Béthune–La Bassée Canal. German

forces immediately entered Arras, a town which had taken them over six weeks to reach in 1914. This Horch was pictured in the Rue du Cardinal on May 24. Behind, then as now, Saint-Baptiste church.

back in a somewhat confused situation under cover of darkness. Rommel had already called his Pz.Rgt. 25 back and ordered it to strike west of Arras at the flank of this troublesome counter-attack. He described the fierce fighting that raged during the night south of Agnez as 'tank against tank, an extremely heavy engagement in which the panzer regiment destroyed seven heavy tanks and six anti-tank guns and broke through the enemy position, though at the cost of three PzKpfw IVs, six

PzKpfw IIIs and a number of light tanks'. According to the location given by Rommel these anti-tank guns were British but the tanks could only have been French.

Men from the 8th Durham Light Infantry holding Walrus were surrounded and could only be extricated with the help of six French Somua S-35s which arrived just at the right time with two armoured personnel carriers. In these they succeeded in breaking past the Germans holding the road to

Duisans. After a hectic withdrawal, what remained of Frankforce was back behind the Scarpe — the starting point — that afternoon.

Once again Rommel emerged from the event with even greater glory through his flair for publicity. His photographs told the story of how he, personally, had saved the day, his communiqué on May 21 referring to his being attacked by 'hundreds of the enemy's tanks' and suggested that only the SS-Totenkopf-Division had given

The Boche are back. Twice in a lifetime the streets echo to the tramp of the jackboot . . . Café Chez Paul has seen it all before.

Today this corner of Arras has seen considerable change with the rebuilding of the station.

In 1914 the German occupation of Arras had lasted for barely a fortnight, but now their tenure was to last for over four years. The picture *above* was taken on May 24 outside the Hôtel de Ville — the French name for the town hall. *Below:* A memorial plaque to the Resistance movement in Arras has since been affixed on the rear of the cloister.

With 'Krisis Arras' averted, the march westwards was now resumed. This convoy has reached Pont-du-Gy, some eight kilometres west of Arras on the N39, a small village which suffered grievously from the ruthlessness of total war, for it was here that the SS-Totenkopf-Division had summarily shot 23 civilians and set fire to five houses on May 23.

ground. Although outfits of the SS division did panic and withdrew in haste, this also applied to men of Rommel's own division. In the same way, although his 7. Panzer-Division bore the brunt of the fighting against the British tanks, outfits of the SS-Totenkopf-Division fought back determinedly with their 37mm anti-tank guns.

British losses had been heavy with 16 of the Mark IIs and 39 of the Mark Is having been lost. The commanders of the two tank battalions, Lieutenant-Colonel James Fitzmaurice of the 4th Royal Tank Regiment and Lieutenant-Colonel Hector Heyland of the 7th Royal Tank Regiment had been killed; Major Gerald Hedderwick who commanded a Matilda company of the 7th RTR was also killed and Major J. S. Fernie, who had taken command of the 4th RTR on the death of Lieutenant-Colonel Fitzmaurice, had been taken prisoner. The 6th Durham Light Infantry had all but disappeared, the 8th was badly depleted and in complete disorder and the 4th Royal Northumberland Fusiliers had lost most of its reconnaissance vehicles.

All in all, the counter-attack of May 21 had not achieved a great deal. The first day's objective, the Cojeul river, had been reached at one only point and for a very short time before the entire operation had been cancelled. Gort

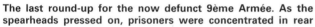

The last round-up for the now defunct 9ème Armée. As the spearheads pressed on, prisoners were concentrated in rear areas ready for the march east to Germany. These French prisoners are being assembled in the army barracks in Cambrai.

may have been correct in later stating that the operation 'imposed a valuable delay on a greatly superior enemy force against which it had blocked a vital road centre', but this was to overlook the fact that the War Cabinet had originally conceived the operation in an offensive, not a defensive, spirit. Costly as it was, the defence of Arras and the delay imposed were small compensation when what the War Cabinet had in mind required Gort to force his way through the gap created by the panzers in order to join up with the French in the south.

The Germans had also lost quite heavily. About 20 panzers had been disabled, many vehicles destroyed, some 300 men killed and wounded, and more than 400 taken prisoner.

But the real success of the British operation was psychological. This un-suspected counter-attack had come as a shock to the Germans who saw it as much more powerful that it actually was. In Guderian's words, 'the English did not break through, but they did make a considerable impression on the staff of Gruppe von Kleist which suddenly became remarkably nervous.' General Franz Halder, the Chief of the Army General Staff, noted in his diary on May 23, that von Kleist had reported

the panzers being down to half their nominal strength and in his view everything should be stopped until the crisis at Arras was solved. Von Rundstedt was impressed too and he declared after the war that 'for a short time it was feared that our panzer divisions would be cut off before the infantry divisions could come up to support them'. The 'Krisis Arras' had disconcerted the higher echelons far more than the forward units, who had quickly been able to gauge the operation for what it was, but it might have been one of the reasons behind the surprising 'Halt Order' issued to the panzers on May 24.

Today the French Army has vacated the complex which is being restored as a cultural centre.

The Weygand Plan

For three days XI. Armeekorps had been putting pressure on British positions near Louvain; now on the morning of May 17 they entered the city unopposed.

By May 15, the situation on the front of the 9ème Armée was such that Général Billotte, acting in his rôle of 'co-ordinator' given to him on May 12, had to issue orders directing the withdrawal of the whole left wing of the Allied front — from the Dyle line to the line of the Escaut. This movement was carried out in three stages; the first on the Senne river, the second on the Dendre river and then on the Escaut by the evening of May 18. It was found that the planning carried out six months before on the 'Escaut Plan' had not been wasted and the move was carried out without too much difficulty as the German Command was then wholly committed to the Heeresgruppe A breakthrough. Also the troops of Heeresgruppe B did not push too strongly in Flanders. Once on these new

The general retreat in Belgium had been ordered on May 15 when the extent of the German breakthrough in the south necessitated pulling back the northern flank of the Allied line in a series of pre-planned steps from river to river. Louvain, the last large town east of Brussels, was evacuated by British troops on the night of May 16. Here German infantrymen march down Bondgenotenlaan the next morning — in the background the memorial to military and civilian victims of the Great War.

Left: **An anti-tank squad enters the marshalling yard at Louvain from its northern end. The leading trooper is carrying a 7.92mm PzB 35(p), an anti-tank rifle of Polish manufacture — hence the** (p) **in the German designation.** *Right:* **The majority of the station service buildings have been demolished or replaced and much of the track altered.**

positions the line was still continuous with the Belgian Army in the north, the BEF in the centre and the 1ère Armée in the south.

There was, however, increasing concern within the French and British Commands about the Belgians who appeared to be losing the will to fight. As early as May 13 the head of the 'Needham Mission' appointed to Belgian Army Headquarters had reported that he felt 'no confidence in them really fighting'. Major-General H. Needham said that 'the C.G.S. is a fussy, windy, yes-man quite unfit for driving a partially unwilling army. I am certain that unless strongly supported by French or British troops this army cannot be relied on.'

Although there was still one line facing east from the mouth of the Escaut in the north to the vicinity of Arras in the south, there was nothing further west to the Somme where the panzers were moving at speed towards the Channel coast. It was therefore necessary to establish, out of what was previously the rear area, a new front facing south along the German breakthrough. At this stage the gap between the Allied armies in the north and the Allied force in France was not that wide — being at some points less than 30 kilometres — so that it had not got to the stage of the Allied Command losing all hope of closing it.

Above: **It appears that BEF engineers mined the station before they left. There men from the 16. Infanterie-Division have already marked out a safe path across the tracks.**
Below left: **Without a contemporary caption one can only hazard a guess at the cause of this explosion but the fact that a photographer was on hand to record the blast would seem to indicate that it was pre-planned — possibly a demolition charge or the deliberate detonation of a mine in the station yard.**

TUESDAY, MAY 21
The Ypres Meeting

Général Maxime Weygand, the new Commander-in-Chief, had a clear indication of how bad the situation was in the north when he decided to visit the Allied armies there on May 21. As all the roads in the Somme area were cut or nearly so, he had to travel by air and his party, in two Amiot 354s with their fighter escort of eight Bloch 152s of G.C. II/3, took off at 9.00 a.m. from Le Bourget. They headed north and soon reached the Somme valley and Abbeville, flying at about 300 feet, low enough to see that the panzers were already there. Explosions, flames and black smoke could be seen as well as the bursts left by the flak that exploded near the aircraft. Although Weygand could not see all this for himself inside the aircraft, from time to time the pilot, Lieutenant Henri Lafitte, told him of the appalling scenes he was witnessing below.

The aircraft landed on the deserted airfield at Norrent-Fontes and Weygand

And on to Brussels! Allied troops left the city on the 17th to fall back on the River Dendre leaving the Belgian capital wide open. The 14. Infanterie-Division entered hard on their heels that evening — these pictures being taken on the following morning. *Above:* In the Avenue de la Reine an attempt had been made to demolish the lifting bridge over the Willebroeck Canal but it was still passable.

The post-war replacement bridge was built on a slightly different angle but the tell-tale brickwork on the canal wall remains to indicate the original line.

Another bridge over the canal was well and truly blown with debris scattered all over Place Sainctelette.

At around 6.30 p.m. on the evening of the 17th, the commander of the XI. Armeekorps, Generalleutnant Joachim von Kortzfleisch, met the mayor of Brussels and within half an hour a German flag had been hoisted over the Hotel de Ville. *Above:* This convoy has stopped outside the Citroën garage on the Quai de Willebroeck on the far side of the canal.

Motor cyclists of the Aufkl.Abt. 14 arrive at Bockstael Square; the Laeken Royal Palace is a kilometre to the north.

And in come the cyclists. Pedal-power in front of the Théatre du Parc in the Rue de la Loi.

Maxime Weygand, recalled from Syria to replace Gamelin, took over the reins as French C-in-C on May 20. Weygand immediately decided to check the situation for himself first hand and the following day he set out to visit the northern commanders. Communications were chaotic and although his aircraft managed to safely reach the airfield at Norrent-Fontes, north-west of Béthune, the reception committee had been sent instead to Abbeville where it only just avoided Guderian's panzers. With no transport the Général took off again for Calais only to be told that King Leopold was waiting to see him in Ypres. This picture of the energetic 73-year-old general was taken at around 7.00 p.m. that day when he returned to Bastion 32, the headquarters of Amiral Abrial (behind in the doorway) at Dunkirk (see also page 445).

Weygand met King Leopold and Général van Overstraeten, his Chief Military Adviser, accompanied by Général Champon and Admiral Sir Roger Keyes. At the second meeting Général Billotte and Général Falgade were also present.

The heart of the matters discussed was Weygand's plan for an offensive designed to close the gap, the BEF and elements of the 1ère Armée attacking from the north while elements of the 7ème Armée attacked from the south. Weygand asked the Belgian Army to contribute to the Allied counter-attack, by protecting the British left flank. For this they would have to make a further withdrawal from the Escaut to the Yser and Général van Overstraeten, who did most of the talking on the Belgian side that day, resisted bitterly, explaining that further retreat would risk a new wave of demoralisation for his soldiers, the more so that this move would leave most of the country to the Germans. He said that it was 'absolutely necessary to suspend withdrawal because the divisions were beginning to disintegrate under a succession of night retreats,' and he announced that the Belgian Army would stay put even if this resulted in its separation from the other Allied armies. Weygand retorted sharply, asking for unity and reminding the Belgians that the French and British had come to their aid; now it was their turn to stand beside their Allies. Apart from Belgian opposition to the plan, another difficulty arose when Billotte arrived for the second session only to explain that the 1ère Armée was in a confused situation and incapable of launching any counter-attack.

Meanwhile King Leopold had urged that an effort should be made to bring Gort to the meeting since nothing could be settled without him but all attempts to reach him by telephone failed. Keyes was then sent by car to try to find him.

went off in an old truck in search of a telephone while the aircraft were refuelled. After a lengthy search he found a telephone in order in the post office of the village and succeeded in making contact with the headquarters of Groupe d'Armées No. 1. He returned to the airfield and the aircraft took off at about midday, except for one of the Bloch 152s which had had to make a belly landing in the morning. An hour later, after having once more flown over the battlefield in the Cambrai area, they landed at Saint-Inglevert and Weygand left for Calais where in the town hall he met the head of the French Military Mission at Belgian headquarters, Général Pierre Champon. Lieutenant Lafitte and the fighter leader, Capitaine Victor Veniel, had orders to wait until 7.00 p.m. for the possible return of Weygand but then to take off and return to their base. The fighters complied with the order and took off but the two Amiot 354s waited all night before taking off next morning, returning safely on their own.

Meanwhile Weygand went on by car to Ypres for the inter-Allied conference. At the first meeting that afternoon

Weygand reached Ypres by car at 3.00 p.m. after a tortuous journey along roads clogged with Army transport and refugees. Neither Général Billotte nor General Gort had arrived at the Stadhuis so the meeting began without them. Billotte arrived in the afternoon, but Gort did not appear before 7.00 p.m., after Weygand had left.

The Belgian king, estranged from his own ministers who were excluded from the meeting (which took place in the Council Room on the first floor), refused to agree to Weygand's plan for the Belgians to pull back to the River Yser, thus shortening the flank to enable the British to mount an offensive southwards. At the same time Weygand wanted the French army to attack northwards to meet the BEF and so cut the German forces in two. Even after Général Billotte arrived, and the proposal was gone over once again, no decision could be reached. The fact that Gort only reached Ypres after Weygand had departed further aggravated the situation, just at a time when maximum unity amongst the Allies was paramount.

In the end, no concensus was found, little was decided and the meeting broke up in a very depressed atmosphere. Weygand went back to Dunkirk and left in the evening on a destroyer, *la Flore*, which was bombed by the Luftwaffe as she left the harbour.

Meanwhile Admiral Keyes had at last succeeded in finding Gort at Premesques, where the British commander said he had waited all day for news of Weygand's visit. Gort and Pownall went immediately to Ypres only to find Weygand had already left. A third meeting was then convened between Gort and Pownall, Billotte, King Leopold and van Overstraeten but still nothing concrete could be agreed.

Although Weygand said later that he was 'inclined to draw what seemed to be the only possible explanation — namely that the former (Gort) had purposely abstained from coming to the Ypres conference', the mix-up might have been accidental. The incident was however an indication of the mutual distrust at high level which weakened the Allied cause just at a time when unity was badly needed. The confidence between French and British commanders was deteriorating but this was still comparatively good when compared to the confidence they both had in the Belgians who were already thinking of capitulation.

Returning from the meeting at Ypres, a further blow befell the Allied cause when Général Billotte was fatally injured during the night when his car was involved in an accident. He died two days later. With his death went the one man who might have pulled the Allies through these difficult hours. Général Blanchard of the 1ère Armée now took over command of Groupe d'Armées No. 1 and Général René Prioux, the

command of the 1ère Armée.

Having disembarked at Cherbourg at 5.00 a.m. on May 22, Weygand was back in Paris by midday for a special session of the Allied Supreme War Council, to be held at the French General Staff Headquarters at Vincennes. Both Churchill, who had flown over specially, and the French Prime Minister were present. All eyes were on Weygand; he was back from Belgium where he had seen the battlefields for himself and talked with the field commanders. He started with a report of his meeting with King Leopold and then enlarged on his plan for a pincer attack

developing at the same time from north and south. This was the plan put forward by Weygand at the Ypres meeting, but he had taken little account of what he had been told there by King Leopold and Général Billotte. The plan was thus highly optimistic since it assumed that the Allied forces both north and south of the gap were capable of a counterattack. Churchill reacted very positively to the idea and it was settled after Weygand had asked in no uncertain terms for the entire British air force, bombers and fighters, to be committed in support of this counter-offensive. Churchill then sent a message to Gort, informing him what had been agreed:

1. That the Belgian Army should withdraw to the line of the Yser and stand there, the sluices being opened.

2. That the British Army and the French 1ère Armée should attack southwards towards Bapaume and Cambrai at the earliest moment, certainly tomorrow with about eight divisions, and with the Belgian Cavalry Corps on the right of the British.

3. That as this battle is vital for both armies and the British communications depend upon freeing Amiens, the British Air Force should give the utmost possible help both by day and by night while it is going on.

4. That the new French Army Group, which is advancing upon Amiens, and forming a line along the Somme should strike northwards and join hands with the British divisions who are attacking southwards in the general direction of Bapaume.

After the meeting in Paris, Weygand issued his Operation Order No. 1 in which he stated that 'the only way to hold, and beat, the German is by counter-attack' and ended by saying that 'the Germans panzer divisions must be hemmed in within the arena in which they have so harshly advanced. They must not get out again'.

Having travelled all night on a roundabout route via Dover and Cherbourg, Weygand reached Paris in time to meet Churchill who had flown from England on his second visit to France within a week. The meeting took place in the Grand Quartier Général at the Château de Vincennes in an underground complex beneath the yard in front of the Pavillon du Roi. This wing of the château is today the location of the Historical Branch of the French Army and the former GHQ is now used to store archives.

THURSDAY, MAY 23
The counter-attack
fails to start

By the morning of May 23, the day when the counter-offensive was scheduled to start, Gort had still not received any specific orders or instructions and he sent a telegram to the Secretary of State for War urging that 'co-ordination on this front is essential with the armies of three different nations'. Blanchard arrived at Gort's command post later in the morning and a discussion followed as to the part which British and French troops could play in the northern pincer of the Weygand Plan. It was then agreed that the attack southwards should be made by two British and four French divisions, among them the three D.L.M.s of the Corps de Cavalerie. Gort made known that, as far as he was concerned the attack could not take place before May 26 because the movements then in process made any earlier date impossible. Neither of them knew if this would fit in with plans for the complementary attack from the south, about which they knew nothing, but Gort made it clear that in his view the attack from the north alone would not be strong enough and, if the gap was to be closed at all, the main effort must come from the south. Blanchard undertook to submit these propositions to the High Command to see if this would fit in with plans for the southern attack.

Thus instead of the planned counter-offensive, May 23 saw only a battle of telegrams in which Reynaud, Churchill, Weygand and others were all involved. Churchill sent a message to Reynaud in which he fully backed the Weygand Plan and declared his desire to see the French and Belgians wholly committed to the success of the plan. Weygand, in a personal telegram to Gort, expressed his regret that they had not met and told him that the attack from the south was 'in very good shape'. Weygand's mistaken belief that this was the case was further underlined when Churchill spoke to him and Reynaud on the telephone. Faith in the Weygand Plan

Le Général WEYGAND
Chef d'Etat-Major Général
de la Défense Nationale
Commandant en Chef de l'Ensemble des
Théâtres d'Opérations

P.C., le 23 Mai 1940.

Entrée _____
Sortie _____

ORDRE GENERAL Nº 3
=================================

Appelé par la confiance du Gouvernement au poste de Chef d'Etat-Major Général de la Défense Nationale et Commandant en Chef de l'ensemble des Théâtres d'Opérations, je compte que chacun apportera une énergie farouche dans l'accomplissement de son devoir en toutes circonstances.

Aucune défaillance, d'où qu'elle vienne, ne saurait être et ne sera tolérée.

Résister est bien, rendre coup pour coup est mieux encore, mais seul obtient la victoire celui qui frappe plus fort qu'il n'est frappé.

Signé : WEYGAND

Two days later the French C-in-C issued his General Order No. 3, exhorting all to fight with 'fierce will' stressing that 'to resist is right, to strike back is better still, yet victory is achieved only by those who strike harder than they are struck'.

was however failing in London and a message from the Secretary of State for War to Gort concluded that: 'Should however, situation on your communications make this at any time impossible you should inform us so that we can

Fine words but they meant little in the confused situation on the ground where chaotic conditions by day, followed by forced marches westwards at night, made a mockery of mounting a concerted Allied offensive co-ordinated from north and south. In reality, Weygand's plan was a non-starter from the beginning, especially after the 6. Armee broke through the Belgian

defences on the Lys on the 24th which effectively sealed the fate of the Belgian forces and led to capitulation. *Left:* These pictures were taken in Deinze, about 20 kilometres west of Gent, as troops of the IX. Armeekorps thundered through the town. *Right:* The SdKfz 6 was pictured turning left at the crossroad at the end of Kortrijk Straat.

inform French and make naval arrangements to assist you should you have to withdraw on the northern coast.'

While all this was happening Gort was also concerned by what was taking place in the Arras sector where the situation was now critical. German troops had skirted the town to the east and west and the 11. Schützen-Brigade was now pressing against the town from three sides, supported by heavy air attacks. At 7.00 p.m. Gort sent a message to Major-General Franklyn to the effect that Arras was to be held 'to the last man and the last round' but later in the evening he saw that it would serve no useful purpose to leave the garrison to its fate and decided instead

Their officer, Oberst Ludwig Wolff, having been grievously wounded as they approached the bridge over the Schipdonk Canal, men of the 56. Infanterie-Division pushed a group of civilians in front of them as a shield as they went forward to drag him to cover. The civilians were left in the open and a stray shell, probably German, exploded in Market Square, killing many of them.

to order a withdrawal to a safer defensive line along the Béthune-La Bassée Canal. Franklyn was then ordered to withdraw his force, including Petreforce in Arras, behind the canal which was carried out without serious interference during the night.

Whatever the weakness of the Weygand Plan and its feasibility, the BEF had now retreated so far that any hope of seeing the planned counter-offensive actually close the breach had

gone and the French High Command had found a fitting explanation for the failure of the plan. On May 24 Reynaud wrote angrily to Churchill, reminding him that he had subscribed with enthusiasm to the plan and explaining that Weygand had been surprised to learn that 'contrary to formal orders confirmed this morning the British Army has decided on and carried out a withdrawal forty kilometres in the direction of the ports'.

Further down Kortrijk Straat, the photographer caught other troops pressing on southwards. This street has also been

widened with many of the houses rebuilt. One exception: No. 37 on the right — now a Chinese restaurant.

On the morning of May 24 Hitler motored to Charleville-Mézières to meet with von Rundstedt at Heeresgruppe A headquarters which had been set up in Blairon House (now Maison de l'Ardenne) in Avenue Georges Corneau.

On May 24 Hitler issued his Führer Directive No. 13 in which he made known his strategic intentions for the conduct of the war in the days to come:

'The next object of our operations is to annihilate the French, English and Belgian forces which are surrounded in Artois and Flanders, by a concentric attack by our northern flank and by the swift seizure of the Channel coast in this area. The task of the Luftwaffe will be to break all enemy resistance on the part of the surrounded forces, to prevent the escape of the English forces across the Channel and to protect the southern flank of Heeresgruppe A . . . The Army will then prepare to destroy in the shortest possible time the remaining enemy forces in France'.

To von Rundstedt the first part of this directive — the destruction of the Allied armies trapped in northern France — now seemed to be merely a formality and that from now on he must husband and recondition his battered panzer units for the coming Operation 'Fall Rot'. Thus on the evening of May 23 Heeresgruppe A sent a directive to the 4. Armee which ordered in turn that 'in the main Panzergruppe Hoth will halt tomorrow; Panzergruppe von Kleist will also halt, thereby clarifying the situation and closing up'.

Hitler visited von Rundstedt at his headquarters in Charleville on the morning of May 24 and the Heeres-

It was at this meeting that the so-called 'Halt' order was given although in actual fact Hitler was merely approving von Rundstedt's own prior instruction to stop the armour short on the line Lens–Béthune–Aire–Saint-Omer–Gravelines.

gruppe A war diary made it clear that the Führer agreed with the view that 'the mobile forces could be halted on the line reached, Lens-Béthune-Aire-St Omer-Gravelines, in order to intercept the enemy under pressure from Heeresgruppe B. He emphasised this view in insisting that it was in any case necessary to conserve the armoured forces for future operations and that any further compression of the ring encircling the enemy could only have the highly undesirable result of restricting the activities of the Luftwaffe'.

Nevertheless as Hitler left Charleville, the order to stop the panzers went out under his name although this should not be confused with the Führer's own Directive No. 13 (opposite) issued that same day. Left: His convoy is pictured passing the Gendarmerie barracks which still exist on the Avenue Charles de Gaulle right.

*The Führer and Supreme Commander
of the Armed Forces*

Headquarters,
24th May 1940

Directive No. 13

1. *The next object of our operations is to annihilate the French, English, and Belgian forces which are surrounded in Artois and Flanders, by a concentric attack by our northern flank and by the swift seizure of the Channel coast in this area.*

The task of the Luftwaffe will be to break all enemy resistance on the part of the surrounded forces, to prevent the escape of the English forces across the Channel, and to protect the southern flank of Heeresgruppe A.

The enemy air force will be engaged whenever opportunity offers.

2. *The Army will then prepare to destroy in the shortest possible time the remaining enemy forces in France. This operation will be undertaken in three phases:*

Phase 1: *A thrust between the sea and the Oise as far as the lower Seine below Paris, with the intention of supporting and securing with weak forces the later main operations on the right flank.*

Should the position and reserves available permit, every effort will be made, even before the conclusion of hostilities in Artois and Flanders, to occupy the area between the Somme and the Oise by a concentric attack in the direction of Montdidier, and thereby to prepare and facilitate the later thrust against the lower Seine.

Phase 2: *An attack by the main body of the Army, including strong armoured forces, south-eastwards on either side of Reims, with the intention of defeating the main body of the French Army in the Paris–Metz–Belfort triangle and of bringing about the collapse of the Maginot Line.*

Phase 3: *In support of this main operation, a well-timed subsidiary attack on the Maginot Line with the aim of breaking through the Line with weaker forces at its most vulnerable point between St Avold and Sarreguemines in the direction of Nancy–Lunéville.*

Should the situation allow, an attack on the upper Rhine may be envisaged, with the limitation that not more than eight to ten divisions are to be committed.

3. *Tasks of the Luftwaffe*

(a) *Apart from operations in France, the Luftwaffe is authorised to attack the English homeland in the fullest manner, as soon as sufficient forces are available. This attack will be opened by an annihilating reprisal for English attacks on the Ruhr.*

Commander-in-Chief Luftwaffe will designate targets in accordance with the principles laid down in Directive No. 9 and further orders to be issued by the Oberkommando der Wehrmacht. The time and plan for this attack are to be reported to me.

The struggle against the English homeland will be continued after the commencement of land operations.

(b) *With the opening of the main operations of the Army in the direction of Reims, it will be the task of the Luftwaffe, apart from maintaining our air supremacy, to give direct support to the attack, to break up any enemy reinforcements which may appear, to hamper the re-grouping of enemy forces, and in particular to protect the western flank of the attack.*

The breakthrough of the Maginot Line will also be supported as far as necessary.

(c) *Commander-in-Chief Luftwaffe will also consider how far the air defence of the areas upon which the enemy is now concentrating his attacks can be strengthened by the employment of forces from less threatened areas.*

In so far as the Kriegsmarine is involved in any changes of this kind, Commander-in-Chief Kriegsmarine is to participate.

4. *Tasks of the Kriegsmarine*

All restrictions on naval action in English and French waters are hereby cancelled and commanders are free to employ their forces to the fullest extent.

Commander-in-Chief Kriegsmarine will submit a proposal for the delimitation of the areas in which the measures authorised for the coming siege may be carried out.

I reserve to myself the decision whether, and if so in what form, the blockade will be made public.

5. *I request the Commanders-in-Chief to inform me, in person or in writing, of their intentions based on this directive.*

ADOLF HITLER

Hitler left and von Rundstedt issued a directive which read 'by the Führer's orders, the general line Lens-Béthune-Aire-StOmer-Gravelines will not be passed'. This order, which would later be known as the 'Halt' order, was to have immense consequences as it made an organised withdrawal and the further evacuation of the BEF possible. It puzzled the German field commanders to such an extent that most of their war diaries show their disappointment of the 'Führer Order'. It must be noted however that Hitler had only endorsed a decision taken by von Rundstedt the day before he himself arrived at Heeresgruppe A headquarters.

For all practical purposes the Weygand Plan had been ruled out by May 24 but Blanchard and his chief-of-staff still went to Gort's headquarters in the morning to discuss the plans for the forthcoming Franco-British attack southwards. However, no one drew attention to the fact that the withdrawal from Arras had now made the proposed operation impossible. Lieutenant-General Sir Ronald Adam, commanding the III Corps and Général René Altmayer, commanding the Vème

By now King Leopold and his military adviser, Général van Overstraeten, both seen here in happier days, were convinced that the time had come for Belgium to pull out of the war.

On Saturday, May 25, Generaloberst Walther von Reichenau, commander of the 6. Armee, requisitioned the Château d'Anvaing, ten kilometres north-east of Tournai, as his headquarters and it was here that the final act in the Belgian drama took place. Two days later, Major-Général Jules Derousseaux arrived at the château to seek terms. He was given one simple option: unconditional surrender.

Corps d'Armée, were told to complete plans for the attack by three French and two British divisions on May 26.

Whether Gort and Blanchard actually intended to launch this attack will never be known as the Germans took the initiative once again. On May 24 the 6. Armee had struck the positions of the Belgians on the Lys at the boundary between the Belgian Army and the BEF and succeeded in gaining bridgeheads at Courtrai and Menin. These were enlarged on May 25 and in the evening the Needham Mission at Belgian headquarters reported alarmingly that the 'German attack 5.00 p.m. today drove back Belgian right to Geluwe. Gap exists between Geluwe and Lys which Belgians cannot close. Last reserves already used . . .'

At 6.00 p.m., without waiting to ask permission of his French superior, Gort took the unilateral decision to abandon preparations for the attack southwards and to move at once the 5th and 50th Divisions to the threatened gap between the Belgian and British armies. The gap created between Menin and Ypres was closed in a nick of time but these developments were too much for King Leopold who was now convinced that the Belgian Army should pull out of the war. Some of his Ministers who met him at Wynendaele Castle at 5.30 a.m. on May 25 begged him to relinquish command of the Belgian Army and to go to France or England with them but he refused and instead issued an Order of the Day to the Army in which he announced that 'Whatever may happen, I shall share your fate'.

Early that morning Gort and Pownall went to Blanchard's headquarters to find that orders cancelling the southern offensive had in fact been issued during the night. The Weygand Plan was now officially dead and buried. News from the Belgian front was disquieting and arrangements were made for a with-

drawal behind the Lys but there was no discussion of retirement and they avoided looking any further beyond that. Although the idea of an evacuation could not have been absent from their minds, it was too awful for Blanchard to speak of, and for Gort to have done so, having shown his intention so clearly during the previous week, would have been a provocation.

Under the pressure of events, each of the Allies was thinking, now more than ever, primarily of themselves. When Gort, whose overriding concern was the saving of the BEF, tried to prevail upon the Belgians to withdraw as far back as the Yser, King Leopold, whose main aim was at all costs to put an end to a hopeless battle, called on Gort to launch an attack between the Lys and the Escaut. Neither appeal was listened to by the other. For the French the

problem was simply how to hold out as long as possible with the Belgian and British troops to give enough time for Général Weygand to create a strong defensive line behind the Aisne and the Somme.

The Germans maintained their pressure against the Belgian lines and at noon on May 26 the Belgian Command informed the head of the French Military Mission at the Belgian headquarters, Général Champon, that 'the Army has nearly reached the limits of its endurance'. Général Oscar Michiels wrote that same day to Gort that he was 'compelled regretfully to say that we have no longer any forces available to bar the way to Ypres'. The following morning Gort received a message from Admiral Keyes saying that King Leopold 'wishes you to realise that he will be obliged to surrender before a débâcle'.

THE BELGIANS CAPITULATE

In spite of these warnings, for most of May 27 Weygand, Blanchard and Gort did not appear to realise that the end was approaching and that Leopold was about to surrender. At 3.30 p.m. the King decided to ask for an armistice and at 5.00 p.m. the Belgian parlementaire, Major-Général Jules Derousseaux, left to seek terms. He reached the German lines in the sector held by the XI. Armeekorps more or less at the same time the news reached London and Paris. London had heard it a few minutes before 6.00 p.m., while at Vincennes Weygand had the news a few minutes later. Général Derousseaux returned at 10.30 p.m. with a German demand for 'unconditional surrender'. Within half an hour Leopold had accepted and a cease-fire was ordered for 4.00 a.m. the next morning. Later that day — May 28 — the armistice was signed by Général Derousseaux and Generaloberst Walther von Reichenau at 6. Armee headquarters in the Château d'Anvaing, ten kilometres east of Tournai. The following day Capitaine Abel Devos surrendered the Fort

Today the château and its surrounds remain almost as if time has stood still . . . perhaps almost unwilling to turn the pages from a not so glorious moment in the country's history.

Le Roi remet la Coupe-Challenge de l'Infanterie.

Les épreuves du Challenge royal de l'Infanterie, qui suscitèrent une vive émulation sportive et athlétique entre les unités de cette arme, ont eu leur dénouement, dimanche, au Stade du Centenaire, où le roi Léopold III remet la coupe au chef de la unité...

Just a month before when this picture was published, the King must have felt that his country was safe and secure under the umbrella of his four-year-old declaration of neutrality, in which he put as much faith in the word of Hitler as that of the Allies. Now on May 28 it was all over, and the King, against the advice of his ministers, decided to stay with his people and agreed to accept the German terms. This is a copy of the Belgian response: 'Lay down arms. Cease-fire on May 28 at 4.00 a.m. Belgian time. A parlementaire will cross the German lines at 5.00 a.m. Belgian time'.

de Tancrémont, and the last point of resistance of the Belgian Army was over.

Although the capitulation of the Belgian Army was fully expected, the way it was done surprised both the British and French. Reynaud, understandably bitter and greatly worried, made an emotional speech in which he alleged that the Belgian Army 'had just surrendered suddenly and unconditionally, in the midst of battle on the orders of its King, without warning its French and British fellow combatants, thus opening the way to Dunkirk to the German divisions'. However even if the final decision was taken with only a few hours' notice being given to France and Britain, the writing on the wall had been present for several days.

The repercussions of the Belgian surrender, especially in France, resulted in a brutal awakening. People had seen the breakthrough at Sedan and the defeat of the Netherlands as all part of fighting a war, the retreat in Belgium as a manoeuvre, and the advance of the Germans to the sea as an opportunity to hit them from both flanks. However, they now began to question the wisdom of moving into Belgium in the first place, and a premonition of an even greater catastrophe was spreading.

'Der Krieg ist aus! — La guerre est finie!' Near Zedelgem, five kilometres south of Brugge, a company of Belgian soldiers, still carrying their weapons and equipment, crowd around a car

bearing a flag of truce on the morning of May 28. A German officer announces the fact that their King had surrendered and that for them the war was over.

367

Although the Belgian capitulation had been in the offing for several days, it was the timing which created much bitterness. M. Hubert Pierlot, the Belgian Prime Minister broadcast to the people that morning from Paris: 'Belgians! Overruling the formal and unanimous advice of the Government, the King has opened separate negotiations and has treated with the enemy. Belgium will be dumbfounded, but the guilt of one man cannot be imputed to the entire nation. Our Army has not deserved the fate which has befallen it. The act which we deplore is without any legal validity. It does not bind the country. According to the terms of the Belgian Constitution, which the King swore to uphold, all the powers come from the people. They are exercised as laid down by the Constitution. No act of the King can be valid unless it bears the counter-signature of a Minister. The King, breaking the bond which bound him to his people, placed himself under the power of the invader. Henceforth he is no longer in a position to govern, since obviously the functions of the head of the State cannot be carried out under foreign control. Officers and public servants are, therefore, released from the obedience imposed upon them by their oath of allegiance. The Belgian Constitution provides for the continuity of the powers of the Government . . . The Government will not fail to do its duty. Assembled in Paris and in agreement with the Speakers of the two Houses and with such Ministers of State as could be consulted, the Government, sure of being the interpreter of the will of the nation, is resolved to continue the struggle for the liberation of the country . . . Belgians! we are going through the most painful trial in our history.'

Ypres — the very symbol of the sacrifice and slaughter twenty years earlier — has fallen. It was Churchill, who had served at nearby Poperinghe, who pressed for a great memorial to be erected in the devastated town which meant more than any other battleground of the war. Throughout, it had seen almost continuous fighting and the surrounding countryside had become the graveyard for a quarter of a million British dead. The site for the memorial was well chosen — at the old gateway on the road to Menin through which virtually every man who served in the Salient would have passed. And so it was to be. Begun in 1923, during the next five years a great triumphal archway rose above the ruins, its stone panels inscribed with the names of the missing — over 54,000. It was unveiled by the King of the Belgians in July 1927. Thirteen years later his son, Leopold, caused much bitterness when the Allies once again found themselves at war. King Leopold was held prisoner by the Germans at his royal palace near Brussels until 1944 when he was taken to Austria. His personal decision to surrender, rather than lead his government into exile in London, laid the basis for a post-war controversy over his return to the throne, and in 1950 he renounced his sovereignty in favour of his son Baudouin.

Before we leave the Belgian scene altogether, there is one aspect which must be covered — the battle for the forts on the eastern frontier. The fortress troops at Liège and Namur had been resisting for the past three weeks even though the fighting had bypassed them to the west, and in fact it was one of the forts — that at Pépinster — which was to be the very last element of the Belgian Army to surrender. All told, there were 21 forts: twelve grouped around Liège (called the Position Fortifiée de Liège or P.F.L.) and nine surrounding Namur — the Position Fortifiée de Namur (P.F.N.). All were of pre-WWI construction and all had the same style of entrance. The one illustrated *above* is that of the P.F.L. at Embourg.

Belgian Forts

After the peace treaty signed at Frankfurt-am-Main in May 1871, France and Germany lost no time in fortifying their new border. As early as 1874, the French started to build a powerful fortification system, with strong points at Verdun, Toul, Epinal and Belfort, while the Germans built impressive 'Festen' at Thionville, Metz, Strasbourg and Istein.

Meanwhile Belgium realised that as a successful attack from either France or Germany would be impossible through such a fortified line, the new danger was that the axis of any future attack would lie either northwards, in Belgium, or to the south through Switzerland. In 1882, Général Henri-Alexis Brialmont put forward the necessity for the defence of the Meuse valley and in due course the idea that Belgium had to fortify its eastern border was accepted. In June 1887 a plan was agreed to construct two 'places fortes' on the Meuse, at Namur and Liège, and for the reinforcement of the fortifications at Antwerp which was seen as a national redoubt in the event of an invasion. The organisation of these fortifications was entrusted to the Général.

Général Brialmont planned to build twelve forts around Liège, four kilometres apart and at about six to eight kilometres from the town, the six major forts alternating with six minor forts, and another fort further north of Liège, at Lixhe near Visé. Around Namur, at some five to eight kilometres from the centre, nine forts were to be built, four major alternating with five minor.

The twelve forts of the Position Fortifiée de Liège (P.F.L.) and the nine of the Position Fortifiée de Namur (P.F.N.) were built between 1888 and 1892, but the fort originally planned at Lixhe was never built because of financial constraints.

The forts were originally constructed following the outcome of the Franco-Prussian War of 1871. Each was triangularly-shaped with a central redoubt or 'massif' surrounded by a moat ten metres wide and five metres deep. The long-range armament was installed on the redoubt and consisted of rotating cupolas mounting either a 210mm howitzer or a 120mm gun, or twin 120mm or 150mm guns. Depending on its size, each fort had a 150mm cupola, one or two 210mm cupolas and two 120mm cupolas. Three or four retracting turrets mounting a 57mm gun were also provided for the immediate defence of the fort and these were supplemented by 57mm guns firing from embrasures provided in casemates enfilading the whole length of the moat, usually from the corners. This is the moat at Malonne (P.F.N.), pictured by the Germans after it had fallen into their hands.

On the morning of August 4, 1914, the German Army invaded Belgium and marched westwards, leaving a siege army to deal with the resistance at Liège. Powerful artillery units started shelling the P.F.L., and Barchon surrendered on August 8; Evegnée followed on August 11, then Pontisse, Embourg and Chaudfontaine on August 13, and all the other forts followed one by one, the last two, Flémalle and Hollogne, surrendering on August 16. The Germans then moved their artillery to take on the Namur forts, and five days later the heavies started to hammer the P.F.N., causing much damage. Maizeret was abandoned on August 22, Cognelée and Marchovelette surrendered on August 23, four other forts on August 24, and the last two, Dave and Suarlée, on August 25.

POST-WAR REORGANISATION

Following the example of France, where a commission had been appointed in 1922 to consider how best the defence of the eastern frontier could be achieved, in October 1926 Belgium appointed a committee to decide on this same issue. The construction of defensive fortifications was considered consistent with the Belgian policy of absolute neutrality and, from the outset, they were seen as a first line of resistance which had to contain any initial assault sufficiently to allow the Belgian Army, which needed several days to mobilise, to assemble its divisions. When the commission recommended the modernisation of the fortifications at Antwerp, Liège and Namur, a second body was appointed in December 1927 to deal with the detailed layout of the fortication line. It examined the problem during the following three months and drew up proposals for the new fortifications in April 1928. These were centered on three lines.

First, the Position Avancée (advanced positions), was to be built along the frontier with Germany from north of Antwerp to Arlon, consisting of small casemates to control the roads and railways. These positions were to be manned by border troops and Chasseurs Ardennais.

Then the Position de Couverture (covering positions) ran right along the Albert Canal from Antwerp to the modernised P.F.L., small pillboxes, each with two machine guns or more, being built along the canal bank. At Antwerp where some of the old forts had been lightly rearmed and transformed into infantry positions, further reinforcement was provided by an anti-tank canal and measures for flooding. All the Meuse bridges were to be fitted with demolition charges and a line of blockhouses built along the river, linking the P.F.N. to the P.F.L.

The Position Centrale (central positions) was to run from Antwerp to the modernised P.F.N. through Liers, Louvain, the River Dyle and Wavre. It consisted of blockhouses, anti-tank barriers, trenches and dug-in positions for machine guns and 47mm anti-tank guns. The northern part of this line, known as the K.W. Line, had been completed

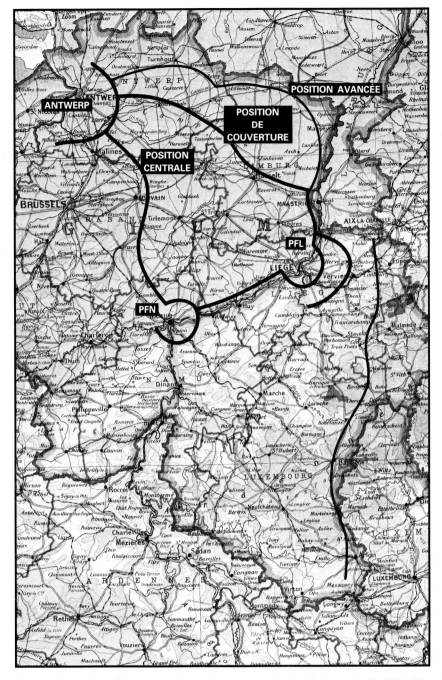

The Belgian defence lines as drawn up after the commission had reported in 1922. The Fortified Positions — the Position Fortifiée de Liège and the Position Fortifiée de Namur — are more usually referred to as simply P.F.L. and P.F.N.

when the attack came in May 1940 but the southern end was virtually non-existent, with its layout not even finalised.

In all these plans, the forts were not looked upon as 'forts d'arrêt' but only as support positions for the infantry units. Both the P.F.L. and the P.F.N. provided a bridgehead south of the Meuse into which troops withdrawing from the advanced positions south of the river would return, and the Belgians had also drawn up plans for counter-attacks being launched from these bridgeheads.

The renewed P.F.L. consisted of eight old forts which had been modernised (the six on the Meuse right bank and two on the left bank), and four new forts built further east of the town at

Eben-Emael, Aubin-Neufchâteau, Battice and Pépinster. Except for Loncin, all the major forts had been modernised, together with three of the minor ones. The three which had not been updated, Liers, Lantin and Hollogne, were to be used for ammunition storage. Loncin had been left as a memorial to its defenders killed in 1914, of whom about 300 were still lying within its walls.

The renewed P.F.N. consisted of seven of old forts which had been modernised — three on the Meuse right bank, two on the left bank and two between the Meuse and the Sambre. The major fort of Cognelée, and the minor one, Emines, were not modernised and were earmarked for storage of ammunition.

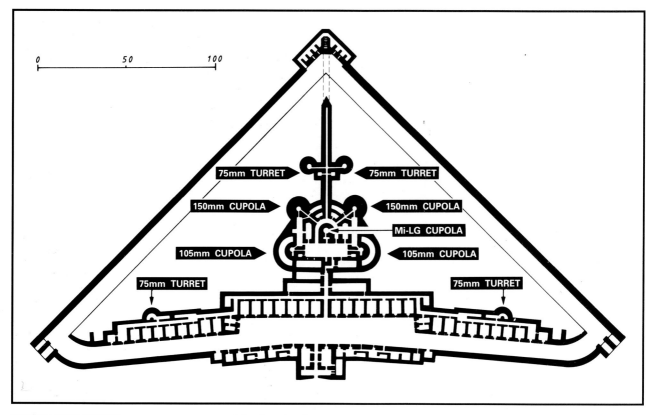

Scale bar: 0 — 50 — 100

Diagram labels:
75mm TURRET — 75mm TURRET
150mm CUPOLA — 150mm CUPOLA
Mi-LG CUPOLA
105mm CUPOLA — 105mm CUPOLA
75mm TURRET — 75mm TURRET

MODERNISATION

Most of the forts captured by the Germans in 1914 had been repaired and re-equipped by them during the war but in 1917 they had begun scrapping them and the Belgian modernisation programme meant a complete reappraisal of armament and equipment. Lessons had been learned from the experience of 1914, a ventilation system was installed to protect the fort in case of gas attack and additional reinforcement was introduced with more concrete under the ceilings and on the walls. New chambers were dug at a deeper and thus safer level although this could not be done at Boncelles where the water table was too high.

The rearmament, mostly carried out between 1928 and 1934, had to make do with what the Germans had left and to compensate for what was missing, some cupolas, turrets and equipment were removed from the Antwerp forts which were not to be rearmed, while others were switched from one fort to another. Consequently the end result was a muddle with each fort receiving different armament.

The only weaponry common to both the P.F.L. and P.F.N. was the 75mm howitzer turret which was made up from the old 57mm turret. Apart from this, nothing was standard: in the P.F.N. the old twin 150mm cupolas were modified and re-armed with a twin 75mm gun (but not at Maizeret where the twin 150mm cupola became a twin 105mm cupola), while in the P.F.L. the 150mm cupolas were transformed as Mi-LG cupolas mounting machine guns and grenade-launchers.

In the P.F.L. some of the 210mm cupolas were re-armed with 150mm guns, while in the P.F.N. the 210mm cupolas were removed completely and the foundations concreted over. In the P.F.L. the 120mm cupolas (either single or twin) were modified to mount a single or a twin 105mm gun while in the P.F.N. the 120mm cupolas were modified to mount either machine guns (Mi cupola) or grenade-launchers (LG cupola).

In the embrasures enfilading the moats, machine guns (ex-WWI 7.65mm Maxims in the P.F.N. and FM-30 in the P.F.L.) were installed in the old 57mm embrasures which were modified accordingly.

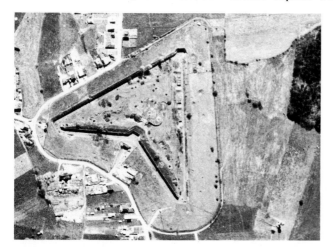

The standard fort design was triangular, the representative plan *(top)* being that of Barchon as it was in 1940. This basic shape can be seen on the aerial shot of Boncelles *(left)*, but where the terrain forbade a full triangle, the tip was cut off to make more of a trapezoidal shape as illustrated by the air view of Pontisse *(right)*. These pictures were taken in the 1970s (and sent courtesy of Francis Tirtiat) — the empty pits showing up clearly where turrets and cupolas had been removed for scrapping. Today Boncelles has completely disappeared under a new housing estate which covers the whole area.

The modernisation programme instituted after the First World War proved half-hearted with a mixture of make-do and mend. Captured German armament was retained, and a variety of other weaponry employed with no thought of overall standardisation. This is the twin 105mm cupola at Flémalle (P.F.L.), pictured after the fort had been captured by German forces for a second time.

ARMAMENT

The basic specifications of the modernised armament was as follows:

75mm turret. A 75mm gun mounted in the old 57mm retractable and rotating turret 1.65 metres in diameter. The origin of this gun is uncertain but it was probably made up from Schneider 75mm guns obtained by Belgium during the First World War. It lobbed a 5kg shell up to 5.2 kilometres. There were 57 such turrets in the P.F.L. and P.F.N.

75mm cupola. Two 75mm guns mounted in the old 150mm rotating cupola 4.8 metres in diameter. The gun, a variation on the Belgian field gun, could fire a 5.5kg shell up to 11 kilometres. There were 6 such cupolas, all in the P.F.N.

105mm cupola. 105mm guns mounted in the old 120mm rotating cupola (or at Maizeret in an old 150mm cupola). These cupolas mounted generally two guns and were about 4.2 metres in diameter, but at Evegnée and Chaudfontaine the 105mm cupolas were 4.5 metres in diameter and mounted a single gun. The 105mm gun, an ex-German piece obtained as war booty, sent a 17.5kg shell up to 13.3 kilometres. Altogether there were 11 105mm cupolas, 7 mounting two guns and 4 one, all in the P.F.L. but one at Maizeret.

150mm cupola. A 150mm gun mounted in the old 210mm rotating cupola 3.6 metres in diameter. The ex-German gun fired a weighty shell of 40kg up to 19.9 kilometres. There were 7 such cupolas, all in the P.F.L.

Mi cupola. 7.65mm Maxim machine guns mounted in the old 120mm cupolas. These cupolas were either 4.2 metres in diameter and then mounted one machine gun or 4.8 metres in diameter and then had two machine guns. There were 6 all told, every one being in the P.F.N.

LG cupola. 120mm grenade-launchers mounted in the old 120mm cupolas, 4.2 metres in diameter and having two grenade-launchers. A close defence armament, this could fire a 2kg bomb out to 350 metres. There were 8 LG cupolas, all in the P.F.N.

Mi-LG cupola. In the P.F.L., the old 150mm cupolas were modified to take a mixed armament of 7.65mm Maxim machine guns and 120mm grenade-launchers. These cupolas were about 4.8 metres in diameter and their armament varied according to the ground they had to cover from their fire, varying from one to two machine guns plus two to four grenade-launchers. There were 5 similar cupolas, all in the P.F.L.

Observation cupola. In each fort, an armoured observation post (Poste d'Observation Cuirassé or POC) was modified from the old armoured searchlight. At Boncelles, which had had all its armoured parts scrapped by the Germans at the end of the First World War, the missing searchlight was replaced by the one taken from Flémalle, adapted for a POC. When at a later date Flémalle was modernised a cupola had to be specially built to provide its POC.

The only anti-aircraft armament was a battery of four outdated 7.65mm Maxims emplaced in trenches in the open air near the fort.

In general, the forts were only partly re-armed and most of them were as a result quite weak, a shadow of their former strength. At Boncelles and Embourg, for example, only the four turrets were re-equipped while the 150mm cupola, the two 120mm cupolas and the two 210mm cupolas were all concreted over. These forts were left with only four 75mm guns, having a maximum range of 5.2 kilometres, as offensive armament.

Besides the weakness of their armament, the gun crews had to cope with design faults. In action, the LG cupolas were easily blocked by concrete fragments thrown up by bomb and shell explosions and, even worse, the powered traverse on the 150mm cupolas failed after only a few hours use, leaving the gun crew the job of moving them by hand. A sizeable number of the 'new' guns installed in the turrets and cupolas were ex-German pieces obtained in 1918 as war booty and several proved unserviceable after only a few shots, forcing the gun crew to change the barrel. At Fléron, one 150mm barrel had to be changed on May 14 and another the following day. At Evegnée the barrel change begun on May 18 had still not been completed when the fort surrendered. Some of the 75mm guns also failed early, one barrel blowing up when fired on May 11 at Barchon and another at Fléron the same day.

On August 16, 1914 and May 16, 1940 the fort had succumbed to its besiegers. This is the 150mm cupola half-buried by the debris thrown up from the Stuka raid on May 15 which disabled three of Flémalle's cupolas and four of its turrets. These pilots have come to inspect the damage for themselves.

Four new forts were constructed in the inter-war period to the east of the inner circle of fortresses at Liège to give forward protection — at Aubin-Neufchâteau, Battice, Eben-Emael and Pépinster. This is the moat at the latter fort (also sometimes referred to as Tancrémont) with the central redoubt on the left. Casemate IV can be seen in the background with its three embrasures: a searchlight to the left; a 47mm anti-tank gun in the centre, and a 7.65mm machine gun on the right.

THE NEW FORTS

The four new forts built in the 1930s east of the town at Aubin-Neufchâteau, Battice, Pépinster and Eben-Emael were given much stronger protection, with the command post, the power house, the barracks and the ammunition storage, all located about 30 metres below ground. They were also better armed.

Aubin-Neufchâteau and Pépinster (often referred to as Tancrémont) were wedge-shaped and similar in external layout to the older forts, a central redoubt being surrounded by a moat 15 metres wide and 6 metres deep. The long-range armament installed on the redoubt consisted of two retracting turrets mounting two 75mm guns. For the immediate defence of the fort, three 81mm mortars and several cupolas mounting 7.65mm machine guns were also added. For the close defence, these were supplemented by 47mm anti-tank guns — three at Pépinster and two at Aubin-Neufchâteau — and 7.65mm machine guns firing from embrasures in casemates built at the corners of the moats. At Aubin-Neufchâteau there were also two cupolas each armed with a 47mm anti-tank gun. These casemates in the moats were also equipped with a searchlight embrasure and tubes down which grenades could be dropped to explode in the moat.

Battice and Eben-Emael were larger and more powerful and somewhat different in shape and layout. As in the other forts, the long-range armament was installed on the central redoubt but the defensive armament was mainly provided in blockhouses built facing the polygone-shaped moat.

At Battice, the longe-range 1ère Batterie controlled A-Nord, Block IV and Block VI, each being armed with a retracting turret mounting two 75mm guns, and B-Nord and B-Sud, each having a rotating cupola mounting two 120mm guns. The 2ème Batterie was responsible for the immediate defence of the fort and controlled eight blockhouses armed with 60mm anti-tank guns firing from embrasures, and machine guns firing from embrasures or in armoured cupolas.

The strongest of the new forts, Eben-Emael, was unique for the Albert Canal ran along one of its sides, forming a huge natural water barrier, while another smaller moat filled with water was dug between the canal and Block II. From Block I an anti-tank ditch with a wall about four metres high surrounded the rest of the fort. The 1ère Batterie controlled the four casemates with triple 75mm gun embrasures; Maastricht 1 and Maastricht 2, facing northwards towards Maastricht, and Visé 1 and Visé 2, southwards on Visé. It also controlled two retracting turrets each with two 75mm guns, Coupole Nord on the top of the fort, and Coupole Sud on Block V. Almost in the centre of the fort was Coupole 120, a revolving cupola housing two 120mm guns.

The 2ème Batterie, intended for defence of the fort itself, controlled Mi-Nord and Mi-Sud on top of the fort and the seven casemates set in the surrounding anti-tank wall. These were referred to as Block I, Block II, Block IV, Block V and Block VI, with Canal Nord and Canal Sud facing the Albert Canal almost at water level. Each of these nine positions was armed with several machine guns, one or two 60mm anti-tank guns and contained observation cupolas and searchlights.

The armoured turrets could be raised or lowered at will. *Left:* This is one of the two 75mm turrets at Pépinster photographed by the Germans in 1940. *Right:* Pictured by JP today! The 75mm turret of Block II.

ARMAMENT

The basic armament of the New Forts was as follows:

75mm turret. Two 75mm guns mounted in a retractable and rotating turret 3.5 metres in diameter. These guns, a Belgian '75 Modèle 1934' adaptation of a Bofors design, fired a 6kg shell up to 10 kilometres. There were nine 75mm turrets in the four new forts.

120mm cupola. Two 120mm guns mounted in a rotating cupola about 6 metres in diameter. These guns, based on the Belgian 120mm field gun of 1931, could lob a 20kg shell to 16.9 kilometres. There were three 120mm cupolas, two at Battice and one at Eben-Emael.

47mm cupola. A 47mm anti-tank gun mounted in a fixed armoured cupola about 2.5 metres in diameter. Two only of which were sited at Aubin-Neufchâteau.

Mi cupola. Two Maxim 7.65mm machine guns mounted in a fixed armoured cupola about 2.5 metres in diameter. There were 26 such cupolas but none at Eben-Emael.

75mm embrasure. A 75mm gun — an adaptation of the 75mm Belgian field gun — was installed in four casemates with three guns each, just at Eben-Emael. This gun could fire a 6kg shell up to 11 kilometres.

81mm embrasure. Three 81mm mortars were installed in a concrete casemate in the middle of the forts of Aubin-Neufchâteau and Pépinster.

60mm embrasure. 60mm anti-tank

One of the two 120mm cupolas at Battice pictured after the battle.

guns armed the defensive blockhouses at Battice and Eben-Emael. There were 16 embrasures all told.

47mm embrasure. 47mm anti-tank guns armed the defence casemates of Aubin-Neufchâteau and Pépinster. There were 7 such embrasures.

Machine gun embrasure. 7.65mm machine guns also armed these casemates and there being 44 embrasures in the four forts.

Observation cupola. Either simply for observation or also to enable a light machine being fired from the embrasure; in total, there were 22 in the new forts.

The new forts were not protected by strong anti-aircraft defences and the only armament provided to repel attack from the air was a battery of six outdated machine guns (ex-WWI 7.65mm Maxims) sited in exposed trenches near the fort or, in the case of Eben-Emael and Battice, on the top of it.

	2×75mm turret	2×120mm cupola	47mm cupola	7.65mm MG cupola	Observation cupola	81mm embrasure	75mm embrasure	60mm embrasure	47mm embrasure	7.65mm MG embrasure
Eben-Emael	2	1			11		12	12		24
Battice	3	2		11	4				4	10
Neufchâteau	2		2	7	4	3			3	5
Pépinster	2			8	3	3			4	5

THE NEW FORTS

The 'new fort' of Battice. Today the fortress has been preserved in fighting order and is open to public view. This is the 75mm turret of Block VI in its retracted position. This same block was also armed with two Mi cupolas.

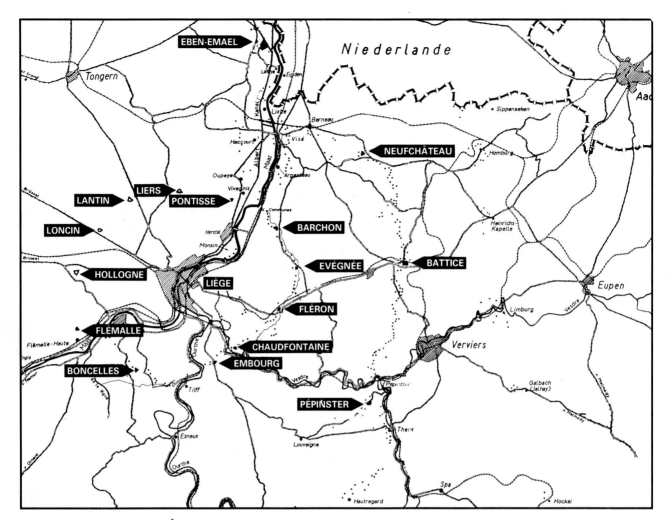

'Festung Lüttich' as depicted in the *Denkschrift über die Belgischer Landesbefestigung*. P.F.L. 1 — the eastern defensive line running from Eben-Emael to Pépinster — can be seen as well as P.F.L. 2 between Barchon and Boncelles.

THE POSITION FORTIFIÉE DE LIÈGE

The P.F.L., which was the major element in the Belgian defensive plan prior to the Second World War, consisted of four lines. In order, from east to west, the first — P.F.L. 1 — was based on the four new forts at Eben-Emael, Aubin-Neufchâteau, Battice and Pépinster. In between the forts, a line of 179 casemates for machine guns but also for 47mm anti-tank guns were built at intervals; from Eben-Emael in the north to the Ourthe valley south of Pépinster. Because of budgetary restraints, the construction of two more forts — one at Sougné-Remouchamps and another near Grand-Rechain — was cancelled; they should have defended the Amblève valley from where the 251. Infanterie-Division attacked the P.F.L. in May 1940.

P.F.L. 2 was based on the six modernised forts on the right bank of the Meuse, with 61 blockhouses for machine guns and observation strung out between the forts with an anti-tank barrier in front.

P.F.L. 3 was the line of 8 strong casemates built to cover the roads east of the town from Jupille on the Meuse to Angleur on the Ourthe south of Liège. These casemates, which were designed to stop any advance on Liège along the main roads, were armed with machine guns and 47mm anti-tank guns and were protected by anti-tank defences.

P.F.L. 4 built on the left bank of the Meuse, was based on the two modernised forts at Pontisse and Flémalle with 10 blockhouses for machine guns. North of the town there were another 31 casemates lining the Meuse and another 9 on the Albert Canal.

The forts of the P.F.L. were manned by men of the Régiment de Forteresse de Liège which had been established in 1928. On the eve of the Second World War, the R.F.L. was under the command of Colonel Maurice Modard and consisted of five groups:

1er Groupe: two batteries at Eben-Emael,

2ème Groupe: three batteries at Pontisse, Barchon and Aubin-Neufchâteau,

3ème Groupe: two batteries at Evegnée and Fléron,

4ème Groupe: five batteries at Chaudfontaine, Embourg, Boncelles, Flémalle and Pépinster,

5ème Groupe: two batteries at Battice.

The R.F.L. was subordinated directly to the IIIème Corps d'Armée under Général Joseph de Krahe whose headquarters were at Liège. After November 1939 the 1er Groupe at Eben-Emael was tactically attached to the Ier Corps d'Armée.

POSITION FORTIFIÉE DE LIEGE (P.F.L.)

	1×150mm cupola	2×105mm cupola	1×105mm cupola	Mi-LG cupola	1×75mm turret
Pontisse		1			4
Barchon	2	2		1	4
Evegnée	1		2	1	3
Fléron	2	2		1	4
Chaudfontaine	1		2	1	4
Embourg					4
Boncelles					4
Flémalle	1	1		1	4

THE POSITION FORTIFIÉE DE NAMUR

The forts of the P.F.N. were manned by men of the Régiment de Forteresse de Namur which had been created in 1932, four years after the R.F.L., an indication of how the P.F.N. ranked second in priority after the P.F.L. Just prior to the war the R.F.N. was under the command of Lieutenant-Colonel Adolphe Drion and consisted of two groups:

1er Groupe: four batteries at Marchovelette, Maizeret, Andoy and Dave,

2ème Groupe: three batteries at Saint-Héribert, Malonne and Suarlée.

The R.F.N. was subordinated directly to the VIIème Corps d'Armée of Général Georges Deffontaine, whose headquarters were at Namur.

POSITION FORTIFIÉE DE NAMUR (P.F.N.)					
	2×105mm cupola	2×75mm cupola	Mi cupola	LG cupola	1×75mm turret
Marchovelette		1		2	3
Maizeret	1			2	4
Andoy		1	1	1	4
Dave		1	1	1	3
Saint-Héribert		1	2		4
Malonne		1		2	4
Suarlée		1	2		4

Another plan from the German intelligence report which was produced by the staff of OKH in 1941. The modernised forts of 'Festung Namur' are drawn in black, while those which were the original ones were outlined only. The individual casemates and blockhouses are shown with black dots.

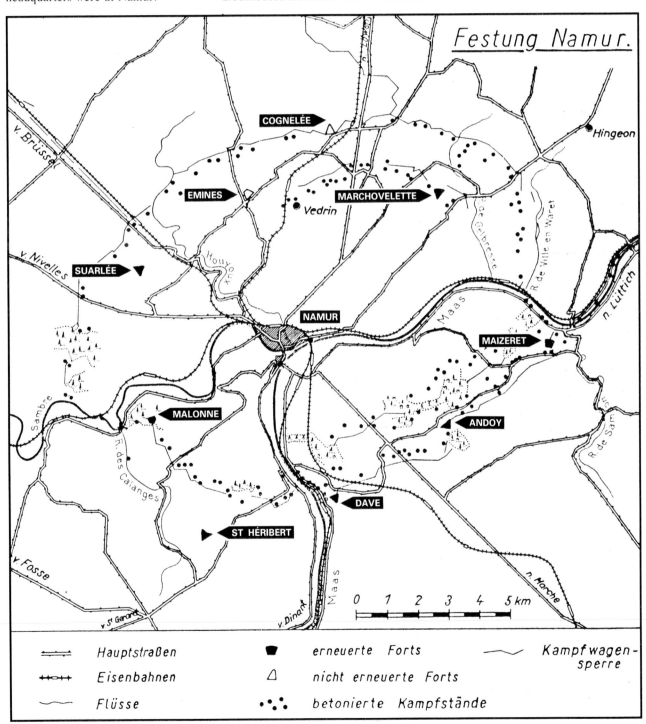

THE SECOND WORLD WAR

The German strategy, Fall Gelb, had placed the 'Schwerpunkt' — Gruppe von Kleist — in the Ardennes, south of the P.F.N., with the intention of crossing the Meuse in France at Sedan, with a feint by the XVI. Armeekorps in the Gembloux gap to the north of the P.F.L. The P.F.N. had no way of intervening with the advance of Gruppe von Kleist, far out of range, but the guns of Eben-Emael did cover the Meuse and Albert Canal crossings in the sector assigned to the XVI. Armeekorps. However, unlike 1914, this time German forces did not hesitate in violating the neutrality of the Netherlands, whose territory lay within a few hundred metres of Eben-Emael, and this enabled them to extend their base of operation for the Meuse crossings. Consequently the Liège sector did not have the importance that it had held in 1914.

An airborne assault by Sturmabteilung Koch was planned to take out bridges on the Albert Canal and Eben-Emael which was thus the only Belgian fort to be singled out for individual attention. The P.F.L. and P.F.N. lay at the junction between the 6. Armee of Heeresgruppe B and the 4. Armee of Heeresgruppe A, the boundary between the two army groups running along Vesdre, then the Meuse between Liege and Namur, and finally the Sambre. The capture of the Belgian forts of both Liège and Namur was the task of either of these armies, depending on which bank of the river the forts lay.

On the left wing of the 6. Armee, after the crossing of the Meuse by the panzers of XVI. Armeekorps and their advance towards the Gembloux gap,

Following the successful capture of the bridges over the Albert Canal, and the capture of the 'new' fortress at Eben-Emael (see page 78), the 6. Armee pressed straight on westwards, completely bypassing Liège to the north. On the army's right wing, the XXVII. Armeekorps probed the northern flank of the P.F.L. These men of the 251. Infanterie-Division watch the effect of an explosive charge detonated above the entrance of Boncelles at 12.30 p.m. on May 16.

the XXVII. Armeekorps had to break through the Liège defences east of the town. It was then to advance towards Namur moving north of the Meuse.

South of Liège and the Meuse river, on the right of the 4. Armee, following the panzers of XV. Armeekorps who were aiming at crossing the Meuse at Dinant, the V. Armeekorps was to advance along the Amblève valley, then across the Ourthe to take the southern wing of the Liège defences before advancing towards Namur on the southern bank of the Meuse.

When we visited the fort in 1986, the in-filling of the moat had just begun, and today all has disappeared beneath a new housing development.

The garrisons of the fortresses of the P.F.L. and P.F.N. were full of confidence in the strength of their positions which were deemed impregnable. However, just as the forts of the Middle Ages had succumbed to new methods of warfare, so even their 20th century versions in steel and concrete were to prove inadequate for modern mechanised attack. Anti-aircraft defences were wholly inadequate, relying on men exposing themselves in a single open position on the top of the fort. Even then, their only weapons were outdated Maxim machine guns. There were no obstacles to prevent landings and at Eben-Emael the gliders had touched down before the AA machine guns had had a chance to open fire!

THE BATTLE OF THE P.F.L.

Apart for the surprise attack by Sturmabteilung Koch on Eben-Emael, May 10 was relatively uneventful for the P.F.L. In the early hours, the various garrisons were put at action stations and at Battice, the fort commander, Major Henry Bovy, currently left in hospital at Liège, immediately left to return to his post, reaching the fort at 4.30 a.m. One hour later, having just ordered the fort to fire its first salvoes, he collapsed and died of a heart attack, his place being taken by his second in command, Commandant Georges Guéry.

Pontisse, Barchon and Evegnée then opened up at Eben-Emael, followed by Aubin-Neufchâteau and Fléron, which started firing at various pre-selected targets. Pépinster, however, did not begin until the evening.

During the night the IIIème Corps d'Armée withdrew across the Meuse leaving the forts south of the river out on a limb. Early next morning, the commander of the R.F.L., Colonel Modard, arrived at Flémalle with two staff officers to set up his headquarters in the fort.

SATURDAY, MAY 11

In the morning Barchon and Pontisse resumed firing at Eben-Emael; Pontisse opened up at Meuse crossings near Eijsden; Fléron fired in support of Battice; then both Battice and Barchon fired to support Aubin-Neufchâteau. Aubin-Neufchâteau first reported an attack by the Luftwaffe early in the morning and some time later both Barchon and Fléron reported their anti-aircraft machine guns had shot down a German aircraft (possibly the same one). Fléron then destroyed with a few 75mm salvoes the aircraft which had force landed near Saint-Hadelin, about three kilometres to the south.

SUNDAY, MAY 12

Barchon was attacked early in the morning by German infantry, whereupon the fort replied, the attackers being beaten back with the support of covering fire from Pontisse. The same story applied in the evening at Pépinster, but there the attack was not as powerful and was easily repulsed. To discourage its renewal next morning, during the night Chaudfontaine, Fléron and Battice shelled the Mazures Wood just north of Pépinster from where the Germans were thought to have started. Fléron, Pontisse and Pépinster all reported light artillery shelling.

Meanwhile 6. Armee was bypassing Liège to the north, the troops claiming the 'capture' of both Loncin and Lantin — in reality not much of a feat for both forts were actually undefended! The XXVII. Armeekorps reported that all the forts of the P.F.L. appeared to be determined to defend themselves.

MONDAY, MAY 13

The panzer divisions were by now far to the west of the Belgian defences at Liège: to the north leading elements of XVI. Armeekorps were west of Hannut while to the south those of the XV. Armeekorps were crossing the Meuse at Dinant. All the forts of the P.F.L. now reported that they were under artillery fire and that the Luftwaffe had entered the battle, having bombed Evegnée and Fléron.

South of the Vesdre, elements of V. Armeekorps had invested Embourg during the night and the fort suffered a whole day of artillery shelling from 150mm howitzers with light 37mm Pak firing in direct sight at the turrets. At about 10.00 p.m. the Germans tried to rush the fort but their attack was repulsed with the help of supporting fire from Chaudfontaine. During the night Chaudfontaine fired more salvoes to try to eliminate some 37mm guns which were firing at the fort from the Embourg quarry.

And then there were the dive-bombers. The Stukas pounded the forts around Liège from May 13 and inflicted impressive damage, collapsing moats, disabling turrets and cupolas and knocking out ventilation systems. This is Barchon, as seen from a German reconnaissance aircraft, most probably on May 16, two days before the fort capitulated. Although four of the cupolas on the central core appear untouched, the fifth has been affected by two very near misses.

TUESDAY, MAY 14

To make up for the weakness of the forts' anti-aircraft defences, plans had been agreed that in case of Stuka attacks the forts would fire at each other using time-fused shells. This arrangement was first tried out on the morning of May 14 when the Luftwaffe attacked Barchon but it was not really successful and the fort suffered considerable damage as a result.

Artillery fire increased, and in the afternoon the Stukas turned their attention to Pontisse, damaging two 75mm turrets. Flémalle was also bombed during the afternoon and severely damaged although no direct hits were scored on the cupolas or turrets.

WEDNESDAY, MAY 15

While advancing towards Namur on both side of the Meuse, both the XXVII. Armeekorps and V. Armeekorps had detached one division to deal with the forts of the P.F.L. The 223. Infanterie-Division from the former kept pressure to bear on the forts east and north of the town while the 251. Infanterie-Division of the latter moved on those on the southern wing. The Stukas returned and pounded the P.F.L. throughout day, attacking Evegnée and Flémalle, followed by Embourg, Boncelles and Chaudfontaine. The damage was impressive, both Embourg and Chaudfontaine suffering a 75mm turret destroyed. At Flémalle, in spite of anti-aircraft, time-fused shells being fired over it by Fléron and Chaudfontaine, four 75mm turrets were disabled as well as the 150mm cupola, the 105mm cupola and the Mi-LG cupola, leaving the fort impotent.

The day was also critical at Boncelles, where 88mm Flak guns had been brought up during the night and emplaced in the village. The 88s opened up on direct line of sight at each turret as they elevated to fire back at 150mm howitzers which shelled the fort. Within a few minutes, three out of the four 75mm turrets had been disabled, whereupon German infantry advanced only to be turned back by machine gun fire. To discourage any further attack under the cover of darkness, the commander at

At Boncelles, the massive explosion (page 378) killed the fortress commander, Commandant Numa Charlier, whose death forced what remained of the garrison to surrender. *Above:* Here the Belgian medical officer, Lieutenant Alphonse Mousny, accompanies German troops as they call on the defenders to come out with their hands up. *Below:* When Jean-Paul took his comparisons in 1986 he was unaware that he would be one of the last to walk in their footsteps. Now all has gone for ever.

Hands held high, the survivors emerge into the daylight. A few seconds later, the soldier on the extreme right, Soldat Georges Joassin, was shot dead out of hand.

More fortunate were Soldats Joseph Reynders and Henri Bodson, both wounded, seen picking their way carefully past the anti-tank obstacles which blocked the main entrance.

Heavily-armed stormtroopers mill around the entrance while another inspects Turret IV, completely blown from its seating.

In 1986 it was still possible to inspect the damage to the façade of the entrance and see the empty mounting for the turret. Today all that remains of Boncelles is the ventilation tower seen in the background. It is sad that, out of all the forts, Boncelles should be the one to disappear as it had fought well, right to the end.

Boncelles, Commandant Numa Charlier, asked for supporting fire to be laid down from the neighbouring forts of Fléron and Evegnée. Together with a volunteer crew, Commandant Charlier himself helped man Turret II, the only turret still serviceable, which was fired throughout the night.

THURSDAY, MAY 16

In the morning the Stukas returned, and again in the afternoon, attacking Aubin-Neufchâteau, Boncelles, Fléron, Embourg and Chaudfontaine, causing much damage. At Boncelles one of the pilots failed to pull out of his dive and the Stuka crashed just in front of the entrance.

In the morning an heartening message from King Leopold to the trapped R.F.L. was passed to the forts: 'To Colonel Modard, to the officers, NCOs and men of the P.F.L. Let us resist to the end for our country. I am proud of you'.

At 10.20 a.m. Commandant Charlier called a conference at which all the officers were of the opinion that it was now time to capitulate as the fort was almost completely incapacitated. Commandant Charlier argued that there was still one turret serviceable and that the ventilation system was still in running order and called for volunteers to man what was left of the weapons. Twenty-five men stepped forward, the others being told they were free to leave. However those that managed to escape from the ventilation tower were soon

Some of the defenders left via the ventilation tower which had been a prominent target for the German gunners. In the background the houses of Les Communes, a part of Seraing.

The commander of the 251. Infanterie-Division, Generalleutnant Hans Kratzert, arrived at Boncelles on the afternoon of May 16 to congratulate his men. With him is Oberst Siegfried von Stülpnagel, the commander of Infanterie-Regiment 451.

captured a few hundred metres away at the edge of a wood filled with German troops.

At about 11.00 a.m., just after a dive-bombing attack, elements of Inf.Rgt. 451 of the 251. Infanterie-Division pressed home an assault and, taking advantage of the destruction caused by the bombs, they soon succeeded in reaching the central redoubt. Grenades were dropped into the openings of the damaged turrets and a heavy charge was exploded above the entrance. This killed Commandant Charlier, and forced what remained of the garrison to come out. It was about 12.30 a.m. . . . Boncelles being the only Belgian fort not to surrender itself in 1940.

Left: This picture of Lieutenant Alphonse Mousny 'surrendering' was a posed shot taken at the tip of Salient I, as German propaganda later claimed that he was the commander of the fort. *Right:* Quite extraordinarily, the memorial to the garrison erected after the war was sited exactly as if the architect had wanted to match up this picture. Perhaps he did.

At Flémalle, although the fort had been completly incapacitated since the previous evening after the bombing, Commandant Fernand Barbieux had decided to hold on for a French counter-attack that might, he hoped, relieve the P.F.L. Following orders from the IIIème Corps d'Armée, Colonel Modard left the fort from the ventilation tower at midday, hoping to regain Belgian lines; he failed but succeeded in reaching Liège, avoiding capture. The Stukas came back again in the afternoon and artillery shelling resumed, shots being aimed at the ventilation tower causing concrete dust to be vented through the fort. At this stage the fort defence council met and decided on surrender and at 2.30 p.m. a white flag was hoisted and elements of Aufkl.Abt. 223, 223. Infanterie-Division, entered the fort. It was 3.20 p.m. The Germans later reported having taken 206 prisoners.

At Aubin-Neufchâteau, three Germans appeared at the entrance block at about 11.45 a.m. with three Belgian civilians brought as hostages and asked to see the fort commander. Commandant Oscar d'Ardenne agreed to meet them providing the hostages were sent back, which was agreed. Oberstleutnant Siegfried Runge, the commander of the Grenzwacht-Regiment 46, a second-rate unit which had taken on the siege

The Luftwaffe inspects its handiwork. Its attacks had been particularly effective at Flémalle where they knocked out all four turrets and three of the cupolas in attacks on May 15. *Above:* A 500kg bomb has collapsed the retaining wall to the moat near the fort entrance. *Right:* The fracture still remains, enabling Jean Paul to produce the perfect comparison.

of Aubin-Neufchâteau, had come in person to propose 'honourable terms'

but these Commandant d'Ardenne refused to discuss.

The author, right, with Francis Tirtiat beside the gaping hole of what remains of Turret IV at Flémalle.

At Chaudfontaine, south-east of Liège, the fort surrendered on the evening of May 17 after the last serviceable turret had been knocked out. *Above:* The garrison have marched down the hill from the fortress and are assembled in front of the local casino. *Below:* Commandant Raymond Clobert bows his head rather than face the camera.

FRIDAY, MAY 17

The Luftwaffe resumed its attacks during the morning at Barchon, Chaudfontaine, Embourg, Fléron and Evegnée, collapsing the moats, disabling turrets and cupolas, breaking communication lines and damaging the ventilation systems. Fléron was in bad shape with the two 150mm cupolas and two 75mm turrets disabled. Although the two 105mm cupolas were intact, all their ammunition had been spent and it was left with only two serviceable 75mm turrets. In the afternoon Commandant Armand Glinne called on the defence council and a decision was made to evacuate the fort. It was about 5.00 p.m. and elements of Inf.Rgt. 425, 223. Infanterie-Division, soon entered the fort. On the following day, Heeresgruppe B noted that Fléron had surrendered though it had not actually been attacked.

At Chaudfontaine the last serviceable turret, Turret III, was disabled by a bomb at 10.10 a.m. and infantry pressed home their attack immediately after the Stukas left, throwing grenades through the damaged observatory. In the afternoon the defence council met and decided to surrender at 6.25 p.m. It was the same story at Embourg, where three 75mm turrets had been disabled by Stukas. There the white flag was hoisted at 8.00 p.m., both forts being captured by Inf.Rgt. 471 of the 251. Infanterie-Division who reported having taken 183 prisoners at Chaudfontaine and 168 at Embourg.

Meanwhile, Battice continued in support of its neighbours but reported that the barrels of the 75mm guns were wearing out at an alarming rate because of the repeated firing of maximum charges to range up to Aubin-Neufchâteau, Fléron or Chaudfontaine.

Embourg has fallen. Today the crossed-cannon badge of the Régiment de Forteresse de Liège makes a nice link with the past.

SATURDAY, MAY 18

Its mission in the Liège sector having ended with the capture of Boncelles, Chaudfontaine and Embourg, the 251. Infanterie-Division now moved west towards Namur, but further north, in the 6. Armee sector, seven forts of the P.F.L. were still to be taken. By now artillery batteries had been brought forward in greater numbers and, early on May 18, the 223. Infanterie-Division launched an all-out barrage on the four forts still holding out. Four groups of artillery from the division's Art.Rgt. 223, i.e. twelve batteries, were backed up for the occasion by a 420mm heavy mortar from Artillerie-Batterie 820. At 5.00 a.m. the 420mm mortar and two of the batteries opened up on Barchon, while seven batteries fired at Pontisse, two at Evegnée and one at Battice. The Luftwaffe also lent a hand in the morning at Barchon and Pontisse.

At Pontisse where only Turret IV remained serviceable, German infantry — elements of Inf.Rgt. 425, 223. Infanterie-Division — began advancing at about 11.30 a.m. and soon reached the central redoubt, engineers blowing charges in front of the embrasures and opening up with flame-throwers. Barchon fired in mutual support of Pontisse until midday, but it was then itself attacked by Stukas and stopped firing. Commandant Fernand Pire then decided to surrender his fort, a white flag was brought out and Pontisse surrendered at 1.45 p.m. The 223. Infanterie-Division reported later having taken 214 prisoners.

At Barchon, all the turrets and cupolas were disabled save a single 150mm cupola, but Commandant Aimé Pour-

His bags packed, the fort's second-in-command, Lieutenant Jean Schiffers, appears resigned to his fate — whatever that is to be.

baix refused to accept an offer to surrender brought to him at midday. At this refusal, German infantry from Inf.Rgt. 344, 223. Infanterie-Division, opened their assault at 5.00 p.m., blowing charges in front of the embrasures and attacking the defences with flame-throwers. The odds were too much and Commandant Pourbaix was forced to surrender at about 7.00 p.m., the 223. Infanterie-Division taking 297 prisoners.

SUNDAY, MAY 19

Of the fortification ring around Liège, there now only remained one fort in operation: Evegnée. It held out for another day but the pressure built up during the morning, until all firing stopped shortly after midday. Emissaries from Inf.Rgt. 344 then arrived and were met by Commandant Laurent Vanderhaegen; he called the defence council together and all decided to surrender. It was about 2.30 p.m.

Jean Paul was excited to find that the spot in the moat just beside the entrance had changed little; even more so when he discovered that the memorial plaque to the fifteen men killed defending Embourg was mounted right alongside. A fitting comparison to those 'Morts pour la Patrie'.

Namur was heavily bombed on Sunday, May 12 and, soon after the Luftwaffe had departed, a photographer from the French 9ème Armée was out and about the city recording the damage. He took this picture in the Place Léopold where a garage was still on fire.

THE BATTLE OF THE P.F.N.

The first days of the German offensive were uneventful as far as the P.F.N. was concerned, except for patrols which were sent in search of German paratroopers reported (wrongly as it happened) to have been dropped in the sector. Lessons had already been learned from the loss of Eben-Emael and some of the forts deployed men out on their central redoubt to oppose any assault from the sky.

The battle opened up for the P.F.N. on May 14, when Malonne was bombed by the Luftwaffe, suffering heavy damage and the loss of a 75mm turret. The same day, Maizeret, Andoy and Dave cupolas saw great activity, firing at men from XV. Armeekorps who were crossing the Meuse in the sector of Houx. The VIIème Corps d'Armée withdrew on May 15, leaving the forts exposed and the pressure on them soon mounted. The ventilation tower at Andoy was assaulted in the evening, then Marchovelette, whereupon both Maizeret and Andoy were called in for support. Following orders from the VIIème Corps d'Armée, Lieutenant-Colonel Drion left Namur with the staff of the R.F.N. and withdrew to Estinnes-au-Val.

MAY 16-18

North of the Meuse, the XXVII. Armeekorps had moved on Namur. Artillery was brought up during the night at Marchovelette and shelling aimed at the ventilation tower began at 7.00 a.m. The fort's 75mm turrets fired back and, together with support from Suarlée and Maizeret, they managed to silence some of the German guns.

Further west, on the northern bank of the Sambre, Suarlée reported both the departure of the last French troops, who were acting in liaison, and an attack by the Luftwaffe. In the evening the fort repulsed an assault by the 269. Infanterie-Division which twice sent in attacks against the vulnerable ventilation tower.

On May 17 an officer of the R.F.L. arrived at Maizeret and was able to explain the tactics that the Germans had used against the Liège forts, this information being circulated to all the P.F.N. forts. The commander of Maizeret, Commandant Léon Hambenne, then put forward a proposal to assemble a combined force from the various forts to mount a raid down into Namur where German troops were reported. However the idea proved impracticable and was not put into effect.

South of Namur, the 211. Infanterie-Division of V. Armeekorps had closed in around the forts, sending forward parlementaries at Dave and Saint-Héribert, although receiving no response.

On the morning of May 18 the Luftwaffe attacked Suarlée and disabled two turrets and one cupola, collapsing parts of the outer wall. At Marchovelette three civilians reached the fort at about 9.30 a.m. with a message from the commander of the third battalion of Inf.Rgt. 469, Major Otto Breustedt, demanding, in poorly-worded French, that the fort be surrendered at midday (Belgian time). If it did, the garrison was promised fair treatment 'as prisoners of war in the most amiable way' but, if it refused, the fort would be destroyed by Stukas. There was no response and the German shelling resumed just after midday.

In the afternoon an heartening message from the King was passed to the attention of the soldiers of the P.F.N., exhorting them to fight 'to the end for our country'.

Maizeret and Andoy brought their guns to bear on the batteries shelling Marchovelette, but their support was weak for Andoy was firing at the limit of its 75mm guns range while Maizeret could only use its 105mm cupola, for which the ammunition supply was already very low. At Marchovelette, Turrets II and III were soon disabled, German infantry assaulted the fort and reached the redoubt. They destroyed the LG cupolas, blew charges in front of the embrasures, and attacked the defences in the moats with flame-throwers. Commandant Georges De Lombaert called on the fort defence council and Marchovelette surrendered at 8.00 p.m., the 269. Infanterie-Division having captured 221 prisoners.

Two days later the battle for the nine forts of the Position Fortifiée de Namur began when Malonne was attacked by dive-bombers. Andoy and Dave were also in action, trying to stop the Germans crossing the Meuse near Houx, a dozen kilometres to the south, at the extreme range of their 75mm cupolas.

MAY 19-21

At Suarlée the crew had worked hard to repair the damage caused by the bombing and succeeded to bring Turret III back into firing order. However the fort remained silent and, at about 10.00 a.m., a German officer and two soldiers approached, possibly believing that the garrison had withdrawn during the night. They reached the central redoubt without even being challenged and, when they were, the Germans demanded the capitulation of the fort. Though Commandant Ferdinand Tislair refused to agree to the offer, nevertheless he was suitably impressed and Suarlée remained silent for two hours before the same German officer — from Inf.Rgt. 469 of 269. Infanterie-Division — returned in the afternoon with a larger group, waving a white flag. Bringing a

Division, at 8.00 a.m. moved up under the cover of a smoke screen. The fort returned the fire and, together with support from Andoy and Dave, succeeded in halting both this attack and another a little while afterwards. Just before 9.00 a.m. 88mm Flak opened fire directly at the turrets and cupolas, knocking them out one by one until the last, Turret IV, was destroyed. As the ventilation system was failing, the fort's defence council was then called together and Commandant Léon L'Entrée decided to surrender at about midday after all documents, instruments, communication and power systems still in working order had been destroyed. Generalmajor Kurt Renner, the commander of the 211. Infanterie-Division, then handed him a document asserting that, 'in view of the brave

MAY 22-24

At Maizeret, both turrets and cupolas successfully fired at German troop movements, as did those at Dave although the latter fort suffered from return German artillery shelling.

At Andoy, 88mm Flak and 37mm Pak guns brought forward during the night began firing at each of the fort's turrets as they raised to fire. These returned the fire, Dave brought in supporting fire, and this combination succeeded in silencing these guns. During the evening, under the protection of a white flag, the Germans spent several hours in searching for their wounded.

At Andoy the shelling resumed at first light with an increased violence, the turrets and cupolas being disabled one after another. However there was no infantry follow-up attack until emis-

Early on May 21, the 211. Infanterie-Division assaulted Saint-Héribert, artillery battering the turrets one by one throughout the morning. With all his guns out and the ventilation system failing, Commandant Léon L'Entrée decided he had no option but to surrender. The following day members of the divisional staff inspected the damage. Here they are examining the Mi cupola. On the left is the POC observatory with one of the twin 75mm cupolas on the right.

written surrender demand, the Germans managed to succeed in misleading Commandant Tislair that the whole fort had been mined. Tislair thereupon signed the surrender at 3.15 p.m., an act which led to him being one of the few fort commanders found guilty by the Belgian Commission set up after the war to examine the reasons for the surrender of the various fortresses.

On May 20 the V. Armeekorps brought forward artillery reinforcements — the first battery of schwere Artillerie-Abteilung 667, equipped with 150mm howitzers, together with I./Flak-Regiment 19, comprising three batteries of 88mm and two of 20mm.

May 21 saw the 211. Infanterie-Division advancing on Saint-Héribert and Malonne. After a violent artillery barrage on Saint-Héribert, infantry from Inf.Rgt. 317, 211. Infanterie-

defence of his fort', Commandant L'Entrée would be allowed to keep his personal sidearm.

At Malonne, under cover of darkness and early morning fog, infantry from Inf.Rgt. 365, 211. Infanterie-Division, approached the fort, crossed the moat partly filled with earth and concrete thrown up by the bombing and reached the redoubt. Machine gun fire from the defenders failed to dislodge them, but fire from Andoy and Dave did. As a result 88mm Flak were brought to bear at 1.30 p.m. which soon disabled Turrets I and III, followed by the LG cupola. The guns were then turned on the ventilation tower causing choking dust to be drawn down into the fort. Thus incapacitated, after having taken the advice of the defence council, Commandant Edgard Demaret surrendered Malonne at 2.15 p.m. on May 21.

saries arrived at the fort at 4.00 p.m. with a surrender offer, announcing the capture of Saint-Héribert and Malonne and the occupation of Namur. The message acknowledged that 'You, my Commandant, and your soldiers had done their duty' but gave Capitaine Auguste Dégehet only half an hour to surrender his fort. He answered that he needed an hour to discuss this with his defence council, which was given. Faced with the fact that the fort was left with only one serviceable 75mm turret, but having no ammunition, it was decided that there was no other option but to surrender. This was carried into force at 5.30 p.m., but not until all weapons and equipment had been destroyed and the ammunition magazine flooded.

At Maizeret the shelling had also resumed at first light on May 23 with the usual 88mm Flak fired point-blank at

Malonne surrendered on the afternoon of the 21st, although these pictures were taken some days later when both captors and garrison had left. *Left:* On the skyline above the entrance can be seen the observation cupola and the two LG cupolas. *Right:* **The fort has been abandoned for years and is now completely overgrown.**

the cupolas and turrets. Maizeret had to fight back alone for Andoy was itself under attack and could not give support while Dave was out of range. Cupolas and turrets were incapacitated one after another until finally Turret I remained the only serviceable weapon. Commandant Léon Hambenne thought of blowing up the whole fort but the ventilation gallery proved to be too small to afford protection to the garrison and the idea was dropped. An attempt to escape from the gallery was thwarted by the Germans and the fort surrendered at 7.00 p.m., all its weapons and equip-

ment having been destroyed. Both these forts had been captured by elements of Inf.Rgt. 317 of 211. Infanterie-Division.

Dave had also suffered from artillery for the whole day and by evening most of its turrets had been badly damaged. The few still serviceable had little, if any, ammunition left and there was only food for one day. An offer of surrender from the Germans, with exactly the same wording of the document brought to Andoy a few hours earlier arrived, but instead the names of Maizeret and Andoy had been added to the list of the

forts which had surrendered. This arrived at 8.45 p.m. but the Belgians wrote back that before answering they wanted to know when Suarlée and Marchovelette had surrendered.

During the night elements from Inf.Rgt. 317 had renewed the attack and by the morning of May 24 they were close to the fort. The ventilation system showed signs of failing and Capitaine Ferdinand Noel decided to surrender after all equipment and weapons had been destroyed. It was at 10.00 a.m. The last fort of the P.F.N. had surrendered.

Left: **In the moat, on the wall facing the entrance, a German photographer pictured this triumphant inscription asserting the capture of Malonne by the second battalion of Infanterie-Regiment 365. (Hülle stood for Oberstleutnant Hülle, the** regimental commander.) *Right:* **At a later date, possibly when the fortress was recaptured in 1944, the wording was obliterated by somewhat violent means, yet amazingly part of the Swastika sign can still be seen.**

THE LAST BATTLES

East of Liège, contact between Battice and Neufchâteau had been lost since May 17, cutting off the latter from the 2ème Groupe on which it depended. The commander of Neufchâteau, Commandant Oscar d'Ardenne, thereupon asked for it to be attached to the 3ème Groupe, a switch which was agreed on May 18 by the group's staff at Évegnée.

On the morning of May 18 a German appeared at the access ramp at Pépinster in the company of the commanders of Embourg and Chaudfontaine which had surrendered the previous day, Commandants Hubert Jaco and Raymond Clobert. Machine guns in Block I opened up at them, and the party turned back in haste but not before Commandant Clobert had been wounded.

On May 19 the last fort of the P.F.L. 2 at Évegnée, surrendered leaving the three forts of P.F.L. 1 east of Liège, against which the 223. Infanterie-Division had now deployed a strong artillery force, fighting in a lost cause.

At Battice (one of the new forts), both ends of the moat debouched into the railway cutting which formed the fort's northern side. The openings were protected by a line of obstacles but they were obviously not as secure as a sunken ditch. This German picture was taken from the top of Block I of the western end — the block on the left is the entrance block.

Battice held out until 6.45 a.m. on May 22 when, acting on a vote of 16-3 in favour of surrender, Commandant Guéry handed the fort over to Infanterie-Regiment 385. *Above:* A bomb has scored a direct hit on the track. In the background Block II which was sited to cover the railway cutting. *Below:* A single line still survives although it shows no sign of recent use.

MONDAY, MAY 20

Early in the morning, Oberstleutnant Runge returned to the entrance at Aubin-Neufchâteau, this time accompanied by a monk of Austrian origin from the nearby Val Dieu Abbey. However Commandant d'Ardenne refused to accept the letter offered to him and the two left. Heavy shelling recommenced with increasing force until about 3.00 p.m. when an all out assault was launched, with German engineers being reported trying to scale the moat walls. The fort fired back with every weapon at its disposal and the agreed code-word 'Tz-Inf' was sent to Battice whose 120mm and 75mm guns opened up in support of Aubin-Neufchâteau. The assault was beaten back but was renewed at 3.30 p.m., and again at 4.20 p.m., followed by a Stuka attack which pounded the fort. At 5.30 p.m. Germans were reported entering Block C-2 whereupon Commandant d'Ardenne immediately ordered it to be blown up.

Battice was also shelled and bombed throughout the afternoon and by evening Heeresgruppe B reported that the attacks mounted by the 223. Infanterie-Division against Aubin-Neufchâteau and Battice had both failed. The report stated also that, in view of the current tactical situation, any further attacks were 'superfluous'.

TUESDAY, MAY 21

At Aubin-Neufchâteau, shelling had not ceased throughout the entire night but the tempo greatly increased in the morning and the Luftwaffe added their contribution around 10.30 a.m., heavily bombing the fort. The turret of Block 2 was damaged beyond repair and was then blown up by its crew. In Block M the mortar embrasures were blocked by pieces of concrete and at 2.30 p.m. the block was destroyed by its crew, as was the turret on Block I.

German infantry pressed on, attacking Block C-1 and the entrance block with flame-throwers, but when support was requested from Battice, there was

Commandant Oscar d'Ardenne, the commander of Aubin-Neufchâteau, shakes hands with Oberstleutnant Siegfried Runge in front of the shattered door of the entrance block just after the surrender of the fort on the afternoon of May 21.

no answer to the emergency 'Tz-Inf' call for help. A final message of thanks and farewell was then sent to Battice.

Commandant d'Ardenne called the defence council together at 3.00 p.m. and, although the gravity of the situation was apparent to all, it was agreed to fire back for as long as the entrance held. The reserves of food, cigarettes and clothing were distributed among the garrison and Commandant d'Ardenne addressed the men who were still in good spirits. However by 4.45 p.m. the last grenades had been expended in the defence of the fort entrance, and a white flag was pushed out followed by Commandant d'Ardenne. He climbed out over the shattered concrete to be helped down the other side by a German officer. It was about 5.00 p.m.

Oberstleutnant Runge then arrived, soon followed by Generalleutnant Paul-Willi Körner, the commander of the 223. Infanterie-Division. Körner addressed his men — elements of Inf.Rgt. 344 — assembled outside the blockhouse and then warmly congratulated Commandant d'Ardenne for the stubborn defence of his fort. In turn, the Belgian asked if 24 hours of rest could be granted to his men before they left for their prisoner-of-war camp to which the Germans agreed.

At Battice heavy shelling had begun at 5.00 a.m., which continued throughout the day with 88mm guns aimed direct at the various turrets and cupolas. The Luftwaffe lent a hand in the afternoon, one bomb penetrating Block I before exploding. This hit ignited explosive charges inside and the block erupting in flames, killing 26 of the crew.

At 4.45 p.m., news came over the radio that Aubin-Neufchâteau had surrendered but although Battice had been shelled all day, by nightfall the fort was still in action. The three 75mm turrets were serviceable, although some of them could not be traversed in certain directions, and of the 120mm cupolas, that on Block B-Nord was still working

while only one gun remained fireable in the one on Block B-Sud. However the fort's 2ème Batterie had been badly damaged: Block I had been destroyed and most of the others covering the moat had their fields of fire badly restricted by pieces of fallen concrete and earth.

At 9.00 p.m. the indefatigable Oberstleutnant Runge arrived at the entrance with Commandant d'Ardenne, the commander of Aubin-Neufchâteau, as interpreter. The defence council agreed to meet them although Commandant d'Ardenne was not required for Commandant Guéry could speak German. Runge proposed a truce until 6.00 a.m. next morning which was accepted. During the night the opportunity was taken to rescue those trapped in Block I and the four gravely wounded were extricated from the outside and taken back inside the fort. Two died later of their wounds.

In reporting the capture of Aubin-Neufchâteau later that evening, the commander of Heeresgruppe B, Generaloberst Fedor von Bock, made known

A shot for the fräuleins back home. Victorious troops of Regiment 344 crowd on top of the entrance block after its capture to view the proceedings going on below.

And our author poses for his souvenir snapshot after capturing Aubin-Neufchâteau yet again — although this time on film.

that 'in order to spare blood' he had ordered that further efforts to take the two forts still holding out at Battice and Pépinster be stopped, the troops having only to sit tight and wait for their inevitable capitulation.

MAY 22-28

As far as Battice was concerned this was not to be delayed for much longer for the defence council had met at 1.00 a.m. and the decision to surrender had been agreed: 16 votes in favour with 3 against. Demolition having been completed, Battice surrendered at 6.45 a.m., to be taken over by men of Inf.Rgt. 385, 223. Infanterie-Division.

The Germans wasted no time and Commandant Guéry was immediately driven over to Pépinster to accompany German emissaries who approached the fort in the afternoon only to be turned back at the entrance. In the evening Heeresgruppe B noted that after the capitulation of Pépinster, expected within the next few hours, 223. Infanterie-Division would be free for further operations in France.

Then the troops fell in to be addressed by their commanding officer who no doubt thanked them for a job well done.

Left: **Generalleutnant Paul-Willi Körner, the divisional commander, also congratulated his adversary, Commandant d'Ardenne** *right* **on his magnificent defence. On the left, wearing the Pour le Mérite, is the roving negotiator, Oberstleutnant Runge.**

However Pépinster was not to surrender as early the Germans had hoped but the tactical significance of this lone fort fighting a lost battle was nil. The 223. Infanterie-Division was moved west regardless, the ring around the fort being left to a secondary unit, the MG-Sperrbataillon 7, attached to the 251. Infanterie-Division.

Since the light attack on May 12, Pépinster had not been assaulted by infantry. It had only been attacked by odd Luftwaffe aircraft, and had only been lightly shelled; thus the fort had suffered only minimal damage and all its armament remained serviceable.

With the fort bypassed, the days passed uneventfully until midday on May 28 when Commandant Abel Devos sent a message to the Belgian High Command and asked for instructions. The only reply he received before communication went dead was: 'Received your message at 12.00 hours'. That evening the defence council met and agreed that the fort should capitulate the next morning.

The picture of the troops on parade was taken looking south. Today the comparison is marred only by the changes wrought by modern agricultural methods which have led to the expansion of field sizes and the demise of hedgerows.

Another fortress inspection tour — this time by a group of Wehrmacht officers visiting Pépinster (another of the new forts), and the last of the Belgian fortresses to give up. Bypassed on May 12 and largely left to its own devices, a

watching brief was maintained by Sperrbataillon 7 for the next two weeks as the fighting moved on westwards. Pépinster, or Tancrémont as it is sometimes called, held out until May 29, more than 24 hours after the formal hour of capitulation.

WEDNESDAY, MAY 29

The following morning Commandant Devos met a German envoy, General-leutnant Karl Spang, in an abandoned house at Tancrémont. Spang at first harangued Commandant Devos, reproaching him for what the Germans saw as a violation of the armistice already signed by King Leopold. Devos, fearing a German trick, held out until Spang swore that the King had surrendered the whole of the Belgian Army and agreed to confirm this in writing. No demolitions were carried out and at 11.00 a.m. on May 29 the last fighting element of the Belgian Army surrendered.

Fighting rearguard actions far from where the decisive battles were being fought, the Belgian forts had resisted, with only the odd exception, until the damage suffered had made them unable to keep on fighting. On May 29 afternoon, when Generaloberst Walter von Reichenau, the commander of the 6. Armee, met King Leopold in his Palace at Bruges, he praised particularly the 'excellent behaviour of the [Belgian] forts'.

Pépinster-Tancrémont came through the battle largely unscathed. This is the access to Block P — the main air intake — and the 'war' entrance to the fort. The block had an observation cupola and two light machine gun embrasures for its own defence.

Left: The same German inspection team pictured beside one of the three camouflaged machine gun cupolas with which Block III was equipped. Right: We were fortunate to be able to include in our comparison ex-Soldat Joseph Natalis of the Regiment de

Forteresse de Liège in front of the Mi cupola in which he had been on duty for those twenty fateful days in May 1940. Today he is one of the volunteers who devote much spare time to the preservation of the fort, now on regular public display.

The 7ème Armée on the Somme

The new 7ème Armée, created on May 17 with units brought back from the north and troops hastily transferred from the south-east, got on with the task of extending westwards the front established behind the Aisne by the 6ème Armée. At first, the army was nothing more than Général Frère and his small staff but they were soon informed of the assignment of the 23ème Division d'Infanterie and the 3ème D.L.I. and, in due course, another five divisions joined the army. The staff set up its headquarters at Amiens, the commander of the XXIVème Corps d'Armée, Général François Fougère, arriving that evening from Longwy with his chief-of-staff, followed by the commander of the Ier

Corps d'Armée, Général Théodord Sciard, who arrived from Belgium with his staff. On May 19 the army had two divisions in hand and the first elements of the 19ème Division d'Infanterie were detraining near Roye and the 4ème D.I.C. near Breteuil. The arrival of the 7ème D.I.N.A. was also imminent in the Montdidier area.

Like the 6ème Armée to the south-east, the army was given some time to prepare its positions as the German units were aiming for the Channel and not southwards. In the German textbook of 'Blitzkrieg' war, each panzer division was quickly replaced by motorised divisions as they advanced westwards, these in turn being relieved by infantry units. As the war machine

rolled on westwards, the process was repeated. At this stage, therefore, the French forces merely lined the southern banks of rivers and canals which the Germans did not try to cross in force, except at a number of bridgeheads in preparation for the next phase of the offensive.

On May 19, the Groupe d'Armées No. 3 was transferred from the quiet French right wing to take charge of the defence of the Aisne and Somme rivers with the 6ème and 7ème Armées. The 8ème Armée there was then subordinated to Groupe d'Armées No. 2. On May 20, Général Weygand met the commander of Groupe d'Armées No. 3, Général Antoine Besson, personally to explain his task.

Top: **Although the motorised elements like this Unic tractor and 47mm Modèle 1937 anti-tank gun could travel the 350** kilometres or so in one or two days, the horsed elements *above* were much slower, taking up to five days to arrive.

Amiens, some 75 kilometres up river from the sea, was a key objective on the Somme and had fallen on May 20. The 7ème D.I.C. counter-attacked south of the town on May 23 but came up against strong oposition and the assault had to be called off after several S-35s of the 7ème Cuirassiers (which was support-ing the infantry) had been disabled. *Left:* Dr Pierre Vasselle, a local keen amateur photographer and historian, took this picture of one of the Somuas lying near Dury on the west side of the N1. *Right:* With little to identify the spot we were lucky that the same small house has survived.

MAY 20-22

The 7ème Armée was hastily extending its line to the north-west, but in doing so was experiencing increasing difficulties. When the trains bringing in the 7ème D.I.C. approached Amiens on the morning of May 20, it was apparent that the 1. Panzer-Division was already threatening the town. As a result the division had to detrain to the west and take up positions facing north. The 4ème D.I.C. was on the right but the situation on the left was badly confused as the German threat had forced the 5ème D.I.C., bound for the army's left wing, to detrain far to the south. It was known that German forces had crossed the Somme, but how strong these were and how far they had advanced was not yet clear. In fact, the 2. Panzer-Division was at Abbeville, its advance elements reaching the coast at the mouth of the Somme that evening.

After a quick refit, what remained available of the French mobile units was hurriedly sent to the Somme. On May 21 the 3ème D.L.C. was subordinated to the 7ème Armée, as were the 2ème D.L.C. and the 5ème D.L.C. during the next few days. These three cavalry divisions had been in action in Belgium or Luxembourg since May 10 and had already sustained from 15 to 20 percent losses before they were ordered west-

The 7ème D.I.C. launched a second attack in the same area four days later, five battalions of infantry being supported by Renault D-2s of the 19ème B.C.C. and Somua S-35s of the 7ème Cuirassiers. Dury was recaptured but the losses were heavy. This Renault 'Marignan' of Lieutenant Averlon was also photographed by Pierre Vasselle just north of the village.

wards. The motorised elements of the divisions travelled more than 350 kilometres on May 23 and were in the Somme area by the next day, but the horsed elements took another five days to arrive.

On the evening of May 21 the commander of the British 1st Armoured Division, Major-General R. Evans, received a message from Gort which instructed him to 'seize and hold crossings of the Somme from Picquigny to

Not far away 'Fleurus', another D-2, had been knocked out just in front of the local cemetery. Its commander, Sergent Maurice Villemin, had been killed when trying to leave his damaged

tank. The 19ème B.C.C. lost eight D-2s on the 27th — 50 percent of its initial strength when the attack started — and it had to withdraw in the evening.

Amiens had been taken after a severe air bombardment by the Luftwaffe. Though there was no real battle for the town, here and there isolated French units fought back doggedly. This Renault FT-17 has been halted in the Route d'Albert, in the northern part of the town, while trying desperately to stop the leaders of the 2. Panzer-Division.

Pont-Remy'. The first elements of the division had landed at Le Havre on May 15 but the harbour had been bombed and mined by the Luftwaffe, and from May 19 the remainder of the division was landed at Cherbourg and assembled to the south of Rouen. They arrived in France with 114 Mark VI light tanks and 143 cruisers but without artillery, with no reserve of tanks or bridging equipment. On the Somme, it was short of one battalion of tanks, the 3rd Royal Tank Regiment, and of all its infantry, which had been sent to Calais on May 20. On May 23 most of the available units had reached the Bresle area and, after conflicting arguments as to how the division should best be used, and clarification that it was not under 7ème Armée control, it was told to get on with the task in hand. General Evans therefore ordered his 2nd Armoured Brigade to push on to the Somme and take the crossings at Dreuil, Ailly and Picquigny.

Taking over the Somme sector from XIX. Armeekorps after it received orders on May 21 to turn northwards, that evening the XIV. Armeekorps relieved the panzer divisions with its 2. Infanterie-Division (mot) from the sea to Amiens and 13. Infanterie-Division (mot) from Amiens to Péronne. Their orders read 'the line of the Somme is to be held, the bridgeheads already seized to be expanded. The Somme bridges are to be prepared for demolition but will only be blown if they can no longer be held in the face of heavy enemy attack.' The bridges at Abbeville, Condé-Folie, Picquigny and Amiens were to be blown only should it become an 'absolute necessity'. The newcomers immediately carried out reconnaissance as far as the Bresle river and their motor cycle patrols were soon reported at Ault, Gamaches and Hornoy.

Some indication of the still more fluid and confused situation on the northern flank of the German breakthrough is contained in this extract from the experiences of Marcel Berger, then a sergeant with the 2ème G.R.D.I. of the 9ème D.I.M. and the commander of a Panhard P-178 armoured car, 'La Drô-lesse'. Three armoured cars from the 2ème G.R.D.I. had been despatched

The wrecked chariots of battle lying in a field near Dury, the place being aptly named Fond d'Enfer — Hell Down. This French Somua and German armoured car were casualties of the battle on the 23rd.

During the winter of 1940, while exploring the battlefield between Amiens and Dury, Pierre Vasselle found scattered French graves beside the Route de Conty.

Time has passed by, yet for this corner of France it has stood still. Henri de Wailly, historian and founder of the 'France 40' Museum at Abbeville, took the picture for us in 1989.

Identified by the oak-leaf insignia of the division, this SdKfz 251 personnel carrier of the 1. Panzers came to grief in Camon, a small village east of Amiens. The stencilling on the rear door also tells us that it belonged to the 8. Kompanie of Schützen-Regiment 1. (We were told that the wheels from this vehicle are still in private hands somewhere in the locality.)

from the Amiens area with orders for the 1ère Armée, and had managed to cut through the mass of German vehicles driving westwards during the night of May 21. One vehicle was then lost to a marauding panzer but 'La Drôlesse' and 'La Gauloise' carried on to Général Prioux's staff near Lens and delivered the orders. They were then instructed to return to Amiens which they were told had been retaken. They left the next day, facing problems with roads packed with troops of the British 17th Brigade and elements of Frankforce withdrawing from around Arras. The two armoured cars and their motor cycle guide drove for a while in the company of a British convoy before turning south near Aubigny. For some time, they were alone in the stillness of the night until, approaching a crossroads, they came upon another road packed with vehicles:

'I fumed when, after only five minutes, I saw that we had driven right back into the British flow of vehicles.' wrote Berger. 'At this new crossroads,

in complete darkness, it was the same column of armoured cars and trucks, as if we had done a complete turn and arrived back with the convoy we had just left. They were going our way so we could do nothing but to go along with them.

'We drove rather slowly for about a quarter of an hour. I felt that we had to leave this convoy that was driving westwards but I saw too late a crossroads that would have been perfect for this. Another crossroads did not materialise. It was now about 3.00 a.m. and we could see nothing but the rear of the truck that we were following at about five metres distance, taking care not to bump into it. I then noticed how much

this British vehicle looked like the German ones. This truck had exactly the same look as the German one we had shelled point-blank at the Sorbais bridge! I thought that after all, this must be normal because all armies had the same requirements. One of these trucks had broken down and our convoy passed the infantry that had got down from it. Leaning from my open turret, I looked at these British soldiers. They trampled in the mud, with the same exhausted faces that I had seen on our infantry. However, they looked taller and younger.'

One of the crew, Michaud, jumped down and climbed back quickly aboard the armoured car, explaining that they

Fifty years later, the half-track (minus its wheels!) has rumbled into the dusty pages of history, yet the Rue du Chevalier de la Barre has survived all.

On May 21 the 1st Armoured Division received a message from GHQ instructing them to drive north and 'seize and hold crossings on the Somme', whereupon the division advanced to the River Bresle within striking distance of the Somme some 15 miles further to the north. These Cruisers from the 2nd Armoured Brigade are parked in front of the château at Foucaucourt, just east of Blangy.

THURSDAY, MAY 23

As from midnight on May 22, the French command structure in the Somme sector was reorganised, with the creation of Groupement A within the 7ème Armée taking over the entire left wing of the army. Placed under the command of Général Robert Altmayer (brother of René — see page 365), Groupement A had the Xème Corps d'Armée under command and was to have the three cavalry divisions as soon as these arrived and the 4ème D.C.R. which was due to reach it on May 25.

To stiffen its line and reduce the German penetrations, the 7ème Armée had ordered 'one step forward' along the whole of its front on May 23. Although this was not too difficult on the right wing, it was impossible on the left as the Germans were determined to hold the bridgeheads they had obtained south of the Somme. The attack in the Amiens area did not get under way until afternoon because many of the troops had not arrived in time. The 7ème D.I.C. came up against strong defences and the attack had to be called off after

were not driving with a British convoy, but with a German one! They tried to leave the convoy when it slowed down in the next village but were shouted back into the file by an angry Feldwebel and the column resumed its advance. Fearing that to force their way out of the disciplined convoy would probably disclose their true identity to the Germans, they chose to trick their way out.

'Approaching the exit of the village, I saw a large sign, saying, in white on black: 'Avesnes-le-Comte, 11 kilomètres'. We should turn left when the convoy was heading right. Could we try to leave? There was only a remote chance of success. Reaching the crossroads, I saw one MP standing, with white gloves and leaning on a motor cycle, directing the vehicles in front of us. He seemed to recognise us, turned, and waved us to the left. Lacombe, who had cat's eyes, suddenly recognised Dandois [their motor cycle guide]. Majestically, 'La Drôlesse' turned, leaving the column. The driver of the truck following hesitated and tried to follow us but Dandois energetically waved him to the right. In a German helmet he had found, I know not where, he stayed there, waiting for 'La Gauloise'. Having repeated the manoeuvre, this time under the interested eyes of a German officer, Dandois calmly mounted his motor cycle, made a perfect turn and followed us'.

The Panhards dodged a further encounter with another German convoy but later came upon the crew of a German armoured car bold enough to question the Frenchmen. This time the game was up, and, in the fight that followed, Dandois was captured and 'La Gauloise' disabled. 'La Drôlesse' escaped, exchanged shots in a running battle with more armoured cars but was badly hit and had to be abandoned by its crew a few kilometres away. Walking by night the three men succeeded in reaching their own lines near Combles on May 25.

Boys will be boys. Little Guillaume de Wailly plays his part today just as French children did in 1940. This is Saint-Maxent, halfway between Blangy on the Bresle and Abbeville on the Somme, where signallers attend to the communications net.

Above: **The commander of the 1st Armoured Division, Major-General R. Evans, arrived at the Château de Foucaucourt on May 26 to meet officers of the 2ème D.L.C. prior to the operation planned for the following morning when his 2nd** Armoured Brigade was to attack under their command. With Evans is his French liaison officer, Capitaine Raymond Vivier de Vaugouin. *Below:* **Entente cordiale indeed at the château today: a British Jaguar with a French number plate!**

several Somua S-35s of the 7ème Cuirassiers supporting the infantry had been disabled.

FRIDAY, MAY 24

The French attack towards Amiens was resumed in the morning but made little progress in the face of the improvised defences. Trees had been blown down to block the roads, mines sown in the nearby fields, and as the French advanced, they were struck by fierce machine gun and artillery fire. From 10.00 a.m. the Stukas added their contribution. About an hour later Général Altmayer came to see the commander of the 7ème D.I.C., Général Louis Noiret, at his headquarters in Essertaux and underlined the importance of taking Amiens as soon as possible to recover the Somme crossings as a base for a future attack by the 4ème D.C.R. The attack continued throughout the afternoon but the losses were heavy and the gains small, and when it was halted in the evening, not even the first objective had been taken.

Tanks and scout cars of the 3rd Armoured Brigade move up to their start positions on the left wing of the attack. *Above:* This Cruiser (with turret reversed) is passing a crude road block in Quesnoy, eight kilometres west of Abbeville.

The photo was taken looking towards Saigneville. The building on the left with the chimney is a beetroot processing plant.

The number '10' signified the 5th Royal Tank Regiment, and the '7' (on the Mk VI) the brigade's headquarters unit.

Left: **German prisoners are marched back in best parade-ground style.** *Right:* **Henri de Wailly located the spot for us at the northern end of Saint-Maxent.**

To the north, the attack of the 1st Armoured Division was equally unsuccessful as the forces committed were small and dispersed. One troop of the Queen's Bays supported by one company of the 4th Border Regiment were employed against each of the three objectives, the Somme crossings at Dreuil, Ailly and Picquigny. At Ailly, two platoons of infantry crossed the river, only to withdraw as the tanks could not follow because of the blown bridge and neither of the other two parties succeeded in reaching the river owing to the strength of the 2. Infanterie-Division (mot) holding the bridgeheads south of the Somme.

SATURDAY, MAY 25

On May 25 news that a German unit had pushed far to the south of the Somme and had reached the Bresle river forced Général Altmayer to shift his attention north. He immediately ordered what had arrived of the three cavalry divisions to move northwards and cancelled for the time being the planned attacks in the Amiens area. Early that morning, Général Noiret was told to consolidate the previous days' gains.

From the War Office came a message indicating that the 1st Armoured Division and, when it arrived, the 51st (Highland) Division, which was being transferred by Général Georges from the Sarre, were to come under French command. Having been required to place himself under the orders of the 7ème Armée, General Evans went to see Général Altmayer at his headquarters and was ordered to prepare his division for supporting a French offensive against the Abbeville bridgehead planned for May 27.

SUNDAY, MAY 26

By now the three French cavalry divisions, or what there was of them — a mere six battalions of motorised infantry, a few recce tanks and armoured cars, some platoons of motor cyclists and six groups of artillery — had reached the lower Somme sector. On the left flank, the 5ème D.L.C., approaching the river between Saint-Valery and Abbeville, was stopped by German forces near Huppy, with the 2ème D.L.C. in the centre also being brought to a halt in the Huppy area but

The original caption to this British official picture stated that it was also taken in Saint-Maxent where this Citroën P-23 'went up in flames' after being 'hit by a German bomb'.

However, Henri and his Jag had to scour the countryside before he located the same street — in Huppy, the next village to the north.

In the battle on the 27th, the lightly-armoured British tanks paid a heavy price to the German anti-tank gun crews. Schütze Herbert Brinkforth, who manned a 37mm Pak 35/36, alone claimed nine tanks destroyed — an exploit which came in for particular mention in the Wehrmacht daily report on May 28.

managing to reach the river between Pont-Remy and Longpré. Over on the right, the 3ème D.L.C. gained the river between Longpré and Picquigny.

That afternoon the 7ème Armée ordered a resumption of the attack at Amiens to bring the line up to Saleux on the south-west of the town. However as the 7ème D.I.C. only received the order at 4.00 p.m., there was not enough time to co-ordinate the operation, and the one battalion which was able to go forward was soon halted by a German counter-attack.

MONDAY, MAY 27

At 9.50 a.m. on May 27 the attack on Amiens was resumed. Five infantry battalions of the 7ème D.I.C. attacked, supported by fifteen Renault D2s of the 19ème B.C.C. and six Somua S-35s of the 7ème Cuirassiers. Once again the fighting was costly and the progress small; Dury was taken but the German artillery replied furiously, soon backed by the Luftwaffe, and at 4.00 p.m. the Xème Corps d'Armée stopped the attack. The 7ème D.I.C. was ordered to consolidate the ground gained. The few Somua S-35s still left to support the division but the 19ème B.C.C., which had lost eight tanks that day, was withdrawn to the rear.

The orders for the attack on the Abbeville bridgehead had been issued on the morning of May 26. The plan was for the 2ème D.L.C., with the 2nd Armoured Brigade under command, to

The 1st Armoured Division lost 65 tanks that day — these two Cruisers were pictured after a further French attack had retaken the area.

Further losses suffered on May 27: two Mark VIs disabled between Saint-Maxent and Huppy. They belonged to the 10th Royal Hussars (unit code '6').

capture the ground overlooking the Somme south of Abbeville, and for the 5ème D.L.C., with the 3rd Armoured Brigade under command, to take the high ground along the Somme from Abbeville to the sea. The French were to supply artillery and infantry support for the British armour but while the 1st Armoured Division was a fresh unit, the two cavalry divisions committed to the attack were exhausted and badly depleted, which limited the support they were able to give. Because of the lack of time, there was only vague information about the German positions and co-ordination between the French and British units was largely ineffective.

The attack was launched at 6.00 a.m. on May 27, an hour late because the French artillery was not ready. On the right wing, the 2ème D.L.C. and 2nd Armoured Brigade made little progress as they encountered well dug-in German outposts and the tanks suffered severely from anti-tank guns in Huppy and Caumont which caught them as they tried to traverse the open ground.

On the left wing, the 5ème D.L.C. and the 3rd Armoured Brigade encountered less opposition and the tanks reached the high ground overlooking the Somme between Cambron and Saigneville and the outskirts of Saint-Valery but they pulled back when it was learned that the French infantry were taking up defensive positions some distance behind them.

By the time that the operation came to an end in the afternoon, nothing effective had been achieved and the German bridgehead at Abbeville had not been dislodged. Losses had also been heavy: the 2ème D.L.C. had suffered painfully; 65 British tanks had been knocked out but of the 50 others damaged, many were recovered over the next few days when further French attacks retook the lost ground.

The Wehrmacht report for May 28 records on that day on the Somme that 'thirty enemy tanks had been destroyed, nine of them by Schütze Brinkforth'.

Herbert Brinkforth manned a 37mm PaK gun with the 14. Kompanie of Inf.Rgt. 25, 2. Infanterie-Division (mot) and later became the first soldier of the rank to be awarded the Knight's Cross in March 1941.

General Evans and other British officers had tried to explain to the French Command the characteristics of the 1st Armoured Division and to point out that the British tanks had not been designed to support an infantry breakthrough but were light, fast cruisers designed to exploit open country warfare. After the division's costly début, the next day Général Georges issued Instruction No. 1809 in which he drew the attention of the French commanders to the 1st Armoured bearing a closer resemblance to a French Division Légère Mécanique than to a Division Cuirassée. Its employment, he insisted, 'should not be contemplated except

within the limits allowed by the nature of its equipment, unless battle conditions make other arrangements vitally necessary.'

Although the British division got on with the task of recovering its disabled tanks, putting repairs in hand and reorganising its remaining forces, in view of these instructions, the French made little use of it in the days that followed as conditions on the Somme front proved less and less favourable to the engagement of the Cruisers.

On May 27 the 7ème Armée informed Groupement A that it was to have the 4ème D.C.R. to 'reduce the bridgehead at Abbeville' and during the night the division, which was assembling in the Poix area, was ordered to move north. The 4ème D.C.R. had been badly shaken in the battles near Laon but had been hastily refitted and given 100 new tanks — 40 Hotchkiss H-39s of the two squadrons of the 3ème Cuirassiers which had not been engaged earlier, 45 Renault R-35s of the 44ème B.C.C. and about 20 Renault B1bis of the 47ème B.C.C. The latter battalion, with only two companies, had replaced the 19ème B.C.C. in the 6ème Demi-Brigade which had left the division and fought in the Amiens sector. That evening the division had, with the cavalry units attached to it, more than 150 tanks: 32 Renault B1bis, 65 Renault R-35s, 40 Hotchkiss H-39s and 17 Somua S-35s. Of these, however, only 140 were in working order and a number of them were dispersed in support of secondary efforts: the Renault R-35s of the 44ème B.C.C. and the Somua S-35s of the 3ème Cuirassiers being near Picquigny.

During the night, the 2. Infanterie-Division (mot) was relieved and the XXXVIII. Armeekorps took charge of the Somme sector from the sea to Amiens with the 57. Infanterie-Division and the 9. Infanterie-Division, the former inheriting the Abbeville bridgehead.

This Mark VI belonged to the 9th Queen's Royal Lancers (unit code '5') of the 1st Armoured Division.

The Abbeville bridgehead

'We were now just in front of the hedge that we riddled with our guns', recalled Lieutenant René Bardel who led his Renault R-35 right into Villers on May 29.

TUESDAY, MAY 28
De Gaulle's tanks attack

Général de Brigade Charles de Gaulle (he had been promoted from Colonel just three days before) and the commanders of the others units involved met at the Château d'Oisemont at about midday on May 28. British officers were there too, among them Brigadier R. L. McCreery commanding the 2nd Armoured Brigade, together with officers from the cavalry divisions and the 5ème D.I.C. The 4ème D.C.R. was to attack in the centre, the 5ème D.L.C. and the 2ème D.L.C. were to support the attack on both flanks but the British units were not involved and held in reserve.

De Gaulle announced the details of the attack he had planned to go in at 5.00 p.m. When it was argued that this was far too early, leaving little time to organise and none for reconnaissance, he said he would brook no delay and insisted the attack go ahead as ordered. The 4ème D.C.R. had now recovered most of its tanks but there was still a shortage of artillery and, although supported by the 22ème R.I.C., few infantrymen to consolidate any ground won.

Because of the lack of time, the operation had not been properly co-ordinated but at the appointed hour the artillery preparation crashed down on the Abbeville bridges and the German positions west of the town. The attack went well, the tanks breaking through the German positions, followed by the infantry. Huppy was taken after a fierce battle and the day ended with a French tactical success. The 57. Infanterie-Division had been pushed back for about four kilometres, 300 prisoners had been taken, Huchenville and Bray were in French hands and six Renault R-35s from the 44ème B.C.C. had reached Mareuil, only to withdraw because no infantry had followed them. However the important objective — the retaking of the German bridgehead — had yet to be achieved.

The 57. Infanterie-Division had only the standard 3.7cm Pak 35/36 in the bridgehead with which to confront the French armour — not a particularly effective weapon especially when pitted against a heavily-armoured tank such as the Renault B1bis — and many a German gun crew was run over, crushed beneath the tracks of an oncoming target. To help bolster the anti-tank defences, during the night the division hastily brought forward batteries of its own artillery and some of the deadly 88mm Flak guns of Flak-Abteilung I./64.

Troops of the 57. Infanterie-Division had dug foxholes in the bank of this road above Caubert waiting for the next French attack. Some of the men cracked and ran when faced with the repeated tank attacks, but their artillery (a 10.5cm lFH 18 can be seen on the bend) fired at them determinedly and the French losses were heavy.

During the attack on May 28, at about 6.00 p.m., the Renault B1bis 'Jeanne d'Arc' had assaulted several German guns and crushed them under its tracks. *Left:* The following morning, Capitaine André Laude of the 47ème B.C.C. pictured the driver of the 'Jeanne d'Arc', Aspirant Guy Aubry de Maraumont, behind a 2cm Flak 30 that he had destroyed by the side of the road near Les Croisettes. *Right:* History was made here on the side of the N28.

WEDNESDAY, MAY 29
The attack resumes

The French attack resumed at about 4.00 a.m. and some of the German infantry, still stunned and shaken from the previous day, initially broke ranks when faced with the tanks they knew they could not stop. The attack progressed, but losses were rising above those of the previous day for, although in places the German infantry had broken, the artillery and Flak batteries were determinedly holding their own. One after another, the French tanks were stopped: 'Eylau', 'Tourville', 'Lodi' and many others being disabled near Villers-Mareuil. Lieutenant René Bardel, of the first company of the 44ème B.C.C., was later to describe the fierce battle for Villers-Mareuil that he took part in his Renault R-35:

'As soon as we started, the khaki coats jumped behind us and followed across the plateau . . . the infantry seemed to be particularly eager this morning. As we passed them, I looked uneasily at the wrecks of two Renault R-35s, still smoking at the edge of the wood. Yesterday, the men who had died riding them were still alive. Whose

Further up the road, Capitaine Laude pictured another of the guns destroyed by the 'Jeanne d'Arc', a 3.7cm Pak 35/36. The body of one of the crew lies on the left of the gun.

Left: Just to the east, on the road between Les Croisettes and Huppy, Capitaine Laude watched and took pictures as the chasseurs of the 4ème B.C.P. brought in some of the 300 prisoners captured by the 4ème D.C.R. between May 28 and 31.

Right: The support of the gate to the pasture was still there by the side of the D25 when Henri de Wailly took this comparison. In the background are the trees lining the N28 just south of Les Croisettes.

Capitaine André Laude of the 47ème B.C.C. took the impressive 'action' pictures shown on the previous pages.

The 'Jeanne d'Arc' was the mount of the commander of the 1ère compagnie, 47ème B.C.C., Capitaine Maurice Dirand, but having destroyed many gun positions, the tank was in turn hit by an 88mm shell and brewed up near Limercourt.

turn today? There was no time for soul-searching, we had a job to do. I fired into a bush, just to the left of a long hedge which stood in front of us and hid the village. The breech recoiled in the turret, spat out the cartridge which clanged onto the tank floor. My melancholy thoughts disappeared, banished by my first shot, and I found myself back in the battle, surprisingly clear-headed and calm.

'Smoke now hid the hedgerow in front of us. The German machine guns hidden there were firing madly, keeping our infantry down on the ground. At full speed, our platoon attacked them — this was a tank's job! The red bursts of our 37mm guns flashed all along the hedgerow; earth, branches flew up. But the enemy held their ground. A sudden shock rang out on my armour and a flame flashed into the turret. We had been hit! I hastily trained the turret to the right and there, between two trees, I saw the white flash of a 37mm AT gun firing at us. Of us two, who was going to die? I would prefer that it was them. One shot after another, I fired three shots, the cases falling down into my tank . . . Suddenly a firework display lit up under the trees. I had probably hit their ammunition box . . . I fired half a charger from my machine gun and another shell . . . I had got them!

'We were now just in front of the hedge that we riddled with our guns. I looked behind me and found that the infantry, still stuck to the ground, had not followed us. They were still under fire from some weapons and were unable to advance. I drove back to get some information. Hiding beside my flank armour, an infantry lieutenant stood up and thumped at my hatch. Opening the hatch, I asked him: "Hey, what is annoying you?" "These two machine guns", he answered, "just to the right of this gate!". We rushed forward at full speed, the engine roaring, and we were soon in front of that gate. Nothing moved. We passed in

front of the hedge, again nothing. We had not gone more than another ten metres when the two machine guns, now feeling safe, commenced firing again just above the ground. Lunain, my driver, stopped the tank suddenly. The turret turned madly and I fired. We were so close that we felt the blast when our shells exploded. One of the two machine guns was blown off its tripod and fell beside the tank. We could see the other after the attack: it was broken and twisted and the upper part of the body of the gunner, cut in two by one of our shells, was still clenched to it.

'I had now spent all my ammunition and we drove back to re-supply. Ten minutes later we were once again in front of this hedgerow and it seemed to me that every machine gun that we had destroyed had been immediately replaced, each of the men we had killed being immediately duplicated. At last, having re-supplied our ammunition racks twice more, and our weapons very hot from having fired too much, we got the infantry into the village. My tank was the first to enter and suddenly Lunain stopped . . . "Lieutenant, look . . . We cannot drive over them!". Alas, we could not crush these bodies, but we had no other possibility. It was not possible to pass beside them. Although I was horrified at the idea of feeling our tracks crushing men's bodies, I knew that we had to pass. "Let's go!". It was horrible! The short flame of a machine gun firing from an air vent suddenly appeared just above ground level. Two shots of 37mm in the cellar, another one into that window. With the machine gun, I fired at the men who rushed out from the door . . . Now to the next house!

There was no visible landmark to identify where the 'Jeanne d'Arc' fought her last battle, but fortunately a local farmer remembered and was able to show Jean Paul the exact spot on the road between Limercourt and Les Croisettes.

The 51st (Highland) Division was inserted on the left wing of the 7ème Armée, occupying the line from Abbeville to the sea. The original caption to this picture states that it was taken 'in the very front line' but this was not really correct as German forces at this time were still a few kilometres further to the east. These men of the 4th Battalion, The Black Watch, were photographed at the eastern end of Toeufles, taking shelter by the side of the D22.

'House to house, street to street, we brought the 22ème R.I.C. up to the opposite edge of the village that was now ours. A lot of Germans had died for it, all of them young men. There were bodies everywhere: in the streets, in the gardens, in the houses. The orchard behind the hedgerow was like a charnel-house. Once again an infantryman thumbed at my hatch and explained that they were being fired at from that cluster of trees. I trained the Reibel to the sky and fired. Chopped by the bullets, leaves and branches flew in every directions until the sniper fell down with his sub-machine gun. With him also fell the chair that he had installed on a fork in the tree: comfort, even for battle!'

At about 5.00 p.m., the attack came to a stop with losses mounting up, fuel running low, and units out of touch with another. Although the day's gains included Bienfay, Villers and most of Mareuil, the troops were exhausted and most of the tanks were disabled or suffering from mechanical trouble. At the same time the German grip on their bridgehead and the Somme crossings had not been loosened. Nevertheless the day was a very difficult one for the 57. Infanterie-Division and General Erich von Manstein, then the commander of the XXXVIII. Armeekorps, later wrote in his post-war memoirs how he had hastened to Abbeville late on May 29 with the commander of the 57. Infanterie-Division, Generalleutnant Oskar Blümm, to rally their forces and turn them around.

On May 30 Général de Gaulle planned to resume the attack at 5.00 p.m. with the forces remaining but the Germans attacked first early in the afternoon, trying to push the 4ème D.C.R. from the ground it had won. The French however held firm and their own attack started as planned but it soon became apparent that the 4ème D.C.R., which had now lost nearly all of its tanks, could do nothing more. In three days the division's casualties, with those of the 22ème R.I.C. attached to it, amounted about 750 men killed, wounded or missing, and it had lost about 105 tanks west of Abbeville.

Reorganisation

Groupement A of the 7ème Armée, was now upgraded to become the 10ème Armée under Général Altmayer; taking the IXème and Xème Corps d'Armée in charge, the army now had the responsibility for the whole of the Somme sector.

Under the IXème Corps d'Armée on the army's left wing was the British 51st (Highland) Division, which had been inserted to hold the line from the sea to the Abbeville area. Then came the 2ème D.L.C. and 3ème D.L.C. from Abbeville to Picquigny. During the night, the horsed elements of these two cavalry divisions arrived, the 3ème Brigade of the 2ème D.L.C. being assembled as reserve for the IXème Corps d'Armée, and the 5ème Brigade of the 3ème D.L.C. entering the line to relieve the tired mechanised units of the division's 13ème Brigade. On the army's right flank the Xème Corps d'Armée, with three infantry divisions, held the Amiens sector as far as the boundary with the 7ème Armée to the west of the town.

Two divisions, the 31ème Division d'Infanterie and the 5ème D.I.C., were on their way to replace the two tired cavalry divisions still in the line. It was planned to assemble them, together with the 5ème D.L.C. already in army reserve, with the 1st Armoured Division and the newly-formed 40ème

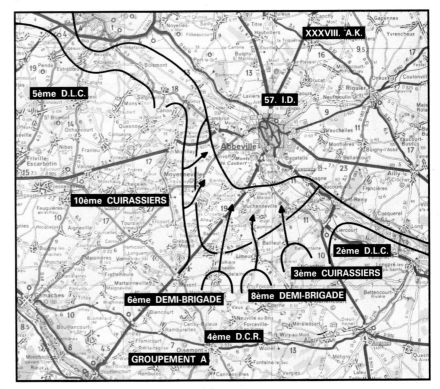

The 4ème D.C.R. renewed the attack against the Abbeville bridgehead early on May 29 and succeeded in breaking through the German defences. Though the day's gains were sizeable the situation in Abbeville itself was critical for the 57. Infanterie-Division. Nevertheless, in the evening the Germans were still holding a solid bridgehead on the south bank of the Somme.

At the beginning of June, the 2ème D.C.R. assembled for a renewed assault against the Abbeville bridgehead. On the eve of the attack, it had a nominal strength of 165 tanks, but of these only 140 were serviceable and battle ready. Out of this total, about fifty were Renault B1bis like those illustrated here of the 1ère Compagnie, Bataillon 8/15, which were pictured on the start line in a wood near Les Croisettes, on the afternoon of June 3.

Division d'Infanterie, in a reserve group ready to strike at the flank of any German breakthrough. The 4ème D.C.R. having clearly shot its bolt, was withdrawn on May 31 except for the divisional artillery.

On May 18 Lieutenant-General Sir Henry Karslake, the commander of the British lines of communication, had ordered that measures be taken to strengthen the defences of the northern district of communications south of the Somme. Two small mobile forces were organised, 'Vicforce' and 'Beauforce', and defensive positions were prepared along the rivers Andelle and Béthune. Bridges were mined for demolition and obstacles were prepared for erection. On May 31 all these improvised forces were formed into Beauman Division under Brigadier A. B. Beauman; the division not being under French command but directly under General Karslake.

In the early morning of Tuesday, June 4, Capitaine Raymond Fissiaux, the commander of the 348ème Compagnie de Chars, led the assault in 'Kléber' as far as the summit of Mont de Caubert. There, in company with 'Maréchal Lefèvre' and 'Crécy-au-Mont', he could see Abbeville down below but they were alone, without infantry, and in the end had to withdraw.

TUESDAY, JUNE 4
The 2ème D.C.R. attack

The French Command continued to be highly perturbed by the German bridgeheads south of the Somme and the 10ème Armée was ordered to attack again to remedy the situation at Abbeville, for which the 2ème D.C.R. was subordinated to the army. After its disastrous committment in front of Gruppe von Kleist, the division had been hastily reconstituted, its original complement of Renault B1bis, down to 17, now reinforced by three new companies of Renault B1bis. The Hotchkiss H-39s, reduced in strength to 23, likewise reinforced by the 351ème Compagnie de Chars with 11 Hotchkiss Hs. The 2ème Demi-Brigade had now two battalions: the 8/15 formed with what remained of the 8ème B.C.C. and 15ème B.C.C. and the three newly arrived Renault B1bis companies; and the 14/27 formed with the remnants of the 14ème B.C.C. and 27ème B.C.C. and the newly arrived 351ème Compagnie de Chars. The 4ème Demi-Brigade had now the two new battalions given to the division, the 48ème B.C.C. and the 40ème B.C.C., both equipped with Renault R-35s and R-40s.

Most of these units had been formed or refitted in haste with tanks and equipment recovered directly from factories or on training grounds and the rate of serviceability was appallingly low. At the end of May, when the division was brought forward for the attack on the Abbeville bridgehead planned for June 4, it had on paper some 165 tanks, about 50 Renault B1bis, 35 Hotchkiss Hs and 80 Renault Rs, but of these less than 140 were actually usable.

Another superb 'action' picture taken around 8.30 a.m. that Tuesday morning by Commandant Michel Malaguti. Two Renault B1bis and one Lorraine personnel carrier have been hit while advancing towards Mont de Caubert along a valley just east of Bienfay. The B1bis burning in the middle is 'Anjou' of the 349ème Compagnie de Chars.

The attack force, units of the 51st Division, the 2ème D.C.R. and the 31ème Division d'Infanterie, were put under the command of Major-General V. M. Fortune of the 51st Division. The plan was for the 2ème D.C.R. in the centre supported by infantry of the 152nd Brigade, with the 31ème Division d'Infanterie on its left, to capture the high ground west of Abbeville. The 153rd Brigade was to take the high ground south of Gouy, while to seaward the 154th Brigade was to keep the German units in the lower Somme valley occupied to prevent them from reinforcing the threatened bridgehead. A composite regiment formed by the 1st Armoured Division out of the remnants of the Bays and 10th Hussars was to be held in reserve. The two French divis-

ions had just moved into the area and were not ready to attack: the 2ème D.C.R., which had to keep its 40ème B.C.C. in reserve, could only field about 100 of its tanks and the 31ème Division d'Infanterie had only one of its regiments at hand, the 15ème R.I.A., some parts of it only arriving ninety minutes or so before the attack.

Again there was little time for detailed preparation and the attacking forces were badly co-ordinated. Reconnaissance was inadequate and the artillery could only fire at what seemed to be likely German positions.

Artillery support for the operation on June 4 was at any rate plentiful: there were the batteries of the two D.C.R., of the three D.L.C. and of the 51st Division.

The barrage which crashed down at 3.30 a.m. on the German positions near Bienfay and Villers was a heavy one. On the left wing, the 15ème R.I.A. advanced between Moyenville and Bienfay supported by Renault Rs of the 48ème B.C.C. but the attack made little progress, the tanks being slowed by an undetected minefield and the infantry being held up almost from the start by strong German positions well dug-in in the woods west of Ménil-Trois-Foetus. At about 8.00 a.m. the tanks repulsed a German counter-attack but only after it had wiped out the few infantry which had succeeded in going forward with the tanks. The situation was badly confused. Allegedly fired on by its own artillery and tanks, and dissatisfied to see so few of the latter, the demoralised

This extraordinary aerial view was taken from a Potez 63/11 of G.A.O. 3/551 on June 1, i.e. after the 4ème D.C.R. attack and before that by the 2ème D.C.R. It shows the fields between Bienfay Wood (top left) and the tree-lined N28 (right) into which the tank attacks were funnelled because of the nature of the terrain. Many tanks were disabled in this area on May 29, and more later on June 4 — a large number of them in a minefield cleverly laid by the Germans at the northern end of this narrow passage. The minefield is just off the top of the picture, above the light-coloured, wedge-shaped field.

infantry started to withdraw in disorder. Their commander, Colonel Jean-Baptiste Favatier, was ruthless in turning them back, ordering the tankers to fire at every French infantryman who moved back of his own accord. As Commandant André Masséna de Rivoli, the commander of the 48ème B.C.C., noted 'from this time on, the dispirited infantry did not act up any more'.

In the centre, the tanks advanced as planned but near Villers they came upon an undetected minefield in a sector which was supposed to be held by elements of the 51st Division. In fact it had been abandoned during the night without the 2ème D.C.R. being informed and the Germans had re-occupied it and laid mines in this vital quarter. A number of tanks were disabled and those which got through took a heavy pasting at very close range from artillery and Flak guns. The Seaforth Highlanders advanced between Bienfay and Villers, clearing enemy posts and striving vainly to reach the tanks and,

Among the tanks lost were 'Ney' and 'Bordeaux' of the 2ème D.C.R. (left). Many others were knocked out by German guns, like the 'Eylau' of the 4ème D.C.R. on May 29 — which can be seen on the open ground between the two woods. On June 4

'Hanoi' (2ème D.C.R.) was to fall into the ravine just beside 'Eylau'. Both tanks can be seen on the picture (right) taken when the Germans recovered the tanks some time later. 'Hanoi' in the foreground with 'Eylau' just behind on top of the bank.

like them, they suffered crippling losses. Three Renault B1bis, 'Crécy-au-Mont', 'Kléber' and 'Maréchal Lefèvre', reached the Mont de Caubert, just to the west of Abbeville, creating havoc among the German units all the way, but all alone, without any support, they had to withdraw, leaving 'Crécy-au-Mont' burning on the hill.

To the south, the 4th Camerons encountered strong German positions and they, too, were prevented from reaching their objective. Two platoons got as far as Caubert, but there they were cut off, only managing to get back, with most of the men wounded, two days later.

Things went better on the left flank, where the 153rd Brigade had reached its objective — the high ground east of Gouy — but with the high ground north of Caubert remaining in German hands, it would have been impossible to hang on to what had been won and the

On the morning of June 4, 'Crécy-au-Mont' had broken through and successfully reached the top of Mont de Caubert in company with 'Kléber' and 'Maréchal Lefèvre'. These last two successfully returned, but 'Crécy-au-Mont' was destroyed. This German photograph shows it just a few metres away from the 88mm Flak gun, being used in its anti-tank rôle, which probably stopped it.

Gordon Highlanders were ordered to return to their starting point.

At about midday it was clear that the operation was not going to succeed and it was stopped, the advance elements being ordered to withdraw.

Sergent Robert Job, the driver of the Renault B1bis 'Crécy-au-Mont' of the 347ème Compagnie de Chars, had survived its brewing-up in such bad shape that the Germans soon released him. Later, he gave the following account of the last morning it went into action:

'At 3.00 a.m. on June 4 we arrived at

the edge of a wood but it was dark and I could see very little of the surroundings. The tank commander, Lieutenant Marcel Blondelet, moved out to get some up-to-date information; he soon came back and ordered "A vos postes!" I drove on, following Lieutenant Blondelet who was walking in front of the tank, guiding me across fields; Caporal-Chef Robert Célérier was fuzing 75mm shells, piling them neatly under the breech, while the tank radio operator, Caporal Marcel Juteau, was singing. "Halte!" cried our Lieutenant who jumped into

Amazingly, the place where the tank burned out could still be seen many years later for the heat must have sterilised the ground. Pierre de Senneville stands where the B1bis was destroyed in 1940. Behind, the Celtic camp of Mont de Caubert.

the tank, slamming the turret hatch and locking it. I could hardly see in front of me but we were behind a small bank that we would have to negotiate in order of battle with the other tanks in a few minutes. We all waited, anxiously looking at the radio operator.

'The order to go arrived and we advanced but my third gear chose this occasion to jam and, moving too slowly, we lost ground with the other tanks. The day dawned and I tried to recover the lost ground in spite of poor visibility due to low hanging fog. A violent jerk suddenly shook the tank and nearly stopped it — we had certainly hit a mine — but it willingly responded to my careful handling even if it now proved unable to increase its speed.

'Our Lieutenant sprayed the edge of a wood with his machine gun. I saw a gun flashing at us, I heard the strikes against the tank and we quickly turned to face this anti-tank gun. I fired two shots from the 75mm gun at some 600 metres while the Lieutenant fired the 47mm from the turret. We must have succeeded in disabling either the gun or its crew as we were not troubled by them any more. It was clear now that we could never rejoin our company and that we had no other chance but to fight on alone. We moved again and after several impressive manoeuvres over deep ditches, we reached high ground and our 'Crécy-au-Mont' stopped in the open between the edges of two woods — quite an uncomfortable situation! The Lieutenant fired machine gun bursts and some 47mm shells from the turret gun to keep the enemy at a distance and I guessed that there was no anti-tank gun there as we received no hits for the five minutes that we stayed there to repair our tank.

'We started again and I fired the 75mm at another wood where enemy units were positioned and I am sure that I disabled another anti-tank gun there. We reached a broken area and the tank bucked up and down across large holes hidden by high weeds. We moved up out of one hole to sink down into another and the light inside the tank went off at each jolt. At last we reached

Though the cost was high, the 57. Infanterie-Division managed to successfully hold the Abbeville bridgehead. In the afternoon of June 4 the last French attack was repulsed and prisoners rounded up. These men of the 15ème R.I.A. are passing through Mautort, just west of the town.

Left: In this shot, Leutnant Franz Arsan, a section commander in 3. Kompanie of Infanterie-Regiment 179 (57. Infanterie-Division) relaxes with his men in Mareuil just south of Abbeville. However, minutes after the picture was taken, a stray French shell hit the garden, wounding six men and killing Schütze Hermann Müller. *Right:* A remarkable comparison. Not only did Henri de Wailly locate the house, he went one better, tracing Franz Arsan and taking him back to the De Facque house.

Franz Arsan took this picture of five of his comrades on Quai de la Douane at Abbeville on May 31. From left to right: Unteroffizier Nitzl, Unteroffizier Josef Maier, Oberleutnant Theophil Braun, Unteroffizier Stöckl and Unteroffizier Josef Krämer, all of the 2. Kompanie of Infanterie-Regiment 199. Braun and Krämer were killed, and Stöckl badly wounded, when the 57. Infanterie-Division attacked to expand the bridgehead on June 5.

Last resting place for Theophil Braun and Josef Krämer in the Bourdon German War Cemetery. Both are in Block 27, Braun in grave 589, and Krämer in grave 593.

a smoother area but a fire had started in the engine compartment. Calmly the Lieutenant ordered Juteau to bring the fire extinguisher into action and, turning to me, he joked: "Il fait chaud dans le coin!" The gauge in front of me showed a very high temperature for the cooling water and I had to drive slowly. Wondering about the problem, we radioed an SOS but at least the fire was out.

'We moved downhill and the Lieutenant suddenly came down from the turret to point out a group of men that we were unable to identify at first. He climbed again into his turret and soon started to fire with the machine gun and the 47mm. They were Germans! I saw a gun abandoned with shells piled beside and I drove for it, intending to destroy it. While the Lieutenant was firing again and again, we approached quickly but a direct hit stopped us a few metres from the gun, the engine stalled and the tank started to burn. It seemed to me that all our fuel tanks were burning this time with at least 150 litres of fuel inside! I cut off the ignition; there was no target that I could engage with the 75mm and I turned just in time to see another direct hit explode in the tank. Everything was burning and the air was suffocating.

'Being unable to breathe, I thought I had been wounded in the chest; I choked and fainted. I woke a few seconds later, opened my hatch and took a breath of fresh air. I tried to look inside the tank but was blinded by the smoke and the flame just behind me. There was nothing to destroy as everything was burning now. I dragged myself to the door. Where were my comrades? I did not know, it seemed to me that they were outside, then I thought I could see them inside ... Before I realised what was happening, two Germans grabbed me and dragged me away. Some others moved out of their foxholes and angrily shook their fists as we passed in front of them. Juteau was brought near me and shook my hand; sadly we thought of our two comrades who had remained in the tank, probably killed by the second shell, the one which had wounded both Juteau and me. 'Crécy-au-Mont' was now completly aflame and could not be approached.' (Sergent Job had been badly wounded: a splinter had lodged in his left thigh, and two in his right; he had a 25-centimetre long wound in his right shoulder, another deep one in his right wrist with splinters inside, plus other minor wounds to the temple and the back.)

The strength of the German bridgehead had been largely underestimated and the operation with insufficient preparation was a complete failure. The 2ème D.C.R. had lost about 40 tanks, 7 Lorraine armoured personel carriers and about 130 men; the 15ème R.I.A. of the 31ème Division d'Infanterie about 250 men, among them Colonel Jean-Baptiste Favatier, the regiment's commander who had been killed when a artillery shell hit his command post. The 51st (Highland) Division had sustained still heavier casualties, the 152nd Brigade alone losing about 570 men.

The final withdrawal

German forces are closing on Boulogne where anxious civilians seek shelter on May 20. Two days hence the panzers would make contact wth the town's defences.

On May 18, when the 7ème Armée was pulled out of Belgium and ordered south to form a front to the north of Paris, the XVIème Corps d'Armée had assumed responsibility for the left wing of the Allied front. On May 21, it had been subordinated to the Belgian High Command, its two infantry divisions having the task of defending the flank to the north-east of Brugge.

Meanwhile the other divisions formerly with the 7ème Armée were hastily moving south but the trains transporting the 21ème Division d'Infanterie to the Somme area were soon cut by the advanced elements of Gruppe von Kleist and the division was hurriedly drawn into the defence of Boulogne. On this same day two battalions of the 20th Guards Brigade were hurriedly shipped to Boulogne from England; it was also planned to reinforce the town with the 3rd Royal Tank Regiment and another infantry battalion, the 1st Queen Victoria's Rifles, from Calais but the situation there was such that this was never attempted. Hopes of the 21ème Division d'Infanterie establishing solid positions were also disappointed when the division was hit by the panzers after only 5 of its 42 trains had arrived. Consequently there would be nothing but improvised French forces under the division's commander, Général Pierre Lanquetot, and the 20th Guards Brigade under Brigadier W.A.F.L. Fox-Pitt, left to defend Boulogne.

Gruppe von Kleist had resumed its advance northwards on May 22 and the 2. Panzer-Division, after having to overcome stiff French resistance at Samer in the early afternoon, reached the outskirts of Boulogne and made contact with the defenders.

British troops evacuated Boulogne on the night of May 23, much to the surprise — and anger — of the French commander, Général Lanquetot, who had not been informed. The French garrison fought on alone until May 25, making a last stand in the Citadel (above). Gruppe von Kleist claimed 2,000 prisoners, many rounded up as they tried to fight their way out.

Left: **Stunned villagers in Ardres look on in despair as armour of the 1. Panzer-Division races through in the direction of Calais,** 17 kilometres to the north. *Right:* **This junction has since been widened, so losing the building line on the left.**

The only two battalions of the 21ème Division d'Infanterie that could be deployed fought back stubbornly and held off the 1. Panzer-Division near Desvres until midday on May 23 but the bulk of the division was attacked when still entrained.

French and British destroyers were shelling enemy gun positions near Boulogne, while the British evacuated their non-combatants and wounded from the harbour. The Luftwaffe made determined attacks on the ships. The commanders of two of the destroyers, the HMS *Keith* and the HMS *Vimy*, were killed and the French destroyer *l'Orage* was sunk.

At 6.30 p.m. on May 23 the War Office ordered that the 20th Guards Brigade be evacuated immediately and destroyers began at once to take off the Irish and Welsh Guards, about a thousand men per ship. The last vessel to reach Boulogne was the destroyer HMS *Vimiera* which entered the harbour early on May 24 in an eerie silence. For over an hour it remained berthed while it was loaded up with 1,400 men before returning them safely to England.

The French had not been informed of the British decision to evacuate their men and Général Lanquetot was both surprised and angry to learn early on May 24 that the majority of the British troops, which he had included in his hastily drawn plan of defence, had gone home during the night. Those that could not be taken off included a party established on the seaward end of the mole under Major J. C. Windsor Lewis, which fought on until May 25. The French garrison barricaded in the Citadel also resisted until May 25 when those inside attempted to escape. They were rounded up and Gruppe von Kleist claimed to have taken 2,000 prisoners overall.

CALAIS

The arrival of British forces despatched hurriedly to France to operate from Calais or Dunkirk and get supply columns through to the BEF was to lead to their being used to defend Calais to the last, but not before the situation there had become thoroughly confused. Units arrived short of vehicles and equipment . . . ships were sent back to England before they had finished unloading . . . contradictory orders came from all directions, one after another. No wonder Commandant Raymond Le Tellier, sent by Général Falgade to command the French forces at Calais, found his ally's intentions 'nebulous'.

The 1st Queen Victoria's Rifles and the 3rd Royal Tank Regiment arrived at Calais on May 22 but off-loading proceeded very slowly as none of the dockside cranes was available because the electricity had been cut off. At 5.00 p.m. the 3rd Royal Tank Regiment,

Mai 23, Ardres, Westfront. **Officers and NCOs of the Kampfgruppe marching in the van of the 1. Panzers are briefed on the latest situation.**

Left: **On the evening of May 23 Gort ordered a withdrawal to a line along the Canal d'Aire. These troops from Frankforce were** **pictured marching through Béthune, just south of the canal, on the following day.** *Right:* **Rue Sadi Carnot 50 years on.**

equipped with 21 Mark VI light tanks and 27 Cruisers, was ordered to proceed to Boulogne but six hours later a liaison officer from Gort's headquarters cancelled the order and sent them instead to Saint-Omer and Hazebrouck. The tanks started to advance in the direction of Saint-Omer but soon met panzers. Although they managed to account for several, after losing 12 tanks it became clear that they could never break through and they fell back on Calais.

On the morning of May 23, when the 30th Brigade sailed to Calais, its commander, Brigadier C. N. Nicholson, had orders to proceed with the 3rd Royal Tank Regiment to the relief of Boulogne. When he arrived at Calais during the afternoon, he found that the regiment had already suffered heavy losses and it was obvious to him that it was no longer possible to move either to Boulogne or to Saint-Omer and that the defence of the town was the urgent task. Orders then arrived from London instructing him to convey 350,000 rations to Dunkirk, and since he was told that this was a priority 'overriding all other considerations' he recalled part of his force from the defence line he had started to organise. While the supply convoy was forming up, the 3rd Royal Tank Regiment sent a squadron of tanks to reconnoitre the road to Dunkirk. These ran into units of the 1. Panzer-Division and all were destroyed except for three which managed to fight their way through to join the troops in Gravelines.

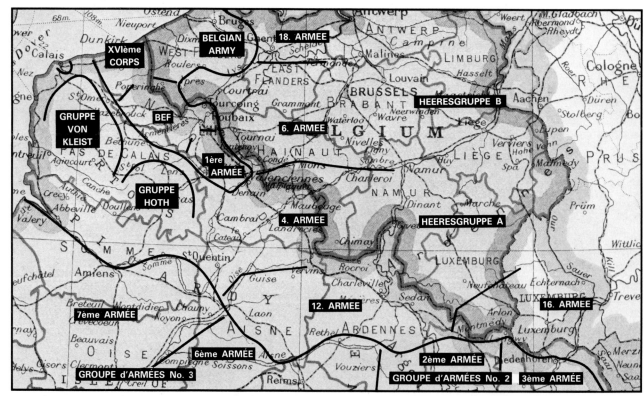

Before we discuss the decision by Gort to evacuate, perhaps this is the point to reflect on the incredible feat of arms achieved by Germany in the space of just ten days. By May 20 the breach south of Arras deepened and widened with German forces driving in two directions: down the valley of the Somme and through Hesdin and Montreuil making for the Channel ports. The Frankforce counter-attack near Arras on the 21st surprised the Germans but failed to achieve a great deal, not gaining its first-day objective — the River Cojeul — before it was called off. By the evening of the 22nd, Boulogne was isolated and armoured columns were nine miles from Calais. On the following day, instead of the planned counter-attack, May 23 saw only a battle of telegrams in which Reynaud, Churchill, Weygand and others were all involved. That night Frankforce abandoned Arras and fell back behind the Béthune–La Bassée Canal. Weygand's idea of mounting a co-ordinated Anglo-French pincer from north and south thus came to naught, and by the 25th the position on the Belgian Army front further to the north had also deteriorated. On the morning of May 26 the position looked like this.

Improvised roadblocks were set up on the routes into Calais. All around lies the detritus of a retreating army.

FRIDAY, MAY 24

On May 24 Général Weygand placed Général Marie-Bertrand Falgade, the commander of the XVIème Corps d'Armée, in command of all the ground forces in the northern sector, under the overall command of Amiral Jean Abrial. Général Falgade reorganised the Calais sector under British command, and the one at Boulogne under French command.

There was a brief interlude for the garrison in Calais when on the afternoon of May 23 the 10. Panzer-Division was once again subordinated to XIX. Armeekorps and Guderian decided to move the 1. Panzer-Division, which was then close to Calais, on to Dunkirk while the 10. Panzer-Division replaced it at Calais. Disengaging from the Calais sector, the 1. Panzer-Division reached the Aa Canal and secured several bridgeheads between Watten and Gravelines. To the south the 8. Panzer-Division had crossed the Aa at Saint-Omer.

Following the 'Halt Order', the panzer units were instructed to hold the line of the canal and they made use of the period of enforced rest for general reorganisation. In spite of this order, SS-Obergruppenführer Josef Dietrich, the commander of the Leibstandarte SS-'Adolf Hitler', decided to force the canal on May 25 to take the vital Mont Watten which, although only 72 metres high, dominated all the surrounding countryside. His initiative met with success and Guderian, his corps commander, decided to move up the 2. Panzer-Division, now freed after the fall of Boulogne, in support.

Nothing had been heard in Calais of the tank squadron sent the previous night to reconnoitre the road to Dunkirk, and another squadron was sent in the morning with a company of the 1st Rifle Brigade. Although the infantry and tanks fought hard to clear a way through, no progress was made and Brigadier Nicholson called off the

A Cruiser Mk III of the 3rd Royal Tank Regiment beside the railway yard. This particular tank belonged to the HQ Squadron as signified by the yellow square insignia on the turret. The bison denotes 1st Armoured Division.

This corner of Calais has seen considerable redevelopment but fortunately the signalbox has survived as a point of reference.

417

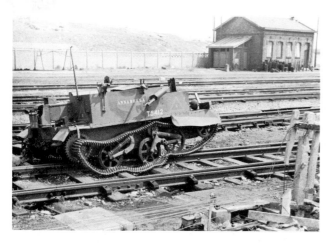

'Annabella' lay stranded across the tracks — a difficult spot to pinpoint today because of the changes.

attack and ordered the troops back to Calais. The 3rd Royal Tank Regiment was by now reduced to 12 Mark VIs and 9 Cruisers.

Early that morning Nicholson had been informed that the evacuation of Calais had been decided 'in principle'. In the afternoon, however, when German pressure against the town had increased, he received a message from London telling him that 'the fact that British forces in your area now under Falgade who has ordered no, repeat no, evacuation, means that you must comply for sake of Allied solidarity'.

During the evening a German aircraft dropped leaflets stating that Boulogne had been taken and calling on the troops at Calais to surrender.

SATURDAY, MAY 25

The German shelling resumed, concentrating now on the heart of the old town. Collapsed buildings blocked the streets, fire raged all over the place and smoke and dust obscured visibility and the movements of troops. Nicholson had established a joint headquarters with the French commander in the Citadel, and the French and British units all around the perimeter fought off all attacks though sustaining heavy losses. A German officer appeared in the afternoon under a flag of truce, accompanied by a captured French captain and a Belgian soldier, to demand surrender. The German envoy went back with Nicholson's negative response — 'it is the British Army's duty

to fight as well as it is the German's' — and an explanation that the other two men had not been sent back because they had not been blindfolded. Nicholson however gave an assurance that 'they will not be allowed to fight against the Germans'.

SUNDAY, MAY 26

The bombardment resumed with even greater violence early in the morning, soon followed by heavy dive-bombing. At midday Guderian asked the commander of the 10. Panzer-Division, Generalleutnant Ferdinand Schaal, what he thought about leaving Calais to the Luftwaffe. Schaal said he would prefer not to, maintaining that bombs would have no effect against the

The Germans broke into Calais, overwhelming one group of defenders after another. This barricade was forced and the troops manning it — British soldiers according to the original

German caption — walked out with their hands up. Note that another barricade had been built further up in the street on the right behind the German half-track.

ancient fortifications and that he would then have to recapture the ground from which his forward units had withdrawn preparatory to the Luftwaffe's attack.

The attack was pressed home during the day and before long the Citadel had been isolated from the town, where the defenders had been split by the German penetrations into groups fighting alone. The attackers broke into the Citadel in the afternoon and captured Brigadier Nicholson, and as evening came, one group after another was overwhelmed and gradually the fighting died out. Calais was in German hands.

At first light on May 27, before it was known that Calais had fallen, the RAF sent twelve Lysanders to drop supplies of water. These were followed later in

The final irony. In a last-ditch attempt to re-supply the besieged defenders, the RAF sent in twelve Lysanders at first light on May 27 on a supply-dropping mission — not knowing that the Germans had overrun the town the night before. More aircraft followed later in an attempt to drop water and ammunition to the troops believed to be still holding out in the Citadel on the west side of Calais. Three aircraft failed to return, this Lysander crashing right on top of Fort Risban which controlled the entrance to the harbour.

the morning by 17 Lysanders which dropped ammunition while nine Swordfish bombed enemy guns near the town — three of the Lysanders failing to return.

This last ditch stand at Calais was not entirely a wasted contribution 'for the sake of Allied solidarity'. The Boulogne and Calais garrisons had tied down two

panzer divisions during the most critical days of the withdrawal to Dunkirk. By the time the 'Halt Order' was lifted — a period which allowed Guderian to regroup — British divisions, freed by the concentration of the northern flank of a shrinking corridor to the sea, had arrived ready for III Corps to stiffen the western rearward flank.

Today the fort is abandoned with a camping site on its roof.

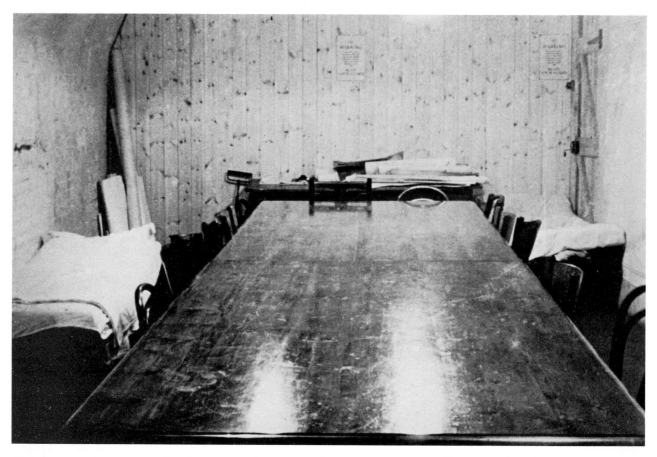

The BEF withdrawal to the coast

The room where history was made: the nerve-centre beneath Dover Castle for Operation 'Dynamo'.

Gort received formal permission to evacuate in a telegram from the Secretary of State for War, Anthony Eden, on May 26. Eden could not see any prospect of a breakthrough from the south and Gort was 'now authorised to operate towards coast forthwith in conjunction with French and Belgian Armies'. Unfortunately, although the policy of evacuation might have been accepted on the highest political level, the French High Command was in two minds about it, and Blanchard still understood that a stand was to be made on the Lys and refused to see the urgency of any further withdrawal. Gort and the French commanders were in disagreement about the feasibility of an evacuation. To the French, and to Gort's superiors in London, the chances of success appeared to be very slim in the face of apparently insuperable odds. For the French there was an additional factor which gave them a different perspective from the British. Even if the evacuation turned out to be a great success, it would inevitably free a mass of German forces and a full-scale attack southwards would soon follow. Every day gained by the armies in the north made it more possible to establish the Weygand Line. The British could view it as winning a breathing space to re-equip their army but the French could see nothing good in it.

Each ally was aware that its own interests conflicted with the others. Despite British claims of having acted in good faith, the decision to evacuate —

The complex of tunnels and casemates dated back to the 1780s, with underground barracks and a 500-bed hospital being installed during the First World War. In 1918 the operations centre was used by Admiral Keyes to plan the raid on Zeebrugge, and 23 years later by Admiral Ramsay for masterminding the evacuation from Dunkirk. In 1959 a complete new floor was added to expand the headquarters into a regional seat of government for use in case of nuclear attack. The government finally relinquished its control in 1986, and in May 1990 English Heritage opened the Casemate Level to visitors. One of the first: forces' favourite Vera Lynn.

420

in fact to withdraw completely from the scene of battle in the north — was not clearly made known to the French at first. The evacuation was well under way before the French Command, under whose orders Gort came, fully understood what their British ally was doing. The French complained bitterly that the decision had been carefully concealed from them, the British answering that any misunderstanding stemmed from the French High Command dithering over whether to go along with it.

Vice-Admiral Sir Bertram H. Ramsay, Flag Officer Commanding Dover, who had been appointed to plan and control an evacuation if it should be ordered, held his first meeting on May 20. Three days later he informed all concerned that, if ordered, the operation would be known as 'Dynamo' — a name believed chosen because his HQ at Dover Castle was above the old dynamo room. The evacuation of 'useless mouths' had been in progress since May 21 and by midnight on May 26 the Navy had already brought back to England 27,936 men who were no longer needed in France through the harbours at Boulogne, Calais, Dunkirk and Ostend. At first it was thought that these same ports could be used if a general evacuation became necessary but by May 26, Boulogne and Calais were in German hands and, with Belgium about to collapse, Ostend was no longer available. Dunkirk alone remained but there the Luftwaffe was already at work, sinking a number of ships in the harbour, among them the French destroyer *l'Adroit* on May 21. Two days later another French destroyer, the *Jaguar*, was torpedoed and sunk off Malo-les-Bains. Admiral Ramsay's plans were well in hand when, shortly before 7.00 p.m. on May 26, the Admiralty sent the signal: 'Operation Dynamo is to commence'. Two hours later the first ship, the boarding vessel *Mona's Isle*, sailed for Dunkirk.

With the failure to implement the Weygand Plan, and the inability of Churchill and the War Cabinet in England to appreciate the desperate situation in which the BEF now found itself, Lord Gort took it upon himself to begin to fall back on Dunkirk and start to evacuate his forces. Général Billotte had still not been replaced and the absence of any clear overall control between the three Allies led each nation to act in its own interest. Belgium, as we have seen, was ready to throw in the towel; now the British decided to save what they could from what they saw as a lost cause. The French, fighting for their homeland, understandably felt that they were being deserted in their hour of need, especially after Arras was abandoned by the British without informing them. Prime Minister Paul Reynaud angrily voiced his feelings in a telegram to Churchill on the 24th, pointing out that the British had pulled out just as the French troops were advancing in the south. When news leaked out that the BEF were beginning to embark from Dunkirk, French feelings towards the English were more than angry. *Above:* June 11: Churchill visits Admiral Ramsey's headquarters beneath Dover Castle.

Churchill's visit to Dover came soon after the end of what has been described as the most successful military evacuation in history. *Left:* Here he looks out from the famous balcony at Casemate Level which overlooks the harbour.

Dame Vera with some of the Dunkirk boys on the same balcony in May 1990. On the left Roger Bellamy, President of the Folkestone Dunkirk Veterans' Association with their Chairman Bernard Whiting, centre, and Secretary Les Tyler, right.

The task of forcing the Canal d'Aire at Béthune (more commonly referred to as the La Bassée Canal) fell to Gruppe Hoth. Facing the 2nd Division was the SS-Totenkopf-Division west of Béthune, the 4. Panzer-Division in the centre, with 7. Panzer-Division to the east of the town. *Left:* Schützen-Regiment 12 (4. Panzers) made their assault crossing just north of Béthune at 8.00 a.m. on the 27th. Here a seriously wounded soldier is brought back from the battle on the northern bank. *Right:* We discovered that the footbridge was built just east of the blown road bridge near Essars.

MONDAY, MAY 27

The Commander-in-Chief, Général Weygand, initiated a meeting at Cassel early on May 27 but Gort failed to appear and sent instead Lieutenant-General Sir Ronald Adam whom he had ordered to leave the III Corps to organise a bridgehead. Général Marie-Louis Koeltz, representing Weygand, and Général Blanchard were there, as were the French commander at Dunkirk, Amiral Abrial, and Général Falgade, commanding the XVIème Corps d'Armée with two divisions of the original 7ème Armée which had remained in the coastal sector. Just before the conference began, a plan for the defence of a perimeter was agreed between Adam and Falgade: the French were to be responsible for the area west of Dunkirk, the British for the area from Dunkirk to Nieuport. At the conference Général Koeltz speaking for Weygand insisted on the necessity to recapture Calais; nobody there pointed out to him that this was impracticable and incompatible with what had been agreed. Weygand later sent a message to Gort making a 'personal appeal' to him that 'the British Army must participate strongly in the necessary general

counter-attacks. Situation demands hard hitting'.

At the far end of the corridor, Général Prioux, the commander of the 1ère Armée, was complying with the French policy and that afternoon issued an order stating that 'the battle will be fought without thought of retreat on the Lys' — nothing about an immediate withdrawal towards Dunkirk.

By midday the bridgehead was nearly a mile wide with German forces expanding rapidly northwards. *Left:* This picture of wounded British prisoners was taken that afternoon in Essars. *Right:* The old square type of milestone (or should we say kilometrestone), not often seen in France today, were originally put up by the Michelin Company. Jean Paul was thrilled to find that this one had survived although the side indicating the direct route to Beuvry had been painted over as the bridge which had been blown over the canal on the D171 was never rebuilt after the war.

Midway between Béthune and La Bassée, Schützen-Regiment 7 (7. Panzers) had established a bridgehead across the canal beside the destroyed road bridge between Cuinchy and Violaines. Here prisoners from the Queen's Own Cameron

Highlanders lend a hand in the construction of a 3-tonne pontoon bridge. Although it was forbidden to force prisoners at gunpoint to carry out such work in the front line, there was nothing to stop the employment of volunteers.

Attacks against the Allied corridor came in from all sides but the Germans found it hard going. The opportunities lost because of the 'Halt Order' were alluded to in the Operations Record of XXXIX. Armeekorps:

'As foreseen, the enforced two-day halt on the southern bank of the canal produced two results on May 27. The troops suffered considerable casualties when attacking across the La Bassée Canal, now stubbornly defended by the enemy, and there was no longer time to intercept effectively the stream of French and British troops escaping westwards from the Lille area towards the Channel.' The Germans troops all around the perimeter knew that men were embarking and Gruppe von Kleist reported on May 27 that 'it is very bitter for our men to see this.'

Meanwhile Dunkirk was violently bombed and with several hundred civilians killed, one third of the town's total civilian casualties for the period of the evacuation, the day ended as one of the worst for the inhabitants.

On the western flank the 62ème Division d'Infanterie was hit by the 1. Panzer-Division and forced to abandon Gravelines during the night; to the south Gruppe von Kleist attacked the line held by the 48th and 44th Divisions, from Bergues to the Lys Canal through Cassel and Hazebrouck, making no real headway.

Further south, between Saint-Venant and La Bassée, the battle reached a crisis for the 2nd Division struck by XV. Armeekorps which attacked to force the Canal d'Aire. The division's 6th Brigade was on the right between Saint-Venant and Robecq; the 4th Brigade in the centre held the line to beyond Béthune, and the 5th Brigade from there to La Bassée. The 7. Panzer-Division experienced some difficulty in forcing the canal on the morning of May 27 at the two small bridgeheads established near Cuinchy in the sector held

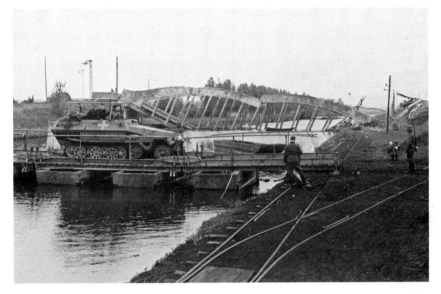

Above: **Transport from the 7. Panzer-Division crosses to the northern bank. The picture was taken looking west towards Béthune.** *Below:* **Today no trace remains of the railway line which originally ran alongside the waterway.**

Further to the west, engineers of Pionier-Bataillon 58 had singled out a site near Cuinchy for another crossing point, just beside a small inlet branching off the main canal.

by the 7th Worcestershire and the 1st Queen's Own Cameron Highlanders, a situation described here by Rommel:

'Prospects did not look too good for the attack across the canal. Elements of the second battalion, Schtz.Rgt. 7, had crossed in rubber boats and were located on the opposite bank in bushes close to the canal. The battalion had not, however, as I had wished, extended its hold deeper on the north bank and dug itself in, nor had it taken the village of Givenchy. It had also omitted to clean up the enemy for a few hundred metres along the north bank to the west, and to get anti-tank guns and heavy weapons across and dig them in.

Rommel wrote how they 'have constructed a number of pontoons in a small harbour just off the canal. However they have built the 8-tonne type instead of the long 16-tonne as the latter would have been too difficult to manoeuvre through the litter of submerged barges.'

'Then, under my personal direction, 20mm anti-aircraft guns and later a PzKpfw IV were turned on the enemy snipers, who were maintaining a most unpleasant fire from the left and picking off our men one by one. While these nests were being engaged, and the sappers were constructing a ramp on the northern bank and with great effort

The 'small harbour' referred to by Rommel is just off the canal through the passage under the footbridge and railway line. Running parallel to the main canal, the U-shaped harbour returns to join the canal further west (see *opposite*).

manoeuvring across the first pontoons, a report came in that a strong force of enemy tanks from La Bassée had attacked the Schtz.Rgt. 7's eastern bridgehead and thrown the Cramer Abteilung (the regiment's I. Abteilung) back across the canal. The enemy tanks, which included several British heavies, were now standing on the northern bank and spraying the southern bank with machine gun and shell fire [in fact these were French tanks belonging to the 1ère D.L.M., six of them, supporting a counter-attack by a company of the 1st Camerons]. We could hear the enemy fire a few hundred metres away to our right and there was a grave danger that the enemy tanks would push on the west along the canal and attack the Bachmann Abteilung [the II. Abteilung], which still had no anti-tank

At the other end of the U-shaped harbour, Rommel's engineers worked furiously to build a bridge suitable for 16-tonne loads. However, because of the sunken barges in the canal, the bridge could not be run in a straight line. The first tank to test the bridge — a PzKpfw III — nearly slid off, so additional work was necessary to strengthen it. Rommel took the photographs and also had one taken of himself on the canal bank wearing his brand new Knight's Cross given to him the day before by his ADC on the express orders of Hitler.

weapon apart from anti-tank rifles on the northern bank and also had no depth. If the enemy exploited his chance, he could be at the western crossing point in a few minutes.

'The situation was extremely critical. I drove the sappers to their utmost speed and had the pontoons lashed roughly together, in order to get at least a few guns and tanks across. With so many sunken barges and other obstacles jammed in the canal, it was impossible for the bridge to take a straight course,

and its structure consequently had little strength. As the first PzKpfw III lumbered over, some pontoons gave noticeably, and it was touch and go whether or not the tank would slither bodily into the canal. While it was crossing, I sent off a PzKpfw IV fifty metres to the east along the high bank on our side of the canal, with orders to open fire immediately on the enemy tanks attacking from La Bassée. The fire of this PzKpfw IV brought the leading enemy tank to a halt. Shortly afterwards the PzKpfw III

425

Left: **La Bassée received a pounding from shelling and bombing and the church tower was badly damaged. These are** prisoners from the 43ème Division d'Infanterie and 2ème D.L.M. *Right:* **We arrived just as a funeral was about to begin.**

La Bassée was no stranger to war, having been totally razed to the ground by Allied bombardments 25 years before. For four years it was a bastion in the German line and the ruins were not recaptured until October 1918. Then in 1940 the Germans came back ... these men are from 7. Panzer-Division on their way north out of the bridgehead while highlanders clear up the street in front of the church.

escape. About a hundred men, all that was left of the two battalions, reached Laventie in the evening with the 2nd Division now reduced to less than the strength of a brigade.

On the eastern flank the four British divisions on the right wing along the frontier — the 42nd, 1st, 3rd and 4th Divisions — withdrew during the night and by morning the bulk of them were behind the River Lys. Not so the French. Only part of Prioux's 1ère Armée had managed to move back in time behind the river as many of the army's units had had to come from much further to the south. Consequently they were in great danger of being trapped in the Lille area when the leading troops of the 4. Armee attacking from the west and those of the 6. Armee advancing from the east joined up behind them.

Already threatened on the east by units of the XXVII. Armeekorps, the 1ère Armée was now confronted with another threat on the west when on May 27 the XV. Armeekorps attacked north of the Canal d'Aire from bridgeheads already established. The corridor at the rear of the army was soon only forty kilometres wide between Menin and La Bassée.

on the northern bank joined in and a few minutes later a howitzer which had been manhandled across. This soon brought the enemy tank attack to a standstill.

'Work was now started on strengthening the 16-ton bridge and before long a steady flow of vehicles began to move one by one across it.'

On this same day, May 27, Rommel was gazetted with the Ritterkreuz which had been awarded him by his ADC, Leutnant Karl Hanke, in Hitler's name.

Rommel massed his strength on the northern bank of the canal and attacked eastwards early in the afternoon. By-passing the town to the north, the panzers attacked La Bassée from the east, almost surrounding the 1st Camerons. Ten tanks of the Royal Tank Regiment attacked the panzers near Violaines, losing all but three, but their action helped the remnants of the Camerons and Worcestershires to

M. Coupet, still selling his curtains from his corner shop, has seen it all before.

At noon on the 27th Rommel was summoned urgently to divisional head-quarters as IX. Armeekorps had transferred Panzer-Brigade 8 under his command for an advance on Lille. (see Rommel's photo on page 425 taken later that afternoon.) These were the tanks from the 5. Panzer-Division which, being one of the pre-war formations, had a panzer brigade of two regiments, each of two battalions, whereas Rommel's division had only one panzer regiment plus a panzer battalion. *Above:* A motorcycle patrol of the 5. Panzer-Division — note the divisional insignia — passes a pair of abandoned French Schneider AMC 29 tanks north of La Bassée. The battered church tower can be seen in the distance. (The 2ème D.L.M. was still equipped with the obsolete Schneider because of the lack of S-35s and H-39s.) *Right:* This P-178 of the 6ème Cuirassiers lay further up the road. A dead crewman lies sprawled outside the door — his last battle over.

The scene pictured by the German photographer was here on the D947 — originally the N347. (Because of the extensive changes in road classifications in France in recent years, we have mostly used current nomenclature to avoid confusion.)

West of Béthune, the SS-Totenkopf-Division had also forced the canal line and advanced to Le Cornet Malo where they clashed with the 2nd Battalion, The Royal Norfolk Regiment. This picture was taken by one of the SS troopers in Le Cornet Malo on the 27th. The SS-Totenkopf-Division was not a panzer unit yet, but this rare shot shows that a captured Somua S-35 has been pressed into action with large German crosses and the division's death's head emblem. Le Cornet Malo was soon in German hands and the SS troops went on to attack Le Paradis, about three kilometres to the north.

DURIES FARM – LAST STAND

ESCAPE ROUTE OF TWO SURVIVORS

CRETON FARM

MASSACRE HERE

PRISONERS SEARCHED HERE

After a fierce battle in which SS-Infanterie-Regiment 2 suffered heavy casualties, the Germans had worked their way across open country and into Le Paradis. The Norfolks had also been heavily depleted, the remaining troops — about a hundred — making a last stand at battalion HQ which had been established in the Duries farm. Major Lisle Ryder posted the men in and around the outbuildings and radioed desperately for artillery support. None was forthcoming and by late afternoon, with ammunition running low, the CO ordered the survivors into the cowshed. He explained that they were completely surrounded and there was no hope of escape. Asking for a show of hands, the decision was made to surrender.

A white flag was tied to a rifle but the first attempt to surrender was answered with a burst of machine gun fire. Five minutes later a second attempt was greeted with cries of triumph as SS troopers from 3. Kompanie ran forward to take them prisoner. The Norfolks were then marched to a nearby meadow where they were searched, the SS holding a summary court alleging that 'dum-dum' bullets had been used against them, contrary to the rules of war. The Norfolks — 99 in all — were then lined up on the lane and marched to the Rue du Paradis and into the yard of the Creton farm. Two machine guns had been set up facing the long brick farm building, the command to open fire being given as the head of the column drew level with the end of the barn. This picture was reputedly taken by a German soldier passing along the road with the Norfolks still lying where they had been mown down. Although the SS went through the bodies, finishing off any soldier showing signs of life, incredibly two men, Privates Bill O'Callaghan and Bert Pooley were still alive and conscious, though wounded. Both men were subsequently captured and taken to hospital in the belief that they were ordinary soldiers wounded in the fighting. Through their evidence, the commander of 3. Kompanie, SS-Hauptsturmführer Fritz Knöchlein, was brought to trial after the war by a British war crimes court and, found guilty, was executed on January 28, 1949.

On May 28 Major Riederer, an officer on the general staff of XVI. Armeekorps, spotted the pile of bodies lying in the farmyard. Examination revealed that it was 'apparently a case of prisoners who had been shot by way of summary execution in the head; which shots must have been fired at very close range. In some cases the whole skull was smashed, a type of wound which can only have been inflicted by blows from rifle butts.' He reported the matter to higher military authority which immediately despatched a medical officer, Dr Haddenhorst, to Le Paradis to report. He arrived at 5.00 p.m. on Wednesday, (the 29th), to find an SS medical company busily engaged in burying the evidence in a pit in the yard. Immediate inquiries were directed to the SS-Totenkopf-Division for an explanation although this was never forthcoming as the division soon afterwards left the corps command area. The French tended the mass grave until May 1942 when the remains were exhumed to be reburied in a special plot behind the local churchyard. By then only 50 bodies could be identified — a fact borne out by the inscription on so many of the headstones today: 'Known unto God.'

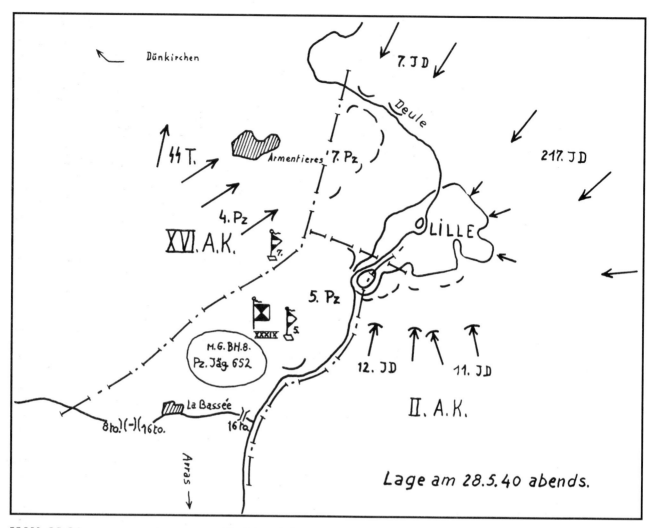

Dünkirchen

7. JD

Deule

SS T.

Armentieres 7. Pz

217. JD

4. Pz

XVI. A.K.

7.

LILLE

5. Pz

XXXIX 5

M.G. BH.8.
Pz. Jäg 652

12. JD   11. JD

II. A.K.

Bko!(-)(16to.   La Bassée
16 ta.

Arras

Lage am 28.5.40 abends.

MAY 28-31
The end of the 1ère Armée

With the BEF having started to pull back northwards, the surrender of the Belgian Army on May 28 only made the plight of the 1ère Armée worse. By that evening the front runners of the 7. Panzer-Division were at Englos and Lomme on the western edge of Lille; those of the 4. Panzer-Divison at Wez-Macquart just to the east of Armentières; the SS-Totenkopf-Division was near Estaires, and the 3. Panzer-Division had crossed the Lys near Mer-

Final despair for the French came on the morning of Tuesday, May 28, with the news of the Belgian surrender. Now, with both her allies having seemingly deserted her, France felt alone, and defeatism began to spread unchecked — coupled with a strong anti-British sentiment. This was the situation at the close of play that evening as drawn up by the staff of XXXIX. Armeekorps. The leaders of the 7. Panzer-Division had just reached the Deule river and joined forces with the 7. Infanterie-Division advancing to reach the north bank. In the pocket around Lille was the 1ère Armée, now completely surrounded. The situation in the area was somewhat confusing as the city was right on the boundary between the 4. and 6. Armees. To simplify matters, on May 30 the sector was subordinated to one corps only — the XXVII. Armeekorps — with the order to clear up the situation 'in and around' Lille.

ville. Alongside were the SS-Verfügungs-Division, the 6. Panzer-Division and the 8. Panzer-Division which had passed Hazebrouck.

Race relations in Wavrin, ten kilometres south of Lille. The author's son, Michaël, stands in for the French soldiers in a

picture which no doubt found a useful place in Dr Goebbels' racial scrapbook.

Abandoned French anti-tank guns stand idle on Wavrin's Place de la République. Meanwhile German forces press on northwards to squeeze the pocket.

The Belgian surrender made it impossible for Gort to postpone an understanding with Blanchard any longer and they discussed the matter of an evacuation when they met at about 11.00 a.m. on May 28. Gort read out one of the telegrams he had received the previous day from the Secretary of State for War which made clear that his 'sole task now is to evacuate to England maximum of your forces possible'. It was evident that although both of them had received orders to establish a bridgehead at Dunkirk, only those issued to Gort had the intention of using it as a base for an evacuation. Gort insisted that the only alternative to surrender was now total evacuation and that time was desperately short but Blanchard refused to take such steps without formal orders from Weygand. While they argued, a liaison officer arrived from the headquarters of the 1ère Armée and made it known that Général Prioux considered that his troops were not in a position to withdraw and that he intended to stand on the Lys. Gort realised that the obstinacy of the French, which would probably result in the total loss of the 1ère Armée, would also cast an odd light on the BEF's evacuation: the image of the French holding their ground, fighting to the last man, covering the withdrawal of British troops who had backed out of the fighting to flee back to their own country.

As the immensity of the tragedy unfolded, Gort, in the words of his later official report, 'begged General Blanchard for the sake of France, the French Army and the Allied Cause to order General Prioux back'. Blanchard then asked Gort formally whether the British troops would pull back further north that night regardless of the situation of the 1ère Armée on the Lys. 'Yes', replied Gort, 'they would', if he was to have any hope of carrying out his government's orders. This withdrawal, they both knew, would leave the northern flank of the 1ère Armée completely exposed. There was nothing more to be said. Blanchard left. His 'parting was not unfriendly', Gort felt able to write.

General Prioux subsequently decided to hold the line of the Lys with his IVème Corps d'Armée while two of his corps, the Corps de Cavalerie and the IIIème Corps d'Armée, would meantime withdraw northwards with their

attached divisions, starting that night. He already regarded his Vème Corps d'Armée still fighting in the Lille area as irredeemably lost. The army staff, and Général Prioux himself, would remain at his headquarters at Steenwerck to coordinate the battle on the Lys.

The next stage of the BEF's withdrawal, on the night of May 28, had left the entire area north of Lille to the Germans. However the Corps de Cavalerie succeeded in bringing back its units that night, covering the IIIème Corps d'Armée which managed to withdraw to Hondschoote — a 60-kilometre night march for the exhausted troops of the, by now, enervated corps, urged on by their commander, Général Benoit de la Laurencie. Further south things had not developed as Prioux had hoped and elements of seven divisions of the IVème and Vème Corps d'Armée were trapped in the area to the south of Lille, all in poor shape, worn out in Belgium although some troops had managed to escape north towards Dunkirk with IIIème Corps d'Armée. Their attempt at breaking out westwards during the

night of May 28 did not stand much of a chance. The 15ème D.I.M. tried to force the Deule Canal from Loos in the direction of Lomme, while the 2ème D.I.N.A. in the Seguedin area and the 5ème D.I.N.A. from Haubourdin pushed in the direction of Santes. The attack was launched at about 7.30 p.m. but none of the three groups got out; only a few armoured cars of the 4ème G.R.D.I. from Canteleu managing to force their way through and reach the Lys. At Haubourdin, the troops assembled there ready to make a break for it came under heavy fire from German artillery which had found the correct range.

Rommel had another close escape after sending out an urgent call for artillery support when it became apparent that the French opposite him near Lomme were steadily increasing in numbers:

'Orders to this effect had just been issued, when a hail of shells suddenly began to fall round the panzer regiment's command post, which was also serving as divisional headquarters.

Smashing the last of the French resistance in the southern outskirts of Lille. This 15cm sIG33 was pictured in action on May 29 in Haubourdin. Unfortunately when we located the spot near the Porte d'Arras, we found that this field had been completely developed, making a comparison meaningless.

The French units trapped in Lille held their ground with fierce determination even though their plight was a foregone conclusion. At Lomme, on the western outskirts of the town, the crew of the 15ème D.I.M. operating this 75mm Modèle 1897 stopped every German attempt to get through on the Avenue de

Dunkerque. Rommel must have been impressed, for he took this and several other pictures in the area although he forgot to leave with them a written location. He probably remembered quite well where he was at the time but it gave Jean Paul a considerable headache to read his mind!

Even as they began we had the feeling that they were our own shells and immediately sent up green flares. I tried to get to the radio to order the cease fire, but the fire was so thick that it was not easy to reach the signals lorry, which was standing behind the house [the command post]. There was no doubt that they were our own shells, probably 150mm, with whose effect we were only too familiar. I was just making a dash for the signals vehicle, with Major Günther Erdmann running a few metres in front, when a heavy shell landed close by the house door near which the vehicle was standing. When the smoke cleared, Major Erdmann, commander of Aufkl.Abt. 37, lay face to the ground, dead, with his back shattered. He was bleeding from the head and from an enormous wound in his back. His left hand was still grasping his leather gloves. I had escaped unscathed, though the same shell had wounded several other officers and men. We continued to send up flares and try by radio to get the fire stopped but it was a long time before the last shell came down.'

Another desperate fire-fight for survival. Further up the Avenue de Dunkerque, Rommel pictured another French road-block with a 75mm gun facing Rue Ronsard, and a second gun trained up the Rue du Moulin.

Left: Rommel would have been in Lille on June 1 or soon after when the 1ère Armée finally surrendered. He inspected the wreck of one of the victims of the 75mm, a PzKpfw II, which had had its turret blown completely off as a result of two direct hits.

Right: Treading in the footsteps of the great warrior, Jean Paul found that the range between the gun and tank had been about 200 metres, the wreck lying outside No. 920 and the gun at the top of the page in front of No. 1000.

Général Prioux and his staff were captured at 1ère Armée headquarters at Steenwerck on May 29 together with Général Henri Aymes, the commander of the IVème Corps d'Armée. What now remained of the 1ère Armée was trapped to the south and west of Lille, where three main areas of resistance were hastily organised. At Haubourdin elements of the 2ème D.I.N.A. and 5ème D.I.N.A. and of the 25ème D.I.M. were assembled under the command of Général Jean Molinié, the commander of the latter. At Loos and in the Faubourg des Postes at Lille were the 15ème D.I.M. with men of the 1ère D.I.M. under the command of Général Alphonse Juin of the 15ème. Then at Lambersart, west of the Citadelle, the 1ère Division Marocaine and elements of the 25ème D.I.M. lay under the command of Général Albert Mellier. Being senior in rank, Général Molinié assumed overall command and sought to co-ordinate their efforts from his command post at Haubourdin.

For the next two days the battle raged as the Germans tried to close the ring. Plastered by the German artillery, the French positions were gradually cut off, isolated groups resisting stubbornly until each had exhausted their ammunition. At the boundary of the 4. Armee and 6. Armee, the battle occupied large German forces. Of the former, the XXXIX. Armeekorps had two panzer divisions engaged just west of Lille and the II. Armeekorps two infantry divisions south of the town. Of the latter Armee. the IV. Armeekorps and the

It is not always easy to figure out the event depicted in a particular photograph and this one at the Heurtebise crossroads in Haubourdin is a good example. It would be nice to think that a guard of honour has been provided for the unfortunate animal. Whatever it is, the crowd is being kept well back.

XXVII. Armeekorps had three divisions north and east of the town, all of which would otherwise have been able to increase the pressure on the Allied divisions withdrawing to the coast.

On May 30 two divisions of the 4. Armee right wing, the 267. Infanterie-Division and the 11. Infanterie-Division, were transferred to the XXVII. Armeekorps of the 6. Armee and the corps was ordered to clear the situation 'in and around' Lille. Early on May 31 the Germans sent aircraft to drop leaflets on the French positions, giving the surrounded troops until 7.30 a.m. to surrender. Thereafter, the artillery began to lay down another heavy barrage. House-to-house fighting took place in Haubourdin, Loos and Lambersart for most of the day but the end was near. That evening, having refused to consider numerous peace offers over the past two days, Général Molinié agreed to talks and at 1.00 a.m. on June 1 he signed the capitulation of the troops in the Lille pocket.

Lille has fallen . . . the battle is o'er. 'Fight the good fight with all thy might' could well be the epitaph for the crew of this gun in the Rue de Solférino who gave their all in a desperate last stand for France.

In recognition of this gallant stand, later that morning the Germans accorded military honours to the surrendering units as they marched past the commander of XXVII. Armeekorps, General Alfred Wäger, and members of his staff on the main square of Lille. The parade at 9.30 a.m. was led by the divisional commanders, followed by three companies — two from the 2ème D.I.N.A. and one from the 5ème D.I.N.A. — all bearing arms but without ammunition, and then by the remainder who had been disarmed. However when they came to hear of this, the German High Command considered it all to be a waste of time and it seems that the Commander-in-Chief of the Army, Generaloberst Walther von Brauchitsch, criticised General Wäger for his old-fashioned chivalry. On June 2 the 6. Armee reported an impressive total of seven generals, 350 officers and 34,600 men taken prisoner and the capture of some 320 guns and 100 tanks in the Lille pocket.

Telephones and taxis — how are the mighty fallen!

A rare gesture in total war. On June 1, 1940, General Alfred Wäger, XXVII. Armeekorps' commander, honours a gallant foe.

Later criticised for his old-fashioned sense of chivalry, General Wäger took the salute with members of his staff in the main square in Lille. Beside him his personal corps commander's standard, with the Nazi flag already flying from the town hall.

The historic parade ground now — like so many main squares in France today — the Place Général de Gaulle.

Dunkirk: the evacuation

Mona's Isle, the first ship to set out on Operation 'Dynamo', had berthed in Dunkirk harbour during an air attack and taken 1,420 troops on board. She was shelled and strafed on the return trip, but arrived safely back at Dover at midday on May 27, 23 of the men on board having been killed and 60 wounded.

Operation 'Dynamo' had got off to an inauspicious start on the first day as a false rumour that Dunkirk was in enemy hands resulted in ships returning empty and by midnight on May 27 only 7,669 men had been brought back. The Luftwaffe had sent about 300 aircraft to raid the Dunkirk sector and the harbour was heavily bombed, several French

ships being sunk, among them two auxiliary minesweepers, *le Dijonnais* and *la Malo*.

On II Corps front, on the eastern flank of the corridor, the main weight of the attacks being made by the IV. Armeekorps south of Ypres (where earlier a gap had opened between the British and Belgians armies as the Belgians had been driven back) were now falling on the 5th Division. As the fighting intensified, artillery and infantry had been brought in to progressively strengthen this flank. Across the corridor to the west, on the III Corps front, the situation was less satisfactory, the 44th and 48th Divisions being widely dispersed. The latter mainly held a

series of strongpoints at Socx, Wormhout, Cassel and Hazebrouck which had been bypassed, but by the evening Socx was lost, Wormhout had become untenable and all contact with Cassel and Hazebrouck had been cut off. The division's commander, Major-General A.F.A.N. Thorne, ordered his troops to retire during the night to the Yser and the move was duly carried out, except by the garrison at Hazebrouck, which was overwhelmed, and at Cassel, which did not receive the order before the next morning. The 44th Division also withdrew during the night to the Monts des Cats, a naturally strong position about six kilometres east of Steenvoorde.

This PzKpfw 35(t) and PzKpfw IV of Panzer-Regiment 11 were pictured on the afternoon of May 27 at the Fort Rouge crossroads, about three kilometres east of Arques on the D933 from Saint-Omer to Cassel.

On the western flank of the corridor south of Dunkirk, along which the BEF was retreating, the 48th Division held a series of strongpoints at Socx, Wormhout, Cassel and Hazebrouck. The latter, where the 1st Buckinghamshire Battalion was surrounded, held out until the evening of the 28th when the stout-hearted garrison was finally overcome. The news that Hazebrouck had fallen would have brought a lump to the throat of all Old Contemptibles for it was a town known to every British soldier who had served in the Great War. Wellington had even used it as a base in 1815, and a hundred years later its Grand Place was a hive of activity, always bustling with troops on their way to or from the lines. It had fallen briefly to the Germans in 1914 but had been recaptured and thereafter remained a major advanced British base. Although the town had been badly damaged, and nearly overrun in 1918, in 1940 the square was spared the worst of the fighting.

Gort's headquarters moved back as well that night and was re-established at De Panne on May 28. Instructions were issued laying down the order of evacuation: III Corps was to go first, II Corps next, then I Corps. With things apparently going better than expected, the Navy's initial task expanded from a hasty embarkation of a part of the force to an effort to bring the whole BEF back home.

Once in the bridgehead Gort came under the immediate command of Amiral Abrial, the French commander of the Dunkirk area. However the command situation was very difficult as the French had not yet come to accept that the British intended to take off the

Looking much the same as it did when pictured after the battle was over, but now another Place Général de Gaulle.

Just to the north was another town with close English military connections — Cassel. It was here that the Grand Old Duke of York had marched his 10,000 men up the hill only to march them down again. That had been in the 1793-94 Flanders campaign against the French. Now, fighting the Germans in May 1940, orders to retire did not reach the 145th Brigade in the town till the morning of the 29th but by then it was under heavy bombardment and none could get out.

Only when darkness fell could the garrison try to make good its escape, but for some it was too late. They lay where they had fallen amid the smoking ruins, entered by the Germans on the morning of the 30th.

that the BEF was embarking 'in force', Blanchard sent a message to Georges at 7.25 a.m. on May 28: 'Numerous indications of embarkation of British troops abandoning matériel. I have not been able to meet General Gort. Urgently request instructions from headquarters.' The answer from Weygand stated that former instructions — i.e. to retrench — were still in force and Blanchard would have to remain 'the sole judge of what must be done to save what can be saved'.

The withdrawal to the bridgehead continued as planned but the traffic problem, which had been partially solved on the previous days, was again complicated as elements of the IIIème Corps d'Armée began to arrive. The French and British both claimed, and still claim today, that the confusion was caused by the other failing to respect the allocation of roads. Morever, both armies were not withdrawing for the same reason: the British, withdrawing to evacuate, were prepared to leave all their equipment behind; the French, withdrawing to hold the bridgehead, needed all of theirs to do so. Whereas none of the French units had orders to leave their vehicles and equipment outside the perimeter, the British had

entire BEF and they were still under the impression that only some rearward elements were to be withdrawn, the bulk of the British troops staying to defend the perimeter side by side with the French. Faced with the evidence

The 4th Oxfordshire and Buckinghamshire Light Infantry formed the advanced guard; the 145th Brigade headquarters, artillery and engineers came next, followed by the 2nd Gloucestershire and the combined carrier platoons of the two battalions, with what was left of the 1st East Riding Yeomanry forming the rearguard. They clashed with strong German forces and when daylight came a series of individual battles led to the men being killed or captured piecemeal. Few escaped to reach friendly lines. The town was a shambles with abandoned gear and equipment everywhere.

orders to prevent any vehicle trying to enter it. Seldom would the French abandon anything unless compelled to at the British control points, and frequently tempers flared. Numerous anti-aircraft guns, anti-tank weapons, truck loads of ammunition — all of which would be badly needed in the days to come — were abandoned at the roadside because of these somewhat short-sighted orders.

Beach discipline was as yet inadequately organised, the military having little knowledge of the handling of boats and the surf during most of the day made the evacuation doubly difficult. However the situation in the harbour had improved, and ships were sent along the mole which had been found the night before to be a practical substitute for the harbour quays. The destroyers HMS *Mackay*, HMS *Montrose*, HMS *Vimy*, HMS *Worcester*, HMS *Sabre* and HMS *Anthony* all entered and embarked large numbers of troops, while other ships lifted men directly from the beaches. Bad weather and smoke haze from the burning installations brought a lull in the Luftwaffe activity over the perimeter. The French minesweeper *Mimi Pierrot* and the British steamer *Queen of the Channel* were sunk and many others damaged but the day went better than the previous one, with more than double the number of men — 17,804 — landed in England.

WEDNESDAY, MAY 29

After the night's withdrawals in the next stage of the contraction of the corridor, early that morning the 50th and 3rd Divisions were on the Poperinge-Lizerne line and the 42nd and 5th Divisions on the Yser, their rearguards having had to fight hard to provide cover. On the Monts des Cats, under heavy mortar fire and Stuka attack for some hours, at around 10.00 a.m. the 44th Division gave up its exposed positions and, although shelled all the way, the division's columns made it into the perimeter. In Cassel, it was 6.00 a.m. before the order to retire reached the 145th Brigade group

Just outside of Cassel — in the small village of Winnezeele — advanced guards of the 6. Panzer-Division have caught a mixed bag of French soldiers — the lieutenant in the middle being from the 2ème D.I.N.A., the others from the 1ère D.I.M.

By the afternoon of May 28 all contact with the men in Cassel had been cut — these soldiers *(left)* of the 145th Brigade having been caught nearby by advanced elements of the 6. Panzer-Division. Further to the north, the Leibstandarte SS-'Adolf Hitler' was pressing on recklessly towards Wormhout and was soon to capture the village, with 150 men of the 144th Brigade being taken prisoner. The events which then took place in Wormhout are but an example of many atrocities of which civilians and fighting men of all the combatants were the victims. On numerous occasions soldiers who had laid down their arms were summarily shot but, in most cases, the perpetrators went unpunished. Le Paradis (see page 429) was certainly the most serious of such incidents during the 1940 campaign, but by no means the only one. Although war often brings out the best in an individual, regrettably it also brings out the worst.

In many instances, particularly on the Somme (see page 479), but also in the Vosges during the last battles in June, German troops behaved harshly towards prisoners, especially if they were black, and shot many of them. There were always alleged 'good reasons': either because dumdum (sawn off) bullets had been found (as the SS-Totenkopf-Division court-martial had alleged at Le Paradis) or because shots had been fired after a white flag had been displayed. Sometimes it was as a result of finding the mutilated body of a comrade, but to separate speculation from fact today is virtually impossible. In many other cases, civilians were the victims. A few days before Le Paradis, the SS-Totenkopf-Division had already distinguished itself in the worst possible way in the Arras sector, shooting 23 civilian hostages at the Hermant Farm in Pont-du-Gy on May 23 (see page 354); 98 others in and near Aubigny, and 45 at Vandelicourt. All were innocent civilians but, on one occasion at least, the SS claimed to have been fired upon by villagers. Though SS troops were predominant in such incidents, Army units were also implicated. At Vinkt in Belgium, 86 civilians were summarily shot after the capture of the town on May 27 by the 225. Infanterie-Division. Also it must not be forgotten or ignored that, although the reputation of the Wehrmacht was stained by such events, Allied troops were also respons-ible for killing men who had surrendered. Inevitably the victors of any war wish to forget their own sins while prosecuting

those of their defeated foe, yet there are many witnesses of the shooting of Ger-man prisoners by French and British troops. When the campaign was over, the Germans investigated such cases and, where locals were involved, they were brought to trial. A typical instance where an Allied misdeed led to such a conviction was when a Heinkel He 111 crash-landed in a field at Vimy (north of Arras) on May 18. British and French soldiers and civilians rushed to the crash

and when the four airmen tumbled out of the wreck, hands up, they were shot. The soldiers left and the aircraft was then looted by the civilians. When the Ger-mans discovered the bodies at the end of the month, enquiries were made and many locals were arrested. Possession of pieces from the aircraft was damning evidence and three people were tried and executed. *Above:* Wormhout lies not quite midway between Cassel and Dun-kirk on the D916.

'I, Charles Edward Daley, formerly of the 2nd Battalion The Royal Warwickshire Regiment (Army number 7342734), and now discharged from the Army say as follows: . . . the Battalion was in the neighbourhood of a place called Wormhout, and was in action for about two days in defence of that place, against a force of Germans who were attacking with overwhelming superiority. By the afternoon of the 27th or 28th May or thereabouts, although we had not yielded our positions we had been surrounded, and our ammunition having given out, we surrendered and were made prisoners of war. A German soldier armed with a revolver shouted at me "Englander schwein" and shot me in the shoulder. From this point, with some other ranks of the Cheshire Regiment and the Royal Artillery, we were marched to a barn *(above)* some distance away . . . According to my estimate there were about ninety altogether who were herded into the barn, more or less filling it. A German soldier at the door stooped to pick a hand-grenade from his jackboot. Captain Lynn-Allen who was commanding "D" Company, and who was the only officer amongst the prisoners, protested against what appeared to be the intention, namely, to massacre the prisoners. He also protested that there were a number of wounded, and that the accommodation was insufficient to give them room to lie down. The German soldier shouted back,

"Yellow Englishman, there will be plenty of room where you're all going to". This man spoke fluent English, with a strong American accent. He and others then threw bombs into the barn. Some of these bombs were smothered by the heroic action of Sergeant Moore and C.S.M. Jennings who threw themselves on them and were immediately killed. One bomb in the direction of Captain Lynn-Allen appeared to wound a man of his Company called Evans, and I saw Captain Lynn-Allen take advantage of the Germans taking cover from the explosion of the bombs, to drag Private Evans out of the barn, and try and make an escape . . . Following this throwing of bombs into the barn, the Germans began taking the prisoners of war out of the barn five at a time and shooting them. I was rather towards the back, having been amongst those first to enter the barn. When the men in front of myself and the others had been taken out of the barn and shot, it came on to rain, and the shooting was finished off in the barn. We were ordered to turn round, and we were then shot through the back. . . . Later on, the Germans fired tommy-guns into the barn, and I was hit again and became unconscious. When I recovered, I found that my right leg had been shattered by a group of bullets from a tommy-gun, and that my left leg had also sustained a wound. I lay in the barn for from two to three days . . . '

'I, Albert Evans, formerly number 5184737: Private Evans of The Royal Warwickshire Regiment, now discharged from the Army, make oath and say as follows: ... I was standing next to Captain Lynn-Allen, just inside the door of the barn, when the Germans began throwing grenades in. I had my right arm shattered by one of the first explosions. Then, while I was still feeling dazed, and as another grenade came in through the door, Captain Lynn-Allen, who was at this time unwounded, seized me and dragged me out through the door, and round the corner, while the Germans who had thrown the grenades were taking cover against the explosions. Captain Lynn-Allen practically dragged or supported me the whole way to a clump of trees, which was about 200 yards away. When we got inside the trees, we found there was a small stagnant and deep pond in the centre *(right)*. We got down into the pond with the water up to our chests. Captain Lynn-Allen was standing some little distance from the edge. I, because of my condition stood closer to the bank, and presumably lower in the water. Suddenly, without warning, a German appeared on the bank of the pond just above us, showing that we must have been spotted before we

gained the cover of the trees. The German, who was armed with a revolver, immediately shot Captain Lynn-Allen twice. Captain Lynn-Allen's body fell forward and disappeared under the surface.

He then fired at me at a range of about three yards. I was hit twice in the neck and, already bleeding profusely from my arm, I slumped in the water. He no doubt thought that he finished me off.'

The perpetrators of the killing at Wormhout were never identified, but they belonged to the II. Bataillon of the Leibstandarte SS-'Adolf Hitler'. The regimental commander, SS-Obergruppenführer Josef Dietrich, had driven to the village in the morning but his car came under fire, killing the driver and forcing Dietrich to take cover in a ditch. There he remained for most of the day, out of touch with his forces. In the belief that their commander had run into a trap, the SS pressed forward only to suffer heavy casualties, amongst whom was SS-Sturmbannführer Schützeck commanding the II. Bataillon who was wounded around 6.00 p.m. The commander of the 5. Kompanie, SS-Hauptsturmführer Wilhelm Mohnke, had then taken over the battalion. Mohnke survived the war and although a case was made out against him, implicating him in the massacre, it failed for lack of evidence as there was no proof that he himself was involved in or aware of what had happened at the barn. In 1972 the events of that day became known to the National Chaplain of the Dunkirk Veterans' Association, the Revd Leslie Aitken, and on May 28, 1973 he dedicated a memorial which had been erected near the site of the barn which had been demolished some time after 1947. A site was donated by Paul Marie de la Gorce by the side of the road from Wormhout to Esquelbecq as being the nearest accessible spot to the barn. Over 2,000 people were present, the British contingent consisting of members of branches of the DVA from all over the world who were in France for their annual pilgrimage. At the time only four survivors of the massacre had been traced: Charles Daley, Albert Evans, John Lavelle and Alfred Tombs, and these men unveiled the memorial *(left)*. *Right:* Just alongside lay the ditch in which Dietrich sheltered for several hours on the morning of the massacre. He survived the war only to be tried by the US Army in 1946 in a controversial trial at Dachau for the murder of American prisoners at Malmédy on December 17, 1944. He served only 10 years of his 25-year sentence, but was promptly re-arrested and imprisoned for a further 18 months for his part in the executions carried out in Berlin and Munich in June 1934 during the Röhm Purge. He died in 1966.

trapped in the town. They had to endure another day's shelling before attempting to pull out after nightfall but not many got through to Dunkirk.

From the King came a message to Gort for the BEF to tell them that 'the hearts of every one of us at home are with you and your magnificent troops in this hour of peril'. Many of the men were almost at the point of total exhaustion after ten days of endless retreat: from the Dyle to the Senne, from the Senne to the Dender, from the Dender to the Escaut, from the Escaut to the Lys. Even though they had reached the coast, their ordeal was not yet over for there were still another 50 miles to go before they reached Dover. In their thousands, they converged on the broad, sandy beaches and the eastern mole to wait; at first without enough food and water, waiting for orders to embark. Warehouses and oil tanks burned nearby, filling the sky with heavy black smoke and it seemed that there was not a single friendly aircraft to oppose the Luftwaffe which attacked Dunkirk again and again.

In the afternoon, three days after the beginning of Operation 'Dynamo', Général Weygand ordered Général Blanchard to 'establish with all available forces a bridgehead south of Dunkerque-Nieuport to provide for a progressive evacuation by sea'. There was still ambiguity about how this policy was to be carried out and Gort asked the War Office that his mission be made clear both to him and the French High Command. Was he to hold the Dunkirk

Wormhout lay not that far from Steenvoorde where Helmuth Ritgen, a Leutnant on the staff of Panzer-Regiment 11 (6. Panzers) photographed two Panzerjäger I halted in front of the village church during the German attempt to wheel against the Allied flank from the Poperinge area. In this case, the troops managed to escape the trap and the pincers closed behind them.

perimeter as long as Amiral Abrial ordered him to do or was he to make good the escape of the BEF?

Organisation on the beaches was improving and the concentration of ships was nearing its peak. By midnight

The nearer one approached to the coast, the more prolific became the amount of abandoned equipment. Vehicles were immobilised by running engines without oil until they seized, or removal of vital parts. We think this is the road to Ghyvelde.

Socx, right on the edge of the perimeter, with an S-35 from the 4ème Cuirassiers of the 1ère D.L.M.

The low-lying ground behind the coast had already been flooded by the opening of sluice gates in early May. This cyclist from 16. Infanterie-Division was no doubt worriedly trying to steer a straight and narrow course along the flooded D916A south of Bergues. In the background the Groenberg Hill topped by Saint Winoc Abbey.

47,310 men had been landed in England and many more were on their way across. Shipping had come under heavy attack and losses were high: the destroyers HMS *Wakeful* and HMS *Grafton* had been torpedoed and sunk, the destroyer *Grenade* bombed and sunk; other sinkings included the passenger ships *Mona's Queen*, *Normandia*, *Lorina*, *Fenella* and *Crested Eagle*.

The destroyers HMS *Gallant* and HMS *Jaguar*, together with the *Intrepid*, *Saladin* and *Greyhound*, and the sloop HMS *Bideford*, had all been badly damaged.

THURSDAY, MAY 30

Early that morning, Rear-Admiral W. F. Wake-Walker arrived to take charge of the evacuation of troops directly from the beaches in an 'armada of small boats' that would ply from the shore. During the morning a long pier of lorries decked with planks stretching into the sea was built on the beach at Bray-Dunes and another was soon ready at De Panne.

The Germans, having followed up the various withdrawals, were now in close contact with the Allied defence line. A degree of confusion still prevailed on the German side as if the 4. Armee and 6. Armee were each waiting for the other to launch the final attack. Guderian, who had bitterly regretted the halting of the panzers, had now seen the ground with his own eyes, and on May 28 he had advised Gruppe von Kleist that he thought a panzer attack across marshy country would be pointless.

On May 29 his XIX. Armeekorps was relieved by the XIV. Armeekorps and his panzer divisions were pulled out with orders that everything had to be done 'to make the divisions fully operationally effective once again'. On May

Death and destruction on the road to Dunkirk. Even this motor cyclist appears to be lost trying to map-read his way through the acres of equipment. Much of the transport was repaired and later impressed into the service of the Wehrmacht.

The Cassel Gate in Bergues on the Canal de la Basse Colme which formed the inland perimeter of the pocket.

30 the operations officer of 4. Armee complained to Gruppe von Kleist that 'nothing is happening today, no one is any longer interested in Dunkirk. Town and harbour must be bombarded, embarkation prevented, panic caused' and in the afternoon von Kleist was ordered to 'attack Dunkirk on both flanks, penetrate right up to the coast and then continue the pursuit east-wards' although his chief-of-staff re-plied that the panzer divisions were unsuitable for this.

All this indecision was to the advan-tage of the troops at Dunkirk. Too late the German High Command decided that it was now urgent to settle the issue. Operations against Dunkirk were placed under the overall command of the 18. Armee of Heeresgruppe B, which was now made responsible for the destruction of all the Allied troops in the perimeter. For this the army had seven infantry divisions, two motorised brigades, the Infanterie-Regiment 'Gross Deutschland', with the 20. Infanterie-Division (mot) and the Leibstandarte SS-'Adolf Hitler' in re-serve. The change-over was to take effect at 2.00 a.m. on May 31. Never-theless von Rundstedt had got his wish — the withdrawal of his armour — to be husbanded for the second phase of the battle in the West, aiming at the com-plete destruction of the French Army.

There was still ambiguity between Abrial's conception of his orders (he felt that they could hold on indefinitely) and those that Gort was carrying out. The War Office's clarification to Gort's request to know exactly what was ex-pected of him was that he was to continue the evacuation, and to nomin-ate a corps commander to whom he was to hand over as soon as his forces were down to the equivalent of three divi-sions. The order for him to return left him 'no personal discretion in the mat-ter'; politically 'it would be a needless triumph to the enemy' for him to be captured. His successor was to 'carry on the defence in conjunction with the French and evacuation whether from Dunkirk or the beaches'. A message from Weygand asking for the co-operation of four or five divisions in the defence of Dunkirk was received on the morning of May 31 by the War Office, but it was not clear whether these divisions were to cover evacuation or to hold out indefinitely. As Gort had

A second key crossing point over the canal lay further east on the D947 at Brouckstraete, just north of Hondschoote. This carrier lay just near the bridge.

already been instructed to 'defend the present perimeter to the utmost in order to cover maximum evacuation', it was not felt that Weygand's request in-volved any change in the orders given the day before.

The area south of the canal between Bergues and Hondschoote was designated as a destruction area for vehicles when the roads within the pocket became clogged. This is the D947 from Hondschoote to Ghyvelde across the inundations.

Within the perimeter all troops, including General Gort, technically came under Amiral Jean Abrial, commanding the Dunkirk area from his bomb-proof bunker, Bastion 32. This was an old casemate built in 1874 beside the Rue Militaire and reinforced just before the Second World War by the addition of armoured steel plates from the decommissioned battleship *Diderot*. (We saw Général Weygand emerging from the bunker on page 360.) *Right:* Here Amiral Abrial is pictured (probably on May 16) in company with Général André Corap, commander of the 7ème Armée from May 15 to 19 when he was dismissed.

French troops were now waiting in large number for embarkation but few French ships had yet arrived and although 'evacuation in equal numbers' was the policy laid down by the British Government, Gort had put only two ships at their disposal. In a telephone conversation with him at midnight, Churchill stressed the importance of this policy being carried out.

In these difficult hours, there were many incidents between the troops of the two nations and tempers flared. French troops congregating on the beaches could see British soldiers leaving while they stayed behind and, protesting that they should both be taken off, the French tried to overcome what they saw as British self-interest. The British responded by accusing the French of indiscipline and blaming them for spreading unnecessary confusion. The British beach teams acted efficiently but harshly, threatening and occasionally firing at French troops, reportedly causing some casualties.

Relatively few ships entered the harbour at Dunkirk that day and, despite an attempt to make up for lost time in the evening, it ended as the only day on which more men were lifted

Centre: These despatch riders are parked outside but today nothing remains for the historic Bastion 32 was razed in 1978 together with many of the other buildings along the street for the extension of the France-Dunkerque shipyard.

Although the panzer formations were still on 'hold' following von Rundstedt's order of May 24, tanks would not have been much use against the pocket with its limited road access across the flooded low-lying ground. There were few main roads leading into the pocket and any panzers using them in single file would have easily been picked off, so blocking the way for those that followed. *Left:* However, there was no 'halt' restriction on the guns and this 15cm howitzer (SFH 18) is being brought forward through Saint Idesbald just north of De Panne. *Right:* A nice comparison, complete with the original tram lines.

Shelling of the De Panne beach — at the extreme eastern end of the encircled pocket — became so intense that it was decided that II Corps should pull back westwards (actually into France as the frontier ran right through the middle of the perimeter). This move was implemented on May 31 and by the following morning the last troops had left this sector.

The King's summer palace on the left has now gone, to be replaced by a Belgian memorial.

from the beaches than from the harbour. In the face of all the difficulties, 53,823 men had now been returned to England and the shipping losses were much smaller than on previous days, only two destroyers being damaged.

The account by J. R. Blomfield, a subaltern in the 23rd Field Company of the Royal Engineers, then with the 1st Division, well describes a typical scene on the beaches for one such unit:

'My section was the last of the company to get to the beach area, my last orders having been to make for Bray-Dunes. As we were approaching the coast, I met the adjutant trying to sort out the most terrific traffic jam. He said that the road was to be cleared of all

What must have been some of the longest, most frustrating queues of all time formed up on the beaches east of Dunkirk. Although two-thirds of the troops embarked from the Continent did so from the port, nearly 100,000 men were lifted straight off the open beach. Apart from De Panne at the eastern end, there were two other loading points: Bray Dunes (above), roughly in the centre for I Corps, and Malo-les-Bains close to the town of Dunkirk for III Corps and the French. Right: Empty beaches and windswept sand — where an army was saved to fight another day.

446

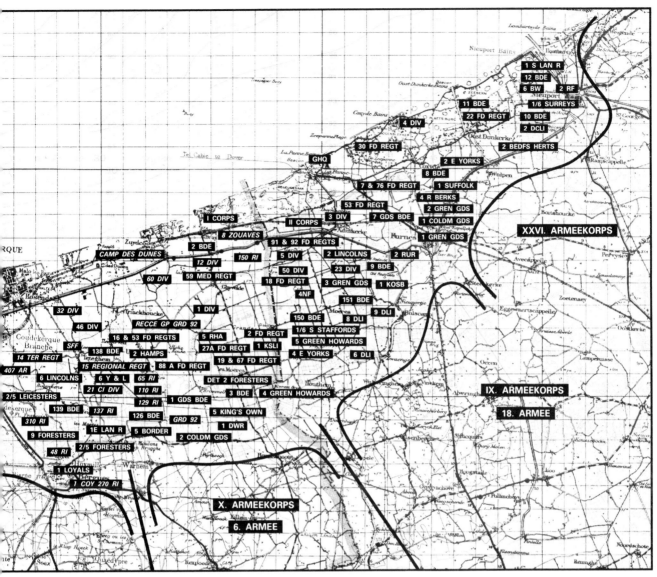

Map labels (reading across the map):

1 S LAN R
12 BDE
6 BW · 2 RF
1/6 SURREYS
11 BDE · 22 FD REGT · 10 BDE
4 DIV · 2 DCLI
30 FD REGT · 2 BEDFS HERTS
GHQ · 2 E YORKS
8 BDE
7 & 76 FD REGT · 1 SUFFOLK
53 FD REGT · 4 R BERKS
I CORPS · 3 DIV · 7 GDS BDE · 2 GREN GDS
II CORPS · 1 COLDM GDS
8 ZOUAVES · 1 GREN GDS
91 & 92 FD REGTS
2 BDE
CAMP DES DUNES · 150 RI · 5 DIV · 2 LINCOLNS · 2 RUR
12 DIV · 9 BDE
60 DIV · 59 MED REGT · 50 DIV · 23 DIV · 1 KOSB
18 FD REGT · 3 GREN GDS
4NF
32 DIV · 1 DIV · 151 BDE
46 DIV · RECCE GP GRD 92 · 150 BDE · 8 DLI · 9 DLI
SFF · 16 & 53 FD REGTS · 5 RHA · 2 FD REGT · 1/6 S STAFFORDS
14 TER REGT · 138 BDE · 2 HAMPS · 27A FD REGT · 1 KSLI · 5 GREEN HOWARDS
407 AR · 15 REGIONAL REGT · 88 A FD REGT · 19 & 67 FD REGT · 4 E YORKS · 6 DLI
6 LINCOLNS · 6 Y & L · 65 RI · DET 2 FORESTERS
2/5 LEICESTERS · 21 CI DIV · 110 RI · 3 BDE · 4 GREEN HOWARDS
139 BDE · 137 RI · 129 RI · 1 GDS BDE
310 RI · 126 BDE · 5 KING'S OWN
1E LAN R · 5 BORDER · GRD 92 · 1 DWR
9 FORESTERS · 2 COLDM GDS
48 RI · 2/5 FORESTERS
1 LOYALS
1 COY 270 RI

XXVI. ARMEEKORPS
IX. ARMEEKORPS
18. ARMEE
X. ARMEEKORPS
6. ARMEE

vehicles except the lorries of the field park company, and I was to help. So, after endless argument, we managed to ditch all the vehicles blocking the road. One Frenchman with a motor cycle and sidecar put up a very strong fight, and he and the adjutant started to wave pistols at each other. However, a sapper waved a Bren gun and he submitted with muttered curses. I detailed a sub-section to do all they could to render the vehicles unserviceable. This they did with great gusto, discovering in the process that pistol bullets apparently bounce off tyres.

'By a miracle, the bridging lorries really did arrive and we went to Bray-Dunes on them. Here we found all the

Left: **British troops march through Dunkirk to the port. This picture was most probably taken on May 26 because the building on the left — the Ronarc'h barracks — was bombed on the following day and burned out. This street, the Rue des Fusiliers Marins, led straight down to the harbour and to the**

Eastern Mole which was to prove a practical substitute for the harbour quays and the easiest place for ships to berth although it was very exposed. It was to be used throughout the evacuation operation. *Right:* **Today there is virtually nothing to relate to the drama of yesteryear.**

447

'On shore we took a lot of notice of bombing and machine gunning and dived frequently into the foxholes with which the beach was pock-marked. In the boats there was nowhere to dive except the uninviting sea, which was covered with the filthiest black oil. During one rest period we collected all the LMGs and ammunition we could find and set them up along the promenade at about ten yard intervals. Anyone who cared was invited to have a shot. The CRE sat in a deck chair with a Bren. He was heard to remark that he did not think he had hit anything but had used an enormous amount of ammunition.

'Finally I was told to go and recce a route to the docks at Dunkirk, where we were to embark that night on a destroyer. This I did and marked the route. We lined up on the beach about 4.00 p.m. and set off. The OC and I were leading. We were both nearly fast asleep. I must have fallen asleep, because just after dark he strode way ahead and I was awakened by a rude cry. He had fallen into a bomb hole which blocked the street. He cursed me roundly for choosing a route with a bomb hole in the middle of it, but was pacified when I assured him that the bomb hole was not there when I had done the recce.

'We stood on the quay for hours and embarked just before dawn. I sat alongside the funnel and woke up in Dover.'

Though the Luftwaffe was a considerable nuisance, sank many ships and destroyed a large part of the built-up area, it failed to stop the evacuation. These townspeople are taking shelter on May 24 — a day when the centre of Dunkirk received a heavy raid.

companies of the division engineers and the CRE inhabiting a particularly insalubrious bit of beach.

'Our working day was organised into shifts, each section doing two six-hour shifts, or till it was dark, or so it seemed. Our magnum opus was building piers to enable us to get chaps into the boats without wading at all stages of the tide. These were about 200 yards long and consisted of 3-tonners end to end filled with sandbags. Decking was lashed to the canopy frames. At high tide, the seaward end lashed about madly, but they helped. The rest of the time we ferried direct to the boats off shore in any available craft. At first we allowed anyone to take a boat, but as the boats never came back we had to put sapper crews in them. Many an irate naval officer was surprised, and peeved, when the crew refused to join his ship. The few motor boats we had were used for towing boats and rounding up abandoned craft.

Firemen at work in the Rue Clémenceau after the raid on the 24th. In the background the tower of Saint-Eloi church. From May 23, when the Germans captured the waterworks at Watten, there had been no supply to the town, and the firemen had to use sea water pumped from the harbour.

FRIDAY, MAY 31

On the morning of May 31 Gort visited Abrial at his headquarters in Bastion 32 to co-ordinate their plans and made known that his I Corps would stay to fight beside the French. He informed them of his own imminent departure and invited Généraux Falgade and de la Laurencie to accompany him to England. They declined, but it was agreed that some members of the latter's staff should sail with the last of the British General Headquarters staff.

Having tried vainly to get permission to remain to the end, Gort issued his final operational order and then delegated Major-General H.R.L.G. Alexander, commanding the 1st Division, to take over the dwindling BEF for the final phase, appointing him to command I Corps. Alexander's instructions were very much on the lines followed by Gort himself during the past fortnight. They stated that he was to act under the orders of Amiral Abrial but to appeal to the Secretary of State for War should 'any orders which he may issue to you be likely, in your opinion, to imperil the

Another major raid hit Dunkirk on May 27, leaving many fires burning fiercely and several hundred civilians reported killed.

This crater was pictured by a French Army cameraman in the Rue de Paris.

Down near the harbour, these French sailors were pictured on top of Bastion 32 in front of the sandbagged parapet which surrounded the anti-aircraft machine guns — but really much too light a weapon to be very effective.

safety of the force under your command'. As well as defence he was to make arrangements with Abrial for evacuation, with French troops sharing 'in such facilities for evacuation as may be provided'. Finally, he was authorised, in consultation with Abrial, 'to capitulate formally to avoid useless slaughter'.

The situation at De Panne had become serious during the day as far more men were there than ships to take them off and German shelling of the beaches as well as the ships offshore was steadily increasing. The 6,000 or so men of the 4th Division were therefore ordered to set out along the sands from De Panne to Dunkirk. An onshore wind with an unpleasant sea did not help although towards evening the weather improved. A number of boats had been sunk or damaged, among them the French destroyer *Bourrasque* mined and sunk off Dunkirk, but losses were far less than the previous day and by midnight a further 68,014 men were back in England, the largest number for a single day during the whole operation.

The wrecks of two of the ships lost at Dunkirk lie on the beach off Malo-les-Bains. *L'Adroit* (left background) was bombed on May 21 and run ashore by her captain while still burning. Later she exploded. The *Chasseur 9* (foreground) was also hit the same day and beached but all efforts to repair her proved fruitless and she had to be abandoned.

When Alexander went to see the French commander that evening Abrial was greatly angered when given to understand that it was only a very much reduced I Corps that was to remain alongside his troops. Pointing out that this was not the commitment Gort had made the previous morning, he claimed that the perimeter should be held until all troops, French and British, were embarked and that both should share the defence of it. This demand Alexander refused, insisting that the front could not be held for more that 24 hours. Abrial and Alexander reported their opposing views, Abrial to Weygand and Alexander to the Secretary of State for War. Weygand received the message at about 7.30 p.m., at the end of a meeting of the Supreme War Council. The matter was then discussed and Churchill, who was forced to admit that only about 15,000

Having embarked from the Quai Felix-Faure with about 800 men on board, the French destroyer *Bourrasque* hit a mine at about 4.45 p.m. on May 30 and started to sink. These pictures were taken from another French destroyer, *Branlebas*, which approached to rescue survivors. Two British drifters lent a hand and all told, about 600 men were picked up.

During the last days of May the atmosphere in Dunkirk was unreal. Troops and civilians were bottled up in a shrinking area with dwindling supplies. People wandered through the burning town searching for food, while at the same time supplies were being burned, guns spiked and transport fired. Then there was a nastier, unsavoury side . . . that of the traitor. Fifth columnists — the phrase had only recently been coined by General Emilio Mola while attacking Madrid during the Spanish Civil War — were feared more than they were a reality as the unknown enemy from within, and Nazi propagandists were only too quick to exploit the chance of fomenting suspicion and distrust. This fellow under arrest is the epitome of the German spy as seen by the French people — but was he really guilty? Appearances deceive — even today.

French soldiers had been evacuated out of a total of 165,000 by noon of May 31, promised that the proportions would be equalised.

The Secretary of State for War replied to Alexander that 'you should withdraw your forces as rapidly as possible on a 50-50 basis with the French Army, aiming at completion by night of 1st/2nd June. You should inform French of this definite instruction.' Abrial and Alexander finally agreed on a compromise, Alexander promising to hold his sector until midnight on June 1. Alexander's view that the line could not be held much longer was probably 'diplomatic' and was proved to be wide of the mark as French troops were to hold off the German attacks for two more days.

SATURDAY, JUNE 1

On the morning of June 1 only about 39,000 of the BEF remained in the bridgehead. There were about 50,000 French troops holding the defensive line and another 50,000 assembled in the dunes, waiting beside the British for evacuation. A further 20,000-odd French troops, not officially accounted for at the time, were dispersed in small groups throughout the pocket. The decision to complete the evacuation by the night of June 1, and the 50-50 rule, would leave more than 30,000 French troops behind and Weygand wired to London on June 1 to insist that British troops should be kept beside the French in order to permit the embarkation to be completed 'as the British Prime Minister promised to the French Premier yesterday'.

Weygand wired Abrial to announce

Above: **De Panne in the east was under increasing pressure, being held by troops of the 4th Division until June 1. The rich haul of captured vehicles included these Panhards of the 8ème Cuirassiers (2ème D.L.M.) parked in the central reservation of the road to Ostend.** *Right:* **This Gefreiter has armed himself with a captured Mitraillette Modèle 34 — a Belgian Army sub-machine gun made at Herstal.**

the official dissolution of the Groupe d'Armées No. 1 and suggest that Général Blanchard, now without a command be evacuated, the Général embarking on the destroyer *Bouclier* that afternoon.

The evacuation continued full swing but the German efforts to disrupt the operation were not unproductive: the destroyer HMS *Keith*, flying Rear-Admiral Wake-Walker's flag, the destroyers HMS *Havant* and HMS *Basilisk*, the minesweeper *Skipjack*, the French destroyer *Foudroyant*, three French minesweepers, the passenger ships *Brighton Queen* and *Scotia* all being sunk. Loss of life could have been greater but as soon as a ship was hit others promptly went to her rescue. The *Brighton Queen* had about 700 French troops on board when she was sunk; the minesweeper *Saltash* picked up 400 French survivors, reporting that they 'behaved steadily and intelligently

Below left: **Troopers of the 56. Infanterie-Division pass one of the 4th Division's abandoned lorries in the main street of De Panne.** *Below right:* **The La Terrasse café trades on throughout . . . whether it be war and peace.**

Ever mindful of the immense publicity to be gained from the British retreat and evacuation, German propaganda teams were alive to every opportunity. And if it was not possible to photograph troops in the front line . . . well . . . why not create a little bit of the action for yourself! The picture of this soldier boy was taken in les Moëres on June 3 — when the French rearguard was still holding out strongly — but his rifle is pointing the wrong way!

though nearly half of them were killed by the explosion'. The *Scotia*, with about 2,000 French troops, was hit by at least four bombs and sunk. The destroyer HMS *Esk* took off a thousand survivors and others ships rescued many more. Thus of the 2,700 men on these two ships about 2,100 were in fact saved and taken back to England. June 1 ended with 64,429 men landed in England, the second largest number transported in one day.

SUNDAY, JUNE 2

Evacuation continued through the night until the early hours of June 2 and many of I Corps who had reached the beach during the night were got away. Admiral Ramsay had called off daylight operations, however, to spare further losses such as those of the previous day.

The coming night's operations were expected to be the last and a demolition party carried out its work on the harbour equipment during the day and measures were taken to block the entance after the last ship had departed.

In the morning Abrial sent a message to Weygand, pointing out that besides the 25,000 French soldiers holding the perimeter, about 22,000 French soldiers remained at Dunkirk. 'The British were all to leave this evening and we may hope to see these 22,000 men evacuated during the night. Tomorrow morning the 25,000 defenders will remain.' He insisted that all the British naval and air support be given to him the following evening 'to evacuate these 25,000 soldiers who had fought and made the evacuation of the last of the British elements possible.'

Movement across the Channel began at 5.00 p.m. The ships entered the port and took off all those who had reached the harbour during the night. Co-ordination with the French was again at fault and fewer French troops were taken off than had been provided for, many of the ships returning empty as they had berthed along the Eastern Mole, whereas French troops were waiting on the Quai Félix Faure and on the Western Mole. General Alexander and the Senior Naval Officer ashore at Dunirk, Captain W. G. Tennant, toured the beaches in a launch to determine that no one was left behind before sailing for England in the early hours of June 3. For the BEF the evacuation was over but Abrial's hope to see 22,000 French evacuated was frustrated, with only about 16,000 having got away.

No faking here . . . this is the grim reality. Tens of thousands may have got back to Blighty, but for some of the mothers, wives and sweethearts waiting anxiously in England for their menfolk, he would simply be missing. It would be many weeks or months before news arrived. Sometimes it was inconclusive . . . sometimes it was worse.

By far the greater number of men left from Dunkirk harbour — the official total being given as 239,555 compared with 98,671 picked up from the beaches. Seen from the lighthouse, this was the sight which greeted the Germans when they entered the town on June 4. The base of the Eastern Mole is in the left foreground next to the Tixier sluice gate to the canal. In the background, the evacuation beach of Malo-les-Bains with the wreck of *l'Adroit* hit on May 21.

MONDAY, JUNE 3

The Germans were now closing in for the final battle and even though Heeresgruppe B recorded that French troops were fighting for every house and every piece of ground, the defenders were gradually forced back to the line of the Dunkirk-Furnes Canal, less than two kilometres from the beaches. That afternoon Amiral Abrial conferred with Générals Falgade and de la Laurencie and they decided that the coming night would be the last. Naval operations restarted as it grew dark, 50 vessels making the crossing. There was congestion in the harbour, and some initial confusion, which was sorted out, and the embarkation proceeded quickly. Commander H. R. Troup, who had been directing the evacuation from the inner pier, provides a vivid and moving impression of his last sight of French troops — men of the 32ème Division d'Infanterie — about to be left behind, saluting their commander, Général Maurice Lucas, on the pier:

'About a thousand men stood to attention four deep about half-way along the pier, the General and his staff about thirty feet away; and after having faced the troops, whose faces were indiscernible in the dawn light, the flames behind them showing up their steel helmets, the officers clicked their heels, saluted and then turned about and came down to the boat with me and we left at 2.30 a.m.'

Three blockships had crossed to Dunkirk during the night; one was mined outside the harbour; the others were scuttled in the entrance channel. The destroyer HMS *Shikari* which had led them took off 383 French troops and was the last ship to leave Dunkirk. 52,921 men had been embarked when daylight put an end to operations in the early hours of June 4.

At Dover Admiral Ramsay discussed the possibility of continuing evacuation yet one more night with Amiral Abrial, who had crossed during the night with Générals Falgade and de la Laurencie, but Abrial said that further evacuation was impossible for the Germans were now closing in. At about 8.00 a.m. on June 4, Général Maurice Beaufrère, commanding the 68ème Division d'Infanterie, and Général Gustave Teisseire, commanding the 60ème Division d'Infanterie, made the first contact with the Germans. The remaining French troops in the perimeter surrendered later in the morning, most of those who

454

had fought to hold off the Germans for so long being among them. The Germans claimed to have captured 40,000 troops at Dunkirk and three generals: Beaufrère and Teisseire and Général Auguste Alaurent commanding the infantry of the 32ème Division d'Infanterie. Général Louis Janssen, the commander of the 12ème D.I.M., had been killed at his command post in Leffrinckoucke on June 2.

The fleet of rescue ships was ordered to disperse on the morning of June 4 and Operation 'Dynamo' was officially ended by the Admiralty at 2.23 p.m. In all, 338,226 men had been evacuated; of these 198,315 were British and 139,911 Allied, mostly French. A total of 228 ships had been lost and 45 badly damaged in addition to a considerable number of smaller boats.

Part of the French forces evacuated from Dunkirk had been taken directly to French ports and of those transported to England, most, about 98,000, were quickly shipped back to France to continue the fight. The staff of the Corps de Cavalerie, of the IIIème and XVIème Corps d'Armée were landed back at Brest and Cherbourg on June 6 and immediately returned to the fray. A sizeable part of the 32ème and 43ème Divisions d'Infanterie and of the 1ère, 2ème and 3ème D.L.M.s had been evacuated but only the men. Thus when the divisions were landed back in France at the beginning of June they had to be completely re-equipped, a huge task where the mechanised D.L.M.s were concerned. Only a few thousand men each from the 4ème and 60ème Divisions d'Infanterie, from the 1ère, 2ème and 5ème D.I.N.A.s and the 1ère Division Marocaine, had been evacuated; their divisions now disbanded, they were incorporated in other units when returned to France. It was too late for the men of the 12ème D.I.M. and 68ème Division d'Infanterie; their own turn to embark never came, and they were left behind at Dunkirk with a collection of men from miscellaneous units.

Finally it was all over and the beaches were empty . . . save only for the makeshift jetties and the sinking lorries. De Panne, June 1940.

Of the wounded who stayed in England, some would later join with Général de Gaulle's Free French Forces but the majority were shipped back to France.

Although Dunkirk was a victory for the Germans, it also contained the seeds of their eventual defeat, for Sichelschnitt had failed in one of its objectives — 'to eliminate', as von Rundstedt phrased it, 'the continental sword of the English'. Churchill warned that 'wars are not won by evacuations', but, in ascribing to this 'colossal military disaster' he could rightly proclaim it 'a miracle of deliverance'. For the British people Dunkirk was a shock but it was not the end of the road. British national pride in the remarkable feat which delivered so many men from death or captivity and brought them home ought

not however, to be allowed to undervalue the part played by the French in ensuring the safety of the BEF and for whom Dunkirk meant something very different. There was no 'victory' to be gained from Dunkirk for the French. Dunkirk stunned them and left them feeling isolated in the face of a renewed German assault: after losing the Netherlands and Belgium, the evacuation from Dunkirk meant that France had virtually lost Britain as an ally too. There was no breathing spell after the evacuation ended on June 4 and when the Germans attacked southwards on June 5 there was only one British infantry division and one British armoured division left in France.

There were two Dunkirks, the British and the French, and they were as different as victory and defeat.

And on a beach in summer what does one do . . . ? Play, of course, and the toys were free for the taking.

Part IV
FALL ROT

The two alternatives

It was on May 24 that Hitler (seen here with Keitel and von Brauchitsch after their promotion to Generalfeldmarschall rank in July) made known his next move: to finish France.

'Fall Gelb' had been an outstanding success. In three weeks, the Wehrmacht had defeated two nations, wiped out six armies and rounded up more than a million prisoners, Dutch, Belgian, British and French. The French Army had suffered badly during this first phase of the battle and had lost about twenty-five infantry divisions, and among these were six of its seven motorised divisions; seven of its thirteen cavalry or armoured divisions — the 1ère and 4ème D.L.C.s, the 1ère, 2ème and 3ème D.L.M.s and the 1ère and 2ème D.C.R.s — had disappeared as organised units.

The extent of the success achieved by the Wehrmacht in so short a time had surprised the Germans themselves. Two alternatives were now offered to the German High Command, either to pur-

sue the mortally wounded French Army or to commit the Wehrmacht to an invasion of England from the Channel ports?

Although Britain now lay virtually defenceless, no serious thought had been given to the possibility of invading England in June 1940. The survivors of the BEF brought back from Dunkirk were no longer an army; almost all their equipment had been left on the Continent, most of them were physically spent. It would take weeks to rearm and reorganise them into fighting units. On the other hand, the Wehrmacht had no experience of seaborne operations, apart from Operation 'Weserübung', the invasion of Norway, a much smaller operation, nor did it have the thousands of boats and barges to hand that an invasion of England would require.

Also with the Royal Navy to contend with, the price of crossing the Channel was bound to be high.

At the same time, France still remained to be conquered. With the memory of the 'Miracle of the Marne' of September 1914 at the back of their mind, von Moltke's successors were determined that there should be no such miraculous recovery this time. No chances were to be taken on the French Army managing somehow to recover and threaten the German rear, and in Führer Directive No. 13 issued on May 24, Hitler decided that the next object of the campaign in the West was, 'to destroy in the shortest possible time the remaining enemy forces in France'.

On May 31, OKH issued the operational orders for 'Fall Rot'. In these, General von Brauchitsch made known

In his May 24 directive (see page 365), Hitler ordered that the next objective was 'to destroy in the shortest possible time the remaining enemy forces in France'. With the initial goals achieved in grand style, the Wehrmacht was now reorganising for this next phase, code-named 'Fall Rot' (Plan Red). *Left:* Near

Péronne, Generalmajor Rudolf Sintzenich, the commander of the 33. Infanterie-Division, and his staff study their maps as did Generalmajor Erwin Rommel, the commander of the 7. Panzer-Division near Flixecourt, between Abbeville and Amiens, with officers of Panzer-Regiment 25 *(right)*.

On June 6 the Führerhauptquartier moved from FHQu Felsennest forward to FHQu Wolfsschlucht (Wolf's Glen) in the small Belgian village of Brûly-de-Pesche, which lay about 25 kilometres north-west of Charleville. Hitler arrived there at 1.30 p.m. Here he is pictured with Hauptmann Gerhard Engel, his army adjutant, in front of the village school.

that the next phase of the campaign was to involve defeating the remainder of the French Army and the few British troops still on the Continent. 'The intention of the Supreme Command is to destroy the allied forces still remaining in France by means of an operation following the battle in Artois and Flanders as rapidly as possible. Operational enemy reserves in substantial numbers need no longer be expected. It will therefore be possible to break down under heavy assault the hastily constructed enemy front south of the Somme and Aisne and then, by rapid, deep penetration, to prevent the enemy from carrying out an ordered retreat or forming a defence line in rear.'

THE FRENCH POSITIONS

Général Weygand, who had inherited the basic set-up from Gamelin, did not have time for drastic changes before the beginning of the second phase of the battle. Gamelin had begun the process of moving forces from the Maginot Line and the rear and Weygand directed these new divisions to establish defensive positions along the Somme, the Crozat Canal, the Ailette and the Aisne. To man this new front from the sea to the western end of the Maginot Line near Longuyon Weygand had only about 60 divisions, some of them still in the course of formation and others greatly reduced in strength after the May battles. Behind the Maginot Line

Groupe d'Armées No. 2 was now down to 15 divisions other than the fortress troops. And whereas on May 10 Gamelin had had 25 divisions in reserve in France, at the beginning of June Weygand was left with only 15.

Weygand speeded up the organisation of new infantry divisions which were formed in haste as 'light divisions' and he was also hoping to reorganise in time those French elements, most of them first-rate troops, evacuated at Dunkirk. What remained of the 1ère, 2ème and 3ème D.L.M.s were thus brought back to France and hastily refitted, on a far lighter scale than the original divisions, in the Evreux area. Two new light mechanised divisions,

Göring used his personal train 'Asien' as a mobile headquarters during the campaign, commuting by light aircraft to Wolfsschlucht. Although there was an established airfield 20 kilometres away at Gros-Caillou, Hermann liked to drop right in on

the spot. A field next to the Wolfspalaast (quarters for some of the FHQu staff — now the Hôtel de la Fontaine) was quite adequate for the short take-off and landing distance required by the Storch.

To man the Weygand Line, which ran from the sea to the western end of the Maginot Line near Longuyon, Weygand had only about 60 divisions. He speeded up the movement of forces from the rear and the creation of new divisions, and nearly 100,000 French troops evacuated from Dunkirk were hastily brought back to France and reorganised.

the 4ème and 7ème D.L.M.s, were created out of the remnants of the 1ère D.L.C. and 4ème D.L.C. which had disappeared in Belgium, and the 1ère D.C.R., which had also been lost there, was being reconstituted. All this took time however, far more time than the French actually had left.

The French forces were hurriedly assembling along the Weygand Line, thrown together behind rivers which the Germans had still not yet really tried to cross in strength, except at a number of bridgeheads which greatly weakened the new French defence line. These bridgeheads, particularly those across the Somme at Péronne, Amiens and Abbeville, were to be the jumping-off areas for the German attacks to come.

On May 26, while he was still fighting against the British leaving, Weygand had issued an operational order which set forth new general principles of defence against the Blitzkrieg. Based on the concept of aggressive defence in depth, the essence of the strategy was that of strong points organised to hold out alone, the troops digging in for protection against tanks and aircraft, and to emerge determined to attack once the danger had passed. Tanks — Weygand still had about 500 modern tanks, although most were dispersed in

Although most of the French armour was scattered about the battlefield in small units, nevertheless at the beginning of June Weygand was still able to field about 500 modern tanks. A sizeable number were Hotchkisses; these three H-39s being named after various winds in France: 'La Bourrasque', 'Le Mistral' and 'La Bise'.

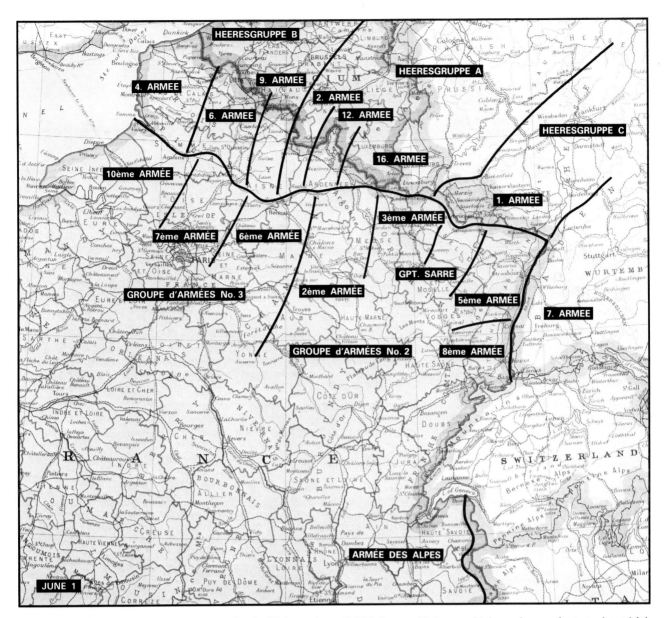

'Fall Gelb' had been an outstanding success for the Wehrmacht. Within three weeks the Netherlands and Belgium had been defeated, the French Army dealt a mortal blow, and most of the British Army withdrawn with heavy losses of men and matériel. For 'Fall Rot', facing Weygand's 60 divisions, the Germans had deployed 143, seven more than for 'Fall Gelb' on May 10.

small units here and there — were to deal with the panzers which might manage to break through and with whatever armoured and mobile troops there were. Weygand lost no time in organising three shock groups and placed them in reserve to strike at any breakthrough. By early June, he planned to have Groupement Petiet — the 2ème, 3ème and 5ème D.L.C.s, the 1st Armoured Division and the 40ème Division d'Infanterie — assembled in reserve behind the lower Somme; Groupement Audet (the 4ème D.C.R. and two infantry divisions) was to be in the area south of Beauvais; while Groupement Buisson, comprising the 3ème D.C.R., the newly created 7ème D.L.M. and two battalions of tanks, was to assemble south-east of Rethel. The 2ème D.C.R. was in the Somme area where it was reorganising after its costly efforts to reduce the Abbeville bridgehead and the 1ère D.C.R. was being rebuilt north of Senlis after its catastrophic engagement in Belgium.

The initiation of new tactics and the number of fresh instructions issued by the French High Command goes to show that the experiences in Belgium and northern France had not been lost on them. However, with only a week left to the French after a major defeat in the field, there was neither the time nor adequate forces available for these tactics to stand a chance of acting as much more than a brake. Although the Germans, by attacking without respite, deprived themselves of a part of their strength, this turned out to be to the Germans' advantage; for the French, who needed time to move divisions from the Maginot Line or elsewhere and to reorganise their shattered units, were deprived of even more. Except on paper, the defence in depth on the Weygand Line was never really achieved. The new French defensive line soon came to be called the 'Weygand Line', suggesting a degree of preparation which none of these efforts possessed.

On June 3 the French Command decided to reorganise the North-East Theatre of Operations and created the Groupe d'Armées No. 4, to take over the 2ème Armée and 4ème Armée in the middle of the defensive front. This new army group was to come into being at midnight on June 6, Général Charles Huntziger, formerly commander of the 2ème Armée, being placed in command.

Groupe d'Armées No. 3, with the 10ème Armée from the sea to the west of Péronne, the 7ème Armée as far as Coucy and the 6ème Armée as far as Neufchâtel, was to defend the line of the Somme and the Aisne between the sea and the area north of Reims. Groupe d'Armées No. 4, with the 4ème Armée from Neufchâtel to Attigny and the 2ème Armée as far as Longuyon, was to ensure a link with Groupe d'Armées No. 2 which held the Maginot Line from Longuyon to Switzerland with the 3ème, the 5ème and the 8ème Armées.

461

The Weygand Line was hurriedly thrown together behind the Somme, the Ailette and the Aisne which the Germans, still occupied in the north, had not yet tried to cross. Incursions were numerous and clashes many. In this sharp encounter, a cavalry patrol of the 87ème G.R.D.I., 87ème Division d'Infanterie d'Afrique, surprised a German patrol south of Laon at the beginning of June, killing three and capturing one wounded. After a lieutenant gave some water to the wounded German, the Spahis left, abandoning one of their horses killed during the engagement.

On June 5, Prime Minister Reynaud carried out another shake-up of his government. Daladier was removed and Reynaud became his own Foreign Affairs and Defence Minister. As Under-Secretary for Foreign Affairs Reynaud appointed Paul Baudouin and for his Under-Secretary for Defence he hastily recalled the recently promoted Général de Gaulle from the battlefield. Although there was never any doubt what de Gaulle stood for, unfortunately Baudouin was increasingly to reveal himself to be a defeatist.

THE GERMAN PLAN

As outlined by Hitler himself in his Directive No. 13, 'the operation will be undertaken in three phases' and Fall Rot was to be fought in three sectors of the front. First an attack from the lower Somme area aiming westwards in the direction of Rouen and Le Havre, then further west and southwards; the main offensive on either side of Reims, between (but excluding) Paris and the Argonne in a south-easterly direction and, in due course, a supporting attack to break through the Maginot Line.

From the sea to the Laon area, Heeresgruppe B, with the 4. Armee, the 6. Armee and the 9. Armee, had 34 infantry divisions and two panzer groups available. Subordinated to 4. Armee, Gruppe Hoth was to spearhead the attack in the lower Somme area with two panzer and two mobile divisions making for the crossings of the Seine. Under the 6. Armee, and forming the western arm of the two-pronged main attack, Gruppe von Kleist was to attack from the Péronne area with four panzer and two mobile divisions, force the

462

For the ten days prior to June 5 a somewhat strange situation prevailed all along the Weygand Line. Apart from the numerous patrols which brushed against one another in no man's land, the front remained more or less quiet and inactive. In Corbeny, 15 kilometres south-east of Laon, this German sentry blocks a road marked 'Caution. The enemy is there.'

Marne, then the Seine, to advance southwards in the direction of Dijon.

From Laon to the Moselle valley was Heeresgruppe A, with the 2. Armee, the 12. Armee and the 16. Armee, which had 40 infantry divisions plus Gruppe Guderian. This panzer group, under the 12. Armee with four panzer and two mobile divisions, was to be the eastern arm of the main attack. It was to assault the area between the Marne and the Argonne to reach Langres and Besançon.

Away to the east, Heeresgruppe C was to deploy its 24 divisions for the attack at a later date through the Magi- not Line. The 1. Armee, when so ordered by OKH, was to force the Line in the Sarre and advance southwards while the 7. Armee, with weaker forces, was to cross the Rhine either side of Colmar and advance through the Vosges in accordance with the general situation.

In fifty years nothing has changed in Corbeny where the N44 still runs seemingly endlessly southwards, as straight as a die.

The same houses ... the same wall ... only the holes have been stopped up.

Paris bombed! Although it was reported at the time that 250 people had been killed, Operation 'Paula' against the city on June 3, was more a psychological success. We have already seen how Rotterdam collapsed within hours of the big air raid although in the case of Paris it was aimed at military targets around the city. The Luftwaffe lost 26 aircraft, the French 17.

Hauptmann Werner Mölders of JG53 added his 22nd and 23rd victories while his contemporary in JG26, Hauptmann Adolf Galland, added a Morane to bring his tally to 12. *Left:* This house is on the corner of Rue Poussin and Rue Girodet (16ème Arrondissement) — the repair work *(right)* being so beautifully done that no clue has been left to the drama of June 1940.

The 18. Armee, under the direct control of OKH, was to carry out occupation duties in Artois and Flanders, protect the Belgian and French coasts against enemy action, and be responsible for the prompt location and utilisation of captured matériel.

Against Weygand's badly reduced forces, the number of divisons available for Fall Rot came to 143, which was seven more than for Fall Gelb on May 10. Three of them had been transferred from the east, where the attitude of the Soviet Union was quite friendly.

PARIS BOMBED

After the bombing of Marseille on June 1, and of Lyon the following day, it was now the turn of Paris under the operational code-name 'Paula' as a preliminary to Fall Rot and the attack against the Weygand Line. About 500 aircraft were brought together for Operation 'Paula', to attack in three waves and deliver the coup de grâce to French fighter bases and installations around Paris. Notwithstanding these objectives, it is likely that the effects of the bombing on civilian morale also figured highly.

On the afternoon of June 3, accompanied by a large escort of Messerschmitt Bf 109s and 110s, the bombers went in to attack 13 airfields, 22 railway junctions and 15 factories. The Armée de l'Air was already badly weakened but the French fighters fought back and managed to account for some of the attackers. From the Germans' point of view, the operation was not a great success: none of the railway yards was put out of action for longer than 24 hours and the factories suffered only minor damage, although it did hinder French preparations to meet the forthcoming battle. Also over 250 people were reported killed and the bombing had a considerable psychological impact even if it was not successful in causing civilian panic. Sixteen French fighters were destroyed on the ground and 17 more in the air but 26 German aircraft had been lost.

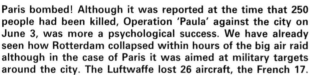

The original caption passed by the French censor for this picture stated that 'A huge bomb crater in a Paris street and cars overturned during the Nazi air raid on the capital yesterday, June 3, when over 1,000 bombs were dropped.'

At 5.00 a.m. on June 5 Heeresgruppe B launched the second phase of the battle, attacking the armies of Groupe d'Armées No. 3 from the sea to the Aisne.

Following Weygand's instructions the French units had organised their sectors into strong points. Villages were fortified, barricades built to block the panzers' advance, and trenches dug for protection against dive-bombing. These tactics promoted by Weygand, although carried out in a hurry, proved to be efficient and the German initial advance was slow and costly.

For a day on the lower Somme, and for two on the 6. Armee front, this unexpectedly firm and effective resistance held the Germans and caused the Heeresgruppe B commander, General-oberst Fedor von Bock, concern over apparently being brought to a standstill between Amiens and Péronne. In some places, the panzers were almost cut off and might have been 'starved out' as Weygand intended, had the French had sufficient strength to hold the 'Weygand Line'. However the defences lacked depth, so that when one sector of the front was broken, a whole stretch of the line gave way as a vacuum developed to its rear.

The 4. Armee from the Somme to the Seine

On the Somme front the 4. Armee had been reinforced after the fall of Dunkirk and received new units, among them the XV. Armeekorps — Gruppe Hoth — with two panzer and one mobile divisions. The army had carefully concealed all its preparations north of the river and any move by day had been forbidden. The artillery was ordered not to fire before the given time, reconnaissance was not to be made beyond the German outposts, and reconnaissance detachments sent out by the panzer divisions were not to wear black panzer uniforms.

The II. Armeekorps was on the right flank, near the sea, with three infantry divisions and the 11. Schützen-Brigade. In the centre, between Pont-Remy and Hangest, lay the XV. Armeekorps with the 5. Panzer-Division, the 7. Panzer-Division and the 2. Infanterie-Division (mot). Over on the left flank, in the Amiens area was the XXXVIII. Armeekorps with two infantry divisions in the first line. Although the II. Armeekorps had two bridgeheads with road crossings south of the Somme, one at Saint-Valery, the other at Abbeville, the XV. Armeekorps had no intact road bridges in its sector and only a small bridgehead beyond two railway bridges spanning the river near Condé-Folie. (Because of their own plans for a

counter-stroke north of the Somme, the French Command had not ordered these to be blown in time nor the two bridges that carried the lines over the road east of Condé-Folie.)

Facing this powerful army, the 10ème Armée, which had exhausted itself trying to wrest the German bridgeheads south of the Somme, had only about ten divisions from the sea to the sector west of Péronne. On the left wing of the army, the 51st (Highland) Division was positioned on the coast, the IXème Corps d'Armée in the centre with five divisions, some of them badly worn out by repeated engagements. Then came the Xème Corps d'Armée with three

Due to their own plans for a counter-strike north of the Somme, the French had refrained from demolishing the two railway bridges over the river at Condé-Folie, midway between Abbeville and Amiens. However, on the morning of June 5, the 7. Panzer-Division stole a march on them and crossed over, in spite of frenetic attempts by the French artillery to stop them. The aerial view *(top)* is an amazing discovery as it was taken just a few seconds after that *(left)* from the ground. *Right:* The railway line is now disused and the crossing site much overgrown but the same bridge still stands.

Having crossed the Somme, the leaders of Schützen-Regiment 6 had to assault the steep slope of the valley, along the top of which a thin line of fox-holes was manned by men of the 5ème D.I.C. *Left:* While their comrades climb the hill, a mortar team prepares to shell the weak French positions. *Right:* Although the secondary railway crossing the Somme is now disused, the main line from Paris to Calais, via Amiens, Abbeville and Boulogne, still runs all along the Somme valley.

divisions. The 40ème Division d'Infanterie and the tired 5ème D.L.C. were in reserve just behind the line. In this sector were also two other British forces: the 1st Armoured Division, which was on the Bresle river, and further to the rear Beauman Division holding a defensive line along the Andelle and Béthunes rivers. The 51st Division and 1st Armoured Division were under French command but Beauman Division was under the orders of General Karslake, commander of the British lines of communications, who was under direct orders of Général Georges.

WEDNESDAY, JUNE 5

The night passed quietly except for some desultory artillery fire but at 3.30 a.m. on June 5 the German artillery started to shell the Allied positions west of the river and the infantry moved forward between Amiens and the coast. Despite their dispositions west of the

A few hundred metres further west, the track passed over the road and this bridge had also not been blown. *Left:* As this SdKfz 222 armoured radio car of the 7. Panzers displayed a 'WL' registration (standing for 'Wehrmacht Luftwaffe'), it was quite probably the mount of the 'Flivo' — the Luftwaffe liaison officer attached to the division. The rails and sleepers had been hastily removed by Pionier-Bataillon 58 to enable the bed to be used as a road. Behind rises the steep slope assaulted by the infantry. *Right:* When Henri de Wailly took this comparison 15 years ago part of the bridge still remained in situ, but when Jean Paul re-checked for this book he found that all had since been demolished.

And this is another shot of the same bridge. With the trackway cast aside, traffic began rolling at 6.00 a.m., Rommel's own signals vehicle being the first across. Rommel went forward to observe the advance of Schützen-Regiment 6 but at about 7.30 a.m. the flow of vehicles across the bridge suddenly ceased. Rommel investigated and took this photograph: 'A Panzer IV had shed its right track and was blocking the entire passage and preventing any other tanks or vehicles from passing. Attempts were being made to drag the tank bodily forwards,

with little success as the sleepers were jamming in the rubber rollers and pushing the ballast along in front of them. A good half-hour was lost while the Panzer IV was pulled and pushed across the bridge by other tanks. Then the crossing gradually began to move again.' In the picture there appears to be some debate going on as to whether to try to tow '321' forward using the PzKpfw 38(t) '613', with '311' behind to give it a helping hand, or pull it straight down the embankment using a third PzKpfw IV.

Left: As we can see from this picture, taken after the road/ railway had been cleared and traffic was moving again, '321' was pulled down the bank to the lower road. One might think that, with the aircraft in the picture, it was taken from another machine, but in fact they are all ground shots from the top of the hill. It gives a good impression of the task the Germans had in assaulting the high ground while being overlooked by the French positions. The bridge on page 465 across the river can be

seen in the left background, and the main railway on the page opposite in the foreground. The plane is a Henschel Hs126 from Aufklärungsstaffel 1.(H)/11, the reconnaissance unit attached to the 7. Panzer-Division. *Right:* This is another comparison taken in the 1970s by Henri when the railway embankment still remained largely as Rommel's men had left it in 1940. Now it has gone, swept away in its entirety when the bridge was dismantled.

467

Once across the bridge, the panzers had to continue straight along the left-hand side of the main railway line before finding a suitable place to cross the tracks and return to the other side. *Above:* Eric Borchert — we last saw him in Thulin — pictured

the massive dog-leg. *Below:* One of Jean Paul's favourite comparisons, taken by his friend Henri some years ago. But for the taller trees and thicker undergrowth in the marshland bordering the river, it is a timeless landscape.

Above: Having made the turn, the column is now travelling back on the direction from which they had come but now on the right-hand (or southern) side of the railway. The division still had to reach the plateau (on the left of the picture) but fortunately a valley — the La Grande Vallée — cut through the steep slope and provided a convenient way up to the top. Below: Retracing the steps of Borchert who was covering the 7. Panzer-Division attack, this was another spot dear to the heart of the author. His comparison shows the extent of the growth in fifty years.

river being too widely separated to form a cohesive 'line', the Allied units fought back with determination. To the north, the 51st Division and the 31ème Division d'Infanterie offered considerable resistance and the II. Armeekorps progressed very slowly. However further south, the XV. Armeekorps' attack fell on the 5ème D.I.C. just when it was in process of relieving the tired 2ème and 3ème D.L.C.s. The men had marched more than thirty kilometres on June 4, with full kit and under a fierce sun, to reach their new positions late in the evening, and had only had a few hours

'All in the Valley of Death rode the six hundred' immediately springs to mind to put with these incredible pictures by Borchert of armour massed in La Grande Vallée. Rommel noted in his diary how 'the bridgehead west of the Somme continued to fill with units of all arms and soon became overcrowded.' Here, we are looking east — then and now — with the Somme valley in the background. 'From 12 o'clock onwards,' wrote Rommel, 'heavy enemy artillery began to bombard the area of our Somme crossing . . . the hills . . . and hollows in which we were forming up for the attack were also the target of intermittent heavy shelling . . . I was able to give the orders verbally, undisturbed by the enemy fire . . . At 16.00 hours sharp, the tanks moved to the attack. The various arms worked in such perfect co-ordination that it might have been a peacetime exercise. The French colonial troops opposing us, who were dug in . . . with large numbers of field and anti-tank guns, defended themselves desperately.'

to recover and organise their positions. Thus the attack fell on exhausted men and unco-ordinated defences.

While his engineers worked hard, unbolting rails and clearing away sleepers on the rail bridges, to prepare them for the panzers, Rommel had sent his Schtz.Rgt. 6 into the small bridgehead near Condé-Folie. The signals vehicles crossed the Somme at 6.00 a.m., and artillery and Flak batteries soon followed. The panzers then started to cross. To the north, the first panzers of the 5. Panzer-Division crossed at Pont-Remy at about 7.30 a.m. only to be stopped at the edge of the river valley by anti-tank guns of the 2ème D.L.C. which disabled about 15 panzers.

At midday, with the bridgehead overcrowded with units, Rommel was informed that the 5. Panzer-Division would not be able to resume the attack before 3.00 p.m. He thereupon ordered his own units to be ready at the same time. The break-out went as planned in

470

Meanwhile, ten kilometres downstream, the vanguard of the 5. Panzer-Division had crossed the Somme at Pont-Remy, but were soon stopped in their tracks by devastating fire from the anti-tank guns of the 2ème D.L.C. By the evening, the division's

engineers had completed this 16-tonne bridge on the site of the destroyed road bridge, these pictures being taken on June 6 after the division had finally succeeded in breaking out of the bridgehead.

the afternoon and the panzers rolled westwards, bypassing all resistance. Nevertheless the 7. Panzer-Division's engineers were not able to build the planned bridge near Hangest as the work was delayed until the evening by a company of the 44ème R.I.C., which fought back in the village until forced to surrender when all ammunition had been exhausted.

At villages like Franleu, Hangest, Quesnoy, Airaines and Hornoy, surrounded units were to fight on, some for one or two days, but others like a unit of the 53ème R.I.C. for three days at Airaines. Some isolated groups held out even longer. The 'hérissons' — hedge-

hogs — tactics of Weygand's initiated because of the weakness of the Allied positions in front of the panzers, proved to be an effective method and it materially slowed down the German advance. The German units had to move round these positions until the French, their ammunition exhausted, were forced to surrender. This hopeless resistance frustrated the Germans who, on numerous occasions, reacted strongly and shot many of those they had taken prisoner who had resisted for 'too long'. The black troops of the 5ème D.I.C. were particularly prone to this sort of treatment, unquestionably war crimes.

THURSDAY, JUNE 6

On the right wing of the 10ème Armée, the 51st Division, the 31ème Division d'Infanterie and the 40ème Division d'Infanterie moved in from the reserve, were holding their ground along the Bresle river which offered a good defensive line. Apart from the Highlanders' efforts to eliminate a penetration south of the river near Eu, the day was comparatively quiet.

Further south it was a different picture. Here the panzers had outflanked the Bresle line and were advancing rapidly towards Rouen and the Seine. The XV. Armeekorps recorded how 'avoiding woods, roads and adjoining

While the engineers who laboured to build the bridge take a well-earned break, a section of PzKpfw IIs move out across it.

villages, and favoured by the gently undulating country practically free from ditches, the corps advanced southwards across country, deployed with tanks in front and infantry in vehicles in rear'. In short, the panzers had broken through the front of the 10ème Armée on the right wing of the IXème Corps d'Armée; the 5ème D.I.C. had been brushed aside, the 13ème Division d'Infanterie had been forced to withdraw southwards and the corps was in great danger of being cut off.

FRIDAY, JUNE 7

General Hoth, the commander of the XV. Armeekorps, went forward in the morning to meet his unit commanders. He saw Rommel at Eplessier and, in agreeing to his proposed advance, even suggested that he thought it might be possible to thrust forward as far as Rouen that day. Rommel visited Oberst Rothenburg who was to lead the attack, and stressed the main points to be observed: 'avoidance of villages,

Damage caused in the initial barrage is evident in these shots of the main street in Pont-Remy. Inevitably, midst the rubble and wreckage, a log-jam built up on the western bank before the breakout could begin. Crossings of the Somme took place at a dozen places on a wide front of some 100 kilometres, the Germans advancing straight across country, avoiding main roads and by-passing villages to take them in the rear.

472

To the east at Picquigny, Pionier-Bataillon 81 had grabbed the opportunity provided by the lock, which considerably reduced the width of the river, to throw across a short length of bridge. These horsemen are from the 45. Infanterie-Division.

Nevertheless one of the hardest nuts to crack was Hangest. It was badly knocked about . . .

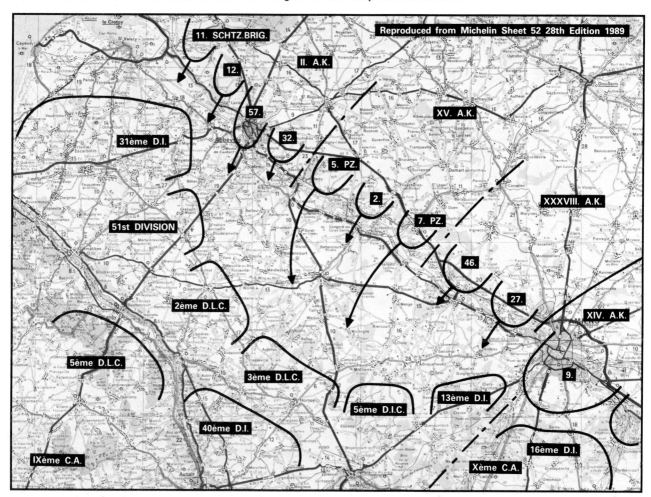

11. SCHTZ.BRIG.

12.

II. A.K.

57.

31ème D.I.

32.

XV. A.K.

5. PZ.

2.

51st DIVISION

7. PZ.

XXXVIII. A.K.

46.

2ème D.L.C.

27.

XIV. A.K.

5ème D.L.C.

3ème D.L.C.

9.

5ème D.I.C.

13ème D.I.

40ème D.I.

16ème D.I.

IXème C.A.

Xème C.A.

. . . so badly, that virtually everything had to be rebuilt, leaving nothing of 1940 recognisable today.

Rommel, June 5: 'By nine o'clock the attack to the south-west had made good progress. To eliminate the enemy force in Hangest, which had long been preventing us from bridge-building there, a whole panzer battalion was launched against the western outskirts of the village. Their orders were merely to shoot up the enemy in the western outskirts, without becoming involved in a fight for the village itself, which was to be cleaned up later by an armoured engineer company which was being sent up for that purpose. We watched the battalion approach closer and closer to the village and very soon heard their fire. Then the tanks turned off up the hill to the west, but only a few surmounted the topmost ridge. Most of them stuck on the hill. This route up the steep side of the hill was not very well chosen. The crews, who dismounted from their tanks,

were suddenly fired on by the enemy machine guns and suffered casualties in the coverless terrain. Meanwhile, a detachment of self-propelled guns under Hauptmann von Fischer came up and bombarded the western outskirts of Hangest. All other troops were directed into the bridgehead position with orders to take up positions in preparation for the forthcoming attack.' The defenders of Hangest, the 5ème Compagnie of the 44ème R.I.C. (a black colonial regiment) fought off every attack throughout the day — even point-blank fire (above) from the 150mm self-propelled guns of sIG Kompanie 705. In these two dramatic pictures the gun is firing at Château Favelle. The building was demolished and subsequently the site was cleared. Today a bridge replaces the level-crossing, making a comparison photograph meaningless.

most of which were barricaded, and all major roads; movements straight across country, thereby ensuring a surprise appearance in the flank and rear of the enemy'. The attack kicked off at 10.00 a.m. and by late afternoon the panzers had cut the main road from Dieppe to Beauvais.

The 1st Armoured Division had been placed under the orders of 10ème Armée the day before and on June 7 General Evans went to army headquarters and met Général Altmayer. Faced with the latest news that the panzers were already south of Aumale, it was decided that what was available of the division should move to Gournay

to strike at the flank of the panzers from there. For this, the division was able to assemble a force of 37 Mark VIs and 41 cruisers. In the evening, when the moves were well under way, Général Weygand arrived at 10ème Armée headquarters and saw Altmayer and Evans. Proclaiming the army's fight 'the decisive battle of the war', he ordered the 1st Armoured Division instead to hold to the last man on the Andelle river while French units were to counter-attack from the south. Evans once again pointed out that his tanks were quite unsuited for a static defence but Général Weygand stuck to his orders, the counter-attack against the

flank of the panzers had to be cancelled and the units moving up to attack were called back.

Meanwhile the panzers had continued their advance, inexorably forcing back the 2ème and 5ème D.L.C.s on their right flank and the 3ème D.L.C. on their left. That evening, the panzers were in contact with the British positions on the Andelle. The 10ème Armée was cut in two, the army headquarters had to retire to the south, while all communication with its IXème Corps d'Armée had been broken.

The confusion was widespread and the Beauman Division was scattered and mixed up with units of the 1st

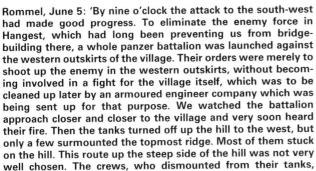

'The cleaning up of Hangest was still giving a lot of trouble and I finally put in Kradschützen-Bataillon 7 under Hauptmann von Hagen', wrote Rommel. The battalion formed up in extended order for the attack on foot, and was on the point of moving off when I drove back to them again to give a further quick order to von Hagen. Before I could do so, my armoured command vehicle was fired upon by machine guns from Hangest. The bullets clanged against its armoured walls but fortunately did

not penetrate, though direct hits were scored on the aerial and machine gun mounting. An NCO in the eight-wheeled armoured signals lorry behind us was too slow getting his head down and was seriouly wounded. The enemy in Hangest continued to cover the road . . . but finally the Kradschützen-Bataillon attacked and reached its objective.' Above: One of the last strongpoints to give way was the village school, which held until all ammunition had been exhausted.

The 10ème Compagnie of the 53ème R.I.C. also held out until the evening of June 5 at Le Quesnoy. The troops were dug in behind the outer wall of the grounds of the château, just east of the village. Its capture was also the responsibilty of Rommel's men: 'The Panzer-Regiment mopped up the enemy in its usual style, in spite of the fact that they had installed themselves very skilfully round the outskirts of the village. This was particularly true of the wall round Château du Quesnoy, which was held by a battalion of coloured troops. Stones had been wrenched out all along the wall to make loopholes from which large numbers of machine and anti-tank guns poured their fire into the oncoming tanks. But even here they had no success, for the rapid fire of our tanks, particularly the shells of the Panzer IVs, soon smashed the enemy forces. While one battalion of tanks moved round Le Quesnoy to the west, Rothenburg took the main body forward close alongside the wall. The armoured cars, following up behind, then held the enemy in check long enough to allow the leading infantry units to come up.' Rommel commented rather disparagingly that many of the prisoners taken were 'hopelessly drunk', but no doubt a measure of intoxication was helpful in settling the nerves of those colonial troops standing up resolutely against advancing tanks.

Armoured Division and French troops, of whose plans and positions nothing was known. The difficulty of maintaining direct communciation and control led General Beauman to issue conditional instructions that troops would hold on 'as long as any hope of successful resistance remained'. These orders placed heavy responsibility on local commanders and resulted in further complication and confusion. In the evening of June 7 Général Altmayer had to send a message to Général Ihler (commanding 9ème Corps d'Armée) in which he urged him to take measures to stop the Beauman Division 'from blowing bridges and roads behind you before the passage of yours troops'.

SATURDAY, JUNE 8

In the morning the Germans attacked the Andelle line at Forges and Sigy. A continuous stream of refugees and stragglers had made it impossible for Beauman Division to hold the road blocks they had built and the panzers broke through, allegedly led by a few captured French tanks. Serqueux was lost, recovered by a counter-attack only to be lost again. Sigy was attacked and gradually the British defenders were overcome and forced back and the Andelle line broken in many places.

Rommel described the crossing of the Andelle as follows: 'Although there was over three feet of water near the eastern bank, the first tanks crossed without

any trouble and soon overtook the infantry. However, when the first PzKpfw II attempted it, its engine cut out in midstream, leaving the crossing barred to all vehicles. Meanwhile, several British soldiers had waded across to us with their hands up, and, with their help, our motor cyclists started in to improve the crossing. Great pieces of the demolished bridge nearby were thrown into the deepest part of the ford. Willows alongside the river were sawn down and similarly used to improve the passage across the ford. One of the PzKpfw IIIs which had already crossed was brought back to tow out the PzKpfw II. At that moment I received a wireless signal saying that Oberleutnant

Finally, around 6.00 p.m., the tanks reached the wall and crashed through. However, the significance of this picture is not so much its similarity to an entertainer bursting through a paper hoop but that the nearest panzer is revealed to be our old friend '321', last seen on page 467 stranded at Condé-Folie some twelve hours previously. The engineers of Panzer-Regiment 25 must have pulled out all the stops to repair the track and get her back on the road. She would then have had about a three-mile drive to catch up with the battle at the château.

Sauvant's reconnaissance troop had succeeded in preventing enemy preparations to blow the bridges in Normanville. Sauvant had both bridges firmly in his hands and was creating a bridgehead across the river with his reconnaissance troop. At this good news, I at once broke off the action at Sigy and switched all forces south at top speed to cross the Andelle at Normanville'.

Although it was now far too late, Général Weygand finally agreed to the retirement of the 10ème Armée on the Seine and sent a personal message to the CIGS telling him of the orders

Surely one of the seven wonders of the Blitzkrieg battlefield — the original breaches sealed up roughly with concrete blocks.

Right: **In Airaines, about four kilometres west of Le Quesnoy, elements of the 53ème R.I.C. fought on until the evening of June 7. This picture was taken in the afternoon when the panzers of 5. Panzer-Division finally succeeded in entering the village. This is a PzKpfw II. The Hotchkiss just visible at the far end of the street belonged to the 2ème R.A.M., which abandoned it there when it broke down on June 5, and for the next three days it was manned as a static pillbox.** *Bottom:* **After the war the opportunity was taken to benefit from the damage by modernising the junction.**

'given this morning to commander IX French Corps who commands 51 British and 31 French Divisions to withdraw these divisions to the area Les Andelys-Rouen'. The orders conflicted with the situation on the ground: whereas the IXème Corps d'Armée could have retired behind the Seine whilst it was on

The strenuous defence put up by the black troops manning the Somme positions, and the delay it caused to their programme, annoyed the Germans intensely and it brought a racial element into the fight which tarnished the image of — Division. The battle over, these Germans appear to something to smile about. Not so their prisoner.

the Bresle, now it was supposed to move through a sector occupied by the Germans.

Général Ihler met his divisional commanders during the afternoon and outlined the plans for the withdrawal to Rouen, the idea being first to move behind the Béthune river and then to Rouen on June 12. Yet even as he spoke of his intention of withdrawing to Rouen in four days time, the panzers were already within four hours of the city!

Further to the south, what remained of the 3ème D.L.C. pulled back across the Seine that afternoon followed by the 1st Armoured Division and Beauman Division during the night. Of the British troops, only the 51st (Highland) Division were now left north of the Seine with the IXème Corps d'Armée.

In the morning the units of the IXème Corps d'Armée began to retire as planned towards the Seine but the panzer divisions were now preparing to turn north to intercept them. All contact with the 10ème Armée had been lost and the corps had nothing but vague rumours about the Germans' progress to work on. General Fortune sent a message via a despatch that he was 'now out of touch with everyone owing to the fact that I am not in possession of the recent code. All communications to me should be in clear or in French code'. In any case, with or without official notification, the danger was clear enough to those threatened by the panzers. When Général Ihler realised that the focus of the withdrawal had to be switched from Rouen to Le Havre, General Fortune quickly organised what troops were available into 'Arkforce' to protect Le Havre.

The Germans were anxious to get moving, and French prisoners — especially if they were coloured — were in great danger of being shot. After resisting bravely for so long against such odds, some are known to have received short shrift for their pains. Rommel all but admitted the fact when he wrote that 'any enemy troops were either wiped out or forced to withdraw'. *Above:* Bodies lying side by side — tell-tale sign of a summary execution — on a street corner in Hangest.

SUNDAY, JUNE 9

During the night Rommel attempted a surprise raid south of Rouen to seize the bridges at Elbeuf. The 7. Panzer-Division skirted Rouen to the east and at about 1.00 a.m. on June 9 the leading panzers reached the Seine at Sotteville-sous-le-Val. They immediately turned west towards Elbeuf only to have the bridges blown in front of their noses. Other explosions followed as the French blew up all the bridges in the area and the panzers withdrew northwards to spend the rest of the day reorganising. 'I was extremely angry over the failure of our enterprise,' admitted Rommel. In the meantime, elements of the 5. Panzer-Division had entered Rouen unopposed, to find that all the bridges had been destroyed and that French and British troops had left that part of the city north of the river.

The Germans reacted particularly badly at Airaines, where elements of the 53ème R.I.C had fought back for three days, and they had many prisoners shot for the only known reason that they had resisted 'too long'. *Left:* Most were black like Soldat Mamadou Boly, now buried in the French Military Cemetery at Condé-Folie. *Right:* This memorial in Airaines is in remembrance of the death of Capitaine Mésany N'Tchoréré, a coloured officer killed on June 7 and those who died 'pour la France'.

Air attacks on the Allied defence line increased following the 4. Armee attack across the Somme with the intention of disrupting communications. Blangy-sur-Bresle was hit twice — on June 5 and again the following day, the first raid catching this crew of the 1st Armoured Division by surprise as they repaired a broken track on their Cruiser.

Following the Supreme War Council meeting between Churchill and his advisers and members of the French government in Paris on May 31 at the height of the evacuation, French requests for air support increased by the day. Desperate for more air cover, during the first week of June Weygand had appealed several times for more fighters to be sent to France, but with the beginning of the Somme offensive on June 5, the demand was for ten squadrons immediately, followed 'as soon as possible by ten further squadrons'. Churchill received a report the next day giving the total picture as regards the relative strengths of the British, German and French air forces. As at May 24, British fighter strength stood at 1,668 aircraft with 194 having been shot down since May 10, and 138 built, a net loss of 56. The French had 1,224, having lost 354 and built 154 — an attrition rate of exactly 200. The total joint strength of the Royal Air Force and Armée de l'Air was 7,621 of all types, whereas the Luftwaffe was estimated to have 11,675 aircraft available. French telegrams to the British government for more fighters to be sent continued throughout June 7, with demands to know the exact number of aircraft engaged over France the previous day. This annoyed Churchill who reluctantly agreed that Reynaud could be told — for his personal information — that 144 British fighters had been engaged in France on June 6. As Churchill pointed out to colleagues, 'This was the equivalent of 12 squadrons and more than they had originally asked for'. On the 8th two squadrons clashed with a strong Messerchmitt formation and ten of the eighteen British aircraft were shot down,. This more or less decided the issue, and Churchill succinctly summed up the position at a Defence Committee meeting later that afternoon. There were, he said, . . . 'two alternatives open to us at the present time. We could regard the present battle as decisive for France and ourselves, and throw in the whole of our fighter resources in an attempt to save the situation, and bring about victory. If we failed, we should then have to surrender. Alternatively, we should recognise that whereas the present land battle was of great importance, it would not be decisive one way or the other for Great Britain. If it were lost, and France was forced to submit, we could continue the struggle with good hopes of ultimate victory, provided we ensured that our fighter defences in this country were not impaired; but if we cast away our defence the war would be lost, even if the front in France were stabilised, since Germany would be free to turn her air force against this country, and would have us at her mercy. One thing was certain,' Churchill added. 'If this country were defeated, the war would be lost for France no less than for ourselves, whereas, provided we were strong ourselves, we could win the war, and, in so doing, restore France to her position.' He felt, in conclusion, that it would be 'fatal to yield to the French demands and jeopardise our own safety'. The minutes of the meeting recorded unanimous agreement, and it only remained to inform Reynaud of the conclusion.

The question remained — how much could the French be told of the mood of the British War Cabinet. At first Churchill proposed a fairly honest and frank reply which included the sentence: 'It would be madness for us to cast aside the entire future, and the surest hope of our common victory, for the sake of what could only be a comparatively minor intervention.' However, after further discussion it was agreed to send a more noncommittal version: 'We are giving you all the support we can in the great battle short of ruining the capacity of this country to continue the war.' Nevertheless, behind locked doors, the same belief remained: that Churchill and the Cabinet believed that the war in France was now lost. All this, of course, was unknown in France although, perhaps, the Tommies at the sharp end felt much the same. On June 6 it had been decided to assemble what remained of the 1st Armoured Division (opposite) and strike at the flank of the leading panzer columns, now reported past Aumale, more than 30 kilometres south of the Somme. Some 80-odd tanks were available from the 3rd Armoured Brigade and Queen's Bays, supported by lorry-borne personnel from the 10th Royal Hussars (2nd Armoured Brigade). That evening Général Weygand arrived at 10ème Armée headquarters at Lyons la Forêt with orders for the 1st Armoured to hold 'to the last' fifteen kilometres of the next river line to the south, the Andelle. Meanwhile the infantry had been slugging it out, trying to hold the Bresle river line. On June 5 the 7th Argyll and Sutherland Highlanders suffered grievously with 23 officers and nearly 500 other ranks killed, wounded and missing when the Germans attacked their positions towards the seaward end of the line. On the 8th the survivors marched into Millebosc (right), about five kilometres west of Gamaches after the retirement from the Bresle had begun. Below: The 51st Highland Division, having been shunted across France by road and rail, found themselves back in the line with the 9ème Armée holding a position from just north of Abbeville to the sea. By June 6 the Division had been forced to retire to the line of the Blangy-Le Tréport road. However, a further withdrawal became necessary in the face of incessant German attacks from dive-bombers on the 7th.

This piper is playing outside the Divisional headquarters in Le Coudroy, a tiny hamlet eight kilometres west of Blangy, just prior to the move back to the Béthune river which runs from Dieppe south-eastwards to Saint-Vaast.

MONDAY. JUNE 10

The French High Command, still unaware of what was actually happening north of the Seine, continued to believe that the IXème Corps d'Armée could cross the Seine and Weygand issued instructions to 'fall back on the Seine below Caudebec inclusive'. These orders were transmitted to the War Office with a request for them to be passed to the 51st Division for delivery to the IXème Corps d'Armée.

The situation had changed for the worse in the morning as the vanguard of the 7. Panzer-Division advanced in between Arkforce and the bulk of the IXème Corps d'Armée and reached the sea near Veulettes.

Before long German guns were installed on the cliffs and the ships which for some days had been operating off the coast found themselves under fire, the destroyer HMS *Ambuscade* being hit that evening.

The Royal Navy had meanwhile started Operation 'Cycle' for the evacuation of the troops north of the Seine and, while shipping began assembling off the coast, Admiral Sir William James, Commander-in-Chief Portsmouth, arrived at Le Havre in the afternoon to see the situation for himself. Realising that it was unlikely that the majority of the IXème Corps d'Armée would ever reach Le Havre, he moved the small craft flotillas to Saint-Valery 'so as to be in a good central position if evacuation takes place'. Général Ihler had also come to the conclusion that his troops would never be able to reach Le Havre and, in agreement with General Fortune, he gave orders for a withdrawal towards Saint-Valery. This move began during the night. In places it was chaotic; the allotment of roads was not adhered to; French and British columns became stuck in interminable jams and rumours flew around that the Germans were approaching.

On the 10th the advance party of the 7. Panzer-Division reached the coast at Les Petites-Dalles, a small seaside hamlet fifteen kilometres east of Fécamp. One of the tanks, a PzKpfw III coded 'BO1', immediately smashed through the sea wall to drive down onto the shingle. It was the tank of the commander of Panzer-Regiment 25, Oberst Karl Rothenburg who we recently came across at Le Quesnoy (page 476). 'The sight of the sea with the cliffs on either side thrilled and stirred every man of us', Rommel was to write, 'also the thought that we had reached the coast of France. We climbed out of our vehicles and walked down to the water's edge until water lapped over our boots'.

On the morrow the division resumed the advance eastwards along the coast through Veulettes towards Saint-Valery.

TUESDAY, JUNE 11

During the morning, what remained of four divisions, the 51st Division, the 2ème D.L.C. and 5ème D.L.C., the 31ème Division d'Infanterie and the 40ème Division d'Infanterie, had drawn together a perimeter round Saint-Valery from which it was now hoped to embark. Early that morning the War Office, concerned that the Highland Division should not be regarded as acting contrary to Weygand's intentions, had sent a message to General Fortune, reminding him of the 'importance of acting in strict conformity' with any orders General Ihler might issue. In his reply Fortune referred to the 'physical impossibility corps approach the Seine. In same boat as me'.

Although the orders for the evacuation arrangements were issued by General Fortune, the 7. Panzer-Division was now too close. Artillery started to shell the town and at about 2.00 p.m. panzers attacked the western edge of the perimeter, forcing their way to the cliffs overlooking Saint-Valery from the west, cutting off the 2nd Battalion, Seaforth Highlanders, in Le Tot and Saint-Sylvain. The capture of this high ground threatened the whole evacuation plan as the embarkation points were now under direct fire. In addition, the 5. Panzer-Division and the 2. Infanterie-Division (mot) were now probing the eastern edge of the perimeter which the Luftwaffe bombed in the afternoon as a prelude to an assault from the east.

Admiral James signalled in the afternoon to the destroyer HMS *Codrington* that 'the evacuation from Saint-Valery is to commence this evening' and that 'all available transports are being sent', and General Fortune informed the War Office that he considered the coming night as the last chance of evacuation. However, his repeated efforts to communicate with the ships off the coast were unsuccessful and from these failures Général Ihler assumed that the ships would never come in time. These doubts were to be confirmed. That evening, under cover of darkness, all the men not actually engaged in the front line made their way to the harbour and beaches to wait for the ships to take them off but none arrived.

On the high ground east of Veulettes a surprise party was waiting and the Germans were caught in a heavy barrage from artillery and anti-tank weapons. Near Le Tot resistance was so spirited that hand-to-hand combat developed at many points. Meanwhile Panzer-Regiment 25 had bypassed the worst of the fighting and had arrived on the high ground north-west of Saint-Valery 'using every gun to prevent the embarkation of enemy troops'. *Above:* Rommel claimed that they succeeded in 'persuading about a thousand men to surrender in the northern part of Saint-Valery . . . most were French, and there were comparatively few British.'

There were believed to be over 40,000 men bottled up in the town and they were not going to give up without a fight. As attempts were made to get men away by boat, German guns fought a duel with ships offshore while the panzers slowly edged their way closer. Finally they entered the built-up area and reached the harbour. Rommel followed the infantry to the market square: 'Shortly afterwards an NCO reported to me that

a high-ranking French general had been taken prisoner on the eastern side of the town and was asking to see me. A few minutes later the French Général Ihler came up to me wearing an ordinary plain military overcoat. His escort officer fell to the rear as he approached. When I asked the General what division he commanded, he replied in broken German: "No division. I command IXème Corps d'Armée".'

WEDNESDAY, JUNE 12

With daylight approaching, it was realised that the men could not be left exposed on the beaches or crowded in the town and plans were drawn up to reorganise the defence of the perimeter. This required the recapture of the cliffs west of the town. Many of the guns and vehicles had already been rendered useless in preparation for the embarkation during the night and Général Ihler soon came to the conclusion that further resistance was impracticable. He decided to surrender but General Fortune disagreed as he considered that a faint possibility of withdrawal still remained. He made it known that he would only accept the order to surrender when he was certain that there was no alternative. However by now there was none. The Germans were already well inside the planned line of defence in many places and a despatch rider then arrived with a message from Général Ihler that a cease-fire would come into effect at 8.00 a.m.

Rommel, as usual, was in on the action: 'The tanks, concealed by the undergrowth, rolled slowly down the narrow winding roads, nearer and nearer to the first houses, until finally they entered the western quarter of the town. Fifty to a hundred yards away from us on the opposite side stood a number of British and French soldiers, irresolute, with their rifles grounded. Close beside them were numerous guns, which appeared to have been damaged by our bombardment. Fires were blazing all over the farther side of the town and there was war material lying about

Centre: **Rommel listens as an interpreter speaks to Général Ihler; General Fortune stands on the right. On Rommel's right is Oberst Georg von Bismarck, commanding Schützen-Regiment 7, with Major Otto Heidkämper, the divisional chief-of-staff, on his left. On Fortune's right is Leutnant Karl Hanke, Rommel's ADC. The bareheaded Luftwaffe Oberleutnant has just been liberated from captivity.**

everywhere, including large numbers of vehicles. The panzers rolled on steadily yard by yard to the south, with their guns traversed east, past rows of captured vehicles parked on the western side of the harbour. Meanwhile we tried to persuade the enemy troops facing us to lay down their arms and walk across a narrow wooden bridge towards us. It was some minutes before the British could bring themselves to it. At first they came across singly, with long intervals between each man, then gradually the file began to thicken. Our infantry now went across to the other side to receive British and French prisoners on the spot'.

The last organised resistance — by men of the 40ème Division d'Infanterie near Houdetot, about ten kilometres inland — lasted until 10.00 a.m.

The exact number of prisoners taken at Saint-Valery is not known but Rommel told of a total of about 46,000, 8,000 of these being British troops. He counted 12 generals among them, including Général Marcel Ihler and the staff of IXème Corps d'Armée, General

The last troops holding out in the area were at Houdetot, eight kilometres outside the town, where men of the 40ème Division d'Infanterie did not give up until mid-morning. Here Général André Durand has just been captured.

Left: The last organised resistance had been overwhelmed and the survivors were rounded up in the afternoon of June 12. The chap in the beret wears the rank of a battalion commander.

Right: With no location on the original, Jean Paul did well to locate the spot — the yard of Clos des Cadets farm at La Gaillarde, not far to the north-east of Houdetot.

V. M. Fortune and his staff, Général Marie-Jacques Chanoine of the 5ème D.L.C., Général Arsène Vauthier of the 31ème Division d'Infanterie, Général André Durand of the 40ème Division d'Infanterie and Général Paul Gastey of the 2ème D.L.C. The latter has just taken command of the division after its commander, Général André Berniquet, had been killed the previous evening. The booty was equally impressive and reports announced the capture of 58 tanks, 1,133 trucks, 56 guns and 368 machine guns.

A few small parties had been lifted from along the coast, and ships managed to get in to Veules-les-Roses and take off 2,137 British and 1,184 French troops and 34 seamen and civilians.

Meanwhile Arkforce had reached its destination at Le Havre and there the evacuation went well, the Navy bringing back 2,222 British troops to England and carrying 8,837 more to Cherbourg to continue the fight. No ships had been lost but three destroyers, HMS *Ambuscade*, HMS *Boadicea* and HMS *Bulldog*, had been damaged.

The same scene was pictured in another farmyard, this time with troops of the 51st (Highland) Division.

The 6. Armee from the Somme to the Marne

The 6. Armee was to attack on a 120-kilometre-wide front from Amiens to the Ailette river. Subordinated to the army, Gruppe von Kleist was to be the western arm of the two-pronged main German attack, the eastern one being implemented by the 12. Armee of Heeresgruppe A. At first, Gruppe von Kleist's two corps were to attack abreast: the XVI. Armeekorps from the Péronne bridgehead, the XIV. Armeekorps from the Amiens bridgehead. After the breakthrough, the two corps were to be rearranged south of Montdidier and Gruppe von Kleist was then to dash south-eastwards. So as not to risk his panzers, General von Kleist wanted to employ only his infantry divisions to achieve the initial breakthrough but the 6. Armee commander, Generaloberst Walther von Reichenau, disagreed and the panzers were engaged from the start. This was to prove a costly decision.

The attack by the 6. Armee was to strike at the positions held by the French 10ème and 7ème Armées. In the Amiens sector, the XIV. Armeekorps attack — by two panzer divisions, two infantry divisions, one of them motorised, and the Infanterie-Regiment 'Gross Deutschland' — fell on the Xème Corps d'Armée of the 10eme Armée. The corps had only three infantry divisions but the odds were stacked still higher as the 'schwerpunkt' was to

With the capture of Saint-Valery and the inevitable retreat to the next river line, the Seine, we must now switch our attention further east to see how the battle was progressing in the 6. Armee sector. The French put up such a good show of resistance on this part of the front that, three days after the attack had begun, Hitler was forced to issue Directive No. 14 to try to cope with the problem.

The Führer and Supreme   *Führer Headquarters,*
Commander of the Armed Forces   *8th June 1940*

Directive No. 14

1. The enemy is offering stiff resistance on our right flank and in the centre of 6. Armee.
2. Therefore, according to the proposal of Commander-in-Chief Army, I approve the orders given this morning by Heeresgruppe B, viz.:

(a) Merely to hold down the enemy on the 6. Armee front.
(b) To transfer XIV. Armeekorps to the left flank of 4. Armee.
(c) To strike a crushing blow at the strong enemy forces on the 6. Armee front by increasing the pressure exerted by the bulk of 4. Armee south-eastwards and by the left flank of 6. Armee south-westwards.

3. I further order:
(a) The basic intention, as laid down in Directive No. 13 [see page 365], viz.: to destroy enemy forces in the Château-Thierry–Metz–Belfort triangle, and to bring about the collapse of the Maginot Line, remains valid.
    However, since Phase 1 of the operation is not yet ended and extremely strong resistance is being offered north of Paris, stronger forces must be employed on the lower Seine and against Paris than had originally been contemplated.
(b) Heeresgruppe A will move to the attack on 9th June south-south-westwards as ordered in Directive No. 13.
(c) 9. Armee will thrust southwards towards the Marne. It will be reinforced as soon as possible by XVI. Armeekorps (including attached SS units and the SS-Totenkopf Division). Strong reserve forces must back up the juncture of the two Heeresgruppe.
(d) I reserve to myself the decision as to the direction of any further thrust by 9. Armee or whether it is to be left with Heeresgruppe B or put under command of Heeresgruppe A.

4. The task of the Luftwaffe, in addition to what has been laid down in Directive No. 13, is as follows:

(a) To support the concentric attack on the flanks of the main enemy forces facing Heeresgruppe B.
(b) To keep under observation and under strong fighter cover the coast on the right flank of Heeresgruppe B and the area south-west of the Bresle sector.
(c) To help the advance of Heeresgruppe A at the focal point.

ADOLF HITLER

hit only one of them, the 16ème Division d'Infanterie, which was to bear the brunt of the assault on its 15-kilometre front. The division had arrived in the sector at the begining of June and had had only four days to try to create a defensive system of the kind that Général Weygand had laid down for the coming battle. Weygand himself had paid a visit to the division's commander, Général Eugène Mordant, on June 4 to see how the situation was.

In the Péronne sector, the XVI. Armeekorps attack by two panzer divisions, two infantry divisions, the SS-Verfügungs-Division and the Leibstandarte SS-'Adolf Hitler', was to strike at the sector held by the Ier Corps d'Armée of the 7ème Armée, this corps having four divisions. The 'schwerpunkt' was to strike at the boundary between the 19ème and 29ème Divisions d'Infanterie.

WEDNESDAY, JUNE 5

In both sectors, the attack started at about 3.00 a.m. with heavy shelling, the four panzer divisions in the lead followed by infantry. The panzers advanced through the French positions, some being crippled by mines and a good many others being accounted for by the French 25mm and 47mm anti-tank guns, but the Germans bypassed any point of resistance and broke through behind. Despite this threat of panzers to their rear, the French strong points fought back and stopped the follow-up troops. A company commander of the 16ème Division d'Infanterie in position near Dury described how 'the 81mm mortar group was the main contributor in stopping the attack as in spite of our repeated demands for a general barrage to the artillery, nothing arrived. Our artillery positions at the rear were already under attack by the panzers'. Although the gunners managed to turn their howitzers and disable some of the panzers, they could not prevent some batteries being overrun.

The battle raged throughout the day

On May 22, the V. Armeekorps had become responsible for the sector south of Péronne and was charged with the task of seizing as big a bridgehead as possible across the Somme Canal. The 3ème Division Légère d'Infanterie held this section of the front and they fought tenaciously to protect bridge sites, stopping every German attempt to cross. When elements of Infanterie-Regiment 190 (62. Infanterie-Division) got across the canal on the 24th at a spot twelve kilometres south of Péronne at Epénancourt, a section of the 40ème B.C.C. backed the 141ème R.I.A. in a counter-attack. Although three Renault R-40s were lost *(above)*, the Germans were successfully thrown back across the canal.

Following the re-commencement of the offensive on June 5, renewed German attempts to cross the canal between Pargny and Ham were all repulsed. This time it was Infanterie-Regiment 183 who were sent back across the canal with their tails between their legs, the 140ème R.I.A. taking more than a hundred German prisoners. *Left:* At Verlaines, the enemy, with hands on heads, is marched before the commander of the regiment's third battalion, Commandant Jean-Marie Bernard.

However, the change of rôles was be be short-lived. Although the new French tactics came as a rude awakening to the Germans, by now used to having everything their own way, the failure of the French to hit hard at the armoured spearheads lost all that had been gained. The panzers erupted from the Péronne bridgehead and the 3ème Division had to withdraw on the night of June 6. *Right:* Now it was the French who were the prisoners, this picture being taken near Voyennes.

German infantry marching through Péronne on their way to the front. On the house on the right, a symbolic plaque tells them that this house had been destroyed in 1870 but was rebuilt in 1873 only to be destroyed again in 1916.

and the next. Strong points bypassed by the panzers and surrounded by the infantry fought on until ammunition supplies were exhausted while further to the rear other positions, including the artillery batteries, tackled with the panzers. The situation was confused, with numerous isolated skirmishes being fought by small cut off French units summed up in the words of Hauptmann Ernst von Jungenfeld, of the 4. Panzer-Division: 'Behind us is the glare of a vicious battle where one fights not only for each village, but for each house. We are not therefore surprised to find ourselves under fire from all quarters, and one could say: "Nobody knows which is the front and which is the rear". When summoned to surrender, the enemy refuses and redoubles his fire. These are soldiers from the Active (regular) troops, they do not know hesitation or weakness'.

'The French', as the Heeresgruppe B commander, Generaloberst Fedor von Bock, noted in his diary that evening, 'are defending themselves stubbornly' but the French well knew that they

Rebuilt in 1924, it was a sobering reminder for the warriors of 1940 of the conflicts that this part of France had suffered. Having survived a third war, what an indictment on society that its loss was finally brought about by so-called 'progress'!

Liancourt-Fosse, 20 kilometres south-west, was assaulted early on June 6 by the second battalion of Panzer-Regiment 35 (4. Panzer-Division), and a counter-attack by Renault R-35s of the

1er B.C.C. failed to dislodge them. This picture was taken later in the day when the panzers were already much further southwards . . . beyond Roye and across the Avre river.

could not hold out much longer against the forces arrayed against them. The Germans, however, could take little satisfaction from the day's progress. Although they had made penetrations through the French positions — the panzer vanguards of XIV. Armeekorps having advanced for about 10 kilometres and those of the XVI. Armeekorps for about 15 kilometres being only 6 kilometres north of Roye — they had achieved no sweeping success and they had paid dearly for those gains in men and machines.

The French units fought back for most of June 6, their strength ebbing. By evening the 16ème Division d'Infanterie had lost 2,000 men and a large part of its artillery, the 19ème Division d'Infanterie the whole of its 117ème R.I. and most of its guns and the 29ème Division d'Infanterie its 112ème R.I.A., two battalions of chasseurs and almost the whole of its artillery. A company of Renault R-35s of the 1er B.C.C. had counter-attacked early that day to try to relieve the staff of the 6ème Demi-Brigade of the 29ème Division d'Infanterie trapped in Liancourt but this had failed.

Although a relative success for the French, these two days showed both the validity of the concept of defence in depth adopted by Général Weygand and the limitations inherent in the speed and resources with which the Weygand Line was put together. In theory, armoured counter-attacks should have dealt with the panzers which ventured far in front of their infantry but there were no French tanks at hand, or too few, to do so in the threatened sectors. Tanks of the hurriedly reconstitued 1ère D.C.R. — Renault R-35s of the 25ème B.C.C., Renault B1bis of the 28ème B.C.C., and Renault R-35s of the attached 34ème B.C.C. — did counter-attack to support the Ier Corps d'Armée on the morning of June 6, but these were immediately set upon by the Luftwaffe, suffered losses and made no headway. They were anyway far too few — only about 75 — to stop the 4. Panzer-Division. What remained of the 2ème D.C.R. also advanced to take on the panzers in the Xème Corps

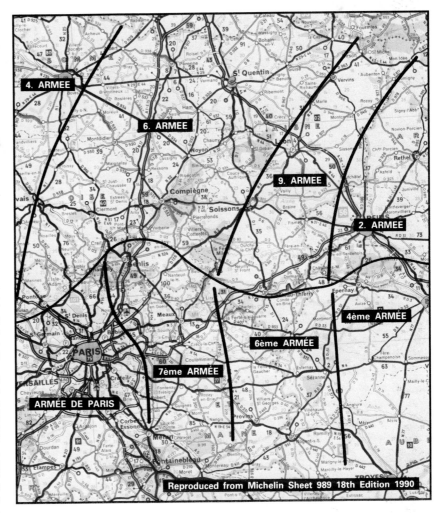

Reproduced from Michelin Sheet 989 18th Edition 1990

Twenty-six years earlier this whole swathe of France had been overrun in a week as the Allies fell back 200 kilometres in the 'heroic retreat' from Charleroi to the Marne. There the line was stabilised and Paris saved in the 'Miracle of the Marne'. This time, although it took the Germans a month to reach the river, there was no chance of a final Allied stand to stem their advance. Weygand's new tactics had held the German onslaught for two days but by June 10 6ème Armée had been forced back and the next day German bridgeheads were established across the Marne.

d'Armée sector. Only a shadow of its former self with about 60 tanks, it arrived too late when the battle was almost lost and had to withdraw.

For the Germans, the experience had been new and unpleasant. General-

oberst von Bock summarised June 6 in his diary as 'a hard day, rich in crises! It seems that we are brought to a standstill!'. Going to the XIV. Armeekorps command post to see for himself and dissatisfied with the results achieved by

These two photos taken in Soissons purport to show the action north of the river, but would a photographer really have stood in such an exposed position if the enemy were just ahead? A

probable explanation is that it has been staged after the battle — as are so many 'action' war pictures — just for the benefit of the photographer.

Units of the 9. Armee reached the Aisne river in the neighbourhood of Soissons on June 6. These two Germans are gingerly approaching the bridge along the N2 from the north under the protection of a white flag, their caution possibly having something to do with the dead bodies lying in the road up ahead.

Further down nearer the river an exchange of fire appears to be taking place between these grenadiers and French snipers.

Perhaps the bodies lying on the N2 were Germans picked off by marksmen and now they are taking no chances.

Unlike September 1914, this time there was no Général Gallieni with an army in taxicabs to halt von Kluck's June 1940 successor. The 6ème Armée had been unable to stop the advance of the 9. Armee and on June 11 units of the 25. Infanterie-Division succeeded in getting a bridgehead across the Marne near Château-Thierry. *Above:* Work began immediately on the construction of a 16-tonne bridge running off the Jean de la Fontaine square. These engineers were pictured on the 12th filling a crater left from the artillery bombardment to give easier access to the crossing site.

either of his panzer corps, he decided 'with a heavy heart' that he would have to disengage his XIV. Armeekorps from the Amiens area and move it behind the XVI. Armeekorps in the Péronne area and orders were drawn up to this effect. Nevertheless the move was never carried out, for that afternoon von Bock and his staff heard that they had at last succeeded in breaching the Weygand Line. This was due to the decisive success of the 4. Armee, which had by now achieved a large, deep breakthrough on the lower Somme, and the progress of the 9. Armee in the Soissons area, where the commander of the French 6ème Armée, Général Robert Touchon, had been forced to order the withdrawal of his left wing on the Aisne. For the Germans, the crisis had been overcome but the stiff resistance which had been encountered — stiff enough to stop the panzer divisions for nearly two days — took its toll, the commander of the 6. Armee, General-oberst Walter von Reichenau, reporting for example that the potential of the XIV. Armeekorps was now down to 45 percent for the panzers and about 60 percent for the infantry.

Some time later the same photographer pictured an SdKfz 222 armoured car of the 3. Panzer-Division as it crossed over the newly-completed pontoon bridge. The 2cm KwK 30 and the coaxially-mounted MG34 are elevated at maximum ready to deal with any threat from the air.

Having crossed the Marne, this PzKpfw I of the 3. Panzer-Division clatters off through the eastern suburbs at Chierry. In the former war, Château-Thierry remained well behind the line until the German advance in 1918. The town had fallen that year on May 31 but it became the scene of the first American offensive of the war and was retaken by them on July 21. In 1940 vestiges of trenches and craters still remained in the surrounding woods, the town itself being dominated by the American cemetery and memorial on Hill 204 established in 1922, completed in 1935 and dedicated on May 30, 1937.

Above left: **Port-à-Binson on the river 30 kilometres to the east. Its bridge — like all those on the Marne — had been blown, leaving these French vehicles abandoned on the northern bank.** *Above right:* **This is an interesting comparison for although the bridge has been rebuilt, the opportunity was taken to straighten the approach road, leaving the original one much as it was, including the old-style overhead electric poles.**

JUNE 7-10

After its hasty withdrawal on the Aisne, the 6ème Armée could not prevent the Germans from forcing the river in the Soissons area. On June 7 the 7ème Armée held its ground in the centre but was now in great danger of being cut off after the collapse of the 10ème Armée front on its left and the withdrawal of the 6ème Armée on its right. On June 8 the commander of Groupe d'Armées No. 3, Général Antoine Besson, ordered the withdrawal of his entire left wing for the coming night, bringing the 10ème Armée and 7ème Armée to behind the Seine and the Oise. On the Aisne, the 6ème Armée had to hold its ground.

On June 10 the 10ème Armée was behind the Seine after a hurried and difficult withdrawal; having lost its IXème Corps d'Armée cut off near Saint-Valéry, it could not prevent the 4. Armee from gaining a bridgehead across the river near Les Andelys. To the east the 7ème Armée had withdrawn with some difficulty on the Oise. To take command of the sector between these two armies, the French High Command now created an Armée de Paris, its commander, Général Pierre Héring being made responsible for the defence of the front along the Seine from Vernon, on the west, to the Oise, north of the city. Further to the east, the 6ème Armée had been unable to stop the advance of the 9. Armee on the Aisne and on June 10 the XVIII. Armeekorps reached the Marne near Château-Thierry. The next day both the corps' 81. Infanterie-Division and 25. Infanterie-Division had succeeded in getting bridgeheads across the river. While his two corps were ordered to assemble south of Soissons to be ready to rush southwards, General von Kleist went to the XVIII. Armeekorps command post to co-ordinate the panzers' attack from this bridgehead.

Above: **Travelling further to the east, this was all that remained to be seen of a French ammunition lorry after it had exploded near Cormoyeux on the edge of the Forêt de la Montagne.** *Below:* **When our author found the correct spot, little Céline Pallud found that the old fence had now been replaced with sections of 'PSP', the pierced steel planking used by the Allies in great quantities for matting on roads and airfields in France after the 1944 invasion. However, in June 1940, having failed to break through in the Amiens-Péronne area, the two corps from Gruppe von Kleist were soon to be shifted eastwards to the 9. Armee sector to take advantage of the bridgehead gained at Château-Thierry.**

Breaching the Weygand Line had not been easy, and the French had exacted a high price. *Above:* **This PzKpfw IV — or what is left of it — was stopped in its tracks on the Boves-Sains road, nine kilometres south of Amiens, on June 5, killing two of the crew: Leutnant Jürgen Hoesch and Obergefreiter Robert Preis. One year later the wreck still remained beside the road when Hoesch's brother returned to erect this memorial on the exact spot.** *Right:* **Not expecting such an unusual monument to have survived — especially in view of the anti-German sentiment after 1944 — Jean Paul was pleasantly surprised to find it intact and unmarked, a credit to local tolerance.** *Below:* **Hoesch having been transferred to a family grave in Germany, Preis remains at Bourdon (Block 31, grave 192).**

The 12. Armee on the Aisne

On June 9 Heeresgruppe A joined Fall Rot, launching its powerful forces at the front held by Groupe d'Armées No. 4 in the Aisne sector. The attack hit mainly the French 4ème Armée, which had left the Sarre sector at the end of May and had assumed responsibility for the front between Neufchâtel and Attigny only three days earlier. Also involved to the east was the left wing of the 2ème Armée and to the west the right wing of the 6ème Armée.

The Aisne was not 'tank country' and the initial attack on June 9 was made only by infantry. The 12. Armee, whose four corps of infantry were to open the way for the panzers of Gruppe Guderian, had devised an elaborate plan for this, each corps being responsible for

two 'panzerstrasse'. On the right flank, between Neufchâtel and Blanzy, the III. Armeekorps was to open Panzerstrasse 1 and 2 for the 2. Panzer-Division, while from Blanzy and Rethel the XIII. Armeekorps was to initiate Panzerstrasse 3 and 4 for the 1. Panzer-Division. Between Rethel and Givry the XXIII. Armeekorps was to establish Panzerstrasse 5 and 6 for the 8. Panzer-Division and the XVII. Armeekorps Panzerstrasse 7 and 8 between Givry and Voncq for the 6. Panzer-Division on the left flank of the attack. Each of the corps had been assigned strong engineer units, with the job of throwing bridges across the Aisne as soon as bridgeheads were gained by the infantry.

SUNDAY, JUNE 9

The odds were heavily stacked against the defenders whose seven divisions faced twice as many German. Nevertheless the French units held their ground and, in spite of some promising gains at first, the German attacks made only disappointing progress. The French counter-attacked with determination and in some places recovered the bridgeheads achieved on the left bank of the river by the Germans and captured a number of prisoners. General Albrecht Schubert, the commander of the XXIII. Armeekorps which had lost a thousand men trying to breach the positions of the 14ème Division d'Infanterie of Général Jean de Lattre de Tassigny, noted: 'The attack ran up

'The attack ran up against an enemy whose morale was unshaken . . . in a manner which recalls the attitude of the best French troops of 1914-18 at Verdun.' This compliment was paid by the commander of the XXIII. Armeekorps, General Albrecht

Schubert, to his enemy in the Aisne sector where German attacks made little progress on June 9, particularly east of Rethel. His corps alone lost a thousand men, either killed or missing, wounded (left) or taken prisoner (right).

The Germans had reached the Aisne at Rethel on May 16, but the 'Sichelschnitt' was aiming westwards and the troops were left at Rethel to fight it out as best they could. In the face of dogged French resistance, it took five days just to take that part of the town north of the river. Up until the beginning of 'Fall Rot' on June 9, the front in this sector remained fairly static, save for much patrolling by both sides. At Sault-les-Rethel, just south of the Aisne, a German commando team comprising two men dressed as civilians slipped a mine under the Renault B1bis 'France' (above), which was covering the bridge on the afternoon of May 20. The tank caught fire, one of the crew, Caporal Maurice Gautheron, being killed.

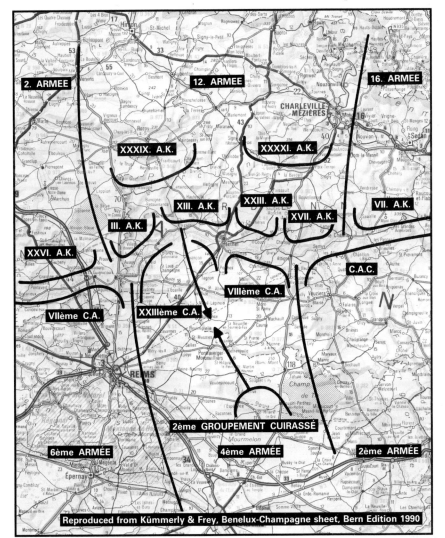

Reproduced from Kümmerly & Frey, Benelux-Champagne sheet, Bern Edition 1990

Four corps of infantry were to open the way for the panzers across the Aisne river, each being assigned strong engineer units for the task. However, the French defenders held their ground and by the afternoon of June 9, only one corps, the XIII. Armeekorps, had succeeded in establishing a firm footing across the river and had built bridges for Panzerstrasse 2 and 3. None of the other six 'tank roads' were operational. The XXXIX. Armeekorps attacked out of the bridgehead on the morning of June 10 but the leading elements of the 1. Panzer-Division were soon counter-attacked by the 2ème Groupement Cuirassé. The battle raged throughout the afternoon near Juniville and in the end the French tanks were forced to withdraw.

against an enemy whose morale was unshaken . . . on June 9 and 10 the 14ème Division d'Infanterie fought in a manner which recalls the attitude of the best French troops of 1914-18 at Verdun'. Just to the east the XVII. Armeekorps experienced the same difficulties and near Voncq, on the Ardennes Canal, the 26. Infanterie-Division lost about 600 men killed or wounded and 500 taken prisoner by the 36ème Division d'Infanterie.

None of the four panzerstrasse assigned to XXXXI. Armeekorps had been opened but to the west of Rethel the German attacks were more successful and neither the 10ème nor the 2ème Divisions d'Infanterie succeeded in throwing the Germans back across the Aisne. Panzerstrasse 2 and 3 were opened, the bridges were being put in place and the panzers of the XXXIX. Armeekorps were able to cross the river at a bridgehead gained by the infantry of XIII. Armeekorps near Château-Porcien in the afternoon of June 9 to assemble on the south bank ready to move on southwards the next morning.

The XIX. corps commander, General Guderian, descibes how 'in the course of the afternoon two shallow bridgeheads had been formed to the west and east of Château-Porcien. These could be used for getting the 2. Panzer-Division over the river, together with further elements of the 1. Panzer-Division (which had crossed at Château-Porcien).

'The attack by my tanks was to start at 6.30 hours on the 10th of June' wrote Guderian. 'I was at the front by then and managed to get the 1. Schützen-Brigade which was too far back, moving forwards. I was surprised to be recognised by the front-line infantry, and when I asked how they knew my name, I discovered I was amongst the Infanterie-Regiment 55, whose home station was Würzburg; the officers and men remembered me from the days when I commanded the 2. Panzer-Division in that once beautiful but now totally ruined city. We were delighted to see each other.'

495

The 4ème Armée had planned a counter-attack south of Rethel by the 2ème Groupement Cuirassé which comprised the 3ème D.C.R., the 7ème D.L.M. and other odd elements. These pictures were taken on June 9 in Cauroy, about 20 kilometres south of Rethel, when the force was assembling before the attack — as it turned out, the last major French attack of the whole campaign. This Laffly S20 lorry is towing a 25mm Hotchkiss anti-aircraft gun northwards in the direction of Juniville.

MONDAY, JUNE 10

Meanwhile the 4ème Armée had planned a counter-attack for June 10 by elements of the 2ème Groupement Cuirassé (also known as Groupement Buisson, after the 3ème D.C.R. commander, Général Louis Buisson) which had the 3ème D.C.R. and the 7ème D.L.M., despatched to this sector as a mobile reserve for the 4ème Armée. The 3ème D.C.R. was still a potent unit, with three of its original four tank battalions intact — the 49ème B.C.C. having been removed to reinforce the 41ème B.C.C. The battalion had been replaced by the 10ème B.C.C. equipped with Renault R-35s. On June 10 the division had some thirty Renault B1bis, fifty Hotchkiss H-39s and forty Renault R-35s.

At the beginning of June a new unit, the 7ème D.L.M., had been hastily created from what remained of the 4ème D.L.C. which had been disbanded after its costly engagement in Belgium. Among these remnants were the 8ème Dragons, which had suffered heavy losses in Belgium, losing more men after being evacuated from Dunkirk when the *Scotia* was sunk on June 1 by the Luftwaffe. The survivors had arrived at Plymouth on June 2; were immediately turned around and rushed back to Brest on June 4 and re-assembled at Evreux on June 5. That same day the 4ème D.L.C. was officially disbanded and the 7ème D.L.M. came into being. The 8ème Dragons was reconstituted as a tank cavalry unit with four squadrons, the first two being equipped with worn out Hotchkiss H-35s taken from training fields, the two others with brand new Hotchkiss H-39s fresh from the factories. Altogether the 8ème Dragons had about forty Hotchkisses and, with the fifteen Renault AMR-33 and ten Panhard P-178 armoured cars of its recce regiment (the 4ème R.A.M.), the 7ème D.L.M. had about 65 armoured fighting vehicles. Assembled in haste as it was from tired

It was followed by a Latil KTL and 105mm Modèle 1913 field gun. This road ran westwards to La Neuville but a track branched off northwards and reached Juniville across country.

Note the hastily-built road-block to which Guderian later referred when he wrote: 'Our infantry had to fight hard for the barricaded streets and houses of the villages.'

Above: **Renault B1bis of the 41ème B.C.C., 3ème D.C.R., rush northwards through Cauroy to counter the panzers at Juniville. The leading tank is Lieutenant Henri Jacquelin's 'Tavel'.** *Bottom:* **This is 'Chambertin' of Lieutenant Robert Godinat.** Both had belonged to the 49ème B.C.C. and had been transferred to the 41ème. They both came through the battle on June 10 only to be knocked out two days later at Mourmelon by panzers of Gruppe Guderian.

survivors of the 4ème D.L.C. and by men and officers scraped together, the new division lacked cohesion.

The XXXIX. Armeekorps attack went in as planned and Guderian describes how 'the advance was rapid through Tagnon to Neuflize. Once in the open the panzers met hardly any resistance, since the new French tactics concentrated on the defence of woods and villages, while the open ground was abandoned out of respect for our panzers. Consequently our infantry had to fight hard for the barricaded streets and houses of the villages, while the panzers, only slightly inconvenienced by the French artillery firing to the rear from the positions they still held on the Rethel front, broke straight through to the Retourne and crossed that swampy stream at Neuflize.

'The 1. Panzer-Division now pressed forward,' continues Guderian, 'attacking along both flanks of the Retourne, with the 1. Panzer-Brigade to the south and Balck's riflemen to the north of the stream. Juniville was reached in the early afternoon, where the enemy counter-attacked with strong armoured forces. A tank battle developed to the south of Juniville, which lasted for some two hours before being eventually decided in our favour. In the course of the afternoon Juniville itself was taken. There Balck managed personally to capture the colours of a French regiment. The enemy withdrew to La Neuville'.

In the afternoon the 2ème Groupement Cuirassé had tried to stop the panzers breaking out from the bridgehead over the Aisne. The units concerned were the 7ème D.L.M. south and west of Juniville and the 3ème D.C.R., with one squadron of Hotchkiss H-35s and one regiment of carrier-borne infantry from the 7ème D.L.M., north of Juniville. South of the Retourne river the 7ème D.L.M. had reached Ménil-Lépinois and cut Panzer-

Above: Motor cyclists of the 6ème G.R.D.I., the recce detachment of the 3ème D.I.M. followed, passing another barricade. Note the 6ème G.R.D.I. insignia, a jousting knight, on the side of the combination on the left. *Below:* We found Cauroy almost exactly the same as it was fifty years ago, with only slight changes here and there. The shell damage which is visible on the wall on the right, just in front of the road block, can still be seen today.

Reims, symbol of France, has fallen. The city so entwined with the history of France was occupied on June 10. With the streets still barricaded, two NCOs wander down Avenue Jean Jaurès from Place Aristide Briand, named after one of the great statesmen of France, eleven times its premier including the critical period of 1915-17.

strasse 3. To the north of it, the 3ème D.C.R. forced its way to Perthes to facilitate the withdrawal of elements of the 127ème R.I. trapped there and had at the same time cut Panzerstrasse 4. After battling with the 1. Panzer-Division, the French tanks withdrew in the late evening. They had caused Guderian to have to admit to 'heavy casualties' but the losses were equally bad on the French side, particularly for the 7ème D.L.M. as many of its worn out Hotchkiss H-35s had suffered also from mechanical failures.

At night, the 4ème Armée ordered Général Buisson to pull back, which was done during the night. His tank group was disbanded the next day, the 7ème D.L.M. being put under command of the XXIIIème Corps d'Armée and the 3ème D.C.R. under the VIIIème Corps d'Armée.

The day was only half a success for Gruppe Guderian, and for the XXXXI. Armeekorps of General Reinhardt. The second corps of the panzergruppe had not yet been able to cross at the points allotted it because of the French resistance (the last troops in Voncq were not overwhelmed until the morning of June 11) and parts of it were switched to cross behind the XXXIX. Armeekorps. However, this was not disastrous as the withdrawal of the whole of the French line on the next day gave the corps the opportunity of still crossing at Attigny as planned.

The situation of the 4ème Armée was made even more serious as to the west the 9. Armee had crossed the Aisne in the Soissons area and forced the 6ème Armée back on the Marne. This gravely endangered the whole left wing of the 4ème Armée and in the evening of June 10, alarmed by the advance of the Germans on his left wing, the commander of Groupe d'Armées No. 4, Général Huntziger, had no option but to order a withdrawal of his 4ème Armée and 2ème Armée on a line running from Reims to the Maginot Line near Montmédy.

Since the start of Fall Rot, the French High Command had committed most of its reserves, and by the evening of June 10 there were now only five divisions left in reserve in the whole of France.

In September 1914, the Germans occupied the city and the German Crown Prince made the Grand Hôtel his headquarters, but his stay was short-lived. Although Reims remained in French hands for the next four years, it was always within range of German artillery and virtually every building was badly damaged, including the cathedral where the Kings of France had been crowned — seen here in the background. This German convoy is parked on Place Royale where stands the statue of King Louis XV, but Reims would have the last word five years later when it was host to the signing of the German surrender.

499

The Defeat

After the defeat in Belgium and in northern France which had left tens of thousands of prisoners in German hands, the failure to stop 'Fall Rot' at the beginning of June resulted in the capture of many more thousands of dispirited soldiery.

First there had been the battle on the Somme, lost on June 6. Then came the battle for Champagne, lost on June 10. Now already the second defensive line based on the Seine and Marne had been broken. The situation was so grave that Général Weygand sent a note to the Prime Minister: 'The events of the past two days oblige me to inform you that a definite break of our defence lines may occur at any moment. If such an eventuality should come about, our armies would continue to fight until their resources and strength were exhausted. But their dispersion would only be a matter of time'.

There was also a development in the wider strategic picture with the declaration of war by Italy on France and Britain on June 10.

Considering the seriousness of the situation, and with German troops crossing the Seine at Andelys and Vernon, Reynaud and his Ministers in Paris had to decide where to move the French government to avoid the possibility of its capture. There were three possibilities: Brittany, Bordeaux or North Africa.

As early as May 31 Reynaud had written to Weygand about the possibility of forming a 'national redoubt' in the neighbourhood of a naval base which would enable France to remain in close touch with England. In this respect, the Brittany peninsula seemed ideal. Although de Gaulle, who hoped for a phased withdrawal to North Africa, favoured the idea, Weygand regarded the plan as impractical. For him it was a 'romantic' notion, dreamed up without

Exactly one month after the Blitzkrieg had commenced, the situation for the Allies was catastrophic. On June 10 German forces were crossing the Seine west of Paris; Italy had decided to go the whole hog and declare war on Britain and France, and Prime Minister Paul Reynaud had evacuated the French government to Tours, over 200 kilometres south of Paris. Général Weygand had already advised him that a break in the defence lines could happen at any moment. Reynaud had tried hard to keep France going but within the next two weeks the meteoric advance of the German armies, and the increasingly defeatist attitude by members of his government, were to overwhelm him.

Since the Blitzkrieg began, the roads of Belgium and France had been alive with civilians fleeing the oncoming panzers. Moving ever southwards, all the misery and despair of a people caught in another war are seen here in these pictures taken in Champagne at the beginning of June. There was no hope . . . and no place to go.

military advice, and on June 11 he made it clearly known to Churchill what he thought of the idea of the Brittany 'redoubt', insisting that it was unreasonable 'to base any hopes upon devices of that sort'. On June 10 he had effectively

told Ministers that he did not believe that the Allies could hold out for more than two or three days in Brittany. Instead Reynaud went for a compromise, Tours, which was almost midway between Bordeaux and Britanny.

Président Lebrun left Paris for Tours and by midnight on June 10 the entire government was on the road. Générals Weygand and Georges also withdrew their headquarters and moved them to Briare with their staffs.

On the evening of the 10th, as Churchill prepared to fly once more to Paris, news came that the French government had already evacuated the Capital — 'a good omen' Churchill thought, because it showed that they intended to go on fighting. He reached Briare, where the French High Command had moved, in the late afternoon and was driven to the Château du Muguet. The château, and the room where the conference was held, remained unchanged for nearly 50 years but was then sold and most of the contents dispersed. A plaque on the entrance gate recalls the two fateful days of June 1940.

TUESDAY, JUNE 11

A meeting of the Supreme War Council was held on June 11 at the Château du Muguet, near Briare, attended by Reynaud and Pétain, with Généraux Weygand, Georges and de Gaulle representing the French side and Churchill, Eden and Attlee, and Generals Dill, Ismay and Spears the British. The meeting lasted from 7.00 p.m. to 9.30 p.m. during which time the British leaders were left in no doubt as to the gravity of the situation. Churchill's soaring faith in ultimate victory was small comfort to the French, to whom the vital and immediate need was for the rest of the RAF fighter squadrons held in England to be committed to the battle on the continent. To this Churchill would not agree. He held out the promise of 25 more divisions, but only at the end of the year or the beginning of the next. Reynaud remarked that 'this was a little like talking about rain to a traveller lost in the Sahara'. For the time being all that Britain could manage was the 52nd (Lowland) Division which had just disembarked and the 1st Canadian Division which was, even then, coming ashore at Brest. A third division was to follow after June 20.

Churchill appealed to Weygand and reminded him of his experience in the First World War when desperate situations were followed by sudden recoveries. Weygand answered: 'No doubt you refer to the rupture of the British front in the spring of 1918. I would like to remind you that we immediately sent twenty-five divisions, then fifteen more; and we had ten others in reserve. Today

I have altogether and for all intents and purposes one division in reserve and it will be used up tomorrow in the first hour. This afternoon we are throwing our last tanks into the battle. They are leaving directly from the factory and are not yet tested.'

After the meeting Reynaud had a private word with Churchill at which he was informed that Pétain had already decided that France would have to seek an armistice.

WEDNESDAY, JUNE 12

Another meeting — it was to be the last — of the Supreme War Council was held on the morning of June 12 at the Château du Muguet and Churchill took the opportunity to approach Amiral Darlan to ask him about the fleet, expressing his hope that it would never be surrendered. Darlan affirmed that no ship would ever be surrendered and that 'scuttling orders will be issued in case of danger'.

A Cabinet meeting was held at the Château de Cangé near Tours at 7.45 p.m. at which Weygand reported on the military situation. It was, he said, worse than dreadful: it was hopeless. Acting now more as a politician than as the Commander-in-Chief of the Army he told the Ministers: 'I will continue the resistance if the Cabinet orders me to do so. From now on, I am obliged to say clearly that a cessation of hostilities is compulsory. We will only be fighting henceforth for the honour of our arms

The fourteenth meeting of the Supreme War Council began in the dining room at 7.00 p.m. According to Ismay, Reynaud was 'friendly, militant and a bundle of energy' despite the hopelessness of the situation and the defeatism which surrounded him, but Weygand seemed 'to have abandoned all hope' while Pétain looked 'more woebegone than ever'. Weygand described the military situation, stating that there was no hope of halting the German drive on Paris or beyond. There were no reserves left. 'C'est la dislocation', he declared, the break-up. Although the British delegation tried to raise the spirits of the French, they had little to offer in the way of positive support when the French need was immediate. Churchill was pressed for every fighter in England to be sent to France, but his answer reflected the view already agreed by the War Cabinet; that if Britain sacrificed any more aircraft she would be unable to counter the German offensive against the British Isles when that began. The meeting ended with no firm conclusion and Churchill was then told by Reynaud that Maréchal Pétain 'had informed him that it would be necessary to seek an armistice'.

and our flags. The war is definitively lost. Morever, as Commander-in-Chief and as a Frenchman, I am worried about assuring order in the country. I do not want France to run the risk of anarchy which follows a military defeat. That is why, as much as it hurts me as a soldier to say so, an armistice is imperative'.

The Cabinet heard the words in silence; for the first time an armistice had been openly demanded. Pétain and two others backed Weygand in a few sentences but their contributions were met by a storm of protest. The situation was grave, yes, but the Germans were not yet in Paris. Paris was not all of France and there was still the French Empire. The old soldiers knew that the battle in France was hopelessly lost, but a number of Ministers, among them César Campinchi, Yvon Delbos, Raoul Dautry and Georges Monnet, strongly opposed the idea of giving in and argued that resistance was always possible on the Loire, on the Garonne or, if all else failed, from the Empire.

The defeatists failed to carry the day. Reynaud determined his policy to be that of continuing the struggle whatever the cost. He said he would consult Churchill before making the final decision about how and where the government would go but he made it known that the first step was to be Britanny. A start was made with the requisitioning of chateaux and hotels in and around Quimper but, dissuaded by the defeatists who repeatedly pointed to Weygand and the Army's disapproval of this 'romantic' idea, Reynaud changed his mind and decided that the government should instead move to Bordeaux.

By now the forces opposing the Germans were down to the equivalent of about 30 divisions covering a front of 450 kilometres from the Seine estuary to the shoulder of the Maginot Line at Longuyon. With reserves now only five divisions, of which four were already spoken for, Général Weygand was faced with the imminent danger of seeing the whole line crumble away.

In the vain hope of holding the Germans at bay somewhere in the heart of France, and to save as many units as possible, he therefore decided to abandon the existing defence line and withdraw his forces to a new one. On June 12 at 1.15 p.m. he sent a telegram to Général Georges. Its message was simple: 'IPS No. 1444/FT3 of June 11 to be executed', the order for a general withdrawal of all the French armies to a line running from Geneva to Caen, through Dôle and the middle reaches of the Loire from Cosne to Tours. On the right flank, all the units of the Groupe d'Armées No. 2 were to move out of their positions on the Maginot Line, which was to be abandoned, while on the left flank, the Groupe d'Armées No. 3 was to withdraw southwards on the Loire. The 10ème Armée was to be subordinated directly to the High Command and ordered to defend Brittany. Paris was to be declared 'ville ouverte' — an open city.

Although Weygand had hardly any choice in the matter, there was little to

A further conference took place the following morning, the overnight news being even worse with Paris expected to fall within the next 24 hours. Although Reynaud was prepared to fight to the end, Pétain's absence was an ominous portent. Before taking his leave, Churchill insisted that the French government inform the British if there was 'any change in the situation' in order that they might come back for a final meeting. On the steps of the château, he said goodbye to Général Georges, who bade him farewell saying that 'an armistice would soon be inevitable'. (No pictures appear to have been taken at these vital meetings, our illustration being attributed to an earlier conference in January 1940.)

commend such a move. The new front was to be longer than the previous one and, even allowing for the troops withdrawn from the Maginot Line, the number of divisions available was still no more than about 45. In the event the retreat was so drastic, and the German advance so rapid, that the new front was never really established. The fortress troops withdrawn from the Maginot Line were not trained to move, the means of transportation were badly lacking and there were neither enough trains nor trucks. The men marched at night and fought by day and, like all retreats, it was to be prove a more costly exercise than a decision to stand and fight, and the abandonment of the unvanquished Maginot Line was psychologically bad for France.

That evening at the Château de Cangé at Saint-Avertin, just south of Tours to where the French government had moved, the most tragic meeting of the French Third Republic took place, when Weygand finally asked ministers to seek an armistice. *Above:* Today the château is only a shadow of its former self, post-war neglect and a fire having taken their toll. Now it is owned by the local town council who will rent out a section of it for conferences, although no plaque or marker mentions its fateful rôle on June 12, 1940.

THE GERMAN INTENTIONS

On June 14 Hitler issued his Directive No. 15 in which he defined the strategic intentions for the further conduct of operations.

'Our relative strength and the condition of the French army now make it possible to pursue henceforward two objectives at the same time:

a) To prevent enemy forces withdrawing from the Paris area, and those on the lower Seine from establishing a new front.

b) To destroy enemy forces in the areas facing Heeresgruppe A and Heeresgruppe C, and to bring about the collapse of the Maginot Line.'

The same day OKH issued the operational orders for driving deeper into France and for cutting off the French armies to the east, as Heeresgruppe C was about to launch the first of the two attacks to breach the Maginot Line and cross the Rhine.

Heeresgruppe B, which had been given the 18. Armee on June 10 and had inserted it between its 4. Armee and 6. Armee, was to force the Loire and advance along the Atlantic coast to conquer the whole of western France.

Heeresgruppe A was to advance southwards in the direction of the Rhône valley and the Alps, cutting off the French armies to the east while Heeresgruppe C was to attack and destroy these large forces. 'They will destroy the enemy in the enclosed area of north-eastern France, ensure the collapse of the Maginot Line, and prevent the withdrawal of forces there towards the south-west', Hitler had decided. This involved command of the 9. Armee and Gruppe von Kleist being transferred from Heeresgruppe B to Heeresgruppe A, the army group boundaries being shifted westwards on June 14.

Paris having been declared 'ville ouverte', messages requesting that the

Weygand's order confirming that Paris be declared a 'ville ouverte' was telephoned to the Military Governor of the Capital on June 12; two days later German forces entered the city. *Above:* They immediately deployed troops to take up defence positions at all key points — the most central being at the foot of the Arc de Triomphe.

Strategic locations like railway stations were also occupied. This is the Gare de l'Est, the gendarme somewhat dismayed at the unwelcome reinforcements. If the clock was correct, this picture was taken at 6.30 p.m. on the 14th.

Directive No. 15

1. The **enemy**, compelled by the collapse of his front, is evacuating the Paris area, and has also begun the evacuation of the fortified triangle Epinal–Metz–Verdun behind the Maginot Line.

Paris has been declared an open city by means of posters. It is not inconceivable that the main body of the French Army may withdraw behind the Loire.

2. Our relative strength and the condition of the French Army now make it possible to pursue henceforward **two objectives at the same time**:

(a) To prevent enemy forces withdrawing from the Paris area, and those on the lower Seine from establishing a new front.

(b) To destroy enemy forces in the areas facing Heeresgruppe A and C, and to bring about the collapse of the Maginot Line.

3. I therefore issue the following orders for the further conduct of the **operations of the Army**:

(a) Enemy forces on the lower Seine and in the Paris area will be vigorously pursued by the advance of the right flank of the Army along the coast towards the Loire estuary and by turning movement from the Château-Thierry area towards the Loire above Orleans. Paris will be occupied in force as soon as possible. The naval bases of Cherbourg and Brest, and also Lorient and Saint-Nazaire, will be occupied.

(b) Forces at the centre, up to approximately the area of Châlons, will continue, for the time being, in the general direction of Troyes; their armoured and motorised divisions will thrust forward in the direction of the plateau of Langres.

Infantry divisions will first reach the area north-east of Romilly–Troyes. Preparations will be made for their later use in the central Loire area.

(c) Orders for other formations of the Army remain unchanged. They will destroy the enemy in the enclosed area of north-eastern France, ensure the collapse of the Maginot Line, and prevent the withdrawal of forces there towards the south-west.

(d) The 'Saarbrücken Shock Group' will move to the attack across the Maginot Line on 14th June in the general direction of Lunéville. The timing for 'Attack Upper Rhine' will be decided as soon as possible.

4. The **Luftwaffe** has the following tasks:

(a) To keep up the momentum of our advance towards the Loire by means of air attacks. At the same time the advancing troops are to be supported by anti-aircraft artillery and protected against air attack.

The enemy's retreat by sea is to be made impossible by smashing ports and shipping on the north coast of France.

(b) The withdrawal of the enemy facing Heeresgruppe A and C is to be held up. The focal point in this respect is in front of the tanks on the right flank of Heeresgruppe A.

Enemy transport by rail running south-west towards and beyond the line Neufchâteau–Belfort is to be prevented.

At the same time the breach of the Maginot Line by Heeresgruppe C is to be supported.

Anti-aircraft artillery is to facilitate the attack by the right flank of Heeresgruppe A and, in particular, the penetration of French fortifications.

ADOLF HITLER

Military Governor of Paris send envoys to receive surrender terms were broadcast by the Germans on June 13 and the first contacts were made late that evening. At about 5.30 a.m. on June 14 the first German troops, men of the 9. Infanterie-Division, entered the French Capital and an hour later they had reached the heart of the city.

An agonising scene for all Frenchmen: German troops in the heart of their Capital. At the end of the Arcole Bridge, a German photographer took this symbolic picture: a veteran, who has lost both his right arm and leg in the Great War, despairing at the sight of a horsed troop passing the Town Hall.

The ceremonial entry was made later in the day, elements of the 8. Infanterie and 28. Infanterie-Division marching past the Arc de Triomphe under which a huge swastika flag had been hung. The commander of Heeresgruppe B, Generaloberst von Bock, lost no time in heading there himself. After meeting the Military Governor of Paris, Général Henri Dentz, and his staff he went to Les Invalides to see Napoleon's tomb. He also breakfasted

Above: **Beating the French at their own game! At the Trocadero, this motor cycle patrol of the 87. Infanterie-Division has lost no time in getting to know the local talent.** *Below:* **The honour of being the first troops to march ceremonially through the French capital went jointly to the 8. and 28. Infanterie-Divisions. This 29. Infanterie-Division (mot) staff car has halted on the Place de la Concorde on the afternoon of June 14 waiting for the parade to pass. Before the French Revolution, this square was called Place Louis XV and the obelisk, given by Egypt to King Charles X in 1829, marks the site of a statue of Louis XV removed by the révolutionnaires.**

at the Ritz — 'Sehr gut' as he commented in his war diary. Halder wrote 'A great day in the history of the German Army. Since 9.00 hours this morning, German troops have been entering Paris'.

A command post was soon established in Hôtel Crillon on the Place de la Concorde and General Alfred von Vollard-Bockelberg was appointed military governor. Preparations were made for a major victory parade by the 30. Infanterie-Division to take place on June 16, Generalleutnant Kurt von Briesen, the division's commander,

Two days later the Germans held their victory parade — this time by the 30. Infanterie-Division. The saluting base was located in the Avenue Foch, midway between the Arc de Triomphe and the Porte Dauphine. The mounted officer is the divisional commander, Generalleutnant Kurt von Briesen.

taking the salute on the Avenue Foch along with General von Bockelberg.

Heeresgruppe B from the Seine to the Loire

After its hasty withdrawal on the Seine, the 10ème Armée could not prevent the 4. Armee from forcing the river. This the II. Armeekorps did downstream of Rouen and the XXXVIII. Armeekorps further east near Vernon. On June 13 a breach was opened between the 10ème Armée and the Armée de Paris. The 3ème D.L.C. counter-attacked near Louviers and managed to halt the Germans but things were not so favourable just to the south where German troops were advancing further west. The risk of the 10ème Armée being completely separated from Groupe d'Armées No. 3 was now so grave that the High Command was forced to commit what armoured elements it had been possible to regroup and refit. Thus the new Corps de Cavalerie, with the 1ère, 2ème and the 3ème D.L.M., were subordinated to the 10ème Armée, and together with the 3ème D.L.C., were entrusted to keep a link open between the Armée de Paris and the 10ème Armée. The former was retreating to the Loire, under Groupe d'Armées No. 3, while the latter was retreating on an axis Rouen, Argentan, Rennes, with the intention of reassembling in Brittany. Thus the two French armies were on diverging courses and

The action now switches to the west where the leaders of 5. Panzer-Division had just reached the suburbs of Rouen (on the Seine) at Bois-Guillaume *(top)*. The panzer column pushed straight on into the heart of the city, the PzKpfw III *(below)* being pictured on the Route de Neufchâtel, the main access road from the north.

the Corps de Cavalerie in the centre faced a major problem in trying to maintain contact with the Armée de Paris.

The 4. Armee brought the panzers of XV. Armeekorps forward behind the infantry on June 16 and, while the infantry corps pressed their advance southwards towards the Loire, the panzers were launched westwards to Brittany to where the bulk of the 10ème Armée was trying to withdraw. On June 17 the panzers were at Laval and Le Mans at which point all contact between

Left: **This PzKpfw I has reached the Place de la République, having advanced along the northern bank of the river.** *Right:* **This part of Rouen, already badly damaged in 1940, was** completely flattened in August 1944 when Allied bombers attacked the Seine crossing sites. Remarkably, the Café Le Commerce on the corner has come through it all.

that army and the armies of Groupe d'Armées No. 3 was lost.

Lieutenant-General A. F. Brooke had arrived back in France at Cherbourg late on the evening of June 12 to assume command of all the British forces upon which it was hoped in London to build a new expeditionary force. Brooke's orders were modelled closely on those issued to Gort when appointed to command the BEF. He was to come under French command but had a right of appeal to London should he be given orders which appeared to him to imperil his forces.

On June 14 he met Weygand, who gave him a frank assessment of the gravity of the situation. Weygand was mistakenly under the impression that the Allied governments had made definite arrangements to organise a redoubt in Brittany and, although he left Brooke

in no doubt that he did not think much of the idea, both signed a note confirming the decision taken afterwards with Général Georges for the employment of British forces. It was agreed that the troops disembarking, the Brooke Corps, elements of the 52nd (Lowland) Division and the 1st Canadian Division, were to concentrate at Rennes, while those fighting with the 10ème Armée were eventually to regroup there with them.

Having signed, Brooke immediately sent a message to the War Office in which he made known that in his opinion it was unwise to try to hold Britanny and that 'He [Weygand], Georges and I are in complete agreement as to military impossibility of this'. He also recommended that the British military missions to Weygand's and Georges' headquarters be withdrawn as the two gene-

rals 'will have no effective control'. What this implied was that the British forces in France ought no longer to be under French command.

On the telephone Brooke made it clear to the new CIGS, Lieutenant-General Sir John Dill, that he was against committing the rest of the 52nd (Lowland) Division with the 10ème Armée. The question that now had to be addressed in London was whether to continue with efforts on the Continent or to evacuate all personnel and stores. The answer hinged on one of a number of telephone conversations that evening between Brooke and the CIGS, when Churchill came on the line. The Prime Minister was insistent that the British must support the French as much as possible but Brooke finally managed to convince him that sending the rest of the 52nd Division into action would not

Left: **Just a few yards to the right, curious German soldiers inspect a Renault FT-17 light tank which was part of a barricade built at the northern end of the Corneille Bridge. The sky was darkened by smoke from burning buildings, and the twin spires of St Ouen's Church can barely be seen in the background.** *Above:* **The house on the left is the reference point in both comparisons.**

Left: Generaloberst Günther von Kluge, the commander of 4. Armee, arrived to view the situation for himself from a vantage point overlooking the city. *Right:* We discovered that the

General had been standing in the centre of the Rue d'Ernemont, close to the spot where the PzKpfw III on page 508 had been pictured. (The Rue de Neufchâtel is on the right of the picture.)

make any difference to what happened to the 10ème Armée and that it would simply be throwing away more good troops for nothing.

Late that night Brooke received a signal from the Secretary of State for War: 'You are no longer under French command but will co-operate with any French forces which may be fighting in your vicinity. In view of your report stating that organised resistance has come to an end you must now prepare for the withdrawal of your force to the U.K.'. The decision was notified to Paul Reynaud and Général Weygand.

General Brooke ordered all British troops still under the command of 10ème Armée to fall back to the Cherbourg area and informed Général Altmayer, the army commander, of the decision. Air Marshal A. S. Barratt, commanding the British Air Forces in France, took similar measures and the remaining squadrons flew to England except for four fighter squadrons which were to cover withdrawal operations. The 3rd Brigade of the 1st Armoured Division (about 50 troop-carrying lorries, 26 tanks and 11 scout cars) covered some 350 kilometres by road to get there. The tanks of the division's 2nd

The top of the Rue d'Ernemont was a splendid spot to observe the advance into the city. This command car from the 5. Panzer-Division (note the triangular divisional pennant on the bulkhead and insignia of an inverted Y with a single dot) has halted to let the officers orient themselves although the squaddie on the left appears to be mildly unconcerned with it all.

As soon as the coast was clear, von Kluge and his staff drove down to the city centre. This picture shows the party on the Place de la Cathédrale, most probably about to have a look

inside the cathedral. The SdKfz 222 in the background is from the 7. Panzer-Division; the building behind dates from the 16th century.

After having rounded up the prisoners at Saint-Valery, Rommel moved on to Le Havre. 'It all went without bloodshed,' he wrote, and he took this picture on the sea front at Sainte-Adresse with the burning port in the distance.

Left: In Sainte-Adresse he paid a visit to the superb Hôtel Nice Havrais overlooking the sea where he was pictured for his personal album. Right: From 1944 to 1946 the hotel was taken over by the American forces for use as their port headquarters for embarkation purposes. It still stands virtually unchanged from Rommel's day on Place Frédéric Sauvage.

June 15 was spent resting and reorganising and the following morning the 7. Panzer-Division set off southwards to cross the Seine south of Rouen where a bridgehead had been achieved near Vernon and Les Andelys.

Above: What remained of the 1st Armoured Division and Beauman Division north of the Seine withdrew across the river on the afternoon and night of June 8. This Cruiser, 'recovered from forward position' according to the original caption, is seen being trundled through Neubourg, 50 kilometres south of Rouen, 'amidst refugees and traffic from Rouen which had fallen that morning.' *Below:* Place Aristide Briand today, with the statue of Jacques Dupont de l'Eure (native of the town who became French Minister of Justice in 1830). Closer inspection reveals that he is no longer in the same pose as in 1940; after the German occupying forces removed the original for smelting, the post-war replacement was carved in stone.

512

Brigade, however never arrived and nothing more was ever heard of the train on which they were loaded.

On the afternoon of June 17 Brooke learnt from the CIGS that the French had asked for an armistice. By then the evacuation was proceeding well, almost all of the 52nd Division had left, and all that had landed of the 1st Canadian Division. Over 40,000 men had been evacuated from Brittany in the past two days and the remaining troops were coming in. The 157th Brigade of the 52nd Division arrived at Cherbourg on June 17 and were embarked in the evening, a few hours after the last elements of Beauman Division had left and General Brooke himself boarded the armed trawler *Cambridgeshire* at 11.30 p.m., the last troopship leaving at 4.00 p.m. when the German vanguards were on the outskirts of the town. More than 30,000 men had been evacuated from Cherbourg and more than 21,000 men, mostly the 1st Canadian Division, from Saint-Malo, all without loss. At Cherbourg, French engineers carried out demolitions, helped by a British demolition party which was brought off by the destroyer HMS *Broke*.

The gravity of the situation comes through the expressions on the faces of these senior British officers pictured at Neubourg on June 9. They are Lieutenant-General James Marshall-Cornwall, appointed liaison officer to the 10ème Armée staff, Lieutenant-General Sir Henry Karslake, commanding the lines of communication, and Major-General Roger Evans, commanding the 1st Armoured Division.

Having abandoned their vehicles on the outskirts of Cherbourg in makeshift roadblocks *(above)*, British troops marched through the port *(below)* to the quayside. The Field Cashier's office, a welcome sight in happier days for those going on leave, now closed for the duration. More than 30,000 men were successfully evacuated from Cherbourg, and another 21,000 from Saint-Malo.

Meanwhile the French Navy had made a concerted effort to salvage all that was possible from its ports threatened by the panzers, ordering all ships to sail for Oran or Casablanca, or for England if they were not able to make it to the Mediterranean. Many ships escaped, including the not-yet-completed battleship *Jean Bart* which managed to leave Saint-Nazaire only a few hours before the arrival of leading elements of the 11. Schützen-Brigade which entered Nantes and Saint-Nazaire on June 19. Although she was in an incomplete state and badly lacking power, the warship succeeded to make her way safely to Casablanca. All those ships that could not sail were sunk in the harbours or blown up while in docks or on slipways. A destroyer, the *Cyclone*, was scuttled at Brest together with four submarines while another three submarines were scuttled at Cherbourg as well as three sloops, three fleet tankers and several smaller boats.

On June 18, the 7. Panzer-Division entered Cherbourg, as the 5. Panzer-Division reached Rennes and continued westwards towards Brest.

All was now over regarding the Brittany 'redoubt' and while the last of the British troops were leaving the field of battle, the French 10ème Armée had all but disappeared, save for a few units which had managed to get away. Some elements of the army's right flank, among them Groupement Petiet and the Corps de Cavalerie, managed to escape the trap and retreated on the lower Loire to join with the Armée de Paris.

On June 15 the French High Command had ratified the collapse of Groupe d'Armées No. 4 in the centre and on the right flank had transferred the 2ème Armée to Groupe d'Armées No. 2 while on the left flank what remained of the 6ème Armée was subordinated to Groupe d'Armées No. 3.

'We reached the neighbourhood of Montreuil at about 5.30 p.m.,' noted Rommel, 'where I ordered an hour's rest.'

The Groupe d'Armées No. 3 had welcomed those elements of the 10ème Armée which had managed to escape but Général Besson's plans to pull back and re-position his forces behind the Loire were becoming almost impossible, the more so as threat on the right flank was soon aggravated with the failure of the 4ème Armée to contain the Germans. On the evening of June 16 they had reached Nevers and Autun and had managed to force the Loire near La Charité.

As the shattered 4ème Armée could not prevent the Germans from establishing a new bridgehead across the Loire south of Nevers on June 17, German elements were now on the right bank of the river as far as Moulins. In the centre, where vanguards of the 33. Infanterie-Division reached the Loire near Orléans, they jeopardised the contact between the Armée de Paris and the 7ème Armée. The establishment of Groupe d'Armées No. 3 on the upper Loire was now obviously impossible and the army group commander, Général Antoine Besson, was forced to plan the withdrawal of his right wing on the Cher river, which was ordered to start on the next day.

On the lower Loire, from Tours to the sea, the Armée de Paris was trying to establish what forces were at hand behind the river. Elements of the 1ère and 3ème D.L.M.s were in the Angers sector, remains of the 2ème D.L.M. near Tours, with miscellaneous units scattered here and there. In the Saumur sector, the cadets of the world-famous French cavalry school were in charge of about forty kilometres of front. When ordered on June 14 to withdraw, the school commander, Colonel François Michon, had asked, and received, permission to defend the town with his cadets. Altogether, he had about 1,300 men, of whom 776 were cadets, a few Hotchkiss H-39s from the 19ème Dragons and some armoured cars.

On June 18 the High Command made known that the French government had decided to declare the status of 'ville ouverte' to all those towns larger than

On the afternoon of June 18 the leaders of the 7. Panzer-Division reached the western outskirts of Cherbourg where Rommel set up his command post. Here his staff congregate at the end of the Rue de la Paix in Equerdreville.

In the yard of the Préfecture Maritime, Rommel found the 'officers of the 7. Panzer-Division assembled on one side and the officers of the Cherbourg garrison on the other' (out of the picture to the left).

20,000 people. Although the order was intended to save lives, it applied to scores of cities all along the front line and was a move which was to provide the Germans with unblown bridges and free access across all rivers.

Downstream at Orléans, units of Groupe d'Armées No. 3 fought back all along the Loire to deny any crossing of the river but these troops were soon overwhelmed and on June 19, in the midst of the incredible disorder resulting from the civilian exodus, the Germans had forced crossings of the river at Sully, Orléans and Beaugency. Things went from bad to worse for the French as those German elements which had crossed the Loire between Orléans and Blois reached the Cher river before the 7ème Armée had had time to establish itself. As a result Général Besson was forced to order his right wing to form on the Indre river; also the French High Command disbanded Groupe d'Armées No. 4 and took direct command of what remained of the 4ème Armée.

On June 20 German advance units were moving forward south of the Loire between the Armée de Paris and the 7ème Armée, others were crossing at Nantes and between Saumur and Tours, and it was soon apparent to Général Besson that his Groupe d'Armées No. 3 was in great danger of being completely shattered. Those units still fighting on the Loire were ordered to pull back and it was made known that the general withdrawal was not to end on the Indre, but farther to the south on the Creuse and lower Vienne along which rivers the Groupe d'Armées No. 3 now hoped to re-establish itself. At Saumur, the Germans had forced a crossing over the Loire and the cadets had launched small counter-attacks to try to throw them back. In this they succeeded but their inferiority in numbers made itself felt and they were ordered to fall back on the town during the night. Next morning saw them digging trenches and building barricades in the town.

'With Heidkämper I visited the Fort du Roule which stood on a hill commanding the town and harbour.'

Gruppe Guderian closes the ring

In the van of Gruppe Guderian (note the letter 'G') — armoured cars of the 2. Panzer-Division.

The 2ème Groupement Cuirassé having been disbanded on June 11, the 3ème D.C.R. now came under the VIIIème Corps d'Armée and it moved during the night to the south-west of Suippes. On the morning of June 12 columns of panzers were reported to the east of Reims, moving southwards in the direction of Châlons-sur-Marne and Suippes, and the 3ème D.C.R. was ordered to contain their advance until the evening to enable the withdrawal of the 14ème Division d'Infanterie and 3ème D.I.M. At about 10.30 a.m. elements of the 42ème B.C.C. and 10ème B.C.C. engaged the panzers and early in the afternoon they were followed by the 41ème B.C.C. and the 45ème B.C.C. advancing northwards, the former on the right wing, the latter on the left.

After four hours of battling wildly against anti-tank guns and panzers the French tanks were ordered to withdraw, the 45ème B.C.C. without too much difficulty. However the commander of the 41ème B.C.C., Capitaine Louis

For Fall Gelb in May, the XIX. Armeekorps had been subordinated to Gruppe von Kleist, but for Fall Rot in June, General Guderian's corps was released and upgraded: thus XIX. Armeekorps became 'Gruppe Guderian'.

Left: 'A difficult passage across the Suippe river,' said the original caption to this German picture. 'French prisoners were called upon to help on June 13.' In addition, it gave the location as Bétheniville which proved to be wrong when Jean Paul reached the village. Somewhat dispirited, he drove out southwards, passing through Saint-Martin but, as his son who was navigating had fallen asleep, he missed the main road and accidentally arrived in Saint-Souplet (right) . . . and there it was!

A moment of high drama on the road to the Marne. At half-past twelve on the afternoon of June 12, the leading elements of the 2. Panzer-Division reached Châlons-sur-Marne and within five minutes reported that the bridge across the river had been captured. En route, the troops had surprised this Citroën staff car in the Avenue de Saint-Menehould which had promptly been fired upon, killing the two occupants in their seats. The driverless vehicle then careered to a violent stop beside this café-bar — still recognisable as the same corner but now modernised with traffic lights and a neon sign.

At Suippes, 20 kilometres north-east of Châlons-sur-Marne, the leaders of the 1. Panzer-Division had also surprised this Renault D-1 of the 67ème B.C.C. and destroyed it in front of the village church. Though armed with a 47mm and two machine guns, the Renault D-1 was ungainly, under-powered and quite obsolete for the fast-moving war of 1940.

Cornet, was not sure that the message he had received over the wireless for 'withdrawal as planned' was genuine and he waited for confirmation. This came at 6.40 p.m. and, in heavy rain, the Renault B1bis started to move back. However, by now they were surrounded by dozens of guns and panzers, and most of them were knocked out and Capitaine Cornet killed. The battle raged on until about 8.00 p.m. when the last tanks still fighting were immobilised by their crews at which point the 41ème B.C.C. had ceased to exist.

At 7.00 p.m. four Hotchkiss H-39s of the 45ème B.C.C. went in to enable infantry of the division's 16ème B.C.P. surrounded at the Ferme de Vadenay, to get clear, which they did. After a last sharp engagement, the 3ème D.C.R. withdrew eastwards during the night, some elements escaping southwards through Dijon although much of the division was destroyed during the next four days.

On June 12 the panzers of Gruppe Guderian were at Châlons-sur-Marne and in the afternoon of June 13 the vanguard of the 1. Panzer-Division reached the Marne-Rhine Canal near Etrepy. The commander of XXXIX. Armeekorps, Generalleutnant Rudolf Schmidt, wanted the units behind to close up with them and ordered Oberstleutnant Hermann Balck, the commander of the leading elements, not to cross the canal yet.

Guderian, who knew nothing of this order, arrived at Etrepy in the evening and, meeting Balck, asked him whether he had secured the bridge. 'He replied that he had', wrote Guderian. 'I asked

Fifty kilometres to the west, and probably two days later, this column of horse-drawn transport looks more in keeping with a John Ford Western movie than Hitler's Blitzkrieg war! It was pictured in Soizy-aux-Bois, just north of Sézanne, movin' out south. Though this was another misleading caption, giving the

place as 'Sens' (80 kilometres away as the crow flies), the road sign on the left gave the clue as to the true location. Jean Paul found that the picture had been taken from a window in the local Hôtel de Ville but, as it was closed, the roof of his car sufficed to give a similar height.

At Pogny, 12 kilometres south of Châlons, two Renault B1bis of the 41ème B.C.C. with an FT-17 hastily took up positions at the southern end of the bridge over the Marne. It was June 12 and the leading tanks of the 2. Panzer-Division soon appeared on the northern bank. A duel broke out across the river, the French tanks being repeatedly hit.

During the night the Germans brought up heavier guns and 'Beni Snassen' was soon struck and set alight. Another shell exploded just as the crew tried to escape, killing all of them, save for the radio operator who was badly wounded. 'Aisne' alongside was hit in turn, its commander, Lieutenant Robert Homé, being killed.

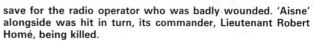

Having crossed the Marne, now the next major river obstacle east of Paris, the Seine, had been breached. On June 15 at Méry-sur-Seine, 25 kilometres north of Troyes, a tank-hunter team of the SS-Verfügungs-Division have set up a 3.7cm Pak 35/36 to guard the bridge . . . but, it's pointing towards their rear!

Perhaps marauding French tanks have been reported still to the north. (Incidentally, Soldat Sylvain Pallud, the author's father, had been captured at La Belle Etoile crossroads, five kilometres to the south, at 6.00 a.m. on the previous day by troops of the 4. Panzer-Division.)

Jean Paul: 'This panzer crewman taking the sun on a chair purposely installed on the engine deck of his PzKpfw II was photographed at Romilly on June 14. It belonged to the 1. Kompanie of Panzer-Regiment 35 in 4. Panzer-Division and

might well be the one — the probability is quite small but the thought is moving — which had menaced my father and forced him to surrender! Since that day there have been many changes and only one house could be recognised today.'

Also on June 14, ten kilometres to the west, at Pont-sur-Seine, a PzKpfw I of the 3. Panzer-Division was pictured in the middle of the level crossing near the village station. It is difficult to say

whether it is stationary or not, but from where it stands it was in an ideal position to cover the bridge over the canal which lies just ten metres in front of it.

'German troops relentlessly push forward in order to hasten the decision in France' was the German caption to this picture taken in Ferreux, ten kilometres south-east of Romilly, on the

14th. This particular PzKpfw I displays on its turret the lopsided 'E' device (probably a stylised version of the Brandenburg Gate in Berlin) denoting it as belonging to the 3. Panzers.

While the panzers were pushing southwards beyond the Seine, support and supply units were following on as fast as they could like this SdKfz 10/4 mounting a 2cm Flak 30. This particular picture gives a good illustration of the groundwork necessary back at base to find such comparisons, as in this case there was no wartime caption available at all. The broken road sign provided the first clue. Although only '-E-Champenoise' is readable, a little detective work suggested 'Fére-Champenoise'. Then there is no substitute for driving the roads in the vicinity, radiating outwards until the scene materialises itself and one gets a wonderful sense of achievement in establishing an accurate location. In this case it was Gourgançon, a little village in the back of beyond north-east of Romilly. Suddenly it is no longer just a simple picture of a half-track.

him if he had also established a bridge-head on the far side. After a pause he answered that he had done that too. His reticence surprised me. Was it possible, I asked, to drive over to his bridgehead by car? Looking at me with deep distrust, he rather timidly said that it was. So over we went. In the bridgehead I found a capital engineer officer, Leutnant Weber, who had risked his life to prevent the demolition of the bridge, and commander of the rifle battalion

Another road sign enabled us to trace the photographer's route and follow him through Vendeuvre-sur-Barse, about twenty

kilometres west of Bar-sur-Aube, where we took this comparison in Rue de le Porte Dorée.

Unfortunately no clues with this one. Two panzerjägers of an unidentified unit — there were five Panzerjäger-Abteilung employed during Fall Rot — moving through a French village.

Each tank-hunter detachment was equipped with 18 panzerjäger: basically a 4.7cm Pak(t) on the chassis of a PzKpfw I. (The 't' stood for 'tschechish' — the gun being of Czech origin.)

Further to the east, at the sharp end of Gruppe Guderian, 1. Panzer-Division was first to reach Chaumont early on June 15. Followed by motor cycle outriders, Major Alexander von

Scheele, the commander of Aufkl.Abt. 5 (the division's recce detachment), stands triumphantly in his command car as they proceed — significantly — along Rue de la Victoire de la Marne.

Meanwhile, over on the right flank of Gruppe Guderian, the 2. Panzer-Division drove into Bar-sur-Aube also on June 15. This particular PzKpfw III was pictured at Soulaines-Dhuys some 20 kilometres to the north.

which had formed the bridgehead, Hauptmann Franz-Josef Eckinger. I was delighted to be able to decorate these two brave officers with the Iron Cross First Class on the spot. I then asked Balck why he had not pushed farther forward; it was only then I learnt of XXXIX. Armeekorps' order to stop. This was the explanation of Balck's

Above: **A PzKpfw II of the 1. Panzer-Division entering Langres citadel through the west gate. The 'I07' inscription identifies it as belonging to the recce platoon of the I. Abteilung, Panzer-** Regiment 1. *Bottom:* **Of the four figures of the date of construction which once adorned the gate, only an '8' remained in 1940. Fifty years later, that same '8' is still there!**

An SdKfz 6, with a 10.5cm IFH18 in tow, follows the signpost for the 'Poids Lourds' route (heavy vehicle bypass) while the command car peels off left to enjoy a 'Touriste' view of Langres and enters via the old town.

At Quitteur, just north of Gray, the 1. Panzer-Division succeeded in capturing the bridge over the Saône intact on June 16. However, the sector was later bombed by the Luftwaffe causing considerable delay but, as Guderian later wrote, 'Since they apparently came from Heeresgruppe C, there was no way we could get in touch with them to tell them of their mistake.' This PzKpfw II is the mount of the signals officer of I. Abteilung of Panzer-Regiment 1.

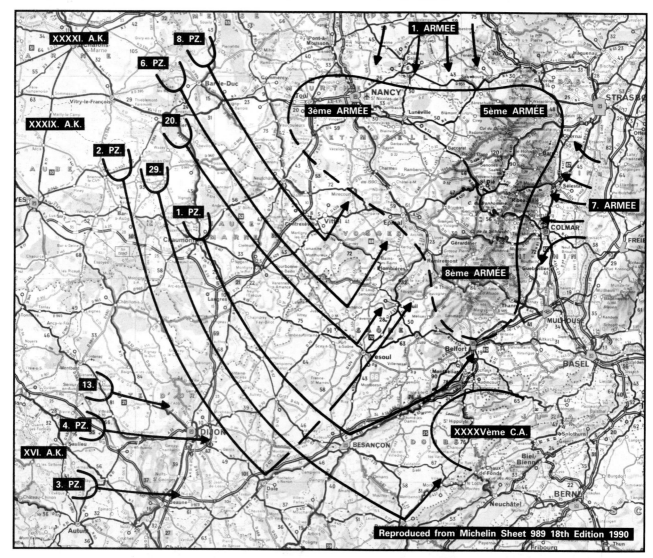

Reproduced from Michelin Sheet 989 18th Edition 1990

Referring to Hannibal's famous victory over the Roman army at Cannae in 216 BC, General Franz Halder, the OKH Director of Operations, noted in his diary on June 10 that 'Cannae tritt in der Vordergrund' (Cannae comes to the fore). The front held by Groupe d'Armées No. 4 had fallen apart after the breakthrough and on June 15 the leaders of Gruppe Guderian had reached Bar-sur-Aube and Gray-sur-Saône, while the armour of Gruppe von Kleist was at Saint-Florentin and Tonnerre. On June 17 the right wing of Guderian's XXXIX. Armeekorps reached the Swiss border at Pontarlier, while the corps' left wing was approaching Belfort. Further north, Guderian's XXXXI. Armeekorps had also turned northwards and was threatening Charmes and Epinal. On this same day the leaders of Gruppe von Kleist had taken Dijon and reached the Saône valley. OKH then transferred command of Gruppe Guderian (and the 16. Armee too) from Heeresgruppe A to Heeresgruppe C which had by then the means to crush the three armies of the stricken Groupe d'Armées No. 2.

extraordinary reticence: he had already gone farther than he should and expected me to reprimand him for doing so.'

This was no time for pussy-footing around — the Blitzkrieg principle of 'go for it' (the 'Auftragstaktik') was still paramount and Guderian immediately overruled the order. The advance south-eastwards resumed at once. In the van, the 1. Panzer-Division reached Saint-Dizier during the course of the night of June 14 and were at Langres by the following morning. By the evening of June 15 the forward units of XXXIX. Armeekorps were at Gray and those of the XXXXI. Armeekorps at Bar-le-Duc.

On June 16 XXXIX. Armeekorps forced the Saône and the 1. Panzer-Division soon reached Besançon while the 29. Infanterie-Division (mot) advanced towards Pontarlier and the Swiss border. To the north, with the 20. Infanterie-Division (mot) ahead of the panzer divisions, the XXXXI. Armeekorps reached Vesoul and Bourbonne.

At Langres on June 17, to wish Guderian a happy birthday, his chief-of-staff had collected together all the Panzergruppe staff on the little terrace between their quarters and the wall of the old fortress.

Having crossed the river, a road-block in Quitteur village has been swept aside as the armour heads for its next goal: Besançon.

A self-propelled gun (a 15cm sIG 33 on a PzKpfw I chassis) of sIG Kompanie 702 is singled out by the photographer as the convoy presses on southwards through the village. The road-block can be seen in the background.

Left: The road to the south. With its commander dressed up to kill, no doubt very proud of his brand new model Ausf G of the PzKpfw III, armour from Panzer-Regiment 1 pushes on in the direction of Besançon. The city is now barely five kilometres ahead. Right: The D67 has been modernised since 1940 with many of its curves straightened out, but this particular bend between Pouilley-les-Vignes and Besançon is an almost perfect match.

527

The leading panzers reached Besançon on the afternoon of June 16 and found that all the bridges across the Doubs river had been blown by French engineers. The evening was spent clearing the town and by the end of the night 1. Panzer-Division reported about 10,000 prisoners in the bag. The following morning, Kradschützen-Bataillon 1 was despatched to the Swiss border. By midday they were at Ornans (above), with the frontier just 40 kilometres away. *Below:* In this case the mountains helped us pinpoint the correct stretch of road along the D67.

After day after day of push, push, push, Gruppe Guderian was at last about to reach its goal — the Swiss border — and thus seal the fate and close the ring around the three armies of Groupe d'Armées No. 2 trapped in the north. Though dusty and tired, these men from Gruppe Guderian are elated by their success.

'As a birthday present', Guderian recounts, 'he was able to hand me a message which stated that the 29. Infanterie-Division (mot) had reached the Swiss frontier. We were all delighted by this success, and I set off at once in order personally to congratulate the brave troops on the day of their great achievement. At about midday, I met Generalmajor Willibald von Langermann in Pontarlier, after a long drive during the course of which I passed most of his division advancing along my road. We sent a message to supreme headquarters informing them that we had reached the Swiss border at Pontarlier, to which Hitler signalled back: "Your signal based on an error. Assume you mean Pontailler-sur-Saône". My reply, "No error. Am myself in Pontarlier on Swiss border", finally satisfied the distrustful OKW.'

Later that same day a Wehrmacht bulletin proudly announced that 'the Swiss border has been reached southeast of Besançon. The ring is thus closed around those French troops withdrawing from Lorraine and Alsace.'

Guderian had established his command post in Langres, some 80 kilometres back from Besançon, and here he is pictured with Generalleutnant Mauritz Wiktorin of 20. Infanterie-Division (mot). On June 17, Guderian's 52nd birthday, his chief-of-staff presented him with the best present of all: a message reporting that his advance guards had reached the border with Switzerland.

Later that day Guderian drove to Pontarlier (the nearest large town to the frontier) to meet Generalmajor Willibald von Langermann whose troops of the 29. Infanterie-Division (mot) had been first at the post. Here Guderian chats to some of the men in the main street, the Rue de la République. Having signalled the success to OKW, at first Hitler refused to believe the news until a second message arrived from Guderian stating that he was himself standing on the Swiss border!

Heeresgruppe C attacks the Maginot Line

On June 14, the day the first German troops entered Paris, the panzers were racing through the French rear and the Maginot Line had been well and truly turned. Gruppe Hoth was crossing the Seine, Gruppe von Kleist had crossed the River Aube and was threatening Troyes and Gruppe Guderian was at Chaumont.

The issue of the campaign in the west was already decided as the drive deeper into France developed and the German High Command ordered Heeresgruppe C to launch the third phase of Fall Rot. Outlined by Hitler in his Directive No. 13 as a 'subsidiary attack on the Maginot Line with the aim of breaking through with weaker forces at its most vulnerable point between Saint-Avold and Sarreguemines', the attack on the Maginot Line by the 1. Armee was to involve seven divisions in the Sarre in Operation 'Tiger'. In the same directive Hitler had also made known that 'should the situation allow, an attack on the upper Rhine may be envisaged, with the limitation that not more than eight to ten divisions are to be committed'. Consequently the 7. Armee was ordered to launch Operation 'Kleiner Bär', an attack across the Rhine.

Facing Heeresgruppe C along the Maginot Line, from Longuyon to the Swiss border, was Groupe d'Armées No. 2 with three armies and one makeshift fourth. The 3ème Armée was on the left with the fortress troops of the Fortified Sectors of La Crusnes, Thionville and Boulay with a strength of only four infantry divisions to support them. In the Sarre was Groupement de la Sarre, with the fortress troops of the Fortified Sectors of Faulquemont and Sarre and two infantry divisions. On the 'corner' of Alsace, from the Sarre to

south of Strasbourg, was the 5ème Armée with the Fortified Sectors of Rohrbach, Vosges, Haguenau and the 103ème D.I.F. and three infantry divisions. On the extreme right wing, up to the Swiss border, was the 8ème Armée with two fortress divisions, the Fortified Sector of Altkirch and four infantry divisions.

Following Weygand's order of June 12 for a general withdrawal, the commander of Groupe d'Armées No. 2, Général Prételat, was to pull back his

armies of some half a million men to reassemble about sixty kilometres to the south on what was to be the right flank of the new French line running from Geneva to Caen.

For two days the left wing of Groupe d'Armées No. 2 had been in great danger of being outflanked when the 2ème Armée of Groupe d'Armées No. 4 had been forced to give ground in the west after Gruppe Guderian's breakthrough on the Aisne. Général Huntziger had then ordered the Montmédy

With German forces having well and truly outflanked the Maginot Line, on June 12 Général Weygand had ordered a withdrawal to a new defensive line from Geneva to Caen. Manning the fortifications facing Germany proper *(top)* was Groupe d'Armées No. 2 of some half a million static troops who were hastily improvised into so-called 'march divisions'. *Above:* Lacking transport, or the training necessary for route-marching, the withdrawal was not going to be easy.

Kerbach, ten kilometres north-west of Sarreguemines, lay isolated in no-man's-land. This German patrol was pictured in the main street on May 13; one month later the area was to be the jumping-off position for the 75. Infanterie-Division in Operation 'Tiger' — the assault against the Line.

sector fortifications to be abandoned on June 11 and 12, the last of the rearguards leaving the sector's three fortresses and dozen casemates during the night of June 12 after having done their best to wreck them.

Groupe d'Armées No. 2 issued orders for the first of the movements of its withdrawal to begin on the night of June 13, the plan being that all the troops were to be behind the Marne-Rhine Canal between Toul and Sarrebourg within four days. A handful of troops — part of the fortress crews and a few interval troops — were to remain in position to mask the withdrawal of

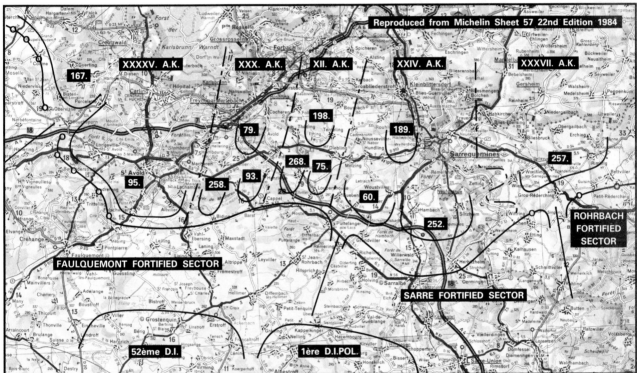

The situation at the beginning of 'Tiger' when three German army corps, each with two divisions up front and a third just behind, attacked in the Sarre gap (see also pages 20-23).

the rest as they pulled out in stages. It was intended that these last troops were to leave during the night of June 17, the much vaunted fortresses of the Maginot Line would then be left empty, their guns out of action, vital machinery and equipment rendered inoperable, ammunition supplies blown up and their lower levels flooded.

Withdrawal, however, was not going to be easy as these were mostly static troops, lacking transport and experience of route-marching. Organised into improvised 'march divisions' they had to adapt to their new rôle literally overnight.

531

The plan to take out the weakest part of the Maginot Line with a frontal assault was referred to by Hitler in his Directive of May 24 (see page 365). For the attack, 1. Armee had amassed a considerable amount of artillery, the heaviest of which were the two 420mm mortars manned by schwere Artillerie-Abteilung 800. (They also had a 355mm howitzer.) The large mortars were designated 42cm Haubitze(t) having been built by Skoda and taken over from the Czechs. With a weight of 105 tons, each piece could hurl a one-tonne shell over 14 kilometres.

OPERATION 'TIGER'

For Operation 'Tiger' the 1. Armee had three army corps, each with two divisions in front and a third just behind, which were to try to force the Line in the relatively weak Sarre sector. For this attack the 1. Armee had amassed an impressive amount of artillery in addition to the normal artillery complement of the divisions. Arko 302 had six groups of 21cm Mörser (heavy mortars), ten groups of 10cm Kanone, about twenty groups of 150mm howitzers and eight batteries, each with two pieces, of heavy railway guns. The heaviest were brought in by schwere Artillerie-Abteilung 800, which possessed three batteries, each of these having one piece. Two batteries had a 420mm heavy mortar, this giant having been built by Skoda, one of the small number taken over from the Czechs (German designation 42cm Haubitze (t)) and one battery had a 355mm howitzer (35.5cm Haubitze M-1). The V. Fliegerkorps was also to support the attack.

In the Sarre gap the Faulquemont Fortified Sector was responsible for the western part and the Sarre Fortified Sector for its eastern part on both sides of the Sarre river. The former sector

had only five minor fortresses, the latter only one east of the river, and these covered only both flanks of the gap whose main defences were about 300 blockhouses and inundations.

In recent weeks responsibility for the defence of both sectors had belonged to Groupement de la Sarre, constituted on May 29 when the XXème Corps d'Armée had been upgraded to take command of this part of the front from the 4ème Armée when it was placed in reserve on the Marne. On June 14 the group commander, Général Louis Hubert, had under him on June 14 the two regiments of fortress troops of the Faulquemont sector and the four regiments of the Sarre sector. Behind these, Général Hubert had only two infantry divisions, the 52ème Division d'Infanterie and the 1ère Division d'Infanterie Polonaise.

Preparations for the army's general withdrawal were under way and Général Hubert met his divisional commanders on the evening of June 13 to work out the details with them for the pulling out of Groupement de la Sarre which was to start the next evening. For this the fortress troops of the Faulquemont sector were organised into a

Groupement de Girval and those of the Sarre sector into a Groupement Dagnan. Indications of something being prepared by the Germans facing them were numerous and it was pointed out that the Germans might well attack the next morning. Hubert urged his commanders to hold their positions if that should happen. And it did.

The French artillery, which was still very powerful as their withdrawal had not yet started and they had plenty of ammunition to use up, fired harassing salvoes at every suspect target and the night was made even more miserable for the German troops assembling for Operation 'Tiger' by heavy rain.

The operation opened in the early hours of June 14 with a very strong artillery bombardment. Arko 302 had arrayed its heavies along the frontier between Völklingen and Saarbrücken from the beginning of June. The 355mm howitzer of Mörser-Batterie 810 was at Freyming, the 420mm giant mortar of Mörser-Batterie 830 was at Merlebach, while that of Mörser-Batterie 820 was at Sitterswald just north of Sarreguemines. In addition, four batteries of railway guns were between Carling and Merlebach, two at Grossrosseln and two north of Sarreguemines. Ballon-Batterie 5 was in the centre near Morsbach for observing.

In spite of this and the employment of the whole V. Fliegerkorps in support of the attack, progress was minor and costly. The battle raged the whole day but the French advanced posts held their ground and the German assault groups paid a high price. The confusion resulting from the drastic withdrawal order was such that the Armée de l'Air only appeared very late in the evening in spite of renewed demands from Général Hubert. It was not as if all the aircraft were engaged elsewhere: the G.C. II/5 which had about thirty Curtiss H-75s at Dijon was not ordered into the air at all that day while the Luftwaffe bombers were hammering the positions of Groupement de la Sarre.

By nightfall although some of the French positions had fallen, the main line had been breached at only one place, near Kalmerich Woods, where a company of the 174ème R.I.F. had been destroyed. Oberleutnant Otto Schulz, the commander of the third company of Inf.Rgt. 125, was referred to in the army bulletin for 'his renewed extraordinary courage' but the price paid for this breach by the regiment had been heavy. Oberleutnant Willy Heldmann, the commander of one of the assault groups, later testified that of the fifty or so men that were with him in the morning there were only a dozen left at 6.00 p.m., all of them physically and mentally exhausted.

For the French it was a neat tactical victory — enough for Général Hubert to write in his war diary that night 'This is a true victory!'. Nevertheless it had a bitter taste to it as the troops began to move out under cover of darkness on the first leg of a withdrawal of more than forty kilometres, just after having won the day. Caporal Robert Dime of the 41ème R.I.C. later testified how frustrated they all were at having to give up the ground they had just regained in a counter-attack near Holving, after treating the Germans to a bad mauling.

At the same time the commander of the 1. Armee, General von Witzleben, was looking with dismay at the reports sent in by his corps commanders: for only small gains, the three corps had suffered more than 1,000 dead and about 4,000 wounded. After the success of Fall Gelb, as the operation was not really a vital one, the long-held attitude towards a direct assault on the Maginot

their radios and telephones, the Groupement de la Sarre had withdrawn its infantry divisions and the two groupements of fortress troops during the night, leaving small detachments behind to make plenty of noise and create the impression that they were still there. The next morning the Germans resumed their advance, having nothing in front of them except these small rearguards, some of which fought until they were annihilated, others managing to fight their way back to their own lines.

tions in the sector. Crushed by the hammering of the 210mm shells, the 24 defenders of the outpost were soon overwhelmed and Oberleutnant Gerd von Ketelhodt, the commander of the 9. Kompanie of Inf.Rgt. 472, who had led his storm group to the assault of the Knop was later rewarded with the Ritterkreuz on July 13.

Further to the west, in the upper Meuse valley, the 16. Armee was advancing southwards and the battle for Verdun began on June 14. West of the Meuse the 3ème D.I.C. was trying to

'Tiger' began early on June 14 but by the evening of the first day the only section of the Line to have been breached lay in the Kalmerich Woods near Puttelange. *Left:* Here Gefreiter Giloj of Infanterie-Regiment 125 demonstrates for the Press how he attacked one of the casemates with hand grenades. This particular blockhouse had been defended by Aspirant Jacques Miller and his section from the 174ème R.I.F. commanded by Capitaine Daubenton. *Above:* Jean Paul found the heavily-damaged casemate near the Hostebach river about a kilometre west of Puttelange.

Line re-asserted itself. The army staff were debating whether it was really worth risking such high casualties and if it would not be better to dig in and let the battle spreading across France run its course, when a captured French document arrived which made up their minds for them. It was an order sent by the commander of the second battalion of the 174ème R.I.F. to his company commanders for them to withdraw as planned during the night. Captured near Kalmerich by Inf.Rgt. 125, this order was probably the one sent to the 6ème Compagnie, whose commander, Capitaine Jean Daubenton, had been badly wounded and captured when fighting off the German troops assaulting his command post.

Having destroyed their weapons,

German propaganda did its best to enlarge on what was in reality a small tactical success, and on June 15 the Wehrmacht bulletin made known that 'on June 14 the air units had sent powerful attacks at the Maginot Line in the Sarre sector. For the whole day fortifications, casemates, artillery and infantry positions and columns were covered with bombs of every calibre. Meanwhile, under strong artillery support, troops from the army had broken through the fortified defences of the Maginot Line and disabled the enemy's numerous fortified positions. The strong position west of Sarralbe has been captured'. This latter position was referred to as the Knop, an advanced post on the crest of a hill which overlooked Sarralbe and the French posi-

stop three divisions of VII. Armeekorps while east of the river the Division Burtaire was opposed to the 71. Infanterie-Division. The French fought back doggedly on a battlefield on which each landmark was already famous . . . Cote 304 . . . Mort-Homme . . . but they suffered heavy losses and could not stop the Germans for long. On June 15 the vanguard of Inf.Rgt. 211 reached the Fort de Vaux at 9.12 a.m., Fort de Douaumont at 11.45 a.m. and the van of Inf.Rgt. 194 entered the Verdun Citadelle at 12.30 p.m.

The commander of the 71. Infanterie-Division, Generalleutnant Karl Weisenberger, was awarded the Ritterkreuz at the end of the month, with particular emphasis on the division's action in capturing historic Verdun.

533

From Karlsruhe south to the Swiss border at Basle, the Rhine forms the frontier between France and Germany, but the need to make a direct attack across the river declined in importance as time went on. Nevertheless the crossing was put into effect on June 15, albeit on a much smaller scale than originally

envisaged, in Operation 'Kleiner Bär'. *Right:* Generalleutnant Anton von Hirschberg, the commander of the 554. Infanterie-Division, and Oberst Franz Vaterrodt, commanding Infanterie-Regiment 623, watch the assault from the top of the Eckartsberg, a hill overlooking the river south of Breisach-am-Rhein.

OPERATION 'KLEINER BÄR'

Of the ambitious plans considered for a powerful attack across the Rhine, some of which even envisaged the participation of about thirty Italian divisions, not much was left at the beginning of June. Italian hesitations about entering the war had caused the Germans to turn away from what they had in mind at that time and the success of Fall Gelb was such that the plans for a Rhine offensive were constantly toned down. Operations 'Panther', 'Lüchs' and 'Bär' were all cancelled and the final plan had a name more suited to its reduced rôle: 'Kleiner Bär'.

The 7. Armee had only four static divisions (Stellungsdivision) on May 10 whose role was solely to guard the river. At the beginning of June the army was reinforced with four infantry divisions and one mountain division. The XXVII. Armeekorps which had been transferred from the Lille area was to launch the main assault with the 218. Infanterie-Division and 221. Infanterie-Division — about 10,000 men — going across in the first hour of the assault. On the left wing of the corps the 239. Infanterie-Division of Höheres Kommando z.b.V. XXXIII was also to force

Only three divisions were committed in the first wave, while on both flanks the static divisions which previously guarded the river were involved in diversionary attacks. To the rear (not shown) were the 213. Infanterie-Division and the 6. Gebirgs-Division. Facing the Germans was the French XIIIème Corps d'Armée with two fortress divisions in the first line and a reserve division, the 54ème Division d'Infanterie, further back.

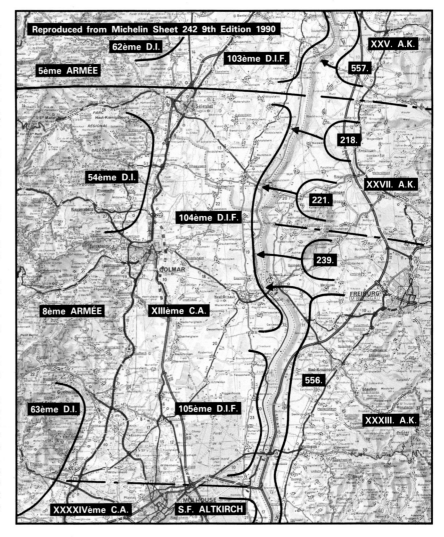

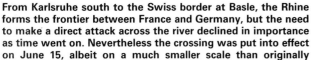

Reproduced from Michelin Sheet 242 9th Edition 1990

62ème D.I.

5ème ARMÉE

103ème D.I.F.

XXV. A.K.

557.

218.

54ème D.I.

XXVII. A.K.

221.

104ème D.I.F.

239.

8ème ARMÉE

XIIIème C.A.

FREIBURG

63ème D.I.

105ème D.I.F.

556.

XXXIII. A.K.

XXXXIVème C.A.

S.F. ALTKIRCH

The crossing was preceded by a bombardment, mainly from anti-tank and Flak guns, firing point-blank at the French casemates lining the river bank. *Left:* This 3.7cm Pak 35/36 commands a superior firing position high on the Eckartsberg. *Right:* The rail bridge across the river at this point had been blown but it was rebuilt after the war as a road bridge.

the river, sending six battalions in the first wave. On the right flank the two static divisions of XXV. Armeekorps were meanwhile to launch diversionary attacks across the Rhine in the Strasbourg area.

A short but fierce artillery bombardment was to open the assault and for this the army was allotted a large number of Flak batteries, whose powerful guns were silently emplaced on the bank of the river to fire straight at the French casemates and blockhouses on the river bank. A whole Flakbrigade Veith has been brought in and the XXVII. Armeekorps thus received seventeen batteries of 88mm Flak guns. Numerous engineer units were also at hand to throw three pontoon bridges across the river as soon as possible.

Holding the Rhine front, the 8ème Armée of Général Emile Laure had three corps at its disposal. The whole of the Rhine front had been weakened since May as numerous units had been transferred westwards to man the Weygand Line. The general withdrawal order had weakened it even more as the 8ème Armée has been ordered to withdraw its infantry divisions on the Vosges to cover the withdrawal southwards of the 3ème and 5ème Armées. On the first stage the infantry divisions had been moved to the foot of the Vosges, leaving the fortress troops alone, with no interval troops and no artillery support on the Rhine bank.

Along the 8ème Armée front on June 15, to the north, from the boundary with the 5ème Armée near Diebolsheim, was the XIIIème Corps d'Armée with two fortress divisions and the 18ème B.C.C. with one battalion of obsolete FT 17 light tanks. To the rear was the 54ème Division d'Infanterie. In the centre was the XXXXIVème Corps d'Armée with the Fortified Sector of Altkirch and the 63ème Division d'Infanterie behind it. To the south, on the Swiss border, was the XXXXVème Corps d'Armée with elements of fortress troops, the 67ème Division d'Infanterie, the 2ème Division d'Infanterie Polonaise and the 2ème Brigade de Spahis. This southern corps was relatively strong for, even at the time when

the panzers were surging deep into France, the French Command was still thinking that the Germans might thrust through Switzerland.

The main German attack was to fall on the XIIIème Corps d'Armée whose 104ème D.I.F. was now alone following the departure of the 54ème Division d'Infanterie for the foothills of the Vosges, about 20 kilometres to the rear, on June 13.

The 104ème D.I.F. had been created in March 1940 when the Colmar sector was reorganised and became a fortress division which held the Rhine frontier from Diebolsheim (north-east of Sélestat) to Geiswasser (south of Neuf-Brisach). On its left flank was the 103ème D.I.F. of the 5ème Armée — also on its own like the 104ème D.I.F. as the 62ème Division d'Infanterie had also pulled back to the Vosges on June 13. To its right was the 105ème D.I.F. From left to right of the division the

regiments along this part of the frontier were the 242ème R.I., 42ème R.I.F. and 28ème R.I.F.

As far as the CORF fortifications were concerned, the front of the former Colmar Fortified Sector was defended by about fifty casemates with a dozen infantry support shelters. The CORF had protected only the weakest points on the Rhine, with three lines of casemates. The first was on the river bank, the second some hundred metres or so behind and the third was along the main road lined by villages, hence its name of 'village line'. When the money to build the Line ran short there still remained an area to be protected along the Rhine and these gaps were hastily fortified by the construction of numbers of blockhouses named Block Garchery from the then commander of the 8ème Armée. Several of these had not yet been completed when operation 'Kleiner Bär' commenced.

This GFM cupola has been completely torn from its seating by repeated hits from 88mm Flak.

THE ASSAULT

On June 15, a day earlier than the chosen date because the Germans had noted that the French were withdrawing in order to establish new defences on the Vosges, the 7. Armee launched Operation 'Kleiner Bär'. The weather was poor the night before and it was raining when the Germans brought assault boats and Flak guns down to the river bank as quietly as possible. On the French side, the nerves of men who had been waiting for an attack they knew would come, were tense in the extreme. They had been alarmed by the noise but when the light came they could see little because of the early morning mist. All was still. At 9.00 a.m., by which time the French were convinced that this was going to be a day like any other — another quiet day — the whole of the German bank erupted with artillery fire. The Flak guns brought down and concealed on the river bank began firing directly at the casemates on the bank of the river, pounding them with shell after shell. After a ten-minute barrage, the assault boats started to race across the river.

The 218. Infanterie-Division forced a crossing near Schoenau although the casemates of the first line held fast and stopped them, but the line was breached further to the south. In the evening the 218. Infanterie-Division had achieved a bridgehead about six kilometres wide and three kilometres deep. To the south, just opposite Marckolsheim, the 221. Infanterie-Division forced its way across the river either side of Sponeck and as early as

The defences silenced, pioneer battalions began to construct the pontoon bridges. This Brückengerät B is being built at Breisach protected by a 2cm Flak 30. However, assaulting their 'own' river from their own territory against an enemy who was already pulling out, was still not quite the push-over the Germans anticipated.

11.00 a.m. the engineers had started to erect a bridge at Limbourg, at a spot where the river was only about 200 metres wide. By evening, the bridgehead had been enlarged to eleven kilometres wide and two kilometres deep.

On the corps' left flank, the 239. Infanterie-Division crossed the river near Breisach but met stiff opposition. Following three counter-attacks in the afternoon, the French might have succeeded in pushing the Germans into the Rhine if only their forces had been a little stronger. In the evening, the situation did not look good for the 239. Infanterie-Division, whose bridgehead was only four kilometres wide and 500 metres deep, while the 221. Infanterie-Division was still three kilometres away to the north.

Having forced the first line of defence the vanguard of Inf.Rgt. 360 of the 221. Infanterie-Division approached Marckolsheim on the afternoon of June 15 but dug-in for the night after a few thrusts to probe the French positions. During the night 88mm Flak guns were brought across the river and manhandled into position. Early next morning Stukas attacked and bombed the casemates at Marckolsheim. One 88mm Flak opened fire against 'Blockhaus 703' — the name on the German maps for Casemate 35/3 — and scored some direct hits on the observation cupola before French machine gun fire forced the German gunners to take cover.

The Stukas bombed the casemates again in the afternoon. With the AM cupola buried under a mound of earth

thrown over it by the explosion of the Stuka's bombs and the GFM cupola disabled by direct hits from the 88mm, the casemate was soon blind. German engineers then managed to reach the superstructure of 'Blockhaus 703' and threw several explosive charges down into the casemate. Driven out by the explosions and the smoke which soon filled the interior, the occupants opened the door and, with their gas masks covering their faces, made a dash for Casemate 34/3. A few machine gun bursts put paid to that and they were taken prisoner. Their commander, Lieutenant André Marois, refused to phone to his comrades in 'Blockhaus 702' — Casemate 34/3 — to suggest that they surrender. Meanwhile, the latter had already launched an unsuccessful counter-attack in an attempt to relieve Casemate 35/3, but succeeded in getting their machine gun into position at the very edge of the road, about 100 metres to the north.

On the morning of June 17, with the corps commander himself, General Alfred Wäger, looking on from the vicinity of the captured 'Blockhaus 703', the attack on 'Blockhaus 702' resumed. A number of 88mm Flak and 37mm Pak were firing straight at the casemate, which stubbornly returned fire until all embrasures and cupolas had been smashed. A battery of 150mm entered the scene and the casemate was soon smoking badly. Led by the casemate commander, Adjudant-Chef Raymond Guilbot, an assault party rushed outside to try to drive the German engineers

away from the casemate but they were forced back, half of them being killed. Among them was Guilbot. German engineers then managed to climb onto the roof of the casemate and drop charges into it but still the occupants refused to surrender. More charges were dropped inside until the door opened and the defenders stumbled from the smoke-filled casemate. The casemate was completely ruined, everything was on fire inside and the ammunition was exploding in the inferno.

The capture of Marckolsheim soon followed. Leutnant Werner Krockzek and Leutnant Martin Bouclier of Inf.Rgt. 360 were both awarded with the Iron Cross First Class, the former for the capture of Casemate 35/3, the latter for that of Casemate 34/3.

It was soon apparent that the gravest menace to the French was to the south where Gruppe Guderian was threatening to cut the lines of retreat for the whole of Groupe d'Armées No. 2, and on June 16 the commander of the 8ème Armée, Général Emile Laure, ordered his XXXXVème Corps d'Armée to move southwards and to keep this line open. At the same time he also ordered that both the 104ème D.I.F. and 105ème D.I.F. be withdrawn behind the line established on the Vosges. This was done during the night, under cover of some elements left in the front line. Some units had major difficulties in extricating themselves, some others did not get the withdrawal orders in time and fought on for most of June 17. The last casemate surrendered on June 18.

The epitome of French defeat. Smashed bunkers of the Maginot Line on the banks of the Rhine near Neuf-Brisach.

The same sights of wrecked armour which we have been seeing right across northern France, now a part of the scene in the east. Fifteen kilometres beyond the Rhine, the 21ème B.C.C. clashed with 6. Gebirgs-Division in Ville, just west of Sélestat. 'Le Taon' was just one of the many French tanks lost in the course of that day.

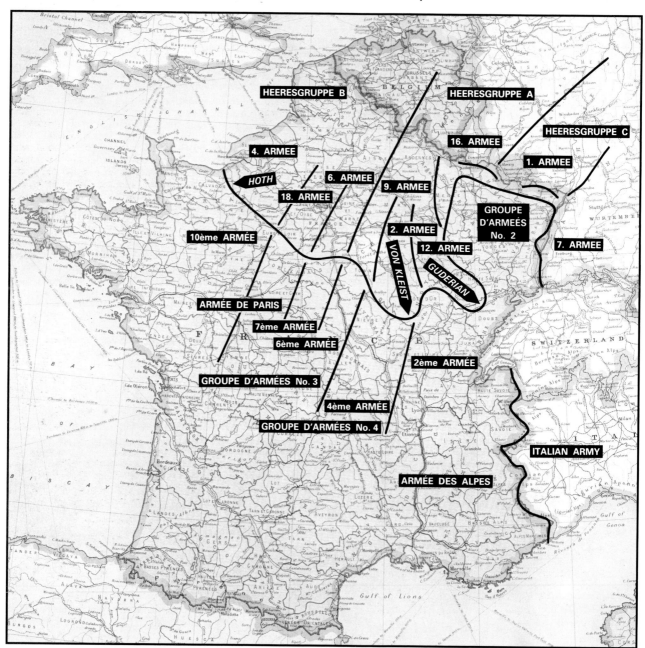

On June 16 the battle was hopelessly lost. German forces were inexorably advancing on all fronts and the successful thrusts of Gruppe Guderian and Gruppe von Kleist were on the point of eliminating the whole of Groupe d'Armées No. 2.

Alsace-Lorraine is once again German. After the defeat of France in the Franco-German War of 1870-71, the area west of the Rhine with its large German-speaking population was incorporated into the German Empire. Many residents who considered themselves French subsequently emigrated westwards, adding to the anti-German feeling in France before the First World War. Victory over Germany in 1918 led to the territory being ceded to France in 1919, a move which caused the German inhabitants to press for home rule and fuelled increasing resentment against what was seen as the punitive penalty clauses of the Treaty of Versailles. Alsace-Lorraine was re-annexed by Germany in 1940 but returned again to France in 1945. *Above:* Victory parade in Mulhouse, June 19, 1940. Against the backdrop of St Etienne Church, Generalmajor Ferdinand Neuling, the commander of the 239. Infanterie-Division and his staff, together with citizens of the long-disputed territory, await the men of Höheres Kommando z.b.V XXXIII which recaptured the city for Germany.

Strasbourg had been evacuated during the night of June 17, all the bridges being blown as the last troops withdrew. Unaware of this evacuation, it was not before the morning of June 19 that Generalmajor Artur Schmitt, commander of Infanterie-Regiment 626, took over the city.

On June 16 von Bock noted in his war diary how the three symbols of France's defence had now been taken: 'Heeresgruppe A has taken Verdun, the Maginot Line is broken through near Saarbrücken, the Rhine is crossed near Colmar'.

PART V
THE END

Reynaud plays his last cards

By mid-June, France was well and truly beaten, with hundreds of thousands of French soldiers prisoners-of-war.

On June 13 Churchill returned to France for a meeting with Reynaud at the Préfecture de Tours. The other French Minister present was Paul Baudoin, the Under-Secretary for Foreign Affairs, who fervently believed that it was now time to seek an armistice. During the conference between the two Frenchmen and the eight-strong British mission, Reynaud posed the question, albeit hypothetically, as to whether Britain would agree to release France from the agreement between the two countries that neither would seek a separate peace. Churchill's response, though negative, was sympathetic enough towards France's plight for Baudoin to interpret it as aquiescence (an interpretation which Reynaud later did all he could to quash when some of his colleagues reproached him for considering pulling France out of the war). Churchill urged Reynaud to appeal to President Roosevelt to intervene; if that failed, they woud have to look at the question again. Both men knew that they were really clutching at

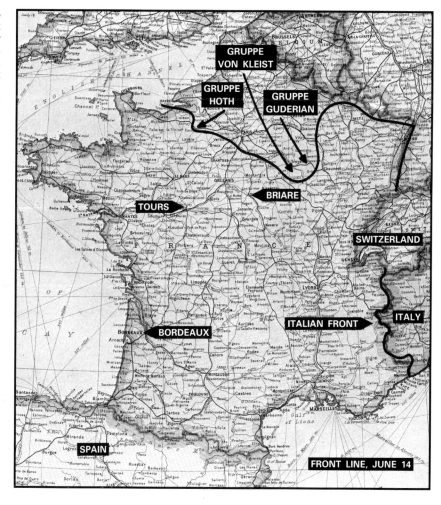

Churchill had been back in England barely twelve hours on June 12 when Reynaud 'phoned again from France. It was just after midnight and Churchill was just preparing to go to bed after having flown back from Briare that morning (see page 502). The line was bad and his secretary, John Colville, took the receiver. Eventually the picture emerged: the French Prime Minister had already moved west to Tours, and he wanted to see Churchill again that afternoon.

Churchill reached Hendon mid-morning only to be informed that bad weather was forecast and the flight should be postponed. With the knowledge that the French government was on the point of giving up, his comment was typical: 'To hell with that . . . This is too serious a situation to bother about the weather!' His party landed at the heavily-cratered airfield at Tours amid thunderstorms and rain. There was no sign of life save for a group of French airmen. The Prime Minister introduced himself in his best French and asked for the loan of a 'voiture' to reach the Préfecture *(right)*. Reynaud was late in arriving, and the meeting finally got under way with just the French Prime Minister and the War Cabinet Secretary, Paul Baudouin. Churchill's mood was defiant: 'England would fight on. She had not and would not alter her resolve: no terms, no surrender.' Reynaud's response was that it was now too late and he asked if Britain would acknowledge that France had given 'her best, her youth, her lifeblood; that she can do no more, and that she was entitled . . . to enter into a separate peace.'

straws, and Reynaud warned Churchill that if Roosevelt's reply was unfavourable they would be in 'a new situation with grave consequences'.

At a Cabinet meeting later that afternoon at Cangé, Weygand was asked for his situation report and then took it upon himself to castigate those ministers who wanted to fight on, if necessary from Africa, for ever having left Paris. The atmosphere was tense. Lebrun tried to reason with Weygand who repeated his position before suddenly leaving the room. On a sombre note, Pétain proceeded to read out a statement ending with the words that an armistice was 'the necessary condition for the perpetuity of France'. It was then decided that the government was to move to Bordeaux the following morning.

On the morning of June 14, before leaving Tours, Reynaud despatched his appeal to President Roosevelt. Stating that the Germans had already entered

Paris and that the French Army was going to withdraw in order to fight new battles, Reynaud stressed that it was doubtful that this could be accomplished, since they were at grips with an enemy which was constantly throwing in fresh troops. 'At the most tragic hour of its history,' Reynaud declared, 'France must choose. Will she continue to sacrifice her youth in a hopeless struggle? Will her government leave the national territory as not to give itself up to the enemy and in order to be able to continue the struggle on the sea and in North Africa? Will the whole country then live abandoned abating itself under

the shadow of Nazi domination with all that that means for its body and its soul? Or will France ask Hitler for conditions of an armistice?'

Reynaud then closed with a final dramatic plea: 'I must tell you at this hour, so grave in our history as in yours, that if you cannot give to France in the hours to come the certainty that the United States will come into war within a very short time, the fate of the world will change. Then you will see France go under like a drowning man and disappear after having cast a last look towards the land of liberty from which she awaited salvation.'

As Churchill was driving back to the airfield, Baudouin, one of the pessimists in the French ranks, announced to journalists that Churchill understood the French position and had acquiesced to France entering into a separate peace. De Gaulle, not present at the first part of the meeting, asked Major-General Sir Edward Spears, who had been there, if this was true. Spears, concerned at the disastrous effect such a statement would have at such a critical stage, decided he must convey the news to Churchill before he took off. He rushed to the airport and arrived just as the aircraft were running up their engines.

The eight Englishmen faced the two Frenchmen in the first-floor conference room *(right)*. Churchill was not prepared to give Reynaud an easy escape route from the recent pledge that neither of the two allies would surrender independently. instead he proposed an approach to President Roosevelt, which he would support with a message of his own, asking outright for American help, up to and including, if possible, a declaration of war. After a short adjournment, the meeting reconvened, now with the addition of a new man, Général de Gaulle. Churchill reiterated the British position that there could be no question of France making a separate peace. However, Reynaud now responded with new-found courage and read out the draft of his proposed appeal to be sent to America, stating that Britain and France could yet achieve victory if the United States were to take 'a further step forward'. In a mood of renewed optimism, the conference then broke up.

General Spears: 'I told Churchill of Baudouin's effort, and got from him absolute and categorical confirmation that at no time had he given to anyone the least indication of his consenting to the French concluding a separate armistice. "When I said 'Je comprends', that meant I understand. *Comprendre* means understand in French, doesn't it? Well," said Winston, "when for once I use exactly the right word in their own language, it is going rather far to assume that I intended it to mean something quite different. Tell them my French is not so bad as that." He beamed. "Shay — " But I did not hear the rest, lost in the roar of the engine. He clutched his hat, bent his head to the draught of the propellers, waved his stick, and the precious, lovable man was off. I gazed upward, in a moment the Flamingo and its escort had disappeared.' It had been Churchill's fifth and final visit to France since becoming Prime Minister, and he would not set foot on the Continent again for four years — almost to the exact day. This picture was taken on his return from one of the earlier trips to Paris. (His bodyguard, Detective-Inspector W. H. Thompson, right.)

This same day, June 14, Président Lebrun and the Cabinet moved from Tours to Bordeaux where they installed themselves amid a general confusion.

At the meeting of the Cabinet on June 15 Weygand again insisted that an armistice had already been delayed too long. A motion was then put forward advancing the defeatist cause, which now gained the support of the majority of the Cabinet. It proposed that the French government should ask 'the Reich to make known the terms on which it would cease hostilities and the terms which it proposes for a peace'. If the terms were reasonable, it was believed that Britain would doubtless agree to the French considering them, and if they were not, it would strengthen the government's hand carrying

on the fight. Reynaud protested that this was the same as asking for an armistice and threatened to resign but Président Lebrun persuaded him to stay on and wait for Roosevelt's reply to the appeal for immediate help sent the previous day.

Meanwhile, on June 14, Reynaud had sent de Gaulle to London to discuss, among other points, how the Royal Navy could help to transport French troops from France to North Africa. De Gaulle arrived the following evening but could not see anyone before the next morning. By then, things had changed for the worst and the atmosphere in London was gloomy as the British Cabinet had just received Reynaud's note.

On the morning of June 16 de Gaulle

met Charles Corbin, the French Ambassador in London, and learnt of a decisive plan drawn up by Jean Monnet and René Pleven, of the French economic mission in London, and Sir Robert Vansittart, the Foreign Office's chief diplomatic adviser. This was a proposal of a 'Franco-British Union' with joint portfolios of defence, foreign affairs, financial and economic policies. There would be a single War Cabinet, the two parliaments would be associated and every French citizen would become a British citizen and vice versa . . . All the energies of the two nations, proclaimed this 'declaration of indissoluble union', would be concentrated 'against the power of the enemy, no matter where the battle may be. And thus we shall conquer'. De Gaulle conferred

Reynaud left Tours for a Cabinet meeting at the Château de Cangé, 35 kilometres away. This was the moment of decision for France: whether to continue the fight or give in. The French Ministers had been assured by Reynaud that the next time Churchill came to France they would have the opportunity to see him. However, Reynaud had made no mention of this to Churchill; one of the greatest enigmas behind the fall of France. Churchill, when he later heard of it, speculated whether he could have swayed the French Cabinet, but what *is* certain is that the 'bad impression and the ill-temper caused by the disappointment of not seeing Churchill . . . undoubtedly played its part in swaying the majority of the Cabinet towards surrender'. After being subjected to the negative views of Weygand and Pétain, the Cabinet gave up all hope of continuing the fight from Brittany, as favoured by de Gaulle, and instead decided to move again, this time to Bordeaux — to the Préfecture in Rue Vital Carles *(left)*. It was here that the final act of the tragedy was played out.

with Eden and Vansittart, the War Cabinet took the final decision in the afternoon and de Gaulle met Churchill.

Roosevelt's reply to Reynaud's appeal had arrived during the night of June 15. Roosevelt spoke of his admiration for France's courage but explained firmly and regretfully that nothing he might say could imply the slightest implication of a military committment. Reynaud may have expected little else but in view of this response he now had a note sent to the British government asking their consent to the French enquiring of the Germans as to the terms of an armistice.

THE DEFEATISTS WIN

At the Cabinet meeting in the morning of June 16 at the Préfecture in Bordeaux, Reynaud read out Roosevelt's answer, which had a depressing effect on the assembled Ministers and told of his request to Churchill. The President of the Senate was brought in to endorse, both on his own and of the behalf of the President of the Chamber, Reynaud's proposal to transfer the government to North Africa. Pétain stood up and announced that he could no longer remain a member of a government which refused to bring an end to hostilities and which contemplated leaving the soil of France. Reynaud appealed for time to at least enable the British to reply and Lebrun asked Pétain to withdraw his resignation, and wait for a last conference with Churchill. The Marshal agreed to the delay but things were now crystal clear for Reynaud: if Pétain resigned, Reynaud's Cabinet would fall and Président Lebrun would call on someone of the defeatist faction, quite possibly Pétain himself, to form a new government.

The British answer had been telephoned through to its Ambassador in Bordeaux, Sir Ronald Campbell, during the morning and immediately passed to Reynaud. The Ambassador brought the textual answer of the British government to him after lunch. It consented to France ascertaining the terms of an armistice 'provided only that the French Fleet is sailed forthwith for British harbours pending negotiations'. Later in the afternoon, at 3.10 p.m., while the War Cabinet was in session drafting the terms of the proposed Franco-British Union, the Foreign Office despatched a further message which expanded the previous answer and pointed that by

putting the Fleet out of the German's reach, it would be in France's interests too, strengthening 'the hands of the French Government in any armistice discussions'.

The suggestion was not well received, not even by Reynaud, for whom the thought of removing French ships from the Mediterranean was stupid when this would mean the Royal Navy having to send more ships to contain the Italian Navy. To the French this was a sound argument, and it is conceivable that Reynaud might have been hoping to capitalise on it to close the door on any British acceptance of separate negotiation and thus reinforce his own position in Cabinet that France was honour bound not to seek an armistice on its own. However, Reynaud's attempt to stake all on France's moral obligation was weakened by the fact that Britain, which retained a part of its forces for its own defence instead of risking all in the common fight, had lost the moral authority to refuse to free its ally from their joint agreements. Most of the French Ministers, including the most firm friends of Britain, were by now bitterly disappointed in the actions of their ally.

It was about 4.30 p.m. when de

Gaulle, still with Churchill in London, telephoned Reynaud to give him the exact terms of the Franco-British Union proposal. Reynaud was enthusiastic yet could hardly believe it and an equally elated Churchill took the telephone from de Gaulle to confirm the offer. They agreed to meet at Concarneau the next day to work out further plans with their military and naval advisers.

In view of the dramatic offer of union, the British War Cabinet decided to suspend their conditional agreement to the French demand for an armistice and Sir Ronald was asked to delay presentation of the two previous messages. This was impossible for he had already conveyed them verbally and by the time this demand had reached him, even the second message had been given to Reynaud. A messenger was therefore sent after him to say that the two meassages should be considered 'cancelled'.

The French Cabinet met at about 5.00 p.m., for the second time that day, in a very depressing athmosphere; a message from Général Georges had just arrived, telling of the gravity of the military situation and ending with a firm request that 'you must absolutely take a decision'. At 5.15 p.m. Reynaud played his last card and disclosed the proposal of the Franco-British Union. Surprise was total but the idea was so far apart in tone and content from the message about the Fleet which had just arrived that it merely left a damaging, confused impression, almost the opposite of what was intended. Most of the Cabinet saw it as a totally unrealistic idea — the answer to everything except the immediate problems faced by France. Instead of strengthening Reynaud's position, it gave the defeatists, who did not hesitate to maliciously misread it, still more ammunition. Some described it as a plot to turn France into a British dominion; others twisted the wording to mean that Frenchmen were only being offered citizenship of the British Empire outside Britain itself. The high-sounding but improvised proposals to bolster the French and keep them in the war had come too late.

The bold British effort to give to the French Cabinet a reason to keep on fighting had failed to attain its goal. The discussion was heated but in the end the vote was in favour of the defeatists, 14 to 10 in their favour, and at 8.00 p.m. Reynaud handed his resignation to Président Lebrun, who immediately asked Maréchal Pétain to form a government. This was done at 11.30 p.m. and the new government held its first meeting; ten of Reynaud's former Ministers who had voted for the armistice had places in the new administration, all the other important figures were military, Weygand becoming Minister of National Defence.

Frenchmen. At the request of Président Lebrun, I assumed, as from today, the direction of the French Government, certain of the affection of our admirable Army, which is fighting with a heroism worthy of its wonderful military tradition against an enemy superior in number and armaments. Certain that by its wonderful resistance it has fulfilled its duty towards its Allies, certain of the support of the war veterans whom I had the honour to command, certain of the confidence of the whole people, I give myself to France to help her in her hour of misfortune. In these painful hours, I think of these unfortunate refugees aimlessly wandering about our roads in the utmost destitution. I extend to them my compassion and my concern.

It is with a heavy heart that I tell you today we have to cease the fight. I appealed last night to the adversary in order to ask him whether he is ready to discuss with me, as between soldiers and in honour, the means to end hostilities.

Let all Frenchmen rally round the Government over which I preside during these difficult trials and affirm their whole faith in the destiny of their country.

MARÉCHAL PHILIPPE PÉTAIN,
BROADCAST, JUNE 17, 1940

During the scenario for the last two fateful days for France, there were changes not only in the venue and the plot, but also to the principal players. However, once the director, Reynaud, was ousted on the evening of June 16, no time was lost by the new leading man, Pétain, in bringing down the final curtain.

Little time was lost in asking for an armistice. Paul Baudouin, the new Minister of Foreign Affairs, telephoned the Spanish Ambassador at 1.00 a.m. on June 17, and asked him to transmit the French request for an armistice to Germany.

Later that day, at 12.30 a.m., Pétain came on the radio and told the French people that he had asked the Germans to discuss an armistice. Not choosing his words very wisely, for he was asking for an end of the fighting but not calling on the troops to stop fighting, he used the words 'with a heavy heart I tell you today that we have to cease the fight.' Although very few of the troops actually heard him speak, the news was on all their lips. Commanders in the field all issued orders informing their men that, until further instructions, the battle continued and no ground would be abandoned, but the impact of what Pétain had said, on troops and civilians alike, was that it was all over for France.

And what of the foreign production, already playing to unwilling audiences throughout the country? Its performance, although only having run a bare five weeks, had been outstanding — a box-office success the like of which the world had never seen. Here, one of the stars of the show, General Erich Hoepner of the XVI. Armeekorps of Gruppe von Kleist, checks his programme in Dijon, 250 kilometres south-east of Paris, which was entered by 4. Panzer-Division on June 17 against little opposition. Hoepner had already received one award — the Ritterkreuz — for his rôle in Poland in 1939.

While the French government was agonising over the fate of France in Tours and Bordeaux, the German spearhead of the 9. Panzer-Division was about to take the earlier location at Briare on the Loire. This was the last natural defensive line in central France at which a stand could be made, and by June 17 the division had reached Joigny, 60 kilometres short of the Loire. *Above left:* The bridge over the Yonne was captured intact and the town suffered little *(right)* in the swift advance.

Twenty-five kilometres to the south, a cavalry patrol crosses the Yonne via another bridge captured at Auxerre.

And over the Loire! Gien, just downstream from Briare, had been attacked repeatedly by the Luftwaffe to soften up the French defences, in this case manned by the 23ème Division d'Infanterie. When German ground forces came into contact, there was a fierce exchange of fire for several hours before the French withdrew to the south bank whereupon the bridge was blown. However, the solid stone structure withstood the blast and the craters were quickly spanned by 1. Gebirgs-Division engineers. Thus the last credible defence line had fallen, heralding the end of the struggle for France.

The success of Fall Gelb in May had seen the extension of the Maginot Line easily forced at some of its weakest points. At Sedan and Monthermé, Gruppe von Kleist had broken through the 2ème Armée defences on the Meuse in the thinly protected Ardennes Defensive Sector. Further to the north the XV. Armeekorps had brushed off the French units in Belgium before the 9ème Armée had time to build its main line of resistance on the Meuse. In the Solre-le-Château gap the panzers had no difficulty in breaking through the line of casemates, thinly-held by men of the 101ème D.I.F., left on their own with no artillery support after the infantry divisions and their artillery had advanced into Belgium.

The panzers had rushed westwards but the infantry following soon turned to the fortified sectors on either sides of the breakthrough. On the left, to the south, the fortress and casemates of the Montmédy Fortified Sector controlling the Chiers valley prevented the widening of the base of the breakthrough and threatened its flank. It had taken the VII. Armeekorps five days to capture the troublesome casemates and the minor fortress of La Ferté, this having fallen on May 19. *(See page 292.)*

To the north, units of the VIII. Armeekorps had dealt with the four minor fortresses of the Maubeuge Fortified Sector where, following a six-day battle, the last one, Les Sarts, surrendered on May 23. *(See page 297.)*

The fortifications of the adjoining Escaut Fortified Sector to the north — comprising one minor fortress at Eth, the old fort of Maulde rejuvenated by some STG casemates built onto its superstructure and 14 casemates — were all overwhelmed on May 26.

At the end of May most of the northwards extension of the Maginot Line had disappeared but the 'old fronts' stood unchallenged and the Line still ran continuously from the casemates west of Le Chesnois, now the westernmost fortress of the Montmédy Fortified Sector, to the Swiss border.

When Fall Rot broke through the front which had been temporarily stabilised along the Somme and Aisne rivers, a general withdrawal was then ordered. At the western end of the fortifications, the Montmédy Fortified Sector (and Marville Defensive Sector which was attached to it) were abandoned. On June 14, the westernmost fortress of the Line was thus the minor fortress at Ferme Chappy, just east of Longuyon.

The 3ème Armée then issued orders for the timing of the successive withdrawal of the other sectors: the interval troops and part of the fortress crews to move back during the night of June 15, the fortress and their reduced crews maintaining the illusion of a strong defence; the garrisons of the casemates to pull out the following day, and the last of the crews at 10.00 p.m. on June 17 after wrecking everything within.

The idea of giving up the Maginot Line without a fight came as a total shock for the French troops. In every unit, but particularly in the fortresses themselves, the men heard of this order

'Übung an der Maginot Linie.' This nice action shot from German propaganda files was most probably taken 'attacking' Czech fortifications — the bloodless coup handed to Hitler on a plate following the Munich agreement in 1938.

The Battle of the Fortresses

with frustrated disbelief which often resulted in outright anger. They knew that apart from La Ferté, the Germans had not taken a single one of the fortresses of the Maginot Line proper. In the knowledge that they had not been beaten, the men could not understand why they should therefore abandon their fortresses to the Germans.

The fortress troops were mostly static units, lacking transport and fitness, and were not prepared for evacuation. To overcome the problem, each fortified sector organised into 'march divisions' those units of fortress troops which were to leave first. These 'march divisions' departed as planned but the remaining sections of the garrisons were destined not to leave.

By June 16 the situation of Groupe d'Armées No. 2 had become critical: while the 1. Armee was now advancing in the Sarre sector, Gruppe Guderian had reached Besançon from the west and the 7. Armee was across the Rhine to the east. With German troops now advancing on the rear of the Maginot Line, the latter stages of the withdrawal became impossible for the remainder, and on June 17 the 3ème Armée commander, Général Charles-Marie Condé, issued his Order No. 4200/3 stating that further withdrawal was over; the fortresses would hereafter resist.

LA CRUSNES

The La Crusnes Fortified Sector was responsible for the frontier from Marville to Dudelange, about twenty kilometres north of Thionville. The fifty kilometres of front were protected with three major fortresses, four minor fortresses and 36 CORF casemates, stretching from the minor fortress of

Ferme Chappy (A1) to the west to another minor fortress, Aumetz (A7), to the east. There were also one shelter and five observatories.

In January 1940, the La Crusnes Fortified Sector Command had been disbanded and tactical control of this sector on the left flank of the 3ème Armée was taken over by the XXXXIIème Corps d'Armée de Forteresse.

Following the general withdrawal order, some of the fortress troops were organised in a Groupement de Fleurian and attached to the 51ème Division d'Infanterie. Together with the interval units, they started withdrawing at 10.00 p.m. on June 13 but there was soon no chance of conducting the later phases of the stage-by-stage withdrawal of supporting troops and garrisons. The commander of Latiremont fortress, Commandant Max Pophillat, took command of the fortress line on the left wing of the sector and Commandant Maurice Vanier, the commander of the Bréhain fortress, that of the right wing.

As the French pulled back, the 169. Infanterie-Division flanked the fortress line and moved eastwards to its rear, aiming at Metz, while the 183. Infanterie-Division which followed advanced in the direction of Thionville.

On June 15 the Germans found the main electricity supply for the fortress at Xivry-Circourt and cut it off, forcing the fortresses to start up their own generators. The 161. Infanterie-Division then took on the left wing of the Line and advanced eastwards on the rear of the fortresses.

On June 17 an 88mm Flak, which had been brought up to the rear of the fortress and concealed east of Longuyon, suddenly started to shell Block 4,

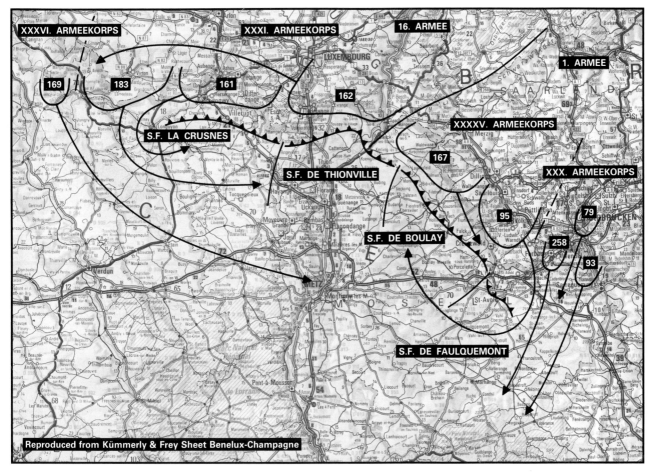

As the 1. Armee pressed southwards on Operation 'Tiger' in the Sarre gap (on the right of the map), the 16. Armee maintained contact with the French as they pulled back. Each German army allocated one army corps to deal with the unbroken part of the Maginot Line which still controlled some 100 kilometres of the frontier. In the west, the XXXI. Armeekorps (16. Armee) sent its 183. Infanterie-Division to flank the fortress line and advance against its rear, while the XXXXV. Armeekorps (1. Armee) to the east did the same with the 95. Infanterie-Division. Both divisions soon made contact at the rear of the Thionville Fortified Sector.

one shell crashing every three minutes on the same spot between guns 1 and 2. The mist and the glare of the sun made it impossible to see precisely where the German gun was positioned, but the defenders were not unduly perturbed as the concrete was 1.75 metres thick. The shells kept on smashing onto the same spot until at midday one broke through and landed near a rack packed with 75mm shells without exploding. Bits of concrete flew about but there was no one nearby and no casualties. By chance, possibly because the Germans realised that they no longer had the sun behind them and could expect more accurate return fire, or perhaps because they felt they stood little chance of making much of an impression on the evidently solid blockhouse, the gun crew decided after this very shell that it was time to find a new target. Thus Block 4 was spared as its ammunition would very likely have gone up with the next shell. During the night, the breach in the concrete, two metres in diameter on the outside and one metre inside, was patched with a couple of iron plates and filled with concrete.

The Germans now decided that it was time they took care of this troublesome fortress and on June 21 a massive artillery bombardment opened up against Fermont, lasting for two hours. At 6.00 a.m. the intensity of the shelling decreased and the watch climbed quickly into their cupolas to see German infantry approaching through the barbed wire blown open by the explosions. The 75mm turret of Block 1 fired shrapnel, the 81mm turret of Block 5

lobbed its bombs, and every machine gun hammered away. Block 6 of Latiremont, firing in support, brought its three 75mm howitzers into action. Fermont's turrets too fired in support of its neighbour to the west, the fortress at Ferme Chappy, which was also attacked. Suffering heavy losses and failing to get near any of the blocks, in the late morning the Germans withdrew. In the afternoon, they approached Fermont with white flags, asking for a cease-fire in order to collect their dead and wounded lying all around the fortress, to which Capitaine Aubert agreed. Apart from the periodic shelling, the next few days until the armistice passed uneventfully.

THIONVILLE

The Thionville Fortified Sector was responsible for the frontier from Dudelange, twenty kilometres north of Thionville, to Launstroff, about ten kilometres east of Sierck. With the Moselle valley running through its centre, the sector was highly vulnerable and it had been well protected with seven major fortresses, four minor fortresses and 17 CORF casemates. The fortifications stretched from the major fortress of Rochonvillers (A8), in the

west, to another major fortress, Billig (A18), to the east. There were also 18 infantry shelters and four observatories.

In May 1940 the VIème Corps d'Armée of the 3ème Armée had assumed tactical control within the Thionville Fortified Sector, and for all this part of the Maginot Line the early weeks of the campaign were uneventful except for desultory shelling.

Following the general order to pull back, sections of the fortress troops were organised into Division de Marche Poisot which started to withdraw with the interval troops at 9.30 p.m. on June 13. Command of the troops remaining in the Thionville sector fortifications passed to Colonel Jean-Patrice O'Sullivan, formerly in charge of the sector's infantry units.

The first part of the withdrawal went as planned but the situation rapidly worsened and on June 15 the reduced garrisons were informed that they were to fight to the end. The 183. Infanterie-Division were soon at the rear of the fortress line and took Thionville. The pressure began to mount in the days that followed, and German patrols got close enough to fire machine guns at the cupolas but were driven off by return fire from the GFM cupolas.

549

In view of the fact that many of the fortress troops had left the relative security of their underground forts to fight in the streets, this German roadblock was set up in Garche, just north of Thionville. The rear of Sentzich fortress, on the right wing of the Thionville Fortified Sector, lies just a few kilometres away.

BOULAY

The Boulay Fortified Sector was responsible for the frontier from Launstroff, about ten kilometres east of Sierck, to Coume, about five kilometres north-east of Boulay. The sector was protected with four major fortresses, eleven minor fortresses and seventeen CORF casemates, from the major fortress of Hackenberg (A19), to the west, to the minor fortress of Mottenberg (A33), to the east. There were also fourteen interval shelters and two observatories.

In May 1940 the VIème Corps d'Armée assumed tactical control within the sector. The 51st (Highland) Division of the British Expeditionary Force held the part of the line in front of the Hackenberg fortress until May 22 when it was relieved and assembled near Etain.

The 75mm turret of Block 2 at Hackenberg, to the west, opened fire for the first time on May 13.

After the general withdrawal order, the interval troops and elements of the infantry in the fortress, having been organised into Division de Marche Besse, began to pull out on June 13. On that same evening the 5,000 or so troops remaining in the sector's fortresses were placed under the sector's infantry commander, Colonel Raoul Cochinard, with the task of covering the withdrawal before they too left. Reorganisation involved the commander of the Hackenberg fortress, Commandant Henri Ebrard, taking over of the whole Hombourg-Budange area from Casemates C53 and C54 at Hummersberg, in the west, to the minor fortress of Hobling, in the east.

From June 15 German reconnaissance patrols were spotted and the general situation made it impossible for the second stage of the withdrawal to be carried out. As a consequence Colonel Cochinard ordered the fortresses to fight to the end and installed his command post in the Anzeling fortress.

On June 15, when the 135mm heavy mortars of Block 9 fired to repel German infantry trying to advance between the Billig fortress and the Hummersberg casemates, a malfunction disabled the turret. In spite of duplicate security systems, the right-hand gun of the turret somehow fired when it was retracted, the resulting explosion destroying the piece.

During the night of June 16 German patrols probed above the fortress and near the entrances, throwing smoke grenades to conceal their movements. A more powerful move between the two casemates at Hummersberg was shelled by the Hackenberg's artillery. The following day a German patrol was surprised in the barbed wire in front of Block 25; two men got back, driven off by machine gun fire, while an officer, Oberleutnant Paul Siebold of Inf.Rgt. 315, was wounded and taken prisoner. In the evening the fortress shelled woods to the north where enemy concentrations had been observed.

Early on June 18 the watch reported mysterious signals being flashed from the vicinity of a nearby chapel, and during the day German troops were spotted in the villages to the rear of the fortress. These were the first elements of the 95. Infanterie-Division which had turned westwards to occupy the rear of the fortress line after the 1. Armee breakthrough in the Sarre.

For the next four days Hackenberg suffered from the attention of the German artillery which fired repeated barrages at the fortress but with no visible results. The fortress's artillery fired co-ordinated barrages with the guns of the neighbouring fortresses to shell any suspected places within range.

On June 22 the Germans concentrated on the Michelsberg fortress and during the afternoon, after a battery of 88mm Flak guns had fired more than 200 shells at its Blocks 2 and 3, emissaries approached the fortress under white flags. The commander, Commandant Jules Pelletier, met them at the entrance and in reply to their demand for surrender informed them that he intended to carry out orders and 'fight to the end'. To show what that meant, Commandant Ebrard ordered a coordinated barrage to be fired by six turrets at areas occupied by the Germans.

The artillery duel continued on June 23 and 24, the German infantry making determined attacks on the neighbouring fortresses at Coucou and Mont des Welches but to no avail. At 10.15 p.m. news of the armistice came over the radio and of the cease-fire which was to come into effect at 12.35 a.m. This was confirmed some time later by Colonel Cochinard, who made it clear that 'until further orders' there was to be no movement out of the fortresses and that any emissaries that might appear must be sent to him at Anzeling, where he had his command post. Meanwhile, Hackenberg was heavily shelled and together with its neighbours fired co-ordinated barrages in return. Commandant Ebrard stated that he would call a halt only when the Germans themselves did so. At the appointed hour, silence descended over the fortifications.

FAULQUEMONT

The Faulquemont sector was responsible for the frontier from Coume, five kilometres north-east of Boulay, to Kerbach, north-west of Sarreguemines. The sector was protected with five minor fortresses and eight CORF casemates, from the one at Kerfent (A34), to the west, to that at Teting (A38), to the east. Its responsibility had been extended to the east in March and the sector then inherited the western end of the Sarre gap only defended by flooded sectors and blockhouses which covered these.

With the withdrawal of the IXème Corps d'Armée on May 27 and the 4ème Armée on May 29, the Faulquemont Fortified Sector passed under the XXème Corps d'Armée soon taken over by the 3ème Armée.

At the end of May German patrols had made contact with the advance posts but nothing significant occurred before the night of June 13, when in accordance with the orders for a general withdrawal, the interval troops and part of the fortress's infantry began to leave, the latter organised into Groupement de Girval. Commandant Adolphe Denoix, who established his command post in the Laudrefang fortress, then took command of those who remained in the Faulquemont sector's fortifications, who were to cover the withdrawal until their turn came to pull out on the night of June 17.

The situation in the Faulquemont sector was soon to become critical as just to the east the 1. Armee was advancing on the heels of the retreating Groupement de la Sarre. On June 15 the casemate garrisons concentrated in the fortress as planned but the next phase of the withdrawal could not be carried out as German troops were now on the ridge to the rear of the fortress line. These were the first elements of 167. Infanterie-Division which had turned the line after the breakthrough in the Sarre and moved behind the fortifications. In next to no time the Germans had discovered Bambesch's Achilles' heel: with its rear at the edge of a dense wood, the fortress could be easily approached. They had no difficulty in bringing their artillery batteries forward, among them 88mm Flak, in a direct line of fire behind the fortress. On June 20 they opened up, concentrating on Bambesch's Block 2.

Above: Men of Infanterie-Regiment 339 have set up a machine gun in a ditch beside the access road to Kerfent, bringing fire to bear on the embrasures of Block 2. *Right:* Unlike the massive casemates, the lightly constructed barracks have disappeared, with only the foundations remaining.

Early on the morning of the attack (June 21), two 88mm Flak guns opened up on Block 3, firing shot after shot on the same trajectory. The defenders attempted to hit back with their 50mm mortar in the LG cupola, but in the end the crew were forced to evacuate this blockhouse. One of the Flak guns was then turned onto Block 2, repeating the same process until a shell penetrated the casemate and exploded inside. French fire from other positions and the Mi turret of Mottenberg gave close support. The defenders were successful in preventing the attackers from approaching the undamaged casemates, and the Germans suffered heavy losses. Finally, however, Capitaine Georges Broché, the commander, called his officers together and a joint decision was made to surrender. In this picture, Capitaine Broché (carrying the coat over his arm) is seen leaving Block 2.

A battle won . . . a battle lost. Block 2, half a century later.

The Bambesch commander, Lieutenant André Pastre, knew that his fortress was beyond the range of both Einseling and Laudrefang but requested supporting fire from their machine guns and 81mm mortars. After two hours of intense shelling, 88mm shells managed to breach Block 2 and forced the crew to abandon it. Meanwhile, the air inside the fortress had become more and more polluted; aware of what had happened to the men at La Ferté, Lieutenant Pastre discussed the situation with his NCOs and on the afternoon of June 20 they decided to surrender to an assault troop of Inf.Rgt. 339.

The infantry regiment's commander, Oberstleutnant Reisner von Lichtenstern, was killed the following day whilst making preparations for an attack on Kerfent. This surrendered after intense shelling, an 88mm Flak being brought up to within about 100 metres of Block 2. Einseling, Laudrefang and Teting held out against four days of heavy shelling and renewed attacks which were defeated thanks to the support of Laudrefang's 81mm mortars. These, the last three fortresses of the Faulquemont sector, would surrender on June 30 after the sector commander, Commandant Denoix, had met Colonel Marion and put his signature to the document drawn up at the headquarters of Höheres Kommando z.b.V. XXXXV.

Stunned troops of Infanterie-Regiment 339 carry their gravely wounded commander, Oberstleutnant Reisner von Lichtenstern, to the rear on June 21. He was soon to die.

Kerfent now lies abandoned, the wind whistling through the shattered cupolas and casemates. The damage to this GFM cupola on top of Block 2 was caused by repeated hits from 88mm Flak shells, the gun firing from a range of a couple of hundred metres. (The same cupola can be identified in the pictures on page 551.)

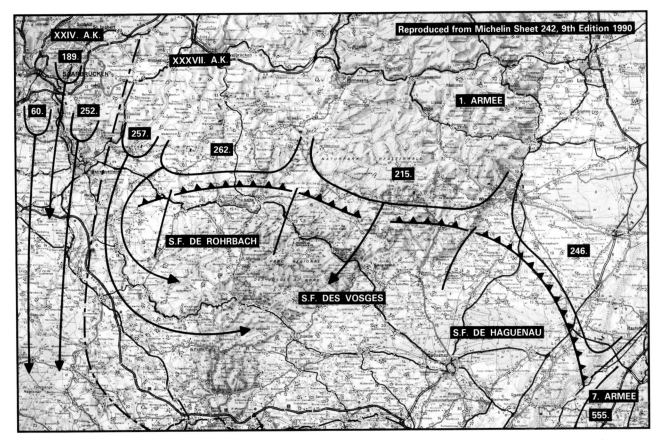

LA SARRE

The Sarre sector was responsible for the frontier from Kerbach, eight kilometres north-west of Sarreguemines, to Obergailbach, ten kilometres east of Sarreguemines, the Sarre river being right in the middle of the sector. Most of the sector was thinly protected by blockhouses covering flooded areas, only the eastern bank of the Sarre being fortified with one lately built minor fortress, Haut-Poirier, and five CORF casemates.

Originally a 'defence sector', La Sarre became a 'fortified sector' in March 1940 when the area for which it was responsible was reapportioned with the sectors on either side. On the left flank the boundary was shifted eastwards and the Faulquemont sector took in over the western half of the gap; on the right flank, the boundary was moved beyond the Sarre river and the Sarre sector took over the right bank of the river with the Haut-Poirier minor fortress and the five casemates built there. There were also nearly 200 blockhouses covering the flooded areas that constituted the main defence of the sector's centre and left wing but the Sarre gap remained the weakest point of the Maginot Line in this area.

Towards the end of May the 4ème Armée staff were moved out and on May 30 the XXème Corps d'Armée, which had been in the area since the winter, was upgraded to Groupement de la Sarre and took over. At the beginning of June the advanced posts exchanged fire with German patrols, the civilians were evacuated from the villages and the flood measures were all improved. On June 13 the Groupement de la Sarre was subordinated to the

The shoulder of the Maginot Line at its eastern end (see page 27). With the German breakthrough in the La Sarre Sector, Höheres Kommando z.b.V. XXXVII was given the task of taking this sector of the Line from the rear.

3ème Armée and given orders for the general withdrawal. The fortress troops of the sector were then organised into a Groupement Dagnan and the withdrawal began but the pull back of the main force was delayed as the men had first to fight back the German attack on June 14 before withdrawing as planned during the night.

Commandant André Jolivet arrived at Haut-Poirier on the afternoon of June 14, having been sent to take command of the Haut-Poirier fortress and the five casemates east of the Sarre with orders to resist until June 17 at 10.00 p.m. and then pull out the last of the fortress troops. However the arrival of this unknown officer, who seemed to know nothing about the fortifications, took the fortress garrison by surprise. In such a confused situation he was looked on with distrust, one of the garrison officers even stating later that he had thought Commandant Jolivet might be from the 'fifth column'.

After the 1. Armee breakthrough in the Sarre on June 15, Höheres Kommando z.b.V. XXXVII turned its attention to the fortresses flanking the breach to the east and attacked Haut-Poirier which was not covered by any artillery as it was out of range of the Simserhof 75mm howitzers. The 262. Infanterie-Division had left its Inf.Rgt. 462 to the north of the fortifications and moved southwards behind them. In leaving only one regiment to hold an area formerly held by his entire division Generalleutnant Edgar Theissen took no risk as he knew quite well that the

French were not in a position to attack northwards. From June 21 the division pressed on Haut-Poirier, Inf.Rgt. 462 mounting diverting attacks from the north while Inf.Rgt. 486 advanced behind it. Further to the east Inf.Rgt. 482 was advancing behind Welschoff.

From the vicinity of Kalhausen 105mm and 150mm howitzers started firing at the rear of Block 3. For hours the shells exploded at the same place, slowly blasting away the concrete until at 6.30 p.m. a shell finally broke through and exploded in the main firing chamber where 300 47mm shells and 500 50mm mortar shells were stored. The whole lot detonated, killing three men and badly shattering the block's upper storey. As the vital powerhouse was in the lower storey of Block 3, all plans to isolate the block from the rest of the fortress were impracticable.

Commandant Jolivet called a conference with all his officers to discuss the situation. He pointed out that their mission, to resist until June 17, had been accomplished and that there was now no point in more men being killed. Some of the officers disagreed but it was decided to surrender the Haut-Poirier and the five casemates east of the Sarre river, and a white flag was hoisted on Block 1. Two German envoys arrived ten minutes later and were met at Block 1 by Sous-Lieutenant Michel Isnard. Because of the late hour, the garrison was allowed to sleep one last night in their vanquished fortress, departing on the morning of June 22. Now nothing remained of the Sarre Fortified Sector.

ROHRBACH

The Rohrbach Fortified Sector was responsible for the frontier from Obergailbach, ten kilometres east of Sarreguemines, to Volmunster, about fifteen kilometres north of Bitche. This sector was protected by two major fortresses, three minor fortresses and twenty CORF casemates, stretching to the west from the minor fortress of Welschoff to another minor fortress, Otterbiel, to the east. There were also eight shelters.

The VIIIème Corps d'Armée of the 5ème Armée had been in tactical command of the sector since September 1939, but this corps was transferred to the Aisne front at the beginning of June when the XXXXIIIème Corps d'Armée de Forteresse took over.

On June 12, following the general withdrawal order, the sector's interval troops began pulling out. Elements of the fortress troops were organised into Division de Marche Chastenet and withdrew during the night of June 13 while detachments stayed in the fortresses and casemates as cover.

On June 14 German pressure on the advanced posts increased, particularly in the wooded area north of Bitche, and an attack against Gros-Rederching was repelled. The 75mm turret of Block 8 fired two salvoes of twenty shells each in the afternoon. In an order of the day circulated among the crew, Lieutenant-Colonel Bonlarron declared that 'the hour is grave for France, the hour is grave for Simserhof . . . we shall fight . . . take heart, even so!'.

By June 15 all the interval troops had gone; the troops holding the fortifications were on their own. Lieutenant-Colonel Bonlarron assumed command of the whole sector. That morning the advanced posts were forced to start withdrawing to the main line and at Simserhof, which had fired for most of the day in support of them, with all the crews at battle stations.

After the 1. Armee breakthrough in the Sarre on June 15, Höheres Kommando z.b.V. XXXVII had turned its attention to the fortresses flanking the breach to the east and forced the Haut-Poirier fortress to surrender late on June 21. As the 257. Infanterie-Division and 262. Infanterie-Division advanced on the rear of the fortress line, guns of the latter division were brought to bear on the back of Welschoff, now the westernmost fortress east of the German breakthrough. Soon the shells were coming straight at Block 1 and the casemate at Bining. The barrages fired in support of the fortifications by the Simserhof 75mm howitzers could not provide much help, for the guns were firing at the extreme limit of their range, Welschoff being within reach only with a favourable wind.

From June 17, when a barrage from the 75mm embrasures of Block 5 landed close enough to drive off the gunners from a 150mm howitzer which had started to pound Welschoff from Singling, Simserhof fired salvo after salvo to force the German batteries to cease fire.

On June 21 the howitzers of Block 5 called a halt to the efforts of those Germans at Rohrbach who had brought up three 37mm anti-tank guns in front of that small fortress. Rohrbach was in sight of the Simserhof observation posts and within precise range of its guns and, due to its support, the fortress was not taken before the armistice, the Germans being unable to bring their guns close enough.

Late on June 23, German batteries succeeded in piercing Block 1 at Welschoff. Ever since Pétain's 'cease-fire' speech of June 17, the fortress commander, Capitaine Adrien Lhuisset, had only been waiting for the armistice, convinced that there was no point in getting more men killed. With Block 1 disabled, he decided to surrender and, though most of his officers strongly disagreed, they were unable to persuade him otherwise, and Welschoff capitulated on June 24.

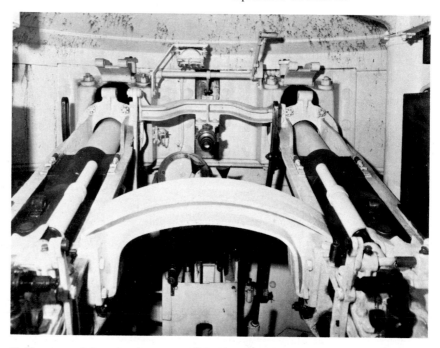

Unlike many of the other fortresses of the Line, Simershof was kept on by the French Army which continued to maintain it in tip-top condition, and today it forms a superb 'living' museum. *Top:* This 135mm heavy mortar fired from an embrasure in Block 4. The fixture behind the breech is to collect the empty cases. *Above:* The interior of the 75mm turret of Block 8 — a view not possible to a present-day visitor.

VOSGES

The Vosges Fortified Sector was responsible for the frontier from Volmunster to the Climbach area, about ten kilometres west of Wissembourg. The sector was protected by two major and one minor fortress and 20 CORF casemates — from the major fortress of Grand-Hohekirkel in the west to Four-à-Chaux to the east. There were also two shelters and 17 CORF blockhouses, plus numerous STG and MOM blockhouses scattered along the Schwarzbach valley.

Its centre being regarded as 'impassable', for about twenty kilometres the sector here was only lightly fortified. On its left wing, from the Grand-Hohekirkel fortress to Windstein, the defence line followed the valley, which had been flooded with a dozen artificial lakes, and was covered by 7 CORF casemates and 15 or so STG and MOM blockhouses. From Windstein to Lembach, on the sector's right wing, the fortifications followed hilly terrain which was so difficult that the CORF had considered it to be adequately fortified with only two casemates and 17 blockhouses. Later, a second line of STG and MOM blockhouses was built behind these. The left wing of the line

Another preserved museum piece is Four-à-Chaux fortress — once part of the Vosges Fortified Sector near Lembach. In this picture the men manning Block 6 overlooking the Sauer valley take a breather outside their casemate.

of casemates as far as Dambach could be supported by the 75mm turret of Grand-Hohekirkel firing from the west; from the east the 75mm turret of Four-à-Chaux could be brought to bear for supporting fire.

The first fortress on the right wing of the Vosges sector, Four-à-Chaux stood on a hill 260 metres high, just east of the town of Lembach. The fortress had six battle blocks and the usual two entrance blocks.

Because of the small size of the hill on which it was built, Four-à-Chaux was far more compact than the CORF principles laid down and the entrance blocks were close to the battle blocks. The personnel entrance led directly into the fortress and was on the same level as the main thoroughfare. The munitions entrance was about fifty metres below this level; from it a gallery 100 metres long ascended a 1-in-4 slope — a unique feature on the north-east front (five other fortresses had galleries sloping down to a lower level). Loads were hauled up and down along the slope on a lift operated by an electric powered

winch, and a 215-step stairway ran alongside. Because of the close proximity of the entrances and the battle blocks, the fortress did not have an electric traction system and the flat-cars were manhandled on the internal railway lines. Cost-cutting caused Four-à-Chaux to be scaled down; a seventh battle block was cancelled and the large M1 main magazine was not built, the ammunition being stored in M2 magazines built at the bottom of each battle block.

In March 1940 the Vosges Fortified Sector was disbanded and tactical control of this sector on the left wing of the 5ème Armée was taken over by the newly-created XXXXIIIème Corps d'Armée de Forteresse.

Not much happened after May 10 except for the 75mm turret of Block 2 firing from time to time at German troops showing too much activity: on May 12 and 13, when German elements encircled French advance posts near the Col de Litschhof and on May 20 when Four-à-Chaux and Hochwald fired at troops reported near Climbach.

The raising and lowering of the 75mm turret on Block 2 is demonstrated to visitors. From the outside, the operation is absolutely silent, and it is an almost magical sight to see the

huge steel dome elevating, turning and retracting without a sound. This particular turret received a Stuka attack on June 19, ending up obstructed by the debris thrown up by the bombing.

After the withdrawal ordered by the 5ème Armée, the interval troops and elements of the fortress troops, the latter organised into a Division de Marche Senselme, started to withdraw on June 13, leaving the fortress and casemate garrisons on their own. On June 15 the troops remaining within the fortifications passed under the command of Commandant Pierre Fabre, the commander of the Grand-Hohekirkel fortress. Reorganisation involved the commander of Four-à-Chaux fortress, Commandant Exbrayat, taking over the whole of the Langensoultzbach area, from the Grunenthal casemates, in the west, to the Schmelzbach-Ouest casemate, in the east, about eleven kilometres of front.

On June 16 the 215. Infanterie-Division was ordered to prepare to break through the 'thinly fortified woods between Bitche and Lembach'. The division had great difficulty in bringing its artillery into position in this wooded and hilly terrain, particularly the heavies. Reconnaissance patrols were sent to probe the lines of casemates, one of them made itself too conspicious at the Col de Gunsthal that morning and attracted a barrage from the 75mm turret of Block 2, and events took a similar turn the following day.

After Pétain's radio broadcast on June 17 Commandant Exbrayat ordered the confiscation of all the radio sets in the fortress to prevent the spread of rumours and false information. The orders were approved by everyone and readily complied with.

On June 18 some 7.5cm FK 16 howitzers were brought forward north-west of the Lembach and started to fire at Block 5. Block 1 returned fire, its 135mm blowing the daring battery sky high, and in the afternoon the 75mm and 135mm of Hochwald-Ouest lent a hand and plastered the Sauer valley north-west of Lembach.

The main German attack started early on June 19, aimed at breaking the lines of casemates and blockhouses between Windstein and Lembach. At 6.40 a.m. a look-out in Block 5 reported an artillery observation balloon floating at a height of about 300 metres north of Lembach and powerful German artillery started to hammer the casemates to the west. For two hours the shells exploded all over the French positions, which were by then hidden under a dense layer of smoke and dust, and the Stukas which arrived at about 9.00 a.m. and bombed the casemates for half an hour added to the destruction. The Stosstrupp of the 215. Infanterie-Division emerged from cover as soon as the last bomb had exploded and launched an assault on the casemates before the defenders were able to fully recover from the commotion created by the bombing.

The defenders fought back and the 135mm, 75mm and 81mm rounds fired at the assault waves by Four-à-Chaux added casualties but the telephone lines linking the casemates to the fortress had been cut by the bombardment and the casemates and blockhouses were quite alone and fell one after another.

Proven in battle — the demise of the impregnable Maginot Line quickly exploited by the advertising department at Junkers in the August 6 edition of *Der Adler*.

At about 10.15 a.m. the Stukas were back and attacked the Lembach fortress just west of the town. Another raid went in at about 12.15 a.m., this time on Four-à-Chaux, its Block 6 being the main target receiving several near hits. The 75mm of Hochwald loosed off above Four-à-Chaux and this improvised anti-aircraft fire was convincing enough to force the Stukas away. When a bomb exploded nearby, the men inside the fortress experienced the dreadful sensation of their huge concrete blocks pitching like a ship riding at anchor. The sight that greeted them as they climbed back into the observation posts at the end of the bombardment was even more impressive: one bomb had exploded on Block 6, another had blown a large crater in front of the block, smashing the radio antenna supports, blowing up elements of the embrasures inside the block and damaging both the 47mm gun and the Reibel twin mountings.

Down below, the roof of the powerhouse fifteen metres or so beneath the surface was cracked and small pieces of paint and cement which had fallen from the roof covered the equipment. However the damage looked worse than it really was and the men were quite confident when another Stuka attack came in at about 2.00 p.m., aiming this time at Block 2 and its annoying 75mm turret. The block was shaken by the explosions and when the Stukas left half an hour later there were huge craters all around it and the turret was obstructed, covered under a thick layer of earth. Two slim men slipped outside through the opening of the JM cupola to clear away the earth and after an hour's strenuous shovelling the turret was back in commission and was immediately elevated to fire 40 shells at Mattstall where German troops were reported.

At about 3.15 p.m. the Stukas were back and turned their attention to Hochwald-Ouest, whose 75mm of Block 12 were also firing to stem the advance of the 215. Infanterie-Division, and Four-à-Chaux returned the favour

This massive 420mm heavy mortar, in German parlance a 42cm Haubitze (t), of schwere Artillerie-Abteilung 800, was emplaced near Oberotterbach, a dozen kilometres north of Schoenenbourg. This weapon opened fire at 4.15 p.m. on June 21, lobbing 14 one-tonne missiles at the fortress and again on June 22 with another 14-shell salvo with two more on the 23rd. Fortunately the picture had been accurately captioned by Adam Heumüller, the German gunner who took it in 1940.

when the 75mm turret of Block 2 fired anti-aircraft fashion at the Stukas. On June 19, Four-à-Chaux fired 970 rounds of 75mm, 260 rounds of 135mm and 450 rounds of 81mm.

To the west, the casemates had fought back throughout the afternoon but hammered by repeated Stuka attacks and fired at from close range by 37mm Pak 35/36 aiming at the embrasures they had been forced to submit one after another. All the casemates and blockhouses from Grafenweiher to Markbach had been captured, the line had been forced and the 215. Infanterie-Division had almost a clear run and its advance elements were soon at Woerth and reached Haguenau at 8.00 p.m. Contact was soon made with the leaders of 257. Infanterie-Division coming from the west, having skirted south of the fortress line after the breakthrough in the Sarre gap, and reaching Nieder-bronn in the afternoon.

On June 21 the right wing of the Vosges Fortified Sector was all but cut off from the sector commander, Commandant Fabre, at Grand-Hohekirkel; consequently, the Four-à-Chaux and Lembach fortresses, and the twenty or so casemates and blockhouses still fighting in the area, were then placed under the command of Haguenau.

That same day German envoys from the 257. Infanterie-Division approached the Glasbronn casemate under a white flag and nearly succeeded in convincing the garrison that the armistice had been signed. In the nearest casemate at Biesenberg, Lieutenant Camille Foll learnt of this and asked Grand-Hohekirkel to send a salvo of 75mm on the Glasbronn casemate as a response, which was done at once. On June 22 the Germans tried the same persuasion at the Biesenberg casemate but were told in no uncertain words to 'go away'! A company assaulted the casemate from a nearby wood in the afternoon but the attack was repulsed with heavy casualties by the return fire.

June 24 saw Four-à-Chaux fire its final round when at 5.00 p.m. the 75mm turret of Block 2 sent a last salvo southwards at the road between Woerth and Soultz.

After the battle: inspecting the damage. This is the crater formed by the explosion of a 420mm shell (a calibre of some 16 inches) alongside Block 3 at Schoenenbourg. Although blasting a crater 12 metres deep, the reinforced concrete suffered only minor cracks.

A bomb dropped by a Stuka has blasted this hole alongside Block 4, but once again damage to the casemate was only superficial. In spite of all the bombing and shelling, Schoenenbourg remained in action right up until the end.

HAGUENAU

The Haguenau Fortified Sector was responsible for the frontier from the Climbach sector, a few kilometres west of Wissembourg, to Stattmatten, on the Rhine, about eighteen kilometres east of Haguenau. With its defence following the terrain at the juncture of the Vosges mountains and the Alsace plain, the sector's only two fortresses were on the left wing, on the final outcrop of the high ground, the protection of the plain continuing eastwards across this area with 39 CORF casemates, a number of them built as couples. There were also fifteen shelters and two observatories. The huge Hochwald fortress — with its eleven battle blocks, three entrance blocks and nine casemates — was on the left wing of the sector, with Schoenenbourg a few kilometres to the east, the last fortress before the plain.

During the phoney war the Hochwald fortress had the honour of firing the Maginot Line's first shots in anger when the 75mm turret of Block 7b at Hochwald-Est fired in support of an infantry attack in the Schweigen sector during the night of September 8, 1939.

In May 1940 the Haguenau Fortified Sector was under the command of the XIIème Corps d'Armée of the 5ème Armée and the Schoenenbourg fortress was commanded by Commandant Martial Reynier.

They had occupied the fortress just ten days before war broke out and the 75mm turrets fired their first trial rounds, twenty shells per turret, on September 10. At the end of January 1940 it was the turn of the 81mm turret on Block 5 to test its mortars. In March a 120mm artillery section was brought forward to take up positions above the battle blocks, and gunners from the 81mm turret were sent to serve the two guns.

Left: Similar treatment from Ju 87s meted out to Hochwald, but Block 6's three 75mm howitzers remained unscathed. *Above:* The same block today with guns removed and crater infilled.

Equally indestructible — the resolve of its commanders. This is Lieutenant-Colonel Henri Miconnet of Hochwald.

Another bomb caused superficial damage to the anti-tank ditch at Hochwald-Ouest. In the background, Casemates 2 and 3 — an area completely covered with trees today, making a comparison photograph meaningless.

Left: The scarred landscape above Block 14 caused by repeated dive-bombing looked impressive, but the forts proved pretty invulnerable to aerial bombardment. In this picture we can see the 135mm turret on the right virtually unscathed. (The cupola

in the foreground is for observation.) In the background lie Blocks 12 and 13. *Right:* Foliage has now encroached on the hillside, restricting the view. Hochwald is another of the preserved fortresses of the Maginot Line open to visitors.

On June 20 storm-troopers of the 246. Infanterie-Division assaulted Oberroedern-Nord, another of the casemates in the Haguenau Fortified Sector. The battle raged all day, five of the attackers being subsequently buried in a crater behind the casemate.

Silent, windswept and mouldering — if only walls could tell their story of brave men's deeds.

On the other side of the Oberroedern-Nord casemate — the side facing the enemy — another German soldier killed that Thursday was buried amidst the barbed wire entanglements.

On May 14 the fortress fired its first rounds in anger, its 75mm howitzers aiming at German movements on either side of Wissembourg. The return fire was not long in coming, and during the evening a 280mm railway gun sent a dozen shells from Bundenthal, out of range of the fortress's guns. These caused no real damage, neither did the twenty shells that were fired on the afternoon of May 15, which blew holes in the anti-tank barrier of sunken railway lines and the barbed wire and blew some large craters on top of the fortress. The 280mm having moved away to attend to another target, a battery of 105mm howitzers had started shelling the fortress from the Wissembourg area on May 16, but these German gunners soon learnt how suicidal it was to attempt this within range of the fortress's guns.

German shelling lessened in the days that followed and the 75mm turrets were occasionally turned to fire at a Henschel Hs 126 spotter aircraft which droned over the fortress. Although they had never been conceived for such a role — and the chances of the emplacements hitting a moving target in the air were almost nil — this anti-aircaft fire was, nevertheless, convincing enough to force the aircraft away, and it was a measure adopted repeatedly by many of the fortresses in May and June. Shelling of the fortress resumed on May 26 with 150mm howitzers joining in, and a soldier on watch in a GFM cupola on Block 5 was killed when the cupola received a direct hit.

During the night of May 27 the fortress was re-supplied with 8,000 rounds of 75mm. On June 4 one of the two 120mm guns on top of the fort was destroyed when a shell exploded prematurely in the barrel; eight gunners were wounded, one of them dying two days later from his wounds. On June 8 another two 120mm howitzers were brought forward near the entrances, making three guns in position outside the fortress. However by June 13 the only one of these that was still capable of being fired was disabled when its carriage failed.

On June 12, following the withdrawal order issued to the 5ème Armée, the interval troops and part of the infantry in the fortress, the latter organised into Division de Marche Regard, started pulling out. Lieutenant-Colonel Jacques Schwartz took command of the troops remaining in the fortresses and casemates of the Haguenau sector and established his command post in the Hochwald fortress. On June 15, the 246. Infanterie-Division attacked in the Hoffen sector a few kilometres east of Schoenenbourg, and the fortress's 75mm turrets responded. As the expenditure of 75mm shells went up, the fortress commander sent out parties to recover supplies left behind in the depots when the interval troops had withdrawn.

On June 19 Hochwald and Schoenenbourg had fired nearly 3,000 shells to repulse the German attacks, the former on the west at the 215. Infanterie-Division trying to break through the

Vosges sector, the latter to the southeast at the 246. Infanterie-Division; of these nearly 1,000 had been fired at bombers attacking the fortresses.

The Germans launched a powerful attack on June 20 and late in the afternoon several groups of Stukas dive-bombed the battle blocks of Schoenenbourg and the casemates in the Hoffen sector. Supported by the 75mm turrets of Schoenenbourg and the 135mm turrets of Hochwald, the casemates at Hoffen, Aschbach and Oberroedern blasted the storm troops which had approached the casemates under the cover of smoke and dust left by smoke shells and explosions. After a whole day of battle the Germans withdrew, having lost about 30 men killed in the attack, of which 18 were found in the near vicinity of the casemates.

At Schoenebourg the bombing had succeeded only in plastering the turrets with earth. This was cleared during the night and the 75mm turrets resumed firing at the German troops the next day. On June 22 the Stukas came back

Like its neighbours at Hoffen and Oberroedern, Casemate East at Aschbach suffered intense shelling although it remained in French hands right up until the end.

Schoenenbourg after the battle. The guns silent, one of the embrasures of Block 6 makes a striking comparison from the era of war . . . to the days of peace.

twice in the morning and again towards evening. When the last of the Stukas departed, they had dropped about 60 heavy bombs on the fortress but had caused no great damage. One direct hit on Block 6 caused some cracks and brought a few chunks of concrete down on the staircase; one hit near Block 1 had twisted a Reibel JM mounting; another had partially exposed Block 4, and a third had blasted earth about a metre thick on to Block 5.

The heavy artillery of schwere Artillerie-Abteilung 800, which possessed two batteries of 420mm heavy mortars and one of 355mm howitzers, was now brought in to deal with Schoenenbourg. The former, which had been installed at Oberotterbach, just north of Wissembourg, opened up at 4.15 p.m. on June 21 by lobbing fourteen one-tonne shells at the fortress, soon joined by the 355mm howitzer. For safety's sake the 75mm turrets were kept retracted while the heavy shells crashed down outside. However, while they were elevating they came under direct fire from 88mm Flak and 105mm howitzers. A hit on Block 3 jammed the turret from retracting fully, so a patrol was sent outside that night to cut away the obstructing piece of metal.

The 420mm opened up again on June 22 and again the following day with the usual 14-shell salvo, and fired another in the evening. Block 3 was hit by one of these great concrete-busters, a few cracks appearing inside but nothing worse. Things were more serious for the 81mm turret of Block 5 as it was hit when firing and could not be fully retracted.

Schoenenbourg fired again at German concentrations on June 24 but its turrets immediately came under violent counter-fire from the batteries of 105mm and 150mm howitzers. When the armistice brought all firing to an end, Schoenenbourg had fired 15,802 rounds of 75mm and 672 rounds of 81mm: more than 80 percent of them between June 14 and the end.

The end in the Vosges

On June 17 the advanced elements of 29. Infanterie-Division (mot) of Gruppe Guderian reached the Swiss border, thus closing the ring around the stricken Groupe d'Armées No. 2.

Along the Maginot Line front held by Groupe d'Armées No. 2, the first stage of the successive moves to withdraw the three armies, amounting to almost half a million men, back behind the Marne-Rhine Canal by June 17 had begun well. By June 14 — Day Two of the operation — the 3ème Armée of Général Condé had drawn back to Metz and was maintaining contact with the 2ème Armée of Groupe d'Armées No. 4 on its left. On June 15, 3ème Armée held a line from Metz to Sarre-Union, south of Sarralbe; 5ème Armée from there to Saverne, and 8ème Armée at the foot of the Vosges, facing the Alsace plain.

To the west, in the centre of the Line, the front held by Groupe d'Armées No. 4 was falling apart after the breakthrough of the panzers, with Gruppe von Kleist advancing along an axis Troyes-Auxerre and Gruppe Guderian along an axis Chaumont-Besançon. The French High Command, which had already thrown in its last reserve division, placed what was left of the 6ème

Monday, June 17 was Britain's first day alone, and Churchill's broadcast that afternoon followed a Cabinet meeting at which the over-riding aspect was now to prevent the French fleet falling into German hands. That same day Gruppe Guderian was transferred from Heeresgruppe A to Heeresgruppe C whereupon Guderian's two corps turned eastwards to complete the encirclement of the three French armies. *Right:* By the evening of June 18, 2. Panzer-Division was nearing Remiremont having advanced more than 100 kilometres in 24 hours.

> *The news from France is very bad, and I grieve for the gallant French people who have fallen into this terrible misfortune. Nothing will alter our feelings towards them or our faith that the genius of France will rise again. What has happened in France makes no difference to our actions and purpose. We have become the sole champions now in arms to defend the world cause. We shall do our best to be worthy of this high honour. We shall defend our Island home, and with the British Empire we shall fight on unconquerable until the curse of Hitler is lifted from the brows of mankind. We are sure that in the end all will come right.*
>
> WINSTON CHURCHILL, BROADCAST, JUNE 17, 1940

Armée on the left under the command of Groupe d'Armées No. 3, while on the right wing the 2ème Armée was given to Groupe d'Armées No. 2.

The 3ème Armée and 5ème Armée were now established behind the Marne-Rhine Canal. By now, most of the 'march divisions' formed by the fortified sectors of the Maginot Line had succeeded in pulling back but all contact had now been lost with the garrisons of the fortresses still fighting to the north. His rear threatened by the advance of Gruppe Guderian, the commander of Groupe d'Armées No. 2, Général Prételat, obtained Général Georges' approval to continue the withdrawal to an intermediate position running from Saint-Mihiel to the Belfort gap. He also moved his command post from Pont-de-Pany near Dijon to Montmorot near Lons-le-Saunier. The trap was fast closing behind him and Général Emile Laure, the commander of the 8ème Armée, ordered his southern XXXXVème Corps d'Armée to advance southwards and try to fight a way open for the army group's withdrawal.

However by now it was too late. On June 16 Gruppe Guderian had reached Gray and Besançon and Gruppe von Kleist was approaching Dijon and every avenue of retreat for the entire French forces fighting east of the Argonne was soon to be cut. On June 17 the advance elements of Gruppe Guderian reached the Swiss border at Pontarlier, so closing the ring around the stricken Groupe d'Armées No. 2.

On June 17, OKH switched command of the 16. Armee and Gruppe Guderian from Heeresgruppe A to Heeresgruppe C. Its commander, Generaloberst Wilhelm von Leeb, had now all the means at his disposal to crush the French armies surrounded in the Vosges. As noted in the war diary of Heeresgruppe C, 'orders for the entrapment of the enemy are: Guderian on the west, 16. Armee on the north-west, 1. Armee on the north-east and 7. Armee on the east'. Accordingly, Guderian ordered his two corps to turn north-eastwards: from the Vesoul area the XXXXI. Armeekorps was despatched towards Epinal and from the Besançon region the XXXIX. Armeekorps was sent towards Belfort. The 29. Infanterie-Division (mot) was to move along the border to the bend in the frontier near Porrentruy and to clear the Jura.

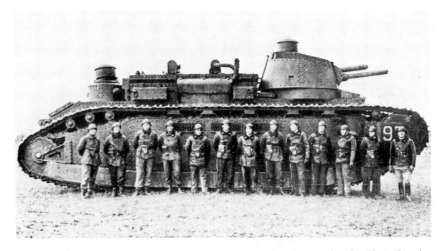

Four days earlier it had been Day One in the withdrawal operation for 3ème Armée. On June 13 the 51ème B.C.C. was ordered southwards with its FCM-2Cs — heavyweight legacies from the First World War. Each tank, armed with a 75mm gun and four machine guns, weighed 70 tonnes and required a crew of 12 to operate it. Loading each monster onto its specially-designed, twin rail bogie took two hours. *Above:* The 51ème B.C.C. possessed seven of the tanks — this is No. 97 'Normandie' photographed with its crew before the war. *Below:* Ready for rail transportation, it came to a sticky end in the little village of Meuse (five kilometres or so downstream from the source of the river of the same name), 20 kilometres north-east of Langres.

What happened was that the two trains got as far as Meuse only to find that the track ahead had been cut during the frequent attacks by the Luftwaffe. It proved impossible to unload the heavy tanks in the confined space alongside the track at the small station and, with German troops reported in the vicinity, the battalion commander, Colonel Georges Fournet, decided to sabotage the tanks, and withdraw. *Below left:* No. 98 'Berry' as a German photographer found it later in June. *Below right:* Meuse as found by Jean Paul 50 years later. The church tower on the left provides the link between 1940 and 1990.

While events on the battlefield were about to reach their foregone conclusion, the wheels of government were turning towards the inevitable end. On Sunday evening (June 16), de Gaulle arrived in France with the text of the proposed Declaration of Union (page 545) but by now it was too late. When a vote of confidence went 14 to 10 against Reynaud, he resigned and was replaced by Maréchal Philippe Pétain, Paul Baudouin becoming the new Foreign Minister.

On the evening of Monday the 17th, German forces reached the ancient fortress town of Belfort, yet the French stubbornly held onto the forts. It was a stance typical of the tradition of the town which had withstood a 104-day siege in the Franco-Prussian War and had been successfully held 45 years later by the French in the First World War. When, next morning, the garrison still refused to surrender, the 1. Panzer-Division organised a Kampfgruppe to deal with the situation. Guderian recalled how 'the first fort to be captured was Basses-Perches, followed by Hautes-Perches and the Citadel'. *Left:* This Renault FT-17 was photographed blocking entry through the Porte de Brisach in the Rue des Mobiles de 1870.

While Gruppe Guderian was moving south of Groupe d'Armées No. 2, the 1. Armee was pressing on in the north. Leutnant Hans Häufler of Bau-Bataillon 158 pictured another Renault FT-17 abandoned on the spot where it had fought its last fight — in the middle of a pontoon bridge it was controlling. This picture was taken at Lutzelbourg, ten kilometres west of Saverne, looking south from the 'island' between the canal (behind the photographer), and the River Zorn parallel to it.

On the evening of June 17, the Marne-Rhine Canal defence line behind which the French had successfully withdrawn with the 3ème Armée on the left and the 5ème Armée on the right, was already breached fifty kilometres east of Nancy at Lagarde, where the 1ère Division d'Infanterie Polonaise had proved unable to hold the weight of the 268. Infanterie-Division. Backed by two companies of Renault R-35s of the 20ème B.C.C., the Poles counter-attacked but failed to dislodge the German engineers who worked all night at rebuilding the bridge over the canal.

The last battle of Groupe d'Armées No. 2 started on June 18 when the 1. Armee attacked and forced the canal line. The French fought back resolutely and the day was costly for both sides on this front but the outcome was inevitable as there were by then some ten German divisions arrayed along the canal. In the French rear, Guderian made swift progress that day, his 8. Panzer-Division reaching Charmes, the 6. Panzer-Division arriving at Epinal, the 2. Panzer-Division at Remiremont and the 1. Panzer-Division at Belfort.

The previous morning, Général Prételat had tried to reach Belfort to rejoin his armies but his small convoy, two cars and a dozen motor cyclists, had had to turn back near Pontarlier when it was apparent that the town was already in German hands. In the absence of the army group commander, on that same day the High Command gave overall control of the trapped 3ème, 5ème and 8ème Armées to Général Condé, the 3ème Armée's commander.

On June 19, the canal line was broken. To the west Nancy, an open town since the morning of June 18 on orders from Général Condé, was abandoned when a vanguard group of the 71. Infanterie-Division, under the command of Oberst Hans-Karl von Scheele, made a surprise entry and reached the centre of the town. To the east the 7. Armee was pressing on to force the Vosges passes defended by elements of the 54ème Division d'Infanterie: the 557. Infanterie-Division aiming at the Col de Sainte-Marie, the 317. Infanterie-

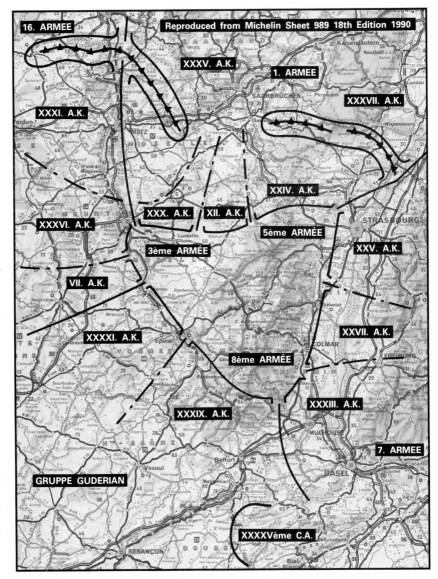

The situation in the Vosges on Tuesday, June 18. Gruppe Guderian is advancing on the pocket from the south-west, with the 1. Armee in the north and 7. Armee to the east. There would be no escape for the French trapped within. To the south, the XXXXVème Corps d'Armée was isolated against the Swiss border and on June 20 the French High Command authorised the corps commander, Général Henri Daille, to cross into Switzerland. Up north, two long stretches of the Maginot Line were surrounded but resisted until the armistice forced them to surrender.

Regrettably, even at this late stage in the campaign when victory was well assured, German behaviour towards their defeated enemy was still far from magnanimous. On many occasions in the Vosges, just as we have seen before in the north, surrendering French soldiers fell victim to summary justice, whether charges such as the use of illegal ammunition were trumped up or not. On June 17 culprits in 1. Panzer-Division executed seven soldiers of the 61ème R.R. who had just surrendered at Sainte-Suzanne near Montbéliard, and two days later men of the 6. Panzer-Division were guilty of a similar offence against ten soldiers of the 55ème B.M. at Dounoux, just north of Epinal. Then on June 20 troops of the 198. Infanterie-Division behaved even worse in Domptail (ten kilometres west of Epinal), shooting many men of the 146ème R.I.F. as they gave themselves up. Oberleutnant August Schrempf was identified as one of the officers of the unit responsible for the shooting of six men in front of a barn and twenty others in a nearby meadow, and he was sentenced to death, in absentia, for complicity in murder by the French in 1959. Later he was traced as living in Stuttgart but was never extradited for trial.

I spoke the other day of the colossal military disaster which occurred when the French High Command failed to withdraw the Northern Armies from Belgium at the moment when they knew that the French Front was decisively broken at Sedan and on the Meuse. This delay entailed the loss of 15 or 16 French divisions and threw out of action for the critical period the whole of the British Expeditionary Force. Our Army and 120,000 French troops were indeed rescued by the British Navy from Dunkirk, but only with the loss of their cannon, vehicles and modern equipment. This loss inevitably took some weeks to repair, and in the first two of those weeks the battle in France has been lost.

When we consider the heroic resistance made by the French Army against heavy odds in this battle and the enormous losses inflicted upon the enemy and the evident exhaustion of the enemy, it may well be that those 25 divisions of the best trained and best equipped troops might have turned the scale. However, Général Weygand had to fight without them.

Only three British divisions or their equivalent were able to stand in the line with their French comrades. They have suffered severely, but they have fought well. We sent every man we could to France as fast as we could re-equip and transport their formation. I am not reciting these facts for the purpose of recrimination. That I judge to be utterly futile and even harmful. We cannot afford it. I recite them in order to explain why it was we did not have, as we could have had, between 12 and 14 British divisions fighting in the line in this great battle instead of only three.

I now put all this aside. I put it on the shelf from where future historians, when they have time, will select their documents to tell that story. We have to think of the future and not of the past . . .

We do not yet know what will happen in France, or whether France's resistance will be prolonged, both in France and in the French Empire overseas. The French government will be throwing away great opportunities and casting away their future if they do not continue the war in accordance with their treaty obligations, from which we have not felt able to release them.

The House will have read the historic declaration in which, at the desire of many Frenchmen and of our own hearts, we have proclaimed our willingness to conclude, at the darkest hour of French history, a union of common citizenship. However matters may go in France, or with the French government, or with another French government, we in this island and in the British Empire will never lose our sense of comradeship with the French people. If we are now called upon to endure what they have suffered we shall emulate their courage and, if final victory rewards our toils, they shall share the gains — aye, and freedom shall be restored to all. We abate nothing of our just demands — Czechs, Poles, Norwegians, Dutch, Belgians, all who have joined their causes to our own, shall be restored.

What Général Weygand called the Battle of France is over. I expect that the 'Battle of Britain' is about to begin.

WINSTON CHURCHILL,
HOUSE OF COMMONS, JUNE 18, 1940

Meanwhile in England, at the very moment on Sunday evening, that the Reynaud government was ousted, Churchill was preparing to return to France, via ship from Southampton, for a meeting at sea with the French Prime Minister to discuss the proposed union. He was actually sitting on board his train at Victoria station when news arrived that the French government had fallen. On Tuesday he addressed the House of Commons and later broadcast the same speech to the nation.

De Gaulle, who had returned to France on the evening of June 16, learnt of the change of government as he stepped from the aircraft at Bordeaux and he had lost no time in deciding his own position. The next morning he left with Major-General Sir Edward Spears, British liaison officer, in the same British aircraft that had brought him the previous evening. After a stop at Jersey for refuelling, he was in London that afternoon. The next day, he broadcast over the BBC. The new French government promptly ordered him to return and on August 2, a military tribunal at Clermont-Ferrand condemned him to death for desertion.

The generals who for many years have commanded the French armies have formed a Government. That Government, alleging that our armies have been defeated, has opened negotiations with the enemy to put an end to the fighting.

We certainly have been, and still are, submerged by the mechanical strength of the enemy, both on land and in the air. The tanks, the aeroplanes, the tactics of the Germans astounded our generals to such an extent that they have been brought to the pass which they are in today.

But has the last word been said? Has all hope disappeared? Is the defeat final? No. Believe me, I speak with knowledge and I tell you that France is not lost. The same methods which have brought about our defeat can quite well one day bring victory.

For France is not alone. She is not alone — she is not alone. She has a vast empire behind her. She can unite with the British Empire, which holds the seas and is continuing the struggle. She can utilise to the full, as England is doing, the vast industrial resources of the United States.

This war is not limited to the unhappy territory of our country. The war has not been decided by the Battle of France. This war is a world war. In spite of all our mistakes, all our deficiencies, all our sufferings, there are in the universe sufficient means to enable us one day to crush our enemies. Shattered today by mechanical force, we shall be able to conquer in the future by stronger mechanical force. The fate of the world depends on it.

I, Général de Gaulle, now in London — I invite all French officers and men who are on British soil, or who may arrive here with or without their arms, I invite all the engineers and the skilled workmen of the armament industries who are now on British soil, or who may arrive here, to get into touch with me. Whatever happens the flame of French resistance must not and shall not be extinguished.

GÉNÉRAL CHARLES DE GAULLE,
BROADCAST FROM LONDON,
JUNE 18, 1940

Division at the Col du Bonhomme and the 221. Infanterie-Division at the Col de la Schlucht. The ring around the trapped armies was firmly closed when the 1. Panzer-Division advancing from Belfort met up at Montreux with elements of the 7. Armee advancing from Mulhouse.

The next day the French forces were cut into two smaller pockets when the 8. Panzer-Division coming from the south linked up with the 258. Infanterie-Division of the 1. Armee near Charmes. The French High Command authorised

Général Henri Daille, commander of the XXXXVème Corps d'Armée now isolated on the Swiss border, to move his troops into Switzerland if, in the last resort, they could not force their way out.

In the days that followed, the Germans continued their advance, fragmenting the trapped French armies until they were reduced to pockets of some 25,000 to 50,000 men, each of which were then approached and induced to surrender piecemeal. In most cases, the Germans tried to lure the

local French commanders, who had no contact with their superiors, into believing that an armistice had already been signed, or that a surrender had been agreed to by their army command. They drew attention to Pétain's broadcast that 'France must cease fighting' and promised 'honourable terms' and 'honneurs de la guerre', mainly to persuade French officers not to order the destruction of equipment. On June 22 the High Command gave Général Condé permission to surrender the armies under his command.

Advancing from the Vesoul area, the XXXXI. Armeekorps had closed on the south-west and on June 18, the 6. Panzer-Division had reached Epinal. *Left:* This PzKpfw 35(t) was disabled by three shots from a 25mm anti-tank gun of the 46ème G.R.D.I. on June 19 just as it was about to start crossing the Pont de Pierre, the only bridge left intact in Epinal. The tank commander, Oberfeldwebel Heinrich Krühsmann, escaped with two of his men, though all were badly wounded, but the fourth crewman, Unteroffizier Anton Dröge was killed. *Right:* Epinal, Quai Louis Lapicque, fifty years on.

Above: **Leutnant Otto Dolimar took this picture of a German anti-tank crew from the 6. Gebirgs-Division positioned to stop any escape attempt, however hopeless, by any of the** thousands of the 3ème and 5ème Armées trapped west of Saint-Dié. *Below:* **We found that the photograph had been taken on the N420 at La Bolle, just west of the village.**

The VIème Corps d'Armée of the 3ème Armée, its fighting value reduced to about five battalions, had been overwhelmed near Charmes on June 20. Général Condé himself was trapped west of Saint-Dié with about 50,000 men of both the 3ème and 5ème Armées; with him was his own staff and those of the XIIème and XXème Corps d'Armée. Pressed by Oberst Ferdinand Schörner, the commander of the 6. Gebirgs-Division, who rejected the idea of each side remaining where they were until an armistice was signed, he threatened an all-out attack unless Condé agreed to surrender. This he did at 3.00 p.m. on June 22. He had signed as the commander of 3ème Armée and acting commander of both 5ème and 8ème Armées for 'the troops he was still able to command,' but by this astute wording both Général Jean Flavigny of the XXIème Corps d'Armée and Général Fernand Lescanne of the XXXXIIIème Corps d'Armée were left out and thus remained free to fight on and eventually agree better terms.

Behind the Moselle, to the south-east of Toul, Général René Dubuisson, previously in charge of the defences in the Verdun area and now the commander of Groupement Dubuisson, had nearly 70,000 men under his command. These were elements of eight divisions, mostly from the XXXXIIème Corps d'Armée and XXIème Corps d'Armée and the Corps d'Armée Colonial. Groupement Dubuisson was soon split into two main pockets, one to the south near Vaudemont containing the XXIème Corps d'Armée and the Corps d'Armée Colonial, under Général Flavigny. Faced with a hopeless situation, Général Dubuisson decided upon talks with the Germans and dispatched an envoy on the evening of June 21 without consulting Général Flavigny. A document was signed by the envoy, Colonel René Cuzin, on June 22 at the headquarters of Höheres Kommando z.b.V. XXXVI for the group's surrender next morning. When Général Dubuisson read what it contained, he wrote to Generalleutnant Hans Feige to protest at some of the terms to no avail.

The XIIIème Corps d'Armée and XXXXIVème Corps d'Armée of the 8ème Armée surrendered near Gérardmer on June 22. The army commander, Général Laure, was captured at his

The encircled French troops were nominally under the command of Général Condé of 3ème Armée and he sent a request to the commander of the 6. Gebirgs-Division to ask if he would agree to keep the status quo until the armistice came into effect. Oberst Ferdinand Schörner refused, threatening an immediate attack unless the men under Condé's command were surrendered forthwith. *Left:* Here Schörner is seen with General Karl von Prager, commanding XXV. Armeekorps, on the Rue Stanislas in Saint-Dié on June 23 — the day after Général Condé had surrendered with upwards of 50,000 of his men. Both Germans wear the Pour le Mérite from the First World War.

headquarters near La Bresse that day, as were the staff of the 5ème Armée and its commander, Général Bourret.

What remained of the 5ème Armée, the XXXXIIIème Corps d'Armée was isolated with two weary fortress divisions on the Donon plateau. Early on June 23 Général Lescanne heard from a French officer sent by the Germans as a mediator that an armistice had been signed. Having no contact with his superiors, he was unable to check but, even after talking with the German envoys for most of the day, he refused to sign anything. Nor did he succumb to the fullsome praise for the stand his troops had made, from the commander of the 60. Infanterie-Division, Generalmajor Friedrich-Georg Eberhardt, when he arrived that afternoon. Two more envoys, sent by Heeresgruppe C also arrived that evening. Only next morning, after a heavy air attack was threatened before a resumption of the

fighting, did Général Lescanne agree to put his name to a surrender.

To the south, moving on Besançon with orders to keep the line of retreat open, the XXXXVème Corps d'Armée (8ème Armée) had encountered the XXXIX. Armeekorps on June 17 and the 67ème Division d'Infanterie which had been badly mauled. The remnants, the 2ème Division d'Infanterie Polonaise and the 2ème Brigade de Spahis, had been trapped on the Doubs and had fought back on the Maiche plateau for two days. On the evening of June 19, Général Daille ordered those units which were able to do so to enter Switzerland. Following the order, a regiment of the 2ème Brigade of Spahis, a company of Renault R-35s of the 16ème B.C.C., most of the 2ème Division d'Infanterie Polonaise, but only a few elements of the 67ème Division d'Infanterie, managed to get away that night and the following day.

Another stand before yet another withdrawal. On June 20 the 1ère Division d'Infanterie Polonaise was holding positions north of Baccarat with the 52ème Division d'Infanterie on its left and the Groupement Dagnan (formed out of elements

withdrawn from the Sarre Fortified Sector) to its right. This 25mm anti-tank gun was successful in halting the leaders of the 75. Infanterie-Division as the vehicles approached down the narrow, tree-lined road just north of Merviller.

The staff of XXXXVème Corps d'Armée also entered Switzerland on June 20 and Général Daille asked for the internment of his troops. Most of the 67ème Division d'Infanterie were trapped west of the Doubs for all bridges had been blown. Unable to escape they fought back until June 23 when they were captured; their commander, Général Henri Boutignon,

Backs against the wall — in this case the frontier of neutral Switzerland. On the evening of June 19, Général Daille, the commander of the XXXXVème Corps d'Armée, ordered those units which were able to do so to cross the border, even though this would inevitably mean internment for the duration. The 7ème Régiment de Spahis, a company of the 16ème B.C.C., most of the 2ème Division d'Infanterie Polonaise, and a few elements of the 67ème Division d'Infanterie, were allowed across under the supervision of the Swiss Army. *Above:* This picture of French soldiers — actually it seems that they were Poles of the 2ème Division d'Infanterie Polonaise — was taken at Goumois on June 20. All such troops were interned until the beginning of 1941. *Below:* Fifty years later all is quiet in the valley of the Doubs.

A sizeable part of their equipment was gathered at the arsenal at Lyss, 20 kilometres west of Berne. This picture of horse-drawn supply carts passing two Renault R-35s of the 1ère

Section (identified as such from the spade insignia on the turret), 2ème Compagnie, 16ème B.C.C., was taken on the road just in front of the arsenal entrance.

who was wounded being taken near Fleury. A few more troops crossed into Switzerland on June 24 and the last fighting units, among them the garrison of the Joux fortress, surrendered the next day. All told, about 42,300 men had entered Switzerland and were interned; among them were about 12,150 Poles and 99 men from the 51st (Highland) Division.

The 'final count' for the 8ème Armée on June 25 was about 2,500 men, most of them belonging to the 105ème D.I.F., isolated on the Vosges, about 1,000 metres up, under the command of Général Pierre Didio, the division's commander. They had weapons and ammunition but food was scarce. They heard of the armistice on the radio and knew that having not laid down their arms, this meant that they would not be taken prisoner. Général Didio waited another day but the weather was now wet and cold and he decided to order his men down into the valley on the morning of June 26. The French naïvely believed that they were not prisoners-of-war and started to discuss with the Germans how they should make for the unoccupied territory in the south of the country. The Germans were not averse

Général Daille and his staff entered Switzerland on June 20 but this picture of him chatting with a Spahi was actually taken at the beginning of 1941, a few days before his men were repatriated to France.

Left: French crews drive into the arsenal before being marched away to hastily-organised internment camps. With German approval, all French troops interned in Switzerland were allowed to return to the unoccupied zone of France (under the control of Pétain's government in Vichy) in January 1941

although their weapons and equipment were sent to Germany. (Some 900 vehicles purchased by the Swiss remained in Switzerland.) Right: Although photography is strictly forbidden in the arsenal today, the Director kindly turned a blind eye for Jean Paul to take this comparison just outside the entrance.

The leading Spahi smiles with relief at the Swiss cameraman as he enters Switzerland. This famed French cavalry corps was created in Algeria in 1834, although in later years it recruited men from the French colonies of Tunisia and Morocco. About 30,000 French and 12,000 Polish soldiers entered Switzerland, together with 5,500 horses.

to stringing them along. They separated the troops from their officers . . . talked on and on about observing the proper honours and proprieties of war . . . at the end of which the French were all made prisoner!

Apart from the troops interned in Switzerland, a large number of men escaped captivity by walking at night across country to eventually reach the unoccupied zone to the south. Many of these were members of the 1ère Divi-sion d'Infanterie Polonaise, which on June 21, on the instructions of the Polish government-in-exile in London, had been ordered by their commander, General Bronislaw Duch, to disperse and try to reach a port and get back to England. A large number succeeded in doing so.

Heeresgruppe C noted proudly that 'the success of the group's attack is greater and larger that any success achieved to date'. A Wehrmacht bulle-tin of June 23 claimed that more than 500,000 men had been captured and announced that 'a considerable booty of weapons and war matériel of every kind, still to be assessed, has fallen into our hands'. Among the prisoners were the 3ème Armée's (and overall) com-mander, Général Charles-Marie Condé, the commander of the 5ème Armée, Général Victor Bourret, and the commander of the 8ème Armée, Général Emile Laure.

More than 2,000 vehicles and 100 artillery pieces were recorded in the inventory by the Swiss authorities. These 75mm AA guns

are temporarily parked in front of the Berne Gate in Morat, 30 kilometres west of Berne, the Federal Capital.

The Final Evacuation

Scorched earth tactics at Brest *(above)* and Saint-Malo *(below)* as the second great evacuation from France gets under way from Cherbourg in the north to Nantes on the Bay of Biscay.

While Admiral James was carrying out Operation 'Aerial' to evacuate what remained of the BEF in France from harbours in Brittany, naval operations to take off all the men and stores that could be cleared from the ports on the Bay of Biscay were entrusted to Admiral Sir Martin Dunbar-Nasmith, the Commander-in-Chief Western Approaches, at Plymouth. Although it was thought that between 40,000 and 60,000 British and Allied troops were converging on Nantes, neither the exact numbers nor the times of arrival were known and the general situation was highly uncertain. Admiral Dunbar-Nasmith had a large concentration of ships available, including the destroyers HMS *Havelock*, HMS *Wolverine* and HMS *Beagle*, four liners, a number of cargo vessels and two Polish ships. These were assembled offshore in Quiberon Bay, ready to evacuate men and stores from Saint-Nazaire and Nantes. As no anti-submarine defences existed this was a risk but no safer anchorage was available.

Embarkation began on June 16 but the first Luftwaffe attacks on the ships in Quiberon Bay caused damage to only one of them, the liner *Franconia*. Over 12,000 troops were evacuated that day and the loading of stores went on all night as additional ships joined the flotilla, including the destroyers HMS *Highlander* and HMS *Vanoc*.

Wing Commander MacFadyen described something of these confused hours at Saint-Nazaire during the night of June 16:

'I gave instructions for my party to sleep in the streets of the docks for that

The greatest tragedy of the entire evacuation, Dunkirk included, and the greatest single loss of life during Blitzkrieg in the West, occured on June 17 off Saint-Nazaire. The 16,243-ton troopship *Lancastria* was a Cunarder which had been launched as the *Tyrrhenia* in 1922 but was taken out of service in 1924 for conversion to cabin class. Dropping the handicap of her awkward name, she reappeared as the White Star liner *Lancastria (left)* and, with the outbreak of hostilities, was pressed into service as a troopship. On the 17th, loaded with upwards of 5,000 men (the exact number has never been determined), she was attacked by the Luftwaffe *(right)* while off the Loire estuary.

night, and unfortunately I was not one to take literal advantage of my own instructions! During the night we were frequently treated to an amazing display of pyrotechnics caused by the discharge of every possible French light firearm at enemy aircraft which must have been quite three times out of range. The danger to personnel in the docks was much greater owing to the law of gravity, and I personally received a portion of the French defences on my steel helmet.

'At 4.30 a.m. the following morning, my party was ready to move off, but I had still received no further instructions. I then noticed that another party had skirted mine by coming down a side street and was marching towards the pier from which embarkation was to take place. I enquired of a military policeman if he knew of any instructions, and on receiving a negative reply I also marched my party to the pier. On arrival at the pier, I discovered that the last 100 yards or so were completely packed with troops and that nobody was present in charge. I halted my party a short distance from the mass of troops in order to have some area for dispersion if necessary, but it was necessary to spread part of my party right across the pier to prevent other troops passing us. Once again I felt considerable anxiety in case of enemy air action, as personnel at the end of the pier could have been simply mown down by machine-gun fire. At about 5.15 a.m. some responsible army officers appeared but embarkation into the tenders did not commence until after 6.00 a.m. Personnel were conveyed in tenders to ships lying about 10-15 miles to seaward from Saint-Nazaire, and my party was embarked in the *Lancastria* at about 8.00 a.m.'

Operations continued without difficulty, fighters of the RAF patrolling at intervals over the harbours to keep the Luftwaffe away, until 3.45 p.m. when German aircraft appeared and attacked the ships assembled at the mouth of the

Flight Sergeant Chadwick of No. 73 Squadron recounted what happened: 'We boarded the *Lancastria* about half-past six on the morning of the 17th June, after having waited about four hours on the quayside. A nice breakfast was supplied for all who were on board; this was particularly appreciated by all, after the snacks we had recently been having. Troops continued to board the boat until lunchtime; there must have been over 5,000 soldiers and airmen on board; also over 400 crew. Most of the troops were weary and took to their bunks or bed spaces for a rest, but were disturbed at about 15.50 hours by the whine of two bombs which landed in the water about twenty yards off the port side of the ship. Nearly everyone then came on deck; those who had lifebelts brought them with them. We saw the aircraft which had dropped the bombs come over the ship again, so we took what cover we could and hoped for the best. This time the bombs hit the ship, and I fear a number of people were killed outright. The ship very quickly took a list to port, so we all went to the starboard side to help right the ship. This was satisfactory for a few seconds only; then the ship listed heavily to port and her nose went down.'

river. Every available anti-aircraft weapon opened up but the *Lancastria*, with about 5,800 on board, including many of the RAF, was hit. In the fifteen minutes she took to sink, nearly 3,000 perished, survivors being picked up and brought back to England. Among them was Wing Commander MacFadyen.

After another night spent loading, soon after dawn on June 18 ten ships sailed for Plymouth with some 23,000 men on board. Because of alarming reports of the Germans getting close, twelve other ships left in haste at about 11.00 a.m. with the last of the assembled troops. Some 4,000 men, and a large amount of equipment had to be left behind but, when it was realised that the report was a false alarm, six destroyers and thirteen transports were sent to Saint-Nazaire that afternoon but only 2,000 men were found and brought away.

About 10,000 men were evacuated from La Pallice on requisitioned cargo ships on June 18. Some 4,000 Polish troops were brought to England the next day by ships from Admiral Dunbar-Nasmith's flotilla but on June 20 the two ports were virtually empty of men to be taken off and there were now virtually no more British troops left in France.

Meanwhile, many thousands of mainly Polish and Czech troops seeking to leave were taken off including 4,000 Poles from Bordeaux on June 19, among them the President of Poland and many of his Ministers who boarded the destroyer HMS *Berkeley*, while embarkation also continued from Le Verdon at the mouth of the Gironde. Another 19,000 Poles were taken off from the southernmost ports of Bayonne and Saint-Jean-de-Luz.

Officially the last troopship to leave for England sailed at 2.00 a.m. on June 25, operations having been brought to an end by the French in accordance with the armistice, although in the event ships continued to take off troops from French Mediterranean ports until August 14. The final total of troops evacuated from France, including the 338,226 of Operation Dynamo (plus

'Most people on board had commenced to disrobe, realising that the ship was going to sink. Before hardly anyone had left the boat, the enemy aircraft came over the ship again and machine-gunned the troops. After this attack, people began to dive or jump off the side of the ship, which was at that time about seventy feet out of the water. As the ship listed more and more to port, many slid down the ropes and the sides of the boat into the water, but unfortunately chairs and other articles were thrown to the people in the water to act as rafts, and actually did more harm than good, as they struck the heads of those who were in the water. As the lifeboats and rafts moved away from our ship, enemy aircraft again came and machine-gunned these unfortunate people. I sat on the side of the ship and stripped off everything but my trousers, and waited a little longer, until I could just spring into the water from the ship's side. For about fifty yards I swam in oil which had come from the *Lancastria*, and then got into clean water. I made for a boat that was about half a mile away, but halfway there I stopped as I saw another enemy aircraft above the boat I was making for, and saw two bombs leaving the aircraft. I remember experiencing a quaking feeling in my stomach, which at the time I could not understand, but later realised must have been caused by the bombs entering the water. My last glimpse of the fated ship was a crowd of men sitting on the keel singing *Roll Out the Barrel*.'

27,936 non-essential troops and casualties evacuated just beforehand) came to 558,032. Of the 191,870 taken off after Dunkirk, 144,171 were British; 24,352 were Polish, 18,246 French, 4,938 Czech and 163 Belgian.

A large amount of equipment and stores were left behind, particularly in the Nantes area, and in a big British

depot in the Gâvre Forest, about forty kilometres north of Nantes, the Germans reported capturing nearly 500,000 artillery shells, among which were 141,300 75mm and 100,300 105mm; more than 30 million rifle and machine gun rounds; 6,000 aircraft bombs — from 50lb to 500lb — and several hundred thousand incendiary bombs.

As the ship had foundered within sight of the shore, help was soon forthcoming. The RAF dropped lifebelts, and the Navy was swiftly on the scene. Eventually, some 2,500 survivors were plucked from the sea and landed in Britain, but the death toll was believed to be nearly 3,000. When Churchill received the awful news during the afternoon, he wrote later that he 'forbade publication', saying that 'the newspapers have got

quite enough disaster for today at least'. He went on to explain that 'I had intended to release the news a few days later, but events crowded upon us so black and so quickly that I forgot to lift the ban.' In fact it was not until July 25 when *The Times* quoted a report in an American newspaper describing the sinking of the *Lancastria* that the Ministry of Information finally announced the loss of the ship.

Since the beginning of June, when the scale of the disaster that loomed ahead was apparent to all, it had become clear that the French fleet, powerful and eager to fight, was to be France's trump card in the continuation of the war. It was also clear that the fleet would be one of the major problems not only between France and Germany, but also between France and Great Britain, in any discussions that came about for an armistice. On June 13, Général Weygand had suggested that all ships of the French Navy be ordered to British ports before opening any discussion with the Germans, in order to prevent them putting forward unacceptable terms concerning the fleet. When it was pointed out to him that the departure of the French squadrons from Toulon or Bizerte would leave North Africa, Corsica and even the southern coast of France exposed to the Italian Navy, the idea was dropped.

When its bases in Brittany were threatened by German forces, the French Navy made a concerted effort to save what it could, ordering all ships away and sinking all those that could not leave. Those which could not reach French bases in Africa or Mediterranean waters were ordered to sail for England. Two elderly warships, *Courbet* and *Paris*, two large destroyers, the *Léopard* and *Triomphant*, eight destroyers, thirteen sloops, seven submarines and about 200 smaller ships reached England before this order was countermanded as a result of the armistice. The Germans seized nothing of value in the Atlantic ports. Most of the French ships in British harbours were boarded by the British on July 3.

Monday June 17 was also the day that Maréchal Philippe Pétain sued for peace. Having given himself 'to France to help her in her hour of misfortune', he took the reins at the worst possible moment . . . to end a catastrophic war . . . to accept German terms . . . to shake hands with Hitler . . . Unfortunately he was soon to find that this was the road to collaboration. This picture was taken of him (left) with Amiral François Darlan, commander of the French Navy, at Toulon later in 1940.

The French fleet was still a potent weapon and Churchill was extremely worried lest it should fall into German hands. He urged in a telegram to Pétain on that Monday morning that England demanded that the ships should sail to England should the French government seek an armistice. By this stage such threats were meaningless, and the majority of the Navy left for French bases in North Africa. (Those unable to make the long journey from the Atlantic ports did sail to England.) However, Churchill was not satisfied that the ships there would not somehow bolster the German war arsenal, and on July 3 the Royal Navy shelled those French ships at Mers-el-Kebir near Oran and boarded those in British ports.

The Alpine Front

The French Alpine troops, and the 'Alpini' (Italian Alpine soldiers) who faced them, were the elite military forces of both sides. This French recce team of an S.E.S. (Section d'Eclaireurs Skieurs, Ski Scout Section) are 'in action' late in 1939.

Since the signing of the Axis pact in 1936 the French Command had been concerned about Italy. At the very beginning of the war Gamelin was convinced, as were most Allied politicians and commanders, that it was necessary to adopt a defensive strategy towards Germany but he was one of those who thought that the Allies could take the offensive against Italy and deal with her first. He was to be disappointed and all offensive plans ruled out when Mussolini hid Italy behind the protective armour of 'non-belligerency'.

After the Allies' declaration of war on Germany, the French forces facing Italy were gradually reduced by a continuous transfer of troops northwards; from the 550,000 men being available to the 6ème Armée on this front in October 1939, this figure had reduced to 206,000 in June 1940. In November 1939, the staff of the 6ème Armée who were responsible for the Alpine front had been moved into reserve in the Bourgogne area and an improvised command staff under Général René Olry had taken over under the name of Armée des Alpes.

A plan had been discussed in March 1940 between the German and Italian staffs which contemplated a force of about twenty Italian divisions on the Rhine sector taking part in Operation 'Grün'. After crossing the river behind German forces, they were to advance southwards in the direction of the Lan-

gres plateau. The Italians were not too happy with this plan, which gave them only a secondary role; the Germans were not either, as they calculated that it would take at least twelve weeks from mobilisation for the Italian divis-

ions to arrive at their starting area in the Oberrhein and in May the idea was dropped. On May 20 Jodl noted in his diary, 'it is better that the Italians attack the Alps front and keep French forces away from the Oberrhein'.

Following the declaration of war in September 1939, contact between French and Italian patrols in the Alps was friendly. Consequently the strength of the Alpine front was gradually reduced as troops were transported to the more vulnerable sectors facing the German threat in the north. This picture was taken in the Mont Cenis Pass in October 1939 as two officers of the Divisione No. 59 'Cagliari' exchange pleasantries with an officer of the 28ème Division d'Infanterie.

A French sentry of the 102ème B.A.F. in Saint-Véran, a small Alpine village only six kilometres from the Italian frontier. It is May 1940 and by now the frontier zone facing Italy had been dangerously denuded, the French relying on sweet-talk with Mussolini and the offer of territory in Africa to keep him from entering the war.

Mussolini waited for an opportunity but was not yet confident enough to move when the Germans attacked in the West on May 10. The capitulation of Belgium made him more courageous, but although bold enough to adopt a more belligerent attitude, he continued to wait even when the French High Command was forced to withdraw forces from the south to reinforce the battered northern front. The French government was aware of this stiffening of the Italian attitude and tried to buy off Mussolini by offering him as much as he could hope to gain by entering the war so late. Proposals involving Jibouti, the Chad and some sort of a condominium in Tunisia were accordingly drafted. The French Cabinet were split, some opposing talks of any kind, others wishing to appeal to the Pope as an intermediary, while some held out for a direct approach, the latter having the approval of Lord Halifax, the British Foreign Secretary, whose proposals for concessions were utterly rejected by the members of Churchill's War Cabinet with the exception of Chamberlain. When a proposal was put to the Italian ambassador in Paris on May 30, the idea of refusing to 'bargain' had triumphed and most of the concrete proposals initially proposed had by now been withdrawn. It was too late anyway, as Mussolini, eager for glory for his country and his régime, was more than ever determined to enter the war now that Italy stood to lose so little in exchange for a seat at the peace table to share the spoils.

On May 31 Mussolini unveiled his plan of action against France to King Victor Emmanuel III and the High Command and also wrote to Hitler telling him that he would declare war on France by June 10 at the latest. He met opposition from all the Italian military chiefs who pleaded that the Italian Army was totally unprepared.

Crown Prince Umberto of Piémont, who Mussolini had placed in command of the army group along the frontier in September 1939, had two armies facing France's now badly weakened Alpine front. From Mont-Blanc to Mont-Viso opposite the XIVème Corps d'Armée was the 4a Armata of Generale Alfredo Guzzoni. With nine infantry divisions, two groups of Alpine troops and one cavalry group, the army had Moutiers as its first objective. From Mont-Viso to the sea was the 1a Armata of Generale Pietro Pintor. With thirteen infantry divisions, two groups of Alpine troops and a cavalry group, its first objective was Nice, and secondly Marseille. Behind this first wave was the 7a Armata held in reserve with five infantry divisions and elements of three motorised divisions. Its task was to exploit the breaches made along the front.

His force further reduced since the begining of June, Général Olry had now about 185,000 men: on his left wing, facing Switzerland, was the weak force, about 4,500 men, of the Secteur Défensif du Rhône and the 1ère Brigade de Spahis, the latter brought in on June 5 after its initial engagement in the north. In the centre was the XIVème Corps d'Armée with two infantry divisions and the troops of the Fortified Sectors of Savoie and Dauphinée. On his right wing was the XVème Corps d'Armée with one infantry division and the troops of the Fortified Sector of Alpes-Maritimes. The situation on the northern front was by then catastrophic and Général Olry could not hope for any reinforcements, and he was soon to have to take measures to protect his rear from far-reaching panzers.

About 185,000 French troops thus faced some 450,000 Italians shortly to be hurled at them by an impatient Duce, although the mountainous terrain did act in the favour of the defenders.

The village lies 30 kilometres east of Briançon, some 2,000 metres up in the Alps. One of its charming features is an abundance of sundials, one of which can be seen on the end wall of the church.

In for the kill. In one of the war's worst examples of opportunism, on June 10 — at the beginning of the last round — the Duce declared war on France, already battered senseless from frequent body blows in the north. Now she was up against the ropes after four weeks of Blitzkrieg war. However, Mussolini held back for a further ten days before launching his jab from below the belt just moments before the final bell. By this time his enemy was down on the canvas, and just days away from the knockout, but to his great surprise his adversary still had the energy to get up and give him a bloody nose. Marching in the van of the Divisione No. 1 'Superga', these Alpini ascend a pass leading to France.

THE STAB IN THE BACK

At 6.00 p.m. on June 10, Mussolini announced that 'The world is witness that Italy has done everything which was humanly possible to avoid war, but all in vain' and he declared that a state of war was to exist between France and Italy from midnight. In a radio broadcast Reynaud commented, 'Signor Mussolini has chosen this time to declare war on us. How can this be judged? France has nothing to say. The world will judge'. President Roosevelt gave his judgement on the way Mussolini had waited for an appropriate moment to attack a weakened France in the rear. Despite having been strongly advised not to jeopardise the 'Italian vote' by being too outspoken, his condemnation was scathing: 'On this tenth day of June, 1940, the hand that held the dagger struck it into the back of his neighbour'.

As soon as war was declared Général Olry, had ordered all demolition charges to be blown. As yet, however, Mussolini did not dare order an immediate attack, and the instructions issued to Crown Prince Umberto were strictly defensive.

On June 17 the situation of the French armies on the main front further to the north was critical. The Groupe d'Armées No. 2 was now trapped in the east of France, the panzers were advancing on Lyon and the Rhône valley and Général Olry was forced to take measures to protect his rear. France's defeat being now only a matter of time, Mussolini threw caution to the winds and on June 17 he ordered the Prince of Piémont to attack at once, right across the front. This was a sharp reversal of the previous defensive strategy, and Mussolini severely rebuked Maresciallo Pietro Badoglio when he pointed out that it would require at least 25 days' preparation.

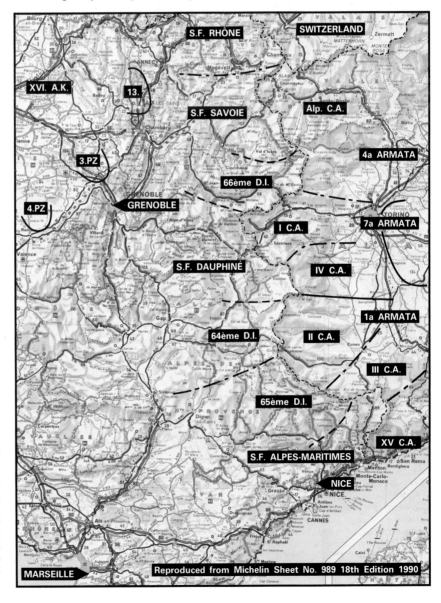

Reproduced from Michelin Sheet No. 989 18th Edition 1990

On June 20 the Italians launched a general attack, starting in the south and extending the next day to the rest of the front. The weather was mostly poor, with fog everywhere and snow falling on the mountains. In places, the Italian Alpini performed remarkable feats and scaled near impossible heights, but so too did the French Alpine troops. In the Tarentaise valley, the Italians moved down from the Petit-Saint-Bernard Pass but were stopped and could not capture the Redoute-Ruinée fortress they had surrounded. In the Maurienne valley, they tried repeatedly for five days to force the French defences but had only reached the line of advance posts on June 24. On July 1 the garrisons of both the surrounded Redoute-Ruinée and Turra fortresses left their unconquered forts to return to the French lines, the men carrying all their weapons, and a company of Italian soldiers saluting them as they left.

Further to the south, the Divisione No. 26 'Assietta' did manage to take the old Chenaillet fort, defended by only twenty men and two light machine-guns, two days before the armistice. The way to Briançon was blocked by the Janus fortress, which was far more powerful, but despite a ten-to-one advantage in this sector, the Italians made no headway, only reaching the advance posts line. The French artillery did a superb job on June 21 when four 280mm heavy mortars of the 6ème Batterie of 154ème R.A.P., secretly installed a year before for just this engagement, disabled the Italian fortress of Chaberton which, 3,100 mètres up, controlled the entire area and threatened Briançon. With only 100 shells the French gunners blew off six of

The conditions under which the fight was held were harsh, the weather being particularly poor in the Alps that June with icy winds, thick fog and falling snow. These are men of the Divisione No. 1 'Superga' in the Maurienne valley. The Italians suffered badly with over 2,000 cases of frost-bite and more than 600 men reported missing or captured.

In contrast to the Italian losses of 631 killed and 2,631 wounded, French casualty figures were incredibly light: only 40 killed, 84 wounded and 150 missing or captured. A patrol of the 92ème B.A.F. climb to meet the challenge.

the fort's eight 149mm turrets and silenced it.

The same story of failure applied to the south where the 1a Armata advanced no more than a few hundred metres. On the coast the attack on Menton by the Divisione No. 5 'Cosseria' was supported by an armoured train of the Italian Navy which fired about 200 152mm shells at the French positions on June 22 until it was forced to take refuge into the Garavan tunnel to avoid counterfire from the Mont-Agel fortress. In the afternoon the train re-emerged to resume shelling but the French gunners were quicker and the 75mm of Mont-Agel disabled three of the train's four turrets. Back into the tunnel went the train, post haste, and it was not heard of again.

On June 22, Mussolini urged his generals to take Menton 'regardless of losses'. As the town was just on the border, in front of the French defence line, it was soon evacuated by the defenders but the advance posts east of the town fought back until the armistice. The garrison of the Saint-Louis fort, which controlled the only road on the coastline, refused to leave until two days after that, upon receiving direct orders to do so. They walked back to the French line, with their weapons and supplies, taking with them the keys of the fort, having carefully locked it up behind them!

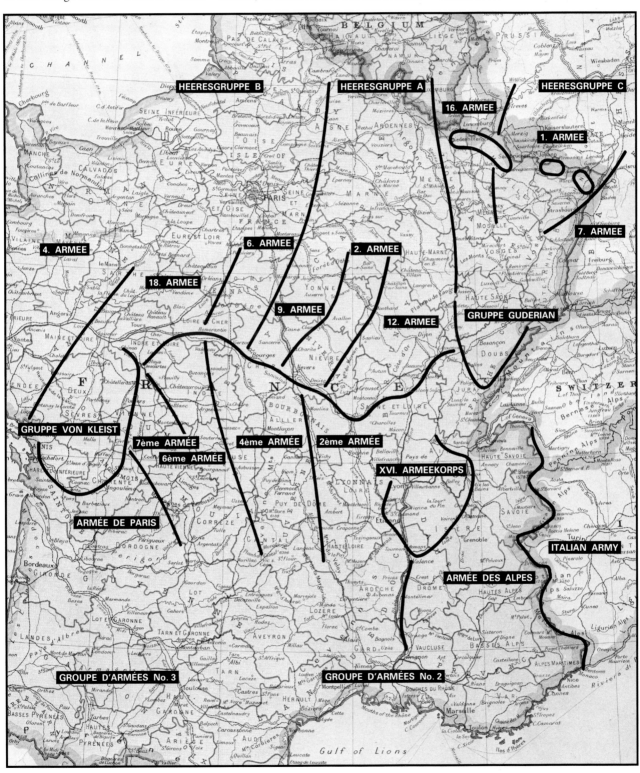

The battlefield as it appeared on the eve of the armistice. Save for the XVI. Armeekorps which was to withdraw, and Gruppe von Kleist which had yet to march southwards to occupy the whole of the Atlantic coast, the battle line at this point was the same as the eventual agreed demarcation line which left the southern part of France unoccupied.

'HADDOCK' FORCE AND THE FRENCH NAVY

Plans for bombing Italian industrial centres had been drawn up since May as the possibility of Italian intervention had long been foreseen, despite Mussolini's claim of 'non-belligerency'. On May 31, the Allied Supreme War Council had decided that if Italy declared war, industrial targets and oil plants in northern Italy should be attacked at the earliest possible moment. On June 3, Group Captain Field and the No. 71 Wing headquarters personnel, who had been at Nantes since their withdrawal from operations on May 17, were detailed to proceed to the Marseille area, where two airfields about fifty kilometres north of the town, Salon and Le Vallon, had been placed at RAF disposal. The plan was that one squadron of Wellingtons should fly out from England, operate for two nights before returning, and be replaced by another squadron. The code-name of the operation was 'Haddock'.

Italy entered the war on June 10 and an operation was ordered for the night of June 11. Whitleys of No. 4 Group flying from England were sent to bomb targets in Turin and Genoa but severe icing conditions forced most of the 36 aircraft to turn back, only a dozen of them claiming to have attacked their targets. Some of them had actually bombed Switzerland, bombs being dropped at Geneva, Renens and Daillens.

Meanwhile at Salon, where twelve Wellingtons of No. 3 Group had arrived in the afternoon, the night was spent in confusion. Orders cancelling the mission were followed by ones saying that it should proceed, and the French, who were anxious not to encourage the Italians to greater activity, were requesting that everything be stopped for the time being. When the first Wellington of the 'Haddock' Force began to taxi into position for take-off, the local French air commander immediately sent a number of lorries onto the airfield to prevent any aircraft taking-off.

Two of the more unusual aspects of the campaign occurred during the battle against Italy when the French Navy (*above*: the *Algérie* of the 3ème Escadre) carried out a bombardment of the Italian coast in the Gulf of Genoa while the RAF mounted raids against inland targets . . . but ended up dropping bombs on neutral Switzerland!

After some 'fairly bitter recriminations' had been passed between the Allies and instruction given to recall the 'Haddock' organisation to England, Air Marshal Barratt was informed on the afternoon of June 13 that the operation could now proceed. It had become apparent that the Italians were bent on something more vigorous than a mere paper declaration of war and the French, who had now abandoned hope of Italy remaining more or less passive, had revised their opinion.

The French Navy struck at Italy and at dawn on June 14, the 3ème Escadre — two squadrons of cruisers (each of two cruisers) and four squadrons of destroyers — carried out a bombardment of the Italian coast from the Gulf of Genoa. One group, with the *Algérie* and the *Foch* and two squadrons of destroyers — the 1ère D.C.T. and 5ème D.C.T., with three destroyers each — set the Vado oil tanks and the Savona refineries alight, while another group, with the *Colbert*, the *Dupleix* and a further two squadrons of destroyers — the 3ème D.C.T. with three destroyers and the 7ème D.C.T. with two — shelled the Ansaldo factories at Genoa. The surprise was complete and the raid was a success, only one ship, the destroyer *Albatros* of the 7ème D.C.T., being slightly damaged, but the destruction caused to the Italian targets was minimal.

It was during the first raid on June 12 that bombs fell on Geneva, on Renens just west of Lausanne, and at Daillens, 15 kilometres to the north-west. *Above:* This is the railway station at Renens on the morning afterwards where stunned townspeople find that their precious neutrality has been rudely shattered.

'Haddock' Force struck its first blow during the night of June 15 when eight Wellingtons were directed against the Piaggio and Ansaldo works at Genoa. The weather was poor and only one aircraft reported hits on the Ansaldo works, nearly all the remaining bombs being brought back. 'Haddock' Force launched another raid the following night, 22 Wellingtons setting out to bomb industrial targets in Milan and Genoa; once again the weather was bad and only half of them claimed to have bombed their targets. This was the last British bombing operation from French soil for by then France was seeking armistice terms and placed an embargo on any aggressive action and 'Haddock' Force was ordered back to England.

The same restriction applied to the French Navy and the French sailors, elated by their successes on June 14, were very disappointed when Admiral Darlan forbade any more offensive operations against Italy. Later, when the armistice negotiations were in process, it was feared that Mussolini might have exhorbitant demands and Darlan planned an all out attack of the fleet on the Italian coastline. On June 22 he asked his commanders to make preparations but Mussolini's demands turned out to be reasonable and the operation was cancelled.

For all Mussolini's huffing and puffing the Italian Army had barely dented the French front in the Alps. Nowhere had they succeeded in breaking through, and they had paid a high price merely to approach the French main line of resistance. In order to 'win' some more ground, to be able to claim a chair at the armistice negotiations about to begin with the French, the Italians were prepared to go to any lengths, and on the morning of June 24, XVI. Armeekorps was informed that 25 Italian aircraft were to land at Lyon with about 300 Italian soldiers on board. Armeegruppe List cancelled all this an hour later and Halder noted in his war diary: 'The morning brought in an interesting variation. The Italians are stopped in front of the French fortifications and unable to advance further. They want to claim occupation of as large an area of France as possible at the armistice discussions and for this they have proposed to transport by air some of their battalions, some to Munich, some others directly to Lyon, then advance these at important points behind the front held by Armeegruppe List, points up to where they want to extend their claims of occupation. The whole idea is an imposture of the poorest sort. I have made clearly known that I do not want my name to be associated with such an affair. It turns out that the whole proposition came from General Mario Roatta [second Chief-of-Staff of the Italian General Staff] but that Marschall Badoglio has refused to approve it. OKW would have to assume that the idea does come from a lower level of command and thus the reasonable Marschall Badoglio, quite probably the only decent soldier in this whole affair, could reject it as shameful'.

It would appear that at least two of the Whitleys of Nos. 10, 51, 58, 77 and 102 Squadrons mistook Lac Léman for the sea (more than 300 kilometres to the southeast), releasing at least eight bombs on Renens and six on Daillens. By the size of this crater in the Rue du Simplon in Renens it would appear that only small-calibre bombs were dropped. Nevertheless, a lady was killed and six people wounded in the mobile home in the background.

Then on June 24 came the French High Command's announcement of the cease-fire from 12.35 a.m. the next morning.

The Italian Army had suffered badly in their ignominious and ill-advised offensive. The men fought well but they were not adequately equipped and the operation was improvised and poorly led. According to the Italian Army Historical Branch figures published in 1949, 631 men were killed in the offensive, with 616 missing or captured and 2,631 wounded. There were 2,151 cases of severe frost-bite.

Piercing the shadows of defeat, the worst ever in French military history, the success of the Armée des Alpes in beating off every attack by the numerically far superior Italians was like a shaft of light. It was brighter still for having been achieved at the cost of 40 killed, 84 wounded and about 150 captured or missing.

In all, two people were killed in Renens and two in Geneva, with up to 80 injured. Naturally the Swiss protested at the violation although there was little they could do after the event. The British extended their 'deep regret for this incident and its tragic consequences'. One bomb exploded in the middle of Rue de Lausanne, the explosion damaging many buildings. This is the badly-damaged façade of the Grand Hôtel. The second casualty in Renens — a man asleep in bed — was killed nearby at No. 1 Rue du Midi.

The Last Act

On June 20 panzers were at Cherbourg, Brest and Nantes; further to the east the 6. Armee had forced the Loire and was already on the Cher. The French armistice delegation had crossed the front line that evening for their appointed rendezvous at Tours.

The German High Command now regrouped its armies for the final blow. On June 20 Gruppe von Kleist was ordered to assemble one of its two

corps, the XIV. Armeekorps, and the divisions attached to it and prepare their transfer to Heeresgruppe B. General von Kleist and his staff were also transferred to Heeresgruppe B, in whose sector they would take charge of the newly-arrived XIV. Armeekorps (the 9. Panzer-Division, 10. Panzer-Division, SS-Verfügungs-Division and SS-Totenkopf-Division). The XV. Armeekorps — 7. Panzer-Division and

2. Infanterie-Division (mot) — would also join the dash southwards along the Atlantic coast from the Loire to the Spanish border.

In eastern France Heeresgruppe A was also to organise a vanguard group for an advance southwards in the direction of the Rhône valley and the Alps. On June 20 OKH gave orders for the XVI. Armeekorps, now released from Gruppe von Kleist, to assemble near

On June 20, General Ewald von Kleist *(left)* and his staff of Gruppe von Kleist were transferred to Heeresgruppe B to lead the units dashing southwards from the Loire to the Spanish border. (This picture was taken on the Eastern Front in 1942 after his promotion to Generaloberst.) That same day, the

12. Armee was upgraded to Armeegruppe List and transferred to Heeresgruppe A to lead the advance down the Rhône valley to the Alps. Its commander was the then-Generaloberst Wilhelm List, pictured *(right)* in 1942 when Generalfeldmarschall commanding Heeresgruppe A in the East.

South of Orléans, the leaders of the 33. Infanterie-Division were approaching the River Cher on the evening of June 18 when three Renault D-2s of the 350ème C.A.C.C. under Lieutenant Hervé Le Roy counter-attacked and hit them at Millancay, ten kilometres north of Romorantin. The French tanks inflicted painful losses but the Germans reacted swiftly: '2084' (pictured) was hit and brewed up with Aspirant Henri Fraisot, the tank commander, and his two crew being killed. The two other tanks were also knocked out with their crews being either killed or captured.

Macon, while the 12. Armee was ordered to transfer to Heeresgruppe A. The army, upgraded to Armeegruppe List, was to take charge of the reinforced XVI. Armeekorps comprising the 3. Panzer-Division, 4. Panzer-Division, Leibstandarte SS-'Adolf Hitler' and Infanterie-Regiment 'Gross--Deutschland'. On June 22 OKH also transferred the 1. Gebirgs-Division (a mountain division) to Heeresgruppe A for employment with Armeegruppe List. As the pass in the Alps was one of its targets, this was a wise decision, but the division was then in the Bourges area and, though they started eastwards immediately, the first element did not reach Lyon until June 24, too late to be of any use.

With orders to start out on June 23, Armeegruppe List was to advance southwards along the Rhône valley, then eastwards towards the Alps to take the French units then holding off the Italians in the rear. It was hoped that the leaders would soon make contact with the Italians and, to avoid any mistakes, orders were issued to ensure that the Stukas would only strike at targets clearly decided upon by XVI. Armeekorps. On June 21 the Heeresgruppe A war diary noted that Italian-speaking interpreters were on their way to join the Armeegruppe staff.

Général Antoine Besson was soon compelled to pull his planned defence line back to the Indre, then even further south to the Creuse. Capitaine André Lande pictured this battle group of the 4ème D.C.R. crossing the river on June 22. In two days time, when the armistice was due to be sounded, what remained of the division was assembled just west of Limoges.

585

THE END IN THE ALPS

After the rupture of the Groupe d'Armées No. 4 front, with the three armies of Groupe d'Armées No. 2 cut off in the east, a huge gap had now opened between the Swiss border and the Loire and the way was open for the panzers to roll into Lyon, the Rhône valley and on to the Alps. Gruppe von Kleist had reached Dijon and advanced southwards in the Saône valley. On June 18 the panzers arrived at Lyon and threatened the rear of the Armée des Alpes which was then successfully resisting the Italian attacks. Refusing to take troops from his already weakened force facing the Italians, Général Olry improvised a defence facing north from odd units brought into the line. Stop lines were organised in the Rhône valley to prevent units and stragglers withdrawing southwards. Hastily reorganised, these makeshift fighting units were sent straight off to take up positions in the line beside elements combed out of local barracks.

On June 18 Général Olry requested the urgent assistance of the Air Force and Navy. The Navy, which had to maintain its ships ready for a possible new operation against Italy, could only send about forty naval guns, 47mm and 65mm in about equal numbers, which could be used as anti-tank guns and about 250 men as gun crews. The Armée de l'Air sent about 1,200 men from its airfield defence companies. Six Renault B1bis were taken directly from the FCM factory at La Seyne and were moved into army reserve near Bollène, crewed by the men who had built them. There was even a group of gunners from the 104ème R.A.L. who had ended up there by a somewhat round-about route. They had been badly knocked about in Flanders with the Vème Corps d'Armée, had withdrawn to Dunkirk, where they destroyed the last of their guns, been evacuated to England, and then re-embarked for Brest and transported to Lyon. There they had been given some 105mm guns built by Schneider for a Rumanian order; the guns were without their laying equipment but as the panzers were arriving at Lyon the gunners had to get cracking again!

From the upper Rhône near Geneva and along the Isère to Valence, the hastily built front of the Armée des Alpes was held in the north by XIVème Corps d'Armée, with the Secteur Défensif du Rhône. Then came Groupement Cartier along the Isère up to Saint-Nazaire, and in the south, in the Valence area, the makeshift Groupement de l'Isère. On the army's left wing, was the XVIIIème Corps d'Armée, of the 2ème Armée, which had the mission to 'plug in' the Rhône valley.

During the night of June 20-21 all the demolitions prepared on the Isère downstream of Voreppe and on the Rhône from Vienne to Valence were carried out. The opening of sluices on the Isère and its tributaries upstream in the mountains, doubled its flow, creating a really impressive barrier. The naval guns were brought into position

On June 23, Armeegruppe List began its drive southwards along the Rhône valley and eastwards towards the Alps. This Bren Carrier, impressed into service with the 4. Panzer-Division, was pictured on the Rhône river bank in Lyon.

along the south bank of the Isère, and others along the Rhône below its confluence with Isère. Lacking any mountings, they were simply set up on concrete 'gun-carriages' out in the open.

Between the Loire and the Rhône all German advances had now halted along the future 'demarcation line' but at 7.00 a.m. on June 23 Armeegruppe List began its drive southwards in the Rhône valley and eastwards in the Alps. Three advance groups had been organised. Gruppe A with the 13. Infanterie-Division (mot) and some mobile elements was to advance from Bourg-en-Bresse in the direction of Chambéry and Annecy. Gruppe B, comprising the 3. Panzer-Division and some mobile elements, was to advance from Lyon in the direction of Grenoble. Gruppe C — the 4. Panzer-Division plus Gruppe

Schmid-Dankward composed of motorised elements from 7. Infanterie-Division, 253. Infanterie-Division and 269. Infanterie-Division — was to cover the left flank of the main attack eastwards and advance southwards in the Rhône valley. Further west, the Leibstandarte SS-'Adolf Hitler' was to march on Saint-Etienne. After reaching these objectives, both Gruppe A and B, by then reinforced with elements of the 1. Gebirgs-Division, were to advance further east and reach the passes at Saint-Bernard, Mont-Cenis and Mont-Genèvre, where the French outposts were still blocking every attempt by the Italians to get past them.

The initial advance was swift and at 10.00 a.m. the 13. Infanterie-Division (mot) was on the Rhône, south-west of Saint-Genix and the 3. Panzer-Division

Cours Lafayette today, little changed save for the absence of the cobblestones and tram lines which were removed in 1957. The Lafayette bridge over the river lies just out of the picture to the right.

was near Moirans. Things then became more difficult as they had reached the French improvised defence line and in the evening the war diary of Heeresgruppe A noted how 'the XVI. Armeekorps was on the Isère, fighting with strong French covering units of Alpine troops'.

When the German attack had started, the positions held by the XIVème Corps d'Armée were already breached at one point in the north as the explosives placed for the destruction of a Rhône road bridge near Culoz on June 21 had failed to detonate. By the time the truck which had been rushed to Annecy to fetch new detonators had returned, the Germans had forced their way across. Six LeO 451 bombers from G.B. 6 had tried to bring down the bridge on June 22 but they failed and the XIVème Corps d'Armée was unable to bring up heavy artillery in time because of the speed of the German advance the following day. The leading elements of the 13. Infanterie-Division (mot) advanced eastwards, entering Aix-les-Bains, but were stopped in front of Chambéry. Général Louis Michal, the commander of the Secteur Défensif du Rhône, was later cited in the army bulletin for having 'precluded a flanking manoeuvre and maintained intact the position he had to defend'.

To the south, duels were fought at close range between the French Navy's guns positioned along the Isère and the panzers. The panzers had the advantage of being mobile, but not that of surprise, and the guns managed to knock out a number of tanks and vehicles before being neutralised themselves. In some places, the concrete 'gun carriages' which had been poured only a few days before were not strong enough and fractured after a few shots, rendering the guns useless.

A column of the 3. Panzer-Division which was approaching Voreppe paid a heavy price for its over-confidence when caught in the open by French guns. These, although hastily emplaced, had their fire directed by observers who had a superb view from the hills, and the Germans were forced to withdraw

At Saint-Genix, 20 kilometres west of Chambéry, the bridge over the Guiers had been blown by the French at 4.00 p.m. on June 23. This picture was taken the following morning as engineers of the 13. Infanterie-Division (mot) inspected the damage.

Unfortunately for the French defence, at least one of the Guiers bridges was not blown in time — that at Saint-Albin — as the destruction of the bridge was delayed to enable the withdrawal of the last elements of the XIVème Corps d'Armée still lying west of the river. When the leaders of the 3. Panzer-Division approached on the morning of June 24, the defenders panicked and failed to set off the charges. *Left:* This column is from the I. Bataillon of Schützen-Regiment 3. *Right:* The bridge was spared destruction in 1940, 1944 and in the 1950s when there was a move to modernise it with a wider replacement.

Another snapshot from the 3. Panzer-Division's battle album showing II. Bataillon of Schützen-Regiment 3 marching through Moirans, (20 kilometres north-west of Grenoble) on the afternoon of June 24. This was the furthest point reached by the division on their advance to the Alps for that evening they received a message advising them that a cease-fire would come into effect at 00.35 a.m. next morning heralded in the Isère valley by the trumpet call 'Das Ganze halt!' (All to stop!).

sn a hurry. In the evening the French artillery counter-fired at German batteries firing at Grenoble from near Moirans and silenced them.

In the Rhône valley, the XVIIIème Corps d'Armée fought the 4. Panzer-Division to a halt, while on the right bank of the river the 1ère Brigade de Spahis counter-attacked and stopped Gruppe Schmid-Dankward near Andance and Sarras. The Rhône bridge at Saint-Vallier was lost but successfully blown on June 23 before the Germans could remove the charges. With the help of artillery the French successfully contained the Germans for three days, limiting their advance.

On June 24 the Germans were at Saint-Etienne, at Saint-Valliers just to the north of Valence and were threatening Chambéry. That evening, at 9.00 p.m., a telegram went out from Army General Headquarters putting an end to hostilities at 00.35 a.m. next morning.

When that moment arrived, Général Olry could be proud of his Armée des Alpes. The German Armeegruppe List had got no further than a line Aix-les-Bains, Voiron, Romans, and the Italians were still stopped more or less on their start lines. The Armée des Alpes, while it was battling to stop dead every Italian attack on its front, had also

Meanwhile the leaders of the regiment's I. Bataillon had been held up all day when it came up against the solid French defenders of Les Echelles, 20 kilometres south of Chambéry. In the evening the news of the armistice was received and contacts made with the enemy. Here Capitaine Jean Baptiste Tournier, commanding the 9ème Compagnie of the 25ème R.T.S. is led blindfolded to the I. Bataillon's command post by Oberleutnant Möll, the battalion adjutant.

succeeded in containing the German advance on its rear and had done all this without suffering total casualties on both fronts of more than 70 killed, 200 wounded and some 400 taken prisoner or missing.

Left: On June 26 — the day after the armistice came into force — a German photographer in the Valence area pictured the demolished railway bridge nine kilometres to the north at Pont de l'Isère. Right: After the war, a hydro-electric plant was built on the Rhône (just south of its confluence with the Isère) resulting in an increase in the water level upstream of the dam.

France has fallen and in Bordeaux, last-ditch refuge of the government, the 7. Panzer-Division mount their own victory parade.

THE END ON THE ATLANTIC COAST

On June 19, disaster befell Groupe d'Armées No. 3 when German forces crossed the Loire and reached the Cher. As a result Général Besson was forced to move the right of the planned defence line from the Cher to the Indre. That same day the French High Command disbanded Groupe d'Armées No. 4 and took direct command of the 4ème Armée.

On June 20, with Germans on the right flank and others advancing south of the Loire between his Armée de Paris and 7ème Armée, Général Besson saw that his Groupe d'Armées No. 3 was in great danger of being completely shattered and he had no choice other than to order his armies to pull back. Thus they ended up not on the Indre but further south on the Creuse and lower Vienne.

After another attempt on June 22 to establish a defence line on Angoulême-Rochefort, the next day Général Besson, his three armies now down to about 65,000 fighting men, was forced to order a withdrawal of the whole line of Groupe d'Armées No. 3 on the Dordogne.

On the morning of June 24, Gruppe von Kleist started to move southwards, the XV. Armeekorps on the Atlantic coast and the XIV. Armeekorps on the left. The 9. Panzer-Division of the latter faced east to cover the left flank of the two corps as they advanced southwards; the move went on until late in the evening when Gruppe von Kleist radioed that the cease-fire was to become effective at 12.35 a.m. the next morning.

When the firing stopped on June 25, the XV. Armeekorps was approaching the Gironde with the vanguards of 2. Infanterie-Division (mot) at Marennes and those of the 7. Panzer-Division at Saintes. The XIV. Armeekorps was on a line Cognac-Angoulème, its SS-Verfügungs-Division at Cognac, the SS-Totenkopf-Division at Angoulème with the 10. Panzer-Division just behind.

Held early morning (the long shadows from the east denote a sun still low on the horizon), the parade was taken by the XV. Armeekorps commander, General Hermann Hoth (in the forage cap). His corps pennant — the black and white square device — stands above the 7. Panzers' triangular divisional sign.

The saluting base was situated mid-way along Quai Louis XVIII, the same three steps facing the Place des Quinconces still remaining.

Starting from Angoulème on the afternoon of June 27, the recce detachment of the SS-Verfügungs-Division reached the Spanish border near Béhobie at 5.00 p.m. on June 28. This picture was taken in the middle of the barricaded bridge across the River Bidassoa as a German officer exchanges a few words with the Spanish frontier guards.

On June 26 the German forces started their moves to adjust to the agreed demarcation line. Although over to the east this resulted in a drastic withdrawal for Armeegruppe List from the Lyon area and the Alps, on the Atlantic seaboard it meant a further advance for Gruppe von Kleist along the coast up to the Spanish border. The XV. Armeekorps was to occupy the coast in the Gironde sector down to the Bassin d'Arcachon, while its 10. Panzer-Division would extend the line from the sector east of Angoulème to the Garonne river. Meanwhile the XIV. Armeekorps was pushing its two SS divisions southwards along the coast. These two divisions were to man the shore and the demarcation line from the Garonne and Arcachon sectors down to the Spanish frontier.

These moves were completed within two days. The reconnaissance batalion of the SS-Verfügungs-Division which started out from the Angoulème area on the afternoon of June 27 had soon passed Bordeaux and reached the Spanish border near Béhobie at 5.00 p.m. on June 28. After a warm greeting by Spanish frontier guards, the Germans were invited to drive straight on to Irun, where the Spanish commander of the Northern Military Sector, General Lopez Pinto, awaited them at his command post. The reconnaissance batalion's commander, SS-Sturmbannführer Wim Brandt, then drove there with some of his officers. The next day General Pinto went to the border crossing at Hendaye to welcome General Wendt von Wietersheim, the commander of XIV. Armeekorps.

We had some difficulty in matching this shot, not least because the bridge at Béhobie was moved and the old one demolished in the 1960s! We offer two pictures taken for us by Francis

Sallaberry on the Franco-Spanish border. *Left:* The view from the French bank of the river across the divide once spanned by the bridge and, *right*, from the Spanish end.

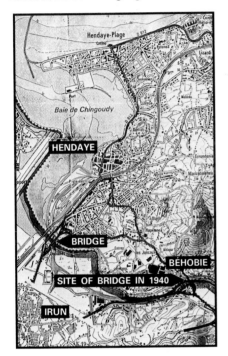

The following day the formal welcoming ceremony took place at Hendaye. At 11.00 p.m. (German time) on June 29, General Wendt von Wietersheim, commanding the XIV. Armeekorps, was met by General Lopez Pinto, the commander of the Northern Military Sector of Spain.

More hello's at Hendaye, this time as Luftwaffe and Spanish officers meet. Four months later the border town was to witness an even greater historic event when the dictators of Germany and Spain met at the local railway station. It was on October 23 that Hitler travelled to meet General Franco to endeavour to persuade the Caudillo to go beyond mere expressions of goodwill and give a more solid military commitment to Germany in response to her assistance to Franco during the Civil War. In the event, Hitler came away empty-handed and Spain was to remain neutral throughout the war.

The Armistice

On June 18 a conference was hastily held at Munich between Hitler and Mussolini, each accompanied by his Foreign Minister and members of the High Command. The idea was to adjust their respective positions so that France could not play one against the other in the coming armistice negotiations. It appears that Hitler moderated some of the Italian demands, particularly for the surrender of the French fleet. He explained that the French would never accept this and that such a demand might well cause the French Navy, who were certainly not prepared to scuttle all their ships, to take them into British ports; it would be far wiser to demand their disarmament in French or even neutral ports. It also seems that the 'dissidence' announced on June 18 by Général de Gaulle had been noted by the Germans at any rate and helped curb their appetite as there was a real risk of much of the Empire siding with de Gaulle if a legitimate government in France was not left with even a façade of responsibility.

At 6.30 a.m. on June 19, the Spanish ambassador communicated the German answer requesting the French government to send plenipotentiaries to be informed of the conditions for ending hostilities. The Cabinet met at 9.00 a.m. and appointed Général Charles Huntziger, commander of Groupe d'Armées No. 4, to head the delegation.

Meanwhile France was acting as if the war was still going on. Amiral Darlan ordered all French warships to continue the war and head for British ports or ports of the French Empire and Général Joseph Vuillemin ordered the French Air Force to fly to North Africa. The three persons who embodied the sovereignty of France, the President of the Republic, Albert Lebrun, the President of the Chamber of the Deputies, Edouard Herriot and the President of the Senate, Jules Jeanneney, were all determined to get to North Africa. The defeatists, Laval at their head, made every effort to impede their departure and managed to compel them to remain at Bordeaux. The question of their departure to North Africa was re-opened at the Cabinet meeting of June 23 but by then it was far too late.

Bordeaux was bombed by the Luftwaffe during the night of June 19 and the next day. From any military standpoint these bombings were pointless; in

Left: **Forêt de Compiègne, November 11, 1918. Amiral Wemyss, flanked by Général Weygand (left) and Maréchal Foch (right), French signatories, descend from a coach of the Compagnie des Wagons Lits after the signing of the armistice which ended the First World War.** *Right:* **June 19, 1940. After having removed it from its museum building which had been built over the old railway track, German engineers return Foch's coach to the exact spot that it had occupied in 1918 — indicated by a marble slab between the rails. Hitler's dream of reversing the rôles had come true; now the stage was set for a moment of high drama.**

French people! I have asked the enemy to put an end to hostilities. The Government yesterday appointed plenipotentiaries to receive their conditions. I took this decision with the stout heart of a soldier because the military situation imposed it.

We had hoped to resist on the Somme-Aisne line. Général Weygand had regrouped our forces, and his name alone presaged victory. The line yielded, however, under the pressure of the enemy and our troops were forced to retreat. From June 13 the request for an armistice was inevitable. The blow surprised you, and, remembering 1914-18, you sought the reasons for it. I am going to give you them.

On May 1, 1917, we still had 3,280,000 men under arms, in spite of three years of murderous fighting. On the eve of the present battle we had 500,000 fewer. In May 1918, we had 85 British divisions; in May 1940, we only had 10. In 1918 we had with us 58 Italian divisions and 42 American divisions.

The inferiority of our material was even greater than that of our effectives. French aviation has fought at odds of one to six. Not so strong as twenty-two years ago, we had also fewer friends, too few children, too few arms, too few allies. This is the cause of our defeat.

The French people do not deny the blow. All peoples have known ups and downs. It is by the way they react that they show themselves to be weak or great. We will learn a lesson from the battle which has been lost. Since victory the spirit of pleasure has prevailed over the spirit of sacrifice. People have demanded more than they have given, they have wanted to spare themselves effort. Today misfortune comes.

I was with you in the glorious days. As head of Government I will remain with you in the dark days. Stand by me. The fight still goes on. It is for France, the soil of her sons.

MARÉCHAL PHILIPPE PÉTAIN,
FRENCH PRIME MINISTER,
BROADCAST, JUNE 20, 1940

Left: On June 16 Hitler had been driven to Château de Lausprelle at Acoz, south of Charleroi, from the Führerhauptquartier at Brûly de Pesche. He reached the château at about 4.30 p.m. to meet with General Juan Vigon, Chief of the

Spanish General Staff. Should the French make peace overtures through Spain, the lines of communication were thus assured. *Right:* The château, which was owned by Baron de Dorlodot in 1940, still belongs to the family.

Following the resignation of Reynaud that evening, and the appointment of Maréchal Pétain as his replacement, a request was made through Spanish channels for terms for an armistice. The German Foreign Office in Berlin immediately relayed the request to Walter Hewel, von Ribbentrop's envoy at the

Führer's headquarters. A film cameraman, Walter Frentz, captured the precise instant when Hewel joyfully gave the news to Hitler. Momentarily ecstatic that France had been brought to her knees in six weeks, Hitler raised his right leg and stamped his foot sharply.

The brief sequence contained only eight frames as reproduced here. However, when the film was released outside Germany a Canadian film technician, John Grierson, realised that he could convert a seemingly natural reaction into a ridiculous jig! By looping and duplicating the film, he scored a propaganda

success for Western newsreels which was only revealed by Grierson in *Esquire* magazine long after the war was over. Often repeated as fact that Hitler danced a jig when France surrendered, the fallacy is sometimes compounded by authors stating that the dance took place at Compiègne.

fact, timed to bring home the full reality of war to the French government, all a part of the carefully applied political pressure.

The credentials of the armistice delegation were signed and it left for Tours at 2.30 p.m. on June 20. With Général Huntziger were the former French ambassador to Poland, Léon Noël, an admiral, Vice-Amiral Maurice Le Luc, a general of the air force, Général Jean Bergeret, and a general of the army, Général Henri Parisot. Delayed by the streams of refugees blocking the roads, the ten-car convoy flying white flags was late when it arrived at Tours and did not cross the front line near Amboise until about 4.00 a.m.

Under German escort the armistice delegation were whisked northwards to Paris where they arrived in the early hours of June 21. They were almost immediately led some eighty kilometres north-east of Paris, to Rethondes, in the Compiègne Forest, to the very place where the German delegation had been brought in 1918 to discuss the armistice. Engineers had torn down the wall of the museum where the railway carriage in which the armistice had been signed was preserved and pulled out the carriage on tracks they had laid, bringing it to the centre of the clearing, to the exact spot where it had stood in 1918.

Hitler arrived by car at 3.15 p.m. accompanied by an entourage which included Göring, Ribbentrop, Hess and Keitel. Their cars stopped in front of the Alsace-Lorraine statue, which had been draped with a German flag to hide the stone image of the German eagle being run through by the golden sword of the Allies. Hitler glanced at the monument and passed by. Arriving near the great granite block on which was engraved, in French, 'Here on the Eleventh of November 1918 succumbed the criminal pride of the German Empire, vanquished by the free peoples which it tried to enslave', Hitler walked to it and read the triumphant words. The American news correspondent William Shirer was there, and described what he saw in his diary:

The monument was removed after the ceremony and taken to Germany where it was found at the end of the war still stored in packing cases. It was later restored to its original position at the beginning of the avenue leading to the clearing.

Later on June 17 Hitler flew to Frankfurt where he boarded his personal train, 'Amerika', for Munich for consultation with Mussolini who had only that day consummated his declaration of war on the 10th with his attack in the Alps (page 577). They met in the Führerbau, the same building where the Munich agreement had been signed two years before *(left)*. *Right:* Today the Führerbau is used by the State High School for Music. Hitler then returned to Wolfsschlucht at 2.15 p.m. on the 19th as preparations began for the signing ceremony at Compiègne.

June 21. With the offending Alsace-Lorraine Memorial hidden behind German war flags, Hitler arrives at the Clairière de l'Armistice after having motored the 150 kilometres from Wolfsschlucht. From left to right: Admiral Karl Raeder (C-in-C Kriegsmarine); Joachim von Ribbentrop (Foreign Minister); Rudolf Hess (Deputy Führer) shaking hands; Generaloberst Walther von Brauchitsch (C-in-C German Army) and, partly hidden, Generalfeldmarschall Hermann Göring (C-in-C Luftwaffe).

'Here on the Eleventh of November 1918 succumbed the criminal pride of the German Empire — vanquished by the free peoples which it tried to enslave.' As a young man bent on seeking revenge for what he called the Diktat of Versailles, under which Germany was to suffer harsh reparations for the damage she had caused in Belgium and France in 1914-18, Hitler would no doubt have heard of the unveiling of a great memorial at Compiègne in 1922. Ten years later, on the eve of his ascent to power, Hitler would have read of the ceremony at Compiègne held on November 11, 1932, to commemorate the establishment of the historic site as a French national memorial. Little could he have known that he had less than ten years to wait before he could personally show his contempt. After the ceremony the slab was blown up, as was the railway shed (which had been financed by an American benefactor, Arthur H. Fleming, in 1927) and the whole area defaced.

'Hitler reads it and Göring reads it. They all read it, standing there in the June sun and the silence. I look for the expression in Hitler's face. I am but fifty yards from him and see him through my glasses as though he were directly in front of me. I have seen that face many times at the great moments of his life. But today! It is afire with scorn, anger, hate, revenge, triumph.

'He steps off the monument and contrives to make even this gesture a masterpiece of contempt. He glances back at it, contemptuous, angry — angry, you almost feel, because he cannot wipe out the awful, provoking lettering with one sweep of his high Prussian boot. He glances slowly around the clearing, and now, as his eyes meet ours, you grasp the depth of his hatred. But there is triumph there too — revengeful, triumphant hate. Suddenly, as though his face were not giving quite complete expression to his feelings, he throws his whole body into harmony with his mood. He swiftly snaps his hands on his hips, arches his shoulders, planted his feet wide apart. It is a magnificent gesture of defiance, of burning contempt for the place and all that it has stood for in the twenty-two years since it witnessed the humbling of the German Empire.'

Hitler and his entourage then entered the railway carriage, the Führer himself sitting in the chair occupied by Foch in 1918. Five minutes later the French

In 1918 there had, in fact, been two railway coaches drawn up a few yards apart in the forest clearing, one for the German delegation and one — that of Maréchal Foch — for the actual signing ceremony. It was the latter which had been preserved in 1927 and which was drawn out for the 1940 re-enactment. Here the French delegation, led by Général Charles Huntziger, prepares to climb aboard. With him (right to left) are Léon Noël representing the government; Général Jean Bergeret (French Air Force); and Vice-Amiral Maurice Le Luc for the Navy. (Général Henri Parisot, the army representative, did not attend the first meeting.)

With Hitler having taken Foch's old seat (extreme left) facing the four Frenchmen, Generaloberst Keitel stands beside him to read a prepared statement putting the blame for the new war fairly and squarely on the Allies. Göring, Raeder and von Ribbentrop have their backs to the camera, with von Brauchitsch and Hess sitting at the far end.

delegation arrived, led by Huntziger and introduced by Generalleutnant Kurt von Tippelskirch of the OKH. According to William Shirer 'they looked shattered but retained a tragic dignity'. Hitler said nothing, made a sign to Keitel and both delegations then listened to a statement read by Keitel which blamed the Allies not only for the war of 1940 but also for the wrongs of 1914 and gave the French Army credit for its heroic resistance. As soon as this preamble had been read, Hitler and his entourage got up and left.

The discussion went on until dusk and the French delegation soon knew the worst, that there was nothing to negotiate, they were faced with a 'diktat' and the 24 articles of the German terms would have to be accepted as they stood. Late that evening, at about 9.30 p.m., Huntziger got in touch with Bordeaux by telephone and informed Weygand that they were 'under a tent, at Rethondes, beside the carriage'. Huntziger then read the German terms, to Weygand who, in November 1918, had been with Maréchal Foch in this same carriage and who had read the armistice terms to the German delegation.

At 1.00 a.m. on June 22 Pétain called his Cabinet together to hear the German demands. Pétain, Weygand and Paul Baudouin, the Minister of Foreign Affairs, realised that the terms had to

Hitler then left the coach, leaving Keitel in charge of the negotiations. The French tried many stalling tactics and the discussions continued for the rest of that Friday and into

Saturday. Finally, at 5.00 p.m. with his patience at an end, Keitel issued an ultimatum: the French must either accept or reject the terms without further argument by 6.30 p.m.

be accepted but others, among them Président Lebrun and Amiral Darlan, were arguing that they had to be refused. Counter-propositions were drafted during the night and were approved during a new Cabinet meeting at 8.00 a.m.: among these amendments were that Paris be left in the unoccupied part of the country and that the fleet was to be allowed to stay in French ports in Africa.

After having spent the night in the Royal Monceau Hôtel in Paris, the French delegation was brought back to Compiègne at 10.00 a.m. to resume the negotiations. The articles were read and gone over word by word and the discussion dragged on until 1.40 p.m. when the session was brought to a close to enable the French delegation to refer some questions to Bordeaux.

The third act in Compiègne started at 3.40 p.m. After more than an hour of 'negotiations' and an unsuccessful effort to call Bordeaux to clear up some further points, all attempts at formulating amendments were stopped. It was obvious that the Germans would only accept 'yes' or 'no' for an answer. The French delegation was not ready to say 'yes' but were afraid of the consequences of saying 'no'. At about 5.00 p.m. Huntziger asked for more time. Keitel told them they could have until 6.30 p.m. at the latest to come to a decision. The five French delegates gathered in a side compartment of the carriage and after a short conference returned to the main one. After ten more minutes of talking, there was only one thing to be done. The armistice was signed at 5.50 p.m. on June 22.

The armistice was to come into force only when the French had also concluded an armistice with Italy. The next morning the French delegation left Paris for Rome on board three trans-

Realising that they had no other choice, the French capitulated and the armistice was signed at 5.50 p.m. (French time) by Huntziger for France and Keitel for Germany. However, it was not to come into effect until a similar agreement had been made with the Italians. The negotiations in Italy took place in the Villa Incisa near Rome on Tuesday, June 24, finally being signed at 6.15 p.m. (French time). The news was telephoned to the Germans at about 6.30 p.m. and, in accordance with Article XXIII, the cease-fire came into effect six hours later — at 00.35 a.m. (French time) on June 25. (This corresponded with a German time of 1.35 a.m., or 11.35 p.m. June 24 GMT.)

port aircraft provided by the Luftwaffe. The French were not prepared to yield too much to the Italian 'victor' they had just stopped dead in his tracks and, knowing nothing of the Italian conditions but fearing that these might be unacceptable, the French Cabinet ordered, on the evening of June 22, that the Mediterranean Fleet be prepared to attack the Italian mainland. But the

Italian delegation led by Maresciallo Badoglio was conciliatory and the armistice was signed at 6.15 p.m. on June 24 at Villa Incisa near Rome.

The cease-fire was to be sounded at 00.35 a.m. the next day, June 25. The six weeks of France's agony were finally over but a new and greater agony was only just beginning: the four-year occupation of the French homeland.

The coach, which had seen the surrender of both France and Germany, begins its 1,000-kilometre journey to Berlin.

THE FRANCO-GERMAN ARMISTICE

Between the Chief of the High Command of the Armed Forces, Generaloberst Keitel, commissioned by the Führer of the German Reich and Supreme Commander in Chief of the German Armed Forces, and the fully authorised plenipotentiaries of the French government, Général Huntziger, chairman of the delegation; Ambassador Noël, Vice-Amiral Le Luc, army corps Général Parisot and air force Général Bergeret, the following armistice treaty was agreed upon:

ARTICLE I

The French government directs a cessation of fighting against the German Reich in France as well as in French possessions, colonies, protectorate territories, mandates as well as on the seas.

It [the French government] directs the immediate laying down of arms of French units already encircled by German troops.

ARTICLE II

To safeguard the interests of the German Reich, French state territory north and west of the line drawn on the attached map will be occupied by German troops.

As far as the parts to be occupied still are not in control of German troops, this occupation will be carried out immediately after the conclusion of this treaty.

ARTICLE III

In the occupied parts of France, the German Reich exercises all rights of an occupying power. The French government obligates itself to support with every means the regulations resulting from the exercise of these rights, and to carry them out with the aid of French administration.

All French authorities and officials of the occupied territory, therefore, are to be promptly informed by the French government to comply with the regulations of the German military commanders and to co-operate with them in a correct manner.

It is the intention of the German government to limit occupation of the west coast

after ending hostilities with England to the extent absolutely necessary.

The French government is permitted to select the seat of its government in unoccupied territory or, if it wishes, to move to Paris. In this case, the German government guarantees the French government and its central authorities every necessary alleviation so that they will be in a position to conduct the administration of unoccupied territory from Paris.

ARTICLE IV

French armed forces on land, on the sea and in the air are to be demobilised and disarmed in a period still to be set. Excepted are only those units which are necessary for maintenance of domestic order. Germany and Italy will fix their strength.

The French armed forces in territory to be occupied by Germany are to be hastily withdrawn into territory not to be occupied and be discharged. These troops, before marching out, shall lay down their weapons and equipment at the places where they are stationed at the time this treaty becomes effective. They are responsible for orderly delivery to German troops.

ARTICLE V

As a guarantee for the observance of the armistice, the surrender, undamaged, of all those guns, tanks, tank defence weapons, warplanes, anti-aircraft artillery, infantry weapons, means of conveyance, and munitions can be demanded from the units of the French armed forces which are standing in battle against Germany and which at the time this agreement goes into force are in territory not to be occupied by Germany. The German armistice commission will decide the extent of delivery.

ARTICLE VI

Weapons, munitions, and war apparatus of every kind remaining in the unoccupied portion of France are to be stored and/or secured under German and/or Italian con-

trol — so far as not released for the arming allowed to French units.

The German High Command reserves the right to direct all those measures which are necessary to exclude unauthorised use of this material. Building of new war apparatus in unoccupied territory is to be stopped immediately.

ARTICLE VII

In occupied territory, all the land and coastal fortifications, with weapons, munitions and apparatus and plants of every kind are to be surrendered undamaged. Plans of these fortifications as well as plans of those already conquered by German troops are to be handed over.

Exact plans regarding prepared blastings, land mines, obstructions, time fuzes, barriers for fighting, shall be given to the German High Command. These hindrances are to be removed by French forces upon German demand.

ARTICLE VIII

The French war fleet is to collect in ports to be designated more particularly and under German and/or Italian control to demobilise and lay up — with the exception of those units released to the French government for protection of French interests in its colonial empire. The peacetime stations of ships should control the designation of ports.

The German government solemnly declares to the French government that it does not intend to use the French war fleet which is in harbours under German control for its purposes in war, with the exception of units necessary for the guarding of coast and sweeping mines.

It further solemnly and expressly declares that it does not intend to bring up any demands respecting the French war fleet at the conclusion of a peace.

All warships outside France are to be recalled to France with the exception of that portion of the French war fleet which shall be designated to represent French interests in the Colonial empire.

ARTICLE IX

The French High Command must give the German High Command the exact location of all mines which France has set out, as well as information on other harbour and coastal obstructions and defence facilities. Insofar as the German High Command may require, French forces must clear away the mines.

ARTICLE X

The French government is obligated to forbid any portion of its remaining armed forces to undertake hostilities against Germany in any manner. The French government will also prevent members of its armed forces from leaving the country and prevent armaments of any sort, including ships, planes, etc., being taken to England or any other place abroad.

The French government will forbid French citizens to fight against Germany in the service of states with which the German Reich is still at war. French citizens who violate this provision are to be treated by Germany as insurgents.

ARTICLE XI

French commercial vessels of all sorts, including coastal and harbour vessels which are now in French hands, may not leave port until further notice. Resumption of commercial voyages will require approval of the German and Italian governments.

French commercial vessels will be recalled by the French government or, if return is impossible, the French government will instruct them to enter neutral harbours. All confiscated German commercial vessels are, on demand, to be returned [to Germany] undamaged.

ARTICLE XII

Flight by any aircraft over French territory shall be prohibited. Every plane making a flight without German approval will be regarded as an enemy by the German air force and treated accordingly.

In unoccupied territory, airfields and ground facilities of the air force shall be under German and Italian control. Demand may be made that such airfields be rendered unusable. The French government is required to take charge of all foreign aircraft in the unoccupied region to prevent flights. They are to be turned over to the German armed forces.

ARTICLE XIII

The French government obligates itself to turn over to German troops in the occupied region all facilities and properties of the French armed forces in undamaged condition. It (the French government) also will see to it that harbours, industrial facilites and docks are preserved in their present condition and damaged in no way.

The same stipulations apply to transportation routes and equipment, especially railways, roads and canals, and to the whole communications network and equipment, waterways and coastal transportation services. Additionally, the French government is required on demand of the German High Command to perform all necessary restoration labour on these facilities.

The French government will see to it that in the occupied region necessary technical personnel and rolling stock of the railways and other transportation equipment, to a degree normal in peacetime, is retained in service.

ARTICLE XIV

There is an immediate prohibition of transmission for all wireless stations on French soil. Resumption of wireless connections from the unoccupied portion of France requires a special regulation.

ARTICLE XV

The French government obligates itself to convey transit freight traffic between the German Reich and Italy through unoccupied territory to the extent demanded by the German government.

ARTICLE XVI

The French government, in agreement with the responsible German officials, will carry out the return of the population into occupied territory.

ARTICLE XVII

The French government obligates itself to prevent every transference of economic valuables and provisions from the territory to be occupied by German troops into unoccupied territory or abroad. These valuables and provisions in occupied territory are to be disposed of only in agreement with the German government. In that connection, the German government will consider the necessities of life of the population in unoccupied territory.

ARTICLE XVIII

The French government will bear the cost of maintenance of German occupation troops on French soil.

ARTICLE XIX

All German war and civil prisoners in French custody, including those under arrest and convicted who were seized and sentenced because of acts in favour of the German Reich, shall be surrendered immediately to German troops.

The French government is obliged to surrender on demand all Germans named by the German government in France as well as in French possessions, colonies, protectorate territories and mandates.

The French government binds itself to prevent removal of German war and civil prisoners from France into French possessions or into foreign countries. Regarding prisoners already taken outside of France, as well as sick and wounded German prisoners who cannot be transported, exact lists with the places of residence are to be produced. The German High Command assumes care of sick and wounded German war prisoners.

ARTICLE XX

French troops in German prison camps will remain prisoners of war until conclusion of a peace.

ARTICLE XXI

The French government assumes responsibility for the security of all objects and valuables whose undamaged surrender or holding in readiness for German disposal is demanded in this agreement or whose removal outside the country is forbidden. The French government is bound to compensate for all destruction, damage or removal contrary to agreement.

ARTICLE XXII

The Armistice Commission, acting in accordance with the direction of the German High Command, will regulate and supervise the carrying out of the armistice agreement. It is the task of the Armistice Commission further to ensure the necessary conformity of this agreement with the Italian-French armistice.

The French government will send a delegation to the seat of the German Armistice Commission to represent the French wishes and to receive regulations from the German Armistice Commission for executing (the agreement).

ARTICLE XXIII

This armistice agreement becomes effective as soon as the French government also has reached an agreement with the Italian government regarding cessation of hostilities. Hostilities will be stopped six hours after the moment at which the Italian government has notified the German government of conclusion of its agreement. The German government will notify the French government of this time by wireless.

ARTICLE XXIV

This agreement is valid until conclusion of a peace treaty. The German government may terminate this agreement at any time with immediate effect if the French government fails to fulfil the obligations it assumes under the agreement.

This armistice agreement signed in the Forest of Compiègne, June 22, 1940, at 6.50 p.m., German summer time.

(Signed) HUNTZIGER
KEITEL

Victory parade in Berlin, Thursday, July 18. Later Hitler let it be known that 'the expression "Blitzkrieg" is an Italian invention.

We picked it up from the newspapers. I've just learnt that I owe all my successes to an attentive study of Italian military theories!'

The end of the Maginot Line

France having capitulated in the early hours of June 25, sector commanders along various parts of the Line neither trusted what they heard on the French radio nor from the Germans facing them. Against this background of uncertainty, with all communications with the High Command severed, the Commander-in-Chief North-East, Général Alphonse Georges, sent three officers north from Montauban, to where his headquarters had withdrawn, to negotiate the handing over of the fortifications that had not been taken.

Article IV of the armistice terms clearly stated that 'The French armed forces in territory to be occupied by Germany are to be promptly withdrawn into territory not to be occupied and be discharged. These troops, before marching out, shall lay down their equipment at the places where they are stationed at the time this treaty becomes effective. They are responsible for orderly delivery to German troops.' This therefore excluded those French soldiers who had not so far laid down their arms before the cease-fire had come into effect, from being considered prisoners-of-war. The envoys were to negotiate the handing over of the fortifications in exchange for the freedom of their garrisons.

The three envoys, Colonel Pierre Marion, Lieutenant-Colonel Jacques Simon and Lieutenant-Colonel Edouard Durieu du Souzy, left Montauban on June 27 and made contact with vanguards of the 4. Panzer-Division near Vienne in the Rhône valley. Driving northwards, they reached the command post of the XVI. Armeekorps near Macon in the evening and arrived at the headquarters of the 1. Armee at Lunéville just after midnight.

The following morning they met the army chief-of-staff, Generalmajor Carl Hilpert, and soon realised that their mission would be difficult, if not impossible. It became apparent that the Germans had decided upon a straightforward surrender of the fortresses and their occupants. The 1. Armee staff were not willing to argue the point with the French representatives and sent them on to Wiesbaden where French and German delegations were to discuss the finer details of the armistice. There they met Général Charles Huntziger, the leader of the French delegation, and explained the problem to him. Neither the three officers nor Général Huntziger actually knew how many of the fortresses were still in French hands, and they had no idea that the Germans had, in fact, taken so few of them. Consequently, and also because Huntziger had so much else on his plate of top level importance, he did not press the issue as strongly as he might have done with the leader of the German delegation, General Carl Heinrich von Stülpnagel. The Germans knew they were violating the terms they had imposed on the French only a few days earlier, but the only 'concession' the German Armistice Commission made was in allowing the officers of the forces to be taken into captivity to keep their swords. Concerned at the prospect of the Wehrmacht resuming its drive southwards if the French government was seen not to be 'fulfilling all its obligations', Huntziger accepted.

On June 30 he despatched the three envoys with orders for the fortresses to surrender unconditionally. At Sarrebrücken they split up, Colonel Marion travelling westwards to meet the four sector commanders of the Metz area, while Lieutenant-Colonels Simon and Durieu du Souzy headed eastwards. At Ingwiller the two met the commander of Höheres Kommando z.b.V. XXXVII, Generalleutnant Alfred Boehm-Tettelbach, and were then taken on to meet the various fortress commanders:

```
Armeeoberkommando 12
Abteilung      Ic/AO              A.H.Qu.,den 27. Juni 1940.


         Leutnant R ö s s l e r  vom A.O.K. 12 hat den Auftrag,
3 höhere franz. Offiziere zur Heeresgruppe C nach Lunéville zu
geleiten.


                              Für das Armeeoberkommando 12
                              Der Chef des Generalstabes:

                              J.A.


                              Major i.G.
```

Leutnant Rössler (in the centre of the photo *above* with back to camera) of the 12. Armee was instructed to escort the French officers to Lunéville where the 1. Armee had its headquarters as it was in the latter army's territory that the bulk of the unsurrendered fortresses lay.

It soon became apparent that the Germans were going to give scant regard to the important difference between French troops already in German-occupied territory as opposed to those still under arms and still holding out in the various fortresses. Although the provisions of the armistice clearly differentated between the two, 1. Armee was not prepared to argue the point and referred the French envoys on to the headquarters of the Armistice Commission which had been established at Wiesbaden in Germany. Général Huntziger (centre), head of the French delegation which had 'negotiated' the armistice in Compiègne and Rome, was already there but he failed to press this breach of the armistice provisions as firmly as he should have. Consequently the troops in the undefeated fortresses were treated as ordinary prisoners-of-war. This rankled badly with the men of the Line: not only had they been unable to prove themselves in battle but now the privileges accorded them as undefeated troops were to be denied them ... in some cases by trickery.

Simon to the Rohrbach sector and Durieu du Souzy to the Haguenau sector. Like Marion, they were amazed to discover just how many fortresses remained uncaptured and how many men would now be committed to captivity. However it was too late to backtrack and there was nothing else that could be done other than carry out their instructions.

SIMSERHOF

Simserhof had fired its last salvo in support of the Rohrbach fortress at 9.30 p.m. on June 24 before the armistice brought all offensive action to an end, the fortress having fired about 30,000 shells of all calibres since war was declared. On June 25, a day referred to as 'one of national mourning', the fortress commander issued a last order of the day in which he declared that: 'For these last days during which sadness and grave concerns were common to all, I have found among all the garrison the same tenacious hope, the same will of fighting to the end. I am very proud of this and thank you with all my heart'.

Nothing happened for the next five days and it was not until June 30 that the Rohrbach sector commander, Lieutenant-Colonel Bonlarron, and the Vosges sector commander, Commandant Fabre, were taken to the Grand-Hohekirkel fortress where they met the French High Command's envoy Lieutenant-Colonel Simon. He told them that he had just come from a meeting with the 257. Infanterie-

Division commander, Generalleutant Max von Viebahn, and he told them that the fortifications were to be surrendered without being sabotaged and that their men were to be considered as prisoners-of-war.

Intensely angry at the denial of the terms of the armistice, only after much protest did the two commanders agree to sign the necessary documents, and they went so far as to make their feelings known in the comments they added to them. Commandant Fabre was so clearly hostile that the Germans, suspecting that he might disobey orders and have the fortresses destroyed, kept a close eye on him. However, the protests could achieve little and the garrisons left their fortresses and departed for their prison camps on July 1.

The final iniquity — having met Generalleutnant Alfred Boehm-Tettelbach at Ingwiller, the French High Command's envoy, Lieutenant-Colonel Jacques Simon, was taken to the Grand-Hohekirkel fortress in order to pass on the surrender instructions to the commander of the Rohrbach sector, Lieutenant-Colonel Raoul Bonlarron, and the CO of the Vosges sector, Commandant Pierre Fabre, on June 30 at the barracks. *Left:* Lieutenant-Colonel Bonlarron scowls disdainfully as Simon (marked XX on this original print) goes on to elaborate on the details. An outraged Commandant Fabre listens incredulously to the terms of the Line's surrender drawn up contrary to the armistice. He was so angry about it, and protested so vehemently at the notion of surrendering his unvanquished forts, that the Germans had him discreetly watched, just in case he was tempted to disobey his instructions. Generalleutnant Max von Viebahn, the commander of the 257. Infanterie Division, can be seen on the left (X) looking on with interest at the somewhat heated exchanges.

can't fight; They even look

An odd situation and a remarkable picture. Two honour guards, one German, the other French, facing each other at the entrance to the Hochwald fortress (Block 8) waiting for their officers to emerge after the formal hand-over on July 1.

FERMONT

At Fermont, the firing had not ceased at the time set for the end of hostilities (12.35 a.m. on June 25) as a number of Germans remained unaware of the cease-fire arrangements. The fortress returned the fire and it was another hour before the guns of the two sides fell silent. A German emissary appeared on the afternoon but Capitaine Aubert informed him that he would only accept orders from Commandant Max Pophillat. On the afternoon of June 26 he received written orders from Commandant Pophillat to leave the fortress as it was and to proceed to a camp at Doncourt. Fermont was vacated the following day, the officers being permitted to retain their weapons as they marched off with the Tricolour at the head of the column. However disillusionment soon set in when it became apparent that they were to become prisoners-of-war. (Capitaine Aubert, for one, refused to accept his fate and escaped from a PoW cage at Metz at the end of the month to join the Free French in Africa only to be killed in Tunisia on January 21, 1943.)

In surrendering the fortresses of the left wing of the La Crusnes Fortified Sector, Commandant Pophillat had acted on his own initiative in anticipation of the orders that were to follow. He was notified of these by the High Command's envoy, Colonel Marion, on July 1 when, together with the commander of the sector's right wing, Commandant Maurice Vanier, he was called in to see the colonel at Errouville.

Centre: **The commander of the Haguenau Fortified Sector, Lieutenant-Colonel Jacques Schwartz, who had moved his command post into Hochwald on June 16, returns the salute of the German officers at the entrance as he leaves the fortress for the last time.**

IMMERHOF

At 5.45 p.m. on June 26 the fortress received a message from Colonel Jean-Patrick O'Sullivan (whose command post was now in the Métrich fortress), indicating that the fortifications on the left bank of the Moselle river had now been placed under the commander of the Kobenbusch fortress, Commandant Lucien Charnal, and he ordered them to prepare to surrender without destroying anything. Commandant Charnal discussed the handing over of the nine fortresses under his new command with the commander of the 183. Infanterie-Division, Generalmajor Benigmus Dippold, and agreed to their being vacated on June 30. The actual surrender was signed on July 1 when Commandant Charnal met Colonel Marion at the Kobenbusch fortress.

As ordered, Immerhof surrendered to the men of the Inf.Rgt. 351 on June 30. As in all the other fortresses the men thought that they would not be regarded as prisoners-of-war, and the fact that the Germans had allowed their officers to keep their sidearms, albeit without ammunition, had tended to support this mistaken impression. They stayed in a barracks at Hettange for a few days, and it was only as they began to march to the railway station — and captivity — that they finally realised that the Germans did not intend to differentiate between those who had surrendered and those who had not.

HACKENBERG

Early on the morning of June 25 Oberst Fritz Hoffmann, commanding Inf.Rgt. 278, approached the Anzeling fortress where Colonel Cochinard, commanding of the whole Boulay Fortified Sector, had set up his command post. He met Colonel Cochinard but the latter refused to surrender the fortresses under his command without a direct order from the French High Command.

The following day two French soldiers were killed and two seriously injured whilst removing French anti-personnel mines outside Hackenberg.

Colonel Marion arrived at Anzeling on the morning of June 30 bringing with him the instructions for an unconditional surrender to Colonel Cochinard. He then took him to the headquarters of Höheres Kommando z.b.V. XXXXV where, together with Colonel O'Sullivan, commanding the Thionville Fortified Sector, and Commandant Adolphe Denoix, the commander of the Faulquemont Fortified Sector, they met Oberstleutnant Hans von Ziegesar, the corps' chief-of-staff. After much difficulty and discussion, because the French officers absolutely abhorred the idea of their men being made prisoners-of-war when they had not been captured, the commanders of the fortified sectors of Thionville, Boulay and Faulquemont reluctantly signed the surrender of the fortresses under their command. On July 4, except for some 65 men that the Germans detailed to remain behind for essential maintenance, the Hackenberg garrison vacated their unvanquished fortress and marched off into captivity.

Albert Haas, the commander of Hochwald fortress's Block 16, took this picture as the men marched off into captivity as ordinary prisoners-of-war. In the background, the French Tricolour was still flying above Block 8 but the German war flag had already been raised a few metres higher up.

SCHOENENBOURG

After a last duel with German artillery on June 24, all shelling was brought to an end by the armistice early the following day. However for five days nothing further occurred until the afternoon of June 30 when the French High Command's envoy, Lieutenant-Colonel Durieu du Souzy, was driven up to the Hochwald fortress, having come from a meeting with the commander of the 246. Infanterie-Division, Generalleutant Erich Denecke, at his command post at Woerth that morning. At Hochwald he passed on the unpleasant news to Lieutenant-Colonel Schwartz that in surrendering his fortifications, he and his men were to be considered prisoners-of-war. As Fabre and Bonlarron had done earlier, Schwartz signed the surrender as ordered but added his own comments to the document to the effect that 'We are laying down our arms solely on the orders of the French Government and not under constraint from the troops surrounding us. Today, we still have at our disposal sufficient means to sustain a siege of several weeks. I have the honour to request that the French Government point out these facts, which it may not itself be aware of, to the German Government.'

Protests changed nothing and at 7.00 p.m. on June 30 the Germans advised that the troops of the Haguenau Fortified Sector would have to leave their fortresses for 'internment' the next morning.

Fifty years after the surrender, Hochwald is still on the active list with the French armed forces although not in its original rôle! Today it is Base Aérienne 901 (Air Base 901) serving as a radar and communications centre with the aerials mounted on the 500-metre-high mound beneath which the fortress is built.

These two soldiers, Unteroffizier Alois Peltz and Schütze Josef Martin, were killed fighting together at the Isly Farm near Oches, 25 kilometres south of Sedan, on June 9. They both belonged to the 11. Kompanie of Infanterie-Regiment 70, 36. Infanterie-Division, then in conflict with the 74ème R.I. of the French 6ème Division d'Infanterie. Death has not separated them for they now lie side by side in a common grave in Block 1 of the German War Cemetery at Noyers, five kilometrea south of Sedan, which was established after World War I. Now it contains over 12,000 war dead from the Second World War.

Five of the 27,074 who died for the Fatherland in the campaign in the West. These men of Pionier-Bataillon 58 (7. Panzer-Division) were killed fighting the 5ème D.I.C. near Quesnoy on June 6. *Left:* They were buried at Bourdon, five kilometres to the east. *Right:* In 1961 the Volksbund Deutsche Kriegsgräber-fürsorge (German War Graves Commission) began to concentrate other graves from the Départements of Nord, Pas-de-Calais and the Somme at Bourdon to be commemorated in perpetuity, and today the cemetery contains over 22,000 dead. It was formally completed in September 1967.

France suffered dearly in the six-week battle, with 92,000 men killed, another quarter of a million wounded, and almost one and a half million taken prisoner. Soldat Roger Clément, a soldier of the 44ème B.C.P., part of the 47ème Division d'Infanterie, was killed on June 8 at Querbigny, just west of Roye, and now lies in the French Military Cemetery at Condé-Folie. Nearby is the grave of a soldier of the 24ème R.T.S., 4ème Division d'Infanterie Coloniale, identified simply as 'Ali'.

Counting the cost

On June 25, the OKW listed the casualties for the campaign in the West: 27,074 killed, 111,034 wounded and 18,384 missing — most of them probably killed as all the prisoners, save those taken to Britain, were returned after the armistice. For the 136 divisions involved this was a casualty rate per division of 1,000. To make this tremendous victory in the West seem even greater, the German propaganda machine insisted on comparing these relatively low figures with those of the costly battle for Verdun in the First World War when the Kronprinz Army had lost 310,000 men of whom 41,000 were killed.

Another casualty at Condé-Folie is Adjudant Georges Liégard of the 53ème R.I.C., 5ème Division d'Infanterie Coloniale, who lost his life fighting on the Somme on June 6.

Général Paul Barbe, the commander of the 4ème D.L.C., was killed near Dinant on May 15. He is buried in the French War Cemetery established at Chastre, just north of Gembloux in Belgium.

Also 'Mort pour la France' — Soldat Gilbert Ouvrard of the 24ème R.I., 10ème Division d'Infanterie, killed on the Aisne on June 9. His grave is in Floing War Cemetery near Sedan.

Britain, with upwards of 250,000 men involved on the Continent, came out relatively lightly with 3,457 men killed and 13,602 wounded. These two graves lie in Abbeville Communal Cemetery (Extension). *Left:* Private Donald McKenzie of the Seaforth Highlanders was killed on June 4 during the battle against the German bridgehead across the Somme. *Right:* The exact date when Private John Lucas lost his life is not known, nor the precise circumstances, borne out by the unusual dating on his Commonwealth War Graves Commission headstone. However, by far the greater number of graves in this particular cemetery reflect those who died of wounds during 1914-1918 when Abbeville was a hospital area behind the lines.

Three illustrations of Belgian graves in the war cemetery at Boncelles. *Left:* Soldat André Closon of the R.F.L. was killed in the fort at Boncelles on the afternoon of May 15 when an 88mm Flak gun disabled Turret IV. *Centre:* Soldat Théodore Bruneel of the 3ème Compagnie, 21ème Régiment de Ligne, 8ème Division d'Infanterie, was killed at Oostrozebeke (ten kilometres east of Roeselare) on the Lys defence line on May 26. *Right:* Adjudant Oscar Nerenhausen of the 1er Régiment de Chasseurs Ardennais struck down on the Lys front, near Oeselgem, on May 26. In all, Belgium lost 7,500 killed and over 15,000 men wounded — a high casualty rate bearing in mind that they were only in the war for 18 days.

608

With hindsight, an analysis of the casualties of the Wehrmacht might provide some lessons on how the 'Blitzkrieg' might have been defeated. The Wehrmacht had lost about 2,500 men each day from May 10 to June 3, but from June 4 to June 25 this figure rose to about 4,600 men per day. As there were no actual battles after June 18, except in the Vosges sector and in the Alps and these only on a small scale, this meant that the daily casualty list more than doubled between the May and June battles. Statistics can be made to mean anything, but these figures would seem to indicate that the tactical principles adopted by Weygand in the later stages of the battle had met with some success. One can therefore speculate as to what might have happened if his methods had been applied from the beginning with energy and confidence.

The Allied armies had been neither well-prepared nor well enough commanded to overcome a German Army that was superior in these two respects. France had paid dearly for her overconfidence and lack of preparation and 92,000 men had been killed, 250,000 wounded, and about 1,450,000 men made prisoners-of-war. With about 100 divisions involved, the French Army had suffered the highest rate of loss per division of some 3,500 men.

The Dutch had lost 2,157 killed and 6,889 wounded which gave a ratio of about 900 casualties for each of the ten divisions involved.

The Belgian Army sustained 7,500 men killed and 15,850 wounded, also a ratio of about 1,000 each for the 22 divisions committed.

In the two-week battle in the south of France, the Italian Army had suffered 631 men killed, with 2,631 wounded. Another 2,000 were casualties of severe frostbite.

About 1,000 war victims lie in Crooswijk War Cemetery in Rotterdam: 115 Dutch soldiers, 550 civilians killed during the air raid on May 14, and 136 Allied Servicemen, mostly airmen shot down near Rotterdam later in the war. Most of the Dutch soldiers buried there were killed during the battle for the Maas bridges in Rotterdam and the airfield at Waalhaven. *Left:* Marinier der eerste Klasse Gerard Bosma, killed on May 15, was posthumously awarded the Bronze for bravery in action. *Right:* Kapitein der Mariniers Willem Schuiling of the Dutch Marines distinguished himself in the fight for the bridge, and was awarded the Militaire Willems orde, the highest Dutch award for the most conspicuous acts of bravery and devotion to duty. He died in a German PoW camp in 1944 and was buried at Crooswijk after the war. The Dutch lost 2,157 killed and nearly 7,000 wounded in their five-day war between May 10-15.

~~Great~~ Britain had lost 3,457 men killed and 13,602 wounded. For the ten divisions involved this gave a loss rate of around 1,700 casualties per division.

However, unlike France, 'neutral' Belgium and the Netherlands, much of the British force had been saved to fight another day. Much equipment had been lost but many lessons had been learned about a new form of warfare in which the machines had become almost more important than the man.

Nowhere was this more apparent than in the air where the next great battle was about to be fought. The Battle of France may have been over but the Battle of Britain was about to begin.

In the six weeks that Blitzkrieg in the West had lasted, the six combatants lost a total of 152,000 men killed and 400,000 wounded. Exact totals of civilian casualties have never been reliably established, but they must run into several thousands.

Today the fields of France are once again at peace, yet the scars remain. Here on the Somme, the spot where a tank once burned on the field of battle remains impressed in the soil, fifty years after the battle.

609

Glossary

BELGIAN

P.F.L. Position Fortifée de Liège Liège Fortified Position
P.F.N. Position Fortifée de Namur Namur Fortified Position
R.F.L. Régiment de Forteresse de Liège Liège Fortress Regiment
R.F.N. Régiment de Forteresse de Namur Namur Fortress Regiment

DUTCH

BomVA Bombardeervliegtuig Afdeling bomber squadron
Divisie division
Grens-Bataljon border battalion
JaVA Jachtvliegtuig Afdeling fighter squadron
Legerkorps army corps
Lichte Divisie light division
LVR Luchtvaart Regiment air force regiment
N.S.B. Nationaal-Socialistische Beweging National Socialist Movement
PAW Pantserwagen armoured car
RI Regiment Infanterie infantry regiment

FRENCH

Armée Army
B.A.F. Bataillon Alpin de Forteresse Alpine Fortress Battalion
B.C. Brigade de Cavalerie Cavalry Brigade
B.C.A. Bataillon de Chasseurs Alpins Alpine Troop Battalion
B.C.C. Bataillon de Chars de Combat Tank Battalion
B.C.P. Bataillon de Chasseurs à Pied Infantry Battalion
B.C.T.C. Bataillon de Chars des Troupes Coloniales Colonial Tank Battalion
B.L.M. Brigade Légère Mécanique Light Mechanised Brigade
B.M. Bataillon de Mitrailleurs Machine Gun Battalion
B.S. Brigade de Spahis Spahis Brigade
C.A. Corps d'Armée Army Corps
C.A.C.C. Compagnie Autonome de Chars de Combat Independent Tank Company
C.O.R.F. Commission d'Organisation des Régions Fortifiées Organising Commission for Fortified Regions
D.C.R. Division Cuirassée Armoured Division
D.C.T. Division de Torpilleurs Destroyer Division (naval)
D.D. Détachement de Découverte Reconnaissance Detachment
D.I. Division d'Infanterie Infantry Division
D.I.A. Division d'Infanterie Alpine Alpine Infantry Division
D.I.C. Division d'Infanterie Coloniale Colonial Infantry Division
D.I.F. Division d'Infanterie de Forteresse Fortress Infantry Division
D.I.M. Division d'Infanterie Motorisée Motorised Infantry Division
D.I.N.A. Division d'Infanterie Nord-Africaine North African Infantry Division
D.L.C. Division Légère de Cavalerie Light Cavalry Division
D.L.I. Division Légère d'Infanterie Light Infantry Division
D.L.M. Division Légère Mécanique Light Mechanised Division
D.M. Division Marocaine Moroccan Division
Escadre Approximates an RAF Wing
G.A.O. Groupe Aérien d'Observation Tactical Reconnaissance Squadron
G.B. Groupe de Bombardement Bomber Squadron
G.C. Groupe de Chasse Fighter Squadron
G.R. Groupe de Reconnaissance Reconnaissance Squadron
G.F.M. Guet et Fusil Mitrailleur Observation and light machine gun cupola
G.R.C.A. Groupe de Reconnaissance de Corps d'Armée Army Corps Reconnaissance Group
G.R.D.I. Groupe de Reconnaissance de Division d'Infanterie Infantry Division Reconnaissance Group
Groupe Approximates to an RAF Squadron
Groupe d'Armées Army Group
M.O.M. Main d'Oeuvre Militaire Military Labour Force
R.A. Régiment d'Artillerie Artillery Regiment
R.A.L. Régiment d'Artillerie Lourde Heavy Artillery Regiment
R.A.M. Régiment d'Auto-Mitrailleuses Armoured Car Regiment

R.A.P. Régiment d'Artillerie de Position Fortress Artillery Regiment
R.C.C. Régiment de Chars de Combat Tank Regiment
R.D.P. Régiment de Dragons Portés Carrier-borne Dragoon Regiment
R.I. Régiment d'Infanterie Infantry Regiment
R.I.A. Régiment d'Infanterie Alpine Alpine Infantry Regiment
R.I.C. Régiment d'Infanterie Coloniale Colonial Infantry Regiment
R.I.F. Régiment d'Infanterie de Forteresse Fortress Infantry Regiment
R.R. Régiment Régional Regional Regiment
R.T.A. Régiment de Tirailleurs Algériens Algerian Infantry Regiment
R.T.M. Régiment de Tirailleurs Marocains Moroccan Infantry Regiment
R.T.S. Régiment de Tirailleurs Sénégalais Senegalian Infantry Regiment
R.T.T. Régiment de Tirailleurs Tunisiens Tunisian Infantry Regiment
S.D. Secteur Défensif Defensive Sector
S.F. Secteur Fortifié Fortified Sector
S.T.G. Services Techniques du Génie Army Technical Engineering Services
Z.O.A. Zone d'Opération Aérienne Air Operations Area

GERMAN

A.K. Armeekorps Army Corps
Arko Artillerie-Kommandeur Corps Artillery Commander
Armee Army
Art.Rgt. Artillerie-Regiment artillery regiment
Auf.Gr. Aufklärungsgruppe aerial reconnaissance group
Aufkl.Abt. Aufklärungs-Abteilung reconnaissance battalion
Ballon-Batterie balloon battery
Bttr. battery
Bau-Btl. Bau-Bataillon engineer battalion
Fall Gelb Plan Yellow (May 10 attack)
Fall Rot Plan Red (June 9 offensive)
F.J.R. Fallschirm-Jäger-Regiment parachute regiment
Flak Fliegerabwehrkanone anti-aircraft gun
Flakkorps Flak Corps
Fliegerkorps Air Corps
Heeresgruppe Army Group
Infanterie-Division infantry division
Infanterie-Division (mot) motorised infantry division
Inf.Rgt. Infanterie-Regiment infantry regiment
JG Jagdgeschwader fighter wing
Jafü Jagdfliegerführer Fighter Commander
KG Kampfgeschwader bomber wing
Kradschützen-Bataillon motor cycle battalion
Kampfgruppe army battle group or task force
leFH leichte Feldhaubitze light field howitzer
Luftflotte Air Fleet
Mörser-Batterie heavy howitzer battery
OKH Oberkommando des Heeres Army High Command
OKW Oberkommando der Wehrmacht High Command of the Armed Forces
Pak Panzerabwehrkanone anti-tank gun
Panzer-Division armoured division
Pi.Btl. Pionier-Bataillon engineer battalion
Pz.Abt. Panzer-Abteilung tank detachment
Pz.Jg.Abt. Panzerjäger-Abteilung tank-hunter battalion
PzKpfw Panzerkampfwagen tank
Pz.Rgt. Panzer-Regiment armoured regiment
Schtz.Rgt. Schützen-Regiment carrier-borne infantry regiment
SdKfz Sonderkraftfahrzeug special purpose vehicle
sFH schwere Feldhaubitze heavy field howitzer
Sichelschnitt literally the 'sweep of the scythe', the left-hook of the German armies towards the coast
s.IG Kompanie schwere Infanterie-Geschütz-Kompanie heavy infantry gun company
StG Stukageschwader dive-bomber wing
z.b.V. zur besondern Verwendung for special employment
ZG Zerstörergeschwader heavy fighter wing

ITALIAN

Alpini Alpine troops
Armata Army
Corpo d'Armata Army Corps

Index

The battle was still being fought but the German war photographer who took this picture proved to be somewhat of an artist and he could not resist the pleasure of taking this classic shot. These men crossing the Saône river near Quitteur on June 16 belonged to the 1. Schützen-Brigade of the 1. Panzer-Division. The Luftwaffe, which was to bomb this sector by mistake, causing losses and considerable delay, soon put an end to this peaceful scene.

Above: These three Tracteurs Blindées Modèle 37L were disabled with their trailers in Boulevard Vauban in Auxerre, right in the centre of the town. They had probably been the victims of air attack about June 15 as evidenced by the parlous state of the buildings visible on both sides of the street. Below: Many of the shattered trees survived the ordeal, and this comparison was still possible fifty years later on a now-peaceful Boulevard Vauban.

Memorial to the French 12ème Division d'Infanterie Motorisée overlooking the Dunkirk beaches.

LOCATIONS

623

The damage caused to the nearby houses indicates that this Renault FT-17 had held up the crossing of the Loire at Blois for some time before being disabled. One span of the bridge covered by the tank had been blown and German engineers had to deal with this annoying obstacle before beginning to span the breach. This was quickly under way and the bridge was repaired within a few hours of French resistance south of the river being silenced.

Men of Panzer-Regiment 11 (6. Panzer-Division). Leutnant Helmut Ritgen third from right.

PERSONNEL

Abrial, Amiral Jean (French
commander at Dunkirk), *360*, 417,
422, 442, 444, 451, 453; Gort
subordinate to in Dunkirk
bridgehead, 437, *445;* Gort visits,
449; Alexander under orders of,
449; angry at reduced British corps
left to fight, 450; Weygand notifies
of dissolution of Groupe d'Armées
No. 1, 451–452; insists 25,000
French troops be evacuated, 453;
decides on last night of operations,
454; crosses to England, 454; tells
Ramsay further evacuation
impossible, 454
Adam, Bt, Lieut-General Sir Ronald
(III Corps Commander), 365–366; at
meeting with French, 422
Agliany, Général Auguste
(commanding 5ème D.I.N.A.), 306
Aitken, Revd L. (author and National
Chaplain, DVA), dedicates
memorial to massacred British
troops, *441*
Alaurent, Général Auguste
(commanding infantry of 32ème
Division d'Infanterie), captured, 455
Alexander, Major-General Hon.
H.R.L.G. (commanding 1st
Division), takes over 'dwindling'
BEF (I Corps) from Gort, 449; sees
Abrial, 450; instructed by S of S to
withdraw forces 'as rapidly as
possible', 451; agrees to hold sector
to midnight, June 1, 451; with SNO
tours beaches before leaving for
England, 453
Altmann, Oblt. G., 80, *81*, 82, *87;*
decorated, 87, *87*
Altmayer, Général René (commanding
Vème Corps d'Armée), 365–366
Altmayer, Général Robert
(commanding Groupement A, later
10ème Armée), 398, 400, 401, 475,
476, 510
Andel, Luitenant-Generaal Jacob van
(commanding Vesting Holland), 150
André, Colonel S., 315; killed, 319
Apell, Oberst W. von, 144
Arent, Uffz. P., 83
Arsan, Leutnant F., *412, 413*
Attlee, Rt Hon Clement, 502
Aubert, Capitaine D., agrees to truce,
549; escapes but is killed later, 604

Aubry de Maraumont, Aspirant G.,
405
Aufsess, Major T. von und zu,
wounded by Spahis, 105
Auwera, Commandant L. van der, 85
Averlon, Lieut., *394*
Aymes, Général Henri (commanding
IVème Corps d'Armée) captured,
433
Backer, Kapitein J. D., 148; took back
Dutch reply to Rotterdam surrender
ultimatum, *145*, 146, 147
Badoglio, Maresciallo Pietro, 583;
rebuked by Mussolini, 579; leads
Italian armistice delegation, 597
Balck, Oberstlt. H., *218*, 219, 335,
497, 518/522/ 524/527
Barbaste, Lieut. P., killed, 229
Barbe, Général Paul (4ème D.L.C.
commander), *181;* killed, 254, *607*
Barbieux, Commandant F., 383
Bardel, Lieut. R., *404;* describes battle
for Villers-Mareuil, 405–407
Barratt, Air Mshl. A. S. (commanding
British Air Forces in France), 215,
510; French ask for 'maximum air
support', 224; presses for more
fighters, 288; informed Operation
'Haddock' could proceed, 582
Baston, Lieut., wounded, *250*
Baudouin, Paul (French Under-
Secretary for Foreign Affairs, later
Foreign Minister), 462, *544;* present
at June 13 meeting of Churchill and
Reynaud, 542, *543;* new Minister of
Foreign Affairs, 546, *564;* broadcasts
to the French people, 564; hears
German armistice terms, 596–597
Beauchesne, Colonel de G., 142
Beaufrère, Général Maurice
(commanding 68ème Division
d'Infanterie), with Gen. Teisseire,
makes first contact (to surrender)
with Germans, 454; captured, 455
Beauman, Brigadier A. B.
(commander of Beauman Division),
408; orders troops to hold on, 476
Behlendorff, Generalleutnant Hans,
'gravely wounded', 105
Bel, Lieut. R. Le, 161
Bellamy, Roger (President, Folkestone
Dunkirk Veterans' Association), *421*
Below, Hptmn. N., *73*
Berger, Sgt. M., 99, 140, *141*, 396–398

Bergeret, Général Jean (member of
French armistice delegation), 594,
595, 598
Bernard, Commandant J. M., *487*
Bernhard, Prince, of the Netherlands
(see also Dutch Royal Family), *117;*
escapes to England, 150
Berniquet, Général André
(commanding 2ème D.L.C.), killed,
485
Bertin, Capitaine M., 298, 309;
German general congratulates, 313
Bertin-Boussu, Général Paul
(commanding 3ème D.I.M.), reports
100 prisoners, 276
Bescond, Commandant J., 328–329;
killed, 330, *335*
Besson, Général Antoine (commander
of Groupe d'Armées No. 3), 48,
393, 492, 514, 515, *585*, 589
Bessou, Caporal-Chef, survivor of
Denée action, 253
Best, Generaal-Majoor Petrus W.
(Dutch Air Force commander), *109*
Bibes, Lieut. R., describes night
march, 328
Billotte, Général Gaston (C-in-C
North-East Front), 47, *48*, 167, 280,
303, 306, 360, *360;* to co-ordinate
Allied forces in Belgium, 163; orders
Allies to withdraw to Escaut, 167;
Corap asks for reinforcements, 207;
calls for 'every available aircraft'
against Sedan bridges, *223;* informs
Gamelin that 9ème Armée in very
critical situation, 241, visits Gort,
337; Ironside and Pownall visit, 340;
decision to attack, 340; 'co-
ordinator', 356; meeting with Gort
and Leopold, 361, *361;* fatally
injured, 361; 'still not replaced', *421*
Billotte, Capitaine, P., describes
French counter-attack on Stonne,
275
Binkau, Major H. (commander of Pi.
Btl.58), killed, 190
Bismarck, Oberst G. von., *52;* at
surrender of Saint-Valery, *484*
Blanchard, Général Georges (1ère
Armée commander), 43, *48*, 49, 101,
340–341, 366, 420, 422; takes over
Groupe d'Armées No. 1 from
Billotte, 361; visits Gort, 362, 365;
Gort and Pownall visit, 366;

Blanchard—continued
evacuation discussed with Gort, 431;
sends message to Georges, 'British
embarking', 438; to establish
bridgehead for evacuation, 442;
evacuated, 452
Bland, Sir Neville (British Minister to
the Netherlands), travels to England
with Dutch Queen, 150
Blomfield, J. R. (RE subaltern),
describes scene on beaches, 446–448
Blondelet, Lieut. M., 411–413, killed,
413
Blümm, Generalleutnant Oskar
(commander of 57.Infanterie-
Division), 407
Bock, Generaloberst Fedor von, 465,
488, 489/491, 539; Heeresgruppe B
commander, *54*, 55; visits
Maastricht, 156; orders troops to 'sit
tight' at Battice and Pépinster, 390–
391; in Paris, 506
Bodson, Soldat H., wounded, *380*
Boehm-Tettelbach, Generalleutnant
Alfred (commanding Höheres
Kommando z.b.V.XXXVII), French
envoys meet, 602, *603*
Boers, Kapitein C. (commanding
Kornwerderzand fortress), 132, *132*,
133
Boly, Soldat, M., shot after capture;
buried in French military cemetery,
479
Bonlarron, Lieut-Colonel R., 554;
signs surrender of Rohrbach Sector,
603, *603*, 605
Bonnot, Commandant P., 243, *302*
Borchert, Eric (photographer), *318*,
320, 321, 326, 468, 469, 470
Bosma, Marinier der eerste Klasse
(Dutch marine), killed,
posthumously awarded Bronze, *609*
Bouclier, Lt. M., awarded Iron Cross
First Class, 537
Bouffet, Général Jean (commanding
IIème Corps d'Armée), 182; killed,
254, *254*
Bounaix, Lieut. L., 97; describes
action, 245, 247
Bourguignon, Lieut. M., 293; body
found and reburied, 296, *296*
Bourret, Général Victor (5ème Armée
commander), 20; captured with
staff, 569, 572

632

All hope gone, French villagers look on with dismay at a German cavalry squadron crossing their village on June 20. This was a difficult location to find as the original caption incorrectly stated that it had been taken in Châtillon-sur-Loire. In the end, after much discussion with local people, we pinpointed the same street in Cernoy-en-Berry, ten kilometres to the south-west, and established that this patrol had just crossed the Loire and was marching southwards.

Unnamed yet not forgotten. Caught up in a whirlwind and swept along in its path: the civilian refugees.

Photo Credits

Just one of the many war reporters who made this book possible — a Kriegsberichter of the German Armed Forces pictured during the campaign in France in 1940.

Adscene Pub.: 420 bottom, 421 bottom right.
Afdeling Maritieme Historie, The Hague: 128 top, 128 bottom, 133 middle.
A.L.M.A.: 559 top left, 604 top, 604 middle.
Archiefdienst, Rotterdam: 125 top, 148 top left, 149 top.
Archives Fédérales, Berne: 570 top, 571 top left, 571 middle, 571 bottom left, 572 top, 572 bottom left, 582 bottom, 583 top, 583 bottom left.
Associated Press, London: 564 top, 574 bottom, 575 top.
J. van der Berg: 118 bottom.
R. Bruge: 533 middle left.
Bundesarchiv, Freiburg: 199 top, 236 bottom left, 387 middle, 490 top, 538 top left, 539 top, 565 top left, 568 top.
Bundesarchiv, Koblenz: 2–3, 4 top, 8–9, 15 bottom left, 52 bottom left, 52 bottom right, 55 bottom, 58 top, 58 bottom right, 82 bottom, 83 top left, 83 bottom left, 84 top, 84 top left, 84 top right, 85 top, 85 bottom left, 88 bottom, 89 bottom left, 89 bottom right, 90 bottom left, 90 bottom right, 114 bottom left, 118 middle, 122 bottom, 138 top, 146 top right, 150 top left, 150 bottom left, 151 top, 151 bottom, 152 bottom left, 156 top left, 156 bottom left, 166 top, 168 top, 168 bottom left, 169 top left, 169 middle left, 169 bottom left, 170 top left, 170 middle left, 170 bottom left, 171 top left, 171 middle, 171 middle right, 171 2nd middle right, 171 bottom right, 172 top left, 172 middle, 172 bottom left, 173 top left, 173 middle, 173 bottom left, 176 top, 177 top, 178 top left, 178 middle left, 178 bottom left, 179 top left, 179 top right, 179 middle, 180 top, 181 top left, 181 middle left, 181 bottom left, 183 bottom left, 184 top, 184 middle, 185 top, 189 top left, 190 top, 191 top left, 191 bottom left, 192 top, 193 top left, 193 middle, 193 bottom left, 197 top left, 197 middle, 197 bottom left, 198 top left, 200 top, 201 top, 201 bottom left, 202 middle, 203 bottom left, 204 top left, 204 bottom left, 205 top left, 205 middle left, 205 bottom left, 206 bottom left, 207 top, 208 middle, 221 middle, 230 top, 231 top left, 231 bottom left, 233 top, 233 bottom left, 234 top left, 234 middle, 234 bottom left, 237 top, 238–239, 243 bottom left, 245 middle, 246 bottom left, 247 bottom left, 252 middle left, 252 bottom left, 253 top,

256 top left, 256 bottom left, 258 top left, 258 middle left, 259 top left, 259 middle, 259 bottom left, 260 top left, 260 middle, 261 top left, 261 middle, 261 bottom left, 262 top, 264 middle, 265 top left, 265 middle left, 265 bottom left, 266 top left, 266 top right, 281 top left, 284 top, 284 top left, 284 top right, 288 top left, 294 top, 295 top left, 295 bottom left, 306 top left, 306 bottom left, 332 top, 342 top, 342 bottom left, 343 top, 346 bottom left, 348 top left, 348 middle, 350 top, 350 bottom, 352 top left, 352 bottom left, 353 top, 354 top, 362 bottom left, 363 top, 363 bottom left, 373 top, 373 bottom, 374 bottom left, 375 top, 378 top, 380 top, 380 bottom left, 380 bottom right, 381 top left, 381 top right, 382 top left, 382 middle, 382 bottom left, 383 top left, 383 middle, 384 top left, 384 middle, 384 bottom left, 385 top, 388 top left, 388 bottom left, 389 top, 389 middle, 392 top left, 392 bottom left, 423 top left, 423 top right, 424 top, 430 bottom left, 431 top left, 431 bottom, 434 top, 434 bottom left, 435 top, 463 top, 471 top left, 471 bottom left, 472 top, 472 bottom left, 473 top, 483 middle, 485 top, 485 middle left, 485 bottom, 492 middle, 499 top left, 499 middle, 504 top, 504 bottom, 505 bottom left, 506 top left, 506 bottom left, 508 top, 508 bottom, 509 top left, 510 top left, 510 middle, 510 bottom left, 516 top, 516 middle, 517 top, 519 top left, 519 middle, 519 bottom left, 520 top, 522 top, 523 top left, 523 middle, 524 top, 526 top left, 527 bottom left, 529 top, 534 top left, 535 top left, 535 bottom, 536 top, 536 bottom, 547 middle, 547 bottom left, 550 top, 562 top, 562 bottom, 566 top, 569 bottom left, 584 top, 598 top, 611, 614 top, 619 top, 627 top, 634 top.
J. Defize: 45 top, 64 top left, 64 top right.
J. van Dijke: 122 middle, 124 bottom right, 125 middle, 125 bottom right, 126 middle, 126 bottom right, 127 bottom, 137 top, 138 middle, 138 bottom right, 141 bottom right, 142 top right, 144 bottom, 145 top, 145 bottom, 148 bottom, 149 bottom, 150 top right, 150 bottom right, 152 top right, 152 bottom right, 153 middle.
ECPArmées, Paris: 10 top, 11 top, 11 bottom left, 14 top, 14 bottom, 16 top, 16 middle, 16 bottom, 17 bottom right, 18 top, 19 top left, 19 top right, 19 bottom left, 20 top, 21 top, 22 bottom, 23 top, 24 bottom, 25 top, 25 bottom,

638

26 top, 26 bottom, 28 top, 29 top left, 29 top right,
29 bottom left, 29 bottom right, 30 top left, 30 bottom,
32 bottom left, 32 bottom right, 33 bottom, 37 top right,
39 top, 39 bottom left, 39 bottom right, 40 top, 40 bottom,
42 top left, 42 top right, 42 bottom, 43 top left, 43 bottom,
46 top, 46 bottom, 47 top left, 47 middle, 47 bottom left,
48 top left, 48 top right, 48 bottom left, 48 bottom left,
48 bottom right, 49 top left, 56 top, 56 bottom, 57 top,
57 bottom, 59 bottom, 60 top, 60 middle, 61 top,
61 bottom left, 61 bottom right, 62 top, 62 2nd top right,
66 top left, 68 top, 68 bottom, 69 top, 69 middle, 70–71,
81 top, 81 bottom, 92 top, 93 top, 96 top, 96 bottom, 98 top,
98 bottom left, 99 top, 99 bottom, 100 top left, 100 top right,
102 top, 102 bottom, 104 top, 105 top, 106 top left,
106 middle, 106 bottom left, 120 middle, 131 top, 139 top,
139 bottom, 140 top, 140 bottom left, 141 top, 142 bottom,
143 top, 158 top, 158 bottom, 159 top, 159 bottom, 163 top,
163 middle, 164 top, 165 top, 174 top, 175 top,
175 middle left, 186 top left, 186 middle left,
186 bottom left, 187 top left, 187 middle left,
187 bottom left, 194 top, 194 bottom left, 195 top,
196 bottom, 198 middle left, 198 bottom left, 210 top,
211 top, 211 bottom, 212 top, 212 bottom, 214 bottom left,
215 top, 217 top, 217 middle left, 220 top, 221 top left,
221 bottom left, 222 top, 223 middle, 225 top,
225 middle left, 225 middle right, 226 top, 226 bottom,
227 top, 227 bottom left, 242 top, 246 top, 248 top, 249 top,
249 bottom, 250 top, 251 top left, 251 top right,
254 bottom left, 254 bottom right, 263 top, 263 bottom left,
264 top left, 266 middle, 267 middle, 267 bottom left,
271 top, 271 bottom, 272 top, 273 bottom left,
273 bottom right, 274 top left, 274 bottom left, 278 top,
278 bottom left, 279 top, 280 top, 280 bottom,
281 bottom left, 285 bottom, 287 top, 287 bottom,
288 top right, 288 bottom, 289 top left, 290 top, 297 top,
298 top, 298 middle left, 299 top, 300 top left,
300 middle left, 300 bottom, 301 top left, 301 bottom left,
302 top, 302 middle left, 303 top, 304 top left, 304 top right,
304 middle, 304 bottom left, 305 top, 307 top,
307 middle left, 311 top, 312 top, 312 middle left, 313 top,
313 middle, 314 top, 314 bottom left, 315 top, 315 middle,
316 top, 316 bottom, 317 top left, 317 middle,
317 bottom left, 318 top, 319 top left, 319 top right,
320 top left, 321 top, 322 top left, 322 top right,
322 middle left, 322 middle right, 323 top, 323 bottom left,
324 top left, 324 middle, 326 top, 326 bottom left, 327 top,
327 bottom left, 328 top, 328 bottom, 329 top, 333 top,
333 bottom left, 334 top, 336 top left, 340 top, 341 top,
341 middle, 345 top, 346 top, 349 top, 351 bottom left,
355 top left, 355 bottom left, 356 top, 356 bottom left,
357 top left, 357 middle, 357 bottom left, 358 top,
358 bottom left, 359 top left, 359 middle, 359 bottom left,
360 top, 366 top, 368 bottom, 369, 386 top, 393 top,
393 bottom, 404 top, 411 top, 412 top, 414 top, 417 top,
417 middle, 418 top left, 426 top left, 426 middle, 427 top,
427 middle, 433 top, 439 top, 442 middle, 443 top left,
443 middle, 444 top left, 444 middle, 445 top, 445 middle,
445 bottom left, 448 bottom, 449 top, 449 middle left,
449 bottom, 450 top, 450 middle, 450 bottom left,
450 bottom right, 451 top, 451 bottom, 452 top left,
452 middle, 452 bottom left, 453 top left, 453 bottom,
454 top, 455 top, 455 bottom, 456–457, 460 top, 460 bottom,
462 top left, 462 top right, 462 bottom, 478 top, 478 middle,
479 top, 488 top, 489 bottom left, 489 bottom right,
490 middle left, 494 top, 494 bottom right, 496 top,
496 bottom, 497 top, 497 bottom left, 498 top, 501 top,
501 bottom, 507 top, 530 bottom, 540–541, 576 top, 577 top,
577 bottom, 578 top, 580 bottom, 582 top, 586 top, 590 top,
596 bottom left, 638, 640.
English Heritage: 421 top.
H. Fendesack: 244 middle.
Fototheek topografische Dienst, Emmen: 146 bottom.
Gemeentearchief, The Hague: 115 top, 115 bottom, 116 top,
116 bottom, 117 top.
H. Guderian: 529 middle, 529 bottom left.
A. Haas: 32 middle, 38 bottom, 555 top, 558 bottom,
559 middle left, 559 middle right, 559 bottom left, 560 top,
560 middle, 560 bottom, 561 top, 561 middle, 605 top.
A. Heumüller: 557 top.
A. van der Hoek: 136 bottom.
J. van der Hoeven: 124 bottom left.
Icare Pub., Paris: 157 top right, 206 top, 224 top left.
Imperial War Museum, London: 17 top, 17 bottom left,
49 bottom left, 50 middle, 50 bottom left, 51 top left,
51 middle, 51 bottom left, 63 top, 63 bottom, 67 top,

67 middle, 67 bottom left, 67 bottom right, 94 top left,
94 bottom, 95 top left, 95 middle, 95 bottom left, 97 top,
97 bottom left, 112 bottom, 156 middle, 337 top,
338 top left, 338 middle left, 338 bottom, 339 top,
339 bottom, 398 top, 398 middle, 399 top, 400 top,
400 bottom left, 401 top left, 401 middle, 402 middle,
402 bottom, 403 top, 407 top left, 421 bottom left,
446 bottom left, 480 top, 480 bottom left, 481 top,
481 bottom left, 512 top, 513 top, 513 middle, 513 bottom,
592 top left.
K.L.M. Luchtfotografie, Schiphol: 117 bottom.
J. A. Laguette: 137 bottom.
A. Laude: 405 top left, 405 middle, 405 bottom left,
406 top left.
Maczek Museum, Breda: 141 bottom left.
National Archives, Washington: 15 top, 15 bottom right,
52 top, 53 top left, 53 top right, 54 bottom right, 58 middle,
58 bottom left, 72 top, 80 middle, 81 middle left, 82 top left,
87 middle, 90 top, 154 top, 155 top left, 155 middle,
155 bottom left, 160 top, 161 top left, 161 bottom left,
162 top left, 162 bottom left, 166 middle, 167 top left,
167 middle, 188 top, 190 bottom left, 202 top left,
202 bottom left, 203 top, 207 middle, 208 top, 209 top,
214 top, 218 top left, 218 bottom left, 219 top, 219 middle,
224 bottom, 226 top, 228 top, 232 top left, 232 middle left,
232 bottom left, 235 top left, 235 bottom left, 236 top left,
236 middle left, 241 top, 243 top, 247 top, 258 bottom left,
267 top left, 273 top, 275 top, 276 top, 276 bottom, 282 top,
286 top, 308 top, 310 top left, 310 middle, 310 bottom left,
336 bottom left, 343 bottom left, 349 bottom, 392 middle,
402 top, 403 bottom, 406 top right, 410 bottom right,
414 bottom left, 415 top left, 415 bottom left, 422 top left,
422 bottom left, 447 bottom left, 459 bottom left,
488 bottom left, 491 top left, 491 middle, 491 bottom left,
492 top left, 509 bottom left, 516 bottom left, 518 top left,
518 bottom left, 521 top left, 521 middle left,
521 bottom left, 523 bottom left, 525 top, 525 middle left,
527 top left, 527 middle, 528 top, 531 top, 542 top,
547 top left, 564 bottom left, 567 bottom left, 569 top left,
587 top, 588 bottom left, 594 middle, 595 top, 595 bottom,
596 top, 599 bottom.
National Archives, Hoffmann pictures, Washington: 12 top left,
12 middle, 12 bottom left, 13 top left, 54 bottom left,
73 bottom left, 86 top, 86 bottom left, 87 top, 87 top left,
87 top right, 87 bottom, 87 bottom left, 87 bottom right,
291 top left, 291 middle, 291 bottom left, 331 top,
364 top left, 364 middle, 364 bottom left, 458 top,
459 top left, 593 top left, 594 top left.
National Archives, Rommel pictures, Washington: 182 top left,
182 bottom, 183 top, 252 top left, 268 top, 269 top,
269 middle left, 269 middle right, 270 top left, 270 middle,
290 bottom, 423 middle, 424 middle, 425 top left,
425 top right, 432 top left, 432 middle, 432 bottom left,
458 bottom right, 465 top, 465 bottom left, 466 top left,
466 bottom left, 467 top, 467 bottom left, 469 top, 476 top,
476 bottom left, 477 top, 482 top, 482 bottom, 483 top left,
484 top left, 484 middle, 511 top left, 511 middle left,
514 top, 514 middle, 515 top left, 515 bottom, 589 top,
589 middle.
A. E. d'Olne: 358 bottom right, 359 top right, 359 bottom right.
V. Paquez: 65 middle, 66 top right.
A. D. von Plato: 189 middle left, 189 bottom left.
R. Potié: 51 top right, 51 bottom right, 417 bottom,
418 top right, 442 bottom right, 443 top right,
443 bottom right, 452 top right, 452 bottom right,
454 bottom.
Admiral H. Ramsay: 420 top.
H. Riebenstahl: 204 middle, 218 middle.
H. Ritgen: 33 top left, 436 top, 438 top left, 438 middle,
439 bottom, 442 top left, 628.
J. L. Roba: 11 bottom right, 101 bottom, 102 middle right,
166 bottom right, 167 top right, 167 bottom, 360 bottom,
361 top.
H. Rössler: 602 top, 602 bottom.
F. Sallaberry: 590 bottom left, 590 bottom right, 591 top right,
591 bottom right.
M. Schmeelke: 548 top.
R. Schulze-Kossens: 73 top.
Sectie Luchtmacht Historie, The Hague: 129 top, 153 top.
Sectie Militaire Geschiedenis, The Hague: 64 bottom, 107 top,
107 bottom, 108 top, 109 top, 111 top left, 118 top, 124 top,
126 top, 126 bottom left, 127 top, 129 bottom, 135 bottom,
136 top left, 136 top right, 142 top left, 147 bottom left.
Service Historique, Armée de l'Air, Vincennes: 41 top, 65 top,
66 2nd top right, 66 bottom.